TALES
OF WAR

TALES OF WAR

Great Stories from Military History for Every Day of the Year

W.B. Marsh AND **Bruce Carrick**

ICON BOOKS

Published in the UK in 2010 by
Icon Books Ltd, Omnibus Business Centre,
39–41 North Road, London N7 9DP
email: info@iconbooks.co.uk
www.iconbooks.co.uk

Sold in the UK, Europe, South Africa and Asia
by Faber & Faber Ltd, Bloomsbury House,
74–77 Great Russell Street, London WC1B 3DA
or their agents

Distributed in the UK, Europe, South Africa and Asia
by TBS Ltd, TBS Distribution Centre, Colchester Road
Frating Green, Colchester CO7 7DW

Published in Australia in 2010
by Allen & Unwin Pty Ltd,
PO Box 8500, 83 Alexander Street,
Crows Nest, NSW 2065

Published in the USA in 2010 by Totem Books
Inquiries to: Icon Books Ltd, Omnibus Business Centre,
39–41 North Road, London N7 9DP, UK
Distributed to the trade in the USA by National Book Network Inc.,
4501 Forbes Boulevard, Suite 200, Lanham, Maryland 20706

Distributed in Canada by
Penguin Books Canada,
90 Eglinton Avenue East, Suite 700,
Toronto, Ontario M4P 2YE

ISBN: 978-184831-074-2

Typeset in 11½ on 13pt Adobe Garamond Pro by
Hands Fotoset, Mapperley, Nottingham

Printed and bound in the UK by
Clays Ltd, St Ives plc

Contents

CONTENTS

vii

CONTENTS

CONTENTS

CONTENTS

Preface

For those of us with an interest in military history, some dates have an instant connection to great events. For example, 11 November signifies the end of the First World War, 18 June the Battle of Waterloo and 15 March the assassination of Julius Caesar. But most days in the calendar no longer conjure up images of past conflicts – even most Americans have forgotten that the American Civil War began on 12 April, when the South fired on Fort Sumter. It is our belief, however, that every day of the year marks the anniversary of some exciting and memorable military action or the story of some great commander.

In surveying the length and breadth of military history – some 3,500 years of it – we have had an enormous selection of events from which to choose. As the writer Arthur Koestler noted, 'the most persistent sound which reverberates through man's history is the beating of war drums'. Hence our task has been to choose events that, in addition to their historical significance, are of interest to our readers because of the strategy or tactics employed, or the figures involved.

The stories in *Tales of War* cover events from almost 50 different wars, over 250 separate battles, and some 30 sieges. The earliest event in this volume is Pharaoh Thutmose III's victory at Megiddo in the year 1479 BC (15 May); the most recent is the heroic action of Private Johnson Beharry in Iraq, for which he was awarded the Victoria Cross in 2004 (11 June).

Many of our stories cover truly momentous occasions, battles that changed history, such as the Greek destruction of the Persian fleet at Salamis (22 September), Henry Tudor's victory at Bosworth Field and the death of Richard III (22 August), the first battles of the American Revolution at Lexington and Concord (19 April), and Montgomery's triumph at El Alamein (4 November). (Some of these world-changing events were covered in our earlier volumes *365: Great Stories From History* and *366: More Great Stories From History*, and versions of those stories are reproduced here.)

Other events may not be quite so momentous but are, we hope, equally gripping. They range from Hannibal's annihilation of the Roman army at Cannae in 216 BC (2 August) to Joan of Arc's relief of the siege of Orléans (8 May 1429) to Chinese Gordon's death at the fall of Khartoum (26 January 1885) to Arab warrior Ibn Saud's surprise attack on Riyadh with only fifteen followers, to create Saudi Arabia (15 January 1902).

But *Tales of War* is not just the recounting of seismic battles, for we wholeheartedly agree with the Arab proverb that proclaims: 'An army of sheep led by a lion would defeat an army of lions led by a sheep.' The great warriors included in the text range from Alexander the Great (13 June) to Charlemagne (2 April) to Wellington (17 March), and hundreds more – about 700 in all. Many of these men died in the wars in which they fought, or in the aftermath, including Richard the Lionheart (6 April), Stonewall Jackson (2 May) and the Napoleonic marshal Michel Ney, shot by firing squad in the court-yard of the Palais Luxembourg in Paris (7 December). In addition to the generals, however, we have also included a number of tales about junior officers and other ranks, like the American film star Audie Murphy (12 July) who displayed remarkable heroism and self-sacrifice under fire.

Soldiers seem not to be a particularly eloquent group – not many can match American general George Patton's pithy summation that 'The object of war is not to die for your country, but to make the other bastard die for his'. But when we have found powerful quotations from history's commanders, we have endeavoured to weave them into the stories.

These range from Caesar's famous 'Veni, vidi, vici' in 47 BC (21 May) to Churchill's splendid rhetoric, 'I have nothing to offer but blood, toil, tears, and sweat' in 1940 (13 May). Some have been straight to the point, like the duc de Guise's disdainful comment to some prisoners he was about to execute: 'My trade is not to make speeches but to cut off heads' (18 February). Others display a more civilised bravado, such as the 18th-century Prussian general Phillip von Neipperg's reply when asked if his men should fall back, 'We'll retreat over the bodies of our enemies' (10 April), or American Marine sergeant Dan Daly's inspirational call (6 June) to his beleaguered men, 'Come on, you sons of bitches! Do you want to live forever?' Some leaders have displayed a princely sense of self-satisfaction, like the Napoleonic marshal Bernadotte, who remarked, 'No one living has made a career like mine' (21 August), while others rued the ephemeral nature of their triumphs, like Saladin, who at his death told his soldiers, 'Go and take my shroud through the streets and cry loudly, "Behold all that Saladin, who conquered the East, bears away of his conquests"' (4 March).

We hope that this combination of great military events and heroic combatants provides 366 stories worth the telling, always bearing in mind Dwight Eisenhower's aside that 'Whoever said the pen is mightier than the sword never faced an assault rifle'.

About the authors

W.B. Marsh graduated from Princeton, was an officer in the US Marine Corps and worked in the advertising business. He now lives in London. On his birthday – 26 October – the American Navy routed the Japanese at the Battle of Leyte Gulf in 1944, the largest naval battle in history.

Bruce Carrick served in the US Army before graduating from Princeton and has worked in book publishing for many years in New York and London. On his birthday – 5 February – in 1856 Britain's highest military medal, the Victoria Cross, was first announced.

1 January

'We were sitting ducks, and our chances
were slim and none'

1945 Two weeks earlier Nazi Germany had unleashed the Ardennes offensive, a last desperate gamble to regain the initiative in the war in Europe, but even this titanic effort would not be enough, as American tanks had broken through at Bastogne (see 19 December). Now, like a wounded animal, cornered but still deadly dangerous, Germany launched Unternehmen Bodenplatte (Operation Ground-plate), a massive air strike intended to cripple Allied air power in the Low Countries and France.

At 8.30 this New Year's morning over 1,000 aircraft – mostly Messerschmitt 109 and Focke-Wulf 190 fighters – took to the sky, hoping to catch seventeen targeted air bases by surprise. One Luftwaffe pilot later recalled: 'To avoid detection by enemy radar, our flight level was on the deck; we flew between chimneys and around church steeples.'

Among the bases to be hit was the American airstrip Y-29 at Asch in Belgium, where one of the most dramatic air encounters of the war would be fought.

Asch was already busy early that morning. The 390th Fighter Squadron was preparing to attack German Panzers at Ondenval, and by 9.20 eight P-47 Thunderbolts were circling overhead, waiting for others to join them. At about the same time, as the haze began to lift, twelve P-51 Mustangs of the 487th Fighter Squadron were rolling down the runway. Their commander, Lieutenant Colonel John Meyer, had feared that the Luftwaffe might try to catch the Allies still groggy from New Year's celebrations and had ordered his men to fly an early morning patrol.

Suddenly from the north-east, FW 190s and Me 109s appeared, screaming in at 1,500 feet. Instantly the American Thunderbolts jettisoned their bombs and attacked, breaking up the German forma-tion. Meanwhile, Meyer was taxiing down the runway with the other eleven Mustangs behind him. As remembered by pilot Lieutenant Alden Rigby, 'We next saw what looked like at least 50 German fighter aircraft about to make their first pass on our field. We could not have been in a worse position. … We were sitting ducks, and our chances were slim and none. It was not a difficult decision to take off, since that was the slim chance.'

All twelve Mustangs throttled forward in near-simultaneous take-offs directly into the oncoming enemy. Meyer later wrote: 'Immediately upon getting my wheels up I spotted 15-plus 190s headed toward the field from the east. I attacked one, getting a two second burst at 300 yards, 30 degree deflection, getting good hits on the fuselage and wing roots. The E/A [enemy aircraft] half-rolled, crashing into the ground.' Another pilot, Captain Alex Sears, reported: 'I was flying White 2 on Colonel Meyer's wing. … One Me 109 came at me head-on and we made several passes at each other, both of us firing. On the third pass I got some strikes on his engine and shot part of the tail section away. He started burning and went into a lazy spiral and crashed.'

The sky was now filled with dogfights around Asch, the Mustangs and Thunderbolts working together in deadly harmony. As Mustang pilot Alden Rigby wrote in his flight log: 'I could see a P-47 in a turn with an Me 109 at about 1,000 ft. … I really needed what ammo I had left for self-preservation, but when the 109 had the advantage, I did not have a choice. As the P-47 mushed to the outside, I came up from beneath, and from very close range fired enough rounds to see hits on the left wing, through the cock-pit, and right wing. The 109 went in from about 500 ft.'

No quarter was given in this ferocious battle, as recounted by Captain William Whisner: 'There were several 109s in the vic so I engaged one of them. We fought for five or ten minutes, and I finally managed to get behind him. I hit him good and the pilot baled out at 200 feet. I clobbered him as he baled out and he tumbled into the ground.'

By the time the surviving German planes finally turned tail for home, in just 30 minutes Meyer's pilots had shot down 23 out of 61 attackers, while the Thunderbolts claimed seven more. Only one Mustang was damaged on the ground, and two more were damaged in the air; one Thunderbolt was shot down. Two of the Mustang pilots – Rigby and Whisner – had downed four enemy planes apiece.

Not all the Allied air bases had been so well prepared or so successful. The Luftwaffe destroyed or damaged 495 Allied aircraft and put several of the bases out of action for at least a week. But the

Germans paid a heavy price, losing over 150 planes to Allied fighters and anti-aircraft guns. Even worse, on their return to their bases in Germany, their planes flew over heavily defended V-2 launch sites, where cloud cover prevented visual recognition of the aircraft seen on radar. To keep Unternehmen Bodenplatte secret, none of the anti-aircraft gunners had been warned of the attack, and, mistaking the returning Germans for attacking Allies, they shot down over 100 of their own planes. In all, the Luftwaffe lost almost 280 planes and over 140 pilots killed and missing, plus 70 captured.

In the end, Unternehmen Bodenplatte was a tactical victory but a strategic disaster for the Germans. While the Allies replaced destroyed planes within weeks, the lost German aircraft and pilots were irreplaceable, and the Luftwaffe was never again able to launch so concentrated an attack.

Other action this day

1586: English admiral and freebooter Sir Francis Drake captures Santo Domingo * 1883: Birth of John Garand, the inventor of the M1, the first semi-automatic infantry rifle * 1962: The US Navy Seals (Navy Sea, Air and Land Forces) are established

2 January

Ferdinand and Isabella capture the last Moorish stronghold in Spain

1492 'They are yours, O King, since Allah so decrees it', said Boabdil, ruler of Granada, as he handed the keys to the city to King Ferdinand of Aragon after a siege that had lasted nine months.

So on this day over five centuries ago the last Moorish stronghold in Spain surrendered to the crusading might of the Catholic Monarchs, Ferdinand and Isabella. The Moors, who had arrived in Spain almost 800 years earlier in 711, were finally defeated. The Reconquista was complete.

The previous spring, a Spanish army of 80,000 men had arrived outside the walled city, but fighting was at first restricted to occasional sallies by the besieged Moors. Then in July a few daring Spaniards had slipped into Granada by night and attached a copy of a Christian prayer to the door of a mosque. The following day a

Moor named Yarfe stormed out of the gates and galloped back and forth in front of the Spanish positions with the prayer tied to his horse's tail.

Smarting from the insult, a Spanish knight challenged Yarfe to single combat. The two armoured knights charged each other, first on horseback and then on foot, until Yarfe was slain. While the knights were fighting, both Spaniards and Moors had watched the struggle but refrained from attack, abiding by the rules of chivalry. But when Yarfe was defeated, the Moorish garrison rushed out to fight, only to be shattered by the Spanish cavalry; they left 2,000 casualties outside the walls before scurrying back inside the city.

It looked like a victory for Christ, but that night Allah seemingly took a hand when a candle set fire to Queen Isabella's tent and the conflagration burned most of the Spanish camp. The following day King Ferdinand marched his army around the city walls to show that despite the fire, he still controlled the siege. King Boabdil once more sent his soldiers on the attack, but after a number of skirmishes they were forced to retreat again into the city. From that time forth the siege became virtually bloodless, but eventually lack of food and the hopelessness of his position drove Boabdil to capitulate.

On this day Ferdinand and Isabella rode out to a clearing on the Genil River about a mile from the city's walls to receive Boabdil's surrender. According to an eyewitness's letter written only six days later:

> With the royal banners and the cross of Christ plainly visible on the red walls of the Alhambra: ... the Moorish King with about eighty or a hundred on horseback very well dressed went forth to kiss the hand of their Highnesses. They received him with much love and courtesy and they handed over to him his son, who had been a hostage ... with a solemn procession singing the *Te Deum Laudamus*, their highnesses dismounted to adore the Cross to the accompaniment of the tears and reverential devotion of the crowd ... and there was no one who did not weep abundantly with pleasure giving thanks to Our Lord for what they saw, for they could not keep back the tears; and the Moorish King and the Moors who were with him could not disguise the sadness and pain they felt for the joy of the Christians ...

Now the gates of Granada were thrown open and Ferdinand entered, bearing the great silver cross he had carried throughout the crusade of eight years.

Mortified by his defeat, Boabdil rode away with his entourage, never to return. Reaching a lofty spur of the Alpujarras, he stopped to gaze back at the fabulous city he had lost. As he turned to his mother who rode at his side, a tear escaped him. But instead of the sympathy he expected, his mother addressed him with contempt: 'You do well to weep like a woman for what you could not defend like a man.' The rocky ridge from which Boabdil had his last look at Granada has henceforth been called El Ultimo Suspiro del Moro (The Last Sigh of the Moor).

The fall of Granada provoked intense and joyful celebration across all of Christian Europe, much as the fall of Jerusalem to Christian crusaders had almost four centuries earlier. Nowhere was the joy greater than in Spain itself, which, during the process of conquering the Moors, had at last become a unified nation.

Other action this day

1669: While Captain Henry Morgan barbecues a pig on the deck of his warship *Oxford* to celebrate the capture of two French ships, a spark flies into the powderhold, igniting an explosion that blows Morgan through a cabin window and sinks the *Oxford*; 250 sailors and Morgan's treasure of jewels and 200,000 pieces of eight seized at Porto Bello go to the bottom * 1905: The Russo-Japanese war ends when the Russian garrison at Port Arthur surrenders * 1942: Thirty-three members of the Duquesne Spy Ring are convicted of spying for Germany and sentenced to a total of 330 years in prison in the largest espionage case in American history

3 January

A glorious day for the American rebels

1777 In his eight years as commander-in-chief of the Continental Army, General George Washington seldom found opportunities to lead his troops to victory in the field. But at a critical point in the war against the British, after a string of defeats that made it look as if the cause of American independence was utterly lost, he suddenly won two battles in a row that restored to the patriots a sense that they might after all prevail. The first of the two victories was at Trenton, New Jersey at the end of 1776 (see 26 December); the second occurred just eight days later at nearby Princeton.

After Trenton, Washington took his army across the Delaware River to await the British response. But on 29 December, he made an unexpectedly risky move, taking some 6,800 men and artillery back to Trenton and occupying a position near the river with no easy escape route. His situation was made worse by a thaw and heavy rains that turned the landscape into deep mud. Learning of Washington's move, the commander of the British forces, General Cornwallis, eager to pay the Americans back for their earlier success, sent his battalions marching down the road from Princeton to meet them. He meant to hit the rebels head-on.

On 2 January Washington's soldiers held off the first assaults that the redcoats launched. Then night fell, turning very cold and freezing the mud. With more British troops on the way, defeat seemed likely for the morrow. But after conferring with some of his senior officers, Washington seized upon a radical plan. Leaving his fires burning and some detachments behind to simulate an army at camp, he and his battalions stole away, their artillery wheels muffled, setting off on a back road towards Princeton and the unsuspecting British rearguard.

Nearing Princeton by daybreak, Washington divided his forces, sending one division to cut the bridge on the main road to Trenton. But they were spotted by a British column and a bloody clash ensued. After volleys were exchanged, and while the Americans were reloading, the disciplined redcoats launched a bayonet charge that killed one American general, Hugh Mercer, and threatened to send the entire rebel line into headlong flight. At this juncture, Washington rode onto the battlefield. Only 30 yards from the enemy and a prominent target, he exhorted his troops to hold their positions, setting an example of personal courage that quickly firmed up the crumbling battle line. Then he ordered a counter-attack that drove the enemy from the field. A witness to the effects of Washington's heroism later wrote: 'I shall never forget what I felt ... when I saw him brave all the dangers of the field and his important life hanging as it were by a single hair with a thousand deaths flying around him. Believe me, I thought not of myself.'

Now the American army entered the town of Princeton, defended by a British regiment which held the College of New Jersey's main building, Nassau Hall, a solid stone structure. Artillery was brought up to induce their surrender. Legend has it that the officer who ordered the shots fired that emptied the building was a young captain of artillery named Alexander Hamilton, who had been rejected for admission to the college only four years earlier.

The rebel troops quickly secured the town. It was still early in the day when outposts reported a large body of redcoats advancing up the road from Trenton. This was Cornwallis, in full knowledge and rage that he had been duped in the night. At this point, Washington, who had considered marching on to Brunswick to raid the British depot, found discretion to be the better part of valour and withdrew his forces from Princeton to the north-east, where they would head for winter quarters in the safety of Morristown.

Princeton was a splendid, timely victory that helped restore the faith of Americans in their army, their leader, and their cause. No one expressed the prevailing sentiment of the day better than one young participant who wrote to his wife after the battle, saying: 'O, my Susan! It was a glorious day, and I would not have been absent from it for all the money I ever expect to be worth.'

Other action this day

1833: The crew of the British brig-sloop HMS *Clio* debark at Puerto Luis and seize control of the Falkland Islands ✻ 1944: American Marine Corps fighter pilot and Medal of Honor winner Major 'Pappy' Boyington gets his 26th and last kill but is shot down over Rabaul and captured in an engagement of 30 American fighters against 70 Japanese ✻ 1946: British traitor and Nazi propagandist Lord Haw-Haw (William Joyce) is hanged

4 January

Caesar loses a battle

46 BC It was a rare occurrence for Julius Caesar, meeting defeat on the field of battle. But it happened today in Tunisia, just six days after he landed advance elements of his army on the shores of Africa. And the general whose forces inflicted the defeat was his former right-hand man in Gaul, the brilliant cavalry commander, Titus Labienus.

Three years earlier Caesar had brought his legion across the Rubicon (see 10 January), starting a Roman civil war against the moribund nobility that ruled the state. A year later he destroyed their leader, his one-time friend and son-in-law Pompey, at Pharsalus (see 9 August), and Pompey had been brutally assassinated in Egypt only a month after the battle. But, in spite of Caesar's power, there were still allies of Pompey who were committed to his destruction, among them Titus Labienus.

Labienus had known Caesar for almost twenty years. As a cavalry commander in Gaul, he had particularly distinguished himself during the battles of Sabis, Alesia, and the Sequana River. He was also second-in-command during Caesar's invasion of Britain.

In 51 BC, Caesar had made Labienus governor of Cisalpine Gaul but refused to back him for consul. Now Labienus, who saw himself as Caesar's military equal, became resentful of this lack of recognition. He also became renowned for his cruelty, especially his barbaric treatment of Gallic captives. His relationship with Caesar began to sour. By the time Caesar left Gaul, Labienus was his committed enemy, quickly joining forces with the old nobility led by Pompey. So strong was his hatred that he refused to consider a negotiated settlement, declaring: 'Nam nobis nisi Caesaris capite relato pax esse nulla potest.' ('Stop talking about an agreement; there can be no peace with us unless Caesar's head is brought back.')

After Pharsalus many of Pompey's old allies, including Labienus, rallied in North Africa. On 28 December Caesar followed them there, landing at Hadrumentum with the veteran legion V Alaudae and five other legions of raw recruits. As he stepped from his ship, he stumbled and fell on his face before his assembled troops. Aware that his men would take this as a direful omen, he spread his arms and kissed the ground, dramatically exclaiming: 'Africa, I hold you.' (See 27 September for William the Conqueror's use of the same gambit.)

Caesar then set up a fortified camp near the town of Ruspina (now Monastir in Tunisia). Short of provisions, on this day he set out with 30 cohorts (18,000 men) to forage, but about three miles from camp Labienus suddenly appeared, leading a large force of at least 16,000 Numidian infantry (native troops from the North African country of

Numidia) backed up by 1,600 Gauls and some 8,000 Numidian light cavalry.

Labienus planned a daring assault, interspersing his cavalry with javelin-armed skirmishers to form the front rank. His line was so closely packed that at a distance Caesar thought that only foot soldiers were attacking. He positioned his own troops with infantry in the middle and cavalry on both wings, but the vastly outnumbered Roman cavalry was unable to withstand the charge of the Numidian horse.

The Romans were surrounded, on the verge of breaking ranks, for whenever a cohort charged, Numidian javelin-throwers would catch it in the exposed flanks. But now Caesar formed his single line into two lines standing back-to-back. He then charged in both directions at once, driving off the enemy and pulling back to a nearby hill.

For a moment it looked like stalemate, but suddenly Numidian reinforcements arrived and immediately launched a new attack. Demoralised and exhausted, the Romans were soon fighting for their lives as they retreated towards their camp. Perhaps a third of their force was killed or wounded. But then a Roman javelin brought down Labienus's horse, knocking him from the saddle, slightly wounded. The surviving Romans now escaped back into Ruspina. The battle was over, and Caesar had been defeated.

Soon backed up by eight more legions and 3,000 extra cavalry, Labienus blockaded the Caesarians behind their fortifications; but by the end of the month Caesar was also reinforced by fresh troops from Sicily and turned from defender to attacker. A month after his defeat at Ruspina, he crushed the conservative faction at Thapsus, although once again Labienus lived to fight another day.

By the following year hostilities had moved from North Africa to southern Spain. There at Munda on 17 March, Caesar met the army of Pompey's son Sextus Pompey, whose cavalry was led by Labienus. When the Pompeian left wing was nearly outflanked by Caesar's Moorish cavalry, Labienus moved his men from the front lines to meet the threat, but Pompey's infantry thought he was fleeing the field and broke in panic, to be cut down in thousands by the Caesarian forces. It was the last battle of the Roman civil war. Labienus was killed on the field and buried there, although his severed head was brought to Caesar as proof of his death.

Other action this day

AD 871: King Ethelred of Wessex and his younger brother Alfred (the Great) are defeated with heavy losses by a Danish army at the Battle of Reading * 1913: German field marshal and strategist Count Alfred von Schlieffen dies at 79 * 1951: During the Korean War, North Korean and Communist Chinese forces capture Seoul

5 January

Charles the Bold perishes on the snowy fields at Nancy

1477 Perhaps because he challenged the French, in English we call him Charles the Bold. But the French have always called him Charles le Téméraire, more properly translated as Charles the Rash. The French were closer to the mark.

Charles was a strange and moody man, with dark brown hair cut pageboy style and expressive eyes that could be soft or gay or with 'une dureté métallique' (a metallic hardness). Intelligent and hard-working, he spoke French, Dutch, English, Latin and Italian. He was also a fine musician who both composed and played the harp and may have invented counterpoint. A thoughtful man, he felt keenly the sadness and transience of life. According to his contemporary Lorenzo the Magnificent, he had 'un animo inquieto' (a troubled spirit). But most of all he was ambitious. It was a family tradition.

Just 115 years earlier, Charles's great-grandfather, Duke Philip the Bold, had made Burgundy virtually independent, with only spasmodic and fiercely resisted control from France. During the intervening years the duchy had been ruled by the same talented, determined and ruthless family, father to son: Jean sans Peur, Philip the Good and now Charles. But Charles was even more ambitious than his forefathers, for he dreamed of resurrecting the ancient kingdom of Lotharingia, one of the three parts of Charlemagne's empire. The greatest obstacle in his path was his wily enemy, King Louis XI of France. Although King Louis could hardly match Charles on the battlefield, he was so adroit at political manoeuvring that he was known as the Universal Spider for the deceitful webs he wove. After years of inconclusive (if sometimes bloody) sparring with

Charles, Louis concluded a treaty with Charles's English brother-in-law and erstwhile ally, Edward IV. Then in August 1471 he signed another with René of Lorraine, who hired scores of feared Swiss pikemen to bolster his forces.

In 1476 René and his Swiss auxiliaries defeated Charles first at Grandson (see 2 March) and then at Morat, where Charles lost about a third of his army. Then René occupied Nancy. Despite the onset of winter, Charles was determined to recapture the city.

On Sunday, 5 January of the following year, Charles's army of about 6,000 men was camped outside Nancy, huddling against the driving snow, when René arrived leading a force of 10,000 Lorrainers plus 10,000 Swiss mercenaries. Charles must have known he stood little chance, obliged to fight a far larger army in the bitter cold of winter. But somehow his moody sense of destiny and his famed obstinacy prevented him from retreat.

René could see that a frontal assault against Charles's entrenched position could prove too costly and sent 2,000 Swiss cavalry and 7,000 infantry around the left flank, hidden by snow-covered trees. After two hours of slogging, the Swiss charged from the woods to the rear of Charles's Burgundians, blowing their alpine horns. Stunned by surprise and overwhelmed by superior numbers, the Burgundian line buckled and Charles's troops began to flee in panic.

For two days no one knew what had become of the great duke. But then a captured Burgundian page was led to the barren and frozen battlefield, where he identified Charles's naked body lying near the pond of St Jean. Charles's face had been opened from ear to jaw by the blow of an axe and his body was pierced by two lance thrusts. Wolves had gnawed the bloody remains.

And so died the Burgundian dream of power and with it the 43-year-old ruler, Charles by the Grace of God Duke of Burgundy, Lorraine and Brabant, of Limbourg and Luxembourg, Count of Flanders, Artois and Burgundy, Palatine of Hainault, Holland, Zealand and Namur, Margrave of the Holy Roman Empire, Lord of Frisia, Salins and Malines.

Other action this day

1066: King Edward the Confessor dies, triggering the struggle for the throne of England that ends in the Norman Conquest * 1781: British troops led by American turncoat Benedict Arnold burn Richmond,

Virginia * 1858: Austrian field marshal Johann Josef Wenzel Graf Radetzky von Radetz, for whom Johann Strauss Sr's 'Radetzky March' is named, dies at 91

6 January

Retreat from Kabul

1842 Today, in the bitter cold of an Afghan winter, a British and Indian garrison of 16,500 soldiers and civilians marched out through the gates of Kabul to begin the terrible journey to the Khyber Pass and on to India. The first stage was to be a 90-mile trek through snow-covered passes to the British base at Jalalabad.

Concerned that Russia's southward progress into Afghanistan could eventually threaten their control in India, the British government had propped up a puppet ruler in Afghanistan, only to provoke the local Ghilzai tribesmen into violent revolt. (The Ghilzai were and are one of the largest groups of Pashtuns, the same Islamic fundamentalists who spawned the Taliban a century and a half later.)

The first crisis had come in October 1841 when tribesmen ambushed an Anglo-Indian brigade en route to Peshawar. The brigade finally fought its way through to Jalalabad after sustaining heavy losses.

The next month an Afghan mob butchered a British official and several of his staff in Kabul itself, and in December a British officer was lured to a meeting with Afghan *ameers* (chieftains) and murdered. Commanded by an elderly, indecisive and mildly crippled major general named William Elphinstone, the British hunkered down in their cantonments, afraid to act.

Finally realising their peril, the British gained a promise of safe conduct from the ameers for the hike from Kabul to Jalalabad. Leading the march were 400 soldiers of the 44th Regiment of Foot, about 100 cavalrymen, 3,800 Indian sepoys, 200 British wives and children, and some 12,000 assorted servants, cooks, grooms, blacksmiths, water-carriers, sepoy family members and other camp followers. The soldiers were armed with muskets and their officers with pistols and swords, but the ameers had insisted that they leave all heavy guns behind in Kabul, except for one horse artillery battery and three mountain guns. In spite of the ameers' promise to let the army go unmolested, Ghilzai assaults started almost the moment the group had left the gates of Kabul. It is estimated that some 30,000 tribesmen armed with swords and *jezail* (long-barrelled muskets) were ranged against the desperate column during the eight-day march.

Despite frequent attacks, on the first day the long train of refugees managed six miles through two-foot snowdrifts, but many died of hypothermia that night, sleeping in the open without tents.

As the retreat continued, the ameer of Kabul arrived, demanding hostages and money but offering safe passage – a promise broken almost instantly. On the third day the column trudged through the narrow, five-mile-long Khoord Cabul pass as Ghilzai fired on them from the surrounding heights. Although the British 44th formed a rearguard, some 3,000 bodies were left in the snowy gorge.

On the fifth day the ameer of Kabul took General Elphinstone as hostage – he was to die in captivity three months later. At Jugdulluk the Ghilzai blocked the trail with a thorn barricade manned by riflemen. The 44th finally cleared the obstruction with their horse artillery, but thousands more perished in the attempt. Now, as the battered survivors pushed onward, tribesmen looted abandoned baggage carts and slaughtered stragglers, whose bodies were stripped and mutilated.

By the eighth day virtually the entire force – soldiers and civilians alike – had been massacred, leaving only twenty officers and about 50 British soldiers, with just twelve working muskets among them. When they reached a hill near Gandamak, the Afghans surrounded them and tried to persuade them to surrender, but a British sergeant yelled out: 'Not bloody likely!' The tribesmen then attacked in a series of charges, overwhelming the pitiful remains of the garrison. One British officer prepared for death by wrapping himself in the regimental colours but was instead taken prisoner, as the Ghilzai thought he must be an important official. Six other officers galloped off on the remaining horses, but five were cut down on the road.

That afternoon the British troops in Jalalabad were anxiously watching for the Kabul garrison when a solitary figure rode up to the town gate. He was the sixth horseman, Dr William Brydon, an assistant surgeon in the British East India Company. Wounded by a sword thrust to the back of his head, he had survived only because, due to the severe cold, he had stuffed a magazine into his hat, cushioning the blow. The Afghans had let him live because they wanted him to warn the British government to abandon Afghanistan.

For three days after Brydon had staggered into Jalalabad the British garrison there sounded the bugle once an hour in the hope of guiding further survivors into the city, but no one came – he alone had been spared of almost 17,000 who had marched from Kabul.

When you're wounded and left on Afghanistan's plains,
And the women come out to cut up what remains,
Jest roll to your rifle and blow out your brains,
An' go to your Gawd like a soldier.

Rudyard Kipling

Other action this day

1412: Mystical military leader Joan of Arc is born in Domrémy ∗ 1919: President, Colonel of the Rough Riders and Medal of Honor winner Theodore Roosevelt dies

7 January

Wasted hope and sure defeat

1942 The defence of the Philippines took a new turn today as American and Filipino forces contesting the Japanese invasion of Luzon island were gathered to form a last-ditch defensive line on the Bataan peninsula. For their commander, General Douglas MacArthur, it was the only course left open.

MacArthur's command included the Philippine army, some 100,000-strong, much of it barely trained and inadequately armed. In addition, he had around 13,000 American regular military personnel: soldiers, Marines and an assortment of what one historian described as 'aviators without planes, coast artillerymen without guns, cooks without stoves'. Lacking any air or naval support for its efforts on the ground, this force proved unable to contain the advance of the invaders, who had landed in Lingayen Gulf just sixteen days earlier with two reinforced divisions of the Japanese 14th Army, totalling nearly 50,000 veteran troops.

A Marine officer on the scene described the attempt to stem the Japanese advance. 'The Filipino Scouts held them off for the first eleven days and eleven nights after the Lingayen invasion. It was continuous attacking, retreating to new positions, stopping long enough to slaughter a few hundred more, then being driven back by the sheer force of overwhelming numbers. There weren't enough guns to stop them.'

So MacArthur declared Manila an open city and drew his forces behind a defensive line at the head of the Bataan peninsula, stretching across twenty miles of rugged jungle terrain from the South China Sea to Manila Bay. From the beginning, the defenders of Bataan, known as Luzon Force, were critically low on supplies, ammunition and medicine, a situation greatly aggravated by the presence within their lines of thousands of Filipino civilians fleeing the invaders.

Despite MacArthur's brave (and often misleading) words about the condition of his command, conveyed in frequent radio broadcasts to the outside world from his headquarters on the island of Corregidor, the ultimate outcome was never in doubt, only the timing. The Japanese had expected to take the Philippines within 50 days; even as the defensive line at Bataan was formed against them, they released troops for service in Java. But the resistance of Luzon Force was so fierce that on 8 February General Homma, with losses of 7,000 troops, was forced to suspend the initial Japanese offensive and bring in reinforcements. But the siege continued, and the attacks were renewed, slowly pushing the defenders southward towards the tip of the peninsula. Now they were surviving on less than 1,000 calories a day.

Meanwhile, on 12 March, under President Roosevelt's personal orders, General MacArthur left Corregidor to make his way through enemy-held waters to Australia, where he would become overall ground commander of the Allied effort against Japan. His deputy, General Wainwright, took command in the Philippines and General King took over Luzon Force on the peninsula.

In early April, aided by heavy air and artillery bombardment, the Japanese broke through the line on Bataan. On 9 April 1942, 108 days from the start of the invasion, General King surrendered his battered command to the Japanese, the biggest surrender of American troops since General Lee handed over the Army of Northern Virginia at Appomattox, exactly 77 years earlier.

Corregidor itself, the 'concrete battleship' off the tip of the peninsula, would fall on 6 May, thus adding the Philippines to the long list of Japanese war trophies that already included Guam, Wake Island, Rabaul, Hong Kong, Malaya, and Singapore.

As soon as the surrender document was signed, Japanese soldiers began herding their captives into long columns for the march to prison camps. On this 65-mile journey, known ever after as the Bataan Death March, an estimated 750 Americans and 5,000 Filipinos died of starvation, exhaustion, disease, mistreatment or execution. About their long and gruelling experience on Bataan, an American lieutenant, Harry G. Lee, wrote these lines:

Saved for another day
Saved for hunger and wounds and retreat
For slow exhaustion and grim retreat
For a wasted hope and sure defeat.

Other action this day

1558: The French recapture Calais after 211 years of English rule, the last English possession in mainland France * 1949: After eight months of fighting, Arab forces ask for a truce, bringing Israel's War of Independence to a close * 1979: Vietnamese troops capture Phnom Penh, driving out the Khmer Rouge and their leader Pol Pot during the Cambodian–Vietnamese War

8 January

Andrew Jackson wins a peacetime battle

1815 Today the United States badly mauled their British enemies at the Battle of New Orleans – even though, unbeknown to the combatants, peace had been signed in December of the previous year.

The War of 1812 was the result of what Americans considered unjust and intolerable British conduct at sea during Britain's titanic struggle with Napoleon. Although France had finally agreed not to interfere with American shipping, the British, with the world's most powerful navy, had blockaded all French ports, making it difficult or impossible for Americans to trade. Worse, under the pretence that many American seamen were really disguised British deserters, the Royal Navy blithely stopped American ships and pressed their crews into service. In June 1812 American President James Madison declared war.

The war was a desultory affair, enlivened principally by the British burning of Washington. Weary of fighting, the two adversaries formally ended the conflict by the Treaty of Ghent signed on 24 December 1814, but communications at the time were so slow that two weeks later the two armies facing each other at New Orleans thought they were still at war.

Commanding the British was Major General Sir Edward Pakenham, the brother-in-law of the Duke of Wellington. He anticipated no trouble in taking New Orleans, as his forces outnumbered those of defender Andrew Jackson by three to one. Hoping he could frighten the Americans into submission, under flag of truce he sent in a letter threatening: 'If you do not surrender, I shall destroy your breastworks and eat breakfast in New Orleans Sunday morning.' Enraged rather than intimidated, Jackson replied: 'If you do, you will eat supper in hell Sunday night.'

The British promptly attacked, but Jackson's men were sheltered behind bales of cotton. His Tennessee and Kentucky riflemen cut down whole ranks of the advancing enemy, while his pirate-trained cannoneers devastated the enemy with grapeshot, killing 2,000, including General Pakenham. The Americans suffered just seven killed and six wounded. The entire battle lasted only 30 minutes.

This was the last serious fighting in the War of 1812. From his victory at New Orleans, Andrew Jackson became a hero who, despite having won a battle during 'peacetime', used the fame he earned there to launch a political career that culminated in the presidency fourteen years later.

Other action this day

AD 871: Ethelred, King of Wessex, and his brother Alfred (the future King Alfred the Great) defeat the Danes at the Battle of Ashdown * 1297: Disguised as a monk, François Grimaldi enters Monaco by subterfuge, opens the gates to his troops and conquers the territory, which his family still rules today * 1877: The US Army narrowly defeats Crazy Horse's band of 500 Indian braves at the Battle of Wolf Mountain, Crazy Horse's last battle

9 January

The British abandon Gallipoli

1916 At 3.45 this morning, with a half-gale blowing, boats shoved off from W Beach at Cape Helles carrying the last 200 British soldiers from the Gallipoli peninsula, south-west of Constantinople. Ten minutes later the ammunition dumps on shore erupted in a savage roar, bringing to a noisy and unhappy conclusion the greatest amphibious operation the world had ever seen. It could have been a forerunner of D-Day; instead it was the herald of Dunkirk (see 4 June).

In early 1915 Gallipoli had held great strategic promise: by seizing the peninsula and sending a naval force through the fortified Dardanelles straits into the Black Sea, Britain and France could have knocked Germany's war partner Turkey out of the war, opened up a critical supply line to their ally Russia, and moved up the Danube against Austria. Success might have shortened the First World War by three years.

But in ten months of struggle and at the cost of some quarter of a million casualties – British, French, Australian and New Zealand – the Allies came very close but ultimately failed either to get their warships though the straits or to advance their army up the well-defended peninsula. It was not an operation for the faint-hearted, the inconstant or the unimaginative, all of which types were well represented in the highest levels of British civilian and military leadership. Gallipoli needed a Nelson or a Lee or a Rommel.

In Parliament the setbacks at Gallipoli threatened to bring down the government. Needing a scapegoat for the failure, the Cabinet found one in Winston Churchill, a staunch supporter of the operation. He lost his job as First Lord of the Admiralty. Later, the army commander was sacked. There were calls for reinforcements and a renewal of attacks, but by now there was a shortage of artillery shells, and troops were sent to other fronts. By October the government had decided on evacuation.

The next year a parliamentary commission investigating the failure cleared Churchill of mismanagement for his part in the operation. He took the occasion to deliver this judgement, which time has proved the right one: 'The ill-supported armies struggling on the Gallipoli peninsula, whose efforts are now viewed with so much prejudice and repugnance, were in fact within an ace of succeeding in an enterprise which would have abridged the miseries of the World ... It will then seem incredible that a dozen old ships, half a dozen divisions, or a few hundred thousand shells were allowed to stand between them and success. Contemporaries have condemned the men who tried to force the Dardanelles. History will condemn those who did not aid them.'

Other action this day

1799: British prime minister William Pitt the Younger introduces the first income tax, at two shillings in the pound, to raise funds for the Napoleonic Wars * 1806: With a funeral procession of 32 admirals, over 100 captains and 10,000 troops, Admiral Horatio Nelson is buried in St Paul's cathedral * 1905: In St Petersburg the Russian Revolution of 1905 is triggered by troops firing on petitioners to Tsar Nicholas I * 1945: Under General Douglas MacArthur's command, 68,000 men from General Walter Krueger's 6th Army land on Lingayen Gulf, 110 miles north of Manila

10 January

Caesar crosses the Rubicon

49 BC Today Julius Caesar led one of his legions across a small stream called the Rubicon, thus defying the Roman Senate and breaking the Lex Cornelia Majestatis that forbade a general from bringing an army out of the province to which he was assigned. Turning to his lieutenants just before he crossed, Caesar remarked bitterly: 'Iacta alea est.' (The die is cast.) It was a de facto declaration of war against the Roman Republic.

The Rubicon is a narrow river south of Ravenna that marked the border between the Republic and its province of Cisalpine Gaul, now northern Italy. For the past nine years Caesar had been governor there and also of Transalpine Gaul, most of today's France and Belgium. There he had waged ferocious war on the primitive local tribes, subduing them in the name of Rome. It was said that he had conquered 800 towns while defeating enemy armies totalling

3 million men, of whom a third were killed and another third sold into slavery.

But now the Roman Senate, jealous of Caesar's success and fearful of his ambitions, were determined to bring him to heel. They demanded that he give up command of his legions and report back to Rome as an ordinary citizen. Caesar knew that, despite his enormous achievements, a small clique of senators were not willing to concede to him the honours he thought he deserved, even wanted to destroy him. He believed, almost certainly correctly, that, once he had relinquished his power, his enemies would trump up charges against him and then ruin or even execute him.

Some credit Caesar with loftier motives – the urgent need to rehabilitate the creaking Roman state that was badly misgoverned by a fractious and self-serving nobility. Most agree that he had no desire to start a war, let alone create a dictatorship, but his *amour propre* demanded that the ungrateful senators recognise his achievements and reward him as they had so many other great generals in the past.

When Caesar crossed the Rubicon, the die really was cast. Not only did his action initiate a three-year civil war, but it also led to the end of the Republic and the age of Roman emperors. Many historians consider it the most extraordinary achievement in human history. One man, armed only with a few legions, his own military genius and what Pliny the Elder called 'the fiery quickness of his mind', took over the largest and most advanced empire the world had known.

Other action this day

1738: American revolutionary and guerrilla leader Ethan Allen is born in Litchfield, Connecticut ∗ 1769: Napoleonic marshal Michel Ney is born in Sarre-Louis (now Saarlouis in Germany but then controlled by France) ∗ 1941: President Franklin Roosevelt proposes the Lend-Lease programme, which gives the President the power to 'sell, transfer title to, exchange, lease, lend, or otherwise dispose of' any military resources he deems in the ultimate interest of the defence of the United States

11 January

An unexpectedly rough outing in Zululand

1879 Reveille blew well before first light this morning at Rorke's Drift. By 6.00am troops were crossing the Buffalo River from Natal into Zululand, mounted units splashing across first, followed by British infantry in punts and native infantry wading through the chest-high water, arms linked against the force of the current. By day's end, with the entire column across – 4,500 soldiers, 300 wagons, 1,600 transport animals – and a base camp established, the Zulu War had begun.

The column, accompanied by the overall invasion commander, Lord Chelmsford, was one of three widely separated British forces entering Zululand that day. Their common objective was Ulundi, the royal *kraal* of the Zulu king Cetshwayo, some 70 miles away. The war took barely six months from start to finish – Ulundi was captured and burned to the ground on 4 July in the last big battle – and resulted in the complete destruction of the Zulus (both as a fighting force and as a nation) and the incorporation of their lands into the British empire.

The war was not especially memorable for its ultimate success for the British. But if the outcome seemed pre-ordained in a conflict that pitted the Martini-Henry rifle against the *assegai* spear, there occurred in the course of the campaign a setback for the British so severe and spectacular that for a while the entire enterprise was cast in doubt. It was perhaps the greatest defeat of a British army in the entire Victorian era.

The setback occurred in the shadow of Isandlwana, a huge rock outcrop dominating the landscape, some ten miles by winding road from the border crossing at Rorke's Drift. On 22 January a force of 1,700 British soldiers and native auxiliaries was engulfed and destroyed by 20,000 Zulus attacking in their classic formation, the 'horns of the beast', in which the 'chest' attacks the centre while the two 'horns' sweep around the sides, often hidden by terrain, to encircle the enemy, and the 'loins' stand in reserve to join the attack where needed. The Zulus struck just before noon. The fighting was over by 2.30pm, leaving 1,300 British dead and the rest fleeing to

Rorke's Drift, where a heroic defence took place against further Zulu attacks.

The Zulus attacked all three invading columns that day. Their success against the centre column at Isandlwana left the flanking columns unsupported – the southernmost falling under siege for three months. The invasion came to a sudden halt, leaving the Natal border virtually undefended and vulnerable to counter-attack. But against British rifle fire, the Zulus had suffered heavy losses in all three attacks – 2,000 alone slain at Isandlwana – and were not ready to seize the opportunity to carry the war into enemy territory. Back in Natal, Lord Chelmsford asked London for reinforcements, and with British prestige on the line, the government of Benjamin Disraeli gave Chelmsford everything he asked for and a good deal more.

In late March, with some 23,000 British and native troops in the field, Chelmsford began a second invasion against a weakened enemy. Reaching Ulundi, British battalions went into a classic formation of their own, forming a huge hollow square, with artillery pieces at the corners that fought off repeated attacks and destroyed what was left of the Zulu army. The second invasion was a success, marred only by the death in Zululand of a highly popular figure in England, 22-year-old Louis Napoleon, Prince Imperial of France, son of the former French emperor Napoleon III. Serving with the British army in a voluntary and unofficial capacity, he was killed on 1 June by Zulus ambushing a patrol. His death, one historian reported, 'horrified the population of England as Isandlwana had never done'.

The price of empire was high. In six months of war, an estimated 8,000 Zulus were killed in battle, with perhaps twice that many wounded. The British lost some 2,100 European and native troops. They captured the Zulu king Cetshwayo and sent him into exile near Cape Town for four years, while his country, with its traditional structure broken up into thirteen separate kingdoms under a British Resident, fell into decades of turmoil.

Other action this day

1863: Union general John McClernand's army of 32,000 men, supported by the Navy, attacks and captures Arkansas Post, taking 4,791 Confederate prisoners * 1867: Benito Juarez returns to the Mexican presidency, following the withdrawal of French troops and the execution of Emperor Maximilian * 1942: Japanese troops capture Kuala Lumpur in Malaya

12 January

Leningrad under siege

1943 For 500 days, since late August 1941, Leningrad had lain in the ever-tightening embrace of Hitler's Wehrmacht. The city once known as St Petersburg, the Imperial capital of the Russian tsars, was now starving, under constant bombardment, and its population reduced by death and evacuation to one quarter of its pre-war number. Every attempt to lift the German siege had failed.

But at 9.30 this morning an intense Soviet artillery barrage marked the beginning of Operation Iskra, the 'spark.' Just before noon, as the artillery fire subsided, two divisions charged across the frozen Neva River, meeting fierce resistance and counter-attacks from the Germans, but continuing to advance.

Over the next six days, units of the Soviet 67th Army moved out of Leningrad, heading eastward towards Lake Ladoga, while troops of the 2nd Shock Army moved westward from Volkhov in the Soviet 'mainland'. Their aim was to join forces in an attack on a key anchor of the German siege lines, the fortress city of Shlisselburg. Marshal Zhukov, hero of the fighting at Stalingrad and Moscow, was sent in to coordinate the movements of the two armies.

The German garrison at Shlisselburg was under orders to hold its position to the last man, but the position fell on the 18th. That evening, residents of Leningrad listening to their radios in anticipation of the news heard this from a Moscow announcer: 'Troops of the Leningrad and Volkhov fronts have joined together and at the same time broken the blockade of Leningrad.' The bulletin overstated the operation's actual achievement, but Iskra had 'sparked' hope.

Back in August 1941, Operation Barbarossa, the German invasion of Soviet Russia, had brought General von Leeb's Army Group North to the gates of Leningrad, whose industrial strength, geographical location, and historical significance ('the birthplace of bolshevism', Hitler observed) made it a prime target. For Leningraders there was no avenue of escape north, for strong Finnish positions blocked the Karelian isthmus.

Initially, the German plan had been to take the city by storm, but strong Soviet counter-offensives and difficult terrain stalled the drive with heavy losses. Then, as Moscow became the main focus of the invasion campaign, Leningrad was designated a 'subsidiary theatre of operation' whose fate was to be 'hermetically sealed', then starved into submission and finally, after capture, levelled to the ground. The first of these objectives had been accomplished by the end of 1941; now the second was getting close. Observing from the siege lines in 1942, Field Marshal Erich von Manstein wrote: 'To anyone reconnoitring along the front south of Leningrad, the city seemed to be within clutching distance …'

With all land routes cut off and the Luftwaffe controlling the skies, the only way to get rations, fuel and military supplies to the residents and defenders of the beleaguered city was across Lake Ladoga, which for much of the year meant by a railway built over some 30 miles of frozen lake. In time, Leningraders were forced to eat bread made out of cellulose, sawdust, and flour sweepings.

What Operation Iskra achieved by taking Shlisselburg was to open a narrow land route to Leningrad that hugged the coast of Lake Ladoga, at points only 500 yards from German artillery positions. The roadway soon won the name 'corridor of death'. But it worked, and slowly the meagre flow of supplies into the city increased, slightly lessening the rate of death by starvation, one cynic noted.

At almost the same moment that Iskra won its success came even greater news: the Soviet victory at Stalingrad. Now, truly, there was hope. Through the rest of 1943, the city hung on, even as the German shelling increased in punishment for Iskra. But in mid-January of 1944, a new and larger Soviet offensive forced the Germans to withdraw from their close positions around Leningrad. The *New York Times* correspondent Harrison Salisbury described the scene on 27 January:

> … at 8 P.M., over the sword point of the Admiralty, over the great dome of St Isaac's, over the broad expanse of Palace Square, over the broken buildings of Pulkovo, the dilapidated machine shops of the Kirov works, the battered battleships standing in the Neva, roared a shower of golden arrows, a flaming stream of red, white and blue rockets. It was a salute from 324 cannon marking the liberation of Leningrad, the end of the blockade. … After 880 days the siege of Leningrad, the longest ever endured by a modern city, had come to an end.

1519: In Acle on the coast of Panama, Spanish conquistador Vasco Núñez de Balboa is beheaded on orders of his own father-in-law on trumped-up charges of trying to usurp power * 1583: Philip II's ferocious general, Fernando Alvarez de Toledo, 3rd Duke of Alva, dies in Lisbon after having conquered Portugal * 1962: American planes start Operation Ranch Hand in Vietnam, spraying the countryside with defoliants to deprive the Viet Cong of vegetation, cover and food

13 January

The death of Gaius Marius, the general who saved Rome from the barbarians

86 BC Today the Roman general Gaius Marius died of a stroke in his 70th year, just three months after he had been elected consul for the seventh time. His death came none too soon, because he had suffered some sort of mental collapse and was hardly sane during his final months, unleashing a reign of terror against any he felt had opposed him. Surrounded by a guard of slaves, he walked through Rome ordering instant executions.

Yet Marius had been one of Rome's very greatest generals. He had saved his country from almost certain invasion and changed the very nature of the Roman army.

Marius had been born a *novus homo* or new man, someone without senatorial forebears, in Arpinum, a provincial town 60 miles south-east of Rome. According to Plutarch, when he was a young boy Marius caught an eagle's nest falling from a tree. In it he found seven eaglets that he brought home to his parents, who consulted the augurs to find the meaning of this omen. The augurs foretold that Marius 'should become the greatest man in the world, and that the fates had decreed he should seven times be possessed of the supreme power and authority'.

As a soldier, Marius became both respected and rich through his victories in Spain and North Africa, where – a rarity for Roman generals – he personally led cavalry charges. When he was about 45 he married into the patrician Julii Caesar family. His wife Julia was Julius Caesar's aunt. Three years later he was elected consul for the first time, an enormous honour for a *novus homo*. He was subsequently elected six more times, fulfilling the augurs' prophecy.

During Marius's first consulship in 107 BC, Rome found itself threatened by the Cimbri and Teutones, two fierce tribes that had descended from Germany en masse with 300,000 fighting men plus an even greater number of women and children, determined to conquer Italy. After the tribes had destroyed two Roman armies near Lake Geneva, Marius led his army against them at Aquae Sextiae (now Aix-en-Provence) and Vercellae (between Turin and Milan – see 30 July). He utterly routed the invaders, killing tens of thousands and selling the prisoners and their families into slavery, saving the Roman Republic.

Marius vastly improved the fighting ability of the army. He made the cohort of 600 men the standard unit, and equipped each legionary with the same armament, a *pilum* (a sort of javelin) and a sword. He trained his men ferociously, using techniques from gladiatorial schools, and had them carry their own supplies and shovels, thus eliminating slow-moving baggage trains. From this his soldiers earned the proud sobriquet 'Marius's mules'.

Even more important in the longer term was Marius's change in the way new soldiers were recruited. Previously only Romans who owned land could join, but Marius dropped all property qualifications and instead offered land as reward for faithful soldiers. The result was an influx of poorer citizens who stayed in service even after battle, thus for the first time creating something like a professional standing army. It was Marius who gave each legion a standard in the form of an eagle. Critically, the legions' first loyalty now was to their commander, who alone could reward them, rather than to the Roman state, a change exploited to the full first by Sulla and then by Pompey and ultimately by Julius Caesar.

Although a military genius, Marius was a clumsy politician who made enemies both in the Senate and among rival commanders, especially his one-time subordinate Sulla. Consequently, at one point he had to flee for his life, but was captured and imprisoned in a dark cell. Then a Gallic soldier was ordered in to decapitate him. According to Plutarch: 'The room itself was not very light, that part of it especially where he then lay was dark, from whence Marius's eyes, they say, seemed to [the soldier] to dart out flames at him, and a loud voice to say, out of the dark, "Fellow, darest thou kill Gaius

Marius?" The barbarian hereupon immediately fled, and leaving his sword in the place, rushed out of doors, crying only this, "I cannot kill Gaius Marius."'

Marius escaped and eventually returned to Rome, where, elected consul for the final time, he wreaked havoc among his enemies. By now he was clearly becoming unhinged, drinking heavily, suffering hallucinations and running 'into an extravagant frenzy fancying himself to be a general at war … throwing himself into such postures and motions of his body as he had formerly used when he was in battle, with frequent shouts and loud cries'. Despondent and afraid, he fell ill and died seven days later.

Other action this day

1630: Ming general Yuan Chonghuan, condemned on false charges of treason, is executed by the 'death of a thousand cuts' * 1898: Emile Zola publishes '*J'accuse*' in *L'Aurore*, accusing the French government of a cover-up of the Dreyfus trial, in which Alfred Dreyfus, the only Jew on the army's general staff, had been convicted as a German spy and sentenced to life on Devil's Island * 1942: A German test pilot uses an ejection seat in a Heinkel He 280 fighter, the first use of such a seat

14 January

Murder triggers the Albigensian Crusade

1208 Of all the cruel and senseless persecutions inflicted in the name of religion, few have been as ferocious as the medieval church's crusade against the Cathars in south-west France. It was triggered today by the murder of the Pope's representative.

The word 'Cathar' comes from the Greek *katharos* (pure), which is what believers attempted to be. Cathars thought that the material world was evil and man's task was to free himself from it. The most devout renounced life's pleasures, including meat and sex, in an attempt to find communion with God.

The church in Rome could hardly find fault with such asceticism, but other Cathar doctrines were anathema. Cathars refused to accept the divinity of Christ, and, worse, sternly criticised the church for its nepotism, greed and corruption. Perhaps the most terrible crime of all was the Cathars' refusal to contribute financial support to Rome.

The Cathar cult was particularly strong around Toulouse and Albi (hence the name of the crusade, the Albigensian), and Count Raymond of Toulouse was such a defender of the Cathars that an investigating papal legate, Pierre de Castelnau, was sent to threaten him with excommunication for his failure to suppress the heresy. The Count quietly submitted and swore his allegiance, so, his mission accomplished, Castelnau began his journey back to Rome. But when he reached the River Rhône, a knight in the Count's service, but perhaps not on his orders, stabbed the legate to death with a hunting spear. It was a deed with terrible consequences.

Incandescent with rage when he heard the news, Pope Innocent III immediately launched the Albigensian Crusade, offering participants full absolution for all sins if they served for 40 days exterminating the heresy.

A minor French noble, Simon de Montfort, was given the task of leading the campaign, spiritually supported by another papal legate, the fanatical Arnald-Amaury, who believed in massacre in the service of God. Together they gathered an army and ravaged southern France, slaughtering and pillaging indiscriminately.

Unlike most of the crusades to the Holy Land (one of which was also launched by Pope Innocent), the Albigensian Crusade eventually succeeded in its aims by besieging and destroying city after city in southern France, among them Carcassonne, Albi, Toulouse, Mont Ségur and finally, in 1255, the very last Cathar stronghold, the Castle of Quéribus. With some poetic justice, Montfort himself was killed by a boulder thrown from a *trebuchet* mounted on the ramparts of Toulouse. The few surviving Cathars fled where they could – Spain, Lombardy, England and Germany – or went underground. Three centuries later, the Midi, particularly the area around Toulouse, proved fertile territory for the Protestant Reformation.

The church's experience with the Cathars had wider repercussions. Innocent died in 1216, but his nephew gained the papal throne as Gregory IX. Fully aware of the dangers of heresy, in 1231 the new Pope launched the Inquisition, which lasted in one form or another until 1908.

Other action this day

1797: Napoleon Bonaparte defeats Joseph Alvintzi's Austrian army at Rivoli, just west of Turin * 1890: British field marshal Robert Napier, who fought in both Anglo-Sikh wars and against the Baris in Pakistan, was wounded at the siege of Lucknow during the Indian Mutiny, and saw combat in the Second Opium War and in Abyssinia in defeating Emperor Tewodros, dies in London at 79 * 1943: Franklin Roosevelt and Winston Churchill meet in Casablanca to discuss their war strategy

15 January

Ibn Saud's daring raid captures Riyadh

1902 Today a 22-year-old Arab prince led a daring raid on an enemy tribe that changed the Arab world – and ultimately changed our own.

Abdul Aziz Ibn Saud was the son of the Sultan of Nejd, a central Arabian state whose capital was Riyadh. The al-Saud family had dominated the peninsula since about 1750 and considered itself the standard-bearer of the Wahhabi Islamic sect. But in 1891 the Rashidi, a rival Arab dynasty, had conquered Riyadh and driven the leading members of al-Saud into penniless exile in Kuwait. Now, after ten long years of waiting, Ibn Saud set out to reconquer his family's lands.

Near the end of 1901, Ibn Saud gathered about 50 of his tribe's warriors and rode south along the Persian Gulf towards Riyadh, living off the country and surviving by *ghazu* (an Arab foray in which one tribe raids another for food and booty). By the time he had arrived near Riyadh, then a town of only 10,000, his band had grown to over 100 camel-men, but the Rashidi learned of his presence and withdrew into strong defensive positions in Riyadh's fortress of Mismak. Ibn Saud had neither the men nor the siege weapons for a direct attack.

Stymied, the prince and his warriors disappeared into the Empty Quarter south-east of Riyadh, where they waited in the desert for 50 days, lulling the Rashidi into dropping their guard.

In January 1902 Ibn Saud and about 40 of his men began a stealthy return to Riyadh, travelling only by night. On the last day of

Ramadan, 14 January, they arrived on a plateau overlooking the town. That night Ibn Saud chose his fifteen fiercest fighters. Under cover of darkness, they approached the town and used the trunk of a palm tree to scale the walls.

Slipping through the sleeping streets, they came upon a local Arab loyal to the Saudis. Riyadh's governor, he told them, was spending the night at the Mismak fort rather than at his mansion across the square.

Silently the small band made their way to the governor's mansion, where they found two women, one of them the governor's wife. Quickly they bound and gagged the women and settled down to wait.

At dawn the governor left the fort and headed toward his mansion. Ibn Saud and his men charged out across the square, but the governor turned and ran *back* to the fort. The attackers caught up with him just as he reached the fort's gate and reached out to seize him, but the governor's guards caught his arms and tried to pull him inside. As both sides grappled for their prize, Ibn Saud's cousin struck through the swirl of arms and legs and stabbed him to death. Now leaderless, the fort's garrison quickly surrendered. Riyadh was once again in Saudi hands.

News of Ibn Saud's triumph quickly spread, and former supporters now flocked to his banner. In 1906 he decisively defeated the Rashidi at Rawdat Muhanna, and over the next quarter-century he continued his conquests, taking the rest of Nejd and then Hejaz (the western strip of today's Saudi Arabia). In January 1926, at the holy city of Mecca, he was proclaimed King of Nejd and Hejaz, and in 1932 all of his conquests were unified to form the Kingdom of Saudi Arabia.

So far, so good. The Arabian peninsula was now a single nation rather than a hodge-podge of warring tribes. And in 1938 things became even better when vast reserves of oil were discovered. Ibn Saud was all-powerful and rich when he died in 1953. But part of his legacy was Wahhabism, an extreme fundamentalist form of Islam that believes in the literal truth of the Koran. Ibn Saud had supported this faith and kept Saudi Arabia in rigid conformity to its doctrines. After his death, other Saudis became increasingly aggressive in spreading Wahhabism, funding madrassahs (Wahhabi schools) not only in Saudi Arabia but also in other countries like Pakistan. Here believers were (and are) taught the virtues of *jihad* to establish the supremacy of Islam in the world. From such schools sprang Wahhabi fanatics such as the Riyadh-born Osama bin Laden.

Other action this day

588 BC: Babylonian king Nebuchadrezzar II starts a six-month siege of Jerusalem, after which he will destroy the city and deport much of the population of Judaea to Babylon * AD 69: Roman emperor Galba is beheaded by his Praetorian Guard that had defected to rival general Otho

16 January

Sir John Moore falls at La Coruña

1809 Today in the Spanish port of La Coruña, in the final act of his outnumbered army's arduous retreat, the British general Sir John Moore fell from his horse, mortally wounded by a French cannon-ball that had shattered his left shoulder and collarbone. He died later in the day, but he had already managed to lead his command – battered but intact – to the safety of evacuation by a British fleet.

In October, Moore had taken command of Britain's only field army on the continent of Europe. He had led it out of Portugal into Spain to face an enormous invading French army now commanded by the Emperor Napoleon himself. The Spanish army was in disarray, and when the capital Madrid fell (see 1 December), Moore's forces were left isolated in the north-west of the country. His first instinct was to retreat to Lisbon, but after learning that Spanish resistance to French occupation had broken out in Madrid, he decided instead to move against the French line of communications.

Thus, his army became, to use Sir Charles Oman's phrase, 'the matador's cape that distracted the Gallic bull from its main intention of conquering the rest of Spain and then Portugal'. Surprised at trouble from this quarter, Napoleon detached significant forces to pursue Moore and postponed his advances south and west. 'If the English are not already in full retreat, they are lost,' the emperor wrote to his brother, 'and if they retire they will be pursued right up to their embarkation and at least half of them will not get away …

Put it in the newspapers and have it spread everywhere that 36,000 Englishmen are surrounded ...'

In their 250-mile retreat to La Coruña, over mountains and in fierce winter weather, the British army became a rabble. Nevertheless, with strong rearguard actions and by dint of personal leadership, Moore was able to keep his forces together and ahead of their pursuers, now commanded by Marshal Nicolas Soult. Reaching La Coruña on 11 January, Moore formed his lines of defence. Throughout the fighting, strong French attacks were unable to pierce the British positions.

At last, on the 14th the British fleet appeared, and the evacuation, starting with the sick, the artillery and the healthier horses, began. But before it was completed Moore was struck down. At dawn the next day he was buried in the central bastion of the fortress as he had ordered, wrapped in his military cloak with his sword at his side. Only a day later the last British soldier was evacuated to the waiting fleet, and the French occupied the port.

It was perhaps as well that Moore died, like Wolfe and Nelson, in the moment of victory, for when his army returned to Britain the first public reaction was one of anger and criticism; many armchair strategists at home believed that instead of retreating, Moore should have attacked. It was many years before his feat was recognised for what it accomplished: a severe disruption of Napoleon's plan to conquer Spain and Portugal and the skilful preservation of a British army that would fight the emperor another day.

A granite monument erected on the orders of another gallant soldier, his pursuer Marshal Soult, still marks Moore's grave at La Coruña. Almost two centuries later, in January 2004, the mayor of La Coruña dedicated a bronze bust of Moore at his burial site.

Other action this day

AD 550: The Ostrogoths under King Totila conquer Rome by bribing the Isaurian garrison to open the gates * 1780: Admiral George Romney's British fleet defeats a Spanish squadron under Don Juan de Lángara at the Moonlight Battle, at Cape St Vincent off the coast of Portugal

17 January

A tough-minded empress saves her husband's empire

AD 532 Today one of the most remarkable women in history stood firm in the face of bloody insurrection and saved her husband's control of the Byzantine empire.

The Empress Theodora was hardly born to the purple; she was a prostitute who, according to the contemporary historian Procopius, was sorry that 'God had not given her more orifices to give more pleasure to more people at the same time'.

The daughter of a bear-keeper in Constantinople and by all accounts exceptionally beautiful, by her mid-teens Theodora had been kept and discarded by several lovers, by one of whom she bore an illegitimate child. Highly regarded for her voracious sexual appetite, she was an actress (virtually synonymous at the time with prostitute), famous for her role of Leda in which she lay stripped on the stage, her thighs covered with grains of barley, which a live goose playing Zeus-as-swan picked up with its bill.

But by the age of twenty Theodora had met, charmed and married Justinian, who had persuaded his uncle the Emperor Justin to change the law that prohibited a noble from marrying an actress. She was, however, far more than just a superb sexual partner; she was possessed of both an acute intelligence and nerves of steel. After her husband became emperor in 527, he treated her as a full partner in ruling his realm. An early supporter of women's rights, she also had her own agenda, backing new laws that prohibited the killing of adulterous wives, closing down Constantinople's brothels and outlawing the killing of unwanted children by exposure to the elements.

Justinian's greatest challenge came five years after his ascension, when rioting broke out between the Green and Blue factions at the chariot races in Constantinople's Hippodrome. A city prefect ordered seven hooligans hanged, but during the execution the scaffolding broke, saving two, who fled to sanctuary in a nearby church. When both Greens and Blues petitioned the emperor for clemency, his refusal provoked a full week of chaos, the two factions combining forces under the slogan 'Nika' (Conquer), the catchword usually shouted during the races. They freed the condemned men, conducted a burning and looting spree throughout the city and demanded that the emperor dismiss two of his senior officials.

At dawn on Sunday, 17 January, Justinian publicly agreed to the rioters' conditions, but it was too late. The hostile mob continued its wanton destruction, proclaimed a noble named Hypatius as emperor and drove Justinian into his royal palace in full retreat.

The terrified Justinian called together his panicky counsellors, who urged him to flee the city on the ship that was waiting at the garden stairs of the palace. But Theodora would have none of it, addressing her husband and his advisors with a ringing call to defy the rioters: 'If flight were the only means of safety, yet I should disdain to fly ... may I never be seen, not for a day, without my diadem and purple ... I believe in the maxim of antiquity, that kingship is a glorious shroud.'

Inspired by her courage, Justinian regained his nerve and sent his loyal general Belisarius to lead his soldiers to the Hippodrome. There he slaughtered over 30,000 rebels and executed Hypatius, whose body was thrown into the sea. Without Theodora's stirring call to action, Justinian's reign would have ended in shameful flight. As it was, he ruled for another 33 years.

During the rioting, an old church had been burned to the ground. Just 45 days after the suppression of the revolt, on Justinian's orders work began on its replacement, the magnificent Hagia Sophia that stands in Istanbul to this day.

Other action this day

1746: Charles Edward Stuart (The Young Pretender) and his Jacobite army defeat a Hanoverian army at the Battle of Falkirk Muir, the last Jacobite victory in the Second Jacobite Uprising * 1885: One thousand British soldiers rout a 12,000-man Dervish army at the Battle of Abu Klea in the Sudan * 1961: President Dwight Eisenhower delivers a televised farewell address to the nation three days before leaving office, in which he warns against the accumulation of power by the 'military-industrial complex' * 1991: The United States launches Operation Desert Storm against Saddam Hussein's Iraq

18 January

Germany's first emperor is crowned in France

1871 At noon on this bitter cold day, with the smell of smoke in the air from nearby Paris, burning under the Prussian siege and bombardment, a magnificent and fateful gathering took place in the Palace of Versailles. In the Hall of Mirrors, King Wilhelm of Prussia was crowned Kaiser of the Germans.

It was a moment for which the Prussian chancellor Otto von Bismarck had devoted all his craft and considerable energies: the unification of all German states into a single empire led by Prussia. It had taken two wars over six years – first with Denmark in 1864, then with Austria in 1866 – to establish Prussia's dominant position among the German-speaking states and to bring the northern states into a confederation.

In 1870 he produced a third conflict – this one with France – by provoking Emperor Napoleon III into a declaration of war. French aggression, Bismarck calculated, and the resulting need for a collective German defence, would have the salutary effect of encouraging the still-independent southern states – principally Wurtemberg and Bavaria – to join the northern confederation.

The combined German armies under Prussian leadership defeated Napoleon's forces with unexpected ease and then embarked on an invasion of France. Even as military operations dragged on longer than expected – stubborn Paris refused to capitulate and guerrilla activities mounted against the German occupation – Bismarck knew the time was right to complete an empire and crown an emperor. He made a variety of concessions to the southern states to overcome their remaining reluctance over the loss of sovereignty to the Prussian confederation. One secret arrangement involved furnishing the mentally unstable King Ludwig II of Bavaria with substantial Prussian funds to reduce the considerable debt he had amassed in his mad castle-building spree.

Standing with Bismarck in the crowded hall waiting for the coronation ceremony to begin was that other architect of victory, the great Prussian General von Moltke, the success of whose war plans had made today's event possible. Others in attendance included

General von Roon, the Prussian war minister; the Kaiser's son, the Crown Prince of Prussia (deemed by his soldiers too tender-hearted for the enterprise of war); the crown prince's own son, almost thirteen (who as Kaiser Wilhelm II would prove far less tender-hearted than his father); and a large collection of kings, grand dukes, princes, landgraves, margraves and lesser ranks of rulers assembled from the various states of Germany.

W.H. Russell described Kaiser Wilhelm's entrance to the Hall of Mirrors for *The Times*:

> It is twelve o'clock. The boom of a gun far away rolls above the voices in the Court hailing the Emperor King. Then there is a hush of expectation, and then rich and sonorous rise the massive strains of the chorale chanted by the men of regimental bands assembled in a choir, as the King, bearing his helmet in his hand, and dressed in full uniform as a German general, stalked slowly up the long gallery, and bowing to the clergy in front of the temporary altar opposite him, halted and dressed himself right and front, and then twirling his heavy moustache with his disengaged hand, surveyed the scene at each side of him.

Ten days after the coronation at Versailles, combat operations in the Franco-Prussian War came to an end with the capitulation of Paris. In March, Kaiser Wilhelm returned to Berlin, where standing on the royal balcony with his grandson he was hailed as the conquering hero by rapturous crowds. On 10 May 1871, the Treaty of Frankfurt was signed, by which, in addition to paying an enormous indemnity of 5 billion francs, France was required to hand over to Germany the provinces of Alsace and Lorraine. So, in military triumph, the German empire was born. It lasted not quite a half-century, ending in 1918 with Germany's defeat in the First World War. Kaiser Wilhelm II abdicated to a modest retirement in Holland, and Germany became for the first time but not the last a republic.

Other action this day

1486: Henry VII (of Lancaster) consolidates his final victory in the Wars of the Roses by marrying Elizabeth of York * 1593: Siamese King Naresuan defeats invading Burmese at Nong Sarai by killing Burmese crown prince

Minchit Sra in personal combat on elephant-back * 1919: The Versailles Peace Conference opens to set the peace terms for Germany and other defeated nations * 1943: The Żydowska Organizacja Bojowa (Jewish Combat Organisation) attacks German occupiers in Warsaw to start the first armed resistance in the Warsaw Ghetto

19 January

Civilians are bombed for the first time – by a Zeppelin

1915 Today, Korvettenkapitän Peter Strasser led a small fleet of two German Zeppelins in history's first-ever bombing raid against civilians. His target was the Norfolk coast of England, where, on the ports of Great Yarmouth, Sheringham and King's Lynn, his airships dropped 24 100-pound bombs and a few incendiaries. Four people were killed, another sixteen injured.

The Zeppelin was a cigar-shaped rigid airship (rather than a balloon or blimp) with a framework of triangular metal girders covered with fabric, with separate gas cells to contain hydrogen. It was the brainchild of Graf Ferdinand von Zeppelin, who had been inspired on a visit to the United States during the American Civil War, when he had seen the Union army's aerial reconnaissance balloons. Later during the Franco-Prussian War he witnessed their use by the French to carry mail.

On 2 July 1900 the first Zeppelin took its maiden flight over the Bodensee in Germany, and in 1909, after the bankruptcy and resuscitation of the company, a Zeppelin was used for the first time to transport passengers.

These airships were first used in war just two days after the German invasion of Belgium (see 4 August). Although Zeppelins had been designed for reconnaissance, their crews saw how easy it would be to drop bombs. Attacking fortifications near Liège, they dropped 8-inch artillery shells with blankets attached to them to make them hit nose first. They were also used at Verdun.

By now Zeppelins were 500 feet long and could fly at speeds up to 85 miles per hour and reach an altitude of 6,000 feet. They were refitted to carry a 2-ton bomb load and were armed with five machine guns for protection against enemy fighters. The German high command had high hopes for these airships, which had significant advantages over the planes of the time – they were almost as fast, could carry more bombs and guns, and had a greater range.

From 1915 Zeppelins were increasingly employed to attack civilian targets. After Strasser's initial raid, London was hit on 31 May, followed by seventeen more attacks during the year on places such as Edinburgh, Gravesend, the Midlands and the Home Counties. In total that year the Germans dropped 37 tons of bombs on Britain, killing 181 people and injuring 455.

The number of airship raids increased the next year to 23, causing another 1,000 casualties, but the British were now beginning to find effective defences against them. Field guns were converted to anti-aircraft use, and fighter planes were launched to attack them. Initially, however, the fighters were ineffective since they were not equipped with synchronisation gear that would permit firing through the propeller. Hence pilots developed the technique of over-flying a Zeppelin and dropping bombs on it, a manoeuvre so risky that the first pilot who did it received the Victoria Cross.

By 1916 the British had developed searchlights to pick out the Zeppelins at night and were using shells that could ignite their highly combustible hydrogen, sometimes causing the entire airship to burst into flames in mid-air. (Non-flammable helium was not used in dirigibles until 1923.) In response, the Germans built advanced Zeppelins that could reach 12,000 feet and fly above the clouds to avoid the searchlights. To direct the bombing, an observer would be lowered on a long cable through the clouds.

Despite these improvements, the Zeppelin now became so vulnerable that the Germans flew only eleven raids in 1917. By then 77 out of the 115 Zeppelins had been shot down or disabled. The last raid took place on 6 August 1918 when Peter Strasser, now a Führer der Luftschiffe (admiral second class), led a night attack on Norwich. A British DH-4 biplane intercepted his airship and shot it down. Strasser and his 22 crewmen all died in the crash.

So ended the Zeppelin's role in the First World War. The company was taken over by new management (Ferdinand von Zeppelin having died in 1917) and produced civilian dirigibles, the most famous being the ill-fated *Hindenburg* that in 1937 went up in flames over Lakehurst, New Jersey, killing 36 passengers. Finally, during the Second World War, the Nazis concluded that fixed-wing aircraft were the future while dirigibles were relics from the past, so Reichsmarschall Hermann Göring destroyed all remaining Zeppelins to use their aluminium for the German war industry.

Other action this day

1419: Rouen surrenders to Henry V, completing his conquest of Normandy * 1671: Captain Sir Henry Morgan leads a fleet of 36 pirate ships against the city of Panama, sailing into the port and decimating a significantly larger Spanish force, burning the city to the ground and making off with 400,000 pieces of eight * 1807: Confederate general Robert E. Lee is born * 1942: Japanese forces invade Burma

20 January

Wellington takes Ciudad Rodrigo

1812 Today, in the blackness before dawn, trigger-happy British soldiers shot out windows and doors in the central cathedral square in a Spanish town they had just captured, and subjected its citizens to an orgy of looting and rape.

Such was the ignoble end of the siege of Ciudad Rodrigo, located 200 miles south-west of Madrid, just east of the Portuguese border. Encircled by ancient ramparts, with a Moorish castle facing the Roman bridge over the Agueda River, it had been defended by 1,900 soldiers of Napoleon's army.

In 1808 Napoleon had deposed the Spanish king and placed his own brother Joseph on the throne. The same year he made the first of three invasions of Portugal. In 1809 Portugal's ally, Great Britain, had sent Arthur Wellesley to command the Anglo–Portuguese forces. After two years of back-and-forth fighting across the Iberian peninsula (during which Wellesley was ennobled as Viscount Wellington after the Battle of Talavera – see 28 July), the French had been chased from Portugal for good. Now the British and Portuguese were ready to advance back into Spain. Their first target was Ciudad Rodrigo, garrisoned by the French since Marshal Ney's conquest of it two years before.

Ciudad Rodrigo was a strong but flawed fortress. The 30-foot cut-stone wall around it was 25 feet wide and was protected by a 20-foot *faussebraie*, an outer wall designed to shield the main wall from artillery fire. But just 800 yards away was a ridge called the Grand Teson that was fifteen feet higher than the main wall and thus the perfect position for enemy guns. When Ney had taken the town, he had placed his artillery there, and now the French had fortified the ridge with a strong redoubt.

In early January, Wellington moved on Ciudad Rodrigo with a force of 10,700 men, including a Portuguese brigade. His first task was to take the Grand Teson redoubt.

Under cover of darkness on the night of 8 January, with no preliminary bombardment to alert the French, Lieutenant Colonel John Colborne and 450 of his men crept over snow-covered ground to within 50 yards of the redoubt without being detected. With riflemen providing covering fire from positions all around the little fort, three companies escaladed over the redoubt's walls, over-whelming the defenders and taking 60 prisoners at a cost of only 25 casualties. Despite heavy fire from Ciudad Rodrigo, the British now began to build siege works where they would position their guns to begin battering the walls.

During the next week Wellington's men extended their siege works, even in the face of a French counter-attack that destroyed some of them. By the night of the 14th they were ready for the softening-up bombardment, opening fire with 23 24-pound and four 18-pound siege cannon. One officer described the scene: the shells 'seemed like fiery serpents leaping through the darkness, the walls crashed to the stroke of the bullet, and the distant mountains returning the sound appeared to mourn over the falling city.' After five days the attackers had fired 9,500 rounds and had opened two breaches in the walls, the main one about 30 yards across.

In response, the French fortified the larger breach with *chevaux-de-frise* (portable frames studded with spikes) and aimed in grape-shot-loaded cannon on both breaches.

By 19 January Wellington was ready to launch his final attack. At 7.00pm a battalion of Cazadores (Portuguese mountain fighters) dashed across the Agueda Bridge to take some outworks that protected the main breach. Then the main attack force charged, but it was slowed down by the chevaux-de-frise and immediately came under withering enemy cannon fire. In a heroic head-on attack, the British took one gun at bayonet-point, although many of those who reached the top of the breach were blown away when the defenders detonated some bags of powder they had buried there. Then another British division assaulting the smaller breach brushed off light French resistance and seized the top of the ramparts. These men now caught the defenders of the main breach from the rear, silencing their guns and opening the way into the town. The French, who had pulled back into the cathedral square, surrendered.

It was now, after the French prisoners had been herded away, that the British soldiers, fuelled by drink, ran amok, firing indiscriminately, seizing as much property as they could carry, and, probably accidentally, killing several civilians. (British soldiers were not the only ones to profit from the siege of Ciudad Rodrigo; Wellington was promoted from viscount to earl, and his pension was doubled to £4,000 a year.) Even when one officer tried to stop the sack with the blast of twenty trumpets, the pillage continued, until it finally petered out after twelve chaotic hours.

During the siege, Wellington had lost 195 killed and 916 wounded, more than the French with 529 casualties – although over 1,300 unwounded French were taken prisoner. Even though the battle was now ended, however, there was still more blood to be spilt. Eleven British deserters had been found in the town, and all were sentenced to death. Although Wellington pardoned five of them, six were shot and buried in a single unmarked grave.

The capture of Ciudad Rodrigo was an important British victory, as it opened up the northern route from Portugal into Spain and marked the turning of the tide in the Peninsular War. In March Wellington won a bloody victory at Badajoz, and another at Salamanca in June. Although the war continued even after Napoleon's abdication, the French were never again in the ascendant.

Other action this day

1839: At the Battle of Yungay, a Chilean army under General Bulnes defeats the Peru–Bolivian Confederacy under Marshal Andrés de Santa Cruz, leading to the end of the confederacy and re-establishing the independence of Peru * 1841: Captain Charles Eliot of the British navy occupies Hong Kong island; Britain and China sign the Chuenpi Convention, which cedes Hong Kong to Britain * 1942: Nazi leader Reinhard Heydrich convenes the Wannsee Conference to set in motion the 'Final Solution' * 1945: In the closing stages of the Second World War, Franklin

D. Roosevelt is sworn in for an unprecedented fouth term as US president and commander-in-chief

21 January

The siege of Khe Sanh

1968 At 5.30 this morning, with a massive barrage of rockets, grenades and mortar shells, the siege of Khe Sanh began. The most famous battle of the Vietnam War, it lasted 77 days, and in the end an attacking force estimated at over 30,000 North Vietnamese regulars failed to capture an American combat base held by four battalions of US Marines and one battalion of ARVN (South Vietnamese) rangers – 6,000 defenders in all.

Located in a remote spot in Quang Tri province some fifteen miles south of the demilitarised zone (DMZ) and nine miles east of the border with Laos, the combat base at Khe Sanh was viewed by the American command as a good forward position from which to engage and defeat enemy forces moving into South Vietnam.

Events of the siege were closely reported around the world and became a nightly staple for TV-watchers in the US. Speaking on 19 February, President Lyndon B. Johnson said: 'The eyes of the nation and the eyes of the entire world – the eyes of all of history itself – are on that little brave band of defenders who hold the pass at Khe Sanh.' A week later Walter Cronkite, reporting on CBS television, told his audience that: 'Khe Sanh could well fall, with terrible loss in American lives, prestige, and morale.'

During its course, the siege was frequently compared with the battle of Dien Bien Phu, in which the Communists had surrounded and decisively defeated a French force in Indochina fourteen years earlier (see 7 May). This time, however, the defenders' firepower and mobility proved dominant, particularly with Operation Niagara, which delivered a 'waterfall' of shelling and B-52 bombardment against the attackers' positions. And unlike the French at Dien Bien Phu, the Americans were able to resupply the Khe Sanh garrison by air throughout the siege.

For both sides, the stakes seemed very high. It was the first battle of the war in which the North Vietnamese used armoured units. At one point, the American field commander, General Westmoreland, asked his staff to develop a proposal for the use of a tactical nuclear bomb against the enemy, an initiative immediately quashed by his superiors in Washington.

Then, inexplicably, after two months of heavy fighting, the North Vietnamese reduced the frequency and size of their attacks against the American perimeter. By late March they seemed largely to have packed up and left the field. On 8 April, as a relief force of Marine and Army troops reached Khe Sanh, the American command declared the siege over. In June the battered base for which so much had been expended was abandoned, its remains 'buried by bulldozer, burned, or blown up'.

Afterwards, there never was much agreement on what had been gained – or lost – by the successful defence of Khe Sanh. By body count, the battle should have been labelled a great American victory: some 500 American and ARVN deaths against an estimated (but undoubtedly exaggerated) loss of 10,000 North Vietnamese regulars. While some observers saw the battle's outcome – particularly the enemy's early disengagement – as clear proof of America's ability to prosecute and win the war in Asia, others claimed that the enemy had simply lured Westmoreland into sending US forces to an out-of-the-way place in the north, then launched their Tet offensive against the vulnerable cities in the south.

To complicate the analysis, the enemy commander-in-chief, General Giap, told an interviewer he thought his forces had in fact won at Khe Sanh. And when one US Marine general pronounced the action 'the most important battle of the war', another called it 'an unsound blow in the air'.

In any case, the war in Vietnam changed after Khe Sanh. Never again did the North Vietnamese attempt to go head-to-head with American forces in the field on the same scale. Instead, they returned to their guerrilla, small-unit, hit-and-run style of fighting. Even more important, they adopted a strategy of protracted warfare that the United States, for all its military superiority in the traditional means of war, was never able to counter successfully.

Other action this day

1506: The first group of Swiss Guards arrives at the Vatican * 1793: Louis XVI is guillotined during the French Revolution * 1824: Confederate

general Thomas 'Stonewall' Jackson is born in Clarksburg, West Virginia
* 1954: Mamie Eisenhower launches the USS *Nautilus*, the first atomic-
powered submarine, in Groton, Connecticut

22 January

British and Americans land at Anzio

1944 All roads lead to Rome. But at the end of 1943 none seemed
to. None, certainly, for the Allied armies whose advance up the
Italian boot was stalemated at the chain of German fortifications
known as the Gustav Line with its key stronghold, Monte Cassino.
Which is why another way to Rome had to be found, and why, at
2.00 this morning, 40,000 American and British troops of the US
6th Corps made a surprise and unopposed landing at Anzio, a port
on the Tyrrhenian Sea some 30 miles south of the Italian capital.

Codenamed Shingle, the amphibious landing behind enemy lines
was intended to force the Germans to abandon the Cassino front,
clearing the way for the US 5th Army to move on towards Rome, the
Allies' objective. Churchill had cabled Stalin enthusiastically: 'We
have launched the big attack against the German armies defending
Rome which I told you about at Teheran. The weather conditions
seem favourable. I hope to have good news for you before long.'

But there was no good news. Operation Shingle never got near
accomplishing its goal. Intended by its planners as the strong first
thrust of a two-pronged effort, the landings were carried out more
like a diversion. Moreover, insufficient sea transportation – most of
the tank-carrying landing craft had already been sent west for use in
the invasions scheduled for Normandy and southern France –
affected the size and composition of the 6th Corps, resulting in an
initial deployment of only two divisions with no mechanised units.

German reaction to the landings was swift and severe. Calling
Anzio 'an abscess', Hitler told General Kesselring, his military
commander in Italy, that 'the Gustav Line must be held at all costs'.
Eight divisions were rushed from France, Yugoslavia and northern
Italy to seal off the beachhead and mount a counter-attack that
would drive the 6th Corps into the sea. Perhaps a Patton or a

MacArthur might have made a success of the operation with a fast strike inland, but the competent, cautious Major General John Lucas, whose advice from 5th Army commander Mark Clark was 'Don't stick your neck out, Johnny', spent the first week ashore organising the beachhead. By 30 January, when he attempted a move north to seize the Alban Hills, the key high ground south of Rome, it was too late.

Now, the troops gathered at Anzio, instead of preparing to mount a bold, front-busting flanking movement, suddenly found themselves penned in and under savage attack by an enemy with superior numbers. To prevent them being overrun entirely, Allied forces in front of the Gustav Line resumed the costly frontal attacks that Anzio had been meant to eliminate. It was not until the middle of May, after the destruction of Monte Cassino, that the 5th Army, now joined by the British 8th Army, broke through in the south.

In the end, there was one prospect for redemption at Anzio. On 25 May, 5th Army units heading north linked up at last with the 6th Corps near Valmontone, where they were in a position to cut the escape route and bag the Germans retreating up Route 6. But General Clark, intent on winning for his 5th Army and himself the honours of reaching Rome before the British 8th Army, now redirected his advance on the capital itself, allowing the Germans to dodge almost sure envelopment.

The welcome news that Allied troops had entered Rome on 4 June was soon obscured by bulletins about even greater events in Normandy. General Kesselring, interviewed after the war, called the Allied effort at Anzio 'a halfway measure as an offensive'. Winston Churchill, who had championed the landings, called them 'a story of high opportunity and shattered hopes'.

Other action this day

1879: British troops are massacred by the Zulus at Isandlwana * 1941: The British capture German-held Tobruk in North Africa * 1943: Australian and American forces defeat the Japanese army in Papua, New Guinea

23 January

Rommel pommels the British in North Africa

1942 From its beginning in 1940, the war in North Africa had been a seesaw affair of offensives followed by counter-offensives, fought across the top of the continent in terrain one German general characterised as 'a tactician's paradise and a quartermaster's hell'. In this war, the advancing force inevitably weakened as its supply line lengthened, while the retreating army became stronger as it drew closer to its base of supplies.

Today's action near Agedabia, 800 miles west of Cairo, made clear what General Rommel's Afrika Korps was up to: not just a reconnaissance in force, as it had appeared yesterday, but a full counter-offensive against the British 8th Army, caught off balance, its forward units dispersed and under-strength.

Recently resupplied by convoys carrying tanks, armoured vehicles, and other *matériel* across the Mediterranean to its supply base at Tripoli, the Afrika Korps was once again in motion, leading an Axis drive – the third of the war – towards British-held Egypt and the vital Suez Canal.

With one column sent up the coastal road in the direction of Benghazi, Rommel threw his main strength eastward from Agedabia in an attempt to encircle the British 1st Armoured Division. It was a bold stroke but one that failed to achieve complete success, leaving open a gap through which a part of the division managed to escape – in disorder and with the loss of almost half its tanks. The following day, Rommel's forces pursued the retreating division and destroyed most of what remained, in what a German officer described as 'one of the most extraordinary routs of the war'.

Today's action near Agedabia seemed a good beginning. Rommel was pleased and wrote to his wife a few days later: 'Four days of success lie behind us. Our blows struck home.' Not so pleased was the Italian component of the Afrika Korps, whose commander, General Cavallero, arrived at headquarters to complain that he had not been consulted about the new offensive. He was right about that, for Rommel had kept the plan a secret. 'We knew from experience,' he wrote in his diary, 'that Italian Headquarters cannot keep things to themselves and that everything they wireless to Rome gets round to British ears.'

As the new offensive continued eastward, Benghazi fell to the Afrika Korps on 29 January; and by early the next month, the battered 8th Army had retreated behind defensive lines at Gazala, where Rommel would pause for four months, having outrun his supply line.

During the long stalemate at Gazala, while the opposing armies refitted, the British garrison at Tobruk surrendered and Rommel was promoted to field marshal. Then the German offensive resumed, shoving the 8th Army back into Egypt and by early July reaching a place only 60 miles west of Alexandria called El Alamein, where Rommel's forward progress ended. It was at El Alamein, in early November, that one of the most decisive battles in world history would be fought, producing a great British victory (see 4 November) and beginning the seesaw war's final thrust, one that would bring the 8th Army under General Montgomery all the way to Tunisia and Allied victory in North Africa.

Other action this day

971: Crossbowmen from the Song dynasty army decimate the Southern Han elephant corps at Shao in China as the Song replace the Southern Han as rulers of China ∗ 1942: Japanese troops attack Rabaul to start the war in New Guinea ∗ 1945: German admiral Karl Dönitz launches Operation Hannibal, one of the largest-ever evacuations by sea, which in fifteen weeks transports over 2 million refugees and soldiers across the Baltic to Germany from East Prussia, after Russia cuts off Prussia

24 January

Caligula is killed by his own guards

AD 41 Today in Rome, Emperor Caligula was assassinated by his own guards. It seems ironic that the military, which had named him as a child and helped him become emperor as a young man, had now brought about his end at only 29.

Born to the purple (Augustus was his great-grandfather), Caligula came from impeccable military stock, including three celebrated generals: his father Germanicus, his grandfather Marcus Agrippa, and his great-grandfather Mark Antony. His full name was Gaius Caesar Germanicus, but when he was three his father took him on campaign, where the adoring legionaries adopted him as their mascot and nicknamed him Caligula ('Little Boots') because of his miniature soldier's uniform of armour and tiny military boots.

Caligula was only seven when his father died, and during the next twelve years he was shuttled between various relations while his mother and brothers were banished, imprisoned and eventually killed by the Emperor Tiberius on charges of treason. When Caligula was nineteen, Tiberius brought him to his royal villa on Capri. There he lived for six years, docile and obsequious in the court of the tyrant who caused the death of three of his family. Caligula now became Tiberius's likely heir, but the ageing despot well understood his enforced guest, saying that he 'was rearing a viper for the Roman people'.

In early AD 37, the military once more took a hand in Caligula's fortunes, this time in the person of Macro, the commander of the Praetorian Guard. On 16 March the sick and decrepit Tiberius lapsed into unconsciousness. Believing him dead, Caligula slipped the seal ring from the Imperial finger to show himself to the waiting crowd as the new emperor. But suddenly Tiberius awoke from what was really a coma and demanded food. Caligula stood petrified with terror, but the quick-thinking Macro rushed in and stifled the old emperor with a blanket. Thanks to Macro, Caligula now became Rome's third emperor. He immediately ordered a *donativum* (cash bonus) to the Praetorian Guard, the first recorded in Imperial history. Having bought the Guards' loyalty, however, he now turned on Macro, who he feared was becoming too powerful, and forced him to commit suicide.

Two years after Macro's death, Caligula led his only significant military operation, which instead of glory brought derision. He marched with two legions to the coast of what is now Normandy to invade Britain – but failed to cross the Channel. Instead, he ordered his soldiers to collect seashells as 'spoils of the sea' and then marched back to Rome, where he dressed peaceful Gauls as savage Germanic tribesmen at his triumph. In all, it was a bizarre performance, one that helped turn the army against him for subjecting it to ridicule.

The sickening tyranny of Caligula's reign is all too familiar – suffice to say that he was insane, believed himself to be a god and enjoyed wholesale executions for imagined offences or to seize rich men's property. He had sex with boys and women alike, including his own sisters. Perhaps the most appalling story concerns his sister Drusilla, whom he impregnated and then, in his impatience to see their god-like child, disembowelled to snatch the unborn baby from her womb. (Neither baby nor mother survived, and Caligula had Drusilla deified.) Most famously, he housed his horse Incitatus in an ivory stall, adorned him with a collar of precious stones and said he would make him consul.

By the beginning of 41, Caligula had been emperor for almost four years and had created enemies everywhere, even in his own Praetorian Guard. A special target was Cassius Chaerea, one of the Guard's military tribunes, whom Caligula mocked for his supposed femininity. Unable to bear the constant taunting, Chaerea conspired with the Guard's commander Cornelius Sabinus and co-prefect Arrecinus Clemens. On this day, while Caligula was walking through a secluded passageway at the Palatine games, they struck. The near-contemporary historian Suetonius tells us that there are two versions of what happened:

Some say that … Chaerea came up behind him and cut him deeply in the neck, having first cried, 'Take that!' and then the tribune Cornelius Sabinus, who was the other conspirator and faced Gaius [Caligula], stabbed him in the chest. Others say that Sabinus, after getting centurions who were in on the plot to get rid of the crowd, asked for the watchword, as soldiers do, and that when Gaius gave him 'Jupiter', he cried, 'So be it!' and as Gaius looked around, he split his jaw with a blow of his sword. As he lay writhing on the ground he called out that he still lived, and the others finished him with thirty wounds … Some even thrust their swords through his genitals.

Caligula's death brought the feeble Claudius to power. Just as Caligula had shown no gratitude to Macro for murdering Tiberius, now Claudius followed suit. Instead of rewarding Chaerea, he ordered him put to death. At Chaerea's own request, he was executed with the sword he had used to dispatch Caligula.

25 January

The Burma Road

1945 The siege of China by Japan, which lasted for three years, was broken today with the completion of the Burma–Ledo road, whose construction was the greatest engineering challenge of the Second World War. The road, linking Allied territory – Ledo, in British India – with the city of Kunming in south-western China, opened for through traffic end-to-end this morning. It was a supply route with the strategic purpose of keeping China in the war against Japan. The first convoy bound for Kunming, 113 vehicles carrying aeroplane parts and ammunition, was already on its slow way eastward from Ledo, following the new road over steep grades, endless switchbacks, and some 700 bridges – a journey of 1,120 miles, carried out at a top speed of about 80 miles a day.

By invading Burma in the spring of 1942, the Japanese had outflanked China, cutting off its last land connection to the outside world, the old Burma Road, which was a link to the Burmese port of Rangoon. Now China was truly besieged. Supplies for the Chinese forces, and for the American units operating within China, were flown in from India using a hazardous route over the Himalayas (the 'Hump'), but there were insufficient aircraft and airfields at either end to bring in the tonnage of critical supplies and war *matériel* that China's armies required.

It was an important strategic policy of the United States to make China an active partner in the war against Japan. But China's leader Chiang Kai-shek was a doubtful ally in the enterprise. He considered the Communists of his own country as great a threat to his power as the Japanese invaders, and saw retreat as the best way to preserve his regime. To persuade Chiang to support American war aims, US President Roosevelt sent Lieutenant General Joseph Stilwell to be his military chief of staff, with a mission to reform China's armies and lead them in the field.

Stilwell decided that one answer to the problem of keeping China supplied to fight the war was to build a road from India across the top of Burma that would link up with the old Burma Road near the Chinese border. Construction began in December 1942, starting from Ledo and following the path of the Allied advance to retake northern Burma. The climate and terrain of the region through which the road would have to pass were nightmarish: mountain ranges with passes at 9,000 feet, deep valleys, broad rivers and secondary streams – all liable to quick flooding during the monsoon season – 50 inches of rain a year, and a prevalence of malaria.

As Allied troops moved into upper Burma in 1943, they were followed by surveyors marking the road's route and by engineers in bulldozers clearing the way. In turn came the construction crews: 80,000 labourers worked on the road, half of them Americans, often working around the clock in two twelve-hour shifts. In good weather the construction rate was three-quarters of a mile a day of a single-lane road with passing places. Until a gravel topping was laid down, the road was virtually impassable in wet weather, a frequent occurrence. Pipelines to carry fuel now paralleled the roadway.

As the war, and the road, progressed, Chiang's demands for Lend Lease supplies from America grew increasingly exorbitant, even as it became clear to observers that he had no intention of allowing Stilwell to lead Chinese forces in any serious effort to repel the Japanese invasion. China's relationship with the United States was soon badly strained, and in the resulting clash Stilwell himself fell victim, recalled by Roosevelt at Chiang's demand in late 1944.

Ironically, when the first convoy reached Kunming, on 4 February 1945, 24 days after leaving Ledo, it was met by cheering crowds waving large banners that bore portraits of Chiang, Roosevelt and Stilwell. Chiang's directive for the occasion proclaimed, 'We have broken the siege of China!' and ordered the road named after 'General Joseph Stilwell in memory of his distinctive contribution and the signal part which the Allied and Chinese forces under his direction played in the Burma campaign and the building of the road'. Learning of this honour, Stilwell, now back in Washington, wrote in his diary: 'I wonder who put him up to that?'

By now, however, Allied forces had retaken much of Burma,

which had the effect of opening up shorter, less dangerous air routes into China. In the final months of the war in Asia, as more aeroplanes and airfields became available in the theatre, the famous road for which so much had been expended quickly lost its critical importance as a line of communications. By October of the same year in which it had been completed, the Stilwell road was abandoned as a main supply route.

Other action this day

AD 477: Geiseric the Lame, conquering king of the Vandals, dies at Carthage * 1153: Crusaders, with Knights Templar at their head, start the siege of Ashkelon (in modern Israel) and will take the city after seven months * 1573: Daimyo Takeda Shingen defeats Tokugawa Ieyasu at the Battle of Mikatagahara

26 January

Chinese Gordon goes down fighting

1885 He was of medium height with a square jaw, sandy hair and a clipped military moustache. His power of command came through his pale blue and penetrating eyes as well as his somewhat unworldly righteousness. He was Charles Gordon, a British major general known as Chinese Gordon for his daring leadership in helping to put down rebel Chinese warlords in the Taiping Rebellion twenty years earlier.

A man of iron nerve, Gordon was a classic case of Victorian complexity. When not soldiering he spent much time helping orphaned children. He meditated three hours a day with his Bible, was celibate throughout his life and looked forward to death to meet his God. Queen Victoria's secretary referred to him as 'that Christian lunatic'.

In 1884 the British government sent Gordon to the Sudan, where a Muslim fanatic called the Mahdi was taking over the country with a large army and threatening British interests in Egypt. Gordon soon arrived in Khartoum, where he organised the defending garrison – all Sudanese or Egyptian soldiers except for a handful of British officers.

Soon the Mahdi neared the walled city. Knowing he had no chance of defeating the Mahdi's large army, Gordon still refused to leave. In the meantime, Prime Minister Gladstone had at last author-ised a relief force, but it seemed beset with incessant delays.

Early on the morning of 26 January the Mahdi ordered his 50,000 warriors into the final assault on the doomed city. In rode his fanat-ical hordes, leaving the streets red with blood. Gordon pulled back to the royal palace and there on an outside staircase he awaited his enemies, unarmed. Tearing open his tunic, he faced his attackers and cried out: 'Strike! Strike hard!' He finally fell in a rain of spear thrusts. Then Mahdist warriors cut off his head, placed it on a pike and deliv-ered it to the Mahdi as a trophy.

The relief force arrived two days later, on what would have been Gordon's 52nd birthday, to find they had come too late. Today, Chinese Gordon's effigy lies in St Paul's cathedral in London, but not his body (or his head), for they were never found.

Other action this day

1856: Marines from the sloop-of-war *Decatur*, backed up by *Decatur*'s guns, defeat an attack by Suquamish Indians on the settlement at Seattle, killing 28 and wounding 80 at the cost of two dead settlers * 1880: American general Douglas MacArthur is born in Little Rock, Arkansas * 1907: The Short Magazine Lee-Enfield Mk III is introduced into British military service; it remains the oldest military rifle still in official use (the first version was introduced in 1895)

27 January

The first flight of the fork-tailed devil

1939 Today at March Field just east of Los Angeles, 32-year-old Lieutenant Benjamin Kelsey climbed into a strange-looking new aircraft, the XP-38. Two engines were mounted on the wings in pods that extended back into tail-fins that were connected by a flat tail-plane. At mid-wing between the engines was a short nacelle for the pilot, with plenty of room for armament, although now the plane was to fly unarmed.

Kelsey levered himself into the cockpit and was soon hammering down the runway. Now in the air, he pushed the speed to over 400 miles per hour, about 100 miles per hour faster than any other aircraft then in existence. This was the first flight of the prototype for the Lockheed P-38 Lightning, the dominant American fighter plane of the Second World War.

A month later the XP-38 set a cross-country record by flying from California to New York in seven hours and two minutes, only slightly slower than today's commercial jets. Having definitively proved itself, the plane now went into full-scale production. The first of over 10,000 combat-ready P-38s rolled off the assembly line in October 1941, just in time for America's entry into the war two months later.

The P-38 did everything a fighter aircraft could do. It was often used for bomber escort, and sometimes performed as a bomber, but, thanks to its long range, ability to fly at any altitude and exceptional armaments, it was unsurpassed at air-to-air combat.

The P-38 first tasted enemy blood on 9 August 1942 when two Lightnings of the 343rd Fighter Group, 11th Air Force, cut down a pair of lumbering Japanese Kawanishi H6K 'Mavis' flying boats. Five days later a P-38 and a P-40 Warhawk (a single-engine fighter) shot down a Focke-Wulf 200 Condor (a four-engine long-range bomber) over the Atlantic, the first German plane destroyed by the American air force.

Armed with four .50 calibre machine guns and a 20mm cannon, the Lightning was a formidable fighting machine. Since all the guns were mounted in the nose of the pilot's nacelle (rather than on the wings, as in most fighters), they gave the pilot heavily concentrated firepower. Wing-mounted guns in other planes fired trajectories that were set to criss-cross one another at one or more points in a convergence zone, but the P-38's nose-mounted guns had no need for convergence zones, giving pilots an effective firing range of up to 1,000 yards, compared to about 200 yards for most other fighters.

Lightnings first encountered the Luftwaffe in force in North Africa. In a single day in April 1943, 26 P-38s shot down 31 German planes, establishing air superiority there. So formidable was the P-38 that the Germans called it 'Der Gabelschwanz-Teufel' (the fork-tailed devil). Subsequently P-38s were used extensively to protect Allied bomber raids, especially in the Mediterranean theatre.

But where the Lightning really came into its own was in the Pacific, destroying over 1,800 Japanese aircraft, more than any other Allied fighter. Over 100 P-38 pilots became 'aces' by downing five or more enemy planes, and America's leading Second World War fighter pilot ace Dick Bong had 40 kills in his P-38.

Lightnings also played the key role in the interception of Admiral Yamamoto, the architect of Japan's naval strategy in the Pacific, including the attack on Pearl Harbor. On 18 April 1943, sixteen P-38s took off from Guadalcanal and flew over 400 miles at less than 50 feet over the wave tops to avoid detection. Near Bougainville they sighted Yamamoto's two bombers, protected by six Zeros (a single-engine fighter). In a determined attack, the Lightnings downed two of the Zeros and sent the bomber carrying Yamamoto crashing into the jungle, where his body was found the next day.

So fearsome were the Lightnings in the Pacific war that later the Japanese ace Saburo Sakai, who shot down 64 Allied planes, remembered: 'The Lightning's great speed, its sensational high altitude performance, and especially its ability to dive and climb much faster than the Zero presented insuperable problems for our fliers. The P-38 pilots, flying at great height, chose when and where they wanted to fight, with disastrous results for our own men. The P-38 boded ill for the future and destroyed the morale of the Zero fighter pilot.'

Sakai understood only too well the threat posed by the Lightnings. During the course of the war in the Pacific, their kill ratio was over 10 to 1 – for every ten confirmed kills, only one P-38 was lost.

Other action this day

1595: English admiral Sir Francis Drake dies of dysentery off the coast of Porto Bello in Panama * 1859: German Kaiser Wilhelm II is born in Potsdam * 1973: The Paris Peace Accords officially end the Vietnam War

28 January

Hitler's last gamble – the Battle of the Bulge

1945 After six weeks of savage warfare, Operation Wacht am Rhein came to an end today with the Allied forces in roughly the same positions they had occupied that fateful morning of Saturday, 16 December 1944, when the German surprise offensive – formally the Ardennes campaign but better known as the Battle of the Bulge – sprang to its short but violent life.

For Hitler it had been a last-ditch chance to turn the war around. He planned to send his Panzer armies crashing through the weakest spot in the Allied line, across the River Meuse, on to Brussels, and thence to Antwerp, the Allies' key supply point. With the British–American coalition thoroughly disrupted, he could then face eastward to concentrate his forces against the advancing Russians. His generals told him the plan would never succeed, but hadn't they told him exactly the same thing in 1940, and look what happened then?

That the Allies were so completely surprised was, of course, an intelligence failure of the first magnitude. Viewed from their head-quarters in Versailles, the war looked close to being won. There were indications of a build-up in the Ardennes, but few people read the signs to mean significant trouble. Code-breaking ULTRA gave no such warnings. And no one among the top commanders – not Ike, not Monty, not Brad – believed that Hitler would mount such a desperate attempt to seize the initiative in the west. So, secure in that belief, when the attack began, they were caught flat-footed.

Remarkably, however, as the rampaging Panzers broke through the line and two US divisions crumbled, Allied commanders regrouped their forces and improvised to meet the threat. They threw reserve units into the line on either side of the Bulge, and with the help of courageous stands at places like St Vith and Bastogne (see 19 December) slowed and constricted the German attack. When the weather mercifully cleared, Allied air power joined the fray. By 25 December – Patton described the day as 'a clear cold Christmas, lovely weather for killing Germans' – the offensive had been corralled, short of the Meuse.

Even so, much heavy fighting remained and the cost was horrendous all round. By late January, when the Germans had been thrust back and the line restored, the Allies had lost an estimated 81,000 soldiers, killed, wounded, or captured. For the Germans the comparable figure was well over 100,000; but, worse, they had sustained absolutely crucial losses in armour, planes and other equipment. Now the war would resume its course, once again on Allied terms.

'It is not a disgrace to be defeated,' Frederick the Great is supposed to have said. 'It is a disgrace to be surprised.' But his maxim doesn't fit the case of the Battle of the Bulge. Badly surprised though they were, the battle-wise Allied forces recovered, fought back, and prevailed. At this stage of the war, defeat would have been the real disgrace.

29 January

Napoleon's last roll of the dice

1814 'He's exhausted. He'll crawl under a bed and hide.' So said France's great intriguer, the cynical Talleyrand, of the Emperor Napoleon, who had returned to Paris after the calamitous defeat at Leipzig in mid-October of 1813. The combined forces of Austria, Prussia, Russia, Sweden, Great Britain and some German principalities were now advancing on France, determined to depose the emperor and restore the Bourbon monarchy. But was Napoleon finished? Today he would take to the battlefield once again, the first of eleven pitched battles in just 50 days, in one last glorious roll of the dice to keep his throne.

On New Year's Day of 1814 the Prussian general Gebhard von Blücher had crossed the Rhine with his Army of Silesia, loudly proclaiming that he came as liberator rather than invader. Advancing in support was Austrian field marshal Karl Schwarzenberg's Army of Bohemia, bringing the Coalition forces to 245,000 front-line troops, with perhaps another half a million in reserve, while France's armies numbered but 70,000 men. When the two invading armies split to advance on Paris, Napoleon seized the chance to attack them piecemeal. On this day came the first of his extraordinary string of victories.

Blücher had led part of his army, 25,000 men, to Brienne in the Champagne country 120 miles east of Paris, and taken over the château dominating the town. It was here where Napoleon would strike, in the town where he had gone to school as a teenager. The emperor commanded 30,000, but they were mostly young recruits – so many of his veterans had perished over the past two years.

The French assault was classic Napoleon. Just after dawn his cavalry overpowered Blücher's Cossack outposts. He then brought up his horse artillery to keep the enemy pinned down and sent marshals Ney and Victor to outflank the Prussians. During the heavy fighting Napoleon's horse was shot from under him and he was almost captured by marauding Cossacks. Blücher also nearly lost his life, as a soldier standing next to him was shot dead. Finally Ney took the town after fierce house-to-house fighting, and Blücher was forced to retreat. Although Napoleon had suffered 3,000 casualties, he had inflicted 4,000 on the enemy.

Such was the first battle in the emperor's last desperate bid to save his crown. Three days later he fought Blücher again, this time in the blinding snow at La Rothière, four miles to the north. Although still outnumbered, he managed a bloody draw, with 6,000 casualties on each side.

Then came five more victories – in only nine days. On 10 February he surprised the Russian general Olussiev's men just south of Champaubert, taking only 200 casualties to the enemy's 4,000 killed, wounded and captured (including General Olussiev). One day after that, with a force of only 10,000, he defeated a Russian/ Prussian army 18,000-strong at Montmirail. Then came victories at Château Thierry (12 February) and Vauchamps (14 February), where the French took 5,000 prisoners and inflicted 4,000 casualties against the loss of only 800. Finally, on 18 February, after an exhausting 60-mile march in only two days, Napoleon defeated the Austrians at Montereau with a ferocious artillery bombardment followed by an infantry assault. At battle's end he ordered hundreds of captured shakos (a peaked military cap) thrown into the Seine, to float downstream to Paris to encourage the Parisians.

Outnumbered 4 to 1, Napoleon had fought seven battles in only three weeks, drawing one and winning six, killing, wounding or capturing 36,000 of the enemy while sustaining only 14,900 casualties himself.

Such was Napoleon's brilliance that the Coalition asked for an armistice (although Great Britain's foreign minister Lord Castlereagh was strongly opposed). But now the emperor fell victim to that nemesis of victors – hubris. Feeling he had the Coalition on the run, he refused.

Despite their losses, the Allies still out-manned and out-gunned the French by a wide margin. Soon they were once again on the march. Just two weeks after Napoleon's victory at Montereau, Blücher crossed the Seine at La Ferté-sous-Jouarre, only 40 miles from Paris.

On 7 March Napoleon attacked Blücher's superior force at Craonne, resulting in a bloody draw in which both sides lost 5,000 men. Then came indecisive actions at Laon and Reims. Two weeks later he flung his army of now only 28,000 against 80,000 Austrians at Arcis-sur-Aube. There Napoleon was thrown to the ground when his horse was shot from under him and he had to withdraw after losing 3,000 men, even though he inflicted 4,000 casualties on the enemy.

Despite the emperor's tactical genius – and the stoic heroism of the French troops – the Coalition had not been stopped. On 25 March the Prussians defeated Napoleon's marshals Mortier and Marmont at Fère-Champenoise, seizing a convoy transporting a vast quantity of arms and nearly all of the army's remaining ammunition. Five days later the gallant Marmont, with only 40,000 soldiers and national guardsmen against 100,000 Coalition attackers, was forced to surrender Paris. After having been deposed by the French Senate, on 11 April Napoleon finally abdicated, fourteen years, two months and nineteen days after his famous *coup d'état* of 18 Brumaire (see 9 November). Within a month he would be exiled on the island of Elba.

Other action this day

1916: Paris is first bombed by German Zeppelins * 1928: British field marshal Douglas Haig (the 'Butcher of the Somme') dies at 66 * 1944: The USS *Missouri*, the last battleship built by the United States and the site of Japan's surrender ending the Second World War, is launched

30 January

The greatest maritime disaster in history

1945 By now the course of the war had made clear to Germans that their nation's fate was sealed, but the event that occurred today was nevertheless shocking: the death of some 9,000 of their countrymen – mostly civilians – when a Russian submarine torpedoed a German transport ship in the Baltic Sea off the coast of Poland. Ironically, this tragedy took place on the twelfth anniversary of 'die Machtergreifung', the seizure of power, the day when Hitler had been sworn in as chancellor of Germany.

Only two days earlier, Hitler had lost his last great gamble at the Battle of the Bulge (see 28 January), and the Russians were overrunning East Prussia and hammering into Poland. In the Nazi-occupied port of Gotenhafen (now Gdynia in Poland) over 10,000 German refugees and servicemen were funnelled aboard the *Wilhelm Gustloff*, a converted 700-foot passenger liner built to accommodate 1,900 people. The *Gustloff*, named for the assassinated leader of the Nazi party in Switzerland, was part of Operation Hannibal, the massive evacuation of German soldiers and civilians fleeing before the Soviet advance.

In the dark of this bitter cold evening, the *Gustloff* left Gotenhafen crammed with 1,080 soldiers (of whom almost 200 were seriously wounded), 173 Kriegsmarine sailors, 373 women naval auxiliary helpers and 8,956 refugees, including thousands of women and children. Snow was falling heavily, and the air temperature had dropped to −15°C. The Baltic Sea was a chilling 4°C, with ice floes on the surface.

Headed for Kiel, the *Gustloff* was accompanied by a sole torpedo boat after another transport and its escort had dropped out with mechanical problems. A German Kriegsmarine commander on board urged that the ship should stay in shallow water and run without lights as protection against enemy submarines, but Friedrich Petersen, the ship's civilian captain, headed for deep water, and when he learned of an approaching German minesweeper convoy, he ordered the *Gustloff*'s green and red navigation lights to be lit to avoid a collision in the dark.

By 9.00pm the *Gustloff* was churning through choppy seas about twenty miles off the Pomeranian coast of Poland when the Soviet submarine *S-13* saw her lights gleaming through the dark. Immediately the sub's captain Alexander Marinesko fired a spread of three torpedoes; the first hit the *Gustloff* at the bow, the second and third amidships, destroying the engine room and shattering the hull. The explosions and the onrushing waters killed several thousand of the *Gustloff*'s passengers outright, while many of the survivors were crushed in their panic to climb the stairs to the deck or running for the lifeboats.

As the *Gustloff* leaned to starboard, the crew fired rescue flares and broadcast an SOS. Remaining passengers leaped from the dying ship to the black and icy Baltic, to expire from drowning or the cold. Now the *Gustloff*'s stern rose high above the dark waters, and just 50 minutes after the torpedo strike, she sank beneath the waves. Miraculously, German ships in the area rescued over 1,000 from the freezing seas, but 9,343 perished in the greatest maritime disaster in history.

Although the Soviet commander Marinesko has been vilified for an attack that cost so many lives, his actions were entirely legal according to the laws of war. The *Gustloff* was not marked as a hospital ship, was armed with anti-aircraft guns and was carrying German combat troops. Although after the war Marinesko descended into alcoholism and was even imprisoned for theft, in 1990, on the 45th anniversary of victory in Europe, the Russian government posthumously named him a Hero of the Soviet Union.

Other action this day

1648: By the Treaty of Münster (part of the Peace of Westphalia), the Netherlands and Spain end the Eighty Years' War, with the Netherlands at last fully independent * 1649: In the aftermath of the English Civil War, Charles I is beheaded, and in 1661 his enemy Oliver Cromwell is formally executed – having been dead for two years * 1933: President Hindenburg appoints Hitler chancellor of Germany * 1945: US Army Rangers and Filipino guerrillas operating behind enemy lines in the Philippines liberate 511 American POWs from the Cabanatuan camp, inflicting over 500 enemy casualties at the cost of three dead and 23 wounded

31 January

The German 6th Army surrenders at Stalingrad

1943 Today, the day after the tenth anniversary of his coming to power, Adolf Hitler raised four of his generals to the rank of field marshal. At that very moment, one of those newly created marshals was in the process of surrendering his army to the enemy. For Field Marshal Friedrich Paulus and his 6th Army, and for Hitler and Nazi Germany as well, the tide of Operation Barbarossa, the German army's invasion of Russia, had turned. The high-water mark was at the city of Stalingrad.

Not many months earlier, believing that the Red Army was on its last legs and possessed no sizeable reserves with which to mount a counter-attack, the German high command determined to deal its foe a knockout blow before winter set in. Hitler wanted Stalin's city taken, no matter what. In this spirit, German ground commanders ignored intelligence reports of large enemy forces building up around the Stalingrad position.

So it was that, beginning on 12 September, when Paulus launched what was supposed to be the final attack, 6th Army found itself facing the fiercest sort of close-quarter resistance, as it attempted to claw its way through the rubble of the ruined city, block by block, building by building, even floor by floor. When the offensive petered out in late October, the centre of Stalingrad still lay in Soviet hands.

Snow began falling on 12 November. It was followed by heavy Soviet attacks driving through the flanks of the long German salient stretching back west and south of Stalingrad. Suddenly, on 22 November, 6th Army, 290,000 strong, found itself cut off and surrounded. In the weeks that followed, the Russians hammered in the sides of the German-held pockets. Supplies had to be flown in now, but the Luftwaffe's available air capacity could bring in less than half of what the army needed to keep functioning. From his headquarters in East Prussia, Hitler proclaimed 'Fortress Stalingrad' and forbade any attempt to break out for the safety of the German lines to the west. Men died by the thousands, from wounds, exhaustion, exposure and starvation. Just before Christmas, a rescue mission was fought to a standstill 35 miles short of 6th Army's lines.

On Christmas Day the temperature was −32°C. On New Year's Day Hitler sent this message to Paulus and his command: 'You and your soldiers … should enter the New Year with the unshakeable confidence that I and the whole German Wehrmacht will do everything in our power to relieve the defenders of Stalingrad …' It was not to be. 6th Army had been abandoned.

Surrender discussions began on 31 January. Sick and demoralised, Paulus at one point refused to order the hold-out XI Corps to join his surrender, but it made no difference. By 4.00am on 2 February, the last signs of resistance had flickered out. All that remained of the German 6th Army – 91,000 soldiers, including 22 generals – was marched away to the Soviet lines. Foreign correspondents witnessing these trophies of the great Soviet victory noted how healthy the German generals appeared compared with their under-nourished troops. Of the German soldiers captured at Stalingrad, 95 per cent died in POW camps. Those who survived, around 5,000, were released after the war, the last 2,000 of them in 1955.

Other action this day

1865: Robert E. Lee becomes general-in-chief of the Confederate armies * 1944: At Cisterna in central Italy, 767 American Rangers and 43 Recon troops are ambushed by vastly superior German forces, including seventeen tanks, as they try to seize the town in a surprise attack; all but seven of the Americans are killed or captured * 1968: The Viet Cong launch attacks against major South Vietnamese cities, provincial capitals and military bases to start the Tet offensive

1 February

'A frozen moment that put a wincing face of horror on the war'

1967 Today in Saigon a general in the South Vietnamese police shot dead a bound enemy prisoner, a member of a Viet Cong murder squad. It was a summary execution that would cause revulsion around the world and destroy the man who fired the shot.

The previous day the Viet Cong had launched the Tet offensive, simultaneously attacking 110 South Vietnamese provincial and district capitals, five of the country's six major cities, and more than two dozen airfields and bases. In Saigon, fierce street fighting erupted across the city, with VC hit squads, dressed as civilians, targeting South Vietnamese National Police officers and their families.

One hit squad member named Lém was captured by the police and brought to Brigadier General Nguyen Ngoc Loan, a 36-year-old former jet fighter pilot who had been put in charge of the National Police. Lém had commanded a team that had just murdered one of Loan's officers and his entire family.

Wearing a broad-checked shirt and dark shorts, Lém stood before General Loan, his hands tied behind his back. Suddenly Loan drew a snub-nosed revolver from his holster, extended his arm and fired a bullet directly into Lém's head, killing him instantly. Loan then turned to a watching reporter and said: 'These guys kill a lot of our people, and I think Buddha will forgive me.'

Buddha may have forgiven Loan, but the world at large did not. In the crowd around him that had witnessed the execution were Associated Press photographer Eddie Adams and NBC cameraman Vo Suu. Both caught the killing on camera, but Adams's picture, wrote the *New York Times*, 'was especially vivid, a frozen moment that put a wincing face of horror on the war. Taken almost at once with the squeeze of the trigger, the photo showed the prisoner … in a final grimace as the bullet passed through his brain.' This grisly image of Lém's death was flashed around the world, appalling people everywhere and stoking anti-war sentiment in the United States.

The Tet offensive continued through June. North Vietnam's ability to strike throughout the south proved a psychological triumph, as it demolished the White House's claims that victory was near and persuaded others that the situation was even worse than they had imagined. In pure military terms, however, it was a disaster for the Viet Cong, who suffered up to 100,000 casualties, against 9,000 US and 11,000 South Vietnamese. One of these was police chief Loan, whose leg had to be amputated after being hit by machine gun fire while he was charging a Viet Cong hideout. Loan was taken to Australia for hospital treatment, but the public outcry at his presence forced the US Army to move him to the Walter Reed Army Medical Center in Washington; but even in America he was repeatedly denounced in Congress.

After Loan returned to Vietnam, he seemed a changed man, spending his time trying to care for children made orphans by the war. When the war came to its end in 1975, however, the Americans refused to help him escape, despite knowing that the Viet Cong would execute him. Nonetheless, he found passage on a South Vietnamese plane and eventually moved with his family to Virginia, where this once proud soldier set up a pizza parlour.

But in America no one had forgotten Eddie Adams's riveting photograph of Loan's seemingly gratuitous act of savagery. Attempts were made to indict him as a war criminal, and people ostracised his pizzeria, where someone scrawled on a restroom wall: 'We know who you are.' As the photographer Eddie Adams later said: 'The general killed the Viet Cong; I killed the general with my camera.'

But Adams, who had seen the raw butchery of the Tet offensive at first hand, including the beheading of women and children in Saigon, came to regret the damage his photograph had done to Loan's reputation. When the general died in 1998, he commented: 'The guy was a hero. America should be crying.'

Other action this day

1477: French troops of Louis XI march into Dijon, ending Burgundy's position as an independent European power ∗ 1702: Prince Eugene of Savoy personally leads a commando-style night attack to defeat the French at the Battle of Cremona during the War of the Spanish Succession ∗ 1862: Julia Ward Howe's abolitionist song, 'Battle Hymn of the Republic', is published for the first time, in the *Atlantic Monthly*

2 February

How Portugal became a great naval power

1509 Today on the west coast of the Indian subcontinent, Portuguese warships sailed into the harbour at Diu and opened fire with a heavy artillery bombardment, completely destroying the enemy's much larger but outgunned fleet. The battle gave Portugal control of the sea routes in the Indian Ocean and turned a tiny nation into one of the world's great naval powers.

At the end of the 15th century the Venetians and the Mamluks of Egypt controlled the lucrative spice trade flowing from India to Europe. Goods followed a sea and land route from India to Egypt and up through the territories of the Ottoman empire (to which the Venetians paid an annual tribute of 10,000 ducats for the privilege) and on to Europe via Venice. But ever since Vasco da Gama's voyage in 1498, Portugal had been trying to supplant the Mamluks and Venetians as the dominant power trading with India, and in 1500 they had established a mini-colony at Cochin on the south-west tip of the subcontinent.

In 1505 the Portuguese viceroy Dom Francisco de Almeida and his son Lourenço led a small armada to Cochin to strengthen Portuguese interests. The 55-year-old Almeida was a tough old soldier who had already distinguished himself against the Moors in Portugal and had fought for the Spanish in the conquest of Granada (see 2 January) in 1492. But north of Cochin lay the Sultanate of Gujarat (an independent state bordering on today's Pakistan and Indian Rajasthan), whose sultan was determined to resist the newcomers. Too weak to fight alone, he called for help from the Mamluk sultan of Egypt, who agreed to send a war fleet to protect the trade monopoly he shared with the Venetians.

The first open conflict came in 1508 when Almeida's son Lourenço was heading back to Portugal with eight cargo ships. As he sailed down India's west coast, a combined Egyptian and Gujarati flotilla cornered him at Chaul. Lourenço was killed in the fighting.

Although they had won the battle, the victors knew that their success against transport ships was a far easier task than taking on the main Portuguese fleet: Portuguese warships were heavily armed sailing ships, principally carracks and caravels that carried broadside batteries that could deliver long-range cannon fire, while the Mamluks and Gujaratis still relied on oar-driven galleys that had cannon only at the bow and stern, since guns on the sides would interfere with the rowers, and native dhows that carried only archers rather than cannon. Therefore, after their victory at Chaul they made for the port of Diu on the coast of Gujarat, where they hoped their land-based artillery could counter the Portuguese guns.

On hearing of his son's death at Chaul, Dom Francisco had sworn he would be avenged. Now the moment had come. The viceroy sailed north from Cochin with 22 ships, including fourteen carracks and six caravels, carrying a crew of 1,000, plus 1,500 soldiers. Although his enemies had 100 ships, Almeida's were vastly superior, and his troops were hardened fighters armed with harquebuses and grenades.

Almeida headed directly towards Diu harbour and opened fire with an intense artillery bombardment. The defenders' cannon were no match for the Portuguese, and the few Mamluk/Gujarati warships were massively out-gunned. Meanwhile, Portuguese small arms peppered the native dhows, which could not get close enough to bring their archers within range. In the final stage of the battle, armoured Portuguese soldiers boarded the enemy ships in the harbour and overwhelmed all resistance. The Mamluk/Gujarati force was utterly destroyed, while the Portuguese did not lose a single ship. (They did suffer minor casualties: one of the wounded was a 29-year-old sailor named Ferdinand Magellan.)

Now Almeida took his final vengeance, ordering most of his prisoners executed in the most barbarous of fashions: some were burnt alive, some hanged and some tied over the mouths of cannon to be blown to bits.

The Battle of Diu broke the Mamluk/Venetian spice trade monopoly and was the initial step towards Portugal's dominance in the Indian Ocean, although Dom Francisco was killed before the extent of his victory had become clear. While he was returning to Portugal ten months after the battle, he stopped on the Cape of Good Hope to resupply. There he and 64 of his men were attacked and killed by Khoikhoi natives. But in the coming years other Portuguese soldier/adventurers established bases in key spots like Goa, Ceylon and Malacca to help create the Portuguese empire that was the most powerful in the area for the next century, until the British East India Company defeated its fleet at the Battle of Swally in 1612.

Other action this day

AD 493: After unsuccessfully besieging Italian king Odoacer at Ravenna for three years, Ostrogoth king Theodoric signs a peace treaty and invites Odoacer to a banquet, during which he makes a toast and kills Odoacer with his own hands, thus becoming King of Italy * 1461: Edward, Earl of March (of York) defeats the Lancastrians at the Battle of Mortimer's Cross * 1645: James Graham, 1st Marquess of Montrose's Royalist army routs the Covenanters under the Marquess of Argyll at the Battle of Inverlochy * 1848: At the conclusion of the Mexican–American War, Mexico and the United States sign the Treaty of Guadalupe Hidalgo which draws the boundary between the US and Mexico at the Rio Grande and the Gila River; for a payment of $15,000,000 the US receives more than 525,000 square miles of land (now Arizona, California, western Colorado, Nevada, New Mexico, Texas, and Utah)

3 February

How the butcher of Cesena started the Papal Schism

1377 In 1308 the French Pope Clement V had moved the papacy from Rome to Avignon, principally as a political favour to Europe's most powerful king, Philip the Fair of France. One of the results of this so-called 'Babylonian Captivity' was a revolt of the Papal States in Italy, led by the Guelphs of Florence. But Pope Urban VI was disinclined to let Italy free from his control, and he ordered his legate there, Cardinal Robert of Geneva, to bring the Papal States to heel, if need be by force of arms.

Robert of Geneva was a young man (34) of high cultivation and sophistication. Although both lame and fat, he was also a cousin of the King of France. His manner was highly autocratic and his methods entirely ruthless.

After hiring a band of mercenaries led by a renegade English knight named Sir John Hawkwood, Robert immediately attacked the city-states in revolt. He was at first unsuccessful but then came to the town of Cesena, near the Adriatic coast between Ravenna and Rimini.

To persuade Cesena's citizens to open their city gates, Cardinal Robert promised clemency by holy oath. But once inside the town he summoned his mercenaries and called for 'sangue et sangue' (blood and blood). Beginning on 3 February 1377, the soldiers butchered the town's inhabitants for three days and nights. Women were raped, men slaughtered and hundreds drowned in the moat outside the walls while trying to escape. Almost 5,000 in all were slain, and Cesena was put to the torch.

Cardinal Robert's services to the papacy at Avignon were considered so valuable that in September of the following year he was elected Pope as Clement VII, although there was already another pope on St Peter's throne in Rome. Thus this noble murderer became the first anti-pope in the Papal Schism that was to tear Christendom apart for 71 years.

Other action this day

1706: Sweden defeats Saxony-Poland and their Russian allies at the Battle of Fraustadt during the Great Northern War * 1787: Massachusetts militia defeat rebel Daniel Shays and his followers, crushing Shays' Rebellion, an armed uprising set off by government taxes and local debt * 1795: Venezuelan general and political leader Antonio José de Sucre is born in Cumaná

4 February

The Big Three meet at Yalta

1945 Today, Allied leaders Franklin Roosevelt, Winston Churchill and Joseph Stalin met at Yalta for a week of meetings that would determine the future and structure of post-war Europe.

Yalta is in the Ukraine facing the Black Sea. Once a chic resort where tsars built summer palaces and Russian nobility flocked, because of its beauty and mild climate, now it was battered and forlorn after the depredations of the Nazis and Stalin's deportation of the Tatars. Churchill called it the 'Riviera of Hades'.

By the time of the conference, the war in Europe had almost been won. In the east, Russia was crossing the Elbe, while in the west,

American and British troops were racing for the Rhine, Paris liberated six months before. In total, the Allies had about 25,000 tanks and the same number of aircraft against fewer than 4,000 tanks and aircraft that Nazi Germany could still field.

Plans put forth at Teheran, the previous Big Three meeting of December 1943, to split post-war Germany into four occupied zones were confirmed at Yalta, and further progress was made in defining the functions of the United Nations, the founding conference of which was to be held in San Francisco only two months later. Trials for major war criminals were agreed, and the subject of German reparations was assigned to a commission when it became clear that Russia was determined to beggar Germany, stripping it bare of all heavy industry, including the steel, electrical power and chemical industries. As a sop to Roosevelt, Stalin promised to enter the war against Japan.

The most contentious question was Eastern Europe, where Stalin was determined to establish Soviet satellites, in direct contradiction to Roosevelt's and Churchill's vision of free democratic states. When Churchill pointed out, 'You know, we have two parties in England', Stalin replied: 'One is much better.' To proposals that Allied observers should monitor elections, Russian foreign minister Molotov protested that it would be insulting to the self-respect and sovereignty of newly liberated countries.

Poland was a particularly acrimonious issue, especially for Churchill, whose country had gone to war to defend Polish independence in 1939. Stalin insisted that the Communist-backed Lublin government should run the country, while Roosevelt and Churchill demanded that members of Poland's London government-in-exile be included and free elections be held.

Eventually Stalin agreed to British–American demands for the establishment of 'interim governmental authorities [in Eastern Europe] broadly representative of all democratic elements in the population ... and ... free elections of governments responsive to the will of the people'.

And so, on 11 February the three leaders headed home, Churchill and Roosevelt hoping for the best, Stalin planning the worst. Two months later the exhausted Roosevelt died of a stroke.

In May Germany capitulated after Hitler's suicide (see 30 April), and in August, after the destruction and shock of two atom bombs,

Japan surrendered unconditionally. And now Stalin broke all the promises he had made: there would be no free elections in Poland, Hungary, Czechoslovakia, Romania or Bulgaria. Russia would set up puppet Communist governments that would suppress other parties and rule by force, backed by Soviet tanks. As Churchill so memorably stated the following year: 'From Stettin in the Baltic to Trieste in the Adriatic an iron curtain has descended across the continent.' The Cold War had begun.

When the Yalta agreements were made public in 1946, the American right reacted with fury, aimed equally at perfidious Russia and at Roosevelt, who, they claimed, debilitated by his final illness, had 'given away' Eastern Europe.

The idea of Roosevelt's 'giving away' Eastern Europe was of course patently absurd. At the time of Yalta Russian troops already occupied most of Eastern Europe, including virtually all of Poland and parts of Germany. The only way to evict them would have been by force, something the Americans and British never contemplated – and could almost certainly not have achieved.

Always suspicious of Stalin, even before the conference Churchill had wondered whether 'the end of this war may well prove to be more disappointing than was the last'. And only a month after the conference closed, when the Russians declared the 'free' Poles ineligible for government, Roosevelt came fully to understand Stalin's duplicity. 'We can't do business with Stalin', he said. 'He has broken every one of the promises he made at Yalta.' When challenged on Yalta's outcome, he answered: 'I didn't say the result was good; I said it was the best I could do.'

Although Stalin died in 1953, the execrable system he instituted kept millions in totalitarian oppression until the collapse of the Communist system 44 years after his deceit at Yalta.

Other action this day
1716: After a 44-day failed invasion, James Francis Edward, the Old Pretender, abandons Scotland for France with the hopeful words, 'Nous recoulons pour mieux sauter' ('We pull back better to jump forward'), but he never again touches Scottish soil * 1789: The Electoral College unanimously elects General George Washington American president * 1861: Seven secessionist southern states form the Confederate States of America, in Montgomery, Alabama, setting the stage for the American Civil War

5 February

For 'some signal act of valour'

1856 Today the *London Gazette* reported that 'The Queen [Victoria] has been pleased ... to institute and create a new Naval and Military Decoration to be styled "The Victoria Cross."' She announced that the new medal would 'be awarded to those officers and men who have served Us in the presence of the enemy, and shall have then performed some signal act of valour'. So it was that the VC became Great Britain's highest award for gallantry in combat, a medal that brought with it the rather niggardly pension of £10 a year (worth today perhaps £650).

Since 1853 Great Britain had been heroically engaged in the bloody Crimean War. British troops had defied Russian shellfire at Sevastopol, infantrymen had formed the 'thin red line' against enemy assault at Balaclava, where the Light Brigade had famously charged the guns (see 25 October), and guardsmen had stormed over the walls of the Greater Redoubt at Alma. Now, with the war about to come to an end (peace was signed on 30 March), the government, the Queen and her consort Prince Albert wanted to recognise individual acts of heroism. In addition, as the Duke of Newcastle somewhat cynically wrote: 'The value attached by soldiers to a little bit of ribbon is such as to render any danger insignificant and any privation light if it can be attained.' (In this he was simply echoing Napoleon, who had commented about the French Legion of Honour: 'A soldier will fight long and hard for a bit of coloured ribbon.')

Initially the citation was to have been named 'The Military Order of Victoria', but Albert saw that the word 'order' would suggest an aristocratic fraternity and proposed that it should be called the Victoria Cross, 'which will make it simple and intelligible'. The medals themselves were to be made from the bronze of Russian guns captured in the Crimea. Unhappily, however, the actual cannon melted down came from Woolwich Barracks, which years later were found not to be Russian at all but Chinese.

The next year in June, the first VCs were awarded in Hyde Park, where the Queen, on horseback, pinned a medal on each of the 62 recipients who stood on a dais. As she leaned forward to decorate one soldier, she inadvertently stabbed him in the chest. Demonstrating the bravery that had won him the honour, the soldier stood unflinchingly as she fastened the pin through his flesh.

In all, 111 VCs were given to Crimean War soldiers and sailors. The first action for which it was granted occurred on 21 June 1854, when HMS *Hecla* was exchanging fire with a Russian fortress in the Baltic. According to the ship's captain, twenty-year-old midshipman Charles Lucas showed 'a remarkable instance of coolness and presence of mind in action' when he picked up and threw overboard 'a live shell thrown on board the "Hecla" by the enemy, while the fuse was burning'.

Behind every Victoria Cross is a similar act of selfless bravery. Some of the earlier citations were succinct: 'On 25 October 1854 at Balaclava, Crimea, an officer in the Heavy Cavalry charge was surrounded by Russian cavalry and in great danger. Sergeant-Major [John] Grieve rode up to his rescue, cutting off the head of one Russian and dispersing the others.'

Other VC stories seem like real-life versions of *Biggles Flies Again*, such as that of RAF sergeant Norman Jackson. On Jackson's 31st mission over Nazi Germany, an enemy fighter opened fire on his Lancaster, igniting a fuel tank in the starboard wing. Already wounded from shell splinters, Jackson grabbed a fire extinguisher and climbed out of his bomber onto the fuselage. Then his parachute partially opened, making him slip onto the wing, now wreathed in fire. Seriously burned, he fell 20,000 feet with a partially opened and burning parachute. Further injured on landing, he was sent to a German POW camp but escaped after ten months to be picked up by the US 3rd Army.

But perhaps more typical is the sombre story of the Australian Frederick Birks: 'On 20 September 1917 ... east of Ypres ... Second Lieutenant Birks, accompanied by a corporal, rushed a strong point which was holding up the advance. The corporal was wounded, but Second Lieutenant Birks went on alone, killed the remainder of the enemy and captured the machine-gun. Shortly afterwards he took a small party and attacked another strong point occupied by about 25 of the enemy, killing some and capturing an officer and 15 men ... He was fatally wounded whilst trying to rescue some of his men who had been buried by a shell.'

By the end of 2009 a total of 1,358 Victoria Crosses had been awarded, and three men had won it twice. Twenty-four VCs were earned on a single day during the relief of Lucknow in the Indian Rebellion and eleven for the epic defence at Rorke's Drift in the Zulu War. 634 VCs were given during the First World War, compared to only 181 during the Second. Totals for more recent wars are: Korean War – thirteen; Indonesia–Malaysia – one; Vietnam War – four; Falklands War – two; Iraq War – one. The war in Afghanistan has so far produced two VCs. One was given to Corporal Bryan Budd, who led two assaults on Taliban positions and was mortally wounded in the second attack. According to Budd's citation, 'when his body was later recovered it was found surrounded by three dead Taliban'. Later Trooper Mark Donaldson of the Australian Special Air Service earned the medal for deliberately drawing enemy fire to help comrades to escape and then saving a wounded interpreter during the Afghanistan War.

Other action this day

1782: Spanish and French forces capture the British-held Mediterranean island of Menorca * 1900: The Boers defeat the British under General Sir Redvers Buller at Vaalkrans in his third attempt to relieve Ladysmith, inflicting 333 casualties * 1918: Off the coast of Ireland, German submarine U-77 torpedoes and sinks the steamship *Tuscania*, travelling as part of a British convoy and transporting over 2,000 American soldiers to Europe * 1918: Gunner-bombardier Stephen W. Thompson becomes the first member of the US military to shoot down an enemy aircraft during the First World War when, flying with the French, he downs a German Albatros D.III fighter over Saarbrücken

6 February

The one-two punch

1862 In the ten months since the beginning of the American Civil War, the Northern generals commanding the most critical sectors of the sprawling Western Theater – Henry W. Halleck and Don Carlos Buell – proved unable to reach agreement over where, when, or with whose troops to launch an attack against the enemy forces that lay to their front. As a result of this divided command, the theatre had seen little action of any kind, despite considerable urging for a joint offensive from various quarters in the Union capital at Washington, especially from President Abraham Lincoln.

At last, General Halleck in St Louis, Missouri reluctantly approved a proposal from a couple of junior commanders for an army–navy expedition to probe two weak points in the Confederate line, which extended eastwards across southern Kentucky and northern Tennessee, from the Mississippi River to the Appalachian Mountains. The expedition's first objective was to be Fort Henry, some 60 miles up the Tennessee River from the Union base at Paducah, Kentucky; if the action proved successful, the second objective, only twelve miles overland from Fort Henry, was Fort Donelson, guarding the Cumberland River.

Accordingly, the two commanders, Brigadier General Ulysses S. Grant and Commodore Andrew Foote, brought six ironclads and two infantry divisions upriver from Paducah, and at 11.00 this morning launched the assault on Fort Henry. The Tennessee was in flood, which slowed the infantry's advance up the east bank but allowed the gunboats to steam up close to the fort, poorly sited on a low bank and partly under water, and to open fire at point-blank range. The artillery exchange was heavy – one ironclad was disabled – but surrender came within two hours, even before the infantry arrived. Capitalising on the quick victory, gunboats now steamed further upriver behind enemy lines to destroy a railway bridge, severing a key link in Confederate communications.

'Fort Henry is ours', Grant cabled Halleck. 'I shall take and destroy Fort Donelson on the 8th.' That was optimistic. Bad weather delayed the march to Fort Donelson, and it wasn't until the 13th that Grant's infantry – two divisions, now reinforced by a third – were in position around their objective. In the meantime, while Foote's gunboats retired downriver to Paducah to refit and resupply for the Cumberland effort, the Confederate theatre commander, General A.S. Johnson, managed to reinforce Donelson, whose defenders now numbered around 14,000.

On the 14th, with his naval force in place, Commodore Foote sent seven gunboats against the fort, hoping to duplicate the success of the previous week. Instead, the Navy gunners consistently overshot the enemy's works, while their boats were badly damaged by plunging fire from the shore batteries, which forced them downriver and out of range. Now it was the army's turn.

Even though the repulse of the Union fleet was telegraphed to Confederate headquarters in Richmond, Virginia as a sign of impending victory, the three Confederate generals inside Fort Donelson recognised the plight of their command, surrounded and outnumbered as it was by the Union forces. To avoid sure defeat and capture, they ordered a breakout the next dawn, in the hope that their troops could escape to the safety of Nashville, Tennessee.

After some initial success and much bloody fighting – the body count would reach over 1,000 – the breakout stalled. Arriving late on the field from a conference with Foote, who had been badly wounded in yesterday's action, Grant coolly surveyed the scene, then gave his division commanders orders to retake the lost ground and seal off the escape route. By nightfall it was done. Even so, during the night, two of the three Confederate generals, with 1,500 troops, made their way out by steamer, leaving behind some 12,000 in the command of General Simon Bolivar Buckner.

Next morning Buckner sent a note to Grant – the two were friends from their West Point days – requesting 'the appointment of Commissioners to agree on terms of capitulation'. What he got in response soon became famous. 'No terms except an unconditional surrender can be accepted', replied Grant. 'I propose to move immediately on your works.'

The one-two punch of Henry and Donelson had immediate and electrifying effect around the Union, as described by the historian Doris Kearns Goodwin: 'The North was jubilant upon receiving news of Grant's triumph at Donelson, the first substantial Union victory of the war. Hundred-gun salutes were fired in celebrations across the land.' The capital city was 'quite wild with Excitement'. In the Senate, 'the gallery rose *en masse* and gave three enthusiastic cheers'. Elaborate plans were made to illuminate the capital's public buildings in joint celebration of the double victory and George Washington's birthday.

For the South, with its western line broken, its forces split, and Union gunboats now patrolling the Tennessee River as far down as Alabama, the Henry–Donelson campaign forced a withdrawal of forces southward to a new concentration in the vicinity of Corinth, Mississippi. Not far from Corinth, in less than two months, another riverside battle with the Union would be fought, this time at a place called Shiloh.

The day after Donelson fell, U.S. Grant was promoted to major general, the order signed by a greatly cheered President Lincoln. The public soon became enchanted with the phrase 'unconditional surrender', which happily fitted the first two initials of the general's name. The victorious campaign in the west also raised expectations in the Lincoln administration – and in the public at large – that something similar should happen in the east, quiet since the Union's defeat at Bull Run the previous July. This pressure helped prod a reluctant general-in-chief George B. McClellan into action. On 8 March the Army of the Potomac began preparations for its offensive against the Confederate capital at Richmond.

Other action this day

1778: French and American representatives sign the Franco-American Alliance in Paris, agreeing to help each other in the event of British attack and thus opening the way for French military assistance during the American Revolution * 1817: Argentinian General José de San Martín completes the 'Crossing of the Andes' to liberate Chile from Spanish rule * 1941: The first day of the Battle of Beda Fomm in North Africa in which the British defeat the Italians

7 February

The Winter Battle of the Masurian Lakes

1915 At the end of 1914, after bitter defeat on the Marne but resounding victory at Tannenburg, there were those in the German high command who thought the Eastern Front should now become the priority theatre of the Great War. First among the 'easterners' was the front's commander-in-chief Marshal Paul von Hindenburg, who called for increased forces with which to launch an all-out offensive that would knock the Russians out of the Polish salient and win the war for Germany.

Not everyone agreed that such a change in strategy would work. Leading the 'westerners' was General Erich von Falkenhayn, whose job as the German army's Chief of the Great General Staff

Hindenburg badly coveted. Falkenhayn maintained that the war could not be won in the east, that it was France and Britain whose defeat would bring an end to the conflict, and that Germany's efforts and manpower should be concentrated in the west.

But Austria-Hungary, Germany's war partner, was desperate for German action in Poland that would take the pressure off its own failures in the Carpathians. Moreover, bold action in the east had the likely prospect of deterring Italy and Romania, both nations so far neutral, from joining the Entente.

In the end, it was Hindenburg who had his way. After his feat at Tannenburg, he was a hero to his nation. More important, he had the Kaiser's ear.

So it was that this morning, amid blizzard conditions and temperatures at 40° below zero, a new vision of the war was put to the test, as two German armies launched an offensive against Russian positions in the Masurian Lakes, at the edge of East Prussia. Even before the attack began, Hindenburg predicted that 'the success will be so evident that the world can no longer doubt Germany's final victory in the East'.

To cloak their intentions, the Germans had mounted a diversionary action a week earlier at Bolimov, well to the south, in which poison gas was used for the first time – and unsuccessfully – in the Great War. Today's bad weather further misled the Russians when it prevented a number of German units from reaching the front lines in time to join the opening attacks, giving the impression that what was afoot was no more than isolated probes.

By the offensive's third day, the German 8th Army had got well around the Russian left, while to the north, attacks by the German 10th Army had sent two Russian cavalry divisions into flight. When the corps holding either end of the Russian line retreated to escape encirclement, the Russian XX Corps was left to face the enemy alone. On 21 February, in the Forest of Augustow, General Bulgakoff surrendered the 12,000 troops under his command, most of them wounded. Overall Russian losses in the two-week campaign totalled 56,000 men and 185 guns.

The Winter Battle of the Masurian Lakes, as the offensive was called, was a solid tactical victory for Germany. But, with his army's southern flank now exposed and the bad weather continuing, Hindenburg could not expand his success. Nevertheless, he made sure it was billed to the German public in appropriate terms: a modern Cannae or, even better, a second Tannenburg. To further the cause, he inflated the Russian losses, which he reported as 110,000 troops and 300 guns. And if more proof of great success were needed, the Kaiser now journeyed to Hindenburg's headquarters at Insterburg, to award the marshal Germany's highest military medal, the Pour le Mérite.

But it was Falkenhayn's prediction that proved correct: there would be no knockout victory on the Eastern Front. The war there continued without cease and at great cost to all sides, fought, as Winston Churchill described it, 'in the snow and mud of Poland and Galicia, over enormous fronts swaying backwards and forwards with varying fortunes …'

Italy declared war on Austria in May. Romania joined the Allies a year later. After the German failure at Verdun, Hindenburg got Falkenhayn's job. The Communist government of worn-down Russia signed an armistice at the end of 1917, but in the end it was on the Western Front that the Great War was finally won – by the Allies.

Other action this day

1074: Pandulf IV, Prince of Benevento, is killed at the Battle of Montesarchio against the Normans * 1807: Napoleon fights the Russians and Prussians on the first day of the inconclusive Battle of Eylau in East Prussia * 1950: The United States recognises Vietnam under the leadership of Emperor Bao Dai, not Ho Chi Minh who is recognised by the Soviets, setting the stage for the Vietnam War

8 February

The fall of Singapore

1942 For four days the Japanese had bombarded British defences on Singapore island. At 8.30 this evening the first wave of landing craft carrying 4,000 men from the mainland crossed the Johore Strait – only 600 yards wide at its narrowest point – and landed on Sarimbun Beach on the north-west coast. In only a week 40,000 Japanese would utterly defeat an Allied force of 80,000 Australians, British, Indians and Malays.

For two months it had been clear that Singapore was in peril; on 8 December 1941 Lieutenant General Tomoyuki Yamashita's 25th Army had invaded the Malay peninsula, an attack that actually started an hour before the bombing of Pearl Harbor (because Malaysia is on the other side of the international dateline, it is a day ahead). The British command in Singapore, however, was both woefully unprepared and deplorably complacent. Singapore was thought to be 'the Gibraltar of the East', protected by massive artillery and a large fighting force. Big guns pointed out to sea to the south, to protect against a seaborne landing. No one could imagine that any aggressor could break through the impenetrable swamps and jungles of the Malay peninsula to attack Singapore from the north. But highly mobile, jungle-trained Japanese soldiers, using bicycles and light tanks, managed to do just that. 'By 30 January,' one observer noted, 'the Malay Peninsula was lost. Less than two hundred survivors of the Argyll and Sutherland Highlanders marched across the causeway to Singapore Island with their pipers playing. They were the last; behind them the causeway was blown ...'

Sarimbun Beach was a ten-mile stretch of coast fronting rubber plantations and mangrove swamps, with almost nothing to stop the invaders. There were only a few tank traps and no anti-tank weapons, and Singapore's mighty guns, although they could be turned to face north-west, had to fire over the city at targets they could not see, more than fifteen miles away. Moreover, their shells were armour-piercing, designed to sink enemy ships, but ineffective against infantry. Meanwhile, Japanese artillery pounded the beach as well as targets further inland.

On Sarimbun Beach the Australian 22nd Infantry Brigade, reinforced by the Australian 2/4th Machine Gun Battalion, had greeted the Japanese invaders with bursts of machine gun fire, but they were spread so thinly along the beach that the enemy could infiltrate and outflank them in the dark of night. By midnight the 22nd had been forced to retreat, and an hour later the last Australian reserves were sent forward. By then the Japanese were landing the first of 200 tanks, of which the British had not a single one. At dawn on the 9th the Australians were overrun, with one battalion suffering 50 per cent casualties.

Although the battle for Singapore continued for a week, the outcome was never in doubt. With total air superiority and highly trained and motivated troops, the Japanese captured Tengah airfield on 9 February and two days later seized most of the Allied ammunition and fuel while knocking out the city's water supplies. Despite moments of heroic resistance, mostly by the Australians or the Malays, they moved inexorably south towards the city of Singapore itself. From London a desperate Churchill ordered: 'There must at this stage be no thought of saving the troops or sparing the population … Commanders and senior officers should die with their troops.' To which he added sententiously: 'The honour of the British Empire and of the British Army is at stake.'

By now, however, the Allied forces were battered beyond resistance and totally demoralised – the Australian 22nd Brigade, which had borne the brunt of the Japanese attacks, had been reduced to a few hundred effectives. The British commander, Lieutenant General Arthur Percival, surrendered at five o'clock on the afternoon of 15 February. The Allied forces had suffered 2,000 killed in action, 5,000 wounded and 70,000 captured, the largest surrender of British-led military personnel in history. The cost to the victors was only 1,700 dead and 3,000 wounded. A few days later the Japanese slaughtered between 25,000 and 50,000 Singaporean Chinese in the so-called Sook Ching massacre.

The fall of Singapore, Britain's key defensive position in the Far East, was a devastating defeat for the British, and some historians maintain that this was the first of many losses that would end in the dissolution of the British empire.

Other action this day

1250: The first day of the four-day Battle of Al Mansurah during the Seventh Crusade, in which Ayyubid (Egyptian, Syrian, Yemeni) forces crush the Crusaders led by King Louis IX of France (St Louis) * 1820: American Union general William Tecumseh Sherman is born * 1881: The Boers defeat the British at the Battle of Schuinshoogte during the First Boer War

9 February

Surprise attack from the sea

1904 Shortly after midnight, in the gloom of a snowy winter night, the naval siege of Port Arthur began as Vice Admiral Togo's Japanese battleships and cruisers, standing well out to sea, opened fire on their targets: the Russian fleet anchored just offshore, the harbour behind, and further back the powerful shore batteries. The long-range bombardment was in effect a declaration of war, confirming the intention of a surprise destroyer raid conducted an hour earlier that had caught the Russian warships unaware and damaged three vessels.

So began the Russo-Japanese War, a clash of imperial ambitions for hegemony in the Far East.

The siege of Port Arthur was the first step in the Japanese war plan. Located on the Yellow Sea, it was Russia's only year-round ice-free port in the Pacific and the main base for its Far Eastern fleet. Its only other naval base in the Pacific was Vladivostok, some 1,000 miles away by sea around the Korean peninsula.

Capture of Port Arthur, or at least the trapping of the Russian fleet there, would give Japan command of the seas. This was a matter of strategic importance, for the next step in Japan's war plan was landing armies on the Asian mainland to engage and defeat the Russian forces in Manchuria before reinforcements could arrive from Moscow, some 5,500 miles by railway across the continent of Asia.

Tonight's opening bombardment did not disable the Russian fleet, but the blockade and mine-laying that followed had the effect of intimidating Russian naval commanders from ordering aggressive action. In the one serious attempt to challenge the blockading cruisers, on 13 April, the Russian battleship *Petropavlovsk* hit a mine and sank with all hands. Thereafter, sorties from the besieged port were few and ineffective.

The very morning after the Port Arthur raid, Japanese warships, escorting transports carrying an expeditionary force, seized the Korean port of Chemulpo (Inchon) across the Yellow Sea, where they destroyed two Russian ships. A week later, a Japanese army – the first of three – began the march north towards Manchuria.

The war on land was fought entirely in Manchuria, as Japanese armies advanced, forcing the Russians to withdraw northwards. Over the next year, a series of battles was fought, beginning with the crossing of the Yalu in late April, then at places like Nan Shan, Tashichao, and Liaoyang, culminating in the Russian defeat at Mukden in March 1905.

Meanwhile, at Port Arthur in the south, the Russian fleet continued to be a threat as long as its warships remained afloat and protected by the harbour's guns. Therefore, in May, the Japanese landed a fourth army on the Asian shore to take by land what they couldn't destroy by sea. The siege of Port Arthur, a series of Japanese assaults on the siege works, long and singularly bloody for both sides, lasted eight months until the Russian surrender on 2 January 1905. It pitted 100,000 Japanese troops, of whom nearly 60,000 became casualties, against some 40,000 defenders, of whom nearly half would become injured or sick.

Hoping to redress the deteriorating military situation, Tsar Nicholas II had ordered Russia's Baltic Fleet to sail for the Far East. By the time the fleet reached the Sea of Japan, in May 1905, Port Arthur had fallen and Vladivostok became the destination. Sailing northward through the Tsushima Strait between Japan and Korea, the Russian fleet met almost total destruction, an event effectively ending the fighting on land and at sea.

With Japan having won its limited war objectives and Russia, preoccupied with internal discontent, ready to disengage, representatives of both nations met in Portsmouth, New Hampshire in a conference called by United States President Theodore Roosevelt. There, on 6 September 1905, a peace treaty was signed.

The attack that began the Russo-Japanese war remained an inspiration to the Japanese military – a blueprint, in fact. But it was only after 7 December 1941 that historians would recognise Port Arthur as 'the first Pearl Harbor'. As proof, it was later discovered that the flagship carrier of the Japanese fleet approaching Pearl Harbor early that December morning flew from its bridge the very flag flown from Admiral Togo's battleship the night his fleet opened the siege of Port Arthur.

Other action this day

1097: 700 Crusader knights defeat Ridwan of Aleppo at the Battle of Harenc, forcing him to retreat and abandon his attempt to relieve

Antioch * 1945: The British submarine HMS *Venturer* torpedoes and sinks the German U-boat U-864 off the Norwegian coast, the only time in history that one submarine sank another while both were submerged

10 February

'Now I'll be at them with the bayonet.'

1846 The Sikh empire in the Punjab was the last kingdom in India not under British domination, as the British East India Company had swallowed up the rest of the subcontinent. But now the Sikh army was rapidly expanding, claiming itself to be the Khalsa, or embodiment of the Sikh nation. Meanwhile the British, fearful that the Sikhs were becoming a menace to their territories along the border, started to build up their own forces, a move that the Sikhs construed as the first step towards invasion. By December 1845 the two sides were battling in the First Anglo–Sikh War.

The British commander-in-chief in India was Field Marshal Sir Hugh Gough, a balding 67-year-old Irishman with mutton-chop whiskers and a bristling moustache. He had proved himself in the Peninsular War – he was severely wounded at Talavera and again at Nivelle – and during the First Opium War in China. In combat he invariably wore his conspicuous white 'Battle Coat' so that his troops could see him and to draw enemy fire away from his own soldiers.

Now in India, Gough led a force of British, Gurkha and Bengal regiments. In mid-December he scored a quick but costly victory at Mudki, followed three days later by an even bloodier one at Ferozeshah, where, it was reported, the red and white pennants on the lances of the cavalry were so coated with dried blood that they stiffened as if they had been starched. Today, on 10 February 1846, his army of 20,000 men and 65 guns would meet the Sikhs near Sobraon in the pivotal battle of the war.

The Sikhs had fortified a strong position with 40,000 men on the south bank of the Sutlej River, the border between Sikh- and British-controlled territory. Dressed in European-style red jackets and blue trousers, their infantry occupied a semi-circular ditch at a bend in the river, connected by a pontoon bridge to their 67 guns across the river behind them.

With the dawn came a heavy fog, which dissipated around 6.00am. Then Gough ordered his 35 heavy guns and howitzers to open fire, the Sikh artillery instantly responding in kind. But neither cannonade did much damage, and within two hours the attackers were running out of ammunition. Gough, however, welcomed the shortage, declaring: 'Thank God. Now I'll be at them with the bayonet.' As drums and bugles signalled the assault, his red-coated infantry, armed with bayonet-fitted Brown Besses (.75 calibre flint-lock muskets), charged the enemy line.

While two British divisions made a feint on the enemy left, Sir Robert Dick led his division in the main attack on the right, as horse artillery units galloped to both flanks to open a covering barrage. Despite heavy return fire from the Sikhs, Dick's soldiers stormed over the ditch, driving out the defenders. But then a Sikh counter-attack drove them back, killing Dick in the process. The Sikhs then butchered the wounded British soldiers left on the field.

Incensed by this slaughter, the British and Bengal regiments attacked once more, this time breaking through. On the Sikh right, the 3rd King's Own Light Dragoons, dashing in their navy blue uniforms with a crimson stripe down each leg, crossed the ditch and infiltrated through the enemy position. Armed with swords and carbines, they turned to charge the Sikhs from the rear.

Now under attack from all quarters, the Sikh line began to fold. Individual soldiers turned to escape across the river, but the pontoon bridge collapsed under their weight, throwing hundreds into the torrent and leaving 20,000 others trapped before the British onslaught.

Although mercilessly bombarded by Gough's artillery, the Sikhs refused to surrender – and the British, still enraged by the Sikh massacre of their wounded, shot down even those who tried. Meanwhile, British guns continued to shell the crowd of hapless Sikhs trying to swim the river. By midday the firing finally sputtered to a halt: some 10,000 Sikhs had lost their lives, while the British suffered just 230 killed and 2,000 wounded.

Within two days the British had repaired the pontoon bridge and crossed into the Punjab, headed for Lahore. On 22 February the Union Jack flew from the citadel, and the Sikh leaders negotiated terms for surrender. By the Treaty of Lahore, signed in March, the Sikhs ceded some valuable land to the East India Company – as well as the 186-carat Koh-i-Noor diamond, then the largest known, which now is set into the crown of Queen Elizabeth II.

Although it ended the First Anglo–Sikh War, the Battle of Sobraon did not terminate hostilities, since the Second Anglo–Sikh War broke out on 21 February the following year. This time General Gough routed the Sikhs decisively at the Battle of Gujrat, and on 2 April the British formally annexed the Punjab, to complete their hegemony of the subcontinent.

Other action this day

1258: The Mongols destroy Baghdad ∗ 1763: The French and Indian War ends with the Peace of Paris; Quebec is ceded to the British ∗ 1906: HMS *Dreadnought* is launched, the fastest battleship in the world and the first battleship to have a uniform main battery rather than a few large guns complemented by a heavy secondary battery of smaller guns

11 February

Heraclius – emperor, general and warrior

AD 641 Today died the Eastern Roman emperor Heraclius after 30 years in power. Leading his army in person, he conquered the Persians, and even when he could no longer take the field, the military system he invented saved his Christian empire from the attacks of a new and powerful force from the Middle East – militant Islam.

Blond and grey-eyed, Heraclius grew up in Roman Africa; according to legend, he early showed his prowess by fighting lions in gladiatorial combat. When he was 35, he and his father overthrew the Eastern Roman usurper emperor, Phocas. When Phocas was captured in Constantinople, Heraclius personally beheaded him and ordered his mutilated corpse to be paraded through the city and burned. Heraclius then had himself crowned emperor.

But while Heraclius had been busy bringing down Phocas, the Sassanid (Persian) empire had been ravaging Imperial territories. His first military response failed to dent the Persian advance, and the Sassanids soon captured Damascus and then Jerusalem, damaging the Church of the Holy Sepulchre and making away with its most precious relic, the Holy Cross.

The Persians then completed their occupation of Egypt and swept into Anatolia, threatening Constantinople. But Heraclius decided to bring the war to Persia itself. Wearing the robes of a penitent, in AD 621 he left Constantinople as the faithful prayed for victory, the reconquest of Jerusalem and the recovery of the Holy Cross. In effect, he was leading the first crusade.

Heraclius took personal command of his army, the first Roman emperor to do so since Theodosius some 250 years before, and advanced with 50,000 men into enemy territory. On one famous occasion, his men charged across a bridge to attack a Persian force, only to be ambushed and almost wiped out. As the Persians hurtled back across the bridge, Heraclius single-handedly met their charge, cutting down the Persian leader and enabling his soldiers to regroup and repel the assault.

The war with Persia lasted for almost five years, Heraclius finally winning a seesaw campaign that enabled him to return to Constantinople in 626. There the Persians were again besieging the city, reinforced by 80,000 Avars (a people from the Caucasus who had settled in today's Hungary). Although only 12,000 cavalry defended the capital, the city's massive Theodosian Walls stymied the besiegers, while the Patriarch of Constantinople encouraged the city's inhabitants to ever-increasing zeal in their defence. Finally, both the Persian and Avar fleets were sunk in separate engagements, and the attackers abandoned the siege, convinced that divine intervention had caused their defeat.

With Constantinople safe, Heraclius again moved into Persia. After a march across the Armenian highlands into the Tigris plain, on 12 December 627 he crushed a Persian army of 70,000 men in a day-long encounter at Nineveh (now in Iraq), the climactic battle of the war. Once again Heraclius's personal bravery turned the tide, as he cut down three generals and then rode into the enemy line at the head of his army, killing their commander and forcing the Persians to flee in panic. He then led his men down the Tigris, despoiling the country.

After his victories, Heraclius treated prisoners of war well and did not punish the inhabitants of the conquered towns, a striking contrast with Persian cruelty. As a case in point, when, a month after

Nineveh, he conquered the royal residence at Dastagird, he left the royal treasury intact, demanding only the return of the Holy Cross. In 630, he marched triumphantly into Jerusalem and restored the Cross to the Church of the Holy Sepulchre.

Now at last the Persians were forced to come to terms, but the Sassanid empire's days were numbered. At this point Heraclius started styling himself Basileus, Greek for 'monarch', a title that Byzantine emperors used for the next eight centuries.

Perhaps unnoticed by Heraclius at the time, a new militant cause was gathering strength in the region, led by a 54-year-old Arab named Mohammed whose intense religious vision was attracting followers. Over the next ten years this new religion, backed by an ever-increasing army, would grow into an unstoppable force that absorbed the remains of the Persian empire, terminally weakened by war with Heraclius. The Muslims gave their victims three choices: convert to Islam, pay the *jizyah* (a tax on non-believers) or die by the sword. Inevitably, this growing Muslim power came into conflict with the Christian Byzantines.

Although Mohammed died in 632, the Muslim force he had created continued to expand, in 634 sweeping into Syria. By now, however, Heraclius was too ill to lead his armies, and without his generalship they could not withstand the Muslim assault.

First his brother Theodore was several times defeated, and then on 20 August 636 came the pivotal Battle of Yarmuk in eastern Palestine. Heraclius had raised an army of about 50,000 men, under the command of Vahan the Armenian, the highest-ranking officer in the empire. Details of the battle are sketchy, but apparently a violent sandstorm struck the Byzantine army head-on, and the Muslims destroyed it after cornering it between the Yarmuk River and a tributary. The Arabs then took Syria and eventually Egypt.

Heraclius now urgently reformed the Imperial army and halted the Muslim advance in Anatolia and part of North Africa. In his new system, Anatolian provincial military governors replaced mercenaries with soldiers drawn from local districts and rewarded with land grants. This developed a flexible defence in depth of trained peasants who had a personal stake in defending the empire. Using this system, during the next four centuries the empire could be defeated but not conquered.

By the beginning of 641, however, Heraclius was suffering from what may have been prostate cancer and died on this day at the age of 65.

Other action this day
1659: After besieging Copenhagen for six months, Swedish soldiers try to cross the city's moat and storm the walls, but are forced to retire with huge losses after fierce hand-to-hand fighting and a Danish ambush against part of their attacking force * 1814: Napoleon defeats the Prussians at Montmirail * 1942: The German battleships *Gneisenau* and *Scharnhorst* and the heavy cruiser *Prinz Eugen* escape from the French port of Brest through the English Channel to safety

12 February

The Day of the Herrings

1429 The English army had been besieging Orléans for four months, but they now needed more supplies, especially food, as foraging would produce little or nothing in the midst of winter. Coming to their aid was Sir John Fastolf, who on 11 February had reached the nearby village of Rouvray with a convoy of 300 wagons containing not only cannons, cannonballs and crossbow shafts but also barrels of dried herring, essential for the good Christian attackers since Lent was approaching. Escorting the precious wagons were 1,000 mounted archers and a few foot soldiers.

This was the Hundred Years War, that intermittent conflict between England and France that had already been running for 92 years. At immediate issue was who should be King of France: the seven-year-old Plantagenet, Henry VI, whose father (the conquering Henry V) had forced the French to agree that he would inherit the throne; or the Valois Dauphin Charles, eldest son of the late French king Charles VI. Now the English, with their Burgundian allies, had seized control of most of France and were set on taking Orléans, one of the last cities still loyal to Charles.

Although the besieging force had sprinkled fortified positions around Orléans, they lacked the men fully to surround it, and 50 miles to the south a sizeable French relieving force was camped at Blois. There Charles de Bourbon, comte de Clermont commanded

3,000 men-at-arms and crossbowmen and was accompanied by 1,000 Scots men-at-arms under John Stewart of Darnley. When agents informed them of the English convoy, they were instantly on the march.

On the morning of 12 February, Fastolf set out from Rouvray to cover the last twenty miles to Orléans, but when he had gone only a mile he saw the stronger French army appearing from the south-west. Outnumbered three to one, he halted the convoy and pulled his wagons into a defensive circle. He then ordered sharpened stakes driven into the ground, butts in the earth, points ahead, to prevent the French cavalry from charging, a tactic used by the English with great effect at Agincourt fourteen years before (see 11 August).

Clermont, however, had also learned from Agincourt, and instead of unleashing his cavalry he brought up his culverins (smooth-barrelled cannon about twelve feet long that fired a 17-pound ball) and set to bombarding the wagon train from a distance. Although the culverins were slow and clumsy, their range was considerably greater than the 200-yard capability of the English longbows. Soon they were causing serious damage to the English wagons, smashing several barrels of dried herring and spreading their contents on the field. The cannonade could have continued indefinitely, since the English feared to charge a force so much bigger than their own.

Now, however, the Scottish contingent fighting alongside the French managed to snatch defeat from the jaws of almost certain victory. Flouting Clermont's direct orders, the Scottish constable ordered his 400-strong infantry to assault the English wagon fort. As they neared the enemy, they came under merciless attack from the English longbows, and Clermont had to cut short his artillery barrage for fear of hitting his Scottish allies.

Now Clermont made one last effort to right a battle disastrously gone wrong – and ordered his mounted knights to charge. But the sharpened stakes prevented them reaching the wagons, and English archers cut them down just as they had at Agincourt. Seeing his enemy in disarray, now Fastolf led his own men-at-arms into the attack, striking them on the flanks and rear and putting them to flight.

Some 120 knights and over 500 foot soldiers (mostly Scots) perished on the field, including the Scottish constable. Clermont was wounded but made his way back to Blois. The English lost just four men-at-arms and a few members of the wagon train.

The battle had a devastating effect on French morale and marked the low point in the career and hopes of Dauphin Charles. It has gone down in French history as La Journée des Harengs (the Day of the Herrings), ironically remembered not so much by its dismal outcome but by the wagon train's cargo left on the battlefield.

But, according to folklore, the Day of the Herrings did have one spectacular result. For on this very day seventeen-year-old Joan of Arc met for the final time with Robert de Baudricourt, the garrison commander at Vaucouleurs, who had previously refused to take her to see Dauphin Charles. This time, however, she told him that 'the Dauphin's arms have this day suffered a great reverse near Orléans'. When news of the French defeat at Rouvray reached Baudricourt a few days later, he was so astounded by her prescience that he at last agreed to escort her to Chinon to see the Dauphin. Although, sadly, this wonderful story is first related 38 years after the event, less than three months after she met with Baudricourt she did relieve the siege of Orléans (see 8 May), and in July she witnessed the Dauphin's coronation as Charles VII.

Other action this day

1814: Napoleon defeats a combined Prussian/Russian army at Château Thierry, where Marshal Ney crushes the enemy rearguard, causing 3,000 casualties to only 600 French ∗ 1893: American general Omar Bradley is born ∗ 1946: The last of 121 surrendered German submarines is scuttled off the coast of Northern Ireland, ending Operation Deadlight

13 February

The bombing of Dresden

1945 Dresden lies in the broad basin of the Elbe just 100 miles south of Berlin. In the late 17th and 18th centuries three electors of Saxony, Augustus I, II and III, turned it into a Baroque bijou whose only rivals in beauty were Vienna and Prague. Exquisite buildings like the Zwinger, the Japanese Palace and the Hofkirche were built, and the electors also assembled outstanding collections of paintings and objets d'art. So brilliant was the city that it earned the nickname of 'Florence on the Elbe'.

That all changed for ever on the night of 13 February 1945 when the first of 773 British Avro Lancaster bombers released its bombs over the city centre. Before the night was over the British had dropped over 2,500 tons of high explosives, of which two-thirds were incendiaries filled with highly combustible chemicals such as magnesium and phosphorus. This firebombing created a self-sustaining firestorm with temperatures over 1,500°C. Almost 90 per cent of the inner city's 28,000 houses were destroyed, including 22 hospitals. Three centuries of architectural magnificence were incinerated in a single night. During the following two days over 500 American bombers joined the attack, although their target area was restricted to the railway yards.

There is still debate on the number of civilians killed. Before the war Dresden's population was about 650,000, but by 1945 the city was teeming with refugees fleeing from the advancing Russian army, bringing the total closer to 900,000. Although Nazi propaganda claimed a quarter of a million had died, modern estimates suggest lesser figures, but these vary from 35,000 dead up to 130,000 killed and wounded, probably the largest number of casualties ever inflicted in a bombing raid, dwarfing the 70,000 deaths at Hiroshima and perhaps twice the 51,509 British civilians killed by German bombing during all of the Second World War.

The primary instigator of the attack on Dresden was the head of RAF Bomber Command, Air Marshal Arthur Harris, who derided the type of precision bombing advocated by the US Air Force. Harris insisted that night-time firebombing raids would undermine civilian morale, in spite of the evidence within his own country that indiscriminate German bombing of civilians at Coventry and London simply stiffened British resolve.

The first German cities to suffer from Harris's tactics were Lübeck, Hamburg, Berlin and Cologne, but Dresden remains a special case because it quartered few German troops, had little war-related industry and was virtually undefended by anti-aircraft guns.

Two months after Dresden, British prime minister Winston Churchill ordered Harris to end the firebombing of German cities 'simply for the sake of increasing the terror' and wrote to the Air Staff: 'The destruction of Dresden remains a serious query against the conduct of Allied bombing.' After the war he conspicuously omitted Harris's name from the list of new peerages, although he awarded them to many less important generals. But perhaps Churchill was a bit disingenuous; there is some evidence that he agreed to Harris's proposed attack in order to intimidate the Russians with the power of Bomber Command.

Although firebombing German civilians was Harris's own invention ('The primary objective of your operations should now be focused on the morale of the enemy civil population and in particular of the industrial workers', he briefed his men), he tried to pass the blame upwards, writing in his memoirs: 'Here I will only say that the attack on Dresden was at the time considered a military necessity by much more important people than I.' Perhaps he realised that his bombing policy had not only wrought unimaginable death and destruction but also failed in its purpose. As historian Max Hastings has written: '... Hitler professed an unconcern, even satisfaction, about the destruction inflicted by bombing: "[it] actually works in our favour, because it is creating a body of people with nothing to lose – people who will therefore fight on with utter fanaticism."' After the war, German armaments chief Albert Speer testified: 'In the burning and devastated cities, we daily experienced the direct impact of war. It spurred us to do our utmost ... the bombing and the hardships that resulted from them did not weaken the morale of the populace.'

Post-war criticism of Harris was so strong that in 1945 he moved to South Africa. In the end, however, perhaps he was lucky. He was never indicted for war crimes, although in 1938 the Geneva Convention had specifically outlawed 'intentional bombings of civilian populations'. Indeed, despite the fervent protestations of the German government, over half a century after Dresden's destruction, Elizabeth, the Queen Mother, led the ceremonies in London at the unveiling of a statue honouring 'Bomber' Harris.

Other action this day

1861: American Army assistant surgeon Colonel Bernard Irwin sets off to rescue 60 men trapped by Apaches under Cochise, a deed for which he is awarded the first Medal of Honor * 1945: German and Hungarian troops unconditionally surrender Budapest to attacking Russians after a 46-day siege * 1960: France tests its first atomic bomb

14 February

'Nelson's Patent Bridge for Boarding'

1797 For most of the night, the sailors aboard the small British fleet had heard the booming of the guns of Spanish ships signalling to each other in the dense fog, which now at dawn was beginning to lift. On board his flagship *Victory*, Admiral Sir John Jervis waited for his captain to count the enemy men o' war as they began to emerge from the haze:

> 'There are eight sail-of-the-line, Sir John,' said the captain.
> 'Very well, sir.'
> 'There are twenty sail-of-the-line, Sir John.'
> 'Very well, sir.'
> 'There are twenty-five sail-of-the-line, Sir John.'
> 'Very well, sir.'
> 'There are twenty-seven sail-of-the-line, Sir John.'
> 'Enough, sir, no more of that, sir ... the die is cast, and if there are fifty sail I will go through them.'

Jervis had just discovered that the number of Spanish warships bearing down on him was almost double the fifteen that he commanded.

It was the midst of the Anglo-Spanish War that had started when Spain had allied itself with revolutionary France. Now Jervis was attempting to prevent the Spaniards from reaching Cadiz to escort a merchant convoy. Here on this day, off the Portuguese headland called Cape St Vincent, he would take on the pride of the Spanish navy, which included the mighty 130-gun flagship *Santísima Trinidad*, the most powerful man o' war afloat.

Despite his inferiority in numbers, however, Jervis had two potent advantages. Very few of the Spanish sailors were trained seamen, the vast majority being pressed and inexperienced landsmen or soldiers, while the British crews were highly trained and battle-hardened. And among Jervis's ships, the 74-gun *Captain* was commanded by a 38-year-old commodore named Horatio Nelson.

Now the British ships cleared for action; gun crews formed up and ammunition was trundled to the guns, as the decks were wetted and sprinkled with sand. Marines climbed into the rigging with their muskets, and below decks surgeons laid out their gruesome tools. The gun ports were flung open and the guns run out, to the rumble of gun wheels on the deck.

The Spanish ships were approaching in two groups with a gap of several miles between them. At 11.00 Jervis signalled his fleet: 'Form in a line of battle ahead and astern of *Victory* as most convenient.' His plan was to take his ships in line ahead straight through the Spanish formation and cut it in two. Nelson's *Captain* was third from last in the British order. Twelve minutes later Jervis ordered: 'Engage the enemy!'

The leading British ship, the *Culloden*, sailed into the gap between the two parts of the Spanish fleet like 'a hawk to his prey', according to one of the British captains, opening fire with double-shotted broadsides. One by one the other British ships followed in her wake, firing salvo after salvo. To break away from the cannonade, the Spaniards turned to escape, but the *Culloden* tacked to follow. Now, however, with the Spaniards dispersing, it became clear that most of their fleet would get away unscathed.

At this point, on his own initiative, Nelson turned the *Captain* hard to port, taking her out of the line, and sailed straight at the Spanish vanguard, attacking the *Santísima Trinidad*. Five more enemy ships now joined their flagship, pouring fire into the *Captain*. Seeing Nelson outnumbered six to one, the *Culloden* and two other British warships sailed to his aid, and all were soon trading broadsides with the enemy, sometimes at ranges of less than ten yards. The disciplined British gun crews fired three broadsides or more to every two fired by the Spanish.

Spanish cannonballs demasted the *Captain*, smashed her wheel, and cut her sails into tatters, so Nelson ordered her run alongside the nearest Spanish ship, the immobilised 80-gun *San Nicolas*, whose rigging had become entangled with the three-decker *San José*. Shouting for a boarding party and brandishing his sword, Nelson jumped on to the stern of the *San Nicolas*, after a British marine. Other soldiers and seamen followed, seven of whom were killed. 'I found the cabin doors fastened,' Nelson later reported, 'and the Spanish officers fired their pistol at us through the windows, but, having broken open the doors, the soldiers fired.' After a vigorous struggle, the captain of the *San Nicolas* surrendered, but now the soldiers on the towering *San José* alongside opened with brisk musket fire.

Although the *San Nicolas* was now on fire, Nelson ordered reinforcements brought on board, crossed her deck and boarded the *San José*. Mounting to the quarterdeck, he received the surrender from the Spanish captain who 'with a bended knee, presented me with a sword'.

By now the remains of the Spanish fleet were scattering, and the heavy damage to the British ships precluded pursuit, but Jervis had captured four enemy ships, including two first-rates (ships of the line mounting 100 guns or more on three gundecks). The flagship *Santísima Trinidad* and several other ships had been badly damaged. Spanish casualties came to about 1,000 while the British had lost 73 dead and a few hundred wounded.

Nelson had acted in the ruthlessly aggressive and decisive manner that was his hallmark. He later referred to his extraordinary capture of two ships by crossing one to board the other as 'Nelson's Patent Bridge for Boarding'. Immediately after the battle he was promoted to rear admiral, and Admiral Jervis was created Earl St Vincent.

Other action this day

1400: King Richard II, a prisoner in Pontefract Castle in Yorkshire, is murdered on the orders of the usurper king, Henry IV * 1779: In Hawaii, in a dispute about a stolen boat, British captain James Cook tries to take the King of Hawaii hostage, but he is attacked by villagers, hit on the head and stabbed to death as he falls on his face in the surf * 1943: German general Erwin Rommel and the Afrika Korps defeat the Allies in Tunisia in the Battle of the Kasserine Pass

15 February

The sinking of the battleship Maine *triggers the Spanish–American War*

1898 Relations between Spain and the United States had been dangerously soured by the continued revolt in Spanish-owned Cuba and the lamentable conditions of the colonised Cubans. Eventually

President William McKinley ordered the battleship USS *Maine* to Havana to reassure Americans living there.

At just past nine this evening the *Maine* was swinging quietly at anchor, most of the crew already gently sleeping in their hammocks while Captain Charles Sigsbee sat quietly in his cabin writing a letter. Then, he later recalled, 'I laid down my pen and listened to the notes of the bugle [playing taps], which were singularly beautiful in the oppressive stillness of the night. ... I was enclosing my letter in its envelope when the explosion came. It was a bursting, rending, and crashing roar of immense volume, largely metallic in character. It was followed by heavy, ominous metallic sounds. There was a trembling and lurching motion of the vessel, a list to port. The electric lights went out. Then there was intense blackness and smoke.'

An enormous explosion had engulfed the front half of the ship, right where most of the men were billeted. The *Maine* settled to the bottom of Havana harbour; of the 350 men on board, 260 died with the ship. The next morning only the ship's charred and twisted stern and bridge could still be seen above the gently lapping waves of the harbour.

Although no one knew who had detonated the blast, the unscrupulous press baron William Randolph Hearst had no scruples about inflaming American public opinion by blaming the Spaniards. His *New York Journal* was in a fierce circulation war with competitive newspapers, and Hearst believed a war against Spain was just what was needed to build readership. The *Journal* even published drawings purporting to show Spanish saboteurs clamping an underwater mine to the *Maine*'s hull. Soon most Americans came to believe that the iniquitous Spaniards had blown up the battleship in a gesture of arrogant contempt for America.

Hearst then urgently dispatched writers and the artist Frederick Remington to Cuba to cover a so-called war between the dastardly Spanish and heroic Cuban rebels. Finding no trace of combat, Remington cabled Hearst: 'There is no war. Request to be recalled.' Hearst's answer was to the point: 'Please remain. You furnish the pictures, I'll furnish the war.'

Hearst was true to his word. Driven by the public's great patriotic fervour, the American Congress soon demanded Spanish withdrawal from Cuba, and by April the Spanish–American War had begun. The United States won a pathetically one-sided contest, in only eight months forcing Spain into a peace treaty by which the US acquired Guam, Puerto Rico and the Philippine islands.

In the pride of victory, the public began to forget about the *Maine*. Also forgotten was the fact that for many years no one really knew why she had blown up or who was responsible. But in 1976 a study by the US Navy indicated that the most likely cause was an accidental detonation in the ship's coalbunker, entirely the fault of the *Maine* herself and her crew.

Other action this day

1942: British-held Singapore falls to the Japanese * 1944: Allied B-17 Flying Fortresses, B-25 Mitchell bombers and B-26 Marauder medium bombers destroy the German-held monastery at Monte Cassino in Italy with 1,150 tons of high explosive and incendiary bombs * 1970: Air Chief Marshal Hugh Dowding, who commanded RAF Fighter Command during the Battle of Britain, dies at his home in Tunbridge Wells, Kent, aged 87

16 February

The Royal Navy captures the Altmark

1940 Tonight in a remarkable feat of naval derring-do, a British destroyer operating under Admiralty instructions intercepted a German supply ship making her way home along the coast of Norway. With searchlights blazing on her target, HMS *Cossack* pursued the *Altmark* into a narrow fjord where the supply ship ran aground. A boarding party killed seven German defenders, then opened the hatches to get at the cargo in the holds. The *Altmark*'s cargo was 300 sailors of the British Merchant Navy, the captured crews of nine merchant vessels sunk the previous autumn by the German raider *Graf Spee*. By midnight *Cossack* was out to sea again, heading with her rescued cargo for the Firth of Forth.

It was, of course, a notable achievement by the Royal Navy and one greatly welcomed by a British public looking for purposeful engagement with the enemy during that trance-like opening period of the Second World War that came to be called the Phoney War or the Sitzkrieg. But the *Altmark* incident had the effect of putting the fat in the fire.

Neutral Norway vehemently protested against the British violation of its territorial waters in vain. To Germany the incident demonstrated that Great Britain was willing to violate Norwegian neutrality and that Norway was unable or unwilling to prevent such action. This state of affairs threatened Germany's supply of Swedish iron ore, so vital to the Third Reich's heavy industries and much of it shipped through Norwegian waters. On 21 February Hitler ordered Exercise Weser – his planned invasion of Norway and Denmark – moved to the highest operational priority, ahead of Case Yellow, the invasion of France and the Low Countries.

In their reporting of the *Altmark* incident some British newspapers included this description from a *Cossack* sailor's account of the boarding: '... Meanwhile our boys were opening up the hatches. One of them shouted: "Are there any English down there?" There was a yell of "Yes!" You should have heard the cheer when our men shouted back: "Well, the Navy's here."' Some days later in London the First Lord of the Admiralty Winston Churchill appropriated this phrase to good effect addressing a large audience at the Guildhall: 'To Nelson's immortal signal of 135 years ago, "England expects that every man will do his duty," there may now be added last week's not less proud reply, "The Navy's here."'

During the night of 6 April 1940, German naval forces and troop ships left their north German ports and sailed for Norway. The Phoney War was almost over. The real war was about to begin.

Other action this day

1519: Admiral of France Gaspard de Coligny, a Huguenot leader in the French Wars of Religion, is born in Châtillon-Coligny * 1804: American captain Stephen Decatur and a small group of men set fire to and destroy the US frigate *Philadelphia*, captured and held by Barbary pirates at Tripoli during the Tripolitan War * 1862: Grant wins the first major Union victory of the Civil War, when Fort Donelson on the Cumberland River in Tennessee surrenders with 15,000 troops

17 February

'Peccavi!'

1843 In London's Trafalgar Square stands a bronze statue of General Sir Charles Napier, the intrepid British soldier whose fame today is based more on his way with words than on his military exploits.

While soldiering in British-controlled India, Napier was admonished by local Hindus for maintaining the British prohibition of *suttee*, the practice of burning widows alive on the funeral pyres of their husbands. 'You say that it is your custom to burn widows', Napier told a delegation of Hindus. 'Very well. We also have a custom: when men burn a woman alive, we tie a rope around their necks and we hang them. Build your funeral pyre; beside it, my carpenters will build a gallows. You may follow your custom. And then we will follow ours.'

Perhaps even more famous was Napier's earlier report on his accomplishments in the province of Sindh (now in Pakistan).

On the morning of this day he entered in his diary: 'It is my first battle as a commander: it may be my last. At sixty, that makes little difference; but my feelings are, it shall be do or die.' He then led his small force of 400 British and 2,200 Sepoys to a crushing victory over 30,000 Baluchis in the Battle of Miani. Napier hurled himself into the midst of the conflict, fighting hand-to-hand. At the end of the battle he finished off the enemy by personally leading a devastating cavalry charge.

Five weeks later he scored a second major victory at Dabo, near Hyderabad, gaining full control of the entire province of Sindh. Entering Hyderabad, he ensconced himself in the Emir's palace and reported his triumphs to headquarters with one of the most remarkable military communications of all time, consisting of a single word: 'Peccavi!' (Latin for 'I have sinned [Sindh]'.)

Other action this day

1461: Henry VI defeats Warwick the Kingmaker at the second Battle of St Albans during the Wars of the Roses * 1814: Napoleon defeats the Austrians at the Battle of Montereau * 1909: Indian warrior chieftain Geronimo dies at Fort Sill, Oklahoma

18 February

Deadly ambush for the duc de Guise

1563 François, second duc de Guise, was the leading member of France's leading Catholic family: proud, reactionary and aristocratic. A general of exceptional talent, he was nicknamed Le Balafré (roughly Scarface) for the scars he received fighting the English when they occupied Boulogne. A lance had struck him between the nose and the right eye, coming out on his neck below his ear. A surgeon had prised it out with a winch, and miraculously Guise had survived.

Guise had been responsible for the bloody massacre of Protestants that had ignited the first French religious war. In March 1562 he was passing through Champagne and stopped in the largely Huguenot town of Wassy-sur-Blaise to hear Mass. There he found the locals defying a royal edict by holding a Protestant service in a barn only a few hundred yards from the Wassy church.

Soon the barn became the scene of a confrontation between Catholics and Calvinists, and Guise and his men attempted to enforce the king's edict by compelling the Protestants to stop their service of worship. In a moment rocks were flying, and the duke found fresh blood oozing from a face wound.

In an instant Guise's men savagely attacked the Huguenots, killing 30 and wounding over 100 more. To top it off, the enraged duke ordered a gibbet constructed from the barn's benches and strung up the Protestant minister. It was the first violence in a religious war that would last 35 years.

So extreme was Guise in his persecution of the Huguenots that during the conflict he executed some prisoners, telling them: 'My trade is not to make speeches but to cut off heads.' So the French Huguenot leader Gaspard de Coligny determined to eliminate Guise – for ever. The opportunity came on 18 February 1563.

Riding towards his military headquarters, Guise had unwisely doffed his coat of mail, unaware that one of his own men, a certain Jean de Poltrot, was a fanatical Protestant and Huguenot spy.

Seeing that Guise was unprotected, Poltrot rode on ahead and then hid behind a hedge. As Guise passed, Poltrot fired. The duke fell senseless to the ground and died a week later at Château Corney, on Ash Wednesday, 24 February, his 44th birthday.

Poltrot was captured the day after his fatal shot at Guise, and under torture confessed to have been working on orders from Gaspard de Coligny, something Coligny strongly denied. Exactly one month later Poltrot paid the price for his treason. Lying on his back in a field, each arm and each leg was securely tied to a different horse – and then the horses were whipped off in a gallop in four different directions. (Some accounts have an even grislier version – that the horses were not able to pull off his limbs, so he was hacked to pieces with cutlasses.) Nine years later Gaspard de Coligny was murdered by Guise's son to start the St Bartholomew's Day massacre.

Other action this day

1268: A coalition of Russian princes utterly rout the knights of the Livonian branch of the Teutonic Order at the Battle of Rakovor * 1294: Mongol conqueror and ruler Kublai Khan dies * 1861: Jefferson Davis is sworn in as president of the Confederate States of America in Montgomery, Alabama

19 February

American Marines land on Iwo Jima

1945 Iwo Jima was nobody's idea of prime real estate – five miles end to end, three miles at the widest point, a low hump of island 700 miles south of Tokyo, covered by rock, sand and volcanic ash, its southern tip dominated by an extinct volcano, 556 feet above sea level, named Mount Suribachi. Taking his first look at it, a young US Marine pronounced it 'not worth fifty cents at a sheriff's sale'. But considering the price paid in blood to gain possession of it, Iwo Jima had to be one of the most costly places on earth.

Within its forbidding terrain, the island held three airstrips and a Japanese garrison of 21,000 troops. One observer said it 'bristled with concealed gun emplacements, pillboxes, mine fields, and an elaborate system of underground caves and shelters'. Artillery pieces and mortars were expertly sited to cover not only the beaches but also virtually every square foot of the interior. For the Japanese, Iwo's strategic value was as part of the home islands' defence cordon; for the Americans it would be as a forward base for B-29s and their fighter escorts taking part in the air offensive against Japan.

Everybody knew Iwo would be tough. Two days before the landings, as US battleships opened up with their pre-invasion bombardment of land targets, rocket-firing minesweepers and gunboats swept close in to scout the beaches where the landings would take place. The tempo of the preliminary operation was so high that the Japanese commander concluded actual landings were underway, and he sent out a communiqué to that effect. That night Radio Tokyo proudly misinformed its audiences that the enemy's first invasion attempt had been repelled.

At 08.59 today – one minute ahead of schedule – the first wave of Marines hit Red Beach One from landing craft. One battalion came across a small sign erected in the sand reading 'Welcome to Iwo Jima'. It was a thoughtful gesture left by Navy Seals two days earlier as they probed the landing area for shoals, reefs, mines and underwater defences.

Two entire Marine divisions went ashore this day. A third would follow. Eventually, there would be 60,000 Marines on the island. Mount Suribachi fell on D+4 (23 February), and the first flag went up at 10.35. From the crowded beaches below came cheers. Staring at the tiny figures high up on the summit, one Marine said: 'Those guys ought to be getting flight pay.' The immortal photograph of the flag-raising ceremony was taken three hours later.

Suribachi was only the beginning. The Marines' advance up the island was bloodily contested every foot of the way. On the tenth day of combat they held less than half the island. Behind every dune, ridge or gully, defenders lay in deadly wait. Iwo Jima was not secured until D+26, and the final act of resistance – a pre-dawn suicide charge – was not quelled until D+35 (26 March). When the Navy released casualty figures for the first three days of combat, press reaction back home was one of shock. In a front-page editorial for the San Francisco *Examiner*, William Randolph Hearst Jr questioned the heavy price in lives lost.

The price was heavy indeed. Among total casualties of almost 26,000 Marines and Navy personnel, there were some 6,000 deaths. Of the Japanese, fewer than 1,000 survived to be taken as prisoners. But even before combat was over, a B-29, low on fuel returning from a bombing mission over Japan, made an emergency landing on one of the landing strips. It was the first of 2,400 B-29s to make use of Iwo during the remaining months of the war. Afterwards, Admiral Nimitz characterised the American effort at Iwo Jima as one in which 'uncommon valor was a common virtue'.

Other action this day

AD 197: In the bloodiest battle between two Roman armies, Emperor Septimus Severus defeats the usurper Clodius Albinus at the two-day Battle of Lugdunum (Lyon) and becomes sole ruler of the Roman empire * 1405: Turkik conqueror Tamerlane (Timur the Lame) dies on campaign against the Ming dynasty of China at the age of 68 * 1408: The revolt of Henry Percy, Earl of Northumberland, against King Henry IV ends with his defeat and death at Bramham Moor in Yorkshire * 1941: The German Afrika Korps is formed

20 February

Execution of an Austrian patriot

1810 Andreas Hofer looked very much the innkeeper that he was – round-faced, bearded and somewhat roly-poly. But beneath his genial exterior beat the heart of a true Austrian patriot, a man who loved his emperor but wanted no truck with either Bavarians or Frenchmen, who were intent on claiming his homeland, the Tyrol in western Austria.

In 1809, when Hofer was 46, under pressure from Napoleon, Emperor Franz I ceded the Tyrol to Bavaria, but Hofer led a local insurrection to return the province to Austrian control. After decisively crushing the Bavarians at Berg Isel, he set himself up in Innsbruck as commander-in-chief of the Tyrol, under the protection of Emperor Franz. In October of that year, however, Franz once again bowed to French pressure and once more relinquished the Tyrol.

Still defiant, Hofer continued to resist the French, causing Napoleon to put a price on his head and dispatch a column of troops to capture him.

Evading his enemies, Hofer fled to the mountains, where he holed up in a deserted herdsman's hut, but his pursuers soon tracked him down, brought him barefoot through the snowy mountain passes and took him to French-controlled Mantua.

There Hofer was subjected to a kangaroo court martial, convicted of treason and sentenced to death. Even though Franz made no effort to save him, he still might have escaped the ultimate penalty had Napoleon not sent a direct order by heliograph from Milan demanding to know the date of execution.

On this day Hofer was led to the city walls to face the firing squad. Refusing a blindfold, he addressed his executioners with the farewell comment: 'Goodbye, wretched world, this death is easy!' Then he ordered the guns, 'Fire!'

Thirteen years later, Hofer's remains were brought back to Austria and interred in Innsbruck. For many years a play celebrating his patriotism was performed each year in Merano, in the Tyrolean part of Italy, and a poem about him was adapted as the Tyrolean anthem.

Other action this day

1753: Born today, Napoleon's chief of staff, Marshal Louis Berthier, who in 1798 took Pope Pius VI prisoner and brought him back to France, participated in most of Napoleon's major battles, including Marengo, Austerlitz, Jena and Friedland, and served in Russia and the Peninsular War but refused to join the emperor at Waterloo * 1809: The Spanish surrender to Napoleon's troops after the two-month Second Siege of Zaragoza during which 64,000 inhabitants die * 1905: The first day of the Japanese victory at the Battle of Mukden, the last major land battle of the Russo-Japanese War, at the time the largest battle ever fought, with more than 400,000 troops on each side

21 February

The Battle of Verdun

1916 At 7.00am German artillery began a bombardment of the French-held salient north of the historic fortress city of Verdun. It was the deafening prelude to the longest and one of the bloodiest battles of the First World War. Erich von Falkenhayn, the German chief of staff and war minister, chose Verdun for the killing ground because it would compel the enemy into costly counter-attacks from which, he promised an appreciative Kaiser, 'the forces of France will bleed to death'.

The shelling from 1,200 artillery pieces paused at 4.00pm, as groups of German infantry edged out of the winter gloom to probe the devastated French forward positions. The battered and deafened defenders just managed to hold on until darkness brought an end to the first day's fighting. Then the bombardment resumed.

And so it went, day after day, savage artillery fire followed by infantry attacks, the French, outgunned and outnumbered, slowly giving way. On the 25th, impregnable Fort Douaumont, the linchpin of the entire French position in the salient, fell to the Germans. Supply routes into Verdun came under fire and were almost severed. Withdrawal to more defensible positions across the Meuse would have been the best military option, but for France, with national honour at stake, withdrawal was unthinkable. Someone would have to organise the defence of Verdun.

The organiser turned out to be Philippe Pétain, an unsung major general who had a talent for defensive warfare and the confidence of the *poilus* that he would not send them out to useless slaughter. He paid special attention to his artillery, co-ordinating its operation into an instrument of punishment for the enemy. He rebuilt and maintained the supply routes, assembling 3,500 trucks that operated day and night, bringing in vital supplies and reinforcements for the Verdun garrison. He restored the fighting value of his troops by rotating his divisions in and out of the line. In time, these prudent measures turned the German tide. The 23rd of June saw the farthest extent of the German advance, almost – but not quite – to Verdun itself. Now, reaching the limits of its reserves, German strength began to ebb. Under French counter-attacks, the front line edged back northward. On 24 October, Fort Douaumont was retaken. In December the fighting subsided into the ordinary, sporadic rhythm of trench warfare.

Verdun bled both armies white. In ten months of battle, the total casualties numbered over 700,000 dead, wounded and missing. For the French it was an act of stubborn heroism, and they hailed it as a great victory, but in truth, as Alistair Horne wrote: 'Neither side "won" at Verdun.' Among its many consequences were these: General von Falkenhayn was replaced as Germany's chief of staff in August after it became painfully clear that his campaign would never prevail; the French commander-in-chief General Joffre was sacked in December, in part for having neglected Verdun's defences; General Pétain, beloved by his troops, was replaced in May as army commander by a more offensive-minded general, but the next year, in even grimmer military circumstances, France turned once again to her 'architect of victory' and this time made Pétain commander-in-chief of the French army; and a young company commander in the 33rd Infantry Regiment, Captain Charles de Gaulle, was captured on 1 March 1916, and spent the rest of the war in a German prison camp.

Other action this day

1431: Joan of Arc's trial begins in Rouen ∗ 1803: Colonel Edward Despard is executed on the roof of the gatehouse at Horsemonger Lane Gaol in London before 20,000 spectators for plotting to seize the Tower of London and assassinate George III ∗ 1849: British General Sir Hugh Gough leads an army of 20,000 men and 100 guns to victory over the Sikhs at the Battle of Gujrat in the Second Anglo–Sikh War

22 February

'Give them a little more grape, Captain Bragg'

1847 Today Mexican dictator Antonio López de Santa Anna, the self-styled 'Napoleon of the West', and an army of 16,000 men faced an American force a quarter their number in north-eastern Mexico. They would begin the decisive battle of the Mexican–American War.

The war had started in the wake of the American annexation of Texas. After a detachment of Mexican cavalry had cut to pieces a small American patrol in April 1846, the United States had dispatched General Zachary Taylor to Mexico. Santa Anna marched north to engage the invaders, prompting Taylor to move his forces to a pass between two mountain ranges at Buena Vista.

Taylor was a tough 62-year-old Virginian, described by one of his officers as 'short and very heavy, with pronounced face lines and gray hair, wears an old oilcloth cap, a dusty green coat, a frightful pair of trousers and on horseback looks like a frog'. The press called him 'Old Rough and Ready'.

Taylor's force at Buena Vista counted no more than 4,500 men, but it included three batteries of 'flying artillery', guns mounted on horse carriages with the entire crew riding horses into battle. In his army were several volunteer units, of which the Mississippi Rifles was commanded by his former son-in-law, Jefferson Davis. (Taylor had opposed the marriage, but his daughter married Davis anyway, only to succumb to malaria three months later.)

On this day Taylor faced the far larger Mexican army but refused to surrender to the haughtily confident Santa Anna, thus setting the stage for slaughter.

The Mexicans opened hostilities with howitzer fire, while attempting to outflank the American left with four battalions of musket-carrying infantry. But the Americans were armed with more accurate rifles and managed to hold off the assault until darkness fell.

At 8.00 the next morning Santa Anna launched his main attack. As priests prayed for victory accompanied by hymns from the general's band, 7,000 green-jacketed infantry advanced on two brigades of volunteers from Indiana and Illinois. About to be overwhelmed, the Indianan line broke in panic, but as the Mexicans charged towards victory they inadvertently exposed a flank to American artillery while the Illinois infantry cut them down with rifle fire. The Mexicans wavered and fell back but were soon attacking once more.

Taylor now ordered Jeff Davis's red-shirted Mississippi Rifles into the fray. Armed with Model 1841 US rifles and known for their marksmanship, they scythed down the Mexican infantry. Then, joined by most of the Indiana brigade, they sent the enemy flying with a determined countercharge.

Now 1,500 Mexican lancers bore down on Davis's Mississippians, but 100 yards from the American line the lancers pulled up, probably expecting the Mississippians to waste an ineffectual long-distance volley. They had forgotten that Davis's men were armed not with muskets, effective only within 80 yards, but with rifles, accurate at six times the range. On Davis's command, a murderous volley rang out, battering the lancers into urgent retreat, as an ecstatic Zach Taylor stood in his stirrups and cried, 'Well done, Jeff! Hurrah for old Mississippi!'

During the shooting a musket ball had caught Davis in the foot. As he was carried to safety behind the lines, Taylor said admiringly: 'My daughter, sir, was a better judge of men than I was.'

By evening threatening clouds darkened the hills, but still the Mexicans came on. Taylor galloped past Captain Baxton Bragg's 'flying artillery' of 6-pound cannon, yanked off his shabby straw hat to swing it around his head and shouted: 'Double-shot your guns and give them hell, Bragg.' The mounted artillery clattered across the battlefield and fired three salvos into the onrushing enemy, shattering their attack just as the skies opened to a torrential downpour that ended the day's fighting. Although the battle had raged for almost ten hours, each army occupied the ground that it had held early in the morning.

That night the Americans slept on their arms, watching the enemy campfires across the hills and expecting to fight again the next day. But at daybreak the field was empty. The fires had been a ruse to cover the Mexican withdrawal during the night.

During two days of battle the Americans had suffered 267 dead and 456 wounded, but Santa Anna had squandered a quarter of his army, losing 3,500 men, including 600 killed. Although he followed the time-honoured path of defeated dictators by declaring victory to his people, he never won another battle during the war.

The war dragged on for almost another year, until the beleaguered Mexicans were forced to sign the Treaty of Guadalupe Hidalgo, which gave America undisputed control of Texas and ceded to the US California, Nevada and Utah and parts of Colorado, Arizona, New Mexico and Wyoming. Zach Taylor gained such prestige from his victory that twenty months later he was elected president, using as his campaign slogan his famous command, bowdlerised to: 'Give them a little more grape, Captain Bragg.' Jefferson Davis parlayed his military fame into a political career that ended with his election fourteen years later as president of the Confederate States during the American Civil War.

Other action this day

1732: President and general George Washington is born * 1813: The British defeat the Americans and capture the village of Ogdensburg, New York * 1932: American War Department General Order No. 3 revives the Purple Heart on the 200th anniversary of the birth of George

Washington, who first established the order on 7 August 1782; originally given for valour in combat, from this point it will be given to those wounded or killed in action

23 February

The creation of a Nazi martyr

1930 For six weeks a 22-year-old Nazi thug named Horst Wessel had lain in a Berlin hospital, his jaw shattered, his tongue an agony, where the bullet had gone through. At first it had looked as if he would survive, but then septicaemia had set in. At 6.30 this Sunday morning he died. Through the propaganda of his patron Joseph Goebbels, he would become a national martyr and inspiration for the Nazi Party.

Son of a Lutheran pastor from western Germany, Wessel had joined the SA (Sturmabteilung or Brownshirts, the original Nazi paramilitaries) when he was only nineteen, recruited by Goebbels, the local Gauleiter (regional party chief). Three years later he was appointed leader of SA Troop 34 in Berlin.

Just prior to his promotion, Wessel had started living with an eighteen-year-old prostitute named Erna Jänicke, whom he had picked up in a bar. The couple moved into a flat in Grosse Frankfurter Strasse (now the rebuilt Karl-Marx-Allee) owned by a certain Frau Salm, whose late husband had been a Communist. While Frau Salm and Wessel detested each other politically, her anger was further stoked by his inability to pay his rent. Now she turned to local Communists for help.

On 14 January, SA thugs had murdered a young Berlin Communist, and Wessel was believed to have been involved. That evening two Communist toughs went to his flat and knocked. The moment he swung the door open they let fire, hitting him in the face, and then disappeared into the night.

It has never been proved whether the Communists killed him on their own initiative, in revenge for their murdered comrade, or in response to Frau Salm's request for help. Although the assailants had fled the scene, one was later convicted of the assault and then murdered in prison by the Nazis.

But the main thing was, Horst Wessel was dead. Quick off the mark to exploit his demise was Goebbels, who described his emotions on hearing of the 'tragedy': 'The telephone rang. I picked up the phone with trepidation … "Horst Wessel has been shot." Trembling with fear, I asked: "Dead?" "No, but there is no hope." I felt as if the walls were collapsing around me. It was unbelievable. It cannot be!' In fact, of course, Goebbels may have been nodding in quiet satisfaction, for now he set out to turn Wessel's timely murder into an abiding Nazi myth.

When Wessel was buried in the Nikolaikirche graveyard, a crowd of 30,000 people, drummed up by the Nazis, came to mourn. There Goebbels delivered the funeral oration. In the audience were Hitler's acolyte Hermann Göring and SA member Prince August Wilhelm, son of the former Emperor Wilhelm II. A few months before his death, Wessel had penned new lyrics for an old German navy song, which Goebbels had published in his propagandist newspaper *Der Angriff* (*The Attack*). The first line ran:

Die Fahne hoch! Die Reihen fest geschlossen!
SA marschiert mit mutig-festem Schritt.

(Raise high the flag! Close the ranks tightly!
With brave firm steps, the SA marches on.)

Now at the funeral a local detachment of Brownshirts sang his song as part of the service. Through Goebbels's skilful manipulation, Nazis all over Germany were soon humming it, and it became known as the 'Horst Wessel Lied'.

But the 'Horst Wessel Lied' was just the start of the Wessel propaganda. The Nazis began to spread the story that Wessel had actually been a sort of secular saint. No, he hadn't taken a prostitute as a girlfriend, he had rescued her from prostitution by inculcating her with Nazi values, only to be murdered by the Communists for his fervent belief in Hitler. The district in Berlin where he was killed was rechristened after him, and another square was renamed Horst-Wessel-Platz.

Then, when Hitler took power in 1933, the Nazis started staging annual pilgrimages to his grave, singing the 'Horst Wessel Lied' in memoriam. It became the Nazi Party anthem, played and sung countless times over the next twelve years. Ceremonially, it almost always followed the singing of the German national anthem, 'Das Deutschlandlied' ('Deutschland über alles'). Typical occasions were 1 August 1936, as Hitler entered a stadium in Berlin to watch the opening ceremonies of the Olympic games, and 18 February 1943, at the Berlin Sportspalas, where Goebbels addressed the party faithful in an attempt to rally the nation growing tense after Stalingrad.

The cult of Horst Wessel as Nazi icon soon went beyond civil adulation to be used by Germany's military, both to honour his 'self-sacrifice' and to motivate men at war. What better than the stirring lines from his song:

Zum Kampfe steh'n wir alle schon bereit!
Bald flattern Hitlerfahnen über Barrikaden.

(We are all prepared for the fight!
Soon Hitler-flags will flutter over the barricades.)

The navy named a training ship the *Horst Wessel*, the Luftwaffe called a fighter wing the Horst Wessel Wing and the 18th SS Volunteer Panzergrenadier Division (motorised infantry) became the Horst Wessel Division.

And so it was that an odious young SA hooligan was transformed into a martyr, ironically such a suitable symbol for the Nazi regime.

Other action this day

1836: Mexican general Santa Anna begins the siege of the Alamo in Texas ∗ 1847: American general and future president Zachary Taylor defeats the Mexicans at the Battle of Buena Vista ∗ 1945: On Iwo Jima, US Marines raise the American flag on Mount Suribachi, a scene that becomes the most famous photograph of Americans in combat of the Second World War ∗ 1946: Japanese general Tomoyuki Yamashita is hanged for failing 'to control the acts of members of his command by permitting them to commit war crimes' during the American retaking of Manila

24 February

A king is captured at the Battle of Pavia

1525 At dawn today, in the great walled park of Mirabello outside the Lombard city of Pavia, the besieger found himself besieged, as King François I was taken prisoner in battle, the first French king to be so humiliated since Jean (II) le Bon was captured at Poitiers 169 years earlier.

François had taken control of the city-state of Milan after his victory over the Swiss in the Battle of Marignano in 1515, after which he had vaingloriously written to his mother: 'There has not been so fierce and cruel a battle these last two thousand years.' But despite François's splendid triumph, the French had been forced out after an Imperial and Papal force defeated them at the Battle of La Bicocca seven years later. Now he was determined to regain all of Lombardy, and in October 1524 he crossed the Alps leading an army of 30,000 men.

When the French arrived at Milan, they occupied it without resistance and then marched on to Pavia, twenty miles to the south. There some 9,000 mercenaries in the employ of Holy Roman Emperor Charles V were preparing to defend the town.

By the beginning of November the French had encircled Pavia, so isolating it that its Spanish commander was forced to melt down the treasures from the town's churches to pay his soldiers. But, despite attempts to storm the town through breaches in its walls, François's men had been forced back with heavy casualties. Unable to take Pavia by force, they determined to starve out the defenders and set up camp in the park of Mirabello just outside.

But soon an Imperial relief army of 19,000 infantry and 4,000 cavalry was approaching under the command of Charles de Lannoy, one of the emperor's generals from the Habsburg-controlled Netherlands. At first Lannoy was hesitant to launch an attack, believing the French force to be both larger and stronger than his own, but by the end of February he was running out of supplies. Unwilling to report back to Emperor Charles that he had arrived but had not fought, Lannoy prepared an assault on Mirabello, hoping that in the confusion he could effect a safe retreat.

In the darkness of evening on 23 February, Lannoy ordered his artillery to pound the French positions while his infantry approached the park. Meanwhile, Imperial engineers blew a hole in a section of the park walls, giving the attackers a way to enter.

Before dawn the next morning, 3,000 of Lannoy's harquebusiers and a squadron of light cavalry had forced their way through the breaches. Soon battle was joined, as French artillery opened up on the Imperial attackers. Now King François led his own contingent of *gendarmes* (heavily armoured cavalrymen of noble birth) into the attack, quickly routing Lannoy's horse but inadvertently masking the fire of his own artillery and separating himself from his infantry.

The trees in Mirabello Park gave François's cavalry no room to manoeuvre and they became encircled by Imperial pikemen and harquebusiers. Then an enemy *condottiere* (mercenary leader) killed the king's horse, and Lannoy's soldiers surrounded him and led him off a prisoner. The remaining French gendarmes were slaughtered piecemeal.

Now the Imperial mercenaries in Pavia's garrison slipped out of the town and overran the French siege lines. Confused and defeated, the French were cut down mercilessly as they tried to flee. The battle had lasted less than four hours.

It was a catastrophic defeat for François. He had lost 12,000 dead or wounded against a mere 500 for the enemy, and he was now an Imperial prisoner. Despite his loss, apparently he retained his appetite, demanding his first food of the day. Legend has it that his captors invented *zuppa pavese* (Pavian soup – a mixture of beef broth, eggs and crusty bread) to feed him.

François was taken away to spend over a year in Madrid as a royal prisoner, en route again writing melodramatically to his mother: 'Tout est perdu fors l'honneur!' ('All is lost, save honour!'). From the Battle of Pavia forth, Emperor Charles V dominated the Italian peninsula. He thought it particularly fitting since this 24 February was his 25th birthday. Perhaps to commemorate the victory, he chose the same date five years later to be crowned by the Pope in Bologna.

Other action this day

1547: Don Juan of Austria, illegitimate son of Emperor Charles V and victor at the Battle of Lepanto, is born in Regensburg * 1942: In a case of

114

war nerves eleven weeks after the Japanese attack on Pearl Harbor, uniden-
tified objects are reported flying over Los Angeles, prompting the 37th
Coast Artillery Brigade to fire 1,400 anti-aircraft rounds starting at 3:16 the
next morning, damaging several buildings and killing three civilians, but
the UFOs are never identified * 1953: German field marshal Gerd von
Rundstedt dies

25 February

Wallenstein is assassinated

1634 Today Albrecht von Wallenstein, one of the 17th century's
foremost generals, met death by violence, not cut down in battle but
murdered by officers of his own army.

Born in 1583 in Bohemia, Wallenstein gained his initial military
experience at 21 fighting for Rudolf II of Hungary against Turks and
Hungarian rebels. His first step towards high command, however,
came not on the battlefield but at the altar, when at 25 he married an
immensely rich widow, inheriting her estate five years later. Three
years after that, he used her wealth to underwrite 200 cavalry for the
Archduke of Styria's war with Venice. Wallenstein gained not only
the command but also the gratitude of the archduke, who would
shortly become Holy Roman Emperor as Ferdinand II.

Wallenstein soon married another heiress, enabling him to equip
a full regiment of cuirassiers in the Bohemian revolt of 1618, the
opening act of the Thirty Years War. In 1621 the emperor gave him
his first independent command against the Hungarian Bethlen
Gábor, who had joined the war on the Bohemian side.

Now Wallenstein went from strength to strength. In 1625 he used
his fortune once more, raising an army of 20,000 men, and two years
later he assembled another army of 50,000 men, giving the emperor
a second substantial force, each commanded by a premier general, as
Johann Tserclaes, Graf von Tilly headed the main Imperial army.
Wallenstein scored a major victory at the Battle of Dessau Bridge,
where he utterly destroyed the German Protestant army of Ernst van
Mansfeld, killing, wounding or capturing a third of the enemy.
Later, when Denmark's King Christian IV entered the war on the

Protestant side, Wallenstein and Tilly together laid waste virtually the entire Jutland peninsula.

Wallenstein's successes had been phenomenal, but his ever-increasing power, his overweening ambition and his arrogance created enemies among the empire's other princes. He started to see himself not as the emperor's loyal subject but as a power in his own right. Fearing he might be planning a coup, in September 1630 Emperor Ferdinand removed him from his command.

In April 1632, however, the Protestants' greatest general, Sweden's King Gustavus Adolphus, inadvertently came to Wallenstein's aid by killing Tilly in the Battle of Rain am Lech, forcing the emperor to recall Wallenstein to fill the void. After raising yet another army, Wallenstein marched into Bohemia, defeated the Saxons and in late summer routed the Swedes at the Battle of Alte Veste in Bavaria, the Swedish king's first defeat. Then came the titanic Battle of Lützen (see 6 November) where Wallenstein was beaten but Gustavus Adolphus was killed.

Wallenstein now became strangely unwilling to attack the empire's enemies but entered into secret negotiations with them instead, perhaps in an attempt to arbitrate between Protestants and the empire. His parleys unsuccessful, he returned to trounce the Swedes at Steinau on the Oder in October, his last victory. Then he once more returned to negotiation.

Now Wallenstein compounded error upon error. His behaviour towards his troops became arbitrary and cruel, ordering executions for trivial reasons and rapidly losing the love of his soldiers. He was winning no victories, and by now rumours of his intrigues were everywhere. For Ferdinand, his conduct was nothing less than treachery: Wallenstein was a general whose role was to do the emperor's bidding, not to treat with the enemy behind the emperor's back. In December 1633 the royal court in Vienna tried him in secret (and *in absentia*) and found him guilty of treason.

At last realising that he was in mortal danger, Wallenstein moved with about 1,000 loyal followers to Eger in northern Hungary, where he hoped to meet the Swedes, no doubt this time truly to turn his coat. Unbeknown to him, however, many of his senior officers had been secretly informing the emperor. Three of them, the Irish general Walter Butler and the Scots colonels Walter Leslie and John Gordon, began plotting his assassination, certainly on the emperor's instigation if not on his direct orders.

On the evening of 25 February, the conspirators invited four officers still loyal to Wallenstein to a banquet and massacred them. One of the victims fought his way out of the banquet hall into the courtyard, only to be shot dead by waiting musketeers.

Later that night the plotters sent an English dragoon captain, Walter Devereux, and a handful of other junior officers to Wallenstein's quarters in the burgomaster's house on the town's main square. Devereaux kicked open Wallenstein's bedroom door and found him asleep and unarmed. Despite Wallenstein's pleas for mercy, Devereux ran him through with his halberd.

Other action this day

1778: Argentine general and liberator José de San Martín is born ∗ 1797: In Wales, a republican French force of 1,400 troops, 'La Legion Noire', surrenders after the farcical four-day 'Last Invasion of Britain' ∗ 1991: The US VII Corps, spearheaded by the 2nd Armored Cavalry Regiment, makes the first major land operation into Iraq during the Gulf War

26 February

Napoleon escapes from Elba

1815 'It's better to die by the sword than in this ignoble retirement.' So counselled the Emperor Napoleon's strong-willed mother Letizia, who shared with him his exile on the island of Elba off the Mediterranean coast of Italy.

Less than a year earlier, on 4 May 1814, Napoleon had arrived on Elba, a beguiling island of pastoral hills and scenic bays covering slightly over 75 square miles. His victorious enemies had treated him handsomely (for a man who had kept Europe almost continuously at war for the better part of fifteen years). He was to be considered an independent ruler of the island, he would retain the title of Emperor, and, to the chagrin of the restored Louis XVIII, France would support him with annual payments of some 2 million francs.

But the emperor was worried. The French government was baulking at paying his yearly stipend, and his agents had learned that many European ministers felt that Elba was too close for comfort, a few mooting the idea of banishing him to some remoter spot. Finally, he missed his wife Marie-Louise, whom he believed his captors were preventing from joining him. (She had in fact no intention of ever seeing him again, as, unbeknown to the emperor, she had taken a full-time lover, the fellow Austrian Adam Adalbert, Count von Neipperg.)

So it was that, taking his mother's advice, Napoleon slipped away from his island prison in the dark of the evening of 26 February 1815. The emperor, 800 loyal soldiers and a few horses boarded some small sailing boats and a brig with the unfortunate name of *L'Inconstant*. On 1 March they landed in what was then a tiny fishing village called Golfe-Juan, just a few miles from Cannes.

First ashore was General Pierre Cambronne, who handed out tricolour cockades to all who would take them. Up went Napoleon's famous proclamation, 'L'aigle, avec les couleurs nationales, volera de clocher en clocher jusqu'aux tours de Notre-Dame.' ('The eagle, with the national colours, will fly from steeple to steeple until it flies from the towers of Notre Dame.') Off to reconquer France, Napoleon marched north towards Paris (you can still drive along his route north from Grasse, proudly labelled the Route Napoléon by the French Ministry of Culture). Hope ran high in the emperor's camp, but Waterloo was only three months away.

Other action this day

1871: Prussia and France sign a peace treaty at Versailles, ending the Franco-Prussian War * 1901: Boxer Rebellion leaders Chi-Hsin and Hsu-Cheng-Yu are publicly executed in Peking * 1915: German soldiers use the first modern flame-thrower for the first time against the French outside Verdun * 1935: The German Luftwaffe is reformed

27 February

Americans defeat the Scots

1776 Today, to the sounds of drums and bagpipes, a Highland army of 1,000 soldiers, kilted, wielding muskets and claymores and yelling Gaelic war cries, met disaster at a bridge in North Carolina. A force of patriot militiamen holding a strategic crossing of Moore's Creek met the Scottish charge with musketry, then routed the survivors. The timely American success had the strategic effect of preventing the loyalist force from linking up with redcoats to retake the region for King George.

It is an irony of history that the Highlanders who fought at Moore's Creek Bridge, most of them recent immigrants to North Carolina, chose to fight as loyalists of the British crown rather than remain neutral or join the rebels of their adopted country. But it was not for love of King George that they fought. Many of them had tasted the fruits of rebellion against England before – in the Stuart uprising of 1745 – and found it bitter. Forced then to take oaths of loyalty in the savage aftermath of the Battle of Culloden, they were not prepared, even 30 years later and in another land, to break their word and once more risk defiance of the crown.

So, when their clan leaders seconded the call of the royal governor for His Majesty's subjects to put down the patriot rising, the Highlanders rallied to the king's colours. For despite their new surroundings, they remained what they had always been: clansmen of strong but narrow loyalties, many still speaking only Gaelic, resolute in their historic enmity towards Lowlanders and Ulstermen, so many of whom had joined the rebel camp.

Some 850 Scots were captured at Moore's Creek. The soldiers were disarmed and ordered to their homes. Officers were sent prisoner to Philadelphia and eventually paroled or exchanged, their properties confiscated. Among these last were the husband, son and son-in-law of one Flora MacDonald, who had achieved everlasting renown after Culloden by leading the defeated Bonnie Prince Charlie to the Isle of Skye and safety from his pursuers, a deed that landed her in a British prison ship. Impoverished like so many of her countrymen after the failed uprising, she and her husband, a leader of the MacDonald clan, sailed for the New World. Now once again they were on the losing side.

If Moore's Creek proved a disaster for the Highlanders, it was heady news for Carolina patriots already inspired by the previous year's events at Lexington, Concord and Bunker Hill. Only six weeks after the battle, South Carolina instructed its delegates to the Continental Congress sitting in Philadelphia to declare their support for the complete independence of the American colonies from

Britain. It was the first such declaration by a colony and would lead to the Continental Congress's Declaration of Independence on the following 4 July.

Other action this day

1814: Wellington defeats a French army under Nicolas Soult at the Battle of Orthez in southern France during the Peninsular War * 1864: The first Union prisoners arrive at the notorious Andersonville prison in Georgia; by the Civil War's end, 13,000 of the 45,000 prisoners held there will die from starvation and disease * 1900: At the end of the ten-day Battle of Paardeberg, Boer commander Piet Cronjé surrenders with 4,000 men

28 February

The siege of Ladysmith

1900 The beleaguered defenders shouted and cheered as just after five o'clock today two squadrons of mounted infantry rode into Ladysmith. Waiting to greet them astride his chestnut mare was the town's elderly commander, Lieutenant General George White. 'Thank God we kept the flag flying', he exclaimed as he leaned forward to grasp the hand of the relief force's chief officer, the young major Hubert Gough. The siege of Ladysmith was finally over, after 118 days.

The Boer War had begun on 11 October of the previous year with the Boer invasion of the British territory of Natal. Predominantly farmers, the Boers hardly looked like soldiers; instead of uniforms they wore everyday work clothes, and, although armed with Mauser rifles, they had no bayonets for close combat. Nonetheless, they quickly drove into Natal and the northern Cape. After besting the British in a number of engagements, they besieged Mafeking (see 17 May) and then Kimberley and Ladysmith, the main British garrison town in northern Natal.

Under the command of Louis Botha, the Boers had begun positioning their men and guns in the hills surrounding Ladysmith on 29 October. The next day White's sortie against them was driven back in disorderly retreat, with 400 killed and 800 taken prisoner. Three days later the Boers cut the railway line to the south, riddling the last train out with rifle fire, as British officers, including Major Douglas Haig, lay on the carriage floor to escape the fusillade. Ladysmith, with 8,000 civilians and 13,500 British soldiers, was now cut off and under siege.

From the Boer positions on a hill four miles to the north, 155mm Creusot howitzers, nicknamed 'Long Toms', lobbed shells into the city, occasionally catching the defenders by surprise; one British officer was killed while bowling at a cricket match. According to the intrepid foreign correspondent Richard Harding Davis, 'The smoke of "Long Tom" ... could be seen for twenty-five seconds before the shell struck in the town, and, in order to warn people of its coming, sentinels were constantly on watch to look for the smoke and give the alarm. At one hotel the signal was the ringing of a bell; the Indian coolies used an iron bar swung from a rope which they beat with another iron bar, and the different regiments enjoyed the services of their buglers. So that the instant a white puff of smoke and a hot flash of fire appeared ... there would be a thrilling toot on the bugles, a chorus of gongs, bells, and tin pans, and the sound of many scampering footsteps. ... But the familiarity soon bred indifference, and after a few weeks only a small number of the people sought refuge under the iron roofs and sand-bags but walked the streets as freely as though the shells weighing a hundred pounds were as innocent of harm as the dropping of the gentle dew from heaven.' In fact, during the entire siege, only 64 people in Ladysmith were killed by artillery fire.

Since November the British relief force under Sir Redvers Buller had repeatedly tried to come to Ladysmith's aid, but each time it was stymied by fierce Boer resistance. In mid-December Buller reached Colenso, just twelve miles away, so close that the besieged could hear the thunder of his guns, only to be driven back with heavy losses. The soldiers in his command began to refer to him as Reverse Buller.

By now supplies in Ladysmith had begun to run short. Two thousand horses were slaughtered for food, and bread was made of bran and bluing starch, originally intended for laundry. Davis reported that 'lack of food and exercise, bad water, and life underground [in bomb shelters] soon bred fever, and its victims outnumbered those of Long Tom nearly ten to one'.

Finally, in mid-February Buller's men began to grind forward, supported by rolling barrages of artillery fire. Despite dogged resistance, on the 25th his soldiers moved through Boer artillery positions at Tugela Heights, capturing one hill with a determined bayonet charge. Outgunned and outnumbered by at least five to one, on the 28th the dispirited Boers retreated in disarray during a huge thunderstorm, trekking away across the veldt in a great column of horsemen and wagons. As one Boer later remembered: 'From the way in which the commandos were hurrying past, it looked that morning as if the Boer cause was going to pieces before our eyes ... it would have taken a bold man to prophesy that the war had still more than two more long years to run.'

Now the British relief column approached Ladysmith. Riding with the South African Light Horse was a 25-year-old war correspondent for the *Morning Post*, who wrote: 'The evening was deliciously cool. My horse was strong and fresh, for I changed him at midday. ... Beyond the next ridge, or the rise beyond that, or around the corner of the hill, was Ladysmith – the goal of all our hopes and ambitions during the weeks of almost ceaseless fighting. ... Ladysmith was within our reach at last. ... The excitement of the moment was increased by the exhilaration of the gallop. Onward wildly, recklessly, up and down hill, over the boulders, through the scrub, Hubert Gough with his two squadrons, MacKensie's Natal Carbineers, and the Imperial Light Horse, were clear of the ridges already. We turned the shoulder of the hill, and there before us lay the tin houses and dark trees we had come so far to see and save.' The enthusiastic reporter was named Winston Churchill.

Other action this day

1476: After the defending Swiss garrison has surrendered during the siege of Grandson, Charles the Bold, Duke of Burgundy has 412 members of the garrison led past him and hanged from trees, or drowned in the lake, in an execution that lasts four hours * 1710: Magnus Stenbock leads his Swedish army to crush the invading Danes in the Battle of Helsingborg, ending Danish efforts to conquer the Scanian Lands * 1833: German field marshal and strategist Alfred von Schlieffen is born

29 February

The Deerfield massacre

1704 Today a band of 48 French Canadian soldiers and over 200 Indian warriors massacred the British colonists of Deerfield, a frontier hamlet of perhaps 40 houses 100 miles west of Boston.

During the so-called Queen Anne's War (a small extension of the War of the Spanish Succession), the French Canadian leader Jean-Baptiste Hertel de Rouville had led this mixed attack force down from Montreal in the midst of winter with the specific objective of annihilating the isolated town, then near the western limits of British territory in North America. For the French, it would be a blow against British interests; for most of the Indians – Pennacook, Huron and Mohawk – a chance for loot or captives to ransom; while the Abenaki, who had once lived and hunted in the Pocumtuck valley around Deerfield, hoped to regain their land.

Today in the small hours before dawn, Deerfield lay silent and deep in snow, at its centre a stockade protected by a high palisade, where drifting snow had made ramps to the tops of the stakes. Unknown to those asleep within, de Rouville's fighters were stealthily approaching from the north.

One of the Indian scouts slipped into the town and found that both its night watch and its small garrison of soldiers must have retired to bed, for the snow-covered streets were empty and still. By now it was approaching 4.00am, and de Rouville ordered the assault.

With hardly a sound, 40 of the attackers climbed over the stockade wall and dropped down inside. But as they moved to open the stockade gate, the watch, at last alert, fired a shot to sound the alarm. But now it was too late to bar the attackers' entry; they were inside the stockade, running and firing, breaking down doors and smashing windows, as Deerfield's colonialists desperately reached for their guns.

Some defenders returned fire, others jumped from windows and tried to escape from the village or hide. Meanwhile, the Indians mercilessly attacked with guns, knives, tomahawks and clubs, slaughtering men, women and children indiscriminately, and especially targeting infants who were too small to survive the trek back to

Canada. Houses were set afire and cows, pigs and sheep were butchered.

In one house the garrison commander, Sergeant Benoni Stebbins, barricaded the doors and organised a strong defence. For over two hours the attackers peppered the building with bullets, but it was made of brick, invulnerable to incoming fire. Trading shot for shot, the defenders brought down four or five Indians, killing a chief and wounding de Rouville in the arm. Ordering his men to take cover, de Rouville bandaged his arm and continued to fight.

Other houses were overwhelmed. In one was the town's minister, John Williams, who later wrote about the horror. Awoken 'by [the Indians'] violent endeavours to break open doors and windows with axes and hatchets,' he grabbed his pistol just as the 'enemy immediately brake into the room, I judge to the number of twenty, with painted faces and hideous acclamations ... Taking down my pistol, I cocked it and put it to the breast of the first Indian who came up, but my pistol misfiring, I was seized by three Indians who disarmed me and bound me naked, as I was in my shirt.' After 'rifling the house, entering in great numbers into every room ... some were so cruel and barbarous as to take and carry to the door two of my children [two sons, one of six, the other an infant of six months] and murder them as also a Negro woman [a family slave].'

Now the attackers, still unable to breach Stebbins's defences, started leaving the town with their captives and plunder. But suddenly a group of some 40 colonists from neighbouring villages galloped into the town, having seen the glow of fire from the burning buildings. 'When we entered at one gate, the enemy fled out the other', one recalled later. Now the colonists were in the attack, charging after the departing force and inflicting heavy casualties. But the pursuers plunged on recklessly, and the French and Indians ambushed them, forcing them to retreat back to Deerfield.

By nine o'clock it was over. Forty French and Indians had been killed and many more wounded, but the toll was far worse for the colonists. Most of Deerfield's buildings had been burnt to the ground, and of the town's 305 residents, 56 were dead, including 25 children. In addition, 109, along with the Reverend Williams and the remains of his family, had been captured and forced on the 300-mile trek to Canada in the dead of winter. The Indians slaughtered any who faltered, including Williams's wife, who was still weak from recent childbirth: 'the cruel and bloodthirsty savage who took her, slew her with his hatchet at one stroke.' Those who survived were kept prisoners in Canada, relentlessly harassed by French Catholic priests trying to convert them, until they were finally ransomed two years later. Eventually, 53 were returned home to Deerfield, including Williams; but one of his daughters, ten at the time of the massacre, married an Indian and spent the remainder of her life living among them.

The Deerfield Massacre, as it became known, was the bloodiest event of Queen Anne's War and a striking victory for the French and their Indian allies, but it hardly settled the war, which dragged on until 1712.

Other action this day

1808: A column of Napoleon's soldiers disguised as a convoy of wounded takes Barcelona by persuading the authorities to open the city's gates * 1864: The Kilpatrick–Dahlgren Raid to free 15,000 Union soldiers being held near Richmond, Virginia fails, thwarted by bad luck and the Union raiding forces' incompetence * 1944: Douglas MacArthur leads Operation Brewer to invade the Admiralty Islands

1 March

Ethiopians crush the Italian army at Adwa

1896 At the end of the 19th century, colonialism was every European nation's favourite sport. In what is known as 'The Scramble for Africa', Britain, France, Germany, Portugal, Spain and Italy manoeuvred with each other and suppressed the natives to colonise an entire continent, until only Ethiopia and Liberia remained independent. (In the midst of this Great Power carve-up, King Leopold II of Belgium, acting as a private citizen leading a group of European investors, wolfed down the Congo, treated the natives like slaves and with appalling irony called the territory the Congo Free State.)

Now, as the century drew to its close, the Italians, who for the most part had stopped being someone else's colony only 30 years before, felt that honour obliged them to carry on the game. Their target was Ethiopia.

Italy had already been at war with the Ethiopian king Yohannes IV, and Italian forces had tasted the future when they were defeated at Bogali on 25 January 1887. But during the next nine years Italy at least nominally controlled much of the country, while armed conflict alternated with diplomacy.

By 1895, however, Ethiopia's new king Menelek II, whom the Italians had helped to gain the throne six years before, was now intent on pushing them out. Italian prime minister Francesco Crispi felt that national honour was at stake and ordered General Baratieri to advance against the king's apparently primitive army at Adwa.

On 1 March 1896, some 17,000 foolhardy Italians, with about 50 artillery pieces and reinforced by a brigade of *askari* (native infantry from Eritrea, then a province of Ethiopia), advanced on Menelek's army of over 100,000 riflemen supported by a significant number of cavalry. First caught in a crossfire and then overwhelmed by sheer numbers, the Italians were annihilated.

Surviving Italian soldiers attempted to escape through difficult terrain while under constant attack. When the battle was over, more than 10,000 had been killed, wounded or captured and held to ransom. Most of the 3,000 prisoners endured their captivity and were eventually released, but 800 captured askari, considered traitors by the Ethiopians, had their right hands and left feet cut off.

Adwa was one of the worst colonial defeats ever recorded, putting an abrupt halt to Italy's efforts to build an African empire. The battle also forced Italy to recognise the independence of Ethiopia – until 1935.

Other action this day

86 BC: Roman general Sulla sacks Athens, killing the captured tyrant Aristion by dragging him from the altar of Athena in the Acropolis and poisoning him ＊ 1562: The duc de Guise and his men kill 30 Huguenots and wound over 100 more during a Catholic–Protestant confrontation at Vassy to trigger 35 years of religious war in France

2 March

Charles the Bold loses his treasure

1476 In all, Swiss pikemen defeated Charles the Bold, Duke of Burgundy, three times, of which the last cost the duke his life.

The first victory, however, was in some ways the most profitable for the Swiss. On this day the two armies met near Lake Neuchâtel at Grandson, where Charles had been besieging the fortress. Determined to break the siege, the approaching Swiss were unaware that, four days earlier, its garrison had surrendered. Then Charles had committed an act barbarous even by the standards of the late Middle Ages. He hanged or drowned in the lake all 412 of the erstwhile defenders.

Now the Swiss vanguard came into view, but the Burgundians mistook it for the main force. Knowing battle was imminent, the Swiss knelt to pray, a sign totally misunderstood by Charles's men, who thought they were offering submission. In no mood to accept surrender, Charles ordered his cavalry back so that his artillery could devastate his enemy. But suddenly the main body of Swiss troops charged from the forest, throwing the Burgundians into total confusion and forcing them from the field. Charles rode among his men, hitting them with the flat of his sword in an effort to turn them around, but in their terror they continued to flee.

There were few casualties on either side in this encounter, but the Swiss captured Charles's chief portable treasures, seizing his gold dinnerware and twelve exquisite enamel apostles, plus an incredible collection of jewels that included:

The 'grand duc de Toscane', a diamond of 139 carats mounted in gold and pearls;

'Le Sansy', a 100-carat diamond;

'Le Federlin', a brooch of five rubies, four diamonds, 70 pearls and three giant pearls, intended for Charles's hat;

'Les Trois Frères', three rubies of 70 carats;

Two huge pearls called 'Non Pareille' and 'La Ramasse des Flandres';

Charles's necklace of the Order of the Golden Fleece;

Charles's hat decorated with sapphires, diamonds, rubies and pearls.

Apart from these incredible jewels, the Swiss also took over an even greater treasure left behind by the fleeing Burgundians: some 2,000 Burgundian *filles de joie*.

Other action this day

1770: Birth of Napoleonic marshal and duke Louis Suchet, who fought at Marengo, the First Siege of Zaragoza, Alcañiz, María, Lleida and Valencia, but lost his title for supporting Napoleon during the Hundred Days ∗ 1916: Captain Charles de Gaulle is bayoneted in the thigh and captured by the Germans near the village of Douaumont during the Battle of Verdun ∗ 1943: American and Australian planes destroy a Japanese troop convoy during the Battle of the Bismarck Sea in South-east Asia ∗ 1962: General Ne Win seizes power in a military coup in Burma

3 March

Inspired during a battle, 'The Star-Spangled Banner' becomes America's national anthem

1931 Today President Herbert Hoover signed a congressional resolution that made 'The Star-Spangled Banner' the national anthem of the United States. Popular among Americans for years – it had been used by the US Navy as the official tune to be played at the raising of the flag since 1889 – the words to the song had been inspired by an unsuccessful British attack on an American fort more than a century earlier during the War of 1812.

In 1814 Baltimore was America's third-largest city, with a population of some 45,000. Since the very beginning of the war it had been a particular thorn in the side of the British, as privateers based there had seized or sunk over 500 British ships. Now the British fleet was determined to pound it into submission.

The plan was to sail into Baltimore harbour and attack the city with cannon fire, but a star-shaped fortress named Fort McHenry protected the harbour's entrance, so the first assault came against the fort on the morning of 13 September.

At 6.30am, the schooner *Cockchafer* opened fire, and during the next 24 hours British warships and bomb vessels fired about 2,000 shells and 800 rockets at Fort McHenry, which was defended by only 1,000 men and 57 guns under the command of Major George Armistead. Over the fort flew an enormous American flag measuring 42 feet by 30 feet, hand-made by Mary Pickersgill, whose mother had made flags for George Washington.

From eight miles away an American lawyer named Francis Scott Key observed the firing from the deck of a British flag-of-truce ship, where he was negotiating the exchange of an American prisoner. As he watched the battle, Key rejoiced when the British finally pulled back at dawn the next day, the flag still waving and the Americans undefeated. Based on what he saw, he wrote the words to 'The Star-Spangled Banner' on the back of a letter he had kept in his pocket. His original title was 'Defence of Fort McHenry'. A few days later his brother-in law scanned it to go to an old English drinking song called 'To Anacreon in Heaven'.

First printed in Baltimore newspapers only a few days after the battle, 'The Star-Spangled Banner' gradually grew in popularity, played at events such as 4th of July celebrations. By 1916 it was being used for special military occasions, on the order of President Woodrow Wilson. Finally Congress reflected popular opinion with its resolution of 1931, and on this day 'The Star-Spangled Banner' took its place as the official anthem of the nation.

1575: Indian Mughal emperor Akbar the Great's army defeats the Sultan of Bengal, ending Bengal's independence after 237 years * 1924: Turkish general Kemal Ataturk deposes Caliph Abdul Mejid II, ending the 1,400-year-old Islamic caliphate of the Ottoman empire

4 March

The great Saladin dies

1193 There is a certain magic to the name Saladin, the legendary Saracen leader who defied Richard the Lionheart during the Third Crusade (particularly if you know what his name means – 'Righteousness of the Faith, Joseph, Son of Job'). It was Saladin who caused Richard to come on crusade in the first place by destroying Christian power in the Holy Land at the Battle of Hattin in 1187 (see 4 July). And although Saladin's armies never bested Richard in open combat, they were in the end too strong for him, and Richard was forced to abandon his crusade without having retaken Jerusalem.

Saladin was born in 1138 in a town called Tikrit in what was then Mesopotamia, today's Iraq. Although best known in the West for his battles against Christians, his first wars were against smaller Muslim states, as he expanded his power. Indeed, fellow Muslims came closer to killing him than Christians ever did. In 1176 during the siege of Aleppo (now in Syria), hired killers from the Hashshashin twice tried to assassinate him, once wounding him in the process.

Although the Christians failed to conquer Saladin, they defeated him several times, most notably in 1177 when Baldwin IV of Jerusalem and Raynald of Chatillon overwhelmed him at the Battle of Montgisard (see 25 November). Of Saladin's army of 30,000, some 27,000 were slain, and Saladin escaped only by vaulting onto the back of a racing camel and fleeing the field. Two years later, however, he destroyed one of Baldwin's garrisons at the Battle of Jacob's Ford.

By 1187 Saladin had conquered almost all the Crusader strongholds in the Holy Land, and finally, after a protracted siege, Jerusalem fell (see 2 October).

By all accounts, Saladin was at least as chivalrous as any European knight. Even while battling with Richard he sent him and his captains chilled wine, pears and grapes from Damascus to ease their life in camp. During the Battle of Arsuf, Richard's horse was killed under him. Saladin saw the English king fall and, instead of ordering his men to finish him off, sent him a fresh horse instead (a gallant act that Saladin may have regretted, since a re-horsed Richard led the final charge that shattered the Muslims).

Richard gave up his crusade in October 1192. Ironically, Saladin died of fever in Damascus only five months later, on this day in 1193.

Dying, he saw the ephemeral nature of all his triumphs. His last instructions to his followers were: 'Go and take my shroud through the streets and cry loudly, "Behold all that Saladin, who conquered the East, bears away of his conquests".'

Other action this day

1152: Frederick I Barbarossa is elected King of the Germans * 1461: Edward IV deposes Henry VI during the Wars of the Roses * 1665: Charles II declares war on Holland to begin the Second Anglo-Dutch War

5 March

Colonial rebels drive the British out of Boston

1776 Morning light revealed the surprise that the American rebels had prepared for General Sir William Howe, the British commander-in-chief in America. During the night they had constructed a fortified artillery position at the top of Dorchester Heights, across the bay from the city of Boston, and, even more remarkable, they had placed in it a battery of powerful cannon that now commanded not only the harbour, where the British fleet lay, but also the city itself, where 6,500 redcoats had been bottled up by the rebel army since the previous spring.

Unknown to the British, the Americans had acquired the cannon when they captured the British stronghold at Fort Ticonderoga the year before. Then, in an epic of winter logistics planned by Henry Knox, the Boston bookseller turned artillerist, the heavy guns, weighing some 120,000 pounds, were put on sledges and dragged by oxen over 300 miles of frozen terrain to the rebel siege lines around Boston.

Sir William knew the jig was just about up. With artillery in such a position, Boston would be untenable. Because the British guns in the city could not be sufficiently elevated to deliver counter-battery fire on Dorchester Heights, Howe's only hope of dislodging the Americans and capturing their cannon was with a night assault. He ordered an attack for that very evening, but it was first delayed by heavy rains and then cancelled, giving the Americans further time to strengthen their defences.

The next day General Howe consulted his commanders in a council of war, at which the decision was taken to evacuate the city. In an agreement with General Washington, Howe promised not to burn Boston if his command were allowed to leave without hindrance. And so it was that ten days later the British garrison and 1,000 American Loyalists boarded ships and sailed away to Halifax, Nova Scotia.

With the evacuation of Boston by the British, round one of the American Revolution – the New England round of Lexington, Concord and Bunker Hill – went to the rebels. But it would be a long war, over six years of fighting, and round two would begin in just four months with a large British army landing near New York City.

Other action this day

1198: The Teutonic Knights are accepted as an official order at the Templars' compound in Acre * 1770: British soldiers fire into a rioting crowd in Boston, killing five, in the so-called Boston Massacre * 1936: The experimental aircraft K5054, the prototype for the Supermarine Spitfire fighter, makes its maiden flight from Eastleigh aerodrome near Southampton

6 March

French cunning captures Richard the Lionheart's impregnable castle

1204 Through inheritance, marriage, treaty and conquest, Henry II hammered together the Angevin empire that included all of England plus roughly half of France, from Normandy in the north through Brittany, Touraine and Poitou, down through Bordeaux to Gascony and the borders of Spain. His son Richard the Lionheart inherited this great empire and fought to preserve it from his hereditary enemy, King Philip Augustus of France.

Richard's most significant contribution to the defence was the massive Château Gaillard, of which the ruins still stand atop a cliff at Les Andelys, about 55 miles north-west of Paris. *Gaillard* in French means strong, large and vigorous, and Richard's fortress was aptly named. With its seventeen massive towers, walls eight feet thick and a moat 45 feet deep, it protected the route the French would have to take to invade Richard's northern possessions. But even such a daunting fortress held no fears for Philip Augustus. 'I should take it if it were made of steel', he is reputed to have boasted. 'I should hold it were it made of butter', was Richard's famous reply.

By the year 1203, however, Richard was dead and his cowardly, incompetent brother John was on the throne. It was then that Philip Augustus moved to conquer Château Gaillard at last.

But the mighty fortress looked just as impregnable now as it had when Richard had built it seven years before. For almost six months the French attackers remained camped outside the walls, suffering daily jeers from the defenders. But while Philip was failing to take the fortress, John was so unsure of his own barons that he could not raise an army to break the siege. It looked like stalemate.

Then Philip learned that the English had over a year's supply of food on hand, so the garrison could never be starved out. Knowing that the only way to victory was by storming the walls, the French king ordered a direct attack.

First the French troops, protected by screens, built a rough path to the moat and promptly filled it with earth and felled trees. Now they could approach the exterior walls, where they mined one of the corner towers, causing its partial collapse.

But still the attackers were unable to force their way in, so the wily Philip sent in a small team of soldiers who entered the fortress through its latrines and quickly lowered the drawbridge leading to the principal keep. Now able to bring in their massive siege machinery, the French hammered a breach in the last remaining walls, compelling the English garrison to surrender on this day in 1204.

The fall of Château Gaillard marks the start of the destruction of the Angevin empire. By John's death twelve years later, English-held territory in mainland France had been reduced to a few small holdings in the south-west, and Philip had earned his name of Augustus, father of modern France.

Other action this day

1836: In Texas, after a twelve-day siege, Mexicans under General Santa Anna storm through a breach in the outer wall of the Alamo courtyard and overwhelm the Texan defenders; of the original force of 198, 189 have been slain, including Colonel Jim Bowie and Davy Crockett * 1940: The Soviet Union and Finland sign an armistice, bringing the Winter War to an end

7 March

Napoleon confronts the king's army

1815 Today the ex-emperor Napoleon added another celebrated chapter to his own legend by facing down royalist soldiers with the dramatic words: 'S'il est parmi vous un soldat qui veuille tuer son empereur, me voilà.' ('If there is among you a soldier who wants to kill his emperor, here I am.')

Napoleon had escaped from Elba after nine months and 22 days of regal confinement (see 26 February). After a night in Cannes, he started his advance towards Paris, almost 600 miles away, with a small corps of 1,200 soldiers.

Knowing that troops loyal to Louis XVIII were to the west in Marseilles and the Rhone valley, he headed straight north through Grasse and, following small trails and mule tracks, climbed into the foothills of the Alps, past Séranon and through the Clue de Taulanne in heavy snow. By nightfall on 4 March he was at the Château de Malijai.

The next day, while Napoleon was lunching in Sisteron, in the royal palace in the Tuileries King Louis received the news of his escape. Frantically, he summoned his generals and sent word to block Napoleon's progress. (Not all royalists were as concerned as the king; the optimistic newspaper *Moniteur* called Napoleon's escape 'an act of madness which can be dealt with by a few rural policemen'.)

When Napoleon reached the hamlet of Laffrey on 7 March, he found that the 5th Battalion of the Royal French Army was waiting there, ready to capture or kill him. On a meadow at the south end of the Lac de Laffrey, the ex-emperor's soldiers nervously faced the royalist troops, all with rifles at the ready. But Napoleon had already seen (and caused) enough French blood spilt. Dismounting from his horse, he directed his guard to raise the Tricolore flag and play the 'Marseillaise', which had been outlawed by the monarchy.

Now he sent 100 of his Polish lancers forward in a slow advance. When the opposing soldiers pulled back, he ordered the lancers to wheel and return. He then stepped forward alone, a proud figure in his grey battle coat and black bicorn hat, and moved within pistol range of the enemy line.

'Fire!' cried out a royalist officer, but there was only silence. 'Fire!' he cried again, but still with no result. Then Napoleon called out: 'Soldats du Cinquième, je suis votre empereur. Reconnaissez-moi.' ('Soldiers of the 5th, I am your emperor. Recognise me.')

Another moment of hush, and then Napoleon dramatically opened his coat to expose his breast and issued his famous invitation for the troops to open fire. The response was an immediate roar of 'Vive l'Empereur!', as the royalist ranks broke and men ran towards him, acclaiming and touching him. Their desperate commander broke into tears and offered his sword to Napoleon, who embraced him.

The same day Napoleon trekked a further seventeen miles to Grenoble, his force now doubled in size, joined by the royalist soldiers from Laffrey. Then north through Lyon and on to Paris, picking up more reinforcements in every town he passed. He reached Paris (see 20 March) the day after Louis XVIII had scuttled off to

Belgium. Arriving at the Tuileries at nine in the evening, Napoleon found himself cheered by 20,000 Parisians. He was emperor once more.

Napoleon had covered a 40-day journey in twenty days, converted opposing troops through a magnificent display of personal courage and regained his throne without a trace of violence or a single shot being fired.

Other action this day

1814: Napoleon defeats a Prussian and Russian army under Blücher at the Battle of Craonne * 1936: In violation of the Treaty of Versailles, nineteen German infantry battalions cross the Rhine to start remilitarisation of the Rhineland * 1945: American troops seize the Ludendorff Bridge over the Rhine at Remagen and begin to cross into Germany

8 March

The Grey Ghost strikes again

1863 It was late in the evening when the Confederate raiders reached their destination, Fairfax Court House, Virginia, some fifteen miles inside the enemy picket lines. The gloom of a rainy night concealed their identity as they rode into town, and melting snow muffled the sounds of their horses. Occasional challenges by sleepy Union sentries were met with the curt acknowledgement, '5th New York Cavalry'.

So it was that Captain John Singleton Mosby, leading a party of 40 guerrillas – 'almost as motley a crowd as Falstaff's regiment', he described his followers – began yet another strike against the Union communications lines in northern Virginia. He was now the 'Grey Ghost', whose spectacular exploits, one historian noted, 'created in the minds of his enemies the impression of a will-o'-the-wisp, of a lurking and mocking spirit, an unseizable force of frustration that might turn up at any moment in any place and interfere with any operation'.

Early in the war, Mosby rode as a cavalry scout in a famous feat of reconnaissance, Jeb Stuart's ride around a Union army that threatened Richmond, the Confederate capital. Then, in January 1863 he organised the Partisan Rangers, a group whose irregular activities soon became a severe and unsettling distraction for the Union Army of the Potomac. One raid halted a Union train and relieved it of a military payroll totalling $168,000 in greenbacks. In another, Mosby single-handedly captured a company of Union cavalry by pointing his pistols at the group and yelling behind him to imaginary followers, 'Charge 'em, boys! Charge 'em!' By 1864 his home territory, Loudon County, in western Virginia, would become known as 'Mosby's Confederacy'. For the ruthlessness with which he carried out his raids, the Union commander-in-chief, U.S. Grant, would give the order: 'When any of Mosby's men are caught, hang them without trial.'

This evening's events at Fairfax Court House resulted in the kidnapping of a Union general, two captains, 30 privates, and 58 horses. Mosby and some of his men managed to enter Brigadier General Benjamin Stoughton's quarters undetected and found him asleep upstairs. Pulling back the covers, Mosby gave his quarry a slap on the backside. In the dim light of the bedroom, recognition was slow, and the following exchange took place: *Stoughton*: 'Do you know who I am, sir?' *Mosby*: 'Do you know Mosby, general?' *Stoughton*: 'Yes, have you got the —— rascal?' *Mosby*: 'No, but he has got you.'

By 3.00am the raiders and their prisoners withdrew, first cutting the telegraph wires, then taking an unlikely escape route to throw off pursuit. By dawn they were clear of the Union lines. Later in the morning, as they rode through Warrenton, the townspeople came out to cheer. The following day, Mosby delivered the prisoners to Confederate general Fitzhugh Lee.

Mosby continued his raids in Virginia until the end of the war, with a number of sensational exploits, including his near-capture in December 1864 by Union cavalry. He was a colonel when the war ended, after which he resumed his law practice, and became friends with General Grant, who called him 'able, and thoroughly honest and truthful'.

President Rutherford B. Hayes appointed Mosby to a US consulship in Hong Kong, where he served for seven years. Herman Melville was so fascinated by Mosby's wartime activities that he wrote a poem, published in 1866, called 'The Scout toward Aldie', about a detachment of Union cavalry that enters a forest in pursuit – ultimately unsuccessful – of the eternally elusive Mosby.

Other action this day

1906: US troops occupying the Philippines massacre 600 men, women and children taking refuge in a crater during the Moro Crater Massacre * 1942: The Dutch surrender to the Japanese on Java * 1965: The first American combat troops, 3,500 Marines, arrive in Vietnam

9 March

The first battle of ironclad ships

1862 The Union ship *Monitor* looked rather like a hatbox on top of a raft, while the Confederate *Virginia* was shaped like a bar of Toblerone chocolate with a smokestack in the middle. Yet when these two peculiar warships met in combat in Hampton Roads, Virginia, they changed for ever the nature of naval warfare. For on this day took place the first battle ever between ironclad ships.

At first blush the ships seemed very different. The *Virginia* had once been a conventional steam frigate named the *Merrimac* and had been built in the North. When Union troops abandoned the Portsmouth shipyard in June 1861, they attempted to burn the ship but failed to sink her, leaving a floating hulk. Salvaged by the Confederates and rechristened CSS *Virginia*, at over 100 yards long, she was twice the length of the *Monitor*, and her crew of 300 was more than five times as large. Further, she was armed with ten guns to her rival's two. The *Monitor*, on the other hand, sported the first naval gun turret in history, so her guns could be aimed in any direction without turning the ship.

The day before the meeting of these metal monsters, off the town of Newport News the *Virginia* had destroyed the Union sloop *Cumberland* and the frigate *Congress* while forcing the *Minnesota* to run aground, all the while remaining impervious to cannon fire.

The Battle of Hampton Roads started about eight in the morning. Both ships fired unceasingly at each other, at so close a range that the vessels actually touched five times during the engagement. The *Virginia* even tried to batter the *Monitor* with her cast-iron ram.

After four and a half hours of fighting the Confederate ship withdrew unharmed. Neither ship had been able to inflict significant damage on the other.

The two ironclads never fought again. The Confederate sailors scuttled the *Virginia* when the South pulled out of Norfolk, while the *Monitor* was lost in a storm off Cape Hatteras on the last day of the year. But naval warfare would never be the same. The wooden warship was relegated to history.

Other action this day

1847: American soldiers under General Winfield Scott invade Mexico near Vera Cruz during the Mexican–American War * 1864: General Ulysses S. Grant is appointed commander-in-chief of the Union forces * 1945: The first day of a two-day attack on Tokyo in which American B-29s drop 1,665 tons of incendiary bombs, killing more than 100,000 civilians, destroying 250,000 buildings and incinerating sixteen square miles of the city

10 March

The story of the French Foreign Legion

1831 France's King Louis-Philippe needed some hardened but perhaps expendable troops to pacify Algeria, and he met the need by creating a new military unit. On this date his minister of war Marshal Nicolas Soult formed the French Foreign Legion, specifying that it 'should not be employed in the continental territory of the kingdom'.

The Legion's officers were recruited from veterans of Napoleon's army who had been mouldering on half pay since Waterloo. The enlisted men were drawn from all over Europe, often desperate men who could find no employment or were wanted by the law. Within a year, Legion strength was 5,500 officers, NCOs and legionnaires.

The Legion first saw combat in April 1832, when two battalions of mainly German and Swiss troops stormed a village called Maison Carrée east of Algiers. Since then, legionnaires have fought in hundreds of wars and brush fires around the world. They were at the siege of Sevastopol during the Crimean War, and supported the puppet emperor Maximilian during his ill-fated reign in Mexico. Their African conflicts have included Dahomey, Madagascar, Tunisia,

Chad, Lebanon and Algeria. They also served in Vietnam, in Bosnia during the civil war there in 1993, and in the first Gulf War.

Over the years, the Legion has boasted some famous names (although not all of them bore those names when they were legionnaires). There have been two Napoleons – the emperor's nephew who was a captain in 1863, and Prince Napoleon, the Bonaparte pretender to the French throne, who served under the name of Blanchard in 1940. Napoleon/Blanchard must have been amused to find a fellow pretender to the throne serving with him – the comte de Paris, who was a direct descendant of King Louis-Philippe, the man who created the Legion. An earlier royal officer was the future Peter I of Serbia, who used the name Kara as his *nom de guerre* in 1870.

The most illustrious Legion officer undoubtedly was Patrice de Mac-Mahon, who served in 1843–4, went on to lead the French army at the great victory at Magenta in 1859 and rose to be president of the Third Republic in 1873. Two other Legion members have become prime ministers of France. Edouard Daladier was prime minister for several years in the 1930s (and co-signer with Neville Chamberlain of the Munich Pact with Adolf Hitler's Germany), and Pierre Messmer was prime minister under de Gaulle and Pompidou.

The Legion also boasts some cultural lions. The American poet Alan Seeger spent three years in the Legion during the First World War and was killed in action at Belloy-en-Santerre, and the Hungarian-born English author Arthur Koestler, writer of *Darkness at Noon*, was in service in 1940. Indeed, the Legion's reputation for hard-bitten souls with a chequered past has been seen as so glamorous that even an American boulevardier like Cole Porter maintained that he had been a legionnaire, although historians now universally debunk the claim.

Today the Legion boasts soldiers of fortune from some 99 countries, usually tough, sometimes criminals on the run. There are no Frenchmen in the Foreign Legion except for officers, all of whom are graduates of the French national military academy of St-Cyr. This combination of French leadership and foreign troops has created a formidable fighting force. The British Second World War field marshal Viscount Alanbrooke called it 'the grandest assembly of real fighting men that I have ever seen, marching with their heads up as if they owned the world, lean, hard-looking men, carrying their arms admirably and marching with perfect precision'.

The Legion remained stationed abroad for 131 years, until the liberation of Algeria forced it to move, for the first time, to France. Today it boasts between 8,000 and 9,000 men. Each year there are about 500 candidates to join, but less than 10 per cent are accepted.

Should the Foreign Legion's history and glamour tempt you to sign up, if you're not French you will have to become a legionnaire, for whom the rules can be daunting:

The minimum term of service is five years
You cannot have a bank account
You are not permitted to live off barracks
You may not own a car or motorcycle
Marriage is forbidden until you attain the rank of sergeant or have served for nine years.

Other action this day

241 BC: The Romans sink the Carthaginian fleet near the Aegates Islands, ending the first Punic War * 1813: King Friedrich Wilhelm III of Prussia establishes the Iron Cross (*Eiserne Kreuz*) on the birthday of his wife Luise, during the Napoleonic Wars

11 March

General MacArthur leaves the Philippines

1942 In the gathering evening darkness, General Douglas MacArthur, commander of United States forces in the Far East, stepped off Corregidor island's North Dock onto the deck of PT-41. Minutes later the motor torpedo boat rumbled away on the first stage of a journey that would take him from the Philippines through the Japanese naval blockade to Australia. In Adelaide a week later he told reporters, 'I came through', then added the phrase that would become famous: 'and I shall return.'

Left behind was a looming defeat whose dimensions were still unknown to the American public. Against a strong Japanese invasion force that landed two weeks after Pearl Harbor, MacArthur had quickly organised his forces in a stubborn, retreating defence.

But he knew, as did his superiors in Washington, that without reinforcements buttressed by air and sea power the defence of the Philippines was a lost cause.

No one would have known the cause was lost from the communiqués issued by MacArthur's headquarters on Corregidor, messages one historian described as 'gripping though often imaginary accounts as to how MacArthur's guile, leadership, and military genius had continuously frustrated the intentions of Japan's armed forces'. For the American public, he became the first hero of the war.

From Washington, President Roosevelt promised MacArthur help. In January, Army chief of staff George Marshall radioed: 'President has seen all of your messages and directs navy to give you every possible support in your splendid fight.' But in the five-month siege of the Bataan peninsula and Corregidor, no planes, no ships, no reinforcements reached the Philippines. There were none to spare.

Now the question was whether to risk MacArthur's almost certain death or capture with his troops, or bring him out. John Curtin, the Australian prime minister, helped decide. In late February, facing the increasing threat of Japanese invasion, the Australian government demanded of British prime minister Winston Churchill either the return of three Australian divisions now with the British 8th Army in North Africa, or the appointment of an American general as supreme commander of an expanded Allied force for the south-west Pacific theatre. Churchill, who had earlier expressed his admiration in the House of Commons for 'the splendid courage and quality of the small American army under General MacArthur', used his influence with FDR.

Initially, MacArthur refused the President's order to leave his command, but Roosevelt persisted, and the general finally agreed. Boarding PT-41 with him this evening for the dangerous voyage were his wife and four-year-old son.

On 9 April the Philippine defence force – 10,000 American soldiers and some 60,000 Filipino troops, out of food, ammo and medical supplies – surrendered to the Japanese. A month later Corregidor – the 'Gibraltar of the East' – fell, adding the Philippines to the lengthening list of Allied defeats, which by now included Dunkirk, Pearl Harbor, Tobruk, Guam, Wake and Singapore.

By then, however, MacArthur, at Allied headquarters in Melbourne, had taken charge and begun to organise the measures that would in time roll back the Japanese tide. After a brilliant series of air and amphibious operations that leap-frogged across the top of New Guinea, he arrived back in the Philippines on 20 October 1944. Wading ashore on Leyte island, he reminded the assembled press corps: 'I have returned.'

Other action this day

1425 BC: Death of the warrior pharaoh Thutmose III, who ruled Egypt for 53 years, ten months, and 26 days ∗ 1387: Fighting for Padua, *condottiere* John Hawkwood triumphs at the Battle of Castagnaro against *condottiere* Giovanni Ordelaffi fighting for Verona ∗ 1507: Italian prince and mercenary Cesare Borgia, illegitimate son of Pope Alexander VI, is killed in battle near Viana in Spain while fighting for Jean d'Albret, King of Navarre

12 March

Belisarius' magnificent defence of Rome

AD 537 Today the beleaguered troops of the great Byzantine general Belisarius cheered and jeered from the walls of Rome as the Ostrogoth king Witigis and his downhearted men burned their camps and withdrew towards their capital in Ravenna. In one of the most astonishing defences in history, an army of only 5,000 men had held the city against enemy forces of over 100,000 for a year and nine days.

With its capital in Constantinople, the Byzantine empire controlled the eastern half of the old Roman world. In the west, the Ostrogoths had ruled Italy since AD 493, when their legendary king Theodoric had completed his conquest. But now the Byzantine emperor Justinian was determined to wrest back the old western part of the Roman empire and dispatched his greatest general to do it.

During the previous seven years Belisarius had defeated the Sasanian Persians in Mesopotamia and the Vandals in North Africa. He had also saved Justinian's throne by massacring the rebels during the Nika insurrection in Constantinople (see 17 January). He was about 30 when he advanced on Italy.

His first major operation came in the summer of 536 when he besieged and occupied Naples. Then, on 9 December of the same year, he entered Rome virtually unopposed. The city had been in decline for over a century, ever since the Visigoths had sacked it in 410. Many inhabitants had abandoned it, many buildings and monuments lay in ruins, and cows grazed in the old Roman forum. But Rome was still the largest city in Western Europe, and Belisarius knew that the Ostrogoths would soon counter-attack. Less than three months later, King Witigis arrived with a massive army.

Belisarius's exiguous force had to defend circuit walls twelve miles in circumference against an encircling enemy. To strengthen his defences he placed catapults on the city walls and ordered a deep ditch dug beneath the walls. To prevent the Ostrogoths from using boats to row up the Tiber he had a chain drawn across the river, and he garrisoned Hadrian's tomb, the fortress known today as the Castel' Sant'Angelo.

Stymied by Belisarius's defensive tactics, Witigis attempted to force surrender by diverting the city's aqueducts, but his plan backfired when his own camps were turned into malaria-breeding swamps.

Witigis then ordered four siege towers with battering rams to be drawn up by teams of oxen against the Roman walls. As Belisarius watched the enemy's approach, he borrowed a bow from one of his soldiers and killed an Ostrogoth officer at a great distance. He then ordered his bowmen to fire, not at the enemy soldiers but at the oxen. As the oxen fell pierced by arrows, the siege towers were left standing in the open, never having reached the walls.

The Byzantine army's greatest strength was its cavalry of armoured archers. According to the historian Procopius, who was there: 'Their bows are strong and weighty; they shoot in every possible direction, advancing, retreating, to the front, to the rear, or to either flank.' Infantry armed with axes, spears and swords supported the cavalry.

Unable to man all points along the walls, Belisarius mounted a series of surprise sorties. First the horse archers would put the enemy cavalry to flight and then Byzantine infantry would close in to slaughter the unprotected Ostrogoth infantry. In spite of the numerical odds, such attacks were almost invariably successful.

While battling the enemy outside the city, Belisarius also had to guard against treachery from within. At first he feared that the Roman citizens, foreseeing eventual Ostrogoth victory, might throw open the city gates, but with continued Byzantine success, the Romans gained confidence in Belisarius and even volunteered to join the fight. One surprise betrayal, however, was that of Pope Silverius, who wrote to Witigis offering to surrender the city. Belisarius dressed the Pope as a monk and sent him into exile.

Eventually some 4,000 reinforcements reached Rome and entered the city during a truce, bringing with them a large quantity of supplies. Having already lost some 30,000 men, Witigis saw the situation was hopeless and abandoned the siege.

Other action this day

1881: Turkish general and president Kemal Ataturk is born * 1930: Canada's top First World War fighter ace (almost 40 enemy planes and balloons destroyed) and Victoria Cross winner William George Barker dies when he crashes his biplane trainer at Air Station Rockcliffe, near Ottawa * 1938: Hitler's troops march into Austria; he declares the Anschluss (annexation) the next day

13 March

Mata Hari springs full-grown into the world

1905 Before the four-armed statue of Shiva she danced, her arms and calves encircled by bracelets, her breasts covered only by small bejewelled cups. The other dancers snuffed out the candelabra, leaving the stage in the dim light of a flickering oil lamp. Then, with her back to the audience, she threw off her sarong and moved towards the statue, writhing with passion, apparently nude. As she knelt before the statue, another dancer flung a gold lamé cloak over her shoulders. Rising, she turned to face the stunned crowd as the curtain rang down at the Paris cabaret.

Such was the 'birth' of Mata Hari, the notorious dancer and courtesan who made her first stage appearance today under her assumed name, a Malay term for the sun, literally meaning 'eye of the day'. Twelve years later she would be shot as a spy by a French firing squad.

Mata Hari was born Margaretha Zella, a dark-haired, olive-skinned Dutch girl of middle-class parents. She had been raised in the Netherlands and had later moved to Java with her mean and dissolute husband whose beatings and philandering eventually drove her to divorce.

When M'greet, as she was called, returned from the Far East she was nearly 30. Unable to find either another husband or a suitable job in Amsterdam, she moved to Paris. There she invented a mysterious new identity for herself, claiming that she came from India, daughter of a temple dancer, and had been raised in the service of the god Shiva. Calling herself Mata Hari, she soon landed a role at the Musée Guimet cabaret, where she found instant fame after her début. Shortly she was triumphantly touring Europe, titillating audiences with her risqué routine and taking lovers along the way.

But by the time she was in her late thirties Mata Hari's body was thickening with age, and she progressively earned her keep more as a *demi-mondaine* than as a dancer. Superbly adroit at lovemaking, she found dozens of rich partners, including celebrities such as a Rothschild baron and Giacomo Puccini. At this time, on the eve of the First World War, she also began her career as a spy.

The details and extent of Mata Hari's espionage remain murky. She claimed that she was enlisted by French Intelligence to seduce German officers to learn their secrets, and in at least one case she was successful. But in late 1916 the French intercepted a coded German message referring to her as their 'agent H 21' and were convinced that she had become a double agent.

The French army quickly brought Mata Hari to trial on charges of espionage, and convicted her in a travesty of justice that was held 'in camera' and during which the defence could not cross-examine witnesses. Mata Hari's choice of a 74-year-old corporate lawyer to defend her primarily because he had once been her lover did not help. The jury of six French officers wasted no time in finding her guilty and condemning her to death.

At dawn on 15 October 1917, Mata Hari was led to the internal courtyard of the Parisian prison at Vincennes. There she faced her fate bravely, telling an attendant nun: 'Do not be afraid, sister. I know how to die.' Refusing a blindfold, she faced the twelve riflemen confronting her and blew them a kiss just before the fusillade ended her life.

Such was the finish of the famed Mata Hari, whose body was given to a French medical school so that student doctors could practise their dissecting skills. The last physical trace of her disappeared in 2000 when her mummified head was stolen from the Museum of Anatomy in Paris.

AD 565: Byzantine general Belisarius dies in Constantinople * 1519: Hernán Cortés lands in what will become Mexico, the first step in destroying the Aztec empire * 1900: British forces occupy Bloemfontein in the Orange Free State during the Boer War

14 March

Admiral John Byng faces the firing squad

1757 The start of the French and Indian War three years earlier had pitted England against France as each attempted to gain control of ever larger slices of North America. Once started, hostilities were hard to stop, and both nations continued to spar with each other in Europe on the eve of the Seven Years War.

In May 1756 the British feared a French attack on their base in Menorca and sent a small fleet under the command of an indolent and indecisive admiral named John Byng to counter French aggression. But by the time he arrived, the base had fallen.

The irresolute Byng launched an attack but in such a desultory manner that he was soon driven off, at which point he decided that he was facing insuperable odds and sailed off to the British base at Gibraltar, leaving Menorca to the mercy of the French.

On hearing the news back in London, British prime minister Thomas Pelham-Holles, Duke of Newcastle, bristled with indignation and resolved to punish Byng for his apparent lack of zeal. Charging the admiral with dereliction of duty, Newcastle guaranteed a biased court martial by announcing publicly that 'he shall be tried immediately; he shall be hanged directly'.

Brought back to Portsmouth in disgrace, Byng was tried and convicted on his own flagship *Monarch* and on this day taken on deck and shot by a firing squad of marines.

No other British admiral had ever been executed for such a crime, and all of Europe was bemused by the news. Two years later, Voltaire published his masterpiece *Candide*, which includes the celebrated observation: 'Dans ce pays-ci il est bon de tuer de temps en temps un amiral pour encourager les autres.' (In this country [England] it's good to kill an admiral from time to time to encourage the others.)

15 March

The Ides of March

44 BC 'Beware the Ides of March!' the augur Spurinna had warned some days earlier, but Julius Caesar had brushed him aside. Now 55, he had been dictator for five years, after having decisively defeated the coalition of nobles who had tried to destroy him. Caesar knew there were senators who hated him, who in fact were plotting to kill him, but so sure was he of his position, of the awe (and perhaps, he hoped, the love) in which he was held, that he had dismissed the troop of Spanish bodyguards that normally escorted him.

So at mid-morning Caesar set off for Pompey's Theatre, where the Senate was meeting. En route a friend handed him a note with the details of the assassination plot, but Caesar simply put it with the other letters he was carrying, having no time to read it.

Entering the theatre, he saw Spurinna among the crowd. 'The Ides of March have come', he mocked. 'Yes,' replied the augur, 'but they have not yet gone.'

Caesar took his seat, quickly to be surrounded by conspirators who pretended to be paying their respects. One seized him by the shoulder, and Caesar shook him off, but as he turned away one of the Casca brothers central to the conspiracy stabbed him just below the throat. Grabbing Casca's arm, Caesar stabbed it with his stylus and tried to escape the ring of murderers now surrounding him. But suddenly he realised it was hopeless. Since Casca's first thrust he had not uttered a word, but when he saw his protégé Marcus Brutus among his assassins, he murmured in Greek, 'You, too, my child?' He then drew the top of his toga over his face; no one should see him powerless and dying.

The murderers struck out in a frenzied attack, sometimes

wounding each other in their eagerness for the slaughter. Twenty-three knife blows struck home as Caesar stood there, defenceless, before he fell lifeless to the floor.

Caesar was dead, but his assassins' triumph was short-lived. Virtually all were killed within three years of the murder or, like Marcus Brutus, committed suicide.

Caesar had been one of the greatest of all generals, equalled perhaps by only Alexander the Great, Hannibal, Genghis Khan and Napoleon. He first saw combat at nineteen in Cilicia (modern Turkey). There, during the siege of Mytilene, he was awarded the *corona civica* (civic crown) Rome's highest decoration for gallantry. Six years later he again achieved renown when he was captured by pirates. After being ransomed he raised a fleet at his own expense, tracked down the pirates and had them crucified.

During his years commanding Roman legions, Caesar achieved a spectacular record of victories. In Hispania he conquered the Lusitani and the Callaici, for which he was awarded a triumph. He then fought in Gaul from 58 BC to 51 BC, where he defeated the Helvetii, the Belgae, the Suessiones, the Tigurine, the Suebi, the Eburones and the Averni. It was against this last enemy that he overcame their leader Vercingetorix in his brilliant triumph at Alesia. In his final Gallic victory at the siege of Uxellodunum, he showed his usual tactical brilliance – realising that the fortress could not be taken by storm, he diverted the sources of a spring to cut off the water supply. Here he also demonstrated his complete ruthlessness. Determined to put an end to local rebellions, he cut off the hands of the defeated warriors, who were then freed to wander throughout Gaul as a warning. Plutarch wrote that during these wars, Caesar's army killed 1 million Gauls and enslaved another million while destroying 800 cities and subjugating 300 tribes.

Caesar's victories were not only over warring tribes. During the Roman civil war he lost to Pompey at Dyrrhachium but then annihilated his larger army at Pharsalus (see 9 August). He also lost to his former lieutenant Titus Labienus at Ruspina (see 4 January) but then defeated and killed him at Munda. Other Caesarian victories included one over a Ptolemaic army at the Battle of the Nile and another over Pharnaces of Pontus at the Battle of Zela (see 21 May). According to Pliny the Elder, Caesar fought 50 pitched battles, more than any other Roman commander.

Caesar was not only a brilliant military leader but also an extraordinary writer. His *Gallic Wars* is considered a literary classic; innumerable commanders in the future would be inspired by it, and the US Marine general Chesty Puller carried it in combat for over twenty years. Caesar was the greatest of all Romans, perhaps, according to Macaulay, the greatest of all men. He changed the world. He replaced the corrupt and incompetent rule of the Roman nobility with an autocracy that endured for half a millennium in the west and 1,500 years in the east, and he gave to France the Latin civilisation that replaced tribal barbarism and that has lasted to this day.

Other action this day

1493: Soldier and statesman Anne de Montmorency, who was Constable of France under François I, Henri II, François II and Charles IX, is born in Chantilly * 1767: American general and president Andrew Jackson is born * 1941: British ships under Captain Donald MacIntyre sink the German submarine U-99, capturing the legendary captain Otto Kretschmer, who had sunk 47 Allied ships

16 March

Creating America's Army officers

1802 Fifty miles north of New York City, the high ground at West Point overlooks the Hudson River. Should it fall to the British, they would control the river valley and could split the American colonies in two. Recognising its strategic importance, in 1778 American rebels fortified the point, and a year later General George Washington established his headquarters there.

The US Army has never relinquished this base (although the treasonous general Benedict Arnold tried to sell it to the British in 1780), and West Point therefore remains the oldest continuously occupied military post in the United States. In 1802, however, it took on a special new purpose – turning young Americans into Army officers.

In 1783 Washington had been one of the first to propose an American military academy, but newly independent Americans had rejected his call, fearing that such a training school might lead to a military aristocracy.

Two decades later, however, Congress had seen the wisdom of Washington's idea and drew up a bill that President Thomas Jefferson signed on this day, establishing the United States Military Academy at West Point. Appropriately, the academy opened for business on Independence Day.

America was not the first country to establish a military academy. The oldest still-extant military academy is the Theresian Military Academy, founded in 1751 by Maria Theresa of Austria. Otherwise, America was among the first countries to establish a formal training school for officers. The British Royal Military Academy at Woolwich was founded in 1741, but the current British officer training school at Sandhurst opened to train staff officers in 1800 and first admitted cadets only in 1802. The French École Spéciale Militaire de Saint-Cyr was set up by Napoleon in 1803, and the Prussian Kriegs Akademie (War Academy) in Berlin was established in 1810.

As one would expect, West Point has produced the preponderance of the country's most illustrious soldiers, but never more so than during the Civil War, when Southern graduates agonised over whether to stay loyal to the Union or to join the forces of their home states. In the end, 638 West Pointers fought for the North, compared to 259 joining the Confederacy. The most famous Northern generals were Ulysses S. Grant and William Tecumseh Sherman, although another Union general and West Point graduate, George Armstrong Custer, gained rather less glorious renown after the war at his Last Stand at Little Bighorn.

The Confederacy's two greatest generals, Robert E. Lee and Stonewall Jackson, were both West Point graduates, as was the president of the Confederacy, Jefferson Davis.

According to one historian: 'The Civil War became a West Pointers' war, with 151 Confederate and 294 Union generals. West Pointers commanded both sides in 55 of the war's 60 major battles, and one side in the other five.'

Other famous West Point graduates include Black Jack Pershing, who commanded the American Expeditionary Force during the First World War, and Second World War generals Douglas MacArthur, Omar Bradley, George Patton, and future president Dwight D. Eisenhower. (Among America's most senior Second World War Army generals, only George Marshall did not attend West Point, receiving his degree from Virginia Military Institute.)

West Point has also produced three heads of state other than American presidents: Fidel Ramos of the Philippines, José Maria Figueres of Costa Rica, and Anastasio Somoza Debayle of Nicaragua, who was forced to resign and was assassinated in exile in Paraguay.

Finally, some fascinating dropouts have also gone to West Point. Edgar Allan Poe was in the class of 1834, but he hated the academy and was expelled during his first year for missing his classes and drills for a week, and the artist James McNeill Whistler withdrew from the class of 1855. Perhaps the most unlikely of all was the psychedelic Timothy Leary, who dropped out of the class of 1943 and later made a virtue of it with his famous catchphrase: 'Turn on, tune in, drop out.'

Other action this day

1812: A 25,000-man Anglo-Portuguese army commanded by Wellington begins the 21-day siege of the 5,000-man French garrison at Badajoz that ends with Allied victory at a cost of 4,800 casualties * 1968: During the Vietnam War, American Army lieutenant William L. Calley Jr. leads his men in the My Lai Massacre during which over 400 unarmed civilians are killed

17 March

The start of the greatest career

1787 Today a young man not quite eighteen years of age joined the British army as an ensign in the 73rd Highland Regiment. He was shy, of indifferent health, and played the violin. Born in Dublin into an old family of the Anglo-Irish nobility now in reduced circumstances, he was a product of Eton and the Royal Academy of Equitation in France, where he had received a year's instruction in riding, swordplay and mathematics.

The young man wasn't looking forward to service in the army – it was a derelict time for that institution after the defeat in North America and before the coming war against republican France – but it was not in his character to protest at his fate. To the contrary, he would make the best of it.

The commission came via the head of the family, his older brother Richard, who had importuned the Lord Lieutenant of Ireland for it. He persevered in the soldier's trade. In 1794, as a lieutenant colonel, he got his first taste of combat leading an infantry regiment in the Duke of York's failed campaign to take the Low Countries from the forces of revolutionary France. The ensign signed his name A. Wesley. It was not until 1798, when the older brother was to be made a marquess, that the family name was realigned for heraldic purposes to Wellesley. In that year he was Colonel Arthur Wellesley. By this time he was in India, where he would in time attain the rank of major general.

But it was in Portugal and Spain, in the period 1808–13, fighting against the French, that Wellesley's remarkable string of battlefield successes laid the basis for his enduring fame and won him the recognition of his countrymen. In 1809, for his victory at Talavera (see 28 July), he was made a viscount. In 1812, after his successful siege of Ciudad Rodrigo (see 20 January), he became an earl, and later the same year, following his triumph at Salamanca, he was raised to a marquess. And for chasing Joseph Bonaparte out of Madrid, he had his portrait painted by Francisco Goya.

Finally, on 3 May 1814, with the Peninsular War won, Napoleon gone to Elba, and King Louis XVIII on the throne of France, Lieutenant General Arthur Wellesley, hailed affectionately as 'Nosey' by his veterans and 'El Liberador' by a grateful Spain, received the title by which the world would know him for all time: duke – the Duke of Wellington. To a letter that he wrote to his brother Henry the next month he added: 'I believe I forgot to tell you that I was made a Duke.' No one else forgot. To his countrymen, as one biographer noted, 'he was henceforth *the* Duke'.

Other action this day

45 BC: In his last victory, Caesar defeats the Pompeian forces of Titus Labienus and Cnaeus Pompey (Pompey the Younger) in the Battle of Munda in Spain, in which Labienus is killed ＊ AD 624: According to the Koran, divine intervention helps Mohammed win a key victory over his Meccan adversaries in the Battle of Badr, leading to the expansion of Islam

18 March

Insurrection in Paris

1871 The people of Montmartre were fed up with their new government, the newly formed Third Republic, for they thought that too many concessions were being made to the victorious Prussians who still occupied large parts of France in the aftermath of the Franco-Prussian War. Worse, they believed that the National Assembly favoured the rich and feared that it might move to restore the monarchy. Sullenly, they collected on street corners, whispered conspiratorially to each other and eyed the paving stones as possible missiles.

In an attempt to stabilise the situation in Paris, Adolphe Thiers, the head of the national government, decided to impound the cannon held by the National Guard, which was thought to be sympathetic to the republican mob. But instead of establishing calm, Thiers's move triggered insurrection; on 18 March Montmartre's doughty citizens commandeered 171 cannons, and when French forces appeared to reclaim them, the crowd dragged one general from his horse and shot him, and shortly seized and shot another. The National Guard quickly joined the insurgents, and the uprising known as the Paris Commune had begun.

In panic, Thiers fled to Versailles, and within ten days the Paris Commune was officially proclaimed, its council ordering revolutionary changes such as giving women the right to vote and decreeing the separation of church and state, while confiscating all church property and banning religion in schools. The Tricolore of France was replaced with the socialist red flag symbolising 'the blood of angry workers'.

In response to the Commune's usurpation of state powers and the slaughter of the generals, French troops began a siege of Paris that lasted two months. By the end of May, forces under General Mac-Mahon had breached one of Paris's city walls and entered the city, summarily executing any National Guardsmen or civilians caught with weapons. In retaliation, the Communards murdered more than 50 hostages, while setting up barricades in the streets and torching the Hôtel de Ville and the Tuileries Palace.

The government's revenge was swift and terrible; during *la semaine sanglante* (the bloody week) that followed the entry of the French army, 20,000 civilians were killed, among them 17,000 who were executed, including women and children. About 750 soldiers also lost their lives. Crushed by the forces of the Third Republic, the Commune collapsed, but the government's reprisals continued. Almost 40,000 more Parisians were arrested, a fifth of whom were deported to New Caledonia.

Other action this day

1793: The Austrians rout a republican French army under Charles François Dumouriez at the Battle of Neerwinden; seventeen days later Dumouriez turns his coat to join the Austrians * 1937: Spanish republicans defeat the Italians at the Battle of Guadalajara during the Spanish Civil War

19 March

Kublai Khan completes the Mongol conquest of China

1279 Today Kublai Khan's navy used a cunning subterfuge to destroy the last fleet of the Southern Song dynasty, giving the Mongols control of all of China.

In 1211 Kublai Khan's grandfather Genghis Khan had led the first Mongol invasion of China, attacking the Juchen state in the north. Although Genghis died in 1227, his sons finally conquered the Juchen in 1234. Inexorably, the Mongols subjugated increasing swaths of China, and in 1250 they began moving into Song territory in the south.

The contrast between the Song and the Mongols could not have been greater. The Mongols had been illiterate until a few years before Kublai Khan's birth, while the Song had ruled south China during one of its most brilliant cultural epochs, as art flourished and literature was driven by the development of moveable type. But, although the Song had initially been a powerful military force, it was no match for the ferocious Mongols in the art of war.

Initially the Song stymied Mongol efforts to invade, holding the line at the Yangtze River, but the Song government became leaderless when the Song emperor Duzong died in 1274, leaving the throne to his four-year-old son Bing. Two years later the Mongols marched into the Song capital of Lin-an (today's Hangzhou) after court officials and the army had fled.

Now, in March 1279, Mongol general Zhang Hongfan's fleet was advancing on Yamen, a port near Canton. Directing the defence was Zhang Shijie, the resolute Grand General of Song.

As the Mongol taskforce approached, some Song officers urged Zhang Shijie to use his ships to block the mouth of the bay in order to protect their retreat route to the west, but the Grand General adamantly refused, fearing that, if an escape route were open, his soldiers might run rather than fight. Instead, he ordered his warships chained together in a long line within the bay, with the boy-emperor Bing in the centre. He then burned all the nearby houses, leaving a shattered landscape with no relief for any retreating troops.

When they arrived before Yamen Bay, the Mongols opened the battle by launching fire ships towards the Song line, but the Song ships had been coated with fire-resistant mud and were little damaged. The Mongols then landed troops to take over the already devastated town, cutting off Song supplies of food and water.

On 19 March the Mongol leader Zhang Hongfan began a naval attack, only to be repulsed by the Song ships. Unable to defeat his enemies by brute force, he now resorted to ruse. He ordered his soldiers to begin playing cheerful music, tricking the Song into thinking that the Mongols had abandoned the fight and were having a banquet. At midday Zhang Hongfan brought his ships closer to the Song line, with his soldiers concealed under large pieces of cloth on deck. Once the Mongols were within striking distance, he sounded the battle horn. His troops leaped from under cover and the Mongol fleet attacked.

The Mongols quickly broke the Song line, and the Song general Zhang Shijie ordered sixteen ships, including the one carrying the emperor, to cut themselves loose and escape. Instantly the Mongols gave chase, cornering the Song as they attempted to flee the bay. Seeing that a breakout was impossible, a loyal Song minister named Lu Xiufu forced his own family to jump overboard and then, carrying the boy-emperor on his back, leaped into the sea. Meanwhile, the Mongol ships carried out a wholesale massacre of the remaining Song fleet. Zhang Shijie evaded capture, only to be drowned in a hurricane.

A week later 'hundreds of thousands' of corpses still floated in the bay. The boy-emperor Bing's body was supposedly found, but the whereabouts of his grave is unknown.

Thus ended the Song empire that had taken control of China in AD 960, was driven from the north in 1127 and now came to an end after 319 years. Kublai Khan's dynasty, named the Yuan, collapsed of its own internal dissensions after only 89 years, the shortest-lived of any major Chinese dynasty.

Other action this day

1314: On the orders of French king Philip the Fair, Jacques de Molay, the last Grand Master of the Templars, is burned at the stake in Paris facing Notre Dame * 1941: The 99th Pursuit Squadron, also known as the Tuskegee Airmen, the first all-black unit of the US Army Air Corps, is activated * 1945: Hitler issues the Nero Decree, ordering all industries, military installations, shops, transportation and communications facilities in Germany to be destroyed

20 March

Napoleon's return to Paris

1815 To the consternation of Europeans everywhere but to the joy of Frenchmen, Napoleon entered Paris today in triumph, borne shoulder-high to the Tuileries by a huge crowd crying 'Vive l'Empereur!' Only three weeks earlier he had escaped his exile on Elba (see 26 February) to land near Cannes and take the Continent by surprise. As he travelled north through a France war-weary but discontented under the restored Bourbon regime, peasants hailed him as their champion, and his veterans, forgetting the realities of recent campaigns, cheerfully disobeyed orders and flocked to his side.

Napoleon's cause seemed to gather strength with every mile of his progress. In Vienna the Congress pronounced him an outlaw. In Paris King Louis XVIII and the royal court decamped for the safety of Ghent.

A handbill caught the spirit of the day.
The Tiger has broken out of his den.
The Ogre has been three days at sea.
The Wretch has landed at Fréjus.
The Buzzard has reached Antibes.
The Invader has arrived in Grenoble.
The General has entered Lyon.
Napoleon slept at Fontainebleau last night.
The Emperor will proceed to the Tuileries today.
His Imperial Majesty will address his loyal subjects tomorrow.

The Hundred Days had begun.

Other action this day

1778: France and the United States sign an alliance against England, after which France provides the US with timely aid during the American Revolution * 1922: The USS *Langley*, a converted collier, is commissioned as the first US Navy aircraft carrier

21 March

The best and worst of Napoleon

1804 History knows few characters as controversial as Napoleon Bonaparte, and today saw him at his best and worst.

The most dramatic event of the day was the execution by firing squad of the duc d'Enghien at the Château de Vincennes east of Paris.

Louis de Bourbon-Condé, duc d'Enghien was an attractive and well-meaning 31-year-old prince who lived in the German castle of Ettenheim in Baden, idly plotting with other aristocratic émigrés the overthrow of the government, of which Napoleon was First Consul. But d'Enghien came from one of France's greatest aristocratic families and thus could be a candidate for the throne should the monarchy be restored. Then Napoleon received intelligence (false, as it turned out) that linked d'Enghien with a serious conspiracy of several generals. Incensed, he sent three brigades of infantry plus 300 dragoons across the Rhine into Germany to seize the poor prince as he lay sleeping peacefully in his undefended house.

Forcibly brought back across the border, d'Enghien was imprisoned at Vincennes. Although Napoleon's wife Joséphine begged her husband to be lenient with the aristocratic prisoner, the First Consul accused him of plotting against France and sent him to a mock trial juried by eighteen generals. Quickly convicted and sentenced to death, he was refused a priest and led into the château's moat, to be summarily shot beside a freshly dug grave. Most of Europe was horrified by this brutal kidnap and murder, while the sardonic Talleyrand quipped: 'C'est plus qu'un crime; c'est une faute.' ('It's more than a crime; it's a blunder.')

On the very same day of the execution Napoleon published a new civil code, the Code Napoléon. This immense body of law was a dramatic improvement over the hodgepodge of existing and sometimes conflicting laws, and it was intrinsically much fairer as well. In later life Napoleon took special pride in his Code, reflecting: 'Waterloo will wipe out the memory of my forty victories; but that which nothing can wipe out is my Civil Code. That will live for ever.' Indeed, even today it remains the basic law of France, Belgium and Luxembourg.

Other action this day

1421: The French and Scots defeat the English at the Battle of Baugé, the first English land battle loss in the Hundred Years War * 1646: After losing the Battle of Stow-on-the-Wold, the last battle of the English Civil War, Royalist general Sir Jacob Astley tells his troops: 'You have done your work, boys, and may go play, unless you will fall out among yourselves' * 1918: At the start of the Second Battle of the Somme, the Germans begin the biggest artillery bombardment of the First World War, firing 1,100,000 high-explosive, poisoned gas and smoke shells in five hours and causing 7,500 British casualties * 1945: British troops liberate Mandalay in Burma from the Japanese

22 March

Stephen Decatur is killed in a duel

1820 Today one of America's most celebrated naval heroes, Stephen Decatur, was mortally wounded in a duel with a fellow officer as a result of bitter acrimony between the two men that had lasted for thirteen years.

Decatur had first gained national renown in 1804 during America's war with Tripoli, a conflict triggered by the piratical pasha's demand for increased tribute in return for not attacking American merchant ships in the Mediterranean. During a night raid, Decatur led 74 volunteers into Tripoli harbour and burned the captured American frigate *Philadelphia* without losing a man. The great British admiral Horatio Nelson called it 'the most daring act of the age'. Decatur's reward for his derring-do was to be promoted to the rank of captain at the age of 25, the youngest captain ever in the American navy.

Eleven years later Decatur, by now a commodore, took on the pirates once again during the Second Barbary War. Leading a fleet of nine ships, he riddled and captured the Algerian frigate *Meshouda*, killing the admiral on board and taking over 400 prisoners. Then, with his guns trained on the harbour of Algiers, he delivered an ultimatum to Omar, the Dey of Algiers. When Omar begged for an annual tribute of 'a little gunpowder' from the United States in order to save face with his people, Decatur replied: 'If you insist upon receiving powder as tribute, you must expect to receive balls with it.' The Dey capitulated in two days, putting a stop for ever to American payment of tribute to pirate states.

Back in 1807 an American officer named James Barron had allowed a British warship to board and search his frigate and carry off four supposed British deserters, one of whom was hanged. A year later Decatur served on the court martial that had expelled Barron from the Navy for five years. From that moment on the two men, who had previously been friends, continued to wrangle and exchange heated letters, a situation made worse when Decatur accused Barron of malingering abroad instead of returning home to fight in the war against Britain of 1812. By 1820 the hostility had become so fierce that Barron challenged Decatur to fight.

The two men met at Bladensburg Duelling Field at what is now Colmar Manor, Maryland, five miles outside Washington, DC. During the preliminaries Decatur remarked to his second: 'I do not desire his life. I mean to shoot him in the hip.' They were to fire at eight paces, but the gentlemanly Decatur did not back up the full distance for safety because of his opponent's poor eyesight.

Both men fired; Decatur wounded his opponent in the hip as planned, but Barron's shot caught Decatur in the stomach. As they lay on the field together, Decatur said that he had never been Barron's enemy, to which Barron replied: 'Would to God you had said that yesterday.'

Taken back in agony to his home on Lafayette Square, Decatur cried out just before he died: 'I did not know that any man could suffer such pain!'

President James Monroe led the mourners at Decatur's funeral, which drew a crowd of 10,000 people and included the entire Supreme Court and most of the Cabinet. Secretary of State John Quincy Adams later described Decatur as 'kind, warm-hearted, unassuming, gentle and hospitable, beloved in social life and with a soul totally and utterly devoted to his country'. Even now there are still eleven American cities named after him, and five Navy warships have been called USS *Decatur*.

Other action this day

1622: Algonquian Indians kill 347 English settlers around Jamestown, Virginia, one third of the colony's population, during the Jamestown Massacre * 1848: The first day of 'Le cinque giornate di Milano' (Five Days of Milan), the Milanese revolt against Austrian rule that liberates the city until it is reoccupied by Austrian general Josef Radetzky four months later * 1943: Russian soldiers massacre 15–20,000 Polish officers at the Katyn Forest

23 March

'Vater' Radetzky tames the Italians

1849 Josef Radetzky was one of the most talented generals ever to fight for Austria, but he achieved his greatest victory – his triumph at the Battle of Novara – when he was 82 years old.

Radetzky had joined the Austrian army when he was nineteen in 1785. His first combat came in the Turkish War of 1787–92, but he rose to prominence fighting the French, first (in 1795) against the Republic and then during the Napoleonic Wars.

In all he fought in over ten battles against Napoleon: in the Italian campaign in 1800 and at Marengo (where he was shot five times), Wagram, Leipzig (where he helped plan the Allied victory), Brienne and Arcis-sur-Aube, Napoleon's last pre-Waterloo battle, where the emperor's heavy casualties virtually forced his first abdication. Radetzky marched into Paris with the triumphant Allies.

By the end of the Napoleonic Wars Radetzky was a lieutenant field marshal, and in 1836 he was promoted to field marshal. He was so venerated by his soldiers that they called him 'Vater Radetzky'. With such a glorious military career behind him, he then retired.

But in 1848 revolution broke out all over Europe. Even reactionary Austria was struck: on 13 March a Viennese mob rioted outside the offices of the obdurate foreign minister Klemens Metternich and forced him into exile after 40 years in power. In December, after fleeing revolutionary Vienna, Emperor Ferdinand abdicated in favour of his eighteen-year-old nephew Franz Joseph.

There were also insurrections in Italy, especially in Lombardy and the Veneto, then under Austrian rule. Now Radetzky, already 81, was summoned from retirement to become commander-in-chief of the Imperial army in northern Italy.

In Milan the famous 'cinque giornate di Milano' (Five Days of Milan) exploded on 22 March, as rebels manned barricades, fought in the streets and fired from roofs and windows. The revolt was so violent that Radetzky withdrew to the Quadrilateral fortresses (the fortified towns of Mantua, Peschiera, Verona and Legnano).

It was then, on 23 March, that Piedmont-Sardinia's king, Charles Albert, attempted to take advantage of the turmoil and declared war on the beleaguered Austrians, determined to kick them out of Italy.

By summer Radetzky was ready to take on the Piedmontese, and, leaving the relative safety of the Quadrilateral fortresses, he marched on Custoza to confront Charles Albert's army. There, during bitter hand-to-hand fighting, both sides lost more than half their troops. At the end, Radetzky captured the city, driving Charles Albert out of Lombardy and forcing him to agree a humiliating truce.

But in March of the following year, Charles Albert renounced the armistice and assembled an army of 86,000 men, significantly more than the 72,000 Austrian troops in northern Italy. On 22 March Charles Albert's army met Radetzky again, this time at Novara, 30 miles west of Milan. The battle revolved around the high ground in Novara's Bicocca district, which was taken and lost several times by both sides. Late in the afternoon Radetzky's light cavalry put the Piedmontese artillery out of action, allowing the Austrian infantry to cross the Agogna River to the west of the town and assault the enemy right flank. During the attack the Austrians took 400 prisoners and caused substantial Piedmontese casualties, including two generals who were killed.

Sporadic fighting continued during the night, and at dawn on this day, Radetzky ordered a sustained artillery barrage against the enemy defenders in Novara and then sent his light cavalry to occupy the town. The battered Piedmontese army was forced into headlong retreat twenty miles north to the foothills of the Alps, and Charles Albert fled into exile in Portugal, to die there only four months later, after having abdicated in favour of his son Victor Emmanuel (who later became king of a united Italy).

Despite his advanced age, Radetzky remained in the army until his death at 91 in 1858. He was so highly celebrated in his time that Johann Strauss the Elder even composed a piece in honour of his victory at Custoza. The rollicking 'Radetzky March' is still played to spectators' rhythmic clapping in performances around the world and closes every New Year's Concert in Vienna.

Other action this day

AD 625: Abu Sufyan leads an army from Mecca to defeat Mohammed at the Battle of Uhud * 1775: Patrick Henry defies the British with his 'give me liberty or give me death' speech at St John's church, Richmond, Virginia, which leads towards the American Revolution * 1821: Greek rebels liberate the city of Kalamata, the first city to be freed after 300 years of Turkish occupation, during the Greek War of Independence

24 March

Wingate crashes in the jungle

1944 Some time in the early evening a Mitchell bomber on a flight from Imphal to Lalaghat in India crashed on a jungle hillside, killing all nine on board. Among them was a British officer recently described by Prime Minister Winston Churchill as 'a man of genius and audacity'. The officer in question was Major General Orde Wingate, a brilliant but controversial military leader, a Bible-quoting mystic, an apostle of irregular warfare, an eccentric man whose successes in the field won him admirers in high places but whose arrogant behaviour brought him enemies on many levels.

Despite his off-putting eccentricities – he sometimes received visitors while nude after a bath; and he often wore an alarm clock on his wrist with which to signal the end of an interview – Wingate, a graduate of the Royal Military Academy, showed a special ability to organise and lead small-scale military operations behind enemy lines. In Palestine in the 1930s his Special Night Squads – British-led Jewish commandos – successfully fought against Arab gangs threatening not only the Jewish settlements and oil pipelines of the region but also the security of the British Mandate itself. In the Sudan in 1940 he organised Gideon Force, a mixed unit of Britons, Ethiopians and Sudanese, with which he raised a rebellion that helped liberate Ethiopia from Italian occupation and restore Haile Selassie to the throne.

In 1942 he was called to India, where he set to work devising a way to combat the Japanese forces that had seized Burma and now threatened India. He took a brigade-sized unit of British and Gurkha battalions and trained it as a long-range penetration group. In the spring of 1943 he led his Chindits, as they became known, into Burma's rugged terrain. In the course of three months, organised into separate columns but connected by radios and supplied by air, they blew up bridges, destroyed railway lines, and played havoc with the Japanese lines of communication, penetrating some 200 miles. But the getting back proved difficult, and when the columns returned to India they had lost a third of their strength, and only 600 of those who made it back were considered fit for active duty.

Whether the expedition was a success – 'worth the loss of many brigades' as Wingate put it, or 'an expensive failure' as General Slim, British 14th Army commander and Wingate's boss, wrote – is still a matter of debate. But the feat was unquestionably a great morale-booster, capturing the imagination of the press, which dubbed him 'Clive of Burma', and of Allied leaders starved for some sign of success on the South-east Asia front. 'Whatever the actual facts,' Slim himself conceded, 'to the troops in Burma it seemed the first ripple showing the turn of the tide.'

Now the man of the hour, even though his unorthodox views of warfare seemed dubious or even threatening to certain quarters of the

British military establishment, Wingate was sent for by Winston Churchill, who brought him to the 1943 Quadrant Conference in Quebec, where the prime minister and President Roosevelt were to meet with their combined chiefs of staff. At the conference, it was agreed to send in a second and larger Chindit force to Burma the following year, bolstered by American air support.

But as the second Chindit expedition got under way in the spring of 1944, with some 20,000 men entering north Burma on foot and by air, Wingate met his fate in the crash of the Mitchell bomber. The operation continued with some success, but without their leader the days of the Chindits as a separate enterprise were numbered, and the unit soon fell under other commands, including that of US general Stilwell, whose celebrated Merrill's Marauders were modelled after them. The early Chindit experiences in the field had at the very least demonstrated that even an enemy as skilled in jungle fighting techniques as the Japanese was vulnerable to the kind of warfare Wingate preached. Ultimately, the combined operations of which they were a part were successful in the 1945 reconquest of Burma, in part because the Allied forces had become, in the words of the theatre commander, Lord Mountbatten, 'Chindit-minded'.

Other action this day

1401: Tamerlane captures Damascus * 1918: During Chief of the General Staff Erich von Ludendorff's Operation Michael, German forces cross the Somme River to open the spring offensive * 1944: To avenge the death of 28 German policemen by partisans the previous day, on Hitler's orders German soldiers under SS officers Erich Priebke and Karl Hass butcher 335 Italian hostages in the Fosse Ardeatine massacre near Rome

25 March

Light Horse Harry

1818 On this date the American general Henry Lee, whose exploits as a cavalry leader in the American Revolution earned him the nickname 'Light Horse Harry', died at the age of 62 on Cumberland Island, off the coast of Georgia. He was on his way home to Virginia from a five-year stay in the West Indies, where he had gone in hopes of restoring his health – or, as his enemies insisted, to escape financial and political embarrassments.

Scion of an old Tidewater family and a graduate of Princeton, Lee joined the Continental Army in early 1776. During the course of the war, he commanded troops in major battles like Brandywine, Germantown, Guilford Court House, and Eutaw Springs. But he craved military distinction – and the public recognition that went with it – and found that the way to achieve both was through independent action: raids, ambushes, and surprise attacks.

He first came to notice in January 1777, while commanding an outpost at Spread Eagle Tavern, near Philadelphia. Surprised by a superior force of British cavalry, Lee, with a small body of dragoons, managed with effective musket fire to hold off his attackers, then bluffed them into retreat by yelling out to hasten the approach of an imaginary force of Continental infantry. Minor though it was, the action impressed the army's commander-in-chief, George Washington.

Lee won a measure of renown – and a Gold Medal from Congress – for leading the 1779 pre-dawn attack on the British outpost at Paulus Hook. As a consequence, he was soon promoted lieutenant colonel and given command of a legion, a battalion-sized joint force of infantry and mounted troops.

In late 1780, 'Lee's Partisan Corps' – highly disciplined, well mounted, and aggressively led – was ordered south to join General Nathaniel Greene's army facing the British advance through the Carolinas. In this theatre, Lee would soon encounter what he would later describe as 'that sanguinary warfare ... which, with the fury of pestilence, destroyed without distinction'.

During Greene's retreat to the Dan River, Lee's legion, the very last element of the American army's rearguard, performed brilliantly to fend off the fierce pursuit of Cornwallis's British army. But in one incident, after discovering that the legion's bugler, a boy of fourteen, had been ridden down and slain by British cavalry, Lee ordered his men to retaliate. In what followed, the legion surrounded an enemy patrol and proceeded to kill eighteen, most of whom had surrendered.

Not a month later, at Haw River, North Carolina, in a bold ploy Lee managed to bring his green-jacketed cavalrymen in among an unsuspecting group of 300 loyalist militia, who had mistaken them for the similarly clad troopers of Banastre Tarleton's British Legion. The result was 90 loyalists shot or sabred to death, nearly all the rest wounded.

In the months of hard fighting to come, Lee's legion fought as part of Greene's Southern Army in large-scale battles, while also conducting separate actions in which five British posts were seized and over 1,100 of the enemy captured. But there were also occasions of brutality and vengeance where his men became involved in the torture and execution of enemy prisoners.

By the spring of 1782, after seven years at war, a badly worn-out Lee left the army and went home, suffering from what might now be diagnosed as battle fatigue. His admiring theatre commander, General Greene, wrote to him: 'I have beheld ... a growing discontent in your mind, and have not been without my apprehensions that your complaints originated more in distress than in the ruin of your constitution.'

In peacetime, Lee was an important leader of the new republic, serving a term as governor of Virginia, then becoming a member of the US House of Representatives. In 1794 President Washington selected him to command the army raised to quell the Whiskey Rebellion, a deed he ably accomplished. But he also made a series of bad land investments, which not only led to scandal and ruin but also to a year in debtor's prison.

Then, in 1812, while in Baltimore defending an outspoken Federalist newspaper editor from an angry Republican mob, Lee sustained the extensive internal injuries that occasioned his retirement to the West Indies.

Although he left a heavily encumbered estate and a family in penury, Lee also bequeathed to posterity three notable items: his memoirs of the Revolutionary War, written while in prison; the famous phrase from his eulogy of George Washington, 'first in war, first in peace, first in the hearts of his countrymen'; and his fourth son by his second marriage, Robert E. Lee, who many years later would lead the Confederacy against the Union that his father had helped found.

Other action this day

AD 101: Trajan invades Dacia to begin the Third Dacian War against King Decebalus * 1802: Joseph Bonaparte and Marquess Cornwallis sign the Treaty of Amiens, ending hostilities between republican France and Great Britain for one year * 1767: Napoleonic marshal and King of Naples Joachim Murat is born in Gascony

26 March

'Drink your blood, Beaumanoir; your thirst will pass!'

1351 Today on a field in Brittany 60 knights in armour and their two captains faced each other in a passage of arms that became widely admired throughout medieval France as a model of martial chivalry.

In 1341 Duke Jean III of Brittany had died without direct heir. Immediately both his niece's husband, Charles de Blois, and Duke Jean's half-brother, Jean de Montfort, claimed the inheritance, touching off the Breton War of Succession, which seesawed back and forth for its first ten years.

In 1351 one of Montfort's captains, an Englishman named Robert Bramborough, held the Breton walled town of Ploërmel, while just seven miles to the west, Charles de Blois's marshal, Jean de Beaumanoir, held the fortress of Josselin.

Although in theory a ceasefire kept the two sides at bay, Robert Bramborough had continued to raid Beaumanoir's holdings. At length, under flag of truce Beaumanoir rode up to the walls of Ploërmel and shouted a challenge – would Bramborough meet him in single combat? The Englishman offered a counter-suggestion: 'God shall be the judge between us. Let each of us choose 30 men to champion his cause. Then we will see which side is in the right.' And so the stage was set for bloodshed.

On Saturday, 26 March, the two bands of armoured knights met at an open field called le Chêne de Mi-Voie (the Midway Oak), halfway between Ploërmel and Josselin. The terms of battle had been agreed as 'combat à volonté', meaning that each of the combatants could pick his own way of fighting, mounted or on foot, with the arms of his own choosing, with no further rules except that all must follow the obligations of chivalry.

Beaumanoir had selected 30 fellow Bretons while Bramborough had assembled a mixed force of twenty Englishmen, six German mercenaries and four Breton supporters of Montfort. When the two contingents arrived at the place of battle, as custom required they heard Mass and exchanged courtesies. Then each group pulled back, facing the other. A signal was given, and the men charged, every man for himself, each eager to bring down the enemy. Swords clanged on armour, spears whistled through the air, and axes crashed against shields, as the charge became a savage mêlée. A Breton squire and a mounted knight were hacked down, and two other knights and another rider were wounded and captured. Beaumanoir's force now numbered only 25, while Bramborough still had 30.

The two sides parted in a momentary truce to bind their wounds and drink some wine. Then one of Beaumanoir's riders cried out to Bramborough: 'You vile pig, you flatter yourself in trying to capture a man like Beaumanoir! Well, I defy you on his behalf, in a moment you will feel the point of my lance!' An instant later he struck Bramborough full in the face with his lance, knocking him to the ground. As the Englishman made a desperate effort to rise, another Breton brought his axe down onto his chest, killing him instantly.

With their captain dead, one of the German knights took charge of Bramborough's men and pulled them into a line, shield to shield, changing the combat from an uncontrolled brawl into a more formal battle. Beaumanoir's attack against the shield wall only brought more wounded, but then his men rushed the two ends of the enemy line, killing four. But Beaumanoir was wounded during the assault and fell to the ground pleading for water. It was then that one of his own men famously called out: 'Bois ton sang, Beaumanoir, la soif te passera!' ('Drink your blood, Beaumanoir; your thirst will pass!')

Now Bramborough's men pulled their line closer together. Seeing his chance, a Breton knight vaulted onto his horse and crashed directly onto the line, striking out with great blows of his lance. After knocking over seven of the enemy he wheeled and trampled three more. Now the other Bretons threw themselves at the line, killing four and taking the others prisoner.

Reports vary on the total carnage, some claiming only three of Beaumanoir's knights died to twelve of Bramborough's. What is agreed is that all the warriors on both sides were wounded and at least nine of the losers were killed. The Bretons treated their prisoners with honour and later released them for a small ransom.

In medieval France this stirring episode seemed to represent all the virtues of chivalry in war, and it gained fame through the repeated telling of wandering *trouvères*, northern France's equivalent of Provençal troubadours. A graven stone was placed at le Chêne de Mi-Voie to mark the spot of the battle, known in French history as Le Combat des Trente (The Combat of the Thirty). But, glorious as it was, the clash failed to end the Breton War of Succession, which dragged on for another thirteen years until Jean de Montfort defeated his enemies at the Battle of Auray, in which Charles de Blois was killed. At last Jean de Montfort was universally recognised as Duke of Brittany.

Other action this day

1554: Birth of French military leader Charles of Lorraine, duc de Mayenne * 1809: The French under General Horace Sébastiani defeat the Spanish at the Battle of Ciudad Real during the Peninsular War * 1917: The British suffer 4,000 casualties in a disastrous infantry assault across 4,000 yards of open ground under continuous Turkish fire in the failed First Battle of Gaza in Palestine

27 March

Operation Starvation

1945 Tonight, under an almost full moon, 102 American B-29 Superfortress bombers flew from the tiny island of Tinian in the Marianas to attack the Shimonoseki Straits, the body of water separating two of Japan's main islands, Honshu and Kyushu, through which 80 per cent of the Japanese merchant fleet passed. But these massive planes – the largest bombers of the war – carried not bombs but mines. It was the first mission of Operation Starvation, designed to disrupt enemy shipping, block Japan's supply of food and raw materials and obstruct the movement of military forces.

Operation Starvation was the brainchild of Admiral Chester Nimitz, who turned to the air force to carry it out. In charge was General Curtis LeMay, who assigned the entire 313th Bombardment Wing of four-engine propeller-driven B-29s to the task.

On the afternoon of 27 March the bombers took off in three groups at 30-second intervals for the six-hour flight to Japan. The planes flew independently at 5,000 feet to a target some 1,500 miles away. Each carried six tons of mines, a mix of 2,000-pound MK 25 mines and 1,000-pound MK 26 and 36 mines, fitted with either magnetic or acoustic triggers, with arming delays of between one and 30 days.

As the planes approached Japan, the moonlight made the target area visible but also lit up the aircraft, forcing pilots to take evasive action to avoid medium concentrations of flak. Although few enemy night fighters took to the air, Japanese searchlights probed the night sky, and warships opened fire to supplement the land batteries. Eleven B-29's were hit, three plunging into the waves beneath.

Flying at speeds of about 200 miles per hour, the bombers now released their parachute-retarded mines, which floated down to the water below. The pilots then turned for the long flight back to Tinian, increasing altitude to about 20,000 feet.

This was the first of 46 mine-laying raids carried out by the 313th. Most of Japan's important ports and waterways were mined, severely disrupting troop and supply movements. The Wing flew over 1,500 sorties and laid over 12,000 mines, to sink or damage 670 enemy ships. Operation Starvation sank more ship tonnage than the American submarine and direct bombing campaigns combined in the last four months of the war. Only fifteen B-29s were shot down. Many analysts believe that, had the operation been started sooner, it alone might have starved the Japanese into surrender.

As it was, the task of compelling the enemy to capitulate was carried out by two other B-29s, both also taking off from Tinian. On 6 August the *Enola Gay* dropped wartime's first atomic bomb on Hiroshima, and three days later the *Bockscar* dropped the second and last on Nagasaki.

Other action this day

1814: Future American president Andrew Jackson's 3,000-man force defeats the Red Stick Creek Indians at the Battle of Horseshoe Bend in Alabama, ending the Creek War * 1836: At Goliad during the Texas Revolution, Mexican general Santa Anna's soldiers shoot 342 Texan prisoners, clubbing and stabbing the wounded to death before Mexican cavalry run down any survivors, and 60 Texans wounded at Coleto Creek ten days earlier are shot or bayoneted on the ground * 1894: French captain René Fonck, the Allies' top fighter ace in the First World War with

75 verified kills and 52 'probables', is born in Saulcy-sur-Meurthe in the Vosges * 1994: At Manching in Germany, the £32 billion European Fighter Jet makes its 40-minute inaugural flight two years behind schedule

28 March

The battles of Ferrybridge and Towton in the Wars of the Roses

1461 On 4 March eighteen-year-old Edward of York had proclaimed himself King of England, even though the doddering Henry VI was still alive. Now, only weeks later, he must prove his claim on the battlefield.

The deposed king and his queen, the implacable Margaret of Anjou, had gathered a formidable army in the north country and were camped outside the walls of York. They were every bit as determined to regain the throne as Edward was to keep it.

By mid-March Edward was marching north from London with his lieutenant and mentor, the Earl of Warwick, and an army of perhaps 30,000 men. Their target was Henry's even larger force, ably commanded by Lords Somerset, Northumberland and Clifford. Edward and Warwick thirsted for revenge; the previous year at Wakefield the Lancastrians under the same commanders had killed Edward's father during the battle and beheaded Warwick's after it. In addition, at the close of the battle John Clifford had personally murdered Edward's brother, a deed for which he was known as 'The Butcher' (see 30 December).

Towards the end of the month, Edward's spies reported that the Lancastrians had moved part of their army under Clifford to a position behind the River Aire across from the town of Ferrybridge, and had established strong defences there to block the Yorkists.

Determined to push forward, Edward sent his vanguard under Warwick to secure a crossing, but Warwick found that Clifford had dismantled the only bridge. As the Yorkists set about laying planks on the piles of the old bridge, Clifford's men let loose a hail of arrows from across the river, killing several Yorkists outright and knocking others into the freezing water to perish. Eventually Warwick managed to force his way across and set up camp for the night.

The next morning, Saturday, 28 March, was bitterly cold, with sleet in the air. At dawn Clifford launched a massive cavalry charge, driving Warwick back across the river with heavy casualties. Warwick himself received an arrow in the leg but dramatically rallied his men by killing his own horse in front of them, vowing he would fight – and if need be die – rather than yield another foot to the enemy.

When messengers alerted Edward to the attack, he immediately sent reinforcements to the beleaguered Warwick, followed up by the main Yorkist army, which arrived on the battlefield at noon. Edward himself joined the battle, dismounting to fight on foot. During six desperate hours of combat, nearly 3,000 Yorkists were slain, including Warwick's half-brother, the Bastard of Salisbury.

By now the Lancastrians had destroyed the planking that Warwick had used to repair the bridge, so Edward dispatched a force under Lord Fauconberg westwards along the river to a ford at Castleford, three miles away. There, amid driving snow and freezing hail, they crossed the river and headed back to outflank Clifford.

Realising his perilous position, Clifford attempted to escape to the main Lancastrian army at Towton, eight miles to the north, meanwhile putting up a heroic defence. He had just arrived within sight of the army when, perhaps exhausted by a day of fighting, he removed his gorget (a steel collar) and was killed by an arrow in the throat. The remorseless Yorkist soldiers hacked his corpse to pieces.

After such a day of carnage, soldiers on both sides might have earned a day of rest, but it was not to be. On the following morning, Palm Sunday, 36,000 Yorkists marched north in the midst of a blizzard to meet 42,000 Lancastrians near their base at Towton. There, as snow swirled in the icy wind, York battled Lancaster for ten hideous hours in the largest battle of the Wars of the Roses.

At first the Yorkists had the wind behind them so that their arrows devastated the enemy while Lancastrian arrows fell short. Between Lancastrian volleys, Yorkist archers would dart forward to collect spent arrows and then pull back to fire them back at their hapless enemy. Finally, in order to stop the terrible slaughter they were suffering, the Lancastrians dropped their bows and charged across what came to be known as the 'Bloody Meadow'. So desperate was the struggle that both Edward and Warwick fought in the front ranks. Edward ordered that no quarter be given, even to common soldiers.

At last, at dusk the Lancastrians were driven back across the blood-stained snow, and then a reserve Yorkist unit crashed into their flank. Now the Lancastrian front disintegrated and every man fled for his life. Most did not succeed, as the ferocious Yorkist cavalry systematically butchered anyone they caught. One bridge over a nearby river collapsed under the weight of armoured soldiers, plunging many into the freezing water. Pursuing Yorkists crossed the river over the bodies of the slain, to hunt the fleeing Lancastrians as far as Tadcaster, three miles to the north.

Estimates of the extent of the carnage vary widely, but the most likely figure is 28,000 killed on the battlefield plus some 12,000 more in the final pursuit, equal to 1 per cent of the entire English population at the time. An equivalent slaughter today would mean 500,000 dead in a single day.

The bloodbaths at Ferrybridge and Towton should have ended the Wars of the Roses, but ex-king Henry VI and his queen Margaret slipped away to Scotland, to fight another day.

Other action this day

AD 845: Norse king Ragnar Lodbrok sacks Paris * 1939: The Spanish Civil War comes to an end as Madrid surrenders to General Franco * 1969: American general and president Dwight D. Eisenhower dies in Washington, DC

29 March

The Rosenbergs are convicted of treason

1951 The trial of American traitors Julius and Ethel Rosenberg touched on three separate wars. They were tried during the Cold War, their crimes had been committed during the Second World War and had, according to the judge, caused 'the Communist aggression in [the Korean War], with the resultant casualties exceeding 50,000 [Americans]'.

On this day a jury of eleven men and one woman unanimously convicted the Rosenbergs of providing Communist Russia with secret information regarding the construction of what the prosecutor termed 'the weapons the Soviet Union could use to destroy us' – the atomic bomb.

The son of a Polish immigrant garment worker from Manhattan's Lower East Side, 33-year-old Julius Rosenberg had long been a member of America's Communist Party, having joined the Young Communists' League at college when he was only sixteen. During the Second World War his wife Ethel's brother David Greenglass had become an Army sergeant assigned to Los Alamos, where the development of the bomb was taking place. Soon Julius and Ethel had persuaded Greenglass to ferret out whatever secrets he could find.

Whenever new information was obtained, it was passed on to a podgy, middle-aged courier named Harry Gold, who served as the liaison with the Soviet vice consul in New York City. From there it made its way to Moscow.

Throughout the war years the Rosenbergs must have believed they would go undetected, but in February 1950 Klaus Fuchs, a British scientist and Russian spy working at Los Alamos, was arrested. Fuchs readily admitted supplying atomic data to the Russians, and he, too, had connections with Gold. The trail soon led to David Greenglass and the Rosenbergs, who were taken into custody.

The trial was one of the most contentious in American history, as it took place while American soldiers were fighting and dying during the Korean War. Both Rosenbergs adamantly denied their guilt, and many left-wingers around the world saw the prosecution as an anti-Communist witch-hunt, possibly with anti-Semitic overtones. But Julius and Ethel were convicted, mostly by the testimony of Ethel's brother, who had admitted his own guilt and turned state's evidence. The case against Julius Rosenberg was clear-cut, but the key proof against Ethel was Greenglass's wife's testimony that she had seen Ethel typing out Greenglass's handwritten notes. Greenglass was sentenced to fifteen years in prison, while Gold drew a term of 30, but the judge sentenced the Rosenbergs to death, declaring: 'I consider your crime worse than murder.' He reasoned that the Russians would never have dared to support the North Koreans and Chinese had the United States retained its monopoly on atomic weapons.

The next two years witnessed an explosion of protest around the world, not so much against the verdict as against the sentence of death. Thousands demonstrated in America and Europe, the Pope asked for clemency, letters of protest rained on the White House, and the Rosenbergs' two sons marched carrying signs reading 'Don't Kill my Mommy and Daddy'. But neither the Supreme Court nor President Eisenhower would intervene. (For several years afterwards, friends, family and assorted left-wingers proclaimed the Rosenbergs' innocence, but in 1997 the Rosenbergs' Russian control officer publicly described his clandestine meetings with Julius in the 1940s.)

Just after 8.00pm on 19 June 1953 in Sing Sing Prison in Ossining, New York, first Julius and then Ethel was strapped into the prison's electric chair. Electrodes were applied to the calf of one leg and the shaven scalp, and dampened with a salt solution to make sure of a good contact. Then a current of some 2,000 volts crackled through the system. Unconsciousness was instantaneous, death virtually so for Julius, but Ethel required three long jolts to die. Ironically, the Korean War, which had so inflamed the trial and caused the judge to issue the death sentence, came to a virtual end with the armistice signed just 38 days later.

So ended the ignoble story of the Rosenbergs, illustrating that not all wars are fought on the battlefield and even cold wars have casualties.

Other action this day

1644: The Roundheads defeat the Cavaliers at the Battle of Cheriton during the English Civil War * 1857: Hindu Sepoy Mangal Panday of the 34th Regiment, Bengal Native Infantry, tries to shoot his British regimental adjutant, is subdued and later hanged, which leads to the Sepoy Mutiny that will break out in May * 1942: Under the direction of British air marshal Arthur 'Bomber' Harris, British bombers attack the undefended city of Lübeck, damaging 62 per cent of the buildings, killing 301 and injuring 783

30 March

The greatest military engineer in history

1707 At 9.45 this Wednesday morning the greatest military engineer in history, Sébastien le Prestre, marquis de Vauban, died at his *hôtel particulaire* in Paris. During his extraordinary career of almost half a century, he had designed and built 33 practically invulnerable fortresses for his master, Louis XIV, including Brest, Toulon and St-Jean-de-Luz, and modified over 300 others.

Vauban's star-shaped forts were surrounded by straight-sided moats that left no blind spots where attackers could conceal themselves: defending musketeers could rake the moats through arrow loops in the fortress walls. Meanwhile, his cannon, mounted behind impregnable stone ramparts, could devastate the enemy whenever they ventured within range.

Even more valuable was Vauban's technique of conducting sieges against fortifications. Using his system of parallel trenches and underground mines, he conducted 47 successful sieges for King Louis. One of his innovations was to aim a cannon along a moat wall or covered way so that the cannonball would ricochet down the length of it, shattering guns and men as it went.

During Vauban's time the most commonly used musket was the unwieldy matchlock, which the musketeer fired by touching a smouldering piece of rope to the gunpowder in the weapon's pan. Vauban encouraged the army to adopt the much more efficient flint-lock musket: the soldier simply pulled the trigger, which caused a flint attached to the hammer to strike the pan and ignite the gunpowder. Vauban also invented the socket bayonet, which was slipped over the muzzle of the musket and so did not have to be removed for firing.

Despite his trade as a soldier, Vauban was a compassionate man who took pity on the defeated. He developed the custom by which, when he breached an enemy's rampart, he would send for the enemy captain and invite him to surrender, thus sparing the defending garrison and reducing the loss of life. He was also the first general since the Romans to provide permanent, well-constructed barracks for his soldiers, of critical importance not only to their comfort and morale but also to their health. The great contemporary memoirist the duc de Saint-Simon described him as 'the most honourable and virtuous man of his age ... incapable of lending himself to anything false or evil'.

King Louis so valued Vauban's advice that he made him a marshal, an unprecedented honour for a man who, although thrice wounded, never commanded an army. He spent up to 150 days a year on the road, riding two or three thousand miles through France, bolstering its defences. When not constructing his own fortresses he could be found besieging someone else's. Even the year before he died he was still in harness, transforming Dunkirk into an impregnable city that could harbour 40 ships even at low tide thanks to an ingenious system of locks.

When he neglected war, however, Vauban fared less well. His travels through France had shown him the poverty in which most Frenchmen lived, and the inequities of the tax system. A few months before his death he published a tract suggesting that all French taxes should be abolished, to be replaced by a 10 per cent levy on all land and trade, which even the nobility would have to pay. King Louis instantly suppressed its publication, shortly after which Vauban died in disgrace, according to Saint-Simon, 'réduit au tombeau par l'amertume'. (Brought to the tomb by bitterness.) (More likely, he succumbed to a pulmonary embolism.) He was 73.

Vauban's disgrace, however, was not permanent. A century later, an admiring Napoleon had Vauban's heart disinterred and reburied under the dome of the Invalides in Paris, where in 1840 it was joined by the emperor's own mortal remains (see 15 December).

Other action this day
1432: Mehmed II the Conqueror, the Turkish sultan who conquered Constantinople, is born ∗ 1282: On Easter Sunday, citizens of Palermo revolt against French occupying troops, starting the massacre known as the Sicilian Vespers ∗ 1856: The Treaty of Paris ends the Crimean War between Russia and an alliance of the Ottoman empire, the Kingdom of Sardinia, France and the United Kingdom

31 March

Gunboat diplomacy opens Japan

1854 Today in Yokohama, under the menacing guns of ten American warships, the Japanese shogunate signed the Treaty of Kanagawa, bringing to an end over two centuries of exclusion (except for the Dutch) of foreign traders from Japan.

Japan's self-imposed isolation had started after the death of the great Japanese shogun Tokugawa Ieyasu in 1616, as successive shoguns attempted to stabilise the country by preventing change. Social classes were frozen, and outsiders – especially Catholic missionaries – came to be seen as a disruptive and threatening influence. By the early 1630s Christianity had been effectively banned, no Japanese was allowed to travel abroad, and the country was closed to foreigners. At times the country's seclusion was so sternly enforced that shipwrecked sailors washed ashore would be summarily executed.

By the mid-19th century, however, North American and European businessmen were yearning for a chance to develop what they were sure would be lucrative commerce. Unable to negotiate through conventional means, American president Millard Fillmore turned to gunboat diplomacy, ordering Commodore Matthew Perry to open Japan to American trade.

In early July 1853 Perry anchored his squadron of four American warships in Edo Bay (now lower Tokyo Bay). His flagship was the USS *Susquehanna*, a two-masted sidewheel steamer armed with two 150-pound Parrott rifles (powerful cannon), twelve 9-inch Dahlgren smoothbores (a type of howitzer) and a 12-pound rifle. The other ships were another sidewheel steamer (the USS *Mississippi*) with two 10-inch guns plus an 8-inch gun, and two sloops-of-war, the USS *Plymouth* and the USS *Saratoga*, which between them carried eight 8-inch guns and eighteen 32-pounders. This small fleet could not only annihilate any Japanese ship but also bring massive destruction on any Japanese port. The Japanese, who had never before seen a steamship, called these vessels the 'black ships' because of the voluminous coal smoke that poured from their funnels.

On 14 July, Perry landed at Kurihama, a tiny village at the entrance to Edo Bay. Haughty, dignified, ponderous and dull, he presented American demands to representatives of the shogun, threatening force if the Japanese refused, and then sailed off to China to await a reply.

In March the following year the Commodore returned, this time with some intriguing presents for the Japanese – a telegraph instrument and a miniature locomotive. But now his fleet was even stronger, numbering ten heavily armed warships. Faced with superior naval power, the Japanese realised that they could no longer fight the inevitable. On the last day of the month they signed the Treaty of Kanagawa (so called because Yokohama is in Kanagawa prefecture), guaranteeing 'a perfect, permanent and universal peace and a sincere and cordial amity' between Japan and the United States.

Perry returned home a hero. Choosing to view his naked threats as skilful persuasion, American merchants in Canton sent him a memorial inscribed: 'You have conquered the obstinate will of man and, by overturning the cherished policy of an empire, have brought an estranged but culturated people into the family of nations. You have done this without violence, and the world has looked on with admiration to see the barriers of prejudice fall before the flag of our country without the firing of a shot.' More practically, Congress awarded him $20,000.

Japan was open at last. As one American observer said at the time: 'We didn't go in; they came out.'

Other action this day

AD 627: Through shrewd diplomacy, Mohammed breaks up an Arab/ Jewish coalition besieging Medina in the Battle of the Trench, and the Muslims kill all the men and enslave the women and children from the enemy Qurayza tribe * 1146: In Vézelay, St Bernard of Clairvaux's sermon to Louis VII persuades him to launch the Second Crusade * 1814: Russian tsar Alexander I and Prussian king Frederick William III march with 230,000 men through the Porte Saint Martin and occupy Paris, the first time Paris had been occupied since the time of Joan of Arc

1 April

The last battle of the Second World War

1945 It was Easter Sunday today when at 08.30 hours four Marine and US 10th Army divisions landed on the west coast of the Japanese island of Okinawa to begin what would turn out to be the final land battle of the Second World War.

Okinawa was to be the springboard for the invasion of Japan, only 200 miles to the west. Now 180,000 ground troops, commanded by Army lieutenant general Simon Buckner and supported by 18,000 Navy personnel on board the invasion fleet, were readying themselves for one of the bloodiest battles in the entire Pacific war.

Prior to the landings, Buckner had ordered a massive softening up of enemy defences; dive-bombers from the fleet's 40 carriers targeted enemy positions while eighteen battleships, 32 cruisers and 200 destroyers mercilessly pounded the island. Meanwhile, the Japanese tunnelled deep into the soft limestone in the rugged south of Okinawa, leaving the north defended largely by conscripted indigenous Okinawans, who had been told to fight to the death or commit suicide rather than suffer the torture and execution that awaited them and their families if captured by the Americans.

The initial landings were relatively easy, and the northern three-quarters of the island fell to the Marines in less than three weeks. The two Army divisions battered their way south, where they encountered ever-increasing resistance from units of the Japanese 32nd Army, 77,000 men backed up by about 40,000 local militia, dug in under ground, often on the reverse slopes of hills and thus largely protected from American bombing and naval gunfire.

Within the Japanese top brass there was disagreement about how to meet the invasion. Some favoured an aggressive policy of banzai charges, while others pushed for a defensive strategy, with pre-planned fields of machine gun and artillery fire that would make the invaders pay for every inch of ground. The Japanese did launch several human-wave banzai attacks, but they were bloodily repulsed with huge loss of life. From then on they opted for stubborn defence. Japanese soldiers, hidden in fortified caves and bunkers, ambushed American troops, and accurate artillery made tanks ineffective.

Meanwhile, the Japanese relentlessly hit the American fleet with waves of kamikaze, and the *Yamato*, the largest battleship ever built, attempted to attack but was sunk by American bombers and torpedo planes before she could get within range. Only 269 of the battleship's crew of 3,332 survived; she carried neither rafts nor lifebelts, which might suggest that salvation was preferable to honourable death in defeat. A light cruiser and four destroyers of the *Yamato*'s screening force also went to the bottom, at the cost of only ten US aircraft.

By the end of April, with the two Army divisions bogged down in the south, Buckner sent for the Marine divisions to join them. Forced to clear out each cave with satchel charges and flame-throwers, the Marines took heavy casualties but kept moving. When the Japanese retreated deep inside their caves, bulldozers sealed off the caves' mouths, dooming the defenders inside.

In May monsoon rains mired troops in mud, and decaying Japanese corpses sank into the quagmire, but the Japanese continued to fight ferociously, even as American warships shelled their positions and Navy and Marine planes attacked them with napalm, rockets, bombs and machine guns. The defenders often blew themselves up with their own grenades rather than surrender.

By early June a vastly reduced Japanese force had holed up at the south of the island, now facing certain defeat. On the 18th, before the final victory, the American commander Buckner was cut down by Japanese artillery, the highest-ranking American killed by enemy fire during the entire Second World War. But by now the battle was effectively over. Just four days later the top Japanese general, Mitsuru Ushijima, committed *seppuku* (disembowelling himself with a short sword, followed by beheading by an aide).

The battle for Okinawa had been extraordinarily costly for both sides. Of about 118,000 Japanese soldiers, some 110,000 had perished, either killed in battle, entombed in sealed caves or by their own hand. In addition, about 150,000 native Okinawans, a third of the population, had been killed or committed suicide. The Americans had lost 8,000 dead fighting on the island, with another 5,000 at sea, and almost 40,000 more had been wounded.

The carnage at Okinawa had a further, perhaps even more important effect. America's new president Harry Truman had been examining plans for invasion of the Japanese mainland. Based partly on the death toll at Okinawa, his staff now projected the invasion's cost at a million American casualties – and an unimaginable number of Japanese, assuming they would defend their homeland with even more ferocity. Then on 16 July in Alamogordo, New Mexico, the first atomic bomb was successfully tested. With the bloodshed at Okinawa fresh in his mind, Truman ordered it dropped on Hiroshima on 6 August.

Other action this day

1865: Confederate general Robert E. Lee begins his final offensive in the siege of Petersburg, Virginia at the Battle of Five Forks * 1918: The Royal Flying Corps and the Royal Naval Air Service are combined to form the Royal Air Force, the first air force to become independent of army or navy control * 1948: The Russians start the Berlin Blockade, which will last eleven months

2 April

Charlemagne, the greatest conqueror of them all?

AD 742 Born this day (although the year is debated): Charlemagne, who must have inherited some warlike genes from his grandfather, the great Frankish commander Charles Martel, who had saved Christian Europe from the Moors at the Battle of Tours (see 10 October).

During his 30 years in power Charlemagne subjugated the Saxons, seized Bavaria, fought campaigns in Hungary and Spain and conquered parts of northern Italy, almost doubling the size of the kingdom that he had inherited. He created one vast realm of practically all the Christian lands of Western Europe except parts of Spain, southern Italy, the British Isles and Ireland. By the end of his life, Charlemagne's possessions, which became known as the Carolingian empire, covered 462,000 square miles, about six times the size of Great Britain.

But how does Charlemagne stack up to other great European conquerors?

Charlemagne vs. the Romans By the time of Trajan (AD 117), the Roman empire covered 2,300,000 square miles, of which about 945,000 square miles were in Europe – but no one man was responsible. It took the Romans some five centuries as a republic and a century and a half during the reigns of thirteen emperors to conquer all their territory.

Charlemagne vs. Attila the Hun In the 5th century Attila the Hun amassed an empire of perhaps 1,600,000 square miles, of which about half was in Europe, far larger than Charlemagne's realm. But although Attila conquered, unlike Charlemagne he never truly ruled the lands he subjugated – he destroyed and plundered. He was finally stopped at the Battle of Châlons in AD 451 (see 20 June).

Charlemagne vs. Suleiman the Magnificent In the 16th century another non-European, Suleiman the Magnificent, built up the Ottoman empire to about 1,700,000 square miles, but only about 10 to 15 per cent of it was in Europe, so his European conquests were less than Charlemagne's. He was famously stymied before the walls of Vienna after an unsuccessful siege.

Charlemagne vs. Napoleon Napoleon's empire, including vassal states, covered about 800,000 square miles, making Napoleon one of Europe's greatest conquerors and possibly its foremost general. The Napoleonic empire, however, lasted but eleven years, collapsing with his army's destruction in Russia.

Charlemagne vs. Adolf Hitler Adolf Hitler's Third Reich totalled some 1,385,000 square miles at its zenith, after he overran fourteen countries plus parts of Egypt and Russia. Although a veteran of the First World War, during the war that he instigated he never saw a battle (except the terminal battle for Berlin from inside his own bunker). His Reich was annihilated after only twelve years, but Charlemagne's empire lasted for 88.

In terms of European territory conquered, then, Charlemagne surpassed only Suleiman the Magnificent, and of course the Carolingian empire is dwarfed by great European empires such as the Spanish at the end of the 18th century (7,300,000 square miles, but most in the Americas) and the British empire (14,100,000 square miles at its peak just after the First World War, but almost nothing in Europe outside the British Isles). Neither of these was largely the work of one man.

Part of Charlemagne's greatness was that he knew when to stop. Attila, Suleiman, Napoleon and Hitler all attempted to continue conquering until they were either defeated or dead. Charlemagne died peacefully in bed at about 71, whereas both Attila and Suleiman died on campaign (see 5 September), Napoleon died in captivity (see 5 May), and Hitler committed suicide (see 30 April). Furthermore, Charlemagne's empire outlasted him by 74 years, but the empires of Napoleon, Hitler and Attila all died with them (or before).

Another famous European empire was the Holy Roman Empire, of which Charlemagne is often considered the first emperor. But as Voltaire once famously pronounced, it was 'neither holy, nor Roman, nor an empire'. Holy Roman emperors were the titular heads of, with little power over, much of their empire. Furthermore, except for Charlemagne's conquests, by and large the empire's territories were amassed not by invasion but through inheritance and marriage.

But Charlemagne was not only a great conqueror but also a great ruler and civiliser, a staunch supporter of the church. After his death his successors tried to persuade the Pope to proclaim him a saint, but, in the words of historian Norman Davies, 'the process was obstructed for 351 years by reports that his sexual conquests were no less extensive than his territorial ones'. Finally, in 1165 Pope Paschal III agreed to canonise him, but, sadly for the Great Charles, he never became a proper saint because Paschal was an anti-pope in competition with the legitimate popes in Rome.

Other action this day

1801: The British defeat the Danish fleet at the Battle of Copenhagen, during which Horatio Nelson puts his telescope to his blind eye and ignores Admiral Parker's signal to stop fighting * 1917: The Canadian Corps opens fire on German trenches prior to the Battle of Vimy Ridge, at that time the biggest artillery bombardment in history * 1917: Woodrow Wilson addresses the US Congress, asking for war against Germany * 1982: Argentine troops invade and occupy the Falkland Islands, starting the Falklands War

3 April

Philip the Fair suppresses the Templars

1312 Today near Lyon, France's King Philip IV (the Fair) and Pope Clement V sat in council, the pontiff on a slightly higher throne as befitted his spiritual seniority. The Pope pronounced the judgement that the king had dictated: Christendom's first and greatest fighting force, the Templars, was formally suppressed.

The Templars had been founded as an order of knighthood on Christmas Day in 1119, when the French nobleman Hugues de Payen had taken vows of poverty, chastity and obedience in the Church of the Holy Sepulchre in Jerusalem. His group of nine fellow knights called themselves 'Pauperes commilitones Christi Templique Solomonici' (Poor Fellow-Soldiers of Christ and of the Temple of Solomon) because their first headquarters was on the spot in Jerusalem where the Temple of Solomon supposedly had stood. Their mission was to guard routes to the Holy Land travelled by devout pilgrims.

The Templar was a sort of warrior monk, whom St Bernard of Clairvaux called 'truly a fearless knight, and secure on every side, for his soul is protected by the armour of faith, just as his body is protected by the armour of steel. He is thus doubly-armed, and need fear neither demons nor men.' Templar knights, who could be distinguished by their white mantles with a red cross over the heart, all came from titled families. They rode huge, heavily armoured *destrier* war horses up to seventeen hands high, which were trained to kick, butt and bite. Templar foot soldiers, dressed in black or brown mantles, came from less exalted families and were divided between archers and axe- and spear-carriers.

Templar knights were the tanks of medieval warfare. They usually fought as units within larger Crusader armies, charging at full gallop through enemy lines to make holes for the infantry to follow. Individual Templars also fought in the Reconquista in Spain.

Templar knights were known for their self-sacrifice and some-times reckless courage. In 1164, when the Franks foolishly attacked the Saracen Nur ed-Din's far larger army in Syria, 60 of 67 Templars were killed. In 1177, at the Battle of Montgisard (see 25 November), 80 Templars ambushed Saladin and his Mamluk bodyguard and started a rout. When Saladin struck back with his seismic victory at the Horns of Hattin (see 4 July), all 230 Templars who were captured were beheaded for refusing to convert to Islam.

After Saladin conquered Jerusalem in 1187 (see 2 October), Christians continually launched new invasions in which Templars invariably participated. During the Third Crusade they formed

Richard the Lionheart's rearguard at the Battle of Arsuf and fought with him again at Jaffa and at Acre, which now became the Temple headquarters in the Middle East. During the Seventh Crusade in 1250 they were among St Louis's defeated force at Al Mansurah.

In 1291 Egypt's new rulers the Mamluks captured the Templars' headquarters at Acre and then drove them from their fortresses at Sidon, Haifa, Tortosa and Atlit; Christianity had lost its last toehold in the Holy Land and the Order its very *raison d'être*. In 1302 the Mamluks captured their last Middle Eastern outpost at Arwad in Syria and put to death the knights who surrendered.

Over the years the Templars had become secretive and introverted, confused by their own rituals and initiations. But the Order had grown phenomenally rich: each knight who joined contributed his wealth, and the Temple had also profited immeasurably through the sacking of Saracen cities. By now the order had over 9,000 manors in Europe and was a tempting target for Philip the Fair, who coveted its wealth.

At first Philip spread harmful rumours about the Order, lies cleverly blended with truth. Then came more outrageous condemnations: the Templars were heretics and idolaters who spat on the Cross; they practised human sacrifice; they were renegades and sodomites. Then, on Friday, 13 October 1307, Philip arrested every Templar knight throughout France. (Some believe that the superstition of unlucky Friday the 13th stems from this day.) He now urged his pet Pope Clement to suppress the Order entirely. (French by birth and elected pope through Philip's manipulation in 1305, Clement was the same pope who had moved the papacy from Rome to Avignon.)

The main evidence against the Temple was the imprisoned knights' confessions, which were induced by torture so severe that 36 knights did not survive their inquisition. When some 500 Templars tried to recant their admissions of guilt, five were beheaded and nine burnt at the stake for 'relapsing'. The remainder quickly recanted their recantations.

Finally, on 19 March 1314, Jacques de Molay, the last Templar Grand Master, was burned at the stake in Paris. At sunset guards took him to the place of execution, dressed only in a cloth shirt. He asked to be turned on the stake to face the towers of Notre Dame, barely visible in the distance. 'God will avenge our death', he said.

'Philip, thy life is condemned. I await thee within a year at the Tribune of God.' Just 31 days later Pope Clement suddenly died, and while his body was lying in state, lightning set fire to the church, reducing his corpse to ashes. On 29 November of that same year, Philip the Fair was felled by a fatal stroke.

Other action this day

1865: After Ulysses S. Grant's army had attacked Confederate lines at Petersburg, Virginia and defeated General Robert E. Lee the previous day, Union forces capture the Confederate capital at Richmond * 1917: Vladimir Lenin returns from exile, in Churchill's words, 'transported in a sealed truck like a plague bacillus from Switzerland into Russia', beginning the Bolshevik takeover of Russia * 1946: Japanese lieutenant general Masaharu Homma is executed in the Philippines for leading the Bataan Death March

4 April

Napoleon's marshals force him to abdicate

1814 Napoleon had been the master of some 70 million people, including 30 million French, and his empire extended to Belgium, Holland, Spain, Portugal, most of Italy and Germany and parts of Poland and Yugoslavia. But then, in 1812, he made the fatal blunder of invading Russia and was finally forced into a humiliating retreat, with most of his Grande Armée left dead on the Russian steppes (see 18 October).

The next hammer blow came in June 1813 when the Duke of Wellington liberated Spain, defeating Spain's nominal king, Napoleon's brother Joseph, at Vitoria, and forcing the French to retreat over the Pyrenees and back into France. At the same time the emperor's former general, Joachim Murat, whom he had made King of Naples, betrayed him by entering into negotiations with the Viennese court.

Then, in October, Napoleon led a reconstituted army of 185,000 unseasoned troops to Leipzig, where it was crushed by a massive force of 320,000 Austrians, Prussians, Russians and Swedes.

Emboldened by their success and unified by their hunger to rid themselves of this turbulent dictator, in March 1814 Russia, Prussia, Austria and Great Britain bound themselves by the Treaty of Chaumont to continue the war until he was overthrown. Despite a remarkable string of Napoleonic tactical victories (see 29 January), the Allies, now 300,000 strong, marched on Paris, entering the city on 31 March as Napoleon hunkered down 40 miles south in the château of Fontainebleau, his far-flung territories reduced to a single grand building.

On learning of Paris's surrender, Napoleon exploded in fury. An eyewitness recorded: 'He raved about punishing the rebellious city; taking it by storm; putting all the inhabitants to the sword; and giving it up to pillage by his soldiers.' But his very anger persuaded even his own most loyal marshals that he must go. Paris, then as now the jewel of France, might be destroyed as Moscow had been, and the generals' own families and property were there.

On this day, a Monday, marshals Ney, MacDonald and Oudinot followed the emperor to his private quarters where they informed him of the French Senate's decision the previous day to strip him of his crown. 'C'est faux!' ('It's false!') declared Napoleon, but the generals showed him the morning's *Le Moniteur Universel*, the official government newspaper that confirmed the action, and told him they would not march on Paris. Now an angry Napoleon insisted that the army would remain faithful to him, but Ney replied tightly: 'The army will follow its generals.' 'What do you want, then?' demanded Napoleon, to which Ney responded: 'Only your abdication will get you out of this.'

Meanwhile, Napoleon's former foreign secretary, Talleyrand, was already hosting the Russian tsar in his Paris *hôtel particulaire*, and then one of the emperor's closest comrades-in-arms, Marshal Marmont, surrendered his VI Corps of 12,000 men to the Austrians.

After vainly trying to leave the throne to his son, on 11 April Napoleon abdicated unconditionally, bringing his ten-year reign to a close. He grandly declared in the third person that: 'There is no personal sacrifice, not even life itself, which he is not ready to make for the good of France.' As if to prove his point, the next day he attempted to poison himself with a mixture of opium, belladonna and hellebore, but recovered after some painful vomiting. Following a tearful farewell to his Old Guard, on 28 April he was en route to exile in Elba, there to wait and plot his brief return (see 26 February).

Other action this day

1884: Japanese admiral Isoroku Yamamoto, the architect of the Pearl Harbor attack, is born ∗ 1918: The fifteen-day Second Battle of the Somme comes to a close with the Germans forced to pull back after suffering 239,000 casualties to 178,000 for the British ∗ 1949: Twelve countries sign the North Atlantic Treaty, creating NATO

5 April

The Battle of the Ice

1242 Today on a frozen lake on what is now the border between Russia and Estonia, the great military leader Alexander Nevsky crushed a crusading army of Teutonic knights, earning himself iconic status in Russia and, eventually, sainthood in the Russian Orthodox Church.

It was a crusading century. Successive popes had urged the faithful on punitive expeditions, first against Muslims in the Holy Land and next against heretics like the Cathars in southern France (see 14 January). Then in 1232 Pope Gregory IX had declared the first crusade against fellow Christians when Frisian farmers from around Bremen resisted the attempts of the local archbishop to levy extra taxes. Now, ten years later, the Crusader target was the Novgorod Republic in north-west Russia, where the Russian Orthodox Church held religious sway.

As always with crusades, the attempt to install doctrinal purity was mixed with ambitions for straightforward territorial conquest. In 1240 the Swedes had tried to invade Novgorod, only to be routed at the Battle of Neva by a nineteen-year-old Rus prince named Alexander Yaroslavich. Commemorating this victory, the prince then became known as Alexander Nevsky (meaning 'of Neva').

Two years afterwards the Teutonic Livonian Order of warrior monks set out to achieve what the Swedes had failed to do – to conquer Novgorod and to extirpate the Orthodox heresy. Recruiting extra troops from Denmark and Estonia, they took Pskov, Izborsk and Koporye and then set their sights on Novgorod itself. During the next year the fight seesawed between German invaders and Rus defenders. Leading the Rus force once again was Alexander Nevsky, who declared: 'Whoever will come to us with a sword, from a sword will perish.' He soon retook Pskov and Koporye.

In the spring of 1242, Bishop Hermann of Dorpat (a bishopric directly across Lake Peipus from Novgorod) led about 1,000 Livonian mounted knights and perhaps 2,000 Estonian infantry to victory over a minor Rus force south of Dorpat. He then set off on his main mission, the conquest of Novgorod.

On this day Bishop Hermann met Alexander Nevsky's Rus army near Lake Peipus, which was still frozen over from the winter cold. Alexander's force numbered approximately 1,000 *druzhina* (select troops serving a chieftain) plus 4,000 Novgorod militia, principally infantry and archers, plus a small contingent of cavalry.

At dawn the two armies faced each other across the expanse of ice-covered lake. Bishop Hermann formed his men into a deep 'boar's head' wedge, with his heavily armoured Crusader cavalry at the point and protecting the sides and his infantry in the centre. This narrow wedge had explosive penetrating power but its narrow frontage made it vulnerable to flank attack.

Alexander countered with three battalions in line, with his druzhina and most of his cavalry behind the lines, unseen by the enemy. Then, judging that the enemy's mounted knights could gain no proper footing on the icy surface, he pulled his army back in order to tempt them into battle on the lake.

The Crusaders took the bait. At the bishop's order, the German knights sang out their war cry and charged into and through the Rus front line, knocking aside Alexander's infantry. They were now certain that victory was at hand, but they had fallen into Alexander's trap: the Rus archers on the flanks moved to enfilade the charging Germans, and the Rus cavalry and *druzhina* swept around their own men and attacked the German rear.

Slipping and sliding on the ice, the Livonian knights first tried to counter-attack but, assaulted from all sides, soon began to retreat. One group managed to get back across the lake to Livonian territory, but another contingent headed north, where the ice was thinner. Under the weight of the heavily armoured knights, the ice began to crack. Suddenly holes appeared and knights and their horses plunged into the freezing water below.

Exactly how many Crusaders perished in the battle is open to debate. According to *The Chronicle of Novgorod*, a near-contemporary Russian record, 'there fell a countless number of Estonians, and 400 of the Germans, and they [the Rus] took fifty with their hands and they took them to Novgorod'. The *Livonian Rhymed Chronicle*, however, maintains that 'Twenty brothers [knights] lay dead and six were captured'.

Whatever the true number, the Battle of the Ice demolished the German crusade against the Orthodox Novgorod Republic. Ten years later Alexander Nevsky became Grand Prince of Vladimir, that is, the supreme ruler of Russia. Over the centuries his triumph attained totemic status, and in 1547 the Russian Orthodox Church declared him a saint. During the Second World War, with the help of Sergei Eisenstein's patriotic and immensely popular film, Alexander Nevsky was used by the Soviet government as a national symbol of Russian victory over invading Germans.

Other action this day

1697: Charles XI of Sweden dies of stomach cancer, bringing Sweden's greatest general, Charles XII, to the throne * 1818: José de San Martin leads South American rebels to defeat Spanish royalists at the Battle of Maipú near Santiago, gaining Chile's independence from Spain * 1975: Chinese warlord and ruler Chiang Kai-shek dies of kidney failure at 75

6 April

Richard the Lionheart's last battle

1199 The tiny village of Châlus lies twenty miles south-west of Limoges. At the end of the 12th century it boasted a minor castle defended by two or three knights and their sons. Nearby a farmer had found a buried treasure of golden coins, probably Roman, and King Richard the Lionheart declared he would have it as his right, since he was overlord of the Limousin. Unwisely, the castle's defenders decided to resist.

Accompanied by a strong troop of mercenaries, Richard laid siege to this insignificant fortress. On the evening of 25 March he decided to inspect the progress his sappers were making in undermining the castle's walls, ignoring the occasional arrow fired by the defenders. Protected by a shield but without his armour, Richard was so nonchalant that he even applauded the efforts of one enemy bowman.

Suddenly through the twilight sped a crossbow bolt, striking the king in his unprotected left shoulder. Richard quickly retreated to his quarters, summoning his captain and his surgeon. The bolt had penetrated deep and was at last recovered only by the excruciating torment of laying open the flesh.

Even without Richard, the king's forces soon reduced the fortress and in the process captured a youth named Pierre Basile who had fired the shot. But by now Richard's wound showed unmistakable signs of gangrene, and the Lionheart knew he would soon die. Perhaps because it was the Lenten season, he performed one last chivalrous act.

Summoning the terrified Basile, Richard demanded to know why he wished him injury. Emboldened, the young man replied: 'Because you killed my father and brother. Do with me as you want. I have no regrets for the vengeance I have taken.'

'Go forth in peace', said Richard. 'I forgive you my death and will exact no revenge.' (Or, according to another account: 'Live on, and by my bounty behold the light of day.')

Twelve days later, on 6 April 1199, the great troubadour-knight-crusader-king was dead, at the age of 41. Ignoring Richard's forgiveness, his army captains had Basile flayed alive and hanged.

Other action this day

46 BC: Julius Caesar defeats a combined army of Pompeian followers under Metellus Scipio and Numidians under Juba at the Battle of Thapsus * 1250: During the Seventh Crusade, the Egyptians defeat the Crusader army of French king Louis IX (St Louis) at the Battle of Fariskur, taking Louis and his brother prisoner * 1800: Austrian soldiers invest Genoa, where French general André Masséna holds out for two months before surrendering due to lack of food * 1945: During the battle for Okinawa, the Japanese begin Operation Kikusui (floating chrysanthemums), the most concentrated kamikaze attack of the war

7 April

'The hope for an easy war and a cheap victory was gone forever'

1862 It was victory snatched from the jaws of defeat. By mid-afternoon today it became clear that the Confederate forces had been shattered by the Union counter-attack and were withdrawing. But 24 hours earlier the shoe had been on the other foot, and General Grant's Army of the Tennessee, reeling backwards from the fierce rebel assault, looked on the verge of annihilation.

The Confederates named this Civil War engagement Pittsburg Landing, after a stopping place on the Tennessee River. The Union army called it Shiloh after a small log meeting-house some four miles from the river. By either designation, it was two days of hell that 'launched the country onto the floodtide of total war'.

As early as 1 April, Confederate cavalry movements and skirmishing near the Union lines indicated an enemy advance was contemplated. Grant's headquarters ignored this evidence. 'The fact is,' Grant wrote later, 'I regarded the campaign we were engaged in as an offensive one and had no idea that the enemy would leave strong entrenchments to take the initiative ...' But Albert Sydney Johnston, the Confederate commander, had a different scenario in mind. Just before the attack, he told his senior commanders: 'Tonight we will water our horses in the Tennessee River.' They came very close in an effort that would cost Johnston his life.

At 5.00am on the 6th, as breakfast fires were being lit in the Union camp, patrols spotted Confederate skirmishers through the woods and underbrush. And suddenly, right behind them, emerged the full Confederate battle line, thousands strong, yelling and firing.

Under the shock of the attack, the Union positions disintegrated. Throughout the long day, the fighting was chaotic and relentless. At dusk, when one more Confederate attack might have destroyed what was left of Grant's army, the rebels halted, exhausted and fought out. During the night it rained and Grant brought up fresh regiments. By daylight today, the Union forces had a sizeable advantage in numbers, and the counter-attack began.

Shiloh was shocking in its carnage: a total of 20,000 men were killed or wounded, about evenly distributed to both sides. Included among the dead was Confederate general Johnston, killed on the first day of battle. That was almost twice the combined losses in all the previous engagements of the war now entering its second year. Bloody Shiloh produced a change in the war, which Bruce Catton summed up this way:

> It had begun with flags and cheers and the glint of brave words on the spring wind, with the drumbeats setting a gay rhythm for the feet of young men who believed that war would beat clerking. That had been a year ago; now the war had come down to uninstructed murderous battle in a smoky woodland where men who had never been shown how to fight stayed in defiance of all logical expectation and fought for two night-marish days. And because they had done this, the hope for an easy war and a cheap victory was gone forever.

Other action this day

AD 451: Attila the Hun sacks Metz * 1842: In a daring sortie from Jalalabad, outnumbered British and Indian troops of the Bengal army drive off Afghans and Ghilzai tribesmen to break a five-month siege * 1939: Italy annexes Albania * 1945: During the Japanese suicide Operation Ten-Go, the *Yamato*, the largest battleship ever constructed, is sunk by American warplanes 200 miles north of Okinawa before she can beach herself near the island and act as an unsinkable gun emplacement to bombard American forces on Okinawa with her 18-inch guns

8 April

Emperor Caracalla is murdered on campaign

AD 217 The Roman emperor Caracalla was in essence a military dictator, fancying himself as the new Alexander and hoping to equal Alexander's conquests in Asia. Although brutal to Rome's citizens, he was generous to his soldiers and popular with them. Who would have thought, then, that on this day he would be murdered by one of his own officers?

The son of Emperor Septimius Severus, Caracalla had been born in Lugdunum (today's Lyon) in AD 188 with the original name of Septimius Bassianus. According to the Roman historian Cassius Dio, his nickname came from a costume he invented – an ankle-length version of the Gallic *caracallus*, a short, close-fitting cloak with a hood.

Caracalla gained his first military experience at 22, when his father sent him to Britain to oversee military operations there and direct the army's campaigns. By the time he returned to Rome in 211 his father was dying. He bequeathed the empire to Caracalla and his brother Geta, but a year later Caracalla murdered his brother, whom he had always hated, and threw himself under the protection of the Praetorian Guard. Septimius Severus had advised him to 'enrich the soldiers, despise all others', advice Caracalla followed by buying his guards' loyalty with a bonus of 2,500 denarii per man, with a 50 per cent raise in the ration allowance. He informed a powerless Senate that he had killed his brother in self-defence.

Now sole dictator, Caracalla ordered the massacre of some 20,000 Romans (including his own wife) whom he suspected of having supported his brother. People were killed in the streets, at the public baths and even in their own homes. (Four years later, on Caracalla's order his soldiers killed a similar number in Alexandria for mocking the claim that in killing his brother he was only protecting himself.)

In 213 Caracalla resumed his military career, leaving Rome to fight the Alamanni along the borders of Upper Germany. There he impressed his troops by marching on foot among them, eating the same food and even grinding his own corn. He also ensured his popularity by raising his soldiers' pay from 500 denarii to 675 denarii, although he had to debase the silver content in Rome's coinage in order to do it. Although he failed to conquer the Alamanni, he defeated them in the campaign's one major battle near the Rhine.

It was now that Caracalla began to model himself on Alexander the Great. He adopted Alexander's dress and weapons and added a corps of elephants to his army. Appending the descriptor 'Magnus' (Great) to his own name, in 216 he set out with eight legions to conquer Parthia (now Iran) as Alexander had done half a millennium before. And, like Alexander, he would perish in the East. Only his ashes would return to Rome.

At first Caracalla's army met only light resistance, as the Parthians pulled back eastwards. After wintering in Edessa (in southern Turkey), he set out once more. On the road to Carrhae, he was struck by dysentery and stepped behind some shrubs to relieve himself. As he lowered his breeches, an officer in the Imperial body-guard named Julius Martialis killed him with a single thrust of his sword. Martialis leaped on his horse to escape but was shot dead by one of the emperor's archer bodyguards.

The reasons why Caracalla was murdered remain debated. Some maintain that Martialis acted in revenge, as the emperor had ordered the execution of his brother a few days before. Cassius Dio, however, insists that Martialis's motive was more mundane: Caracalla had refused to promote him to centurion. Finally, Herodian makes the more likely claim that the commander of the Praetorian Guard, Marcus Opellius Macrinus, instigated the killing in order to take over the empire. (Macrinus did, in fact, become the next emperor, and, perhaps as a belated apology, agreed to Caracalla's deification, but only fifteen months later he was overthrown and executed.)

Caracalla would have wanted to be remembered as a great soldier; ironically, the one memorial for which he is known has nothing to do with war. It is the immense and beautiful Baths of Caracalla in Rome, originally designed to accommodate 1,600 bathers, but now where, on a summer evening, you can hear the triumphant arias of Verdi and Puccini during spectacular performances of open-air opera.

Other action this day

1271: Mamluk sultan of Egypt Baibars conquers the Hospitallers' great fortress, Krak des Chevaliers, in Syria * 1336: Tamerlane (Timur) is born in Kesh near Samarkand, in modern Uzbekistan * 1981: American five-star general Omar Bradley, who during the Second World War commanded the 900,000-man 12th Army Group, the largest group of American soldiers to ever serve under one field commander, dies at 88

9 April

The American Civil War comes to an end

1865 Palm Sunday at Appomattox Court House, a small village in Virginia, the final scene of the American Civil War. At dawn the

Southern rebels had launched one last attack – and failed. Out-numbered, outgunned, worn out, the rebel army was near collapse. The great Southern general Robert E. Lee was making a last desperate attempt to reach Lynchburg, where he could head for the mountains and take up guerrilla warfare, but the huge Union army under the command of General Ulysses Grant dogged their every step.

Suddenly the Southern vanguard ran into a concentrated troop of Union cavalry. Refusing to attack, the cavalry simply opened their lines so that the Confederates could see a solid wall of Union infantry backed by cannon blocking the Confederate path. There was nowhere left to go.

Now Lee knew the end had come. 'There is nothing left for me to do but go and see General Grant, and I would rather die a thousand deaths', he said.

The two generals met in the parlour of a local farmer, Lee immac-ulate in his best uniform and gold-mounted sword, Grant rumpled and scruffy in a second-hand private's jacket, on which he had pinned his general's stars. Grant offered the terms of surrender under which Lee's officers were allowed to keep their side-arms and Confederate troopers their horses and mules to carry out the spring planting. Lee signed his acceptance, shook the hand offered by Grant and stepped out the door.

As Lee rode away, the Union soldiers around the house broke into wild cheers of celebration, but, as Grant recalled: 'I at once sent word, however, to have it stopped. The Confederates were now our prisoners, and we did not want to exult over their downfall.'

The war was over – almost. At the time of Lee's surrender almost 200,000 Confederate troops remained in the field throughout the South. Soon other commanders began to lay down their arms, but not before the last full-scale battle of the war on 12–13 May when the Confederates defeated a Yankee force at Palmito Ranch in Texas.

In all, some 618,000 American soldiers died during the Civil War, almost 60 per cent of whom were from the victorious North. The total is more than the American dead from all other wars combined, from the Revolution through the two World Wars to Korea, Vietnam, the two Gulf Wars and Afghanistan.

Other action this day
1241: The Mongols defeat a Polish army reinforced by Teutonic knights at

the Battle of Liegnitz in Silesia, marking the high-water mark of the Mongol invasion of Europe * 1782: The first day of the four-day Battle of the Saintes, in which British admiral George Rodney defeats French admiral François Joseph Paul de Grasse * 1940: As Nazi Germany invades Denmark and Norway, a single parachute battalion (the first ever employed in warfare) takes the Oslo and Stavanger airfields * 1945: German admiral and one-time head of the Abwehr (military intelligence) Wilhelm Canaris is hanged for plotting against Hitler

10 April

The 18th century's greatest general runs from his first battle

1741 Frederick II had inherited the throne of Prussia only six months before, and now he decided to snatch the province of Silesia from the Austrians, who he supposed would be weak since Queen Maria Theresa had been in power three months less than he had. Marshalling the formidable army left to him by his father, Frederick marched into Silesia, where on this day he met the Austrians in the snows of Mollwitz. Although Frederick had served under the great Austrian commander Eugene of Savoy in the Rhineland in 1734, this was his first real battle, and he had never before commanded an army in the field.

Shortly after noon on a day blindingly white with snow, the two armies formed up lines of battle, the Prussians outnumbering the enemy 21,000 to 19,000. But as the Prussian infantry advanced, Austrian cavalry smashed into its right wing, leaving the Prussian flank dangerously exposed. The battle looked so desperate that the young Prussian king, terrified he would be captured, galloped from the field, leaving command in the hands of his experienced field marshal, Phillip von Neipperg, who quickly rallied the Prussians.

Asked if his men should fall back, Neipperg told his soldiers: 'We'll retreat over the bodies of our enemies.' Ordering a general advance, he soon had the Austrians on the run. Although Prussia won the battle, it was an inauspicious beginning for the king, but it was the last time he would leave the field early. As he later recalled: 'Mollwitz was my school.'

During the next 45 years Frederick made Prussia the foremost military power in Europe and firmly established himself as the greatest commander of his age. If he had run from his first battle, he aggressively attacked in most of the rest, once chiding his Guards when they hesitated to charge the Austrians at Kolin: 'Ihr Racker, wollt ihr ewig leben?' ('You rascals, would you live for ever?') We know him as Frederick the Great.

Other action this day

1500: While Louis XII is besieging Novara in northern Italy, the Swiss mercenaries who are fighting for both sides turn Milanese duke Ludovico Sforza (Ludovico il Moro) over to the French; he will remain in captivity at Loches until he dies eight years later * 1919: Lured to a meeting by government agent Jesús Guajardo, Mexican revolutionary leader Emiliano Zapata is ambushed and shot dead

11 April

The fall of the Thunderbolt

1512 Since 1508, northern Italy had been torn by the incessant fighting of the War of the League of Cambrai, as Pope Julius II allied himself with Venice and Spain in what he grandly termed the Holy League to drive the French out of the region. But in the spring of 1511 French king Louis XII sent a new commander to Italy, his 21-year-old nephew, the tough and energetic Gaston de Foix, duc de Nemours, who would gain the nickname Le Foudre d'Italie (The Thunderbolt of Italy) for his forceful leadership.

By the autumn, Gaston had routed a Papal–Spanish army at Bologna (then part of the Papal States) and pummelled the Venetians at Brescia. After capturing several cities in the Veneto and the Romagna, in March 1512 he was joined by an Italian contingent under the Duke of Ferrara. He then marched with 23,000 men to lay siege to the old Imperial capital of Ravenna, where a garrison of 5,000 Papal soldiers defended the city.

When he learned of the siege, Pope Julius dispatched the Spanish general Ramón de Cardona with his 16,000-man army, reinforced by a company of Papal troops, to go to Ravenna's aid. On 10 April they arrived about a mile south of the French positions outside the city, where they set up a fortified camp, their backs to the Ronco River and their flanks protected by earthworks. As was customary in those days, Gaston de Foix now issued a formal invitation to battle, which Cardona readily accepted.

Leaving 2,000 men to keep the Ravenna garrison bottled up inside the town, the next day Gaston advanced against Cardona. He positioned his men in a large arc, with his heavy cavalry, daunting in their heavy plate armour, on the right flank. His light cavalry held the left, and between them marched his infantry, which included 3,500 crossbowmen and 8,500 German *Landsknechts* (pikemen). Moving to within 200 yards of the Spanish position, he brought his 54 artillery pieces forward to cannonade the enemy, a barrage quickly answered by Cardona's 30 guns.

For two hours the French and Spanish exchanged cannon fire in the largest artillery duel to date. Despite the volume of fire, the Spanish infantry remained well protected by their entrenchments, but the Papal cavalry was relatively exposed and began to take casualties. Meanwhile, the Spanish guns zeroed in on the French bowmen and Landsknechts, killing perhaps 2,000 men. Dazed by the barrage, the bowmen started to pull back, but the Landsknechts kept them in line with their pikes.

Now the Duke of Ferrara's cannon opened fire on Cardona's light cavalry, inflicting heavy losses. Simultaneously, two French heavy guns were moved across the Ronco River where they could fire directly into the Spanish rear. Enfiladed from two directions, Cardona in desperation ordered his beleaguered cavalry to attack the French heavy horse near the river.

The Spanish heavy and light cavalries fell on the French *gendarmes* (cavalrymen of noble birth) under the direct command of Gaston de Foix. For a full hour the two sides hammered at each other in a general mêlée. The Spanish attempted to flank their enemies but, failing, retired from the field, accompanied by their commander Cardona.

Even now, however, the battle was far from over, as the Spanish infantry surged out from the protection of their fortified camp and attacked the French line. Caught from the rear, the Landsknechts almost broke, but then the French cavalry returned and virtually surrounded the Spanish infantry, most of whom fled. But one company of Spanish foot soldiers remained on the field, determined to retreat in good order. Gaston de Foix reassembled a small detachment of cavalry and charged, only to be killed by a harquebus bullet.

The French had destroyed the Spanish and Papal forces, killing 9,000 and inflicting a large number of wounded. The main battle over, they returned to the siege, soon capturing and sacking Ravenna. But they had also lost a large proportion of their force, with perhaps 4,500 killed and an equal number wounded, and their dynamic leader Gaston de Foix had perished.

Although Gaston had conquered much of northern Italy, only four months later the French were forced to abandon it when England's Henry VIII threatened to invade France and troops were needed for its defence.

The War of the League of Cambrai continued for another four years, a senseless conflict of ever-shifting alliances. When it petered out in 1516, territorial boundaries were almost exactly as they had been before the war in 1508.

Other action this day

1241: The Mongol army under Batu Khan utterly routs the forces of Hungarian king Bela IV at the Battle of Mohi * 1713: The War of the Spanish Succession is ended by the Treaty of Utrecht in which England and Holland recognise Philip V as King of Spain and France cedes Newfoundland and Gibraltar to Britain * 1945: Near Weimar in Germany, soldiers from the US 9th Armored Infantry Battalion liberate Buchenwald concentration camp, where 56,000 of the 240,000 prisoners held there during its seven-year existence had died or been put to death

12 April

The South fires the first shot of the American Civil War

1861 Today at 4.30 in the early dawn a huge mortar shell rose from the South Carolina shore and exploded on the small island fortress of Fort Sumter. The newly born Confederacy had started the American Civil War.

America had been at peace – barely. Four months earlier, South Carolina had seceded from the United States, quickly followed by six other southern states. Southerners now considered themselves independent, but America's president Abraham Lincoln was determined to preserve the nation. War was looming, but no battle had yet been fought.

Pentagonal Fort Sumter sits on a small, man-made island commanding the entrance to Charleston harbour, four miles from the city. Still under construction and incompletely armed, Sumter lacked even a garrison until December 1860, when US major Robert Anderson took 80 soldiers from a nearby fort and occupied it. Now, more than ever, it was a thorn in the flesh (and pride) of the South.

In March 1861, the 43-year-old Confederate general Pierre Gustave Toutant de Beauregard took command of the Confederate troops in South Carolina and was soon in Charleston demanding immediate Union withdrawal. As was often the case in this fratricidal struggle, Beauregard was a close friend of Anderson's, having studied artillery under him at West Point.

Anderson refused to budge but sent urgent dispatches up the Union chain of command that provisions were running low. In early April President Lincoln, who had been in office for only a month, ordered a resupply by sea, having notified the Carolina governor that 'no effort to throw in men, arms, or ammunition will be made'. But instead of calming the waters, Lincoln's announcement triggered the attack, as the Confederates tried to force Fort Sumter to surrender before resupplies could arrive.

At first light the initial Confederate artillery barrage came from four directions. Union captain Abner Doubleday immediately ordered the fort's guns to return fire. (Doubleday has a unique place in American history. He not only commanded the gunners that fired the North's first shots of the war but is also considered the 'father of baseball', according to legend having formulated the rules of the game in 1839.) The Union gunners soon ran out of shells, but the Confederate bombardment, some 4,000 rounds, lasted 33 hours, throughout the day and the following night.

Although the fort was solid enough – walls 40 feet high and eight to twelve feet thick – the small garrison there, with supplies exhausted, was finally forced to surrender. A truce was agreed on 13 April, and the North formally surrendered at 2.30 the next afternoon. Two days later, Lincoln called for 75,000 militia troops from the Union states, and on the day after that, Virginia seceded from the US and joined the Confederacy.

Miraculously, no one was killed in the Battle of Fort Sumter, except for one Union soldier who died when a pile of cartridges exploded while the Northerners were firing a final salute as they evacuated the fort. It was a precedent that didn't last long – the war would continue for exactly four more years, less three days. During that time, between them the two sides would sustain well over a million casualties, of whom 618,000 died.

Other action this day

1796: Napoleon Bonaparte wins his first battle in the Italian campaign, defeating an Austro-Sardinian force at Montenotte * 1917: Canadians capture Vimy Ridge from the German 6th Army during a battle in which they suffer 3,500 killed and 7,000 wounded and four Canadians earn the Victoria Cross * 1937: Sir Frank Whittle ground-tests the first jet engine designed to power an aircraft at the British Thomson-Houston factory in Rugby * 1945: American president and commander-in-chief Franklin Delano Roosevelt dies of a stroke

13 April

Mission to Ethiopia

1868 Today, while a British expeditionary force stormed his mountain fortress at Magdala, Ethiopian emperor Tewodros II died by his own hand, the last scene in one of Britain's most famous imperial adventures.

In the 1860s Ethiopia had come under attack from both Egypt and the Ottoman empire. Hoping for European military supplies and expertise, Tewodros, a Coptic Christian sometimes referred to as Theodore by Europeans, wrote to Queen Victoria, confident that she would help a fellow Christian against Muslim aggressors, but the British colonial bureaucracy smothered the letter.

After two years without answer, an infuriated Tewodros imprisoned all British subjects in Ethiopia, including the British consul. Finally the British government dispatched a mission, but it brought no weapons, so Tewodros threw the mission into prison along with the others. Now in Britain the government ordered the 58-year-old Indian Army general Robert Napier to lead a punitive expedition.

In January 1868 Napier landed on the Red Sea coast with 13,000 British and Indian soldiers, 26,000 camp followers, 16,000 mules and ponies, 5,000 bullocks, 8,000 camels and 44 elephants to transport the heavy guns. But the 400-mile route to Magdala was a march through a trackless wilderness without roads or bridges, and each soldier carried over 55 pounds of equipment.

After a trek of almost three months, Napier's army finally arrived before Tewodros's fortress, perched high on a mountain peak. Now it was the emperor's turn to take the initiative.

On 10 April – Good Friday – he ordered an attack on the expeditionary force on the approach road to his fortress. His seven cannon fired down from the mountain, and his 3,500 warriors launched a wild charge. A few had muskets, but most carried only spears, while Napier's men were armed with breech-loading rifles. The 4th Foot, reinforced by two Indian regiments, poured deadly fire into the advancing mass, stopping the Ethiopians and putting them to flight. Over 700 lay dead, with another 1,200 wounded, while the British had suffered only twenty wounded. Soon many of the remaining Ethiopians started to desert.

In a last desperate attempt to arrange a truce, over the next two days Tewodros freed the British captives and sent Napier a gift of cattle to be slaughtered on Easter Sunday. Napier accepted the peace offering while declining the peace, promising only that Tewodros and his family would be well treated. The emperor swore he would never be taken prisoner.

Now, at nine o'clock on this Easter Monday, Napier ranged his 12-pound Armstrong guns and 8-inch mortars on the fortress while his troops advanced to the foot of the mountain. There they came upon the putrefying corpses of native prisoners. Tewodros in his fury had ordered their hands and feet cut off and then hurled them from the 300-foot cliff.

The only path to the fortress led to two fortified gates. Failing to breach them with artillery fire, Napier ordered a frontal assault. Under covering fire from the infantry, sappers approached the walls, only then realising they had forgotten their powder kegs and scaling ladders.

But now two soldiers from the 33rd Foot earned their place in military history – and two Victoria Crosses – by their daring attack. Private James Bergin and Drummer Michael Magner had reached the twelve-foot wall along the lower defences. Bergin hoisted Magner until he could just grip the top. A quick shove, and the drummer scrambled onto the wall. There, ignoring enemy musket fire, he hauled up his companion, who opened up on the Ethiopians, killing several, while Magner pulled up more British and Indian soldiers. As the attackers lowered their bayonets, the Ethiopians fled or surrendered. The battle for Magdala was over. When Napier's troops entered the fortress, they found Tewodros lying dead. He had shot himself in the mouth with a pistol given to him by Queen Victoria.

Now, with Napier's consent, the British and Indian soldiers looted and burned Magdala. On 19 April the expedition headed back towards the Red Sea coast, the soldiers marching behind the colours, led by a regimental band. While the army sailed for India, Napier made for London, to be rewarded with the title of 1st Baron Napier of Magdala. He had brought an army from India to Ethiopia, trudged across perilous territory for almost three months, subdued the enemy and conquered and burned his capital and then marched back across the same dangerous terrain, losing only two men to battle wounds.

Other action this day

1204: During the Fourth Crusade, an army led by the Doge of Venice captures the Byzantine (Christian) capital, Constantinople * 1919: During a religious festival in the Jallianwala Bagh in Amritsar in India, 90 British Indian Army soldiers open fire on a crowd of unarmed men, women and children, killing 400 to 1,000 and wounding 500 to 1,000 more * 1940: A British taskforce of the battleship HMS *Warspite* and nine destroyers sinks eight German destroyers and a submarine at the Battle of Narvik in northern Norway * 1975: Gunmen open fire on members of the Kataeb (predominantly Christian) Party in east Beirut as they leave a church, killing four and sparking a retaliatory killing of 26 members of the Popular Front for the Liberation of Palestine, in turn triggering the Lebanese Civil War in which 80,000 people are slain

14 April

Abraham Lincoln is assassinated

1865 April is the cruellest month – at least it was for Americans during the Civil War. The war had started on 12 April with the South's bombardment of Fort Sumter and had come to its bloody conclusion four years later with the Confederate surrender at Appomattox Court House (see 9 April). And now, once again in April, despite the South's capitulation five days ago, there would be another casualty, the most tragic of the war. The nation's president, Abraham Lincoln, would be shot to death.

On 11 April Lincoln had addressed a crowd from the balcony of the White House. After promising that there would be no revenge against the defeated Confederates, he expressed hope that some blacks – 'very intelligent' men and those who had served in the Union army – would be permitted to vote.

Listening from the lawn below was a sometime actor and Southern fanatic, John Wilkes Booth. A 23-year-old with dark curly hair and a droopy moustache, he had been a militia volunteer in the troop that had hanged the Abolitionist John Brown in 1859 (see 2 November). His hatred of Lincoln and of blacks was visceral. On hearing the president, he exclaimed to a friend: 'That means nigger citizenship! Now, by God, I'll put him through!'

Three days later, on Good Friday, Lincoln and his wife Mary went to Ford's Theater in Washington to enjoy a new play called *Our American Cousin*. There the president's bodyguard, a bored Washington policeman, went into the alley behind the theatre for a drink.

During the third act Booth stepped into the president's unguarded box. Drawing a small Derringer pistol, he shot Lincoln in the back of the head, theatrically crying: 'Sic semper tyrannus!' ('As always to tyrants!' – Brutus's words to Caesar.) He then leaped to the stage, but the spur in his boot caught in a decorative flag so that as he landed he fractured his left leg. Despite his injury, he fled from the theatre.

Mortally wounded, America's greatest president was carried to a house across the street, where he died without regaining consciousness at 7.22 the following morning. He was 56 years old.

Although Booth had escaped from the theatre, two weeks later Federal troops and secret service agents tracked him to a barn in Virginia. They set the barn alight, and as Booth moved from corner to corner in the burning building, one of the soldiers, Boston Corbett, saw him through a crack and opened fire with his Colt revolver, hitting him in the neck. Corbett was later to claim that 'God Almighty directed me'.

Dragged from the barn, Booth lay all night on a nearby farmhouse porch, slowly bleeding to death and sucking a brandy-soaked rag given him by a charitable soldier. At dawn the next day he realised he could no longer move his hands. 'I thought I did it for the best. Useless, useless', he muttered to one of his guards just before he died. His body was whisked to a nearby Federal arsenal and secretly buried under the floor.

Other action this day

AD 69: Vitellius defeats Emperor Otho at the Battle of Bedriacum to become Roman emperor * 1205: At the Battle of Adrianople, Tsar Kaloyan of Bulgaria ambushes and defeats Baldwin I of Constantinople and his Crusaders, killing 300 knights and capturing and blinding Baldwin * 1471: Warwick the Kingmaker is defeated and killed at the Battle of Barnet during the Wars of the Roses

15 April

Mass suicide at Masada

AD 73 Masada – an unassailable fortress of rock on eighteen acres of flat, treeless mesa, baking in the Palestinian sunlight at a height of 1,400 feet. Here, near the Dead Sea's south-west coast, a garrison of Jewish Zealots defied a Roman army of 15,000 men for two years before finally committing mass suicide on this day rather than surrender.

The Zealots were a fanatical group of fundamentalist Jews who were determined to establish a theocracy and destroy the hated regime of the pagan Romans in Palestine. Founded by an extremist with the historically unfortunate name of Judas, the Zealots instigated their first rebellion in AD 6, and in AD 66 struck again, leading a revolt in Judaea during which the Roman governor was murdered and a militant regime was established in Jerusalem.

Within a year, a Roman army under the command of future emperor Vespasian had arrived in Palestine, crushing all rebel resistance. Before completion of the task, however, the then Emperor Vitellius was toppled and killed (see 20 December), and Vespasian left Palestine to take over the empire, leaving his son Titus in command.

By AD 70 the Romans had recaptured Jerusalem, destroying the Second Temple in the process (see 26 September). But the Zealot garrison at Masada, although only 1,000 strong, thought their position could never be stormed and steadfastly refused to submit. They had not counted on the Romans' resolve and formidable siege techniques. The Roman commander Flavius Silva saw that frontal attack was impossible, and Masada's huge aqueduct-fed cisterns could keep the fortress in water almost indefinitely. His answer was to build a monumental siege ramp against the fortress's western face, which finally permitted the attackers to breach the massive defensive walls.

When the Romans at last entered the fortress, however, all they found was corpses, as the defenders, led by one Eleazar ben Jair (a descendant of the Judas who founded the Zealots), had killed themselves to a man, slaughtering even their own women and children. Only after the Romans had occupied the stronghold did two women and five children emerge from a water conduit, where they had hidden to avoid the massacre. They were the only Jewish survivors.

Other action this day

1450: The French defeat the English at Formigny during the Hundred Years War, ending English domination of northern France * 1632: During the Thirty Years War, Swedish king Gustavus Adolphus routs the Catholic League under Graf von Tilly at Rain am Lech in Bavaria, where Tilly is mortally wounded by a cannonball * 1952: The Boeing YB-52 bomber, prototype of the B-52 Stratofortress, makes its maiden flight

16 April

Bonnie Prince Charlie is defeated at Culloden Moor

1746 Today Bonnie Prince Charlie and his Highland troops were crushed at Culloden Moor and all hopes of a Stuart restoration to England's throne were crushed for ever with them.

Fifty-eight years earlier Charlie's grandfather, the inept and arrogant James II, had fled into exile in France, and ever since the Stuarts had been trying to regain their kingdom. In 1745, young Charlie (then only 25) determined to win back the throne for his father, the Old Pretender, who lived in exile as *de jure* James III.

Bonnie Prince Charlie's first efforts were triumphant. Having landed successfully in Scotland, he occupied Edinburgh and led his troops south as far as Derby, well into England.

Then the English army pushed him back into Scotland until this fatal day at Culloden Moor when the Bonnie Prince met a far larger English army of 9,000 men under the Duke of Cumberland, King George II's oversized brother. (He weighed 18 stone – 250 pounds – and was still ten days short of his 25th birthday.)

The night before the battle, the Scottish rebels had attempted a night march to catch Cumberland's army by surprise, but progress had been so slow that it had to be abandoned. At dawn the next morning the weary and famished Jacobites arrived at the battlefield.

The English opened hostilities with intense and deadly cannon fire, their guns loaded with grapeshot, and then attacked Charlie's band of about 5,000 Scots. As the armies closed, each English soldier ignored the man directly in front of him to bayonet the vulnerable side of the man to the right.

This one-sided butchery lasted just over half an hour, the English suffering only 50 dead and 260 wounded. Over 1,000 Scots were killed outright, many slain with bayonets, pistols and clubs as they lay wounded on the field. Another 1,000 were hunted down and slaughtered in the following weeks: any man found bearing arms was hanged on the spot, rebel houses were torched and families left to starve. For ever after the Scots referred to Cumberland as 'Butcher Cumberland'.

The charismatic, charming Prince Charlie finally managed to recross the Channel after five and a half legendary months on the run, a price of £30,000 on his head. During the next 42 years he maintained the Stuart claim without ever being able to raise another army, and he died in France a haughty, disagreeable, dropsical old man at the age of 68.

Other action this day

1797: The English fleet mutinies at Spithead * 1917: Nineteen divisions of General Robert Nivelle's French 5th and 6th Armies attack German positions at the disastrous Second Battle of the Aisne in which the French suffer over 40,000 casualties and lose 150 tanks on the first day alone * 1945: Soviet submarine L-3 torpedoes and sinks the German transport ship *Goya* in the icy waters of the Baltic Sea , killing about 7,000 German troops and civilians either within the ship, or outside by drowning and hypothermia, as only 183 survive

17 April

Chesty Puller – Marine!

1920 Today in Port-au-Prince a 21-year-old American Marine on assignment with the Gendarmerie d'Haiti was awarded his first military decoration, the Médaille Militaire, for nine months of fighting against the Cacos, fierce, jungle-wise Negro tribesmen who were rebelling against the Haitian government. During that time he fought in over 40 engagements, deadly little battles of 20 or 30 men on each side. These ferocious skirmishes were especially lethal for foreigners. If they were captured, the Cacos tortured them to death and ate their hearts to imbibe their courage.

The Marine's name was Lewis Puller, later known as 'Chesty', not only for his bull chest but also for his absolute fearlessness and belligerence. During 37 years in the US Marine Corps he would become the most highly decorated Marine ever.

Puller had joined the Marines in June 1918, but with the end of the First World War he was put on inactive status. Desperate for action, he volunteered for the Gendarmerie d'Haiti, a paramilitary police force set up by a Marine general and staffed largely by Marine officers. It was in Haiti that Puller first saw combat; in his very first action he surprised a Caco band, charged through it and personally shot dead one of the rebels.

During the next 35 years Puller would fight in Nicaragua, the Pacific and Korea. In every conflict he attacked the enemy with unremitting ferocity while inspiring his men with his coolness under fire and his concern for his troops.

In two stints in Nicaragua between 1928 and 1932 Puller fought in nine battles against the notorious rebel Augusto César Sandino, winning two of his five Navy Crosses (the highest medal for bravery after the Medal of Honor). The first citation reads: 'By his intelligent and forceful leadership without thought of his own personal safety, by great physical exertion, and by suffering many hardships, he surmounted all obstacles.' He left Nicaragua in 1931 but returned a year later, prompting Sandino to put a bounty of 5,000 pesos on his head. Puller's response was to win his second Navy Cross for more daring attacks.

In 1942 during the Second World War, Puller earned his third Navy Cross in the jungles of Guadalcanal. Now a lieutenant colonel commanding the 1st Battalion, 7th Marines, one night he inspired his troops by lighting his pipe in the open to draw fire from an enemy machine gun nest to pinpoint its position, so that his men could obliterate it with mortars.

The specific action for which he was decorated was the fight for Henderson Field, where his 800-man battalion was the only American unit defending an airfield against a full regiment of Japanese. After three hours of fierce combat, much of it hand-to-hand, the Marines had killed 1,400 of the 2,000 attackers for the loss of nineteen dead, 30 wounded and twelve missing. Puller himself was shot by a sniper and wounded by shrapnel but personally killed three enemy with his .45.

Puller's fourth Navy Cross was for his leadership on Cape Gloucester in New Guinea in January 1944, when he took command of two bloodied and leaderless battalions, reorganised them while under heavy machine gun and mortar fire and led them in a daring assault against heavily fortified enemy positions. Two years later he commanded the 1st Marines at the battle of Peleliu, where he was almost killed when a shell hit his landing craft. During the bitter fighting his regiment suffered 60 per cent casualties, losing almost 1,800 men.

In the Korean War Puller participated in both the Inchon landing (see 14 September) and the battle of the Chosin Reservoir (see 11 December), where he won his fifth Navy Cross. There, although surrounded by six Chinese divisions, he coaxed, cajoled, bullied and led his men to safety in one of the greatest fighting retreats in history. ('There are not enough Chinamen in the world to stop a fully armed Marine regiment from going wherever they want to go', Puller remarked.)

Chesty Puller retired from the Corps in 1955, but ten years later he volunteered to fight in Vietnam. His request was denied because of his age – he was 67.

During his remarkable career Puller won 52 decorations, including fourteen for personal bravery in combat. Apart from his five Navy Crosses, he was awarded the Distinguished Service Cross, the Silver Star, two Legion of Merits, the Bronze Star, three Air Medals, the Purple Heart and innumerable campaign medals. In addition, Haiti, Nicaragua, China, Korea and the United Nations all honoured him with decorations.

One Marine Corps commandant said of Puller: 'He's about the only man in the Corps who really loves to fight. I'll go further: he's the only man in any of our services who really loves fighting.' But perhaps the greatest accolade he received came from a private on New Guinea, who said: 'We all thought he was a wonderful son of a bitch.'

Other action this day

1864: The start of the four-day Battle of Plymouth in the American Civil War, in which the Confederates defeat the Union * 1895: The Sino-Japanese War ends with Treaty of Shimonoseki * 1942: French prisoner-of-war General Henri Giraud escapes from the German prison Festung Königstein near Dresden to return to Vichy France and eventually join de Gaulle's Free French * 1961: Cuban exiles, supported by American airpower, fail to invade Cuba at the Bay of Pigs

18 April–19 April

Paul Revere's ride and the start of the American Revolution

1775 Over these two days a 41-year-old silversmith named Paul Revere would first create an American legend by his own actions and then witness a seismic event, the first battle of the American Revolution.

By 1775 Revere's home town of Boston had already been the scene of British repression and American resistance for almost ten years. By 1768 the British had stationed a garrison there to control a restive populace, and two years later they had fired into a rioting crowd, killing five protesters, in the so-called Boston Massacre. Then in 1773 came the famous Boston Tea Party (see 16 December), and by 1775 nascent rebellion simmered throughout the whole area.

Now the British military governor General Thomas Gage was preparing to send a force of 700 soldiers from Boston, first to the nearby town of Lexington to arrest two dangerous radicals, Sam Adams and John Hancock, and then a few miles further to Concord, to seize rebel arms and supplies.

Revere, a fervent patriot, was determined to warn his compatriots of the threat. 'One if by land, two if by sea', he is supposed to have said (actually a poetic invention of Longfellow's – see below), referring to the lanterns that two of his confederates would place in the steeple of Boston's Old North Church to signal the movement of the redcoats. In the event, two lanterns were lit, indicating that the British were leaving Boston by boat instead of by land via the isthmus of Boston Neck. Then, at ten o'clock on this moonlit Tuesday evening, Revere galloped off on a borrowed horse called Brown Beauty on the most celebrated ride in American history to alert his countrymen that the British were on the march.

Revere's fifteen-mile run took him west to Lexington to warn Adams and Hancock. Along the way he woke every household he passed and alerted the Minutemen (members of the local militia who promised 'to be ready at a minute's notice') to the British movements. By the end of the night there were about 40 other patriots who set out on horseback to deliver the news around the countryside.

Revere arrived in Lexington around midnight, and, after tipping off Adams and Hancock, he set off for Concord in the black of night at about 1.30 on 19 April. After a few miles, however, he found his way blocked by a British patrol. Here is Revere's account of what happened next:

'I [took] to the right, toward a Wood, at the bottom of the Pasture, intending when I gained that, to jump my Horse & run afoot; just as I reached it, out started six [British] officers, siesed my bridle, put their pistols to my Breast, ordered me to dismount, which I did. One of them, who appeared to have the command there, and much of a Gentleman, asked me where I came from; I told him, he asked me what time I left it; I told him. He seemed surprised, said Sr, may I crave your name. I answered my name is Revere, what said he, Paul Revere; I answered yes; the others abused me much; but he told me not to be afraid, no one should hurt me. I told him they would miss their aim. He said they should not, they were only waiting for some Deserters they expected down the Road. I told him I knew better, I knew what they were after; that I had alarmed the country all the way up [...] and I should have 500 men there soon [...] one of them [...] clapd his Pistol to my head, and said he was going to ask me some questions, if I did not tell the truth, he would blow my brains out [...] he then ordered me to mount my horse [...] He said to me "We are now going toward your friends, and if you attempt to run, or we are insulted, we will blow your Brains ..."

'We rid [back] toward Lexington, a quick pace; they very often insulted me calling me Rebel, &c &c. after we had got about a mile, I was given to the Serjant to lead, he was Ordered to take out his pistol [...] and if I run, to execute the Major's sentence. When we got within about half a Mile of the Meeting house, we heard a gun fired; the Major asked me what it was for, I told him to alarm the country [...] when we got within sight of the Meeting House, we heard a Volley of guns fired, as I supposed at the tavern, as an Alarm; the major ordered us to halt [...] he then asked the Serjant if his horse was tired, he said yes; he Ordered him to take my horse; I dismounted, the Sarjant mounted my horse [...] & rode off down the road. I then went to the house where I left Adams & Hancock, and told them what had happened; their friends advised them to go out of the way; I went with them, about two miles a cross road; after resting myself, I sett off with another man to go back to the Tavern [at Lexington], to enquire the news; when we got there, we were told the troops were within two miles. We went to the Tavern to git a Trunk of papers belonging to Col. Hancock, before we left the house, I saw the [British] troops from the Chamber window. We made haste & had to pass thro' our Militia, who were on the green behind the Meeting house, to the number as I supposed, about 50 or 60. I went thro' them; as I passed I heard the commanding officer [Captain John Parker] speake to his men to this purpose. 'Lett the troops passby, & don't molest them, without they begin first.' I had to go a cross Road, but had not got half Gun shot off when the [British] Troops appeared in sight behinde the Meeting House; they made a short halt, when a gun was fired. I heard the report, turned my head, and saw the smoake in front of the Troops, they imeaditly gave a great shout, ran a few paces, and then the whole fired ...'

The colonial militia at Lexington had assembled on the village green at daylight and now were facing a British advance party of 180. In addition to telling his men not to shoot first, Parker is supposed to have added: 'If they mean to have a war, let it begin here.' Suddenly a shot rang out – no one knows who fired it, American or British – and the redcoats opened fire, followed by a bayonet charge. Eight militiamen lay dead, plus nine more wounded. The rest turned and ran.

Now the British column marched towards Concord, nine miles further west. But, after searching the town and destroying some supplies, a detachment guarding the North Bridge found itself facing about 400 Minutemen advancing from across the Concord River.

Soon both sides were firing and taking light casualties, but to the joy of the Americans and the astonishment of the British, the colonials stood their ground against trained British soldiers. The detachment retreated in confusion, and then the whole British force began to retreat towards Boston, only to be beleaguered en route by an ever-increasing number of militia and Minutemen.

This ignominious flight was a disaster for the British, as Americans sniped at them from behind trees and stone walls along the roadside. By the time they reached safety they had suffered 273 casualties against only 95 for the rebels and the American Revolution was well under way.

Revere rose to the rank of lieutenant colonel of artillery, was put in charge of Castle William defending Boston Harbor, and supervised the manufacture of gunpowder for the Continental Army, but he gained no particular notice. His rise to fame came more than 40 years after his death, when in 1861 Henry Wadsworth Longfellow published his celebrated poem 'Paul Revere's Ride' that over the years cemented Revere's legend in the mind of the American public.

Other action these days

18 April 1942: American general Jimmy Doolittle's sixteen B-25 Mitchell bombers raid Tokyo, Osaka, Kobe and Nagoya, the first Allied bombing of Japan during the Second World War * 1943: Japanese admiral Yamamoto, the architect of the Pearl Harbor attack, is killed when US fighters shoot down his plane over the Solomon Islands during Operation Peacock * 1955: Atomic bomb instigator and inventor Albert Einstein dies in the Princeton Hospital of ruptured arteriosclerotic aneurysm of the abdominal aorta, having opposed surgery to prolong his life

19 April 1587: In an incident known as 'the singeing of the King of Spain's beard', British vice admiral Sir Francis Drake leads sixteen warships into Cadiz harbour and loots, burns or sinks 24 Spanish merchant ships laden with supplies for the Spanish Armada * 1917: The Ottoman empire defeats a British force under General Charles Dobell at Gaza for the second time in a month * 1943: On the eve of Passover, Nazi soldiers enter the Warsaw Ghetto, blow up buildings and kill or deport to concentration camps 56,000 Jews

20 April

The Red Baron's last kill

1918 After two weeks of bad weather, the rain finally stopped today and by late afternoon the cloud cover had lifted enough to send up a patrol. The fighter wing's commander gave the order. Within minutes, six Fokker triplanes were in the air above the aerodrome at Cappy, in the Somme valley. The lead plane was painted entirely red, and seated at its controls was the most famous combat pilot of the First World War, Rittmeister (Captain) Manfred von Richthofen of the German air force, better known to much of the world as the Red Baron or the Red Knight.

Sighting a flight of enemy planes in the distance, the patrol steered towards them. In the brief combat that ensued, Captain Richthofen shot down two RAF Sopwith Camels, giving him his 79th and 80th kills of the war.

The past 30 days had been a highly productive period for Richthofen and his pilots in the celebrated fighter wing, officially Jagdgeschwader No. 1, but now famous as the Flying Circus or Richthofen's Circus, for its colourfully painted planes and for the frequency with which its squadrons and equipment were moved around the front on trucks and railway cars. Flying air operations in tactical support of Erich von Ludendorff's spring offensive, the group had downed a total of 46 British planes, of which twelve had been the captain's personal tally. In a single day – 27 March – flying 118 sorties, the wing had shot down thirteen of the enemy, of which three kills were his.

At dinner that evening, back at Cappy, his pilots raised their glasses to their commander, toasting him as 'the ace of aces'. The Red Baron, not quite 26 years old, retired early to bed on the last full day of his life.

The next morning, after an army band serenaded them to honour Richthofen's success of the previous day, the Flying Circus took off, heading west in search of enemy reconnaissance flights. The wind was from the east, behind them, blowing towards no man's land and the Allied lines. As they drew close to the front, anti-aircraft batteries opened up.

Now the Flying Circus, spotting an RAF squadron flying north-east towards the Somme, turned to close with the enemy. Aaron Norman, a historian of air operations in the war, described the ensuing aerial combat: '... twenty-five German machines, mostly triplanes, and a few Albatrosses, pitted against fifteen British Sopwith Camels. ... [A] chaotic whirligig of planes weaving in and out of one another's track, banking, looping, slipping, rolling, climbing, diving, often almost scraping noses as pilots manoeuvred madly for a fractional moment's advantage.'

Richthofen chased a Sopwith, which dodged and twisted to get away. But the Red Baron remained close behind his prey and one of his machine gun bursts hit the plane, wounding the pilot. Now the Sopwith dived steeply to escape its pursuer. On the ground, held by Australian troops, machine gunners opened up on the red triplane, while artillery men, squinting in the sun, watched the aerial manoeuvring taking place directly over their positions on Marlancourt Ridge.

Richthofen may never have noticed another Sopwith that closed in behind him and fired a burst. While the first Sopwith continued its evasive moves, now the Red Baron's triplane began a mile-long slide towards the ground, finally crashing behind Allied lines, where the pilot's body was recovered and identified and his plane quickly stripped by souvenir-hunting troops. There is argument to this day over whether Richthofen was killed by bullets from the burst fired by Captain Roy Brown or by machine gun fire from the ground.

The next day the RAF buried Richthofen with full military honours. Germany knew only that he had gone missing. On 23 April a British plane flew over Cappy and dropped a photograph of the burial ceremony accompanied by a message from the RAF: 'To the German Flying Corps: Rittmeister Baron Manfred von Richthofen was killed in aerial combat on 21 April 1918. He has been buried with all due military honours.'

The news was flashed around the world. Imperial Germany mourned the loss of its most famous hero. Jagdgeschwader No. 1 was quickly redesignated Jagdgeschwader Freiherr von Richthofen No. 1. On 7 July, as the Allies mounted their war-winning offensive, an order from Berlin confirmed a new commander for the wing, an officer unknown to the pilots, a former squadron commander with twenty kills to date, Lieutenant Hermann Göring.

Richthofen's 80 kills were a record for the war. Among other notable aces were Captain René Fonck, French Air Service, 75; Major Edward Mannock, Royal Air Force, 73; Lieutenant Colonel William Bishop, a Canadian pilot with the RAF, 72; and Captain Edward Rickenbacker, US Air Service, 26.

Other action this day

1744: French and Spanish troops force the pass of Villafranca, defeating its English and Sardinian defenders during the War of the Austrian Succession * 1792: The French Assembly declares war on Austria to start a conflict that lasts on and off until 1815 * 1861: Robert E. Lee resigns his commission in the US Army to command the forces of the State of Virginia * 1945: Soviet troops enter Berlin in the last days of the Second World War

21 April

Babur founds an empire

1526 The great Mughal conqueror Babur may have inherited his talent for war – through his father he could trace his bloodline to the 14th-century conqueror Tamerlane and through his mother to Genghis Khan. On this day he crushed a Hindustani force almost three times the size of his own at the Battle of Panipat and established an empire that would endure for over three centuries.

When Babur was twelve he succeeded to his father's territory of Fergana in the north of today's Uzbekistan. He grew up to be immensely strong, supposedly able to carry a man on each shoulder and then run up a hill. He also swam across rivers, including the Ganges. By the time he was 22 in 1505, he had conquered much of Afghanistan, setting up his capital in Kabul.

In the early 1520s, Sultan Ibrahim Lodhi ruled Hindustan in northern India. He was an unpopular ruler whom his own uncle and cousin repeatedly tried to overthrow. Under the pretext of helping the would-be usurpers, Babur marched into the Punjab in 1524, seizing Lahore. His eye was now set on Hindustan, claiming that he was the true heir to the Sayyid dynasty that had held sway there almost a century before. In January 1526 he set out with a small army of 10,000 Mughals and 5,000 allied Indian troops. He would face an enemy of some 40,000 men, reinforced by over 100 elephants, but Babur's soldiers enjoyed two huge advantages: they were supported by twenty field cannon and were armed with matchlock muskets. Ibrahim's army had no firearms at all.

Babur kept to the foothills of the Himalayas until he descended to the town of Panipat, 50 miles north of Delhi. During the trek he had commandeered about 700 wagons, which he now lined up end to end, tied together with rawhide ropes, but leaving occasional spaces in the line to permit his cavalry to charge through. He positioned his left flank along a ravine, protected by felled trees.

Meanwhile, Ibrahim was marching out to meet the invaders, arriving at Panipat on 12 April. For a week there were only minor skirmishes, each side fearing open battle. On the night of 19 April Babur launched his first major assault with 5,000 men, but the attack foundered in the dark and his men were forced to withdraw. This mini-defeat actually worked to Babur's advantage, since it encouraged Ibrahim to attack, which Babur had been hoping for.

At dawn on this day Ibrahim advanced across an open plain towards Babur's line of wagons. Babur let fire with cannon and then with muskets, inflicting some casualties, but, more importantly, the noise of the firing frightened Ibrahim's elephants, causing them to trample his own men. Then, when the Hindustani infantry reached the wagon line, the soldiers hesitated, giving Babur the opportunity to launch his cavalry through the gaps in his line and around both enemy flanks to attack them from the rear. Now Babur ordered his infantry forward through the gaps, and the Hindustanis were assaulted on three sides at once. As they pressed together, uncertain how to defend themselves, Babur's matchlocksmen and bowmen mercilessly cut them down. Almost 20,000 Hindustanis were killed, including Ibrahim.

Later that same day, Babur dispatched his son Humayun to Ibrahim's former capital at Agra to grab the state treasury. There Humayun found the Raja of Gwalior, who, to guarantee his family's safety, sent to Babur his most precious jewel, the Koh-i-Noor diamond, which remained with Babur's descendants until 1747.

Babur's empire, now including northern India, became known as the Mughal empire (from the Arabic word for Mongol, referring to Babur's forebears). Twenty-one Mughal emperors would hold the throne until Bahadur Shah was ousted in 1857 during the Indian Mutiny.

Babur died only four years after his great victory, still just 47, but his fame has endured. For 200 years the Koh-i-Noor diamond was known as 'Babur's Diamond', and his name is still today a favourite in India. By his autobiography, we know that Babur was a man of both intelligence and self-effacing wit. No doubt he would have smiled at one namesake, 'born' in 1931 – Babar the Elephant.

Other action this day

43 BC: The armies of Aulus Hirtius and Octavian (the future emperor Augustus) defeat Mark Antony at the Battle of Mutina in northern Italy, where Hirtius is killed, leading to a truce between Octavian and Mark Antony and the Second Triumvirate * 1836: In the last battle of the Texas Revolution, Sam Houston defeats Mexican general Santa Anna at the Battle of San Jacinto in just eighteen minutes; Santa Anna is captured the next day

22 April

'Gas! Gas!'

1915 On the Western Front, where the opposing armies had come to realise the cost and futility of attacking trench lines guarded by barbed wire and deadly gunfire, both sides sought a way to break the stalemate.

One way was poison gas, which was used on the front for the first time today in the Ypres salient. At five o'clock in the afternoon a greenish-yellow vapour suddenly appeared, moving across no man's land from the German lines towards the French trenches, where its effect was instantaneous and horrifying. By the thousands, French troops abandoned their positions and headed for the rear, clutching their throats, gagging, stumbling, and turning blue in the face, collapsing. An estimated 1,400 soldiers were killed by the gas, twice that many injured.

Their flight left a gap 8,000 yards wide in the Allied line. But the Germans, unprepared for the success of their experiment, lacked sufficient reserve strength to capitalise on the event, and the line was soon reinforced.

The gas the Germans employed at Ypres was chlorine, released from canisters in front of their own lines and requiring wind from the right direction to carry towards the enemy's positions. A mild dose of chlorine caused irritation of the eyes and lung; a bigger dose resulted in a victim's drowning from liquid filling his lungs.

Gas had been used only once before in the Great War, on the Eastern Front at Bolimov, west of Warsaw. There, on 31 January 1915, the Germans fired shells containing an asphyxiating agent known as T-stoff (xylyl bromide) at the Russian lines. In the sub-freezing temperatures, however, the agent was slow to vaporise, and a shift of wind brought what gas had formed back to the German trenches, with serious effect. Allied intelligence remained ignorant of the event.

Even though there had been recent warnings of such an attack from captured German soldiers, the French, British, and Canadian troops around Ypres had no protection against today's gas, beyond hasty improvisations such as towels and handkerchiefs soaked in water or urine. Soon would come a variety of protective devices: hoods, gauze pads, goggles, masks, and flannel respirators, with chemicals to neutralise the agents in the gas.

At Ypres, the Germans used gas again two days later, then twice again in May. From then on, gas was used by both sides in a number of battles, including Loos, Verdun, the Somme, and Caporetto. Chlorine gas was soon supplemented by phosgene, equally deadly. The most widely used was mustard gas, also the deadliest. Later in the war, gas was more often delivered by artillery shells fired into enemy lines, more effective than having to rely on the force and direction of the wind. But however and wherever used, gas proved to be more a weapon of harassment than a decisive tool of war.

Some months later, the British turned the tables and used poison gas in the fighting near Loos. Robert Graves, serving with the Royal Welch Fusiliers, described the scene from a British trench where an attack was to follow the release of gas towards the German trenches: '... the gas went whistling out, formed a thick cloud a few yards away in No Man's Land, then gradually spread back into the trenches. The Germans had been expecting the attack. They immediately put their gas-helmets on, semi-rigid ones, better than ours. Bundles of oily cotton-waste were strewn along the German parapet and set alight as a barrier to the gas. Then their batteries opened on our lines. The confusion in the front trench was great; the shelling broke several of the gas cylinders and the trench was soon full of gas.'

Perhaps the most vivid description of the effect of poison gas on troops came from Wilfred Owen, in his poem 'Dulce et Decorum Est':

Gas! Gas! Quick, boys! – An ecstasy of fumbling,
Fitting the clumsy helmets just in time;
But someone still was yelling out and stumbling,
And flound'ring like a man in fire or lime ...
As under a green sea I saw him drowning.
In all my dreams, before my helpless sight,
He plunges at me guttering, choking, drowning.

Other action this day

1806: Admiral Pierre-Charles Villeneuve, who commanded the French fleet at Trafalgar, is found dead from six stab wounds at a hotel in Rennes; the police issue a verdict of suicide ∗ 1809: Napoleon defeats the Austrians under Archduke Charles at the Battle of Eckmühl ∗ 1961: Putsch des Généraux: French top military brass in Algeria seize Algiers in a putsch to take over the country and stop negotiations with the Algerian FLN (National Liberation Front), but the next day President Charles de Gaulle addresses the French public by radio, to break the putsch

23 April

St George loses his head

AD 303 Today in Nicomedia (near present Istanbul), Emperor Diocletian watched the beheading that he had ordered of one of his own army officers. The emperor would hardly have guessed that his victim would gain far more military renown than he had ever dreamed of, for he would be celebrated for centuries as St George.

George was a *comes* (count) in Diocletian's personal bodyguard. He had been born to a Christian family in about AD 270 in Cappadocia in modern-day central Turkey, where his father was also an officer in the Roman army. When his father died, his mother moved back to her native Lydda in Palestine (now Lod, near Tel Aviv). There George grew up, joined the army, and was sent to Nicomedia, then the capital of the Eastern Roman empire.

The crime for which George was decapitated was insubordination; in 303 Diocletian issued his first edict against Christianity, which the army was commanded to enforce. George confessed to being a

Christian and refused to obey the order, so Diocletian had him tortured and beheaded in front of Nicomedia's walls. His body was taken back to Lydda, where his tomb quickly became a shrine. You can still see it there today.

Perhaps just an insubordinate soldier when he was alive, George soon made up for that after he was dead. His first victory is surely his most famous one. No longer an officer in the emperor's guard, he was now a lone knight-errant battling with a dragon. We all know the story: a fearsome dragon lived in a lake near Silena (in what is now Libya). In order to draw the lake's water, villagers each day fed the dragon two sheep, but when they ran out of sheep, they substituted beautiful maidens, selected by lot. One day the king's daughter drew the fatal lot, but before the dragon could devour her, George galloped in, clad in shining armour and carrying a lance. Crossing himself, he charged the dragon and skewered it with a single thrust. Having saved the princess, he then converted the king and his villagers to Christianity and rode off to find more battles to fight.

George's next recorded military adventure was in 6th-century England, where he became the patron saint of the knights at King Arthur's Round Table, a military post if ever there was one, even though there is no record of his actually going into combat. But that all changed at the siege of Antioch during the First Crusade in 1098.

Christian forces had just taken the city but were now besieged by a vast army of Seljuk Turks, reinforced by desert Arab cavalry. Hoping for victory through sheer audacity, the Christians charged out from the city gates to take on their enemies. The battle was fierce, with heavy casualties on both sides, when suddenly a company of knights on white horses smashed into the foe's left flank, led by St George, St Maurice and St Demetrius. So inspired were the Christian soldiers that they now attacked with murderous courage and routed the enemy.

A year later St George appeared again, this time at Jerusalem, just as the Crusaders assaulted the city walls, and in 1177 he was seen fighting shoulder-to-shoulder with the Christians when they ambushed and almost killed Saladin at the Battle of Montgisard (see 25 November).

Because of these daring feats, Richard the Lionheart adopted the banner of St George (the red cross of a martyr on a white background) for his soldiers during the Third Crusade in 1189. Such a stalwart battlefield companion was George that in 1344 Edward III made him patron saint of England.

We next hear of George on the battlefield in 1385, when Richard II invaded Scotland. He commanded all his troops to wear the badge of St George and swore to execute any Scottish soldiers 'who do bear the same crosse or token of St George, even if they be prisoners'. Thirty years later Henry V called on George once again, this time before the Battle of Agincourt (or at least so says Shakespeare):

'Follow your spirit; and, upon this charge
Cry God for Harry, England and St George!'

Over the centuries George has continued to inspire not only England's soldiers but also those of other countries; in 1325 Charles I of Hungary founded his Order of St George and in 1769 Catherine the Great established Russia's highest award, the Military Order of the Saint Grand Martyr and the Triumphant George.

Despite these greater honours, George must still have been pleased when in 1908 Robert Baden-Powell chose him as patron of the soldiers of tomorrow, the Boy Scouts, because 'he is the patron saint of cavalry, from which the word chivalry is derived'. And surely George must have been even more thrilled when King George VI established the George Cross (named for the saint, not for himself) for 'acts of the greatest heroism or of the most conspicuous courage in circumstances of extreme danger'.

Other action this day

AD 821: Ethelred the Unready, King of Wessex, is killed at the Battle of Merton against the Danes * 1014: Irish chieftain Brian Boru defeats Viking raiders at the Battle of Clontarf but is killed in the action * 1521: Royalist troops supporting Spain's Charles I (Holy Roman Emperor Charles V) crush the Comuneros rebels at the Battle of Villalar near Valladolid, ending the Comuneros revolt

24 April

Emperor Charles V wins the Battle of Mühlberg

1547 The 47-year-old Holy Roman Emperor Charles V was at the height of his powers. Over two decades earlier he had seen the heretic Martin Luther outlawed; later he had held the King of France in captivity in Madrid for a year; still later he had chased Suleiman the Magnificent and his vast army from the gates of Vienna; and now he was on the verge of crushing the rebellious Protestant princes of Germany, who dared challenge the authority of their emperor.

Charles's army was like its master – of no fixed nationality. There were Netherlanders and Italians, good German Catholics and those prime shock troops, the Spanish *tercios*. Reaching the Elbe near Leipzig early on a misty morning, some valiant Spaniards under the command of the Duke of Alba took their swords between their teeth and swam the frigid river. Soon the rest of the army was across, and the enemy, caught completely by surprise, was shortly scattered in defeat. Of their force of 10,000 men, the Protestant princes suffered 2,500 killed, 4,000 wounded and 1,000 captured. Two of the Protestant leaders, the Elector of Saxony and the Duke of Brunswick, were among the prisoners.

This was the famous Battle of Mühlberg, which gave Charles control of all of Germany. He was then at the pinnacle of his power, master of much of Europe, without challenger. Today, Titian's great equestrian portrait of Charles celebrating the victory hangs in the Prado in Madrid. The armoured emperor rides a prancing horse of unnerving black, the skies overhead are somehow full of menace, and Charles's sad eyes seem to reflect the disillusions of a lifetime rather than triumph. Indeed, within eight years, the great emperor would retire to the Spanish monastery of San Jerónimo de Yuste, defeated by the knowledge that his aim to unite his empire in the religion of Rome could never be accomplished.

Other action this day

1736: Imperial general Eugene of Savoy dies in his sleep at 72 in Vienna, after playing a game of cards * 1877: Russia declares war on Turkey to start the Russo-Turkish War * 1898: Spain declares war on the United States to start the Spanish–American War

25 April

Allons enfants de la Patrie,
Le jour de gloire est arrivé!

1792 Five days earlier, France – not yet a republic but getting close – had declared war against Austria. So it was fitting that at a patriotic dinner, held this evening in Strasbourg and attended by the city's notables and the officers of its army garrison, a rousing new song was given its first public performance.

The song was composed by a young army officer, a captain of engineers with a talent for musical composition, named Claude-Joseph Rouget de Lisle. He gave his song the title 'Chant de Guerre de l'Armée du Rhin' (War Song of the Rhine Army) and dedicated it to that army's commander, whose troops would soon be facing foreign armies invading to restore the French monarchy.

With a soaring melody, stirring march rhythm, and lyrics evoking themes of blood, honour, strife, family, soil, and glory, the 'Chant de Guerre' perfectly caught the spirit of a nation galvanised by the imminent prospect of war. The song proved immensely popular and spread quickly far beyond the region of Strasbourg, greatly helped by the mobilisation of the nation for war, as army volunteers from around the country flocked to Paris.

Three months later, on 30 July, a contingent of 500 provincial volunteers from the city of Marseille marched into the capital, by now an armed camp, bringing with them the song that would take Paris by storm. Soon retitled 'La Marseillaise', Rouget de Lisle's composition joined the *sans-culottes*, the *bonnet rouge*, and the tricolour flag as one of the great and enduring symbols of Revolutionary France.

On Bastille Day in 1795, the National Convention adopted 'La Marseillaise' as the national anthem. The song was banned during the years of Napoleon's empire and under the restoration of Louis XVIII; brought back by the Second Republic in 1830; banned again during the Second Empire; and adopted once more by the Third Republic in 1879.

1644: Rebelling peasants led by Li Zicheng take over Peking, and the sixteenth and last Ming emperor, the Chongzhen Emperor, hangs himself on a tree in the imperial garden outside the Forbidden City * 1707: During the War of the Spanish Succession, a Franco-Spanish army commanded by James FitzJames, 1st Duke of Berwick, routs a British-Portuguese army commanded by the Earl of Galway (born Henri de Massue, marquis de Ruvigny) at the Battle of Almansa, reclaiming most of eastern Spain for the Bourbons, in the only battle in history in which the British forces were commanded by a Frenchman, the French by a Briton * 1862: Union admiral David Farragut captures New Orleans during the American Civil War * 1945: American and Russian troops meet at the Elbe River

26 April

Guernica

1937 At 4.30 this Monday afternoon – market day – Adolf Hitler's Condor Legion, using the Spanish Civil War as a testing ground, tried out some new techniques of blitzkrieg on the residents of the historic Basque town of Guernica.

It was a success. Heinkel 111s, flying over in waves, worked for four hours dropping high-explosive and incendiary bombs on Guernica, whose normal population of 7,000 had been greatly increased by the presence of Republican troops and of civilians getting out of the way of the Nationalist advance. When the bombers finished, most of the town had been destroyed or was on fire. At that point, Junkers took over the action and strafed civilians in the streets.

Two days later Nationalist ground forces captured Guernica. Franco's propagandists reported that Basques had set fire to Guernica as a device to whip up Republican resistance. But the German pilots of the Condor Legion were soon boasting of their success, and the newspapers quickly got hold of the story. There was a great deal of international outrage, but not much in the way of action. When two Basque priests, both eyewitnesses to the bombing, went to Rome hoping to inform the Pope of the atrocity, they were shunted off to

Cardinal Pacelli (soon to become Pope Pius XII), whose only response was: 'The Church is persecuted in Barcelona.'

The Spanish Civil War moved on to produce more bloody events that might have obscured what happened at Guernica, except that Pablo Picasso reminded the world with his most famous painting. Guernica was a preview of what would happen in places like Warsaw, Coventry (see 14 November), London, Berlin, Dresden (see 13 February) and Tokyo.

Other action this day

1478: Conspirators from the Pazzi family attack, wound but fail to kill Lorenzo the Magnificent in the Florence cathedral, and are hunted down and killed in their turn, cementing the rule of the Medici * 1859: Piemontese Count Camillo di Cavour rejects an Austrian ultimatum, starting the Italian War of Independence * 1721: In Leicester House (in today's Leicester Square) in London, Prince William, Duke of Cumberland ('Butcher Cumberland'), royal English general who won the Battle of Culloden Moor, is born

27 April

Magellan the great explorer is killed in the Philippines

1521 Fernão de Magalhães, better known to us as Ferdinand Magellan, was born of a noble Portuguese family in 1480 and raised in the royal household. In his late thirties, Magellan approached the Portuguese king Manuel I to finance a voyage to the Moluccas (today part of Indonesia) by a western route. Manuel had no confidence in his countryman, so Magellan turned to Spain. Luckily for him, and for us, the Spanish king was the future Holy Roman Emperor Charles V, grandson of Ferdinand and Isabella who had financed Columbus. A man of imagination and intelligence, Charles agreed to underwrite the voyage, and Magellan set sail across the Atlantic on 20 September 1519.

A little over a year later, Magellan had crossed the Atlantic; he then bore ever southward along the coast of South America to find a way through to the 'Spice Islands' for which he was searching. On 28 November 1520, having discovered the straits at the tip of South

America that now bear his name, he reached the Pacific Ocean, which he then set out to cross.

As provisions dwindled, conditions aboard Magellan's ships became appalling. His men were reduced to eating putrid and worm-infested biscuit, sawdust and grilled rat. Their only good luck was the weather, which remained miraculously calm for almost four months, without a single storm. Because of this one bounty they named this new ocean the Pacific.

Continuing westward, Magellan landed in the Philippines in March and set out to explore these largely unknown islands. On the island of Cebu, Magellan made friends with Rajah Humabon and his queen and converted them to Christianity. Then Humabon persuaded Magellan to attack his enemy Lapu-Lapu, the chieftain on neighbouring Mactan.

On the morning of this day in April, Magellan and his ships arrived at Mactan. According to the only eyewitness account: 'Forty-nine of us leaped into the water up to our thighs, and walked through water for more than two cross-bow flights before we could reach the shore. The boats could not approach nearer because of certain rocks in the water. The other eleven men remained behind to guard the boats. When we reached land, [the natives] had formed in three divisions to the number of more than one thousand five hundred people. When they saw us, they charged down upon us with exceeding loud cries ... The musketeers and crossbow-men shot from a distance for about a half-hour, but uselessly ... Recognising the captain, so many turned upon him that they knocked his helmet off his head twice ... A native hurled a bamboo spear into the captain's face, but the latter immediately killed him with his lance, which he left in the native's body. Then, trying to lay hand on sword, he could draw it out but halfway, because he had been wounded in the arm with a bamboo spear. When the natives saw that, they all hurled themselves upon him. One of them wounded him on the left leg with a large cutlass, which resembles a scimitar, only being larger. That caused the captain to fall face downward, when immediately they rushed upon him with iron and bamboo spears and with their cutlasses, until they killed our mirror, our light, our comfort, and our true guide. When they wounded him, he turned back many times to see whether we were all in the boats. Thereupon, beholding him dead, we, wounded, retreated, as best we could, to the boats, which were already pulling off.'

So died the great explorer, still only 41. His badly depleted crew, down to a bare seventeen men, finally reached Spain on 6 September 1522 to complete the first-ever round-the-globe voyage.

Other action this day

1296: Edward I defeats the Scots at the Battle of Dunbar ∗ 1522: Italian *condottiere* Prospero Colonna leads the Imperial army of Charles V, allied with Papal troops, to victory over a combined French and Venetian force at the Battle of Bicocca ∗ 1805: US Marines capture Derna, on the shores of Tripoli ∗ 1822: American president and general Ulysses S. Grant is born at Point Pleasant, Ohio

28 April

Mussolini is lynched with his mistress

1945 Caught like a rat and dispatched like one. This is the fate that befell Benito Mussolini this afternoon not far from Lake Como. He was pushed out of an automobile by Communist partisans and shot to death at the side of the road. It is ironic that the man who brought on the downfall of Italy by joining it to the Axis cause in the Second World War should die on a road named Via XXIV Maggio to honour the date in 1915 (24 May) when Italy joined the Allies in the First World War.

Gunned down by his side was his mistress Claretta Petacci. Executed nearby were fifteen members of his fascist government fleeing with their Duce to Switzerland ahead of the Allied advance and anti-fascist resistance. When the partisans stopped the column the day before, they had discovered Mussolini disguised in a Luftwaffe overcoat and helmet. After the shootings, the corpses were trucked to Milan. There in the Piazzale Loreto, the site of a fascist massacre of resistance fighters the year before, the bodies were strung up by their heels at a petrol station and displayed the next day to a jeering mob. Someone tied Claretta's skirt around her legs to preserve modesty. It was a fittingly shabby end for the man whom A.J.P. Taylor described as 'a vain, blundering boaster without either ideas or aims'.

Mussolini's father named him Benito after the Mexican revolutionary Benito Juárez, with whom the elder Mussolini shared an antipathy for Habsburg rule. Benito Mussolini electrified Italy and the world in 1922 with the march on Rome, a propaganda event that bluffed a timid King Victor Emmanuel III into making him prime minister. Mussolini was fascist dictator of Italy for the next 21 years, at one point simultaneously holding the offices of prime minister, minister of foreign affairs, minister of war, minister of the navy, minister of aviation and minister of the interior. He dazzled his countrymen with dreams of empire in Ethiopia and Albania. In foreign policy there were other courses available, but he chose the fatal alliance with Hitler. The realities of war proved his, and Italy's, undoing.

On 25 July 1943, as Sicily fell to the Allies, a majority of the Fascist Grand Council, one that included his son-in-law Galeazza Ciano, the foreign minister, voted to deprive Mussolini of supreme military command. The king, now determined to save his country by suing for peace with the Allies, dismissed Mussolini as prime minister and ordered him from Rome to confinement on the island of Ponza. There he was the object of a daring rescue by SS paratroopers acting on Hitler's orders. He was flown first to safety in Germany, where news of his survival was broadcast to the world. Then Hitler returned him to Italy, to the town of Salvo on Lake Garda, where he was installed as leader of a puppet regime under German protection, intended to maintain fascist control of northern Italy. But in the spring of 1945, with defeat now inevitable, Mussolini and his followers began to pack.

Whatever else he may have been, the Duce was a family man: an Italian historian calculated that by the year 1943 over 300 relatives of Mussolini or his wife Rachele were receiving government handouts. But even family feeling could not save his son-in-law, whom he sent, with others similarly guilty, before a firing squad in January 1944 for the 'treachery' of his vote the previous year.

The Duce died just two days ahead of his partner in crime Adolf Hitler, who, likewise accompanied in death by a mistress (whom he had actually married a couple of days before), committed suicide in Berlin (see 30 April).

Other action this day

1192: During the Third Crusade, Crusader Conrad of Montferrat is stabbed to death by Hashshashin, possibly in the pay of Richard the Lionheart, who resented his growing power * 1789: Fletcher Christian forces Captain Bligh into an open boat to start a mutiny on HMS *Bounty* * 1813: Death of 68-year-old Prince Mikhail Kutuzov, the Russian field marshal who was wounded at Austerlitz, stymied Napoleon at Borodino and harassed his armies on their retreat from Moscow * 1945: German tank commander Kurt Knispel, the Second World War's leading tank ace with 168 confirmed tank kills and 28 probables, is killed in action in the Balkans

29 April

The Moors invade Spain

AD 711 On this day a fierce, one-eyed Berber chieftain from Morocco named Tariq ibn Ziyad landed with a force of 7,000 warriors on the southern point of a tiny mountainous island on the south coast of Spain. It was the first, bold step in an invasion that would eventually put most of the Iberian peninsula under Muslim rule for the next 700 years.

Spain at the time was part of the kingdom of the Visigoths, who had swept down from France in the 5th century. But in AD 710 their king Witiza was assassinated during a coup, and Roderic, the ruling duke of Baetica (roughly, today's Andalucía), usurped the throne. Roderic succeeded in defeating Witiza's son in battle, but legend says that he then made the fatal error of ravishing the daughter of Julian, governor of Ceuta (a city on the Moroccan coast) when she was his ward. Now Julian joined forces with Witiza's son, and together they invited Tariq ibn Ziyad to help overthrow Roderic and restore the rightful ruling family. Julian even allowed Tariq to use Ceuta as a staging ground for his invasion, as there were only ten miles of water between it and the island where the Moors eventually landed.

But it soon became clear that Tariq had no interest in making Witiza's son king. His first act was to burn his ships to show his army (and the Visigoths) that he had come to stay. He then inspired his soldiers with a stirring speech that clearly specified that this was *jihad*, a holy war for Allah:

'Attack this monarch [Roderic]. ... Here is a splendid opportunity to defeat him, if you will consent to expose yourselves freely to death. Do not believe that I want you to face dangers that I won't share with you. In the attack I myself will be in the fore, where the chance of life is always least. ... I shall perish with you, or avenge you. ... The Commander of True Believers, Alwalid [the Umayyad caliph in Damascus, Tariq's ultimate boss] has chosen you for this attack from among all his Arab warriors. ... Such is his confidence in your fearlessness. The one fruit that he desires from your bravery is that the word of God shall be exalted in this country, and that the true religion shall be established here. The spoils will belong to you. ... Should I fall before I reach Roderic, redouble your zeal, force yourselves to the attack and conquer this country, in depriving him of life. With him dead, his soldiers will no longer defy you.'

Now, bringing his army from the island to the mainland, Tariq advanced into Spain. Less than three months later, he defeated the Visigoths at the battle of Guadalete near Cádiz, where Roderic was (probably) killed. (He thus came to be known as 'the last of the Goths'.) The claims of Witiza's son were cast aside, and Tariq set out to subdue the rest of Spain, bringing in reinforcements from North Africa.

Tariq's achievements promised so much that he was soon joined by his immediate superior, Musa ibn Nusair, the Muslim governor of North Africa, who landed with an army of mixed Arabs and Berbers 18,000-strong. By 712, much of southern Spain from Cádiz to Seville to what today is southern Portugal had fallen. Then, a year later, the Moors captured Jaén, Murcia and Granada, while sacking Toledo and beheading all the town's nobles. By 714 they were campaigning in the Ebro valley, near the border of France, and had penetrated Portugal as far north as Coimbra. By the next year almost all of southern Iberia was under Muslim control. Indeed, the Moors continued to grow in power until 732 when Charles Martel finally stopped them near Tours in France (see 10 October). From that time they dominated most of Spain, until finally conquered by the Catholic Monarchs Ferdinand and Isabella in 1492 (see 2 January).

After Tariq's magnificent start in Spain, Caliph Alwalid recalled him to Damascus, probably as a reward. But Tariq's true reward was geographic immortality: the mountainous island where he first landed is still called Gibraltar, derived from Jabal Tariq, meaning 'mountain of Tariq'.

Other action this day

1792: Nine days after the French declare war on Austria, French republican general Théobald Dillon and his force of 5,000 cavalry turn and flee from a small Austrian force at Baisieux; Dillon is arrested, taken to Lille, and lynched by the mob * 1945: US soldiers liberate Dachau concentration camp in Upper Bavaria, freeing 32,000 starving and disease-ridden prisoners * 1945: The German army in Italy surrenders to the Allies

30 April

Hitler commits suicide

1945 The huge 30-room bunker beneath the Reich Chancellery was dim and dank, the electricity faltering under the unceasing bombardment of Russian guns. The twenty or so people inside included two of the most sinister still alive in the crumbling Third Reich: the second most powerful man in Germany, the shadowy Martin Bormann, and the Nazi minister of propaganda, Joseph Goebbels. All waited solemnly, some with dread, others with impatience, for the death of their master Adolf Hitler. They knew that he had sworn to commit suicide with Eva Braun, the 33-year-old mistress he had married only two days before.

Outside the bunker some 100,000 Russian troops were taking Berlin street by street, vastly outnumbering the German defenders, composed of only a few seasoned soldiers leading a ragtag collection of old men and Hitler youths, boys of less than sixteen, armed for this final apocalypse. The Russian tyrant Joseph Stalin had ordered his generals to take the city no later than 1 May at all costs so that its fall could be announced in the May Day parade in Moscow.

Hitler seemed in shock, his face ashen, his left arm trembling uncontrollably as if with Parkinson's disease, his green jacket stained with spilled food. Two days earlier his friend and ally Benito Mussolini had been executed by Italian partisans and hung by his heels in a square in Milan (see 28 April), and Italy had capitulated yesterday. Now Hitler had learned that his most faithful lieutenant Heinrich Himmler had betrayed him by trying to negotiate surrender through neutral Sweden. The last message ever sent from the Führerbunker was an order for the arrest and execution of this traitor.

The first to die was Hitler's German shepherd bitch Blondi, who was fed a capsule of cyanide to test the poison's efficacy. Now in the early afternoon Hitler summoned his last remaining supporters, distractedly shook their hands and bid them a listless goodbye. Just after three o'clock he led Eva to his sitting room in the lower bunker and closed the door. Two loaded pistols and two cyanide capsules were waiting for him there.

Finally at four o'clock Hitler's valet, accompanied by Goebbels, Bormann and two generals, opened the closed door to the room. Eva lay dead from the poison while Hitler slumped in his armchair, a bullet hole in his right temple. Obedient to the last, his supporters carried the bodies to the bunker courtyard, doused them with petrol and set them alight. They then honoured the burning corpses with a final Nazi salute. Shortly afterwards Goebbels and his wife Magda poisoned their six small children and committed suicide, a deluded Magda boasting: 'You see, we die an honourable death.' Bormann made his way out of the bunker but was killed not in the fighting but from having taken poison to avoid falling into Russian hands. His body was buried in the rubble.

At 10.50 that evening Russian soldiers finally seized the Reichstag, but the victorious troops were quickly shouldered aside by agents from SMERSH, a directorate of the Russian state security apparatus. Hitler's burnt skull was secreted back to Stalin in Moscow, and only years later did the Russians reveal that Hitler's body had been found.

One week later, what was left of the Nazi government signed an unconditional surrender. Hitler's Thousand Year Reich was dead after thirteen years.

Other action this day

AD 313: Co-Eastern Roman emperor Licinius defeats rival emperor Maximinus at the Battle of Tzirallum * 1524: While retreating from Battle of Robecco against the Imperial army, Pierre Terrail, chevalier de Bayard, 'the knight without fear and beyond reproach', is hit and killed by a harquebus ball * 1975: Saigon falls to the Viet Cong, signalling the North Vietnamese victory in the Vietnam War

1 May

The first enemy soldiers enter in Venice in 1,100 years

1797 When Lodovico Manin became Doge of Venice, he hoped to preside over the great republic's regeneration. Instead, he found himself in charge of its dissolution.

Manin's family had moved east from the Veneto to neighbouring Friuli in 1312 but had returned in 1651, soon becoming one of the richest in Venice. As the republic was traditionally led by its most prominent citizens, in 1791 the Greater Council nominated Manin as the new doge, the 120th since it had installed its first, Paolo Lucio Anafesto, in the year 697. When the council's decision was announced to the waiting crowd, one onlooker, referring to Manin's family's stay in Friuli a century and a half before, cried out: 'Ga fato doxe un furlan, la republica xe morta!' ('They've elected a Friulian, the republic is dead!') The danger, however, came not from Friuli but from France, where the Revolution was now entering its third year.

For five years Manin ruled well, but in 1796 he could only watch nervously as General Napoleon Bonaparte, commander-in-chief of the French army of Italy, marched on Turin. Despite Austria's attempts to stop him, Bonaparte soon merged Modena, Emilia and Bologna into the Cisalpine Republic. Then, in January 1797, he flattened the Austrians at Rivoli and Mantua surrendered. When would it be the turn of Venice?

Her turn came three months later. On 30 April, 4,000 French troops arrived on the shore of the Venetian lagoon, causing Manin to declare in despair to the Greater Council: 'Sta notte no semo sicuri neanche nel nostro letto.' ('Tonight we're not safe even in our own bed.') It was the first time in the republic's history that enemy soldiers had trod on Venetian soil.

On the following day, 1 May 1797, Bonaparte presented his demands: the doge was to abdicate and the republic to cease to exist. He had offered Venice to the Austrians if they would give up their claims to Bologna, Ferrara and Romagna.

Outmanoeuvred and outgunned, Manin was forced to agree to Bonaparte's ultimatum and the Republic of Venice, La Serenissima, came to an end after a glorious history of 1,100 years. Along with the republic, the office of doge also vanished, although a strange echo of the name would resonate in the 20th century. 'Doge' is the Venetian for the Latin *dux*, or leader, a title to be revived by Benito Mussolini as 'Il Duce'.

After his abdication Manin refused to become governor of the once-proud state and turned into a gloomy recluse. He abandoned good society, refused visitors at home, and never again set foot in Piazza San Marco or the Doges' Palace. On the few occasions when he ventured forth, he was taunted and jeered at in the streets. Five years later he died of dropsy and pulmonary congestion, leaving in his will 110,000 ducats for the insane, abandoned children and poor girls without dowries.

Other action this day

1669: Off Maracaibo, English buccaneer Sir Henry Morgan sails a fireship into Spanish vice admiral Alonso del Campo y Espinosa's 48-gun flagship, the *Magdalen*, which burns and sinks, and captures another Spanish man o' war * 1769: Arthur Wesley, later Duke of Wellington, is born in Dublin * 1802: The French military school for officers at St Cyr is opened * 1898: American admiral George Dewey wins the Battle of Manila Bay in the Spanish-American War * 1945: The German Reichstag in Berlin surrenders to the Russians after frantic resistance by SS troops

2 May

Stonewall Jackson is shot by his own soldiers at the Battle of Chancellorsville

1863 Chancellorsville, Virginia: scene of one of the American Civil War's bloodiest battles. The North suffered 17,000 casualties to the South's 13,000, but the greatest loss to the Confederates was the legendary general, Thomas Jonathan Jackson, known then and now as 'Stonewall'.

Jackson was a slight, wiry man with a high, intelligent forehead and a handsome curly beard. Dour and eccentric, he was an accomplished psychosomatic who (thought he) suffered from constant indigestion, neuralgia, chilblains, tonsillitis and incipient deafness.

He also had poor eyesight, for which his treatment was to immerse his head in cold water with his eyes open and remain submerged until he ran out of breath.

Stern, righteous and God-fearing, Jackson was not liked by his men, but his courage under fire, his cool head and his brilliant tactical abilities made him the kind of general that soldiers willingly follow. As one observer commented: 'He lived by the New Testament and fought by the Old.' His Northern opponent Ulysses Grant remembered him as a 'fanatic ... [who] fancied that an evil spirit had taken possession of him'.

Jackson had earned his nickname at the First Battle of Bull Run when, greatly outnumbered, he resisted a strong Union attack, helping the South to a major victory.

The Battle of Chancellorsville began on 1 May as the Union and Confederate armies faced each other, each manoeuvring for position, but with little combat. The Union commander Joseph Hooker planned to tempt the Southerners into attack, which he felt confident he could bloodily repulse with his superior force of 133,000 men, compared to about 61,000 of the enemy. But the South was led by the brilliant general Robert E. Lee, who decided on the risky strategy of splitting his army to outflank the Northerners.

The next day, 2 May, the cavalry general Fitzhugh Lee, Robert E.'s nephew, led Jackson on a reconnaissance to ascertain the exact location of the Union right and rear. As the two men looked down on the unsuspecting Yankees, Lee observed Jackson intent in prayer. As he later wrote: 'I only knew Jackson slightly. I watched him closely as he gazed upon Howard's [a Union general] troops. It was then about 2 P.M. His eyes burned with a brilliant glow, lighting up a sad face. His expression was one of intense interest, his face was colored slightly with the paint of approaching battle, and radiant at the success of his flank movement. To the remarks made to him while the unconscious line of blue was pointed out, he did not reply once during the five minutes he was on the hill, and yet his lips were moving. From what I have read and heard of Jackson since that day, I know now what he was doing then. Oh! "beware of rashness," General Hooker. Stonewall Jackson is praying in full view and in rear of your right flank!'

Now the Battle of Chancellorsville started in earnest, with Jackson leading the 26,000 men of his II Corps on a bold fourteen-mile march to strike the exposed Union right flank and drive it back in confusion with heavy losses. At dusk Jackson rode out on a moonlight reconnaissance. Some of his own nervous soldiers mistook the general and his aides for Yankees and opened fire, hitting Jackson in the right hand and twice in the left arm, which had to be amputated. The wound looked serious but not mortal. When General Lee heard about Jackson's injury he sent him the complimentary message: 'You are better off than I am, for while you have lost your left, I have lost my right arm.'

The battle, considered a stunning victory for the South, continued until 6 May when both sides withdrew to lick their wounds. But the most serious Confederate wound refused to heal. The amputation gravely weakened Jackson, who contracted pneumonia. Soon he was half-delirious. On 10 May he seemed to wake from his restless sleep and clearly pronounced his last words: 'Let us pass over the river, and rest under the shade of the trees.' When he died the great general was only 39.

Almost a century later, Jackson's enigmatic farewell found an echo in Ernest Hemingway's novel about the death of an officer entitled *Across the River and into the Trees*.

Other action this day

1808: Napoleonic marshal Joaquin Murat crushes a popular uprising in Madrid and the next day executes hundreds of the revolutionaries by firing squad * 1813: Napoleon defeats a combined Russian and Prussian army at the Battle of Lützen * 1982: The British nuclear submarine HMS *Conqueror* sinks Argentine cruiser ARA *General Belgrano* during the Falklands War

3 May

Death comes to the Turkish sultan who brought an end to the Byzantine empire

1481 Today died the Ottoman sultan Mehmed the Conqueror, so named for conquering Constantinople and bringing an end to the Byzantine empire after 1,058 years (see 29 May).

At the beginning of May, Mehmed had complained to his chief physician of abdominal pains, but the doctor's prescription had failed to cure, and two days later the sultan died – probably not from natural causes, but poisoned on orders from his ambitious son Bayezid. It was perhaps a fitting ending for a man who had welcomed the news of his own father's death with public joy and whose first act afterwards was to have his infant brother drowned in his bath.

Mehmed (II) was the son of Murad II by a slave girl, but his father seemed to favour him, and when Murad abdicated after fearful losses to Crusader forces, he placed Mehmed on the throne at the age of twelve. Two years later Murad returned to command the empire's armies, this time victorious, but he died in 1451 when Mehmed was nineteen, and thenceforth until his death Mehmed ruled with a hand of iron.

Mehmed's abiding obsession was the capture of Constantinople, the last stronghold of the Christian Byzantine empire that had been born in AD 395, when Emperor Theodosius I had split the Roman empire between his two sons, never to be reunited.

First Mehmed neutralised Constantinople's Christian allies, Hungary and Venice, by offering them peace treaties on very favourable terms. Then he added a fleet of 31 galleys to his army, hired a Hungarian gunsmith to cast a cannon larger than any then in existence, and, to control the Bosphorus, built the Rumeli Hisari fortress (which still stands in intimidating glory) only a few miles from Constantinople.

Not all agreed with Mehmed's determination to conquer the great city, especially the grand vizier Candarli, but Mehmed would brook no argument and besieged the city on 6 April 1453, himself as commander in the field. After a siege of 54 days Constantinople fell; one of Mehmed's first acts was to order the arrest and execution of the reluctant Candarli.

But there was more to Mehmed than pure military prowess. Immediately on capturing Constantinople he headed straight for the magnificent Hagia Sophia church and converted it into a mosque. He not only fostered the Muslim faith but also brought in an Armenian patriarch and a Jewish head rabbi and re-established the Greek Orthodox Patriarchate. Transferring his capital to the city, he imported Christian merchants and offered guarantees of safety to

Greek and Italian traders. Within 75 years Constantinople (by then increasingly called Istanbul) had become the largest city in Europe.

Nor were these all of Mehmed's accomplishments. He gave the Ottoman empire a new constitution and brought philosophers and scholars to his court while accumulating a huge library of Latin and Greek works. He summoned the Venetian painter Gentile Bellini to paint his portrait (now in London's National Gallery) and to embellish the walls of his palace. Mehmed even penned a collection of his own poems.

Throughout this cultural renaissance, Mehmed remained a merciless tyrant, meting out the harshest punishment to any who opposed his wishes, becoming the prototype for the despotic Ottoman sultans who would rule in the centuries to come. He put in place the basic structures that would sustain the empire for half a millennium, largely the same structures that would bring about its final collapse in 1922.

Other action this day

1814: Wellington is made a duke * 1815: The second day of the Battle of Tolentino in which the Austrians defeat King Joachim Murat of Naples, causing Murat to flee to Sicily * 1945: Four days after Hitler's suicide but before the German unconditional surrender, the RAF sinks the prison ships *Cap Arcona*, *Thielbek* and *Deutschland* in Lübeck Bay carrying 7,000 prisoners from the German concentration camps in Neuengamme, Stutthof and Mittelbau-Dora

4 May

The Battle of the Coral Sea begins

1942 At 6.00am today, carrier-launched American aircraft made a surprise bombing raid on Japanese shipping at Tulagi in the Solomon Islands, doing only minor damage but beginning a five-day naval battle that would be the first check to Japan's bid for supremacy in the Pacific.

In the spring of 1942, flushed with their recent successes against the British, the Dutch, and the Americans in South-east Asia and the

Pacific, the Japanese decided to extend their reach by capturing bases from which they could sever the vital supply line from the United States to isolated Australia. In April they gathered strong naval and invasion forces at their great base at Rabaul, then sent them south-eastward, supported by a striking force of two big aircraft carriers, towards the Coral Sea.

By this time, however, Allied cryptographers had broken the Japanese naval code. Learning that the enemy's first moves would be to take Port Moresby in New Guinea and Tulagi in the Solomons, Admiral Nimitz, the US Pacific commander-in-chief, dispatched a taskforce with the carriers *Yorktown* and *Lexington* to spoil the game. The United States drew first blood when the *Yorktown* launched its surprise attack this morning on Tulagi, seized by the Japanese only the day before.

What followed over the next four days in the Coral Sea was the first naval battle in history in which no ship on either side ever sighted the enemy. It was also an engagement of air attacks and counter-attacks that Samuel Eliot Morison described as 'full of mistakes, both humorous and tragic, wrong estimates and assumptions, bombing the wrong ships, missing great opportunities, and cashing in accidentally on minor ones'. Battle ended on 8 May and both forces withdrew, the US having lost more tonnage sunk, including the *Lexington*, the Japanese more aircraft.

In other circumstances the Battle of the Coral Sea might have been judged a tactical draw. The outcome, however, was a strategic American victory because it forced the Japanese to halt their expansion around the perimeter of Australia. Moreover, ship damage and aeroplane losses sustained in the battle prevented both of the big Japanese carriers from joining their fleet the next month at Midway, where the US Navy achieved an even greater and more decisive victory (see 3 June).

Other action this day

1471: Edward IV defeats the House of Lancaster at Tewkesbury during the Wars of the Roses * 1799: The British East India Company defeats and kills Tippoo, Sultan of Mysore, at the Battle of Seringapatam * 1814: Napoleon arrives on Elba

5 May

Napoleon is murdered?

1821 Today at 5.49 in the late afternoon Napoleon Bonaparte, once emperor of half of Europe and lord to 70 million people, died on the remote island of St Helena a few months before his 52nd birthday, of what was thought to be stomach cancer. His last word was a faintly whispered 'Joséphine', a wistful final thought for his first wife who had died seven years before.

Napoleon spent the last five and a half years of his life on St Helena, an island with a population of only 2,000 but with 1,400 British troops to guard against his escape. Bored to distraction and bitter at both the enemies who had defeated him and the supporters who had betrayed him, he kept a minor court of a few French officers and their wives who had followed him into exile. His last eighteen months were passed in pain and growing weakness, characterised by extreme nausea, headaches, weakened sight, insomnia, deafness and bleeding gums. Although he faced death without flinching, on the evening of 3 May 1821 he lapsed into unconsciousness, apparently paralysed, after taking a huge dose of calomel laxative that his doctors hoped would help him. Two days later he was dead.

Napoleon was buried on the island where he died in a grave twelve feet deep, lined with stone. There he remained for nineteen years until his body was returned to Paris for entombment in Les Invalides (see 15 December).

In the late 20th century, scientific analysis of Napoleon's hair showed residual traces of arsenic, prompting some historians to conclude that he had not died of cancer but had been murdered, probably by one of his courtiers, Count Charles Tristan de Montholon, who had poisoned his wine. Montholon's putative motive was revenge for Napoleon's affair with his wife. Equally likely is the suggestion that the British and the restored French monarchy together persuaded Montholon to administer the fatal dosage, fearing that Napoleon might once again escape and overturn the autocratic monarchies of Europe.

Once the scientists had concurred that the ex-emperor had been poisoned, however, in 2007 a new group of scientists noted that

Napoleon's father had died of cancer and once again postulated that it was cancer that killed him, since there was no evidence of poisoning in his internal organs. And so the debate continues.

Other action this day

1061: Norman Crusader Godefroi de Bouillon, the first king of Jerusalem, is born in Boulogne-sur-Mer * 1860: Garibaldi and his Thousand Red Shirts set sail from Genoa to free Sicily from its king and his 30,000-man army * 1862: The Mexican army defeats the occupying French troops of Napoleon III at the Battle of Puebla

6 May

The duc de Bourbon is killed sacking Rome

1527 Charles II, duc de Bourbon, was the last of France's great feudal lords. Although Constable of France, he had long been at odds with his sovereign François I and even more so with François's mother Louise, whom he had rejected with disgust when she suggested he marry her.

In 1523, Bourbon became an outlaw in France by signing an illegal alliance with Holy Roman Emperor Charles V that, if effected, would have reduced France to a state of feudal anarchy. Abandoning his own country, Bourbon was awarded command of Charles's 35,000-man army in Italy.

By the spring of 1527, however, the army was near mutiny, having been unpaid for months. Ever the opportunist, Bourbon joined the mutineers and on 6 May marched on Rome to perpetrate one of the bloodiest and most violent sacks of a major Western city since Crusaders had sacked Constantinople half a millennium before.

Although surrounded by massive stone walls, Rome was protected by only about 5,000 militia and the papal Swiss Guard. On 6 May, Charles de Bourbon's army attacked and immediately overwhelmed the garrison, but while directing the assault Charles himself was cut down by a harquebus bullet fired by one of the Pope's defenders, the Florentine sculptor Benvenuto Cellini (or at least so claimed Cellini ever afterwards).

Now that their commander was dead, the Imperial troops went on an unprecedented rampage of killing and looting, slaughtering 147 of the 189 Swiss Guards in front of St Peter's as they defended Pope Clement VII. But thanks to their bravery, Clement had time to scuttle down the passetto de Borgo, a secret tunnel inside a wall that linked (and still links) the Vatican with the Castel' Sant'Angelo. (The Castel' Sant'Angelo was originally Hadrian's tomb but by Clement's time had been converted into an impregnable fortress.)

Meanwhile, the invading soldiers were running amok in Rome, executing about 1,000 of the defending militia and pillaging the city with brutality and thoroughness. They killed whoever crossed their path and ransacked the town's palaces, churches and monasteries. Nuns were raped, priests were murdered, and horses were stabled in St Peter's. Some 4,000 people were slain.

The sack of Rome lasted eight dreadful days, but despite the army's best efforts, the Castel' Sant'Angelo resisted all attempts to storm it as Pope Clement cowered in one of the inside rooms. Eventually he agreed to pay 400,000 ducats in exchange for his life and freedom.

Rome now lost its pre-eminence as a Renaissance centre and did not fully recover for half a century, when Pope Sixtus V ordered major reconstruction in 1585.

Other action this day

1622: Marshal Johann Tserclaes, Count of Tilly and Gonzalo Fernández de Córdoba lead the troops of the Holy Roman Empire and the Catholic League to victory over the Protestants at the Battle of Wimpfen ∗ 1757: Frederick the Great's 67,000 Prussians defeat 60,000 Austrians at the Battle of Prague while suffering 14,000 casualties ∗ 1758: Napoleonic marshal Jean-André Masséna is born in Nice

7 May

The fall of Dien Bien Phu

1954 Gabrielle, Huguette, Claudine, Isabelle, Dominique, Béatrice, Eliane, Marcelle. What charming names. So Gallic, so feminine. You can almost smell their perfumes, hear the soft tones of their voices.

But today Gabrielle and all her sisters had fallen. And so, most tragically, had the very centre of their existence, what they were meant to surround and protect: the French base at Dien Bien Phu, in Vietnam, overrun this afternoon by Communist troops after a siege of four and a half months.

And Gabrielle, Claudine, and the others? They were the outlying strongpoints and artillery bases protecting the main position, all named, so it was believed, for the current and former mistresses of the garrison commander, a dashing cavalryman with a fine record in the Second World War, and – it hardly needs saying – irresistible to women.

Dien Bien Phu, scarcely more than a place name on a map, lies in a remote valley some 220 miles west of Hanoi, near the Laotian border. Its strategic value for the French army was as a launching point for operations against the Communist Viet Minh forces, led by General Giap, fighting for the independence of Vietnam from French control. In November 1953, the French sent in paratroopers to occupy the place, built a fortified position, constructed an airstrip, and airlifted in the first of what would eventually be 16,000 men. But the strategy was faulty in several key respects: the French were outnumbered and outgunned, the position could be resupplied only by air, and the French lacked the air power that might change an adverse outcome on the ground.

So General Giap brought up his men, 40,000 of them, and his guns, and Dien Bien Phu turned into a trap for the French. As the weeks went by, the perimeter, entrenched and protected by barbed wire, shrank under heavy Communist artillery fire, tunnelling tactics, and savage infantry assaults. It was Vicksburg, or Stalingrad. The airfield fell to the attackers on 27 March. Now the defenders were forced to rely on airdrops from low-flying planes that proved all too vulnerable to anti-aircraft fire. The strongpoints fell one by one, faithful Isabelle holding out to the very last. Dien Bien Phu now became, in Bernard Fall's phrase, 'Hell in a very small place'.

And so today, 7 May, with the Communist lines only yards away, the French prepared for the end by destroying everything of military value: artillery pieces, engines, rifles, optical equipment, radios. At 17.50 hours the last radio message went out to French headquarters in Hanoi: 'We're blowing up everything. Adieu.' The firing slackened, then ceased. There was no white flag of surrender. Instead, three Viet Minh soldiers hoisted a red flag with a gold star over the command bunker.

Of the 16,000 French soldiers who fought at Dien Bien Phu, only 73 were able to escape. Some 10,000 were captured, many of them wounded, and marched away to prison camps. The rest were dead. Communist losses were estimated at 25,000. The debacle of Dien Bien Phu marked the effective end of French control in South-east Asia, and the beginning of an increasing role in the region for the United States, which within a decade would be drawn into a much-expanded conflict, the Vietnam War.

Other action this day

1104: Seljuk Turks defeat the Crusaders from the principality of Antioch at the Battle of Harran, the first decisive Crusader defeat after their capture of Jerusalem ∗ 1763: Pontiac's Rebellion against the British begins when Ottawa Indian chief Pontiac leads 300 armed braves to Fort Detroit in preparation for a full-scale attack two days later ∗ 1945: General Alfred Jodl signs Germany's unconditional surrender to the Allied forces, to take effect the next day

8 May

Joan of Arc relieves Orléans

1429 The English and their Burgundian allies were intent on placing the English boy-king Henry VI on the French throne, as stipulated in the Treaty of Troyes, which Henry's father, the bellicose Henry V, had forced on the French nine years before. France's true heir, Charles VII, controlled only small pieces of his own country, and since 12 October 1428 the English had been besieging Orléans, the last major city loyal to him. If it fell, nothing below the Loire would be safe. But then came the miraculous intervention of Joan of Arc.

On 6 March 1429 this seventeen-year-old girl had first met Charles at his fortress at Chinon and somehow persuaded him that she had been sent by God and should be entrusted with an army. Just seven weeks later, on 29 April, she arrived at Orléans, which the English had half-surrounded with seven *bastilles* (stone towers) on the west and four more to the south, but holding only a fortified church at St Loup on the east, lacking the men fully to invest the city.

Joan arrived at Orléans by the Chécy road from the east. As an almost-contemporary journal records: 'at eight o'clock of the evening … she entered fully armed, mounted on a white horse; and bearing her standard before her, which was likewise white, which had two angels holding a lily flower in their hands; and on the pennon was painted the Annunciation … she was received by soldiers and burghers and burgesses of Orléans carrying torches in great number, and making such joy as if they saw God descend among them … there was a marvellous press to touch her or the horse on which she rode, so much so that one of those who carried torches approached so near her standard that fire caught the pennon.'

The next morning Joan was up early, riding out to inspect the English positions, then returning to the city to scold its citizens for profanity. (Although a true inspiration to the Orléanais, she must have been tiresome in her endless piety, once banning town prostitutes from her presence on the grounds that 'because of their sins, God would permit the army's defeat'.)

During the next few days Joan sent occasional messages to the English, demanding their withdrawal. One such instruction, shot into the enemy camp with an arrow, was received with the English shout, 'News from the harlot of the Armagnacs!' (the French faction supporting Charles), at which she is said to have wept bitter tears.

On 4 May Joan saw action for the first time, leading an attack on the English-held fortified church of St Loup. There, in a three-hour assault, the French killed 140 of the enemy while taking 40 prisoners. Joan forbade them from pillaging the church and reportedly cried for the English who had died without confession.

Orléans lies on the north bank of the Loire, its south gateway at that time opening directly onto a stone bridge that crossed the river. On the last arch of the bridge was a fortified gateway called Les Tourelles, from which a wooden drawbridge reached to the south bank. There, at the other end of the drawbridge, was a walled monastery called Les Augustines. English garrisons occupied both Les Tourelles and Les Augustines.

The day after Joan's attack at St Loup was Ascension, so she refused to fight, but a day later she led a large French force around the east of the city to attack Les Augustines. After fighting which lasted all day, the monastery finally fell, the surviving English retreating to the fortified gateway of Les Tourelles.

After resting for a night, the French directed their assault against Les Tourelles. Here the English defence was dogged. As historian Albert Bigelow Paine describes the scene: 'the ladders rising against the steep embankment, men swarming up them, only to be beaten back or overthrown; the fighting at the very summit of the defences; the air thick with arrows and stones, missiles of every sort; the intermittent roar and the drifting smoke of the guns, and amid it all a figure in white armour, encouraging her soldiers, lending a hand to the work, her standard, held aloft by a bearer, floating before her on the wind.'

Suddenly, as Joan was setting up a ladder, an arrow fired from above struck her between the shoulder and the throat, piercing her armour and nicking her body. Although she had the wound dressed, she refused to leave the field and, after a quarter hour's prayer, she returned to the attack. Doubly inspired by her bravery, the French now mounted a concerted assault. Meanwhile, courageous citizens from Orléans towed a barge of inflammable material under the drawbridge that connected Les Tourelles with the south bank. Panicked, the English garrison fled across the burning bridge, many to tumble in full armour into the water below.

The English had now lost three of their strongholds, but their force was still in place in the other bastilles to the west of the city. The next day, 8 May, they assembled their remaining soldiers in full array, while the French also brought up their troops, prepared to fight. But Joan, who had already attended Mass twice that morning, refused to attack because it was a Sunday. The armies nervously watched each other for about an hour, and then the English turned and quietly decamped.

It had been an astonishing performance, the cowed French roused to overcome their powerful enemies by a mystical teenage virgin. No wonder one English commander later explained that she was 'a disciple and limb of the fiend, called the Pucelle, that used false enchantments and sorcery'.

Other action this day
1846: Future American president Zachary Taylor whips the Mexicans at the Battle of Palo Alto in the first major battle of the Mexican–American

War * 1942: During Operation Chariot, British commandos destroy heavily defended docks at St Nazaire in occupied France * 1945: Major 'Bubi' Hartmann, 'The Blond Knight of Germany', scores the last of a record 352 aerial victories during the Second World War when he downs a Russian Yak-9 fighter over Czechoslovakia * 1945: The Second World War in Europe ends as all German operations cease at 23.01

9 May

The oldest peace treaty in Europe

1386 The ancient sheepskin document lies at Windsor Castle, yellowed and wrinkled with age. Written in Latin, it affirms an alliance 'forever' between England and Portugal, as young King Richard II and João I pledged 'an inviolable, eternal, solid, perpetual and true league of friendship'. The so-called Treaty of Windsor is the oldest unbroken alliance in European history – it has now been actively in force for over 600 years and invoked as recently as 1982.

In the spring of 1385 the Portuguese Cortes (assembly) had elected João king, and three months after that he had devastated an invading Spanish army at the Battle of Aljubarrota with the help of a small force of English archers, safeguarding Portugal's independence and greatly enhancing João's value as an ally. Already enjoying warm relations with England, João now agreed the Treaty of Windsor with Richard, which came into force on this day.

Two months after the signing of the treaty, King Richard's uncle John of Gaunt travelled to Portugal and reinforced João in his invasion of Castile. Although the offensive was not successful, the British–Portuguese alliance was further strengthened, and João married John of Gaunt's daughter Philippa the following year. (One of their children was the famous Henry the Navigator, who paved the way for Portugal's Golden Age with his sea voyages of discovery.) João and Philippa are buried side by side in the Abbey of Batalha, their hands clasped in a symbolic expression of the 'harmonious relations between Portugal and England'.

In 1661, almost three centuries after the treaty was enacted, Portugal once again turned to Britain for help, this time against threats from France. The two nations signed a military treaty, and Charles II married the Portuguese Infanta, Catherine of Braganza.

Once more, during the War of the Spanish Succession at the beginning of the 18th century, the Treaty of Windsor was put to the test. France declared war on Great Britain and asked Portugal to close its ports to British ships, but instead Portugal joined Britain and the Netherlands in the 'Grand Alliance'. Then, a century later, when Napoleon invaded Portugal in 1807, the Portuguese invoked the treaty and Britain sent troops during the Peninsular War.

During the Second World War Portugal was neutral, but the treaty was the basis for the Allies setting up bases on the Azores. Finally, England invoked it yet again in 1982 when asking Portugal for airbases during the Falkland Islands War with Argentina.

Other action this day

1846: An American army under General Zachary Taylor defeats a Mexican force twice its size at the Battle of Resaca de la Palma during the Mexican–American War, Taylor's second victory in two days * 1918: French fighter pilot René Fonck shoots down six German planes in a single day * 1936: Fascist Italy captures Addis Abba in Ethiopia and annexes the country * 1941: The Royal Navy captures the German submarine U-110 along with its Enigma machine for encryption and decryption of secret messages

10 May

Hitler invades the West as the seeds of his own destruction are sown

1940 Smug with his achievements and supremely confident of future success, Adolf Hitler stood poised to obliterate all opposition to his plans to dominate Europe. With 122 infantry and twelve Panzer divisions, 3,500 tanks and 5,200 warplanes on the Western Front, he was ready to invade the preposterous French and any other nation that opposed his plans for expansion.

And why not? Four years earlier Hitler had called Europe's bluff in remilitarising the Rhineland. Two years after that he had absorbed Austria without firing a shot. Then he had seized the Sudetenland in

Czechoslovakia, while Continental and British leaders had only wrung their hands in alarm. Then came the non-aggression pact with Russia, effectively ending any Soviet threat, and finally, after manufacturing a spurious border incident, the German army swept into Poland on the morning of 1 September 1939. The German blitzkrieg destroyed the Polish air force in 48 hours, and the last resistance in Warsaw surrendered in only 27 days, after the Soviet Union had joined Germany in invading the country.

Since the invasion of Poland, Germany had, in theory, been at war with France and England, but typically the European powers' words were louder than their actions, as no battles were fought during a period sardonically known as the 'Phoney War' or 'Sitzkrieg'. But while the Allies were dawdling, on 9 April 1940 Hitler sent his armies to occupy Denmark and Norway.

Now the time had come to put Western Europe in its place. Following the brilliant plan of German general Erich von Manstein for a Panzer attack through the Ardennes forest, at dawn today the Wehrmacht began its invasion of Luxembourg, Belgium, Holland and France. By afternoon, German forces had penetrated as far west as Maastricht and Liège.

Now an icily self-assured Hitler knew that Europe soon would be his. Who could resist the mighty German onslaught? He was probably only vaguely aware of a change across the English Channel and discounted its importance, but it would be the first nail in his coffin.

In Great Britain the frail and ageing prime minister Neville Chamberlain, following the advice of his friends in the Conservative Party and the Opposition of the Labour Party, resigned. His successor was a dark horse candidate, Winston Churchill, First Lord of the Admiralty, whose 40 years in politics had convinced many in his party that he was unreliable, mercurial, and a lone wolf not to be trusted with supreme political power. Moreover, he had been in charge of the Royal Navy during its recent failure to prevent the German invasion of Norway. But the younger Conservatives, like the nation at large, were behind Churchill, for they saw that he – virtually alone among the senior leadership of the nation – had been outspokenly right on the great issues of the decade: Hitler, rearmament, and appeasement.

And so it was that at 6.00pm on the same day that Hitler charged into Western Europe, Winston Churchill, the man who would do most to destroy him and his Third Reich, took over the leadership of Great Britain. 'We cannot yet see how deliverance will come, or when it will come,' growled the new prime minister, 'but nothing is more certain than that every stain of his infected and corroding fingers will be sponged and purged and, if need be, blasted from the surface of the earth.'

It was not a moment too soon. The preliminaries were over and the main bout had begun.

Other action this day

1631: Imperial general Tilly captures and sacks Magdeburg, having killed 20,000 during the seven-month siege * 1775: American revolutionary Ethan Allen and 83 Green Mountain Boys take British-held Fort Ticonderoga in northern New York * 1796: General Napoleon Bonaparte defeats the Austrians at the Battle of Lodi * 1865: Thirty-one days after the South surrenders, Union troops capture Confederate president Jefferson Davis after several weeks of flight, near Irwinville, Georgia * 1941: Hitler's deputy Rudolf Hess parachutes into Scotland to try to negotiate peace with Great Britain

11 May

General Jeb Stuart meets his match

1864 Nowhere is the legend of Southern valour, dash and taste for adventure better embodied than in James E.B. 'Jeb' Stuart, the flamboyant Confederate cavalry general during the American Civil War.

Tall and handsome with a full flowing beard, Stuart wore leather hip boots and a red-lined grey cape and sported a plume in his hat. (During the second Bull Run campaign, he lost his hat and cloak to pursuing Union soldiers, but later captured Union general John Pope's full uniform when he ransacked his headquarters.)

Stuart's first notable appearance in history comes in the capture of abolitionist John Brown at Harper's Ferry. Later he led his cavalry in many of the Civil War's most famous engagements, including the Shenandoah Valley campaign, Fredericksburg, Gettysburg, Chancellorsville, Antietam and both battles of Bull Run. He was known for his daring raids behind enemy lines, scouting enemy positions and causing general disruption. In one incursion near the Rappahannock River he inflicted 230 Union casualties while losing only 27 of his own men.

But towards the end of the war, Northern cavalry had at last matched the South in verve and ability – and were far better armed, with rapid-fire carbines. They also had a leader equal to Stuart in Philip Sheridan, who, like Stuart, used his cavalry as an independent offensive weapon for wide-ranging raids rather than just for reconnaissance of the enemy.

In May 1864 Sheridan led a huge contingent of 10,000 men on a long foray through Virginia, hoping to entice Stuart into a head-on clash. Finally, on 11 May, the Southern cavalier met the Yankee at a deserted inn called Yellow Tavern, a few miles outside Richmond. Outnumbered two to one, the Rebels were routed and a dismounted Northern cavalry private brought Stuart down with a pistol at a distance of 30 feet. Dashing Jeb Stuart died the next day at the age of 31. At the end he was heard to whisper: 'I am resigned; God's will be done.'

Other action this day

1745: The French under Marshal Maurice, comte de Saxe defeat an Anglo-Dutch-Hanoverian army at the Battle of Fontenoy during the War of the Austrian Succession * 1857: Indian mutineers seize Delhi

12 May

Mutiny on the Thames

1797 In February Britain had declared war on republican France, and then in April British sailors at Spithead off Portsmouth had done the unthinkable – they had mutinied, pressing for better living conditions and more pay. Within a month, the Admiralty was ready to grant some of their demands, with a royal pardon for the mutineers. It looked so easy it would be called 'the breeze at Spithead'.

So now the crews of British warships anchored at the Nore, a Royal Navy anchorage at the mouth of the Thames estuary, resolved to try their luck in a mutiny of their own. The first to act were the men of the largest of the vessels, the 90-gun HMS *Sandwich*. Today, without violence, they seized control of their ship, and thirteen other ship's crews followed in their wake.

Each ship elected a delegate to represent its men, and then the mutineers chose a 'President of the Delegates of the Fleet' from the *Sandwich*. He was Richard Parker, a dark, handsome 30-year-old with some education who, the rebels thought, could speak 'like a gentleman' with the fleet's admiral. Although he had a history of insubordination, he was not one of the mutiny's ringleaders, but he agreed to represent the others.

By 20 May Parker had drawn up a list of demands, including better pay and rations, more leave, an end to impressments and the removal from the ships of certain cruel or unpopular officers. Meanwhile, however, the most headstrong of the mutineers were crying for more radical concessions. By 23 May, when no response had been received from the Admiralty, they hoisted the red flag of rebellion from their mastheads.

Eventually fourteen more ships joined the mutiny, but the mutiny itself was being commandeered by intransigent hard-liners who insisted that the king (George III) dissolve Parliament and make immediate peace with France. To force concessions, they anchored their ships in a line across the Thames, blocking all traffic to and from London. But instead of giving way, the Admiralty and the government hardened their stance, and the king threatened draconian new laws calling for the death penalty for anyone trying to 'seduce soldiers or sailors from their duty'. In addition, the mutineers' food supplies were running low, with no means of replenishing them.

Now the more moderate men began to waver and insisted that they were loyal subjects, seeking only better pay and conditions. On 4 June, King George's birthday, the entire fleet except the *Sandwich* fired a royal salute after striking the red mutiny flag and displaying the colours. One by one, ships slipped their cables to desert, despite more uncompromising crews futilely opening fire to stop them.

Seeing the chances of success ebbing away, Parker wanted to leave the *Sandwich* with an offer of submission, to be traded for pardons for the mutineers, but radicals blocked his path. Then, in a last desperate attempt to save the mutiny, on 9 June he ordered the fleet to sail for the Netherlands, but not a single ship moved when the signal to sail was given. By 13 June the Union Jack had replaced the red flag on every ship's masthead, and the vast majority of sailors wanted to surrender, provided they were pardoned. The mutiny had failed.

The next day Parker tried to escape the *Sandwich*, but he was held by other mutineers who feared the Admiralty's wrath if they allowed him to flee. The ship then sailed to Gravesend, where he was arrested, taken to Maidstone prison shackled by leg irons and charged with treason and piracy.

On 22 June Parker's trial began aboard HMS *Neptune*. Despite his claims that he was trying to moderate the mutineers' extreme demands, the judges sentenced him to hang.

On 30 June guards brought Parker to a platform beneath the yardarm of the *Sandwich*, where a hanging rope had been fixed. He was hooded, and the noose was slipped over his head, but before the signal could be given, he jumped off towards the sea, breaking his neck.

In the following days 28 other mutineers were hanged, while others were flogged, locked up or transported to Australia. But the government agreed to some of their demands for better pay and conditions and pardoned most of the men without punishment – every one would be needed, for the war with France would last for another eighteen years.

Other action this day

1809: Major General Sir Arthur Wellesley defeats Marshal Soult at the Battle of the Douro during the Peninsular War * 1820: British nurse and heroine of the Crimean War Florence Nightingale is born in Florence * 1865: In Texas, Confederates defeat the North at the Battle of Palmito Ranch, fought 33 days after the South's surrender at Appomattox, the last battle of the American Civil War * 1943: Axis forces in North Africa surrender

13 May

Churchill offers blood, toil, tears, and sweat

1940 Today, with German armour advancing invincibly across the Continent towards the English Channel, Winston Churchill entered the House of Commons for the first time since becoming prime minister of Great Britain three days earlier. In this moment of military crisis, he had come to present his administration's policies and ask for a vote of confidence. We remember the great words he spoke on this occasion and through them we imagine his voice already to be that of a nation united behind him. It was not so. Instead, the new prime minister faced an uncertain, almost hostile political atmosphere in the Commons. As he strode into the chamber, the Opposition Labour benches greeted him with loud cheers, but across the aisle the Conservatives – his party – remained silent. Their hearts were still with his predecessor, Neville Chamberlain, brought down by the fiasco in Norway that many thought should have been laid at Churchill's door.

This first speech was a test. Here are the words he gave them: 'I have nothing to offer but blood, toil, tears, and sweat [...] You ask, what is our policy? I will say: it is to wage war, by sea, land, and air, with all our might and with all the strength that God can give us; to wage war against a monstrous tyranny, never surpassed in the dark, lamentable catalogue of human crime. That is our policy.

'You ask, what is our aim? I can answer in one word: Victory – victory at all costs, victory in spite of all terror; victory, however long and hard the road may be; for without victory there is no survival. Let that be realised: no survival for the British Empire; no survival for all that the British Empire has stood for; no survival for the urge and impulse of the ages, that mankind will move forward towards its goal.

'But I take up my task with buoyancy and hope. I feel sure that our cause will not be suffered to fail among men. At this time I feel entitled to claim the aid of all, and I say "Come, then, let us go forward together with our united strength."'

It was a good beginning. Churchill got a unanimous vote from the House that afternoon, and if some members grumbled that showy rhetoric might be all he had to offer, and others predicted a short life for his administration, he soon proved the doubters wrong on both counts.

Other action this day

1860: After telling his troops, 'Here we make Italy, or we die', Garibaldi and his Red Shirts defeat a 3,000-strong French garrison at Calatafimi in the Kingdom of the Two Sicilies, the first significant battle of the

Risorgimento * 1916: The Lafayette Esquadrille, a squadron of American pilots in the French army, flies its first combat mission in France during the First World War * 1940: Dutch queen Wilhelmina and her government leave the Netherlands for England the day before Dutch commander-in-chief General Henri Winkelman surrenders to the Germans, who had threatened to bomb Rotterdam and Utrecht if resistance continued

14 May

The fortunes of Venice come full circle

1509 Today in northern Italy Louis XII of France led his army to a bloody victory over the outnumbered forces of the Republic of Venice. According to Machiavelli, in a single day the Venetians 'lost what it had taken them eight hundred years' exertion to conquer'. But even Machiavelli couldn't have foreseen that six years later the Venetians would get it all back.

In the early 16th century the hodgepodge of Italian city-states created tempting targets for the great powers of Europe: France, Spain, the Holy Roman Empire and even the papacy vied for more territory in a kaleidoscope of intricate and ever-changing alliances.

Venice now ruled most of north-eastern Italy, as far west as Bergamo. When Julius II became pope, one of his first demands was the return of key cities in the Romagna, once controlled by his predecessor Alexander VI but now owned by Venice. When the Venetians refused to hand them over, in 1508 Julius allied himself with Louis XII of France, Holy Roman Emperor Maximilian I and Ferdinand I of Spain to form the League of Cambrai. Their aim: to snatch from Venice all its territories outside the city itself and parcel them out to the participants.

The first to act was King Louis, who in April 1509 marched east from Milan (then ruled by France) into Venetian territory with an army of 30,000 men. To meet the threat, the Venetians hired a mercenary army of 15,000 commanded by two outstanding *condottieri*, Niccolò di Pitigliano and Bartolomeo d'Alviano. Unfortunately, however, although the two were cousins, they disagreed on how to meet the French invasion. Pitigliano wanted to shadow-box with the invaders, slowing their advance through minor skirmishes, while the younger Alviano favoured an immediate attack.

On 14 May, in the driving rain, Alviano moved his force of 8,000 towards the town of Agnadello, 22 miles east of Milan. There he came face to face with the French vanguard under Milan's governor, Charles d'Amboise, seigneur de Chaumont. The Venetians took defensive positions on a ridge overlooking some vineyards, while Chaumont launched first his cavalry and then his Swiss pikemen into an uphill attack through the vineyards. But the incessant rain had turned the hillside into a quagmire, making it almost impossible for either foot or horse to charge, and the French pulled back after failing to break the Venetian line.

Although momentarily saved by the weather, Alviano knew that another attack was imminent and urgently requested his cousin Niccolò to send reinforcements. Pitigliano, however, wanted at all costs to avoid a pitched battle and kept his troops well away from the field, urging Alviano to withdraw.

But for Alviano, withdrawal was no longer an option: King Louis had arrived with the rest of the French army and could now attack from three sides at once. 'Mes enfants,' Louis cried to his soldiers, 'your king is watching you!' He further encouraged them by assuring them that gunfire could not kill a king of France.

For the next three hours the French mercilessly assaulted the Venetians, and Alviano's mercenary army began to disintegrate. His cavalry galloped away to safety, but some 4,000 foot soldiers were killed, while the rest disappeared into the countryside. Alviano himself was wounded and taken prisoner.

Pitigliano had avoided the main battle, but when his mercenaries heard of Alviano's defeat they started to desert en masse. The following morning the remnants of his force retreated to Treviso.

Victorious, Louis took control of all of Lombardy, while cities like Verona, Padua and Vicenza, now defenceless, surrendered to Emperor Maximilian. Pope Julius, whose contribution to the war had been confined to excommunicating all the Venetian republic's citizens, seized the Romagna. It looked as if Venice was finished as a power in Italy.

But now that he had acquired the territory he wanted, Pope Julius began to feel that his erstwhile French allies had become too powerful a force in northern Italy. Needing help to evict them, whom should he choose but his ex-enemies the Venetians, with whom he formed the Veneto-Papal alliance. Together they succeeded in expelling the French from Italy in 1512. But now Venice felt short-changed by the meagre spoils of war it received and within two years had allied itself with France, the very country it had fought twice in the past six years. Through their triumph at Marignano in 1515 (where Bartolomeo d'Alviano again played a key role, this time on the winning side) the French would regain Milan and the Venetians all the territory they had lost at Agnadello.

Other action this day

1147: Conrad III of Germany and an army of German Crusaders depart from Regensburg on the Second Crusade * 1219: The great English knight William the Marshal, 1st Earl of Pembroke, who served kings Henry II, Richard the Lionheart, John and Henry III, dies at Caversham in Oxfordshire * 1264: King Henry III is captured by his brother-in-law, Simon de Montfort, at the Battle of Lewes * 1955: Seven Communist countries – Albania, Bulgaria, Czechoslovakia, Hungary, Poland, Romania and the USSR – join the Warsaw Pact; the German Democratic Republic joins the next year

15 May

The Pharaoh leads his army into battle

1479 BC Today Egypt's great warrior-pharaoh Thutmose III inflicted a devastating defeat on Canaanite rebels, personally leading his army in the field.

Egypt had long ruled the cities of Canaan (very roughly, today's Palestine), but now they had risen in revolt, led by the King of Kadesh (in today's Syria). But Thutmose, who was to become one of ancient Egypt's greatest commanders, immediately set out to restore his country's supremacy.

To prepare for Egypt's retaliation, the King of Kadesh had gathered his Canaanite allies together at Megiddo, a fortress perched on a hill about sixteen miles south-east of Mount Carmel (now in northern Israel).

At the beginning of May, Thutmose marched out from his border fortress of Sileh at the head of an army of 10,000 men. He headed first to Gaza along the road known as 'The Way of Horus', and then on to Yaman, only sixteen miles south-west of Megiddo. Here the Pharaoh and his generals held a council of war.

They had three choices of attack. The southern and northern routes to Megiddo were longer, and the most direct route was by the Aruna road. But that would be perilous in the extreme because it led through a ravine so narrow that 'horse must follow horse, and man after man', making the Egyptians extremely vulnerable to attack. They could be cut down one by one as they came through the pass.

Thutmose's generals advised taking either the northern or southern routes, but scouts reported that Canaanite chariots and archers were defending both. Apparently, however, the rebels considered the Aruna Pass too difficult for an army and had left it unguarded. The Pharaoh ordered his men into the pass, positioning himself at the head of the column to inspire their confidence. The long line of troops stretched for miles through the defile.

The scouts had been right. The Aruna Pass echoed only with the tromp of Egyptian boots, empty of enemy guards. On the evening of the next day, Thutmose and his soldiers debouched into the Plain of Esdraelon before Megiddo. Caught completely unawares, the Canaanite coalition frantically summoned their blocking units to return to defend the fortress. As night fell, the two armies faced each other, each waiting for the other to attack.

The next morning Thutmose, fearsome in his armour and blue war helmet, ordered his army to pass before him in review. As the soldiers marched by to the sound of war trumpets and the beating of drums, they must have made an intimidating sight to the watching enemy. The infantry were armed with axes, curved swords and shields, while the chariots carried bowmen, all roaring defiance. Thutmose divided his force into three wings in a concave formation, putting himself at the centre in his war chariot of gold and electrum (a pale yellow alloy of gold and silver), and ordered the attack.

According to an Egyptian near-contemporary report: 'The king led his army himself, mighty at its head like a flame of fire, the king who wrought with his sword. He went forth, none like him, killing the barbarians, smiting Retjenu [the Egyptian name for Canaanites and Syrians], seizing their princes as living captives, their chariots worked with gold, bound to their horses.' A single assault scattered the enemy, who fled in panic. When they reached the walls of Megiddo, the defenders there refused to open the gates for fear that the pursuing Egyptians would charge into the city. Instead they lowered knotted sheets to pull at least their high-ranking officers, including the King of Kadesh, over the walls to safety.

At this point the Egyptians could probably have stormed the fortress and overwhelmed the garrison, but they were diverted by the chance to plunder the enemy camp. For the moment the Canaanites were safe, although 83 had been killed.

Thutmose now ordered a moat dug around the city and beyond it a wooden wall. Cut off with no hope of reinforcement and threatened by starvation, Megiddo surrendered after a brief siege. As the Pharaoh entered the gates, the frightened inhabitants brought him gifts of gold, silver and lapis lazuli, hoping for mercy. But Thutmose wanted submission, not revenge: he ordered no executions and restored some of the town's leaders to positions of authority after they had sworn loyalty. (Whether the King of Kadesh would also have been spared is moot; he somehow escaped during the siege.) For the Egyptians there was booty aplenty. They headed home with 924 chariots, over 2,000 horses, 22,000 sheep and a vast hoard of armour and weapons.

The conquest of Megiddo was the first of Thutmose's seventeen military campaigns during which he extended Egypt's borders to their greatest extent. He is said to have conquered 350 cities, creating an empire that stretched from southern Syria through to Canaan and Nubia.

Almost 900 years later, in 609 BC, the Egyptians scored another notable victory at Megiddo, this time against the Kingdom of Judah. And 2,527 years after that, during the First World War, British field marshal Edmund Allenby duplicated Thutmose's daring approach through the Aruna Pass to defeat the Turks at Megiddo. Indeed, perhaps Megiddo will see yet another great battle, for in the Bible the Book of Revelations divulges that at the end of the world the forces of God will meet those of Satan at Armageddon, Hebrew for 'the hill of Megiddo'.

Other action this day

1464: Yorkist troops under John Neville defeat the Lancastrians at the

Battle of Hexham during the Wars of the Roses * 1948: Egypt, Transjordan, Lebanon, Syria, Iraq and Saudi Arabia attack Israel to start the 1948 Arab–Israeli War, one day after Israel declares its independence * 1988: After more than eight years of fighting, the Red Army begins its withdrawal from Afghanistan

16 May

British muskets stop the French at Albuera

1811 The bloody battle fought at very close quarters this morning outside the town of Albuera, Spain, was hardly decisive strategically. But it did have the immediate effect of repelling a French army's attempt to enter Portugal. It would also turn out to involve the largest assault ever launched in seven years of war on the Iberian peninsula.

It happened this way. Early the previous month, Viscount Wellington, with his hands full prodding General Massena's French army out of northern Portugal, decided to send a subordinate general south to address a problem in another quarter: laying siege to the fortress of Badajoz, recently captured by the French, which guarded the Portuguese border with Spain.

Wellington picked General Sir William Beresford and gave him orders not only to retake the fortress but also to be prepared for the arrival of a French army, commanded by Marshal Soult, which might approach from the east with the intention of relieving Badajoz and entering Portugal. To accomplish these tasks, Beresford would command an Anglo-Portuguese force and two Spanish armies with a total strength of 35,000 troops.

Accordingly, when Beresford learned from Spanish scouts that Soult's army was on the march towards Badajoz, he called off the siege to concentrate his forces against the enemy's approach. Further intelligence indicated the French army to be moving along a road that would pass through the town of Albuera, where a bridge carried the road across a small, north-flowing river.

It was along the west side of the river, extending both north and south of the town, that Beresford set his defensive line. To the north there was a clear view across the river to the plain beyond; but to the south, where the river flowed as two shallow tributaries, woods between the streams obscured any view of enemy movement.

Early this morning, Soult's army – 24,000 strong – came into view. At 8.00am a French brigade approached the river just north of the town and launched an attack, while a second, smaller force moved across the bridge and entered the town. But these proved diversions, for the main attack began at 9.30, over a mile south of town, the initial crossing hidden from Beresford's view.

It consisted of two French infantry divisions, one behind the other – 8,400 troops in all – turning northwards along the river, advancing on a front 400 yards wide, intending to roll up the Allied flank. Quickly redeployed to face the attacking column were four Spanish battalions, an insufficient force but able to deliver sufficient musket fire to slow the column's advance.

While British battalions arrived to reinforce the Allied line, a heavy rain suddenly descended on the battlefield, putting muskets out of action for both sides. This gave French cavalry – in the form of Polish lancers – the opportunity to penetrate that part of the line held by Spanish infantry, then break into the rear of their position, doing much damage to the artillery concentrated there, before being driven back by British dragoons.

But the rain ceased and musketry resumed. Seven British battalions (3,700 men) faced an enemy crowded into one enormous column, 200 men wide, 40 deep. By itself, the British line might have prevailed with its concentrated musket fire, but the French more than made up for that by bringing up guns and firing into the Allied ranks from only 300 yards back.

The historian Jac Weller called the confrontation 'a fire fight at close quarters perhaps never equalled in military history'. It was an hour of frightful carnage, targets obscured by smoke and a dank, cloudy atmosphere. Sir John Fortescue's account described the scene in the British line this way: 'The men stood like rocks, loading and firing into the mass before them, though frightfully punished not so much by the French bullets as by grape shot from the French cannon at very close range. The line dwindled and dwindled continually; and the intervals between battalions grew wide as men who were still on their legs edged in closer and closer to their colours.'

All the while, more infantry units crossed from the east side of the river to join the French column, swelling its numbers to some

14,000. But at the same time, a British infantry division was brought forward on the Allied right, adding 4,000 men deployed in a line facing south-east, from which angle they could deliver heavy enfilading musket fire against approaching cavalry and into the infantry column itself.

Now the tide of battle began to change. Reinforced, the Allied line enjoyed a wider front than that of the enemy, allowing the battalions at either end to wrap around the head of the French column and deliver a destructive crossfire. As the front ranks of the column wavered in the face of the concentrated musketry, there came a bayonet charge by three British battalions. Now the French began to retreat in earnest, and in increasing disorder, toward their crossing point.

After a total of four hours' fighting, the French withdrew to the high ground between the tributaries, remaining there through the next day but retiring entirely on the 18th along the road by which they had first come to Albuera.

Beresford had turned back the French advance, but at a heavy cost to the Allied armies. Losses for the day were roughly 6,000 for the Allies, against 8,000 for the French. Criticism of Beresford was immediate and fierce, mainly on the grounds that much of the loss was owed to his slowness in ordering redeployments to meet the enemy's advance.

Wellington himself, however, took a more realistic view of the outcome, writing to Beresford: 'You could not be successful in such an action without a large loss.'

In any event, today's fighting, confused as it was, demonstrated once again the distinct advantage in firepower of the British defensive line, where every soldier could fire his musket, over the attacking French column, in which the muskets were useless in the rear ranks.

Other action this day

1643: Royalists defeat the Roundheads at the Battle of Stratton in Cornwall * 1771: South Carolina governor William Tryon crushes American rebels at the Battle of Alamance * 1943: The Warsaw Ghetto Uprising ends after 27 days of fighting and 13,000 Jewish deaths

17 May

British troops relieve Mafeking

1900 When the war in South Africa broke out in the autumn of 1899, the Boers immediately laid siege to several British-held towns. The longest and bloodiest of these sieges – and the only one to introduce a new word to the English language – took place at Mafeking, finally relieved by a British column at 7.00 this evening after 217 days of constant blockade, intermittent shelling, and occasional raids.

At first, the Boers outnumbered the Mafeking defenders by six to one, but they reckoned without the commander of the British garrison. He was a cool customer, a veteran African campaigner named Colonel Robert Baden-Powell (B-P, he was called) who offered a skilful and imaginative defence throughout the ordeal. For the British, the strategic value of holding Mafeking was simply to draw Boer forces away from the lightly defended Cape Colony until reinforcements arrived from Britain. B-P was the right man for the job.

With the garrison in Mafeking were several newspaper correspondents who filed their stories by telegraph, filling in their readers around the world with the events and atmosphere of the siege: tales of heroism, cowardice, raids, escapes, near misses, and the like. The public was enthralled. On 30 April, the 200th day of the siege, a cocky Boer commander sent a message into Mafeking proposing a cricket match between the two sides, to which B-P responded: 'I should like nothing better – after the match in which we are at present engaged is over. But just now we are having our innings and have so far scored 200 days, not out … and we are having a very enjoyable game.' As it turned out, the game was just about over.

News of the relief of Mafeking produced riotous, hysterical street demonstrations around the British world, especially in London. It also produced this entry in the *Oxford English Dictionary*: 'Maffick. v.i. Celebrate uproariously, rejoice extravagantly, esp. on an occasion of national celebration (orig. the relief of the British garrison in Mafeking, South Africa, in May 1900).'

After the mafficking was over, the Boer War continued for another two years, extracting from all concerned inordinate amounts of human suffering, devastation, and money. In time, B-P went home to England, eventually retired from the army a general, and in 1907, employing the fieldcraft he had learned and taught his troops during his days in the veldt, he founded the Boy Scouts and, a few years later, the Girl Guides.

Other action this day

1742: Frederick the Great defeats the Austrians at the Battle of Chotusitz * 1809: Napoleon annexes the Papal States to the French empire; they will remain under French control until his fall in 1814 * 1943: Nineteen bombers of No. 617 Squadron of the RAF carry out the Dambuster Raids on German dams in the Ruhr, causing a catastrophic flooding of the Ruhr valley while losing eight planes and 53 of the 133 aircrew

18 May

Lee stymies Grant at Spotsylvania Court House

1864 Planned for 4.00am, launched at 8.00am, and called off by 10.00am – that was the fate of the Union army's final assault at Spotsylvania Court House this morning, shattered well short of the Confederate trench line by a deadly hail of artillery fire, and bringing to an end ten days of horrific warfare in the rain-sodden terrain of central Virginia.

The fighting around Spotsylvania was like that on the Somme in 1916. The historian Bruce Catton described it this way: 'Here men fought with bayonets and clubbed muskets, dead and wounded men were trodden out of sight in the sticky mud, batteries would come floundering up into close-range action and then fall silent because gun crews had been killed; and after a day of it the Union army gained a square mile of useless ground, thousands upon thousands of men had been killed, and the end of the war seemed no nearer than it had been before.'

General Ulysses Grant's Union Army of the Potomac had crossed the Rapidan two weeks earlier to begin its advance on the Confederate capital at Richmond. It was to prove a costly road. In the first confrontation with Robert E. Lee's Confederates, fought in early May in the murky nightmare of the Wilderness, the Union army lost some 18,000 men. Despite that, Grant resumed his advance, hoping to catch Lee's Army of Northern Virginia in the open, where it could be destroyed. But Lee fell back and dug in at Spotsylvania, where, in ten days of hard fighting – including this morning's failed assault – Grant suffered another 18,000 killed, wounded or missing.

Spotsylvania was a testing ground, not only for Grant but also for a new style of warfare. A commander of an army so repulsed might have admitted defeat and withdrawn his battered forces to rethink both tactics and strategy. Fredericksburg and Gettysburg were precedents for such a move. But Grant was a different sort of commander, who realised that to end the war, now in its fourth year, you had to keep pushing ahead, no matter the cost, always keeping your enemy on the defensive, never allowing him the initiative. So it was that before dawn on 21 May the Union army was on the march once again, its divisions pulled out of line and sent around the enemy flank. The next stops on the road to Richmond would be North Anna and Cold Harbor: engagements that would add yet another 18,000 to Grant's losses.

By mid-June, Grant would give Lee the slip a final time, taking positions around Petersburg, some eighteen miles south of the capital. But by then the Army of the Potomac's appetite for frontal attacks would be more than sated. Exhausted, both armies built trench lines from which they would face each other until almost the end of the war, which was finally in sight. Richmond itself remained elusive, falling only on 4 April 1865, after the Confederate army had left on its final campaign, which ended in surrender at Appomattox (see 9 April).

Other action this day

1302: Les Mâtines Brugeoises: Pieter de Coninck leads a massacre of French troops stationed in Bruges * 1863: Union troops under Ulysses S. Grant begin the siege of Vicksburg, which ends in Confederate capitulation on 4 July * 1916: Fighter pilot Kiffin Rockwell of the Lafayette Esquadrille (a volunteer squadron of American pilots in the French army) shoots down a German two-seater LVG, the first enemy plane downed by an American pilot in the First World War * 1953: American fighter pilot Joseph McConnell shoots down three MiGs in two separate missions to bring his total kills to sixteen, the highest of any pilot during the Korean War

19 May

The mysterious life of Lawrence of Arabia

1935 Today T.E. Lawrence died in self-imposed obscurity, at the age of 46, from injuries sustained in a motorcycle accident. The obscurity he maintained for thirteen years was shelter from the intense public enthusiasm and media scrutiny that greeted his exploits in the First World War as 'Lawrence of Arabia'. He had suddenly become world famous after the American journalist Lowell Thomas visited Palestine in 1917 and made films of the Arab Revolt, in which Colonel Lawrence, a British intelligence officer, had been instrumental as an advisor and leader.

As the war ended, Thomas's film and lecture presentations, seen by millions in Britain and America, showed Lawrence in Arab dress against desert landscapes, surrounded by fierce tribesmen mounted on camels and waving rifles. For audiences weary of four years' stale-mate and carnage on the Western Front, the scenes were irresistible: a diminutive Englishman leading Britain's Arab allies in a series of daring – and successful – guerrilla raids against the Turks, all in the promise of an independent Arab homeland in Syria when the war was over.

At war's end, however, it became known that Britain had signed a secret wartime treaty with France in which the two nations agreed to carve up between them Turkish possessions in the Middle East. Under the treaty, France was to receive Syria, which the Arabs had helped conquer during the war and fully expected to be within their homeland. Lawrence was dismayed at Britain's betrayal of its original promise to the Arabs. At a private ceremony with King George V at Buckingham Palace, where he was about to receive a DSO and the Order of the Bath, Lawrence unexpectedly refused the decorations. Surprised, the king was left, in his own words, 'holding the box in my hand'. Later, Lawrence told Winston Churchill that the refusal was the only way he knew to make the king aware of what had been done in his name.

In 1919 Lawrence, dressed once again in Arab attire, attended the Versailles Peace Conference to argue the Arab case, but the post-war settlement endorsed the Syrian mandate in France. For a while,

Lawrence worked as an advisor on Middle Eastern matters to Churchill at the Colonial Office, but with the cause betrayed in which he had invested so much of himself and for which he had become a legend, he found the hero's role impossible to sustain.

Seeking anonymity and perhaps the comradeship of his war years – and no doubt as atonement for what he considered his failure – Lawrence abruptly gave up public life in 1922 and under a pseudonym enlisted as a recruit in the Royal Air Force. His cover soon blown by an attentive press, he joined the Tank Corps as a private. He returned to the air force as T.E. Shaw, serving for a time in Karachi where he translated *The Odyssey*. In 1926 *The Seven Pillars of Wisdom*, his account of the Arab Revolt, was published in a limited edition. In time it would be acknowledged a great classic of war writing. Lawrence left military service in 1935 to live in Dorset.

Among those who attended his funeral were Winston Churchill and the poet Siegfried Sassoon. King George V wrote to Lawrence's brother: 'Your brother's name will live in history and the King gratefully recognises his distinguished services to his country and feels that it is tragic that the end should have come in this manner to a life so full of promise.'

Other action this day

1643: Louis of Bourbon-Condé (Le Grand Condé) defeats the Spanish at the Battle of Rocroi, destroying Spanish military supremacy in Europe * 1692: A French fleet, seeking to cover an invasion of England by a French army to restore James II to the throne, is intercepted and defeated by an Anglo-Dutch fleet off Cap Barfleur in the English Channel * 1804: Napoleon creates the first eighteen of 26 Napoleonic marshals of France, including Augereau, Bernadotte, Berthier, Bessières, Davout, Jourdan, Kellerman, Lannes, Lefebvre, Masséna, Mortier, Murat, Ney and Soult; Grouchy will be the last, elevated on 3 June 1815, fifteen days before Waterloo

20 May

Death of a revolutionary aristocrat

1834 Guess who died today. He:

- was an American major general at the age of nineteen.
- once wrote to George Washington that 'I always consider myself, my dear General, as one of your lieutenants on a detached command.'
- fought with distinction at the Battle of Brandywine (see 11 September).
- entrapped the army of British commander Lord Cornwallis at the American Revolution's final battle at Yorktown.
- was spirited, energetic and enthusiastic, but, according to James Madison, had 'a strong thirst of praise and popularity'.
- arrived in America for the Revolution in his own private brig.

If you haven't guessed yet, he also:

- became a French *maréchal de camp* (brigadier general) at 25.
- had Louis XVI brought back from his flight to Varennes.
- drafted the Rights of Man and presented it to the French National Assembly.
- ordered the final demolition of the Bastille after 14 July.
- created the modern French flag by combining the blue and red of Paris with the Bourbon royal white.
- at the age of 73, commanded the French National Guard that helped oust King Charles X and bring Louis-Philippe to the throne.

The answer is Marie-Joseph-Paul-Yves-Roch-Gilbert du Motier, the marquis de Lafayette, revolutionary aristocrat in both France and America, who died today in Paris at the age of 76.

Although he was laid to rest in the Cimetière de Picpus in Paris, Lafayette was, literally, buried in American soil. When he left the United States after the American Revolution, he had become such a fervent Americanophile that he carried with him enough earth to fill a grave. As he had wished, he was buried in it.

1217: William Marshal, 1st Earl of Pembroke, defeats Prince Louis (the future Louis VIII) of France at the Second Battle of Lincoln, called the 'Lincoln Fair' because after the battle the English troops sack the town, slaughtering women and children, because the town had sided with Louis * 1521: Ignatius Loyola is wounded while fighting for the losing side in the Battle of Pamplona between Spanish and French troops * 1631: After a five-month siege, the Protestant city of Magdeburg falls to Imperial generals Tilly and Pappenheim, whose troops run riot and massacre 25,000 of its 30,000 inhabitants * 1802: Consul Napoleon Bonaparte creates France's highest award, the Légion d'Honneur (Legion of Honour), about which he once sardonically commented: 'A soldier will fight long and hard for a bit of coloured ribbon.' * 1941: German paratroops invade Crete

21 May

'Veni, vidi, vici'

47 BC First civil war had engulfed the Roman world, and then, after defeating Pompey, Julius Caesar had sailed to Egypt for his famous affair with Cleopatra. During this turmoil, King Pharnaces of the Bosporan Kingdom in the Crimea had taken advantage of Rome's preoccupations to grab more territory.

Pharnaces quickly subdued Cappadocia, Colchis and Lesser Armenia, but apparently had forgotten – or discounted – that these small kingdoms were under Rome's protection. Soon Caesar's general Domitius Calvinus was marching to their relief, but Pharnaces easily routed him at Nicopolis and then conquered the Roman-allied Kingdom of Pontus in north-east Anatolia, where once his father Mithridates IV had ruled. But instead of befriending his father's former subjects, he sold most of them into slavery and ordered the castration of any Roman male civilian he captured.

Now Caesar, breaking off his idyll in Egypt, headed for Anatolia with four legions to show Pharnaces the folly of challenging Rome.

Learning of Caesar's approach, Pharnaces entreated him to come not as an enemy but as a friend. Caesar's response was to demand Pharnaces' immediate withdrawal from Pontus, the return of all captives and loot, and an enormous sum in tribute. Meanwhile, the Roman legions continued their inexorable advance, soon nearing Zela (now Zile in Turkey), a place of ill omen because Mithridates had defeated a Roman army there twenty years before. Pharnaces had built a fortified camp on a ridge three miles from the town.

Caesar camped with his troops about five miles away, and before daybreak the next day (21 May by our calendar, 2 August by the Roman calendar) he set out with his army, arriving at dawn on a hill two miles across a valley from the unsuspecting enemy. There he set about fortifying his position, leaving only his first line in order of battle.

When Pharnaces discovered the Roman force opposite him, he saw that only the first line was prepared for battle and, spurred on by favourable omens, ordered his infantry and scythed chariots into an immediate attack.

According to a report by one of Caesar's lieutenants, when Pharnaces' soldiers began crossing the valley towards the Roman position, 'Caesar at first laughed at his ostentation, in crowding his army into so narrow a place, where no enemy in his right mind would have ventured: in the meantime Pharnaces continued his march, and began to ascend the steep hill on which Caesar was posted.'

Astounded by Pharnaces' recklessness, Caesar called all his troops into action, ranging them in battle order.

Initially the Romans were disconcerted by the enemy's chariots, but they hurled volley after volley of *pila* (2-metre javelins) at the oncoming foe, hobbling their advance. Then the opposing armies closed with a shout, and Caesar's experienced 6th Legion on his right wing overpowered the enemy left. After giving stiff resistance, Pharnaces' centre and right began to fold under Roman pressure and fled down the slope and up towards their own defences, to be slain in great numbers by pursuing Romans: 'Our victorious men did not hesitate to advance up the unfavourable ground and attack their fortifications, which they soon forced, despite the resistance made by the troops left by Pharnaces to guard it. Almost the whole army was cut to pieces or made prisoners.'

While the Roman legionaries were ransacking Pharnaces' camp, Pharnaces himself managed to escape with some cavalry, but later the same year he was captured and put to death by one of his own governors.

Zela had been a spectacular victory; Caesar had won not just a battle but also a war in just four hours. He announced his great triumph in a letter to Rome in perhaps the most famous battle report in history: 'Veni, vidi, vici' – I came, I saw, I conquered.

Other action this day

1809: Austrian archduke Charles defeats Napoleon at the Battle of Aspern-Essling * 1863: 30,000 Union troops begin the successful 48-day siege of Port Hudson, Louisiana, against 6,500 Confederates * 1881: Clara Barton establishes the American Red Cross based on her experiences as a nurse during the American Civil War * 1916: The Battle of Jutland between Britain's 151-ship fleet and Germany's 99-ship fleet begins, the largest naval battle of the First World War, which ends the next day with a narrow German victory

22 May

The first battle of the Wars of the Roses

1455 Today the English royal army met that of the rebellious Richard, Duke of York, at St Albans, just north of London, in the first battle of that bloody internecine slaughter picturesquely called the Wars of the Roses.

Leading the royal army of perhaps 2,000 men was King Henry VI, son of the great warrior Henry V who had died without ever seeing his infant son. But Henry VI was the very opposite of his cold and belligerent father. A studious and pious loner, who just five months earlier had suffered a nervous breakdown, he was dominated by his wife, the ambitious Margaret of Anjou.

At the head of an enemy force some 6,000 strong was Richard, Duke of York, supported by the Earls of Salisbury and Warwick, the latter known to history as Warwick the Kingmaker (see 22 November).

There was a legitimate question whether Henry or Richard had the better right to the throne, for both men claimed it through descent from Edward III. The House of Lancaster now held it only because Henry's grandfather Henry IV had usurped it from the hapless Richard II.

But Richard of York had no real desire to make himself king. The conflict stemmed from the anarchy caused during Henry VI's long minority, when every baron maintained a private army in a lawless country. During one of Henry's fits of insanity Richard had become protector of the realm, but Henry's wife Margaret had forced him out when Henry regained his senses. Hated by Margaret, Richard feared for his position, his wealth and his head, and took up arms in self-defence.

As the armies jockeyed for position around St Albans, Richard sent word offering to negotiate, swearing fealty to the king. Perhaps enraged by his subject's refusal to submit instantly, Henry sent back a message vowing to hang, draw and quarter any who questioned his authority. Now battle became inevitable.

Richard's first two charges were bloodily repulsed as the king's forces defended themselves behind hastily erected barricades in the town's narrow streets. Warwick then led his troop through unguarded back alleys until he reached the market square, where he found the bulk of the king's troops unprepared for battle, some not even wearing their helmets. Warwick's immediate attack scattered the defenders, and his archers killed several of the king's bodyguard, grazing Henry in the neck. Outflanked, the Lancastrians fled from the town, leaving about 60 dead behind. With his army in flight, Henry could only surrender to the Yorkists. The whole battle had lasted less than an hour.

Now in full command, Richard allowed Henry to remain king, subject to his control, but the uncertain peace lasted only until 1458. The terrible dynastic brawl continued to drench England in blood for 30 years, until the pivotal Battle of Bosworth Field ended the struggle of rival Plantagenets and Henry VII, the last representative of the House of Lancaster, founded the Tudor dynasty (see 22 August).

According to Shakespeare, the Wars of the Roses gained its name one day when Richard of York was walking in the garden of the Inns of Temple in London, where he encountered one of King Henry's advisers, the Duke of Somerset. During an argument, Somerset picked a red rose from a bush, saying: 'Let all of my party wear this flower!' In retort, Richard simply plucked a white rose to represent the House of York.

Although Shakespeare's version is apocryphal, the white rose was certainly one of the symbols of the House of York. Historians disagree, however, on the red rose. Some say it was originally a symbol of Henry's great-grandfather John of Gaunt, while others insist that it was assumed by the House of Lancaster by Henry VII only after the wars were over. In any case, the actual nomenclature – the 'Wars of the Roses' – was coined only in 1829 when Sir Walter Scott used it in his novel *Anne of Geierstein*.

Other action this day

AD 337: Roman emperor and general Constantine the Great dies at Ancyrona in Bythnia (now Turkey) ✳ 1176: Hashshashin assassins try and fail to murder Saracen commander Saladin during the siege of Aleppo ✳ 1939: Italian foreign minister Count Galeazzo Ciano and his German counterpart, Joachim von Ribbentrop, sign a 'Pact of Steel', guaranteeing full military support should either country go to war

23 May

Marlborough wins at Ramillies

1706 The idea of English soldiers fighting on Belgian soil makes one think of Waterloo or the organised butchery of the First World War. But on this sunny Sunday three centuries ago John Churchill, Duke of Marlborough achieved one of his greatest triumphs when he led his allies to victory over the French at Ramillies in Belgium (then called the Spanish Netherlands).

This great battle took place during the War of the Spanish Succession, when France's Louis XIV was fighting to keep his grandson on the throne of Spain, against violent opposition from all over Europe, where governments feared that this would lead to France and Spain united under a single monarch.

Marlborough commanded an Allied force of 62,000 British, Dutch, Austrians, Hanoverians, Prussians, Danes and a few Swiss. Leading the French was the duc de Villeroi, with 60,000 French and Bavarians. The Allied force had an advantage in artillery, with 120 guns and mortars compared to 70 pieces for the enemy.

The first fighting of the day – really just a skirmish – took place at eight in the morning when French hussars encountered an Allied scouting party of dragoons under Earl Cadogan, but after a few volleys from each side the French pulled back. Continuing to reconnoitre enemy positions, Cadogan soon sighted the main French line and galloped back to inform Marlborough. Unwisely, Villeroi had thinly deployed his force in a slightly concave formation along the entire length of a four-mile ridge, on either side of the villages of Ramillies and Offus.

Shortly before noon Marlborough brought his army up into line of battle, and an hour later his artillery opened up, just before British, Dutch and German regiments of foot attacked the enemy left flank. This assault was so successful that Villeroi was forced to reinforce his flank with troops pulled from his centre.

Perceiving Villeroi's now weakened middle, Marlborough moved to attack it. He shifted half the battalions and his cavalry from his right into the centre, their route masked from the French by the hilly terrain and the smoke of battle.

When his cavalry arrived, Marlborough himself plunged into the fight but was set upon by some French dragoons and thrown from his horse when it stumbled. Seeing him fall, a general commanding two Swiss battalions was able to push the enemy back and save his commander, but when an equerry brought up one of Marlborough's spare horses, he was beheaded by a cannonball while helping the duke to mount.

Now Marlborough sent Danish cavalry to sweep around and through Villeroi's right flank while the concentrated Allied infantry, supported by British cavalry, attacked the vulnerable French centre. When Villeroi belatedly tried to reinforce this weak spot with troops from his unengaged left, they became enmeshed with the baggage carts left behind the lines. Then, as the centre started to implode, the whole French/Bavarian force began to crumble, many fleeing the field, others asking for quarter. A retreat became a rout, and Allied cavalry pursued escaping enemy soldiers until Marlborough called them back at midnight.

The tally for the defeated French and Bavarians was appalling – 12,000 casualties plus 7,000 captured and 52 cannon lost, compared to a mere 1,100 dead and 2,600 wounded for the Allies. When he heard the news of this shattering loss, an offended Louis XIV complained: 'God seems to have forgotten all that I have done for him.'

A few days after the battle, Marlborough celebrated the victory in Brussels, toasting the English–Austrian candidate for the Spanish throne, 'Charles III'. But in spite of Ramillies (and of Blenheim which had preceded it – see 13 August), Louis's grandson remained King of Spain as Philip V.

Other action this day

1430: Joan of Arc is captured by the Burgundians during the siege of Compiègne * 1568: The Dutch win the Battle of Heiligerlee, the first battle of the Eighty Years War, the revolt by the Netherlands against Spanish rule * 1618: The Second Defenestration of Prague: Bohemian rebels throw representatives of Holy Roman Emperor Matthias from the first-floor windows of the Hradcany Palace in Prague to spark the Thirty Years War * 1945: While in British custody in Lüneburg in northern Germany, Heinrich Himmler commits suicide by biting into a hidden cyanide capsule while being searched by a British doctor

24 May

A temporary victory: the Bismarck sinks the Hood

1941 Just after dawn this Saturday, a brief but significant naval action took place in the Atlantic Ocean, just south of the Denmark Strait between Greenland and Iceland. In less than ten minutes of combat, the German battleship *Bismarck*, the world's most heavily armoured vessel, sank the battlecruiser HMS *Hood*, the Royal Navy's largest ship.

The *Bismarck*, pride of Hitler's fleet, had left the Baltic Sea five days earlier on her first mission of the war, to join the effort to defeat Great Britain by destroying the convoys that brought vital supplies across the Atlantic. Accompanied by the cruiser *Prinz Eugen*, she sailed for Bergen, a move to which the British Admiralty was alerted by Enigma decrypts. Two days later, the two German ships left Bergen heading north-westwards into the Atlantic, now shadowed by two British cruisers.

Emerging at dawn today from the Denmark Strait, the *Bismarck* and the *Prinz Eugen* found themselves facing a powerful British force sent to intercept them, headed by the *Hood* and the battleship *Prince of Wales*. Salvoes were quickly exchanged, both German ships concentrating their fire on the *Hood*. One of the German shells penetrated the *Hood*'s armour to reach a magazine holding 300 tons of high explosives. A violent explosion split the ship in two. She sank within minutes, leaving only three members of her 1,500-man crew to survive.

The *Prince of Wales* now took heavy fire from her opponents and was quickly forced to withdraw behind a smokescreen, but not before inflicting two hits on the *Bismarck*. The German ships steamed away westwards, still shadowed by British cruisers.

The sinking of the *Hood* was a shocking loss to Britain. It was also a glorious beginning to the *Bismarck*'s war career, and Joseph Goebbels, the Nazi propaganda minister, made sure news of the event was broadcast around the world.

The British Admiralty now gathered all available forces to find, meet and destroy this powerful threat. Battleships, aircraft carriers, cruisers, destroyers and aircraft were summoned from as far away as Scapa Flow, Halifax, Novia Scotia and Gibraltar. The chase was on. C.S. Forester described it as 'a pursuit without precedent in the history of navies'.

Not many hours later, the *Prinz Eugen* left her partner to refuel and head for the French port of Brest. For the next three days, in thick weather and heavy seas, the *Bismarck* attempted to give her pursuers the slip. At times she was completely lost to them, but contact was always re-established – by radar, by aircraft sighting, by radio signal – and it became clear she was headed eastwards for Brest and German air cover. She was also leaking oil, caused by a shell from the *Prince of Wales*. Then torpedo aircraft from the carrier *Ark Royal*, approaching from the south, scored two hits, one that damaged her rudders and propellers, forcing her to steer for a while in circles, and slowing her speed to ten knots.

At last, on the morning of the 27th the net of her pursuers had closed in and blocked her passage eastwards. She was now an easy target for the approaching battleships *Rodney* and *King George V*, whose heavy fire – some 700 shells – finally silenced the battered hulk, now on fire. Two torpedo hits from a cruiser were the *coup de grâce*. At 10.40am the *Bismarck* capsized and sank. All but 100 of her 2,000-man crew went down with her.

Neither the sinking of the *Hood*, nor that of the *Bismarck* three days later, did much in itself to change the course of the war. They were simply dramatic episodes in the long Battle of the Atlantic. Taken together, however, the two deeds – bold thrust and forceful response – illustrated Britain's need – and her ability – to remain in command of the Atlantic sea lanes.

More than many in his neutral nation, President Franklin D. Roosevelt understood the significance of what had occurred over the past five days. Hearing news of the battle's outcome only hours after the event, he had cabled Prime Minister Churchill: 'I hope you will like my speech tonight. … All of us are made very happy by the fine tracking down of the *Bismarck*.'

Addressing his radio audience that evening in a scheduled 'fireside chat', Roosevelt warned that the war 'is coming very close to home'; that an Axis victory in the Atlantic would be a grave threat to the interests and security of the United States; and that greater American involvement must follow if the necessary supplies were to reach Britain. Heard over radios in Britain early in the morning of 28 May, the president's address was welcomed for its directness and its timing.

So it was that just five weeks after the *Bismarck* sank, 4,400 US Marines were dispatched to Iceland to establish a base from which US naval forces could extend their protection of convoys steaming across the Atlantic for Great Britain.

Other action this day

15 BC: Roman general Germanicus is born * 1218: The calamitous Fifth Crusade leaves Acre for Egypt, during which the Crusaders eventually surrender to Egyptian sultan Al-Kamil * 1943: Josef Mengele becomes chief medical officer at Auschwitz

25 May

The Mongols obliterate the Jin in China

1233 Today the unstoppable Mongol armies of Ögedei Khan marched into Pien (modern Kaifeng), the capital of the Jin dynasty that ruled north-eastern China. It not only sounded the death knell for the Jin but was also a major step in a war of conquest that, 46 years later, would see Mongol subjugation of all of China.

The Jin had first come to power in Manchuria in 1115 and twelve years later had pushed into China, sacking Pien, then the capital of the Song dynasty that had conquered China in AD 960. Although most of the Jin's realm was now in China proper, they continued to use their own language and alphabet and banned Chinese clothing in their armies, in which they instilled a fierce warrior discipline. During the next twenty years some 3 million of the Jin moved into their conquered territory, ruling over 30 million Chinese.

But in the beginning of the 13th century the Mongol chieftain Genghis Khan was gathering the reins of power over all of Mongolia. A ferocious warrior, he hammered together an unstoppable army, ordering every soldier, with his family and possessions, to be assigned to a particular unit and forbidden to leave it on pain of death.

In 1206 Genghis attacked the Jin's western neighbour, the Western Xia dynasty, in north-west China, completely overwhelming it three years later. Next he set his sights directly on the Jin.

In 1211 Genghis led some 110,000 soldiers, mostly cavalry, through the Changbai mountains and descended into Jin territory, where he scored a massive victory at a spot called Badger Pass when a Jin messenger defected with his army's battle position. By 1215 he had besieged, captured and sacked the Jin capital at Zhongdu (now Beijing), forcing the Jin emperor to abandon the northern half of his kingdom to the Mongols and move his capital to Pien, the same city the Jin had pillaged 88 years before.

During the next decade Genghis focused his main efforts elsewhere, particularly against the empire of the Khwarezm shahs in Persia, while leaving the subjugation of the Jin to his general Muqali. The Jin somehow managed to hold out, and then in 1227 Genghis died (see 18 August), to be succeeded by his son Ögedei. In 1230 Ögedei renewed the onslaught on the Jin but initially met stiff resistance. In 1233, however, he swept the Jin armies from the field and entered the Jin capital at Pien almost unopposed, as the Jin emperor Aizong fled the city. Pursued by the Mongols, he committed suicide a year later to avoid capture, the ninth and last Jin emperor.

So ended the Jin empire after over a century in power. Perhaps the best testimony to the Jin's military prowess was the undying respect of the invading Mongols, who were amazed at the valour of the Jin warriors who had held out for seven years after the death of Genghis Khan. (The Jin may have been shattered, but their descendants, the Manchus, established the Qing dynasty that ruled China five centuries later.)

The Mongols, however, were far from finished. Although Ögedei died in 1241, his sons continued to conquer for the next half a century, annexing all of China, turning Korea into a vassal state, taking over Persia, and later conquering almost all of Russia, Hungary and Poland to create the largest contiguous empire the world has yet known.

Other action this day

1085: Alfonso the Brave (VI) of Castile retakes Toledo from the Moors * 1734: The Spanish defeat the Austrians at the Battle of Bitonto during the War of the Polish Succession * 2000: The Israeli army withdraws from occupied territories in Lebanon after 22 years of occupation; this date is now celebrated as Liberation Day in Lebanon

26 May

Sacrifice at Calais

1940 Today, after four days of gritty resistance against a vastly larger and more powerful German army, the last defenders of Calais finally threw down their arms. Only yesterday Winston Churchill had signalled to his besieged forces: 'Every hour you continue to exist is of the greatest help to the BEF [British Expeditionary Force]. Government has therefore decided you must continue to fight ... Evacuation will not (*repeat* not) take place.' But the defenders had been overwhelmed, and now those of the 3,000 British and 800 French soldiers who remained alive would be carted off to POW camps, some, like the British commander Brigadier Claude Nicholson, to die there. It was a heavy price, but the sacrifice at Calais had bought the time for the BEF to reach Dunkirk 27 miles up the coast and make their dramatic escape – or had it?

On 20 May General Heinz Guderian's tanks had reached Abbeville on the Somme, cutting off the BEF's lines of supply. Two days later the first British units arrived at Calais to establish new supply lines. The next day three squadrons of tanks ventured five miles south of the port but ran into the German 1st Panzer Division that had been ordered to head for Dunkirk but to try to capture Calais as they went past. After a brief engagement, the British pulled back, but not before the Germans realised they would have to leave Calais for other German units to take.

At 2.00 the next morning, 24 May, the British made their first – and last – attempt to open supply lines to Dunkirk, but a squadron of tanks and a company of infantry were quickly forced back by stiff German resistance. And now the 10th Panzer Division of 15,000 men and about 150 tanks began to move on Calais, breaking through the city's outer perimeter despite fierce British and French resistance and naval gunfire from Royal Navy destroyers. By evening Brigadier Nicholson had been forced to move his HQ to the Gare Maritime on the waterfront. As the defenders huddled behind the bastions of the inner perimeter, many thought of England and hoped for deliverance by sea.

On the 25th the German Panzers struck once more, hammering the inner perimeter, but the defenders, although down to two anti-tank guns and two light anti-aircraft guns, managed to hold on. Now Nicholson moved his HQ one last time, to the citadel, a medieval stronghold on the west side of the town, where he twice rejected German calls for surrender.

That evening Churchill and his war secretary Anthony Eden and Field Marshal Edmund Ironside mulled the terrible dilemma they faced: if the British and French troops in Calais were to be saved, their only hope was evacuation, but if the fighting ended in Calais, the German units there could move up the coast to attack the BEF's west flank at Gravelines, just sixteen miles away. So it was, with terrible misgivings, that Churchill sent his final message: there would be no evacuation.

Now, as the final day of the battle dawned, Stuka dive bombers took up the attack while mortars hammered British and French positions. Then came the German tanks and infantry. The bloodied defenders now had neither tanks nor anti-tank guns nor artillery, but still they fought. Finally the French surrendered Fort Risban, and then at 11.00am the last bastion of the inner perimeter raised the white flag. Six hours later German infantry seized the citadel, and

Nicholson was taken prisoner. The very last fighting took place in the old fisherman's quarter, where at 9.00pm British soldiers were ordered to split up into small groups and try to escape the town. Almost none succeeded.

So the battle for Calais came to an end, with 300 British and French dead, 200 wounded (only these had been evacuated) and the remainder captured. During the fighting they had inflicted over 1,000 German casualties.

As regrettable as it was to have left the defenders to their fate, the British high command long believed their sacrifice had helped make possible the 'miracle of Dunkirk'. Only British and French resistance at Calais, they thought, had stopped the Germans from sweeping into Dunkirk before the BEF got there. It was only after the war that they learned that what stopped the Germans was not Calais but Hitler's inexplicable order of 24 May that not only halted the advance but called German forces back to a line running south from Gravelines, just as Guderian was about to drive on Dunkirk.

Other action this day

1521: Spanish troops under Hernán Cortés attack the Aztec capital Tenochtitlan, which they will capture on 13 August * 1644: The Portuguese defeat the Spaniards at the Battle of Montijo during the Portuguese Restoration War * 1650: John Churchill, the future Duke of Marlborough, is born at Axminster in Devon * 1859: Italian volunteers under Giuseppe Garibaldi defeat the Austrians at the Battle of Varese during the Austro-Sardinian War

27 May

The last ride of SS3

1942 Today two Free Czech agents ambushed Reinhard Heydrich as he rode in his open car through the streets of Prague, eliminating one of the Third Reich's most malevolent leaders but bringing appalling reprisals from Czechoslovakia's German occupiers.

Heydrich was a picture-postcard Nazi – blond, arrogant, intelligent and totally ruthless. According to the German intelligence chief

Walter Schellenberg, 'His unusual intellect was matched by the ever-watchful instincts of a predatory animal'.

Heydrich was both brutal and brave; he claimed to have killed his first man at fifteen, fighting Communists in the streets of his home town of Halle. Later, in Russia, he took unauthorised flights over enemy territory, was shot down and survived for two days on his own before being rescued.

In 1931, when he was 27, Heydrich had joined the SD (Sicher-heitsdienst – intelligence service) of Himmler's SS, the first step in his meteoric rise in the Nazi ranks. He was a key figure in the planning of the 'Night of the Long Knives' when the SS exterminated its rival the SA, and he sent thousands of Jews to concentration camps during Kristallnacht. Later he supplied bogus evidence that triggered Stalin's purge of his officer corps (see 12 June) and masterminded the fake 'Polish' border attack, Hitler's pretext for invading Poland.

In 1939 Heydrich headed the combined SD, Gestapo, and Criminal Police. In Poland he formed Einsatz (Special Action) Groups to round up and shoot leading citizens and crammed over 2 million Jews into ghettos, where half a million died from starvation and disease.

Two years later he was appointed Reichsprotektor (read military dictator) of Bohemia and Moravia (roughly, Czechoslovakia). Four months into the job he took a few days off to chair the infamous Wannsee Conference that set in motion the Endlösung, the Final Solution. He was still only 37.

During Heydrich's reign, Czechoslovakia was outwardly peaceful, but beneath the surface hatred for the occupiers continued to simmer. Now the Czech government in exile in London determined to act.

Working with Britain's SOE (Special Operations Executive – a group responsible for orchestrating espionage and sabotage), the Czechs launched Operation Anthropoid – Heydrich's assassination – assigning Jozef Gabčík and Jan Kubiš to lead the mission.

On 28 December 1941, the two men and five other Czechs parachuted into Czechoslovakia from an RAF bomber and made their way to Prague.

There Gabčík and Kubiš learned that, in a display of fearless arrogance, every day Heydrich took the same route from his home to his office in an open-topped black Mercedes that sported small swastika flags on both front wings and bore the licence plate SS3.

The two Czechs planned to strike on a hairpin bend that would force Heydrich's car to slow down. There on this morning they waited for their quarry, Gabčík concealing a Sten sub-machine gun under his raincoat, Kubiš carrying a modified anti-tank grenade in his briefcase.

At 10.30 the black Mercedes slowed to round the curve, Heydrich in a green uniform in the front passenger seat. Gabčík stepped into the road, levelled his Sten and pulled the trigger – and nothing happened. The gun had jammed. Heydrich shouted to his driver to stop and stood in his seat, drawing his pistol. At that moment Kubiš pitched his grenade, which exploded with a mighty roar, spraying shrapnel into the car and wounding Heydrich in his left side. Kubiš was also injured by the blast, and both he and Gabčík started to flee.

Ignoring his injuries, Heydrich leaped from the mangled car, fired several shots and then collapsed. His driver pursued the Czechs, but Gabčík shot him twice in the leg with his pistol as he and his partner ran from the scene.

At a nearby hospital Heydrich was operated on for damage to his diaphragm, lung and spleen. At first he seemed on the road to recovery, but then septicaemia set in. On 2 June he slipped into a coma, and at 4.30am on 4 June he died.

Even before Heydrich was dead, the Germans had launched savage reprisals, with 21,000 policemen and soldiers searching for the assassins all over Prague. Over 3,000 people were arrested, of whom 1,357 were executed. An additional 637 died under Gestapo interrogation. Then, six days after Heydrich expired, on Hitler's personal order, German soldiers and members of the SD surrounded the nearby village of Lidice, shot all 172 men and sent the women to Ravensbrück concentration camp. The town was then razed to the ground.

Despite this pitiless retribution, the Germans failed to track down Heydrich's actual killers, who had concealed themselves with five others in the Church of Saints Cyril and Methodius in Prague. In mid-June, however, a turncoat Czech partisan betrayed them for 1 million Reichsmarks in blood money.

At 4.10 in the morning of 18 June, 700 SS troops surrounded the church. For two long hours the Czechs traded shot for shot, killing fourteen and wounding 21. In the end, the Germans stormed the church – only to find six corpses. Two defenders had been killed and four, including Gabčík, had shot themselves rather than be captured. The only survivor was Kubiš, who had been severely wounded by a grenade and died as he arrived at the hospital.

Other action this day

1508: Captured by Louis XII at the siege of Novara, the Duke of Milan, Ludovico Sforza, dies after eight years in a French prison at Loches * 1860: Garibaldi lays siege to Palermo in his invasion of Sicily * 1905: The Japanese fleet sinks six Russian battleships, four cruisers and seven destroyers and captures two battleships and two destroyers at the two-day Battle of Tsushima

28 May

Cantigny – America's first major battle in the First World War

1918 At 05.45 today, elements of the US 1st Infantry Division – the Big Red One – launched a surprise attack against the German line, cutting out a salient and seizing the town of Cantigny. Supported by French tanks and artillery, three battalions of the 28th Infantry Regiment advanced a mile into what had been German-held territory, taking some 240 prisoners and suffering only light casualties. Later in the day, with two more regiments brought forward to strengthen the position, the division withstood five determined counter-attacks, losing almost 1,000 men in the process but inflicting almost double that number on the attackers.

The action at Cantigny was the first major combat operation conducted by American troops in the First World War. For the Americans fighting in France, whose leadership and battle-readiness had been questioned by their French and British allies, Cantigny was a major test of military prowess. Trumpeting the victory, General John J. Pershing, commander-in-chief of the American Expeditionary Force, said that it proved 'our troops are the best in Europe'.

Not everyone among the Allied war-planners agreed with Pershing's assessment. And yet, however one rated it, Cantigny became the first step towards the realisation of an important American war goal: the establishment of an independent fighting force. 'In military operations against the Imperial German Government,' Pershing's orders read, 'you are directed to co-operate with the forces of the other countries employed against that enemy; but in so doing the underlying idea must be kept in view that the forces of the United States are a separate and distinct component of the combined forces, the identity of which must be preserved.'

The first American troops – infantry units – began arriving in France in June 1917, just two months after the United States declared war on the Central Powers. By the end of the year, there were nearly 200,000 'doughboys' on the Western Front. As the divisions arrived, they were quickly amalgamated into French and British corps for training. The newcomers lacked almost everything from artillery to transport to aircraft, wrote the British historian John Terraine, 'except enthusiasm and numbers'.

But it was their enthusiasm and numbers that counted most at this critical juncture of the war. The Central Powers, suffering badly under the Allied naval blockade of Europe, needed a decisive victory in 1918 to win the war. With Russia fallen from the Allied ranks since the end of 1917, Germany began transferring divisions from the Eastern Front to France, in order to launch a new series of spring offensives ahead of the American build-up. But it was the Allies who won the manpower race, for by the summer of 1918, some 250,000 American troops were arriving in France each month.

Following the Big Red One's success at Cantigny came favourable actions by other American divisions at Château Thierry, Belleau Wood, and the Marne. Then, in the big Aisne–Marne offensive of July, which blunted the last of the German offensives, eight US divisions totalling 270,000 men fought as parts of three French armies, contributing almost 25 per cent of the troops involved. Meanwhile, Pershing never forgot his orders. So it was that in August, after acrimonious wrangling at the highest levels, Pershing won the reluctant agreement of his fellow Allied commanders – General Haig of Great Britain and Marshals Foch and Pétain of France – to gather fourteen of the 25 American divisions in France and form the 1st United States Army. It was an achievement that Premier Clemenceau of France sourly ascribed to Pershing's 'invincible obstinacy'.

Now the tide of war had turned. In September this new army took a major role in the Allied advances in the St Mihiel and Meuse–Argonne sectors. In October, the 2nd United States Army was formed, and Pershing became an army group commander, joining Pétain and Haig in that elevated status. By this time, there were over 1,200,000 American troops in France.

In early November, with final victory almost assured, the supreme Allied commander, Marshal Foch, paid tribute to the Americans: 'Certainly the American Army is a young army, but it is full of idealism and strength and ardour. It has already won victories and is now on the eve of another victory; and nothing gives wings to an army like victory.'

As to whether the first American victory at Cantigny measured up to Pershing's fevered description, the man who planned the assault, the 1st Infantry Division's operations officer, Lieutenant Colonel George C. Marshall, Jr, who would one day become the US Army's chief of staff and later American secretary of state, had a different view. He described the action that day as a 'small incident'.

Other action this day

585 BC: After six years of war, the Medes and Lydians abruptly disengage at the Battle of the Halys River when a solar eclipse takes place, believing it to indicate that the gods want the fighting to stop ∗ 1644: The Bolton Massacre: a Royalist army under Prince Rupert of the Rhine storms the city of Bolton and slaughters 1,600 defenders and citizens ∗ 1754: Lieutenant Colonel George Washington leads the Virginia militia to victory over a French reconnaissance party in the Battle of Jumonville Glen in the French and Indian War; after the battle, Washington loses control of his troops and they butcher their prisoners, killing all but one of the wounded

29 May

Constantinople falls to the Turk – the end of the Middle Ages

1453 Tradition says that today marked the end of the Middle Ages, as Constantinople finally fell to the Turkish forces of Sultan Mehmed II, the Conqueror.

The siege had started in February, when the Byzantine emperor Constantine XI Palaeologus tried to defend the city with only 10,000 troops against a Turkish army of 150,000 men.

In spite of their numbers, the Turks made little headway during the first months of the siege. Constantinople's massive stone walls, 25 feet high and studded with square towers, seemed unbreachable and a great iron chain shut the Turkish fleet out of the Golden Horn, the narrow body of water forming the north boundary of the old city. Finally, however, Mehmed had 70 of his ships dragged overland from the Bosphorus to the Golden Horn, forcing Constantine to fight on two fronts. Even then the defenders held firm, despite Mehmed's intimidating practice of impaling the occasional prisoner.

But then nature came to the aid of the attackers. Back in the 15th century, all believed in signs and portents, and during the preceding months exceptionally explosive thunderstorms had pummelled the city. By their abstruse calculations Byzantine astrologers took this to signify that Constantinople would hold out against attack. But on 22 May came a very different omen: the moon entered an eclipse so that all that was visible was a thin crimson sickle – the very image of the Turkish crescent moon emblazoned on Mehmed's banners.

Four days later another ominous sign appeared. A dense fog enveloped the city, and when it started to lift, the refracted evening sunlight was reflected in the city's windows and on the great copper dome of the Hagia Sophia church, making it appear to be wreathed in flame. As the Byzantines began to lose heart, Mehmed's men gained confidence. The Turkish sultan ordered three days of massive cannon bombardment, and on 29 May his inspired troops stormed the Romanos Gate to enter the city.

In despair at his plight, Emperor Constantine cried out: 'Is there no Christian to cut off my head?' His own men refused, but shortly Turkish soldiers dispatched him. Mehmed ordered his head to be severed from his corpse and displayed to those few Greeks who had survived the slaughter. He subsequently gave Constantine an honourable burial. The Byzantine empire was no more, and Constantinople was lost for ever to Christendom just 1,123 years after the first Emperor Constantine – the man who legalised Christianity across the Roman empire – had made it his capital.

AD 363: Roman emperor Julian the Apostate defeats the Sassanid (Persian) army at the Battle of Ctesiphon * 1167: With an army of only 1,600 men, Holy Roman Emperor Frederick Barbarossa defeats a Roman army of 10,000 at the Battle of Monte Porzio * 1176: Holy Roman Emperor Frederick Barbarossa is decisively defeated by the Lombard League at the Battle of Legnano near Milan * 1798: British soldiers cut down about 350 surrendering Irishmen during the Irish Rebellion of 1798 at the Gibbet Rath massacre

30 May

The death of a valiant soldier

1431 Today the enemy killed a courageous French warrior who had fought in almost a dozen battles during a year of war against the English and their Burgundian allies. But death came not from the steel of sword or lance or the swift flight of an arrow but in the agony of fire. Burned at the stake for leading inspired resistance against the enemy, this brave captain was no seasoned soldier but a nineteen-year-old girl. She was Joan of Arc.

Joan's astonishing story took place in the midst of the Hundred Years War. English barons were trying to put their boy-king Henry VI on the throne of France, as stipulated by the treaty that his father, Henry V, had forced on the French eleven years before. France's true king, Charles VII, had not been crowned because the English and Burgundians controlled much of the country, including Reims, the traditional place for the coronations of French kings.

Believing she was commanded by the 'voices' of St Michael, St Catherine and St Margaret, in early 1429 Joan set out from her home in Domrémy in the Vosges of eastern France, determined to come to the aid of her country. She famously recognised the disguised Charles at his fortress at Chinon, and persuaded him to fit her with armour and give her an army.

Her first and most famous military exploit came in May when she broke the English siege of Orléans; there she was wounded in the shoulder by an arrow but nonetheless led the final charge (see 8 May). In June came the conquest of Jargeau, where a cannonball grazed her helmet as she climbed a scaling ladder. Three days later with Joan in the forefront the French captured Meung-sur-Loire and two days after that, Beaugency. Then came the great French victory at Patay, although Joan's role there was minor. But this triumph was enough for the French to retake control of Reims, and on 17 July Charles was crowned there, with Joan in attendance.

The war, however, was not over. In August the French and English armies met at Senlis. Although there was no serious fighting, Joan inspired her companions by riding past the enemy position flourishing her banner painted with an image of Christ crucified. Shortly afterwards at Paris a crossbow bolt caught her in the leg, but she continued to lead her troops until they were forced to withdraw. Subsequently she led the assault on Saint-Pierre-le-Moûtier and after that conducted an unsuccessful month-long siege at La Charité-sur-Loire. Then, in April the next year, came Compiègne.

Compiègne was under siege from both the Burgundians and the English. On 22 May Joan entered the town under cover of darkness. The next day she was in the thick of the action, twice fighting off Burgundian attacks but at length forced to retreat. Perhaps foolishly, she remained with the rearguard and was captured when she was unhorsed and, weighted down with her armour, unable to remount.

Her Burgundian captors imprisoned her in a tower in Vermandois, where she tried to escape by leaping from a 70-foot tower into the soft earth of the dry moat below. She was instantly recaptured, and, in one of the most sordid bargains in history, the Burgundians sold her to the English for 16,000 francs.

Transferred to the English headquarters at Rouen, Joan faced her jailers with courage, defying them while showing her knowledge of English swear words: 'You think when you have killed me you will conquer France, but that you will never do. Even if there were a hundred thousand Goddammees more in France than there are, they will never conquer that kingdom.'

Although Joan was judged by the church, her trial was really a political one. To the English, Henry VI was France's rightful king, so to them Joan was guilty not only of fighting against her sovereign but also of playing a key role in getting the pretender Charles VII crowned at Reims.

Joan's trial took far longer than most in a day when justice rarely needed more than a few hours to reach its conclusion. The judges had first been assembled in February 1431, but under the leadership of the infamous Bishop of Beauvais, Pierre Cauchon, these ecclesiastical worthies required three months to find adequate proof against the religious innocent. On 29 May she was found guilty of witchcraft and heresy (although her principal offence was having defeated the English army). She was turned over to civil justice for her punishment, as the church itself could not or would not carry out the sentence.

Twenty-four hours later, on this Wednesday, Joan was brought to the old market place of Rouen, guarded by 700 soldiers. There three platforms had been erected, two for the judges and prelates, a third of plaster surmounted with a post with chains attached. Nailed atop the stake, a placard read: 'Heretic, Relapsed, Blasphemer, Idolatress.'

Joan remained the religious mystic until she died, claiming to the last her faith in the saintly voices that had directed her most of her life. After two soldiers had chained her to the stake, she asked for a cross, which one soldier made for her out of two small sticks. At about noon the fire was lit, and this brave young virgin died in agony. Her executioner threw her ashes into the Seine so that no relic might remain.

So ended the incredible story of an illiterate peasant girl from Domrémy who led an army, restored a king and changed the course of history.

Other action this day

1434: The major Hussite leaders are slain at the Battle of Lipany, ending the Hussite Wars in Bohemia * 1857: The 182-day siege of Lucknow begins during the Sepoy Revolt in India * 1859: Future Italian king Victor Emmanuel of Sardinia defeats the Austrians at the Battle of Palestro, telling his victorious soldiers: 'Do not fear: there is glory enough for all!'

31 May

A Mongol reconnaissance in force

1223 For over twenty years Genghis Khan had been slaughtering any who had opposed him (and indeed many who had not): first his fellow Mongols, then the Chinese, and then the Khwarezm (the

Khwarezm empire was in today's Turkmenistan and Uzbekistan). Now, moving westward through the Caucasus into southern Russia, it was the Russians' turn, although Genghis had given the task to two of his foremost generals, Subutai and Jebe, who led an armed reconnaissance of perhaps 40,000 horsemen. Today, at the Kalka River in the Ukraine, the Mongols and Russians came face to face on the battlefield.

The Mongols' initial target had been the Cumans, a tribal nation located north of the Black Sea. Hearing of the Mongol incursion, the Cumans joined forces with several Russian principalities, of which the most powerful was the Kievan Rus. By March 1223 the allies had started their preparations. Infantry and supplies came by boat down the Dnieper River, while cavalry trotted along its banks, headed for a rendezvous about 40 miles south of Kiev. Together, some 70–80,000 men were now ready to fight.

The Mongols, who were still on the east side of the Dnieper, had no quarrel with the Rus – their prey was the Cumans – so Jebe dispatched ten ambassadors to Prince Mstislav of Kiev to make peace with the Rus, promising not to raid their lands and offering bribes. But Mstislav was loyal to his alliance – or perhaps he welcomed war; he knew his forces outnumbered the Mongols by almost two to one. Whatever his motives, instead of reconciliation, he had Jebe's envoys executed. Now the Mongols declared war.

The alliance plan was to corner the invaders and annihilate them. Splitting their armies, they sent one up the Dnieper and another down it, with the Cumans trying to work their way around to the Mongols' rear.

When Jebe and Subutai learned of the Rus's movements, they headed east, away from the enemy, leaving a 1,000-man rearguard on the east bank of the river to monitor Rus movements. These troops, however, now became the target for the first Rus assault. Under heavy arrow fire, Mstislav crossed the Dnieper and overwhelmed them. Every soldier in the Mongol rearguard was slain. Soon the Rus had thrown up a bridge and more alliance soldiers were crossing the river.

It was now that Subutai hatched a daring plan. His aim was to draw the enemy army into the steppe, the treeless grassland favouring Mongol horse archers, fearsome warriors who each carried at least two bows and about 90 arrows. On the open steppe, this highly mobile Mongol cavalry could harass, encircle and finally obliterate the less agile Rus.

For nine days Subutai orchestrated a series of small attacks followed by feigned retreats, pulling back to the east about 50 miles and each time enticing the Rus to chase after him. At length the Mongols arrived at the Kalka River near modern-day Kharkov. Here on 31 May they turned to face their pursuers, hiding their movement by a screen of black smoke created by smudge pots.

A few Rus units broke even before battle was joined, and then the Mongol heavy cavalry thundered into the enemy ranks, driving the Cumans into full retreat. As the Cumans pulled back, Rus units opened a gap to let them through, but the Mongol horsemen galloped through the gap, breaking the Rus line. Then the Mongol light cavalry swept around the whole Rus army, loosing volley after volley of arrows, while the heavy cavalry continued their frontal assault.

Mstislav of Kiev and some of his army managed to cut their way through the encircling Mongols and retreated to a fortified camp on a hill by the Dnieper. After they had stubbornly held out there for three days, Subutai offered to let them return to Kiev unharmed on payment of a huge ransom. With little hope of fighting his way out and his water supplies running low, Mstislav agreed. But when he led his men from the camp, Subutai ordered a massive attack, killing most of the Rus and capturing Mstislav and five other Rus princes.

The battle had been a catastrophe for the Rus and their allies – casualty reports vary from 10,000 to 50,000 – while the Mongols lost only a few hundred. To celebrate, the Mongols chained Mstislav and the other captured princes under a giant platform on which Subutai, Jebe and their soldiers held their victory banquet, feasting and dancing while the prisoners were slowly asphyxiated.

When he heard of their overwhelming victory, Genghis Khan was full of praise for his generals, but he viewed the raid as a mere reconnaissance in force in preparation for a full-scale invasion in the future and did not follow up their triumph. Since Genghis died four years later, before he had been able to return, the Rus were momentarily spared. In 1237, however, his grandson Batu and Subutai invaded with an army of 120,000 men; by 1240 they had completed the conquest of Kievan Rus, the ancient capital at Kiev totally destroyed.

Other action this day

1864: Ulysses S. Grant's Union army loses 13,000 men as the North is held by Confederate general Robert E. Lee at the thirteen-day Battle of Cold Harbor, while on the same day Confederate troops halt Union general George McClellan's push towards Richmond on the outskirts of the city at the Battle of Seven Pines * 1902: The Peace of Vereeniging ends the Second Boer War, in which British casualties numbered 5,774 killed in action (plus 16,000 deaths from disease) against 4,000 Boer battle deaths and over 20,000 civilians dying in concentration camps

1 June

'Don't give up the ship!'

1813 Today a mortally wounded American naval captain earned immortality for himself by commanding his crew: 'Don't give up the ship!'

James Lawrence had been an unruly youth brought up in Burlington, New Jersey. At seventeen he joined the American navy and soon saw action against Barbary pirates. But it was in the War of 1812 against Great Britain that he gave his life and gained his fame.

When the war started the 31-year-old Lawrence was given command of the USS *Hornet* and sank the British ship HMS *Peacock*. Promoted to captain, he then took over the 49-gun frigate USS *Chesapeake* with a new and untrained crew.

On this day Lawrence was refitting the *Chesapeake* in Boston Harbor when the British 38-gun *Shannon*, commanded by the experienced captain Philip Broke, hove into view. Broke, whose crew was one of the best trained in the Royal Navy, issued a challenge to the American, to meet 'ship to ship, to try the fortune of our respective flags'. Unwisely, Lawrence sailed out to fight.

The battle was over almost before it began, as the *Shannon* battered the *Chesapeake* into a helpless hulk in less than fifteen minutes and fatally wounded her captain. 'Tell the men to fire faster and not to give up the ship,' Lawrence cried, 'fight her till she sinks!' Inspired by their captain's bravery, every officer aboard the *Chesapeake* fought until killed or wounded. Nonetheless, the American ship was captured in less than an hour and taken to Halifax in Nova Scotia under a prize crew. Lawrence died en route three days after the battle.

To pay tribute to the gallant captain a group of women stitched 'Don't Give Up The Ship!' into a flag that was given to the American commander Oliver Hazard Perry, whose flagship was renamed the USS *Lawrence* in honour of Captain Lawrence. Only three months after the capture of the *Chesapeake*, Perry avenged Lawrence's death by defeating an entire British squadron in the Battle of Lake Erie, although the *Lawrence* was so badly damaged that Perry had to transfer his flag to another ship.

After the war, Lawrence's famous exhortation became the motto of the US Navy, and Perry's flag emblazoned 'Don't Give Up The Ship!' is now proudly displayed in the United States Naval Academy. Little mention is usually made of Captain Lawrence's final order on the *Chesapeake*. Seeing the situation was hopeless, he commanded: 'Burn her!'

Other action this day

AD 836: Viking raiders sack London * 1794: 'The Glorious First of June', or Third Battle of Ushant, the first great naval engagement of the French Revolutionary Wars, in which the British fleet defeats a French fleet but a French convoy gets through unscathed, allowing both sides to claim victory * 1879: Prince Louis Bonaparte, the son of Napoleon III and last Bonaparte claimant to the French empire, is killed by Zulus while fighting for the British in Zululand

2 June

Death comes to Giuseppe Garibaldi

1882 South of Corsica, north-east of Sardinia lies the tiny island of Caprera, stony and dry like its neighbours, where the weather is mild but the farmer's life is hard.

Caprera's most eminent resident was the gnarled but still hardy Giuseppe Garibaldi, the great Italian patriot, revolutionary and general. Even in old age he carried a sizeable beard, and his high, noble brow gave him a rather messianic appearance. The most famous man in Europe in the second half of the 19th century, Garibaldi had captured Europe's imagination (and indeed the fear and hatred of many European governments) with his flamboyant leadership.

'Non posso offrirgli né onori né stipendi; gli offro fame, sete, marcie forzate, battaglie e morte', he dramatically told his followers. ('I can offer you neither honour nor wages; I offer you hunger, thirst, forced marches, battles and death.') And they came in their thousands, donning the famous red shirts that became their emblem (although tradition has it that Garibaldi chose the colour so that his followers would know they would be visible if they ran away in the heat of battle). Together they outfought and outfoxed the decaying monarchy of Sicily and forced the papacy to relinquish most of its territorial claims.

Garibaldi had been born on 4 July 1807. His first battles for freedom were not for Italy but for South America, where he spent twelve years fighting in one country or another, striving to throw off Spanish rule. There he learned the business of soldiering and of fighting guerrilla-style. At various times he was shot, imprisoned, starved and tortured. He returned to Italy a formidable fighting man.

More than any other man, Garibaldi created the united Italy of today. He spent his last days in Caprera, and here, at the age of 74, he died on this day. Here also he is buried.

Other action this day

AD 455: Pope Leo I throws open the gates of Rome to an invading Vandal army under King Geiseric, who had promised not to destroy the city nor kill its inhabitants but who nevertheless sacks the city for fourteen days ∗ 1098: With the help of a traitor inside the city, Christian forces conquer Antioch after a 94-day siege during the First Crusade ∗ 1624: John III Sobieski, the King of Poland who routed the Turks at the Battle of Vienna, is born in Olesko, Poland (now in the Ukraine)

3 June

ULTRA wins the Battle of Midway

1942 On this day, in the middle of the vast Pacific Ocean, David met Goliath. Goliath was, of course, by far the stronger of the two and very confident of his ability to prevail. David, however, came to the contest armed, not with a sling and five smooth stones, but with ULTRA.

In the spring of 1942 Allied cryptographers managed to break the Japanese navy's operational code. The ability to read the enemy's coded messages, one of the war's most closely guarded secrets, was known as ULTRA. From decrypts of the radio traffic, US naval intelligence pieced together what appeared to be the Japanese strategy for achieving total victory in the Pacific. Under the cover of a diversionary attack in the Aleutians, the first step was to be the capture of Midway Island, scheduled for 4 June. Forewarned by ULTRA,

Admiral Chester B. Nimitz, commander of the US Pacific Fleet, gathered his carriers under Admiral Jack Fletcher to counter the enemy's main thrust.

Seizing Midway Island, now the westernmost American base in the Pacific, looked to be a pushover for the huge Japanese Combined Fleet, 163 vessels strong and steaming eastward in several groups spread across the ocean. Shortly before sunrise this day, Japanese bombers left their carriers for the initial strike on Midway. Admiral Nagumo, who had led the great raid on Pearl Harbor six months before, had no suspicion that just over the horizon three US carriers – *Yorktown*, *Enterprise* and *Hornet* – carrying 233 planes, were closing in. When he found out, it was too late.

Shortly before 10.00am, while the flight decks of Nagumo's four carriers were jammed with returning aircraft refuelling and rearming for a second strike against the island, the first American attack came in. Three waves of low-flying torpedo bombers were almost entirely destroyed by Japanese anti-aircraft fire and fighter planes. 'For about one hundred seconds,' wrote Samuel Eliot Morison, 'the Japanese were certain they had won the Battle of Midway, and the war.' But on the heels of the first attack, swarming down from 14,000 feet, came 36 Dauntless dive-bombers. Within six minutes three of the Japanese carriers lay in flames, sinking. Later in the day the fourth carrier was so badly bombed that it had to be scuttled. During the evening Nagumo withdrew his invasion force from around Midway to avoid further losses, but hoping the American carriers would follow in the night and encounter the destructive power of Japanese battleships and cruisers converging on the scene. Admiral Fletcher, with his flagship the *Yorktown* fatally damaged and heavy losses in aircraft, declined pursuit.

Thus David, armed with ULTRA, prevailed over Goliath: Midway remained in American hands and the Japanese Combined Fleet withdrew westward, its vital carrier strength crippled. The defeat was so momentous for Japan, which until now had enjoyed almost unbroken success against the Allies in the Pacific, that the Imperial navy did not inform Prime Minister Tojo of the outcome for over a month. Later, Admiral Nimitz acknowledged ULTRA's crucial role in the victory, concluding: 'Had we lacked early information of the Japanese movements, and had we been caught with carrier forces dispersed [...] the Battle of Midway would have ended differently.'

1745: Generalleutnant Frederick von Gessler's 1,500 Bavarian dragoons destroy twenty Austrian battalions and take 2,500 prisoners, 67 flags and four cannon, losing only six officers and 28 men, during Frederick the Great's victory at the Battle of Hohenfriedberg during the War of the Austrian Succession * 1861: After firing a few shots at the advancing Union troops, Confederate soldiers break lines and run, some still in their bed clothes, at the Union surprise attack at Philippi, Virginia, a skirmish thereafter known as 'the Philippi Races' – the first land action of the American Civil War

4 June

Dunkirk: 'Wars are not won by evacuations'

1940 Early this morning, as German armour pressed to within three miles of the harbour, Operation Dynamo – the evacuation of Allied forces trapped at Dunkirk – was abandoned. Left behind in the shrinking bridgehead were the remains of the rearguard, several thousand soldiers of the 1st French Army still defending the perimeter. But brought across the Channel to safety in Britain over the course of nine perilous days were almost 340,000 British and French troops.

On 28 May, when Operation Dynamo began, the situation of the British Expeditionary Force had seemed hopeless, its left flank suddenly exposed by the surrender of the Belgian army. Winston Churchill, prime minister of Great Britain for less than three weeks, doubted whether more than 50,000 troops could be extracted. At the end, however, the rescue effort succeeded beyond all expectation – owing to good luck, German errors, and the magnificent performances of the Royal Navy and the RAF, who conducted and protected the operation.

To a British public understandably relieved at the salvation of its army, the narrow escape became 'the miracle of Dunkirk', almost a triumph in its own right, a way of disguising the magnitude of the Allies' defeat at the hands of the all-conquering Wehrmacht. But later that day, speaking to the House of Commons, Churchill chose these words to describe what had happened across the Channel: 'We must be very careful,' he told the MPs, 'not to assign this deliverance the attributes of a victory. Wars are not won by evacuations.'

In spite of his caution, however, Churchill roared defiance with one of history's most stirring speeches, including the famous lines: 'We shall not flag or fail. We shall go on to the end. We shall fight in France, we shall fight on the seas and oceans, we shall fight with growing confidence and growing strength in the air, we shall defend our island, whatever the cost may be. We shall fight on the beaches, we shall fight on the landing grounds, we shall fight in the fields and in the streets, we shall fight in the hills; we shall never surrender.'

Other action this day

1859: After French Foreign Legion commander Patrice de Mac-Mahon proclaims, 'Voici la Légion! L'affaire est dans le sac!' ('The Legion is here, the affair is in the bag!'), a French–Piedmontese army under Napoleon III and Mac-Mahon routs an Austrian force at Magenta during the Second Italian War of Independence * 1916: Russia launches the two-month Brusilov offensive in the Ukraine against Austro-Hungarian forces, killing, wounding or capturing 1,500,000 in one of the most lethal of all battles in history * 1941: Ex-Kaiser Wilhelm II dies in exile in the Netherlands

5 June

Kitchener goes down with the ship

1916 A great hero and symbol of his nation died this evening in the North Sea.

We remember him from the famous recruiting poster reproduced in history books: his glowering, square-jawed countenance with its bristling moustache and piercing eyes, his forefinger pointing directly at the viewer, and below it the caption, 'Your Country Needs YOU'. He was, of course, Field Marshal Herbert Horatio Kitchener, avenger of Gordon, reconqueror of the Sudan, hero of Fashoda, protector of the North-west Frontier, commander-in-chief in South Africa, Earl Kitchener of Khartoum, and now secretary of state for war in the Asquith government.

When Britain declared war in 1914, the day after Germany's invasion of Belgium, Kitchener's name was on every lip. The

Conservatives in Parliament called for him, the big newspapers demanded him, and Winston Churchill, already in the Cabinet, urged his appointment on Asquith.

'What he symbolised, I think,' wrote the Prime Minister's daughter many years later, 'was strength, decision and above all success. South Africa, Khartoum – everything that he touched "came off." There was a feeling that Kitchener could not fail. The psychological effect of his appointment, the tonic to public confidence were instantaneous and overwhelming.'

For all his immense reputation and military successes, however, he was a warrior of the 19th century facing warfare on an unprecedented industrial scale. He did foresee from the outset, when few others did, what a long war would demand in the way of manpower, and he prepared to meet the enormous expansion of Britain's military strength through the formation of new 'Kitchener divisions'. But he could not find a strategy to break the stalemate on the Western Front. Nor was he in favour of flanking side-shows in other theatres. He flip-flopped badly on the Dardanelles/Gallipoli campaign and ended up by opposing the only part of the operation that was a success: the final evacuation. As the war dragged on with no conclusion in sight, his influence in the Cabinet waned, and his colleagues began to challenge his decisions.

A Chief of the Imperial General Staff was appointed to handle much of the management of the war that had been Kitchener's alone. Asquith, wishing to avoid the political embarrassment of a Cabinet resignation, sent Lord Kitchener off to Russia to assess the situation on the Eastern Front. He was on the armoured cruiser *Hampshire*, sailing from Scapa Flow for Archangel, when on the evening of 5 June 1916 she hit a mine in the North Sea and quickly sank, taking with her virtually everybody on board.

David Fromkin offered this assessment of Kitchener: 'If he had died in 1914 he would have been remembered as the greatest British general since Wellington. Had he died in 1915 he would have been remembered as the prophet who foretold the nature and duration of the First World War and as the organiser of Britain's mass army. But in 1916 he had become the ageing veteran of a bygone era who could not cope with the demands placed on him in changing times.'

1798: The British defeat Irish republican insurgents at the Battle of New Ross during the Irish Rebellion of 1798, massacring hundreds of prisoners and sympathisers * 1857: Rebelling Sepoys besiege Cawnpore during the Sepoy Revolt in India, starting a siege that lasts three weeks and includes the Bibighar Massacre, in which 120 British women and children are hacked to death and dismembered with meat cleavers * 1944: Seventy-seven American B-29 Superfortress four-engine bombers – the largest bombers in the Second World War – take off from India to attack Japanese railway facilities in Bangkok, the first combat mission for B-29s in the war

6 June

Sergeant Dan Daly creates a Marine Corps legend

1918 German armies were stretched out along an endless front anchored in the English Channel east of Calais and extending east and south across northern France. Nowhere was the pressure greater than in Belleau Wood, a small wooded tract just 40 miles from Paris. Should the Boche break through the crumbling French defence there, the capital was theirs for the taking – and perhaps the war.

In early June the French received long-awaited reinforcements – two battalions of United States Marines. Today a legend was born, based on the heroism of 49-year-old gunnery sergeant Dan Daly, a diminutive man of only 5 foot 6 inches weighing just 132 pounds.

The Marines attacked early in the morning, but the attack faltered when it was met by murderous machine gun fire from the entrenched Germans. Daly and his men were pinned down in a wheat field as casualties mounted. A newspaperman present at the battle reported what happened next: '[Daly] stood up and made a forward motion to his men. There was slight hesitation. Who in the hell could blame them? Machine-gun and rifle bullets were kicking up dirt, closer and closer. The sergeant ran out to the center of his platoon – he swung his bayoneted rifle over his head with a forward sweep. He yelled at his men: "Come on, you sons of bitches! Do you want to live forever?"'

Daly's men charged and the Germans fell back, their momentum towards Paris broken, never to be regained. Although the Marines did not capture the wood, it fell nineteen days later to American army reinforcements. But the Marines had made the difference. One hyperbolic US Army general even claimed: 'They saved the Allies from defeat [...] France could not have stood the loss of Paris.' Later the grateful French renamed Belleau Wood the Bois de la Brigade Marine. And to this day every new Marine recruit hears the tale of Sergeant Dan Daly.

Other action this day

1513: The Swiss defeat the French at the Battle of Novara, forcing Louis XII to pull out of Milan and restoring Maximilian Sforza to power ∗ 1865: Confederate bushwhacker William Quantrill dies of wounds received on 10 May during an ambush by Union soldiers in Taylorsville, Kentucky ∗ 1898: American warships attack Spanish positions at Guantánamo Bay, the start of the American invasion of Cuba during the Spanish–American War ∗ 1944: D-Day – two American, two British and one Canadian army totalling 175,000 men land on Normandy's beaches

7 June

The launch of the Lusitania

1906 At 12.30 today at John Brown's shipyard on the Clyde, Mary, Lady Inverclyde, widow of the Cunard Line's late chairman, christened a new ocean liner before thousands of onlookers. The ship was 790 feet long, with four tall stacks that billowed black smoke, the fastest and most luxurious liner in existence. No one among the crowd could have imagined the terrible fate that awaited her. She was RMS *Lusitania*.

The *Lusitania*'s career as a liner started propitiously. On her maiden voyage a year after her launch she won the coveted Blue Riband for the fastest-ever transatlantic crossing, completing the westbound journey at an average speed of 23.99 knots and bettering the record that the German liner *Deutschland* had set four years earlier. In 1909 she upped that record to 25.85 knots. Over the years she continued to ply the Atlantic, crossing no fewer than 202 times on the Liverpool–New York route. But that was before the First World War.

About six months after the beginning of hostilities, Germany upped the ante, declaring that all the seas around the British Isles would be considered a war zone. Now any Allied ship, not just warships, would be sunk without warning by prowling German U-boats.

On 1 May 1915 the *Lusitania* departed from Pier 54 on New York's West Side carrying a crew of 702 plus 1,201 predominantly British passengers, but including 188 Americans. Despite the German warning, no one thought their deadly submarines would attack a vessel carrying only passengers, especially since so many were citizens of a neutral – and powerful – United States.

In the early afternoon of 7 May the liner was nearing the west of Ireland, sailing at only 18 knots due to heavy fog. Unknown to her captain, the German submarine U-20, commanded by Kapitänleutnant Walther Schwieger, was lurking unseen nearby.

Suddenly a torpedo rocked the *Lusitania*, to be quickly followed by a huge second explosion. Within minutes she began to sink. Panicky passengers stampeded for the ship's 48 lifeboats, some climbing into the boats while they were still hanging from their davits. But those boats on the port side could not be lowered due to the list of the ship, and as the liner lurched downward, half-filled lifeboats from the starboard side tumbled into the ocean, passengers thrown into the waves. Only six were eventually launched.

The *Lusitania*'s captain stayed aboard until the water engulfed the bridge. He then jumped overboard, to be buoyed by a floating chair he found in the water. Three hours later he was miraculously saved. But most of the *Lusitania*'s passengers were not so lucky. The ship had gone down in just eighteen minutes – with 1,198 of its passengers and crew, including 128 Americans and 63 children.

As German submarine commander Schwieger recorded in his log: 'Clean bow-shot from 700-metre range. Shot hits starboard side behind bridge. Unusually heavy explosion follows … Many [life] boats crowded, come down bow or stern first and immediately fill and sink … I submerge to 24 metres and go to sea.' (Kapitänleutnant Schwieger himself was killed when his U-boat hit a British mine in 1917.)

The German government insisted to an appalled American public that the ship had been carrying a large quantity of explosives intended for Britain's war effort. Not so, cried the British Admiralty.

High explosives on an ocean liner, endangering hundreds of innocent civilians? An evil German fabrication. By and large the
Admiralty was believed, and although the US stayed out of the war
for two more years, the sinking of the *Lusitania* was a critical turning
point in American opinion.

Ever since the *Lusitania* went down, the debate has raged about
the cause of the second explosion. Kapitänleutnant Schwieger had
fired only one torpedo, so a clandestine cargo of explosives is certainly
possible. Others maintain that the ship's boilers blew up, or that coal
dust in the hold was ignited when the ship was hit. Whatever the true
cause of the second explosion, the *Lusitania* could probably not have
long survived the strike of the German torpedo – but the sinking
would have been much slower, allowing far more passengers to be
saved.

Other action this day

1672: The English and Dutch fight an inconclusive naval battle at Solebay,
the first naval battle of the Third Anglo-Dutch War * 1915: Flight
Sub-lieutenant Reginald Warneford becomes the first man to bring down a
German Zeppelin by dropping bombs on it from his fighter plane, a deed
for which he wins the Victoria Cross * 1917: During the Battle of
Messines in the First World War, the British detonate 21 mines totalling
455 tonnes of ammonal explosive under German trenches, killing 10,000
and destroying the German fortifications and the Belgian town of Messines
(Mesen)

8 June

Death of the Black Prince

1376 On this mild Sunday in June died Edward, the Black Prince, in
his palace south of the Thames in London. Son of Edward III (who
was still alive when the younger Edward died), the Black Prince was
the most notable fighting man of his age.

Edward got his first taste of battle when he was only fifteen during
a campaign in Flanders, and a year later distinguished himself at the
famous English victory at Crécy (see 26 August). (In positioning him
in the thick of the battle, his father said: 'Also say to them, that they

suffre hym this day to wynne his spurres, for if God be pleased, I woll this journey be his, and the honoure therof.' – commonly quoted as: 'Let the boy win his spurs.')

It was at Crécy that Edward won his famous nickname, which came not from his colouring (he was blond and blue-eyed) but from the black armour he wore. It was also after Crécy that he established two royal traditions. During the battle the blind King John of Bohemia had charged into the action against the English, only to be instantly cut down. Edward picked up his helmet and found it lined with ostrich feathers. Admiring the king's courage, he adopted both the feathers and his motto, 'Homout; ich dene' ('Courage; I serve', later shortened to 'Ich dien'). All subsequent Princes of Wales have retained the feathers as their emblem and used 'Ich dien' as their motto.

Edward also played prominent roles at the siege of Calais and the Battle of Winchelsea prior to commanding the English at the great victory at Poitiers (see 19 September) where the French king Jean II was captured. Because of his conspicuous gallantry, he was the first member of the Order of the Garter, created by his father.

Edward later participated in successful actions at Reims and Najera, and his final campaign was the siege of Limoges in 1370.

When the Black Prince died just seven days short of his 46th birthday, he succumbed to a lingering and painful disease, probably dropsy (oedema) or cancer. He left behind a blond-haired son of nine, who would one day gain the throne as the tragic Richard II.

Other action this day

1663: The Portuguese defeat the Spanish at the Battle of Ameixial during the Portuguese Restoration War * 1675: In Plymouth, Massachusetts three Wampanoag Indians are hanged for murder, triggering a bloody war known as King Phillip's War * 1845: American president and general Andrew Jackson dies in Nashville, Tennessee

9 June

Knights in shining armour crush the peasant revolt

1358 To escape the marauding bands of peasants who wreaked havoc across the north of France, today 300 aristocratic ladies and their children barricaded themselves in the fortified market-place of Meaux. Guarded by only a handful of men-at-arms, they huddled in fear as an enraged mob 9,000-strong approached the city, baying for blood. The peasants of France had risen in the brutal revolt known as the Jacquerie.

The Jacquerie had started twelve days earlier when about 100 hate-filled ruffians had armed themselves with pitchforks, knives and clubs and attacked a manor house in Saint-Leu 60 miles to the north, burning it to the ground and murdering the owner and his family. Led by a wealthy peasant named Guillaume Callet, the revolt spread. As many as 100,000 rampaged through the land, torturing and killing as they went. As the contemporary chronicler Jean Froissart reported: 'They slew a knight and after did put him on a spit and roasted him at the fire in the sight of the lady his wife and his children; and after the lady had been ravished by ten or twelve, they made her perforce to eat of her husband and after made her die an evil death and all her children.'

The reasons for the revolt were not hard to find. The Black Death had killed a third of the population and bands of marauding mercenaries called the Great Companies ravaged the countryside. Then in 1356 England's Black Prince had routed the French at Poitiers, capturing the king Jean II and hauling him away to England (see 19 September).

Those who suffered most were the peasants, many of whom already lived at subsistence level, in huts without furniture, water or heat, sleeping on straw and eating little but bread and onions. Further afflicted by the hated *gabelle*, a tax on salt collected by unscrupulous tax farmers, they were filled with hatred and thirsted for revenge on the nobles who contemptuously called them 'Jacques Bonhomme'.

Now the lawless horde had arrived at Meaux, just 35 miles east of Paris, only to be welcomed into the town with meat and drink by the rebellious local citizenry. According to the chroniclers, the ladies in the fortified market-place trembled in anguish at the 'savage cries' of the insurgents.

But then, in the words of historian Barbara Tuchman, 'knighthood errant galloped to the rescue in the persons of that glittering pair, the Captal de Buch and Gaston Phoebus, Count of Foix ... with a company of forty lances'.

The Captal and the Count had been returning from Prussia when they heard of the looming calamity at Meaux. Riding hard, they reached Meaux market and the terrified aristocrats on the same day that the peasant army entered the town. They realised at once that their small force could not hold out for long against the mass of peasants. Their only hope was attack.

At the head of 25 armoured knights, lances levelled, Gaston Phoebus and the Captal ordered the market's portcullis to be raised. Suddenly the cries of the mob were silenced. Then, reports Froissart: 'Those in front began to fall back and the noblemen to charge them, striking at them with their lances and swords and beating them down. Those who felt the blows, or feared to feel them, turned back in such panic that they fell over each other. Then the men-at-arms burst out of the gates and ran into the square to attack those evil men.'

The narrow causeway leading from the marketplace and Meaux's confined streets meant that only a few of the peasants could face the charging knights at a time, nullifying their enormous numerical advantage. The knights 'mowed them down in heaps and slaughtered them like cattle; and they drove all the rest out of the town, for none of the villeins attempted to take up any sort of fighting order. They went on killing until they were stiff and weary and they flung many into the River Marne.

'In all, they exterminated more than seven thousand Jacques on that day. Not one would have escaped if they had not grown tired of pursuing them. When the noblemen returned, they set fire to the mutinous town of Meaux and burnt it to ashes, together with all the villeins of the town whom they could pen up inside.'

Meaux was the turning point in the Jacquerie revolt, with the battle at Mello the following day completing the formal fighting. There the peasant leader Guillaume Callet, who had not been at Meaux, led his peasant force against the much smaller army of King

Charles the Bad of Navarre. Promising safe passage, Charles asked Callet to parley, and the trusting rebel leader left his camp to cross enemy lines. There he was instantly thrown into chains. Now leaderless, Callet's demoralised mob dispersed in panic when the enemy cavalry charged. That evening Callet was crowned with a red-hot iron circlet and decapitated.

By the end of June the Jacquerie was over, and an enraged and fearful nobility drenched the country in blood. According to a proverb of the time: 'Oignez vilain, il vous poindra, poignez vilain, il vous oindra.' ('Spare a villain, he'll cut your throat, show a villain your steel and he'll kneel.') Up to 20,000 peasants were slaughtered. Jacques Bonhomme would have to wait over 400 years for his revenge to begin in Paris.

Other action this day
AD 721: Eudes the Great, Duke of Aquitaine, defeats the Moorish governor of al-Andalus, Anbasa ibn Suhaym al-Kalbi, at the Battle of Toulouse, preventing the Moors from moving west into Aquitaine * 1866: Bismarck's Prussian troops invade Holstein * 1973: German field marshal and strategist Erich von Manstein dies

10 June

Marlborough meets Eugene of Savoy

1704 Today began one of the most productive partnerships in military history, when England's greatest general, John Churchill, the Duke of Marlborough, first met Prince Eugene of Savoy, the greatest general ever to serve the Holy Roman Empire.

Marlborough had first received his commission in the foot guards in 1667, when Eugene was only four years old. During the next four decades he had fought both for and against the French and was made a duke by King William III for his victory at Kaiserswerth two years before his historic meeting with Eugene. His rise to fame and fortune – he was also awarded the Order of the Garter and made commander-in-chief of the Allied armies in Europe – was also furthered by his wife's close connections to Queen Anne, who had succeeded William in 1702 when he was killed by being thrown from a horse.

Eugene had been born in the highest aristocracy, a prince of the House of Savoy, and was rumoured (almost certainly falsely) to be the illegitimate son of Louis XIV, who indeed had had an affair with his mother. Slight, ungainly and somewhat horse-faced, at 40 he hardly looked like a seasoned warrior, but, even though he was thirteen years younger than Marlborough, he was at the time a more celebrated general; he had fought in his first battle at the siege of Vienna in 1683 (see 12 September), had routed the Turks at Zenta in 1687 and had become a field marshal five years later, still only 29.

Now England and the Holy Roman Empire were allied to halt the expansion of Europe's largest and most powerful nation, the France of Louis XIV, during the War of the Spanish Succession. At about five in the evening on this day Eugene rode into Marlborough's camp at Mundelsheim, south-east of Stuttgart, to discuss strategy. Historian Correlli Barnett describes the scene: 'Now in this humble Württemberg village nestling amid tiny vineyards steeply terraced in the local yellow-grey stone, an English duke played host to an Imperial prince with all the ceremony of the baroque age. Military pomp and splendour were followed by a banquet: the table magnificent with Marlborough's campaign silver plate; the Duke's silver candlesticks in profusion as the light faded; and the two great personages themselves, one the most famous of living soldiers, the other with a reputation still to make, exchanging smiling compliments and shrewdly appraising each other from beneath their wigs.' The two generals took to each other instantly; their partnership was to last for almost ten years.

The first fruits of their friendship came just two months later when their combined forces destroyed the French at the Battle of Blenheim (see 13 August), securing Bavaria and all of Germany for the Holy Roman Empire and forcing Louis XIV to pull back behind the Rhine, never again to threaten Germany. Subsequent triumphs included French defeats at Oudenaarde, which eventually led to the recapture of Ghent and Bruges, and Malplaquet, the last great battle of the war. Between the two of them, Eugene and Marlborough demolished for ever Louis XIV's hope of hegemony over Europe.

Other action this day
1190: Holy Roman Emperor Frederick Barbarossa drowns on crusade while crossing the Calycadnus (now the Göksu) River in Anatolia *

1719: British troops defeat a coalition of Jacobites and Spaniards at Glenshiel, the last close engagement of British and foreign troops on mainland British soil * 1944: The 1st Battalion of the 4th Waffen-SS Panzer-Grenadier Regiment seals off the French town of Oradour-sur-Glane and murders 190 men, 247 women and 205 children because French Resistance fighters have kidnapped Sturmbannführer (Major) Helmut Kämpfe, the highest-ranking officer ever captured by the Resistance; partisans execute Kämpfe the same day

11 June

Private Johnson Beharry wins the VC

2004 Today in the Iraqi city of Al Amarah a 25-year-old private in the 1st Battalion of the Princess of Wales's Royal Regiment put his life on the line for the second time in just over a month to earn his nation's highest military decoration, the Victoria Cross.

Johnson Beharry had moved to Great Britain from his native Grenada in 1999 when he was twenty, and a year later joined the army. When his battalion was shipped to Iraq in 2004, he was the driver of an FV510 Warrior tracked armoured personnel carrier (APC), a mini-tank of only 30 tonnes designed to carry troops under protection to the objective and then give them firepower support.

In the early hours of 1 May, Beharry's company was ordered to go to the aid of an outpost in the centre of Al Amarah, under attack from local insurgents.

Moving into the city, the company fought through a series of ambushes to rescue an isolated foot patrol pinned down by enemy machine guns. Some of the Warriors now also came under heavy fire, and Beharry's platoon set off to help.

As the platoon commander looked down the empty, silent road in front of him, he knew they might be moving into an ambush. He stopped the APC to evaluate the situation, but the Warriors immediately came under fire from rocket-propelled grenades.

Violent explosions rocked Beharry's Warrior, wounding the platoon commander, the gunner and a number of the soldiers in the rear. The APC's radio was knocked out, leaving Beharry with no way to communicate with either his turret crew or any of the other Warriors around him.

Closing his driver's hatch, Beharry moved forward through the ambush to try to establish some form of communications, halting just short of a barricade across the road. His Warrior was again hit by a sustained grenade attack from insurgent fighters lying in wait in alleyways and on rooftops.

Now the Warrior caught fire and rapidly filled with thick, noxious smoke. Beharry opened the hatch cover to clear his view and orientate himself. Then, to extricate his vehicle and his crew, he drove directly through the barricade, not knowing if it was mined, and led the remaining five Warriors behind him towards safety.

As the smoke in his driver's tunnel cleared, he was just able to make out the shape of another rocket-propelled grenade in flight heading directly towards him. He pulled the heavy armoured hatch down with one hand, while controlling his vehicle with the other, but the overpressure from the explosion wrenched the hatch from his grip, and the flames and force of the blast passed directly over him and down the driver's tunnel, further wounding the semi-conscious gunner.

The explosion destroyed Beharry's periscope, forcing him to drive through the remainder of the ambushed route, almost a mile long, with his hatch open and his head outside, exposed to enemy fire. He still had no communications with any other vehicle, and rocket-propelled grenades and small arms fire repeatedly hit his burning Warrior. A bullet penetrated his helmet and remained lodged on its inner surface. Despite the weight of incoming fire, he pushed through the ambush, still leading the platoon, until he broke clear.

He then followed another Warrior through the streets of Al Amarah to a different outpost under attack. Without thought for his own safety, he stopped his still-burning APC and climbed onto the turret. Oblivious to incoming small arms fire, he manhandled his wounded platoon commander out of the turret, off the vehicle and to the shelter of the other Warrior. He then returned to his own vehicle and lifted out the gunner and moved him to a position of safety, after which he went back to the rear of his vehicle to lead the disorientated and shocked troops and casualties to safety, all the while exposing himself to enemy fire.

Remounting his burning Warrior for the third time, Beharry

drove into the defended perimeter of the outpost. Only now did he pull the fire extinguisher handles, immobilising the vehicle's engine. After dismounting and moving into the relative security of the back of another Warrior, he collapsed from physical and mental exhaustion.

For most men, this might have been heroism enough, but, after medical treatment, Beharry returned to duty. On this day, 11 June, he was once again in action, his Warrior part of a force attempting to cut off an enemy mortar team that had attacked a Coalition base. In the lead vehicle, Beharry was moving rapidly through the dark city streets when he was ambushed yet again, as insurgents opened fire from surrounding rooftops.

A rocket-propelled grenade detonated on his Warrior's front armour, just six inches from Beharry's head, causing a serious head injury. Other rockets struck the turret and sides, incapacitating his commander and injuring several of the crew.

With the blood from his head wound obscuring his vision, Beharry still controlled his Warrior and reversed it out of the ambush area. When the vehicle struck the wall of a nearby building and came to rest, he lost consciousness from his wounds, but he had driven out of the enemy's killing area, saving his crew.

On 18 March 2005 Beharry was awarded the Victoria Cross for having 'displayed repeated extreme gallantry and unquestioned valour, despite intense direct attacks, personal injury and damage to his vehicle in the face of relentless enemy action'.

Other action this day

1429: Joan of Arc leads the French to victory at the Battle of Jargeau against an English force led by William de la Pole * 1289: The Guelphs (supporters of the Pope) defeat the Ghibellines (supporters of the Holy Roman Emperor) at the Battle of Campaldino, securing Florence for the Guelphs * 1967: Six days after Israel launches a pre-emptive surprise attack against Egypt's air force, the Six-Day War between Israel and its Arab neighbours ends with a United Nations-brokered ceasefire

12 June

Stalin purges his army

1937 Today in Moscow, after the briefest of trials, Marshal Mikhail N. Tukhachevsky, one of the highest-ranking officers in the Red Army and its former chief of staff, was shot to death for treason, espionage and conspiracy. His execution took place in the headquarters of the NKVD, Soviet Russia's secret police. Shot along with him on similar charges were seven other top commanders who, with the marshal, were among Soviet Russia's best and most experienced military officers.

In the 1930s Stalin began a series of purges to 'purify' Soviet Russia of all potential opposition to his regime. By 1937 it was the army's turn. Among the targets of scrutiny were former aristocrats, tsarist officers and anyone associated with Trotsky's command of the Red Army during the Civil War. Despite his elevation to the rank of marshal by Stalin only two years earlier, Tukhachevsky was vulnerable on all counts.

It made no difference that he was also a brilliant military reformer who had led the Soviet armed forces into much-needed innovations in combined arms, armoured formations, airborne units, tactical air support and an independent bomber force. These contributions were evidence of a capacity for 'independent thought', now the deadliest of Soviet sins.

Naturally, there was 'proof' of Tukhachevsky's involvement in a plot to seize the Kremlin and overthrow the Soviet leadership: a faked dossier of correspondence between the marshal and two German generals. Under torture the marshal confessed to all charges against him.

The purge did not stop with Tukhachevsky and his colleagues. Over the next year the 'show' trials resulted in the following losses to the Red Army through death or imprisonment: three of five marshals; fourteen of sixteen army commanders; 60 of 67 corps commanders; 136 of 199 division commanders; 221 of 397 brigade commanders; and some 35,000 lower-ranking officers – in all amounting to about half the officer corps. Their replacements were for the most part unfit or untrained as commanders.

One result of these leadership losses was the Red Army's poor showing in its 1939–40 campaign against Finland, a performance carefully noted by the German military. What followed in 1941 was worse yet: full-scale disaster at the hands of the Wehrmacht in the opening phase of Operation Barbarossa. If there was a silver lining to this defeat, it was the speedy elimination through death or capture of thousands of incompetent Soviet officers to be replaced by better material. And in the nick of time, as the German army neared Moscow late in the year, the Soviet high command reinstated many of Tukhachevsky's doctrinal innovations. It was almost too late.

Other action this day

1215: English barons force King John to sign the Magna Carta at Runnymede * 1758: During the French and Indian Wars, British troops under the command of Lord Jeffery Amherst and James Wolfe seize Lighthouse Point to start the siege of Louisbourg in Nova Scotia, which will end in victory 45 days later, leading to the loss of Quebec in 1759 and the rest of French North America a year later * 1862: Brigadier General J.E.B. Stuart leads 1,200 Confederate cavalrymen around General George McClellan's Union army over three days of hard riding, destroying supplies

13 June

Alexander the Great dies in Babylon

323 BC Towards evening today in the fabled city of Babylon he died, still only 32. In his twelve years and eight months as King of Macedonia he changed for ever the Western world. He was Alexander the Great.

As always in antiquity, when a great man died young, there were stories of plots and murders. Plutarch tells us of the bad omens that foretold a coming calamity. Alexander's pet lion was kicked to death by a donkey, and ravens attacked each other over the walls of Babylon, one falling dead at the king's feet. After Alexander's death a story grew that conspirators had given him poisoned wine. Feeling as if 'an arrow had struck him in the liver', he tried to throw up the poison by forcing a feather down his throat, but the feather, too, had been poisoned, compounding the original dose. Modern historians are sceptical, most believing that, already weakened by alcohol, the great conqueror was finally consumed by malaria.

Alexander had inherited the throne of Macedon from his assassinated father, Philip II, along with an even more valuable legacy, the finest army in the world. In addition, his mind had been trained by one of the greatest of all thinkers, Aristotle.

In late 335 BC or early 334 BC Alexander set out on his fabled conquests – first all of Greece, then Turkey, the Levant, Egypt, Syria and back through modern-day Iraq and Iran, conquering the Persian empire. And still onwards he went, into Parthia, skirting the southern edge of the Caspian Sea into today's Afghanistan and across the Hindu Kush into Pakistan and India, where his troops finally said 'enough' and refused to go further.

Such were the conquests of the great Alexander, the man who founded at least seven Alexandrias, including the one that remains, in Egypt, where he was buried. Alexander's only son was born posthumously and therefore had no real chance to inherit his father's empire, but that would not have mattered to the great conqueror. When asked to whom he left his empire, he answered: 'To the strongest.'

Nonetheless, Alexander did leave behind two dynasties, not in Greece but in the Middle East, and not of his own blood but through two of his generals who had been his boyhood companions.

The first was Seleucus, who was about 32 at Alexander's death. After several years of in-fighting with Alexander's other generals he took control of what today is mostly Syria and Iran to form the Seleucid empire, which lasted for 240 years. The other was Ptolemy, who became King of Egypt. His family ruled for 293 years until his descendant Cleopatra clasped an asp to her bosom in 30 BC.

Shortly before he died, Alexander ordered all Greeks to worship him as a god, which he sincerely believed he was. He had been well prepared for this role; his mother had told him that Zeus rather than King Philip was his real father, and when he conquered Egypt he became Pharaoh and thus officially the son of the greatest Egyptian deity, Amon-ra. He thus established the idea of a god-king in Europe, a concept that reached full bloom in Rome three centuries later with the Emperor Augustus and eventually transformed itself into the divine right of kings.

1655: The English rout the Dutch fleet at the Battle of Lowestoft, losing just one ship to seventeen Dutch * 1777: The marquis de Lafayette lands in his own brig near Charleston, South Carolina to join the rebel cause in the American Revolution * 1786: American general Winfield Scott is born near Petersburg, Virginia * 1808: French marshal and president Patrice de Mac-Mahon is born near Autun in Burgundy

14 June

Death of a traitor

1801 At 6.30 this Sunday morning at Gloucester Place, London, a British general died of dropsy and gout at the age of 60. In debt and out of favour, he was buried without military honours in a church crypt in unfashionable Battersea.

He had once been one of the best combat commanders on either side in the American Revolution, his name linked with such celebrated exploits as Quebec, Valcour Island and Saratoga. In those days, however, he had been an American general, not a British one. His name was Benedict Arnold.

In 1780, Arnold turned traitor and began a secret correspondence with the enemy commander-in-chief in New York City, Sir Henry Clinton. He proposed to give Clinton the strategic American position at West Point in return for £20,000 and a commission in the British army. But the plot was discovered when Major John André, Sir Henry's intermediary with Arnold, was caught in disguise behind American lines, bearing papers that revealed the betrayal. André was hanged as a spy, and Arnold himself narrowly escaped to British-held New York City.

The British paid Arnold only about one third of the promised money, but they did make him a brigadier general. As the war carried on, he led British troops in operations against his former countrymen in Virginia and Connecticut. Then came the notable American victory at Yorktown.

Arnold had counted on the British continuing military operations in North America, thus providing him with a career in the army, perhaps as commander of Loyalist forces in America. To argue that case, he took himself and his family to England in 1782, but not long after his arrival an anti-war Whig government gained office in London. He would find a home neither in English society, where he came to symbolise the now-unpopular conflict, nor in the British army, where fellow officers considered his motives mercenary and dishonourable. Moreover, the loss to the service of the highly popular André was still mourned.

Arnold was forced to spend much of his last twenty years abroad in Canada and the West Indies in search of fortune. In contrast to Arnold's humble interment in Battersea, Major André received a monument in Westminster Abbey on which the inscription proclaimed him 'universally beloved and esteemed by the Army in which he served'.

Other action this day

1645: Oliver Cromwell and Sir Thomas Fairfax rout Charles I's forces at the Battle of Naseby during the English Civil War * 1658: The French under Turenne, supported by 3,000 British Parliamentary troops, defeat the Spanish at Dunkirk in the Battle of the Dunes * 1800 and 1807: Napoleon crushes the Austrians at Marengo and the Russians at Friedland * 1775: The US Army is founded when the Continental Congress authorises the enlistment of riflemen to serve the United Colonies for one year * 1800: In Cairo, Napoleonic general Jean Baptiste Kléber is knifed through the heart by a Syrian student hired by Egyptian rebels * 1940: German soldiers march into conquered Paris

15 June

The Duchess of Richmond's ball

1815 There was danger afoot on the continent of Europe. Napoleon had recently escaped his exile on Elba, had returned to Paris, and this very day was at the head of an enormous army advancing on Belgium. In Vienna, news of these disturbing developments caused the Congress to give up its waltzing, but in Brussels this evening the Duchess of Richmond gave a ball, maybe the most famous ball in history, where the assembled company feasted and danced the night away, 'up to the very brink of battle'.

'There never was, since the days of Darius,' wrote Thackeray, 'such a brilliant train of camp followers as hung around the train of the Duke of Wellington's army in the Low Countries in 1815.' Chief among the attendees at this evening's ball was the cream of British and European military leadership, headed by the Prince of Orange, the Duke of Brunswick and the Duke of Wellington, now commander-in-chief of the Allied armies in Flanders. Ambassadors, military officers and aristocrats thronged the spacious rooms. Beautiful ladies abounded in a dazzling array of wives and daughters that included, in addition to the hostess herself, her daughter Lady Georgiana Lennox, Lady Charlotte Greville – a favourite of the commander-in-chief – and, if we wish to believe Thackeray's account in *Vanity Fair*, that arch-schemer Mrs Rawdon Crawley, better known as Becky Sharp.

The Duke of Wellington came late and left early. At midnight a rider arrived with a dispatch, and when he had finished reading it, the duke began issuing orders to aides and conferring with senior officers. Later, at supper, where he sat next to Lady Charlotte, he was composed and attentive as always, but afterwards he asked the Duke of Richmond for a map, which he consulted in the privacy of the study.

Some time after 2.00am, with the festivities in full swing, Wellington left for his quarters. The French army was drawing very near now – had crossed the Sambre, in fact – and there was much to be done to prepare his own army for events. It was no longer the eve of battle, and the approaching dawn would see the commencement of a great military campaign that would culminate in three days' time at Waterloo.

Other action this day

1219: Danish king Valdemar's army defeats the heathen Estonians at Tallin after a red banner with a white cross falls from the sky to inspire the Christian Danes, who then adopt the *dannebrog* as their national flag * 1330: Edward, the Black Prince is born in Woodstock * 1775: The Continental Congress names George Washington as commander-in-chief of the Continental Army

16 June

Henry VII captures a royal impostor

1487 It was less than two years since King Henry VII had defeated and killed Richard III at Bosworth Field (see 22 August), yet already plots were brewing to overthrow him in favour of the Yorkist faction he had replaced. As a protective measure, Henry had imprisoned the ten-year-old Edward, Duke of Warwick in the Tower of London; Warwick was the son of the dead Duke of Clarence, brother of Richard III, and thus had a strong claim to the throne. But some time in 1486 rumours began to spread that Warwick had escaped.

At about the same time a young Oxford priest named Richard Symonds noticed that a handsome eleven-year-old son of a local joiner and organ-maker bore a resemblance to the deposed royal family. Perhaps this was the opportunity the Yorkists had been waiting for.

The young boy's name was Lambert Simnel. Symonds began to tutor him in kingly speech and manners and then took him to Ireland, declaring him to be the escaped Warwick and the rightful heir to the throne. The pro-Yorkist nobles there believed the subterfuge, and Lambert Simnel was crowned in Dublin as Edward VI.

To counter the plot, King Henry paraded the real Duke of Warwick through the streets of London, all to no avail. Soon an army of dissidents and opportunists grew up around Simnel, including Francis Lovell, 1st Viscount Lovell and John de la Pole, Earl of Lincoln, who himself had been named as heir to the dead Richard III. Further support came from Richard III's sister, the dowager Duchess of Burgundy, who sent 2,000 Swiss and German mercenaries to join rebel English and Irish in an attempt to overthrow Henry VII. Although the key conspirators like Lincoln and Lovell probably had no doubt concerning Lambert Simnel's true identity, they thought they could use him to further their cause.

On 4 June 1487 the Yorkist commander, the Earl of Lincoln, landed in Lancashire with an army of perhaps 6,000 men. He was soon headed south, picking up reinforcements as he went. Meanwhile, King Henry was rallying a force of 12,000 to crush the insurgents.

At nine in the morning of 16 June the vanguard of the royal army met the Yorkists near the town of Stoke, 130 miles north of London. There the rebel force, now grown to 8,000, had taken a position on a ridge with the River Trent protecting their right flank and rear.

Lincoln instantly ordered an attack, even though it meant giving up the Yorkist defensive advantage of holding the high ground. Having heard reports of the size of the full royalist army – significantly larger than his own – he hoped to crush the vanguard before Henry's main force could reach the battlefield.

At the beginning the combat was bitter and evenly matched, Henry's vanguard even forced to pull back. But then Henry arrived with the balance of his army and began to wear down the rebels. Now the Yorkists were desperate, unable to retreat because of the river behind them. The Irish contingent started to panic and flee, but the tougher Swiss and German mercenaries fought it out to the end.

After three hours of brutal fighting, those few remaining Yorkists threw down their arms. Some 4,000 had been killed, including their commander, Lincoln. Of the chief conspirators, only Lovell escaped, to ride hell-for-leather for his house in Minster Lovell in the Cotswolds, there to hide in a secret room. For years no one knew what had become of him, until in 1708 his skeletal remains were found still in the secret room. He probably died of starvation.

Among the captives taken at Stoke was the impostor Lambert Simnel. He must have expected to be executed, but Henry's humour and compassion came into play. Realising that Simnel was merely a puppet for the Yorkists, the king put him to work in the royal kitchens with the lowest of jobs, turning the spit. Simnel eventually rose to become a falconer and 47 years later died quietly in bed.

Other action this day

1826: In Thessaloniki, Turkish sultan Mahmut II directs cannon fire onto the barracks of mutinying Janissaries, killing 4,000, and orders the execution or exiling of survivors, ending for ever the Janissary Corps, founded four and a half centuries before * 1866: Prussia marches under Bismarck against Austria during the unification of Germany * 1940: First World War hero Philippe Pétain becomes French prime minister

17 June

Americans lose a battle but gain heart at Bunker Hill

1775 The first battle of the American Revolution had been fought only two months earlier and twelve miles away (see 19 April), and now rebel soldiers were occupying three hills looking down on Boston Harbor, threatening British ships. The highest of the hills rose to some 110 feet. It was called Bunker Hill.

When cannon fire from the ships failed to dislodge the Americans, the British commander General Sir William Howe led his force of 2,300 men to remove the Yankees. Most of the action actually took place on neighbouring Breed's Hill. As the British advanced, American general Israel Putnam gave his famous order: 'Don't shoot until you see the whites of their eyes.' (Putnam's command was not altogether original. In destroying the Austrian army at Jagerndorf in 1745, Prince Charles of Prussia gave an almost identical order, as did Frederick the Great in 1757 at the Battle of Prague.)

The American soldiers were barricaded behind makeshift barriers of old fences packed with hay and brush. Initially the accurate colonial gunfire stopped the British attack, but eventually the Americans were forced to retreat when they began to run out of ammunition and weapons.

By nightfall the Battle of Bunker Hill was over. Some 226 British lay dead on the field, with another 826 wounded. The Americans suffered 140 killed in action with 301 more wounded. Even though they lost the battle, the Americans were jubilant. They had demonstrated that untrained militia, hastily assembled, could trade blow for blow with professional British soldiers, and American determination was strongly boosted. But the Revolution still had another six years and four months to run.

Other action this day

1462: Vlad III Dracula (Vlad the Impaler) fails to kill Turkish sultan Mehmed the Conqueror during a surprise night attack near Bucharest * 1497: English king Henry VII defeats Cornish rebels at the Battle of Deptford Bridge * 1888: German general and tank strategist Heinz Guderian is born in Kulm, West Prussia (now in Poland)

18 June

The sayings of Waterloo

1815 Today Napoleon's meteoric career crashed into dust at Waterloo in history's most famous battle. Waterloo changed the fate of nations – but also engendered some of history's most noted quotations.

- 'Napoleon has humbugged me, by God; he has gained twenty-four hours' march on me.' *The Duke of Wellington, on learning three days before the battle that Napoleon had moved across the border from France into Belgium, his sudden arrival catching the Allied command unprepared.*
- 'Hard pounding this, gentlemen; let's see who will pound longest.' *Wellington, when the battle began at 11.30 in the morning with a feint by Napoleon at Wellington's right, followed by an 80-gun French bombardment of the Allied centre.*
- 'Give me night or give me Blücher.' *Wellington, during the early afternoon when Napoleon drove hard at the ridge south of Mont-Saint-Jean that sheltered Wellington's main force, while the duke's ally, the Prussian general Prince Gebhard von Blücher, was still advancing from the east but had not yet joined the battle.*
- 'Come and see how a marshal of France can die!' *French marshal Michel Ney, who had five horses shot out from under him during the battle, trying to inspire his troops after his cavalry overran the British cannons but foundered against Wellington's hollow squares of infantry and the French army began to unravel. (Ney survived the battle, only to be shot by a firing squad six months later – see 7 December.)*
- 'La Garde meurt, mais ne se rend pas.' ('The Guard dies but does not surrender.') *Commander of the Old Guard Pierre Cambronne's answer when a few battalions of the Old Guard were asked to surrender when they were the only remaining French resistance.*
- 'Merde!' *Cambronne, who after the battle denied the grandiloquent quotation above, had instead made a one-word reply, the word since known to the French as 'le mot de Cambronne'.*
- 'Blücher and I have lost thirty thousand men. It has been a

damned nice thing – the nearest run thing you ever saw in your life … By God, I don't think it would have done if I had not been there.' *A self-satisfied Wellington after the battle as he reflected on the result.*

- 'The battle of Waterloo was won on the playing fields of Eton.' *Apocryphally attributed to Wellington after the battle, supposedly a tribute to his officers.*
- 'Not a battle but a change in the direction of the world.' *Victor Hugo, in* Les Misérables.
- 'Wellington was the technician of war, Napoleon its Michelangelo.' *Victor Hugo, in* Les Misérables.
- 'Waterloo is a battle of the first rank won by a captain of the second.' *Victor Hugo, in* Les Misérables.

So it was on this day that an Allied force of 68,000 British, Dutch and German soldiers plus 50,000 Prussians defeated Napoleon's 72,000-man army, inflicting 25,000 casualties while suffering 22,000 of their own.

Other action this day

1155: Crusading king and invader of Italy Fredrick I Barbarossa is crowned Holy Roman Emperor in Rome ∗ 1429: The French defeat the English at the Battle of Patay, the first major field victory of the French in the Hundred Years War ∗ 1757: The Austrians defeat Prussia's Frederick the Great at the Battle of Kolin, Frederick's first-ever loss ∗ 1812: The United States declares war on England to start the War of 1812, later described by American president Harry Truman as 'the silliest damn war we ever had, made no sense at all'

19 June

Mexican emperor Maximilian faces the firing squad

1867 At dawn this morning in Querétaro in central Mexico a tall, blue-eyed Austrian with a foot-long golden beard carefully donned his black frock coat in his prison cell and mounted a carriage accompanied by a priest, en route to his execution. By 6.40am he was dead, cut down by the bullets of a seven-man firing squad of Mexican soldiers. Just 34, he had been Emperor of Mexico for three years and nine days. His last words as he faced the rifles were a courageous 'Viva México'.

Maximilian von Habsburg was the younger brother of the Austrian emperor Franz Joseph. A well-meaning lightweight, he had been persuaded by Mexican reactionaries, French emperor Napoleon III and his own ambitious wife Charlotte to accept the Imperial crown of Mexico, a country mired in a ferocious civil war between extreme reactionaries backed by the church and anti-clerical republicans.

Maximilian had thought to impose a 'liberal dictatorship' to restore order and stop the killing. Although so deeply conservative that he called his brother 'Your Majesty' even when the two were alone together, he could see that the priest-ridden society of the Mexican right, with few civil liberties, no religious freedom and a system of peonage that enslaved most of the peasants, should not continue. But he abhorred the Left's attack on aristocracy and the church. So he accepted the poisoned imperial chalice and assumed control of a government held in power solely by a French army.

Napoleon III had invaded Mexico in 1861 for the putative reason of collecting the debts owed to France by the Mexican government, but his real ambitions were to establish French dominance in Latin America and to 'erect an insuperable barrier against the encroachments of the United States'. The timing had been ideal, since the American Civil War precluded armed intervention to back up the Monroe Doctrine, which in effect banned European powers from intervening in the western hemisphere. Napoleon saw Maximilian as little more than his puppet.

Maximilian tried to govern fairly and refused to rescind the confiscation of church land executed by the republican government. But he was financially incompetent: Mexican debt rose from $81 million in 1861 to $202 million in 1866 and Maximilian's own Imperial household expenses came to $1.5 million per year, 50 times the amount spent by his republican predecessor Benito Juárez. During his entire reign, civil war continued as the republicans tried to regain lost power. In retaliation, in October 1863 Maximilian issued the infamous Black Decree that permitted immediate execution of any captured 'rebel' soldiers, with no possibility to petition the emperor or any other authority for mercy.

In April 1865 Maximilian's regime received a death-blow, although the emperor was too complacent to recognise it: the American Civil War ended, and now it was only a matter of time before the Monroe Doctrine would be enforced. Within a year, an army led by Philip Sheridan was massed on the Rio Grande, threatening to intervene. Napoleon III soon ordered his troops to sail for home, leaving Maximilian with a ragtag force of Austrians, Belgians and a few die-hard conservative Mexicans. He vacillated on whether to abdicate but was dissuaded by his wife, his mother and his ultra-conservative ministers who feared for themselves if the republicans should regain power. He took personal charge of the Imperial army but soon was besieged, starved and finally betrayed at Querétaro, where he surrendered on 15 May 1867.

Tried within a month, Maximilian was found guilty of usurping the power of the legitimate government and using a foreign army to wage war against Mexico. Despite strong protests from Austria, France and Great Britain – and petitions from liberals like Victor Hugo and Garibaldi – Juárez refused to commute the sentence of death by firing squad.

On hearing of Maximilian's execution, Napoleon III waxed philosophical about his whole Mexican adventure: 'God did not want it; let us respect His decrees.' Republicans in Europe were jubilant. As future French prime minister Georges Clemenceau wrote at the time: 'Between us and these people [royalty] there is a war to the death. They have tortured to death millions of us and I bet we have not killed two dozen of them.'

Other action this day

1821: At the Battle of Dragashani in Wallachia, Ottoman sultan Mahmud II defeats Greek insurgents seeking independence for Greece * 1918: Canadian ace Billy Bishop downs five German planes in just fifteen minutes on his last day of combat, bringing his total for the war to 72 * 1944: The US Navy's 5th Fleet, with fifteen aircraft carriers, defeats the Japanese with nine carriers at the Battle of the Philippine Sea, the largest aircraft battle in history; some 500 Japanese planes are shot down in 'The Great Marianas Turkey Shoot'

20 June

Europe is saved from Attila the Hun at the Battle of Châlons

AD 451 'They all have compact, strong limbs and thick necks and are so monstrously ugly and misshapen that one might take them for two-legged beasts ... By the terror of their features they inspired great fear ... They made their foe flee in horror because their swarthy aspect was fearful and they had, if I may call it so, a sort of shapeless lump, not a head, with pin-holes rather than eyes ... Like unreasoning beasts, they are utterly ignorant of the difference between right and wrong.' So did a contemporary historian describe the fearful Huns of Attila.

Although their origin is uncertain, the Huns were probably an Asian people called the Hsung-nu, barbarians of such ferocity that six centuries previously the Chinese had built the Great Wall of China to defend against them.

Attila himself was short and stocky with a wispy beard gracing his abnormally large head. He had become joint king of this Mongol horde in AD 433, sharing the throne with his brother Bleda. But by 445 he had murdered Bleda to take sole command.

The Western Roman emperor at the time was Valentinian III, who normally paid Attila an annual tribute to keep him out of his realm. But in 450 his sister Honoria pleaded with Attila to rescue her from a marriage that Valentinian had arranged, sending him her ring as proof of her trust. Attila immediately declared Honoria to be his own wife, with half of Valentinian's empire as her dowry.

In early 451 Attila led a gigantic nomad force composed primarily of mounted archers across the Rhine and laid waste to every town he came upon: Reims, Metz, Amiens, Beauvais, Cologne, Strasbourg. The devastation he wrought justified his boast that 'grass never grows again where my horse has trod'. Even Paris was nearly destroyed, saved only by the miraculous intervention of Saint Geneviève, whose prayers inspired the defenders to hold the city walls. In like manner, Orléans escaped destruction when its bishop Anianus (later St Aignan) restored the city's crumbling battlements by carrying holy relics around them.

With an army mounted on horseback, Attila used speed, surprise, mobility and above all ferocity rather than military strategy. The cruelty of the Huns and of Attila himself was extraordinary, even in this time of cruelty, as the Western Roman empire was staggering towards its end.

But at last the Romans and their sometime allies the Visigoths combined forces under the command of the Roman general Aetius to meet this so-called Scourge of God. The two armies met on 20 June 451 on the fields near Châlons, in what today is the champagne country of France. Attila set the tone for the conflict by exhorting his men: 'Sunder the sinew, and the limbs collapse; hack the bones and the body falls. Huns of mine, rouse your rage and let your fury swell as of old!'

The battle lasted throughout the day, with terrible slaughter on both sides. At dusk the Visigoths finally smashed through the enemy's flank, threatening the Hun centre and almost killing their leader, although the Visigothic king Theodoric I was thrown from his horse and trampled to death. Attila was forced to retreat, the first and only defeat in his marauding career.

The terrible Attila lived for only another year, spending that time laying waste to Italy. But the Battle of Châlons had turned the tide, saving much of Western Europe from the ravages of the Huns. Attila's defeat also enormously boosted the prestige of the Church of Rome, which claimed much credit for resisting the heathen Huns at Paris and Orléans.

Such was the terror that Attila inspired that he appears in the legends of France, Italy and Scandinavia. He is also featured in the German *Nibelungenlied* under the name of Etzel, while he is called Atli in Icelandic sagas.

Other action this day

1596: Walter Raleigh and Robert Devereux, Earl of Essex storm and capture Cadiz; among their soldiers is the poet John Donne * 1791: Louis XVI and Marie Antoinette flee Revolutionary Paris to Varennes, only to be brought back under guard * 1825: Greek revolutionary and patriot Papaflessas is killed in the Battle of Maniaki during the Greek War of Independence

21 June

The Black Hole of Calcutta

1756 At 6.15 this morning at Fort William in Calcutta, 23 dishevelled survivors staggered out through the brig door into the open air.
They were the lucky ones; 123 British soldiers and civilians lay dead
inside, in the infamous Black Hole of Calcutta.

In preparation for a possible clash with the French in India, earlier
in the year the British East India Company had started reinforcing
Fort William, but Siraj ud-Daulah, the Nawab of Bengal, saw this as
a provocative move against his own rule and a threat to his independence. When the East India Company ignored his requests to stop the
build-up, Siraj marched on the fort with an overwhelming force of
30,000 foot soldiers, 20,000 horsemen, 400 war elephants and 80
cannon. After nearly four days of fighting that caused heavy casualties among the defenders, most of the British soldiers fled, along with
their Indian troops, leaving a token force under John Holwell, once a
military surgeon but now a high-ranking East India Company civil
servant. Facing hopeless odds and weakened by more desertions,
Holwell surrendered the fort.

Then Siraj's soldiers, apparently acting on their own initiative,
herded their 146 prisoners into the fort's brig, a 14×18-foot cell that
the British had previously dubbed 'the Black Hole'. Holwell has left
us a memorable account of what followed: 'A hundred and forty-six
wretches, exhausted by continual fatigue and action, [were] crammed
together, in a close sultry night ... shut up to the eastward and southward (the only quarters from whence air could reach us) by dead
walls, and by a wall and door to the north, open only to the westward
by two windows, strongly barred with iron, from which we could
receive scarce any the least circulation of fresh air.'

At first the prisoners tried unsuccessfully to force open the cell
door, while almost immediately 'every one fell into a perspiration so
profuse ... [that it] brought on a raging thirst, which increased as the
body was drained of moisture'. Then one prisoner 'proposed that
every man should sit down on his hams', but every time it was tried,
the weaker ones 'fell to rise no more, for they were immediately trod
to death or suffocated'.

The prisoners tried to bribe their guards to beg Siraj to release them, but the Nawab had retired for the night, and none dared awaken him.

By nine o'clock the sweltering heat had become intolerable and even breathing became difficult. Holwell relates that 'by keeping my face between two of the bars, I obtained air enough to give my lungs easy play'. By now the prisoners were suffering severely from lack of water, and one of the guards, 'taking pity on us, ordered the people to bring some skins of water ... We had no means of conveying it into the prison, but by hats forced through the bars ... There ensued such violent struggles ... to get it, that before it reached the lips of any one, there would be scarcely a tea cup full left in them ... Several ... force[d] their way to the water [and] pressed down those in their way, who had less strength, and trampled them to death.' Holwell was reduced to sucking the sweat from his sleeve and even tried drinking his own urine, but 'it was so bitter, there was no enduring a second taste'.

By dawn most of the prisoners were dead of heat stroke, suffocation, or crushing, and 'the stench arising from the dead bodies was grown so intolerable'. At around 5.30 Siraj finally awoke and, for the first time becoming aware of his prisoners' plight, ordered their release. But 'as the [cell] door opened inwards, and as the dead were piled up against it, and covered all the rest of the floor, it was impossible to open it by any efforts from without; it was therefore necessary that the dead be removed by the few that were within, who were become so feeble, that the task, though it was the condition of life, was not performed without the most difficulty, and it was twenty minutes after the order came before the door could be opened.'

At last, just after six o'clock, the few survivors tottered out of the Black Hole. Siraj's soldiers then dragged the dead bodies out of the cell, threw them into a ditch and covered them with earth.

Siraj's victory at Fort William and the treatment of his captives did not remain long unavenged. A year and two days later, the East India Company decisively defeated him at the Battle of Plassey, and on 2 July he was executed on orders from Mir Jafar, the puppet ruler whom the British had installed in his place.

Other action this day

AD 68: Legio X Fretensis, commanded by future Roman emperor

Vespasian, destroys Jericho as the Romans crush the Jewish Revolt * 1558: Italian condottiere and marshal of France Piero Strozzi dies during the siege of Thionville near Calais during the Italian War of 1551–59 * 1813: The Duke of Wellington routs the French at Vitoria, forcing the Spanish king, Napoleon's brother Joseph, to abandon Spain and return to France * 1942: German general Erwin Rommel captures British-held Tobruk in North Africa

22 June

Americans land on Daiquiri Beach

1898 Today should be observed as D-Day, and a generous-sized Daiquiri cocktail hoisted to honour the US forces that landed this morning on an enemy beach, the vanguard of a great invasion. It wasn't at Normandy or Iwo Jima or Inchon. It was at a remote spot on the long southern coastline of Cuba, where elements of the army's V Corps went ashore at Daiquiri Beach, some eighteen miles east of Santiago.

This was amphibious warfare with a distinctly holiday air about it. From the deck of a troopship the correspondent Richard Harding Davis described the first wave going in: 'Soon the sea was dotted with rows of white boats filled with men bound about with white blanket rolls and with muskets at all angles, and as they rose and fell on the water and the newspaper yachts and transports crept in closer and closer, the scene was strangely suggestive of a boat race, and one almost waited for the starting gun.'

A preliminary naval bombardment had evidently driven away any Spanish troops who might have been around to contest the landing site, which was just as well, for even a few hundred well-motivated defenders could have inflicted a terrible slaughter on the V Corps and changed the course of the war.

During this first day of invasion, 6,000 infantry, accompanied by a few reporters, got ashore in a continuous stream of launches and barges. Horses and mules for the artillery and pack trains were simply shoved out of cargo ports to swim ashore. Later, when cavalry dispatched by General 'Fighting Joe' Wheeler, who had once commanded troops of the Confederacy, raced up a hill behind the beach and raised their regimental flag, a reporter recorded that the entire invasion force, afloat and ashore, began cheering 'and every steam whistle on the ocean for miles about shrieked and tooted and roared in a pandemonium of delight and pride and triumph'.

With the advent of evening, the troops began pitching their tents above the beach. In the words of one historian: 'They were spending their first night in the field of war, in the near presence of the enemy. Whether or not they would even spend another they did not know.' So began the first ground operation of the Spanish–American War.

They don't make invasions like that any more. But you can make a Daiquiri by mixing four parts rum to one of lime juice, sugar to taste, and plenty of ice. Shake well before serving.

Other action this day

168 BC: At Pydna on the north-east coast of Greece, Roman consul Aemileus Paulus crushes the Macedonians, who suffer more than 25,000 dead or captured out of 40,000 * 1476: The Swiss annihilate the army of the Duke of Burgundy, Charles the Bold, at the Battle of Morat * 1815: Napoleon abdicates, proclaiming his son François (the future Duke of Reichstadt) Emperor of the French * 1941: Hitler unleashes Operation Barbarossa, the invasion of Russia * 1944: The 27-day Operation Bagration in Belorussia begins, which clears German forces from the Belorussian Soviet Socialist Republic and eastern Poland and in which the Russians lose 178,000 killed and missing, while the Germans lose 399,000

23 June

Robert the Bruce defeats the English at Bannockburn

1314 On this day near Stirling Castle outside Edinburgh, the Scottish king Robert the Bruce carefully positioned his infantrymen on a hillside above a stream called Bannockburn, taking advantage of cavalry-slowing bogs on one side of his front and an infantry-concealing forest on the other. Then he waited for the vanguard of the English army.

For almost twenty years now the Scots had fought to remain independent from English domination, in a seesaw struggle with England's King Edward I, the 'Hammer of the Scots'. Edward invaded Scotland for the first time in 1296, then again in 1306, after the Earl of Carrick, as Bruce was then, was crowned the Scottish king. So Bruce as king became an outlaw, always on the run, at one point harried clean out of Scotland, his wife, daughters and sisters imprisoned, his youngest brother beheaded.

But Edward died at the beginning of the second invasion, and Edward II proved no match for his father in matters of war. The second campaign languished, and as victories came for Bruce and his growing forces, the Scottish nobility began to favour his cause. Now, however, for a third time, an English army, 25,000 strong, had come over the border, with the intent of relieving the siege of Stirling Castle, the last English stronghold in the north of the country.

On 23 June the English delivered their main attack, the sheer weight of which, Edward was sure, must prevail. His cavalry crowded forward over the narrow front of stable footing but piled up in a congested mass, unable to get past the thick clusters of Scottish pikemen. In the confusion, English archers rained down arrows on their own cavalry as much as on the Scots.

The brutal slogging match might have ended as a bloody draw but for an ingenious ruse that decided the day. A force of Scottish camp followers – grooms, priests, cooks and porters – emerged from the forest on the English left, waving banners and shouting in simulation of a counter-attack. The English, hesitating at what appeared to be a fresh army sent against them, began to withdraw, slowly at first but soon in panic when it became known that King Edward had decamped.

Reinvigorated, the Scots drove their enemy from the field, leaving thousands dead and wounded and capturing hundreds more. Among the English dead were 21 barons and baronets, 42 knights and 700 men-at-arms. The ransoms paid for the prisoners would for a time make Scotland a rich country. The most important of the captives was the powerful Earl of Hereford, whom Bruce exchanged for his wife, his daughters and his sisters.

The great victory at Bannockburn gave substance to the Scots' claim of independence and to Bruce's leadership of his nation. It did not end the war, which dragged on until 1328, when Edward III signed the Treaty of Northampton, the main clause of which read: 'Scotland shall remain to Robert, King of Scots, free and undivided from England, without any subjection, servitude, claim or demand whatsoever.'

Other action this day

203 BC: Hannibal crosses to North Africa from Croton (Cotrone) in Calabria on his way to defend Carthage from invading Romans under Scipio * AD 79: Roman emperor and general Vespasian dies * 1757: Clive of India crushes the forces of the Nawab of Bengal at the Battle of Plassey, establishing British East India Company rule in India

24 June

Two emperors and a king slug it out at Solferino

1859 When a combined Piedmontese–French army met the forces of Imperial Austria at Solferino a few miles south-west of Italy's Lake Garda today, the troops were commanded by two emperors and a king: Napoleon III of France, Franz Joseph of Austria and Victor Emmanuel, already King of Sardinia-Piedmont and soon to be the first king of a united Italy. This was to be the decisive battle in the Second Italian War of Independence.

The battle was fought along a fifteen-mile front in almost unendurable heat, as some 270,000 men met to kill each other in a struggle that lasted from 4.00 in the morning to 7.00 in the evening. In the end, the Piedmontese–French army prevailed, but the cost was frightful. Each side lost some 15,000 men killed or wounded, with some 8,000 Austrians captured or missing.

The victorious Victor Emmanuel recoiled at the slaughter, aware of how near he had come to losing. 'Luck plays too great a role', was his view of war after this battle. As for Napoleon III, although he claimed victory, he was so appalled by the carnage that he pushed for an armistice, which was duly signed eighteen days later, ending the war.

Now most of Lombardy, including its capital Milan, hitherto controlled by Austria, was transferred to the Piedmontese, who shortly occupied central Italy as well. Nice and Savoy were also stripped from the Austrians and awarded to the French.

One other result of Solferino was less apparent at the time. Arriving on the day of the battle was a 31-year-old Swiss named Henri Dunant, who had come not to fight but to seek help from Emperor Napoleon on a business deal. By evening there were over 30,000 injured, dying, and dead on the battlefield, with little attempt to provide care. Some of these wounded headed for the nearby village of Castiglione, looking for food, water and medical help. Many found sanctuary in the local church, and there Dunant and some local women worked for three desperate days and nights trying to save the injured and the dying of both sides.

So shocked was Dunant by the savagery and suffering that in 1862 he wrote *Un Souvenir de Solférino* (*A Memory of Solferino*), a book describing the 'chaotic disorder, despair unspeakable, and misery of every kind' of the battle, and he then went on to help found the Red Cross and gather international support for the establishment of the Geneva Convention.

Other action this day

217 BC: Hannibal defeats the Romans at the Battle of Lake Trasimene, killing 15,000, including consul Gaius Flaminius * 1128: Portuguese forces led by Afonso Henriques (the Conqueror) defeat the army of his mother Teresa de León and her lover at the Battle of São Mamede and he becomes Portugal's first king as Afonso I * 1821: Simón Bolívar defeats Spanish forces at the Battle of Carabobo, leading to the independence of Venezuela

25 June

Custer's last stand

1876 George Armstrong Custer was a tall, rangy man with a hard narrow face, a high forehead, flaxen hair worn long, and a droopy old-cowpoke moustache. Few remember today that he was also a noted soldier. In the American Civil War he was the youngest general in the Union army, and at the war's close it was he who received the Confederate flag of truce and was present at the South's surrender at Appomattox.

By 1876 Custer was 37 years old and now, instead of Southerners, he was fighting a coalition of Indian tribes, including Sioux, Cheyenne and Arapaho. Leading the Indians was the great chief Sitting Bull.

On 17 June the combined Indian forces had defeated American troops in the Battle of the Rosebud in the Montana territory. Shortly after this victory Sitting Bull had driven himself into a trance performing the Sun Dance, after which he reported having seen a vision of soldiers falling to earth like grasshoppers from the sky, accurately predicting the victory that was to follow in a few days.

Meanwhile, Custer was leading the US 7th Cavalry when on 25 June he came upon the Indian encampment by a river called the Little Bighorn. Not realising the number of enemy he faced, he rashly divided his force of some 600 troopers into three groups and attacked.

Custer was personally leading about 225 soldiers as the battle started. Of more than 1,000 waiting Indians was a 26-year-old chief named White Bull. Later, White Bull told his story: 'When I rushed him, he threw his rifle at me without shooting. I dodged it. We grabbed each other and wrestled there in the dust and smoke [...] He tried to wrench my rifle from me. I lashed him across the face with my quirt [...] He let go [...] But he fought hard. He was desperate. He hit me with his fists on my jaw and shoulders, then grabbed my long braids with both hands, pulled my face close and tried to bite my nose off [...] Finally I broke free. He drew his pistol. I wrenched it out of his hand and struck him with it three or four times on the head, knocked him over, shot him in the head, and fired at his heart.'

The general and his force were killed to the last man at Little Bighorn in a battle known as Custer's Last Stand. It was a fitting end for the man who coined the odious phrase: 'The only good Indians I ever saw were dead.'

After his victory at Little Bighorn, Sitting Bull continued to resist American attempts to capture him until 1883, when, his followers devastated by hunger and disease, he finally surrendered and was sent to the Standing Rock Agency to live. Two years later, however, he was given his freedom to join Buffalo Bill's Wild West show. In 1890, amid fears of further Indian uprisings, American troops were sent to arrest him but killed him while his warriors were trying to save him.

Other action this day

1646: The Royalist surrender of Oxford to the Roundheads signifies the end of the English Civil War * 1944: A Finnish force of 50,000 men, reinforced by German air support, defeats a 150,000-man Russian army at the Battle of Tali-Ihantala * 1950: At 4.00am this Sunday, North Korea invades South Korea to start the Korean War

26 June

Emperor Julian the Apostate – done in by a saint?

AD 363 Today Rome's last pagan emperor, Julian the Apostate, died in his tent near the banks of the Tigris River from wounds received in battle against the Persians. His death engendered an enduring myth that strengthened the very Christianity he had tried so hard to undermine.

Julian was a complex man, above all a first-rate general but also a philosopher and accomplished writer of essays, letters and even satires. A contemporary reported that 'his eyes were fine and flashing, an indication of the nimbleness of his mind'. Despite his other achievements, however, Julian is best remembered for his hostility to emerging Christianity only 50 years after his uncle, Constantine the Great, had declared it the empire's religion of choice.

Born to the purple in AD 331, Julian became Caesar of the West at only 24, while his elder cousin Constantius was Caesar of the East. A burly, handsome man with a pointed beard, he was an inspiring leader of men who endured the hardships of military life along with his troops. For six years after becoming the Western emperor, he proved his mettle against Germanic tribes, retaking Colonia Agrippina (today's Cologne) and crushing the Alamanni at Strasbourg. He also scored notable victories over the Salian Franks, the Charnavi and the Attuarian Franks.

On 3 November 361 Constantius died, and Julian became emperor of the entire Roman empire. Now he began his famous attacks on Christians (whom he somewhat contemptuously referred to as 'Galileans'). Although raised a Christian, Julian had converted to Hellenism, believing that Christianity weaned men's loyalty away from the state and the emperor. He saw the religion's fractious sects as divisive, claiming that 'no wild beasts are as dangerous to men as Christians are to one another'. He reopened many pagan temples and made Christian churches return property previously looted from them. He proscribed the veneration of holy relics and even had two of his own bodyguards executed for opposing the ban. He never imposed an outright prohibition of Christianity, but in 362 he revoked its legal primacy, making all religions equal before the law.

In 359 the Sassanid (Persian) emperor Shapur II had launched a campaign against the Romans. In March 363 Julian marched east to meet the threat. Soon deep into Sassanid territory, he arrived with 35,000 men before the enemy capital of Ctesiphon (below modern Baghdad) at the end of May. There, on the 29th of the month, he faced a Sassanid army of infantry, supported by cataphracts (heavily armoured cavalry) and war elephants.

Julian's generals hesitated to tackle such a force, but the emperor positioned his battalions in a crescent formation and attacked the enemy under the very walls of their capital. The wings of Julian's army closed around the Persians, leading to total defeat of the enemy, as Julian lost but 70 men to 2,500 for the Persians.

What was left of the Sassanid army hunkered down within the city walls, but Julian had no siege equipment, and, after camping for two months before the city, he learned that a second Sassanid army was on the way. Unable to consolidate his victory, he was instead compelled to withdraw.

On 16 June Julian's disappointed troops began their retreat along the Tigris, heading for a rendezvous with another Roman force, but ten days later near the town of Samarra his rearguard came under attack from the pursuing Sassanids. Hearing the sounds of battle, Julian grabbed his sword and plunged into the mêlée, so eager to fight that he neglected to don his armour. When the Romans began to drive off the enemy, Julian led the pursuit, only to be struck in the side by a thrown spear, which pierced his liver. His soldiers carried him to his tent, where his personal physician washed the wound with wine and attempted to suture the gash, but he died just before midnight.

As the years passed, apocryphal stories began to proliferate about Julian's death. According to one tale, one of Julian's boyhood friends, Saint Basil of Caesarea, who was languishing in prison when Julian was killed, prayed to Saint Mercurius to help him. Obligingly, the good saint appeared in his cell in a vision, claiming to have wielded the spear that felled the emperor (no nonsense about the sixth commandment here).

Another myth relates that a Christian who was one of Julian's own soldiers threw the fatal spear. (In one version Saint Basil ordered the soldier to slay Julian.) According to this account, the emperor's final words were a mournful 'Vicisti, Galilæe' ('Thou hast conquered, O Galilean'), as he recognised that Christianity would triumph after his death.

Sadly, Julian's purported last words were first recorded by Bishop Theodoret of Cyrrhus in the 5th century, and the story of Saint Basil is first related a century after that. Nonetheless, later Christian historians convinced many a God-fearing Christian that Julian was killed by a saint, a sure sign of God's wrath against the unyielding apostate and a lesson for those who might stand against the True Church.

Other action this day

1541: Spanish conquistador Francisco Pizarro is assassinated by followers of fellow conquistador Diego de Almagro, who had been executed by Pizarro's brother Hernando * 1794: The French under Jean-Baptiste Jourdan defeat the Austrians at the Battle of Fleurus during the French Revolutionary Wars * 1898: Lieutenant General Lewis 'Chesty' Puller, the most decorated US Marine in history, is born in West Point, Virginia * 1918: Allied troops under General 'Black Jack' Pershing defeat the Germans under Crown Prince Wilhelm at Belleau Wood

27 June

Peter the Great crushes the Swedes at Poltava

1709 This day brought mixed fortunes for Russia's Peter the Great. In 1695, when he was 23, Peter experienced his first real battle – and lost – against the Turks at Azov. In 1709 he was 37 and at war again, this time against one of the great soldier-kings of history, Charles XII of Sweden.

Charles had inherited Sweden's throne when he was just fifteen and ruled as an absolute monarch. By the time he was 27 in 1709 he had transformed Sweden into a great European power through a series of wars against Poland, Russia and various German states, which came to be known as the Great Northern War.

On 27 June 1709, Charles's small army of only 17,000 men attacked a Russian fortified camp under Peter's command at Poltava in the Ukraine. The Swedes had two distinct disadvantages. First, their army – already tired and battle-weary – was massively outnumbered by Peter's 80,000 troops; and second, Charles himself could not personally lead his army, as was his custom, because he had earlier sustained a wound in the left foot and had to be carried on a litter between two horses.

The Russians gave way before the initial Swedish assault, then launched 40,000 men in a devastating counter-attack that obliterated the Swedes. The shattered Swedish survivors retreated southwards and finally capitulated at the River Dnjestr, outside the village of Perevolotjna, four days later. Charles himself managed to escape with about 1,500 of his soldiers and took refuge in Turkey, where he was obliged to remain for the next six years.

Peter the Great's victory marked the start of Sweden's decline from being the dominant nation of northern Europe to the lesser nation that it has remained ever since. Poltava also marked Russia's ascendancy, one that it has never relinquished.

Other action this day

1472: Duke of Burgundy Charles the Bold invests Beauvais to begin a 25-day siege that fails because a local butcher's daughter named Jeanne Hachette, armed with her father's hatchet, inspires her fellow citizens by cutting down the Burgundian flag-bearer and seizing his standard * 1795: 10,000 French émigrés returning from England land at the Breton port of Carnac, only to be captured and executed by French republicans * 1800: Napoleon's 'first grenadier of France', Théophile de la Tour d'Auvergne, is killed at the Battle of Oberhausen

28 June

Sarajevo

1914 Why the Archduke Franz Ferdinand, heir apparent to the throne of Austria, chose to visit the capital of Bosnia in this summer of Balkan discontent, we will never know for sure. 'To pay that visit,' wrote Rebecca West, 'was an act so suicidal that one fumbles the pages of history books to find if there is not some explanation of his going, if he was not subject to some compulsion. But if ever a man went anywhere of his own free will, Franz Ferdinand went so to Sarajevo.'

Only eight years earlier Bosnia had been annexed by Austria-Hungary, infuriating the highly nationalist Serbs who constituted a large minority of Bosnia's population and hoped for eventual union with Serbia. Anti-Austrian feeling ran high, now exacerbated by Franz Ferdinand's decision to review military exercises in Bosnia in his role as inspector general of the Austro-Hungarian army.

When the trip was announced, the Serbian government, no friend of Austria, alerted Vienna to the strong likelihood of an assassination attempt by the secret Serbian irredentist group Crna Ruka or Black Hand, officially entitled Ujedinjenje ili Smrt, Unification or Death. This infamous organisation had become so powerful that in 1913 its leader was named head of intelligence for the Serbian general staff.

Deaf to all advice, warnings and good sense, the ambitious and unpopular Franz Ferdinand determined to carry out the military inspection, perhaps viewing the visit as a rehearsal for his own emperorship. Whatever his motive, off he went, more arch-fool than archduke.

After attending two days of Austrian army manoeuvres, provocatively conducted near the Serbian border, Franz Ferdinand, now joined by his wife Sophie, started a processional drive through Sarajevo at 10.00 this Sunday morning – an offensive choice of date since it was Vidovdan, Serbia's national day.

You might have guessed that in such circumstances Austrian troops would have been posted along the route. But there were none, only local police. And surely the tour would have been cancelled after someone flung a bomb that glanced off the royal automobile and exploded under the next car, wounding an aide-de-camp. But the tour proceeded as scheduled to the Town Hall.

There the welcoming festivities were cut short and a route change agreed, but somehow no one informed the chauffeurs. At 11.15 the tour resumed. When the lead car with the deputy mayor of Sarajevo turned to follow the old route, there was confusion among the security detail. The second car, carrying the royal couple, came to a stop while things were sorted out. At this point, Gavrilo Princip, a nine-teen-year-old Bosnian student and member of the Black Hand, stepped from the crowd of onlookers, drew a revolver and fired, one bullet hitting the archduke, another his wife who had thrown herself across the car to shield him. Both died within minutes. It was their fourteenth wedding anniversary.

Princip was instantly captured, tried within four months and sentenced to twenty years in prison, the maximum allowable for criminals under twenty. In less than four years he was dead of tuberculosis.

But one month to the day after the assassination, even before Princip was brought to trial, Austria declared war on Serbia, precipi-tating the First World War.

Other action this day

1098: During the First Crusade, as Raymond of Aguilers carries the Holy Lance before them, Crusaders under Bohemund storm out of Antioch to defeat the Turks under Kerbogha * 1644: Manchus defeat rebels under Li Tzu-ch'eng at Shanhaikuan, as the new Ch'ing dynasty replaces the Ming in China * 1778: The perhaps apocryphal Molly Pitcher takes her fallen husband's place at the cannon during the Battle of Monmouth Court House, which the Americans claim as a victory after the British with-draw * 1855: British field marshal Raglan dies of dysentery during the siege of Sevastopol

29 June

King Charles defeats the Roundheads at Cropredy Bridge

1644 In the twenty months since Charles I had raised his standard at Nottingham to start the English Civil War, he had personally commanded his army in four battles – Edgehill, Turnham Green, the siege of Gloucester and the First Battle of Newbury – and each had ended inconclusively, the king neither victor nor vanquished.

Now, in the spring of 1644, Charles was once again in the field, but two Parliamentarian armies were advancing towards the Royal capital at Oxford; the king was in danger of being surrounded. But then the Roundheads divided their forces, half heading south to relieve Lyme Regis, and Charles decided to seize his chance and draw the remaining enemy army under Sir William Waller into battle.

On Saturday morning, 29 June, the Royalist force of 5,000 horse and 3,500 foot moved north from Banbury, along the main road on the east side of the River Cherwell, to the east of the town of Cropredy. Shadowing their movement from the other side of the river were Waller's 5,000 horse and 4,000 foot. The armies were actually in sight of each other, little more than a mile apart, but neither dared to cross the river in the face of the other's cannon.

Now, suddenly another threat appeared: 300 Roundhead cavalry were descending from the north. With the two forces so evenly balanced, Charles knew that even so small a reinforcement could turn the battle, and he dispatched a vanguard of his own cavalry to intercept the Parliamentarian horse, ordering his infantry to follow close behind. But somehow his instructions failed to reach his small rearguard of two cavalry brigades and some infantry, which now lagged a mile and a half behind the other Royalist units and became dangerously exposed.

From his vantage point on a nearby hill, Waller could see the opportunity unfold. Dispatching two regiments of horse and nine companies of foot across Cropredy Bridge to block the rearguard's northerly advance, Waller himself and 1,000 men drove to cross the Cherwell further south to catch the king's rearguard in a pincer movement.

After routing a small detachment of Royal dragoons at Cropredy Bridge, the Parliamentarian infantry turned south to attack the rearguard, while the cavalry galloped north to confront the main body of Charles's force where they were crossing the Cherwell at Hay's Bridge.

But now Waller made the same error that Charles had made: he allowed his forces to become spread out and dispersed. The king's rearguard offered stiff resistance to the Roundhead infantry attack, and Royalist musketeers, having blocked Hay's Bridge with an overturned cart, now poured withering fire on Waller's horse. Meanwhile, Charles was bringing his infantry back from Hays Bridge, to charge into Waller's infantry and artillery, now unprotected by cavalry.

The Royalist attack forced Waller's men back across Cropredy Bridge, but Parliamentary artillery prevented them from crossing in pursuit. By evening the two armies held roughly the same relative positions that they had occupied in the morning, facing each other across the Cherwell.

The next day Charles tried fruitlessly to persuade Waller to turn his coat. He then learned of the approach of some 4,500 Parliamentarian reinforcements and that night stole away with his army under cover of darkness.

In terms of territory gained, the battle had been yet another draw, but the casualty count made it clear that this time Charles had triumphed. He had suffered only a few casualties, but the Parliamentarians had lost eleven artillery pieces and 700 men, many through desertion immediately after the encounter. In the aftermath of the battle, the morale of Waller's army disintegrated, and by the middle of July his army had collapsed into mutiny and chaos.

Despite this timely victory, the Civil War continued indecisively until June 1645 when the Roundheads shattered the king's army at Naseby. Now defeat followed defeat until Charles sought sanctuary with the Scotch Presbyterian army, only to be turned over to the Parliamentarians, who executed him on 30 January 1649. If the Battle of Cropredy Bridge was Charles's first real victory, it was also his last; indeed, it was the last battle ever won by an English king on English soil.

Other action this day

1149: Syrian ruler Nur al-Din destroys the Crusader army of Raymond of Antioch at the Battle of Inab * 1659: Ukrainians defeat Russian prince Aleksey Trubetskoy at the Battle of Konotop * 1943: US forces land in New Guinea to expel the Japanese

30 June

The Night of Sorrows

1520 Today tens of thousands of Aztec warriors almost annihilated conquistador Hernán Cortés's tiny force of Spanish soldiers as they desperately tried to break out of the Aztec capital of Tenochtitlan. It proved to be the last gasp of the Aztec empire.

In August 1519 Cortés had landed on the coast of Mexico with 500 soldiers, 100 sailors and sixteen horses. After forming an alliance with the Tlaxcalan tribe, he advanced to Cholula, a city allied to the Aztecs. There, after having been told that the Cholula were plotting to assassinate him and his Spaniards, he butchered some 3,000 inhabitants and burned the city.

A month later Cortés's army, along with 3,000 Tlaxcalan allies, reached the Aztec capital, a huge city in the middle of a lake where Mexico City now stands, built on islands connected to the mainland by eight causeways.

Initially King Moctezuma welcomed Cortés, believing him to be an emissary of the god Quetzalcoatl, and offered him a palace to live in. Cortés realised, however, that Moctezuma could at any moment simply call his guards and have all the Spaniards put to death. Accompanied by 35 of his soldiers, he seized the king in his own palace, chained him as a prisoner and hostage against Aztec rebellion, and took an enormous ransom of gold. Throughout, Moctezuma cooperated with extreme passivity, offering no resistance.

But then Cortés had to go back to the coast to head off some more Spaniards sent to arrest him (he converted them to his own cause with promises of gold). By the time of his return, the Aztecs were in open revolt, sparked by the massacre of some Aztec nobles by the lieutenant left in charge in Tenochtitlan during his absence. Warriors now besieged the palace housing the Spaniards and Moctezuma. When Cortés forced the king to appear on the palace balcony to plead with his people for peace, his warriors jeered and hurled rocks, hitting him on the leg, arm and head. Three days later Moctezuma died, Spanish accounts claiming from the wound to his head and Aztec reports insisting that the Spaniards had murdered him.

Now the Aztecs seized the great temple and fought off several attempts to retake it. Determined to annihilate the Spaniards, they demolished bridges around the city to keep their enemy from reaching the mainland. Cortés realised that he was doomed if he stayed in the capital; even, he later recalled, if 25,000 Indians perished for every Spaniard, his men would still be destroyed. He had no choice but to break out.

Shortly before midnight on this rainy, moonless night, Cortés and his soldiers started their clandestine departure, their horses' hooves muffled, the men in silence. Two companies of 50 Spaniards each led the escape, followed by 150 soldiers and 400 Tlaxcalans carrying a mobile bridge and wooden boards to cross the canals. Then came the rest of the army, with 30 Spaniards and 300 Tlaxcalans bringing up the rear. The soldiers were laden with stolen gold, about seven tons of it, with a value today of perhaps £100 million.

The army crossed the first bridges but now came under attack from both sides of a causeway from an 'infinite multitude' of Aztec warriors brandishing spears and loosing arrows from canoes. As spearmen charged down the causeway, Spanish crossbowmen and harquebusiers opened fire, and armoured infantry hacked their way forward through the enemy. Spanish horsemen were dragged from their mounts and soldiers pulled into the water where, weighed down by armour and gold, they sank and drowned.

Cortés and five other horsemen led 500 infantry down the causeway. They charged through groups of enemy warriors, swam gaps where bridges had stood, and finally reached the mainland. Having established a secure base, Cortés then returned with three horsemen and twenty foot soldiers to help the rest of his men cut through the mass of enemy. By the time that the Spanish reached the mainland, two thirds of their original force had been slain or captured, and all the survivors had been wounded. Their Tlaxcalan allies lost 2,000 men. Back in the capital, the captured Spaniards were sacrificed, their living hearts cut out on Aztec altars. In Spain this calamitous flight from Tenochtitlan is called La Noche Triste – the Night of Sorrows. Today, a massive old ahuehuete tree still marks the spot where Cortés is supposed to have wept at his loss of men and treasure.

But Spanish conquistadors were almost as tough as the armour they wore. After six days of retreat, Cortés fought the Aztecs once again, this time on an open plain near the town of Otumba. There his armoured cavalry and infantry annihilated the Aztecs, setting the stage for his final conquest of Tenochtitlan. On 13 August 1521 the capital fell, bringing the Aztec empire to an end.

Other action this day

1422: Italian *condottiere* Francesco Bussone's Milanese crossbowmen enfilade the invading Swiss flank while his dismounted men-at-arms charge the enemy centre to win the Battle of Arbedo * 1643: The Royalists consolidate their hold on Yorkshire in the Battle of Adwalton Moor during the English Civil War * 1708: The Duke of Marlborough and Prince Eugene of Savoy defeat the French at the Battle of Oudenaarde in Flanders * 1934: The Night of the Long Knives – Hitler bloodily purges Ernst Röhm's SA (Sturmabteilung or Brownshirts), killing at least 85, to consolidate his own power

1 July

Teddy Roosevelt's Rough Riders storm San Juan Hill

1898 In the midday Cuban sun, thousands of American soldiers lay along the trough of the San Juan River, waiting for orders, sweltering in the riverbed, low on food, water and ammunition. Ahead of them, past the jungle fringe, they could see open ground leading to their objective, the strong defensive positions atop San Juan Hill and neighbouring Kettle Hill, from which Spanish rifle fire was having effect.

On the far right of the line was the 1st US Volunteer Cavalry Regiment, a picturesque contingent of cowboys and college men who like thousands of their peers had joined the crusade to free Cuba from Spanish tyranny. An appreciative press had dubbed the regiment variously 'Teddy's Terrors', 'Rocky Mountain Rustlers', and finally, still alliteratively and most pleasing to its lieutenant colonel, 'Roosevelt's Rough Riders'.

Not too many weeks earlier, Theodore Roosevelt had been the assistant secretary of the US Navy. But Roosevelt knew an absolutely bully opportunity when he saw one, and with war declared against Spain he resigned his office to raise a regiment of volunteers.

Around 2.00pm, Gatling guns were brought forward and went into action, clearing the Spanish soldiers from the top of San Juan Hill. Now, commanders shouted out orders to advance, and from the jungle beyond the riverbed a long line of blue-shirted figures emerged and started across the meadows. The Rough Riders were in reserve, but when Roosevelt got the message 'Move forward and support the regulars', he decided it called for an all-out charge. Gesticulating with his hat, he led the way, mounted on his horse Texas, followed by a crowd of Rough Riders and black troopers from the 9th and 10th Cavalry. In a rush, they took Kettle Hill.

To his left, he could see the main advance stalled on San Juan Hill some 700 yards away as American artillery, two miles to the rear and so far largely inactive, suddenly opened up on the summit. Frantic waving of hats and flags called off the firing, but the delay allowed Roosevelt time to join the attack for its final drive. In a few glorious minutes it was over, and all along the ridgeline American soldiers stood, firing at the backs of the retreating enemy and gazing down at the city of Santiago.

It was 4.00pm when Roosevelt brought order to the happy confusion of victory, formed up the soldiers on the summit, and prepared to meet the press. One historian wrote of the occasion: 'As the newspaper dispatches went off describing the heroism of the Rough Riders and their lieutenant-colonel, another military genius had been given to American history.'

Hostilities were over by August, and Secretary of State John Hay pronounced the outing 'a splendid little war'. And so it was for the United States, which in acquiring Puerto Rico, Guam and the Philippine islands became a world power; for Cuba, which gained its independence after 400 years of Spanish rule; and for Colonel Roosevelt, his nation's newest hero, who went on to become governor of New York, vice president for President William McKinley, and on McKinley's death on 14 September 1901, President of the United States.

Other action this day

AD 251: Roman Emperor Decius and his son are both killed as the Goths defeat the Romans in the Battle of Arbrittus (in modern Bulgaria) * 1270: Louis IX (St Louis) leaves on the disastrous Eighth Crusade, during which he will die of smallpox * 1690: William III defeats the deposed James II at the Battle of the Boyne in Ireland * 1916: During the first day of the Battle of the Somme, 100,000 British troops advance two miles but 20,000 are killed and 40,000 wounded or captured, the greatest one-day loss ever sustained by an army in history

2 July

The first American soldier-turned-president

1775 Today General George Washington arrived in Cambridge, Massachusetts to take command of the colonial forces assembled around Boston in the aftermath of the Americans' 'encouraging defeat' at Bunker Hill (see 17 June). For the next six years he would lead the army and then retire to his Virginia farm. In 1789, however, he would be called back to lead once more, becoming America's first soldier-turned-president. But he was hardly the last, for 26 of his 42 successors also bore arms for their country.

Besides Washington (who fought in the French and Indian War as well as the Revolution), five professional soldiers won the presidency: Andrew Jackson, William Henry Harrison, Zachary Taylor, Ulysses Grant and Dwight Eisenhower. Together they spent 122 years in the military, with Taylor accounting for 40 and Eisenhower 38. Jackson and Taylor served in eight wars between them: the Revolution, the Creek War, the War of 1812, the three Seminole Wars, the Black Hawk War and the Mexican–American War. One other future president wanted a career in the armed forces but didn't get it – Jimmy Carter attended the US Naval Academy at Annapolis and joined the Navy but resigned after seven years because of the death of his father.

Collectively, American presidents have fought in fifteen wars:

War of Independence Washington, James Monroe, who was shot in his left shoulder at the Battle of Trenton (see 26 December), and Jackson.

Indian wars (the French and Indian War, the Northwest Indian War, Tecumseh's War, the Creek War, the three Seminole Wars and the Black Hawk War) Washington, Harrison, Jackson, Taylor and Abraham Lincoln, who served briefly in the Black Hawk War but saw no action.

War of 1812 Harrison, Taylor, John Tyler, James Buchanan and James Madison, the only president who faced enemy gunfire while in office. He commanded an artillery battery during the British attack on Washington.

Mexican–American War Franklin Pierce, who became a brigadier general, and Grant, who served under Zachary Taylor, whose victory at Buena Vista (see 22 February) propelled him to the presidency.

The Civil War saw six future presidents in service. Grant was the Union's top general. Rutherford Hayes, a brevet major general, was wounded in action. James Garfield, a brigadier general, commanded a brigade at Shiloh. Chester Arthur was never in combat but served as quartermaster general of the state of New York. Benjamin Harrison – the grandson of William Henry Harrison – ended the war as a brevet brigadier general.

William McKinley was promoted to second lieutenant for his bravery at Antietam and was later raised to brevet major.

In the run-up to the Civil War there was one other soldier who became president. Jefferson Davis was a West Point graduate who fought in the Black Hawk and the Mexican–American wars under Zachary Taylor. Chosen president of the Confederacy in 1861, his first act was to send a peace commission to Washington to try to prevent the war.

The Spanish–American War made a hero of Theodore Roosevelt and his regiment of Rough Riders (see 1 July). In 2001 he was posthumously awarded the Medal of Honor, the only president to win one. In 1906 Roosevelt had won the Nobel Prize for his help in settling the Russo-Japanese War, so he was the only person in history to receive both his nation's highest military award and the world's foremost prize for peace.

First World War Although Dwight Eisenhower never got overseas, Harry Truman was a battery commander at St Mihiel and the Meuse-Argonne. His battery did not lose a single man during the war.

Second World War Apart from Eisenhower, who was the supreme Allied commander in Europe, six other future presidents were in uniform:

- A Japanese destroyer sank Jack Kennedy's PT (patrol torpedo) boat near the Solomon Islands, but he led his men to safety, for which he won the Navy and Marine Corps Medal and the Purple Heart.
- Lyndon Johnson became a lieutenant commander in the South Pacific and won a controversial Silver Star. Awarded by Douglas MacArthur, many believe it was the general's way of ingratiating himself with President Roosevelt – Johnson was part of a three-man survey team assigned by Roosevelt to observe operations.
- Richard Nixon was a naval aviation ground officer in the Pacific and rose to the rank of lieutenant commander, but saw no action.
- Gerald Ford became a lieutenant commander on the carrier *Monterey*, which fought at the Gilbert Islands, Kwajalein, Eniwetok, the Marianas, New Guinea, the Battle of the Phillipine Sea and Wake Island. Although never wounded

in battle, he was almost killed when a typhoon nearly sunk his ship.

- George H.W. Bush flew 58 combat missions in the Pacific. During an attack on a Japanese base, his plane was brought down by flak and he was forced to bail out, spending four hours in a life raft before being rescued by an American submarine. He was awarded the Distinguished Flying Cross and three Air Medals.
- Ronald Reagan became an Army captain, but his poor eyesight kept him out of combat, so he spent the war making training films.

The last president to enter the armed services was George W. Bush, who joined the Texas Air National Guard during the Vietnam War. Critics contend that this was not to get into combat but to avoid it.

Of the 27 presidents who served in the armed forces, 20 were in battle. But there was one with no war experience at all who still witnessed two famous military actions. When he was seven, John Quincy Adams watched the Battle of Bunker Hill from the top of Penn's Hill above his family's farm (see 17 June), and in 1812 he was America's ambassador to Russia and observed Napoleon's occupation of Moscow.

Other action this day

1625: The Spanish army takes Breda in the Spanish Netherlands, after nearly a year of siege * 1644: Roundheads defeat Prince Rupert and the Cavaliers at the Battle of Marston Moor * 1704: The Duke of Marlborough defeats the French at the Battle of Schellenberg during the War of the Spanish Succession * 1871: Completing the reunification of Italy, Victor Emmanuel II establishes Rome as his capital, proclaiming 'A Roma ci siamo et ci resteremo!' ('We are here in Rome and here we will stay!')

3 July

Churchill wipes out the French fleet

1940 At 5.46 this evening, after a long day of unsuccessful negotiations, British Vice Admiral James Somerville gave his ships the order to open fire. Within ten minutes most of the powerful fleet anchored at the Algerian port of Mers-el-Kebir lay in ruins: one battleship blown up, two more beached, 1,250 sailors dead. Only a single battleship and a few destroyers managed to escape. What the British destroyed this day, however, was not the fleet of an enemy but that of their close ally, France.

Barely a month after Dunkirk, and facing the prospect of imminent German invasion, Great Britain had to ensure that the fleet of recently defeated France would never fall into the hands of their common enemies, Germany and Italy. Despite assurances from Marshal Pétain, who had led his nation into capitulation to Germany, Prime Minister Winston Churchill ordered his fleet to issue this ultimatum to the French admiral at Mers-el-Kebir: sail your ships to safety, in either England or the West Indies, or scuttle them. Or Britain will sink them for you. Elsewhere, British boarding parties seized French navy vessels in Portsmouth and Plymouth and put their crews ashore. In Alexandria the French squadron disarmed itself under the orders of a British admiral.

Outraged by the humiliating loss of her fleet, France – now reduced by its armistice with Germany to the rump and puppet state of Vichy – broke off relations with Britain. Marshal Pétain complained to President Roosevelt of 'British aggression'. Many Frenchmen around the world now found themselves hating their former ally as much as they detested their conquerors. For General Charles de Gaulle, in London as the leader of the Free French, Mers-el-Kebir created a special problem. In the aftermath of Dunkirk there were thousands of French soldiers and sailors in England. From among these (and from among other Frenchmen in France's African colonies) he had been endeavouring to recruit a military force that would carry on France's fight alongside Great Britain. But after Mers-el-Kebir, could de Gaulle – could any Frenchman – remain on the side of his country's latest attacker?

De Gaulle was disheartened by the 'lamentable event', and all the more so that the British treated it as a victory. Nevertheless, a few nights later, when he spoke to his countrymen over BBC radio, he told them this: 'Come what may, even if for a time one of them is bowed under the yoke of the common foe, our two peoples – our two *great* peoples – are still linked together. Either they will both succumb or they will triumph side by side.'

Vichy France sentenced de Gaulle to death for his 'refusals to obey orders in the presence of the enemy and inciting members of the armed forces to disobedience'. In the end, of course, it was a liberated France that sentenced Marshal Pétain to death for his role as a collaborator with Nazi Germany: a sentence commuted to life imprisonment by General de Gaulle.

Other action this day

AD 324: Although wounded in the thigh, Emperor Constantine and his 130,000-man army defeat rival emperor Licinius's force at the Battle of Adrianople, killing a fifth of Licinius's 165,000 men * 1250: Louis IX is captured by Baibars's Mamluk army at the Battle of Fariskur in Egypt while he is on the Seventh Crusade * 1853: Russia invades Moldavia in the first action of the Crimean War * 1863: The three-day Battle of Gettysburg ends with 23,000 Union and 28,000 Confederate casualties, the bloodiest battle in America's Civil War * 1866: Prussians under von Moltke crush the Austrians at the Battle of Sadowa (Königgrätz) during the Seven Weeks War

4 July

Saladin triumphs at the Horns of Hattin

1187 The two large hills known as the Horns of Hattin lie just a few miles west of the Sea of Galilee in northern Palestine, and it was there that, today, that most famous Saracen, Saladin, totally destroyed the power of the Christian kingdom of Jerusalem.

Like all the Saracen leaders, Saladin was a Kurdish Turk. He had once served as a young officer under Nur ed-Din, the ruler of Syria, and on Nur ed-Din's death in 1174, Saladin became the leader of Muslim orthodoxy in the Middle East.

During the evening of 3 July 1187 Saladin's great army completely surrounded the smaller Christian force under the command of the king of Jerusalem, Guy de Lusignan. An eyewitness tells the tale: 'As soon as they [the Christian army] were encamped, Saladin ordered all his men to collect brushwood, dry grass, stubble and anything else with which they could light fires and make barriers, which he had made all round the Christians. They soon did this and the fires burned vigorously and the smoke from the fires was great; and this, together with the heat of the sun above them caused them discomfort and great harm. Saladin had commanded caravans of camels loaded with water from the Sea of Tiberias [today known as the Sea of Galilee] to be brought up and had water pots placed near the camp. The water pots were then emptied in view of the Christians so that they should have still greater anguish through thirst and their mounts too ... When the fires were lit and the smoke was great, the Saracens surrounded the host and shot their darts through the smoke and so wounded and killed men and horses.'

By the next morning the Christians were dying and desperate. King Guy had no choice but to attack the larger enemy force. A division of knights 'charged at a large squadron of Saracens. The Saracens parted and made a way through and let them pass; then, when they were in the middle of them, they surrounded them. Only ten or twelve knights ... escaped them ... After this division had been defeated, the anger of God was so great against the Christian host, because of their sins, that Saladin vanquished them quickly; between the hours of tierce and nones [9.00am and 3.00pm] he had won almost all the field.'

Most of the European nobles who survived, including the king of Jerusalem, were captured and held to ransom. The Christian army was totally destroyed and 15,000 foot soldiers were sold into slavery. The Knights Templar and Hospitaller who were taken prisoner were given a grim choice: convert to Islam or face execution. Some 230 Templars and a smaller number of Hospitallers refused and were beheaded as Saladin watched, seated on a dais in front of his army. Three months later Jerusalem fell to Saladin after 88 years of Christian rule (see 2 October).

When the news reached Europe, the Christian world went into shock. According to contemporary testimony: 'Pope Urban [III] who was at Ferrara died of grief when he heard the news. After him was Gregory VIII, who was of saintly life and only held the see for two months before he died and went to God.'

Other action this day

1190: Kings Richard I (the Lionheart) of England and Philip II (Augustus) of France leave on crusade * 1546: Turkish admiral and pirate Barbarossa (Barbarossa Hayreddin Pasha) dies in his seaside palace near Istanbul at 68 * 1807: Italian nationalist revolutionary and military leader Giuseppe

Garibaldi is born in Nice * 1916: Fighting with the French Foreign Legion, American poet ('I have a rendezvous with death') Alan Seeger is killed by machine gun fire near Belloy-en-Santerre while cheering on his fellow soldiers in a successful charge

5 July

Napoleon's last victory

1809 A map of Paris is virtually a monument to the Emperor Napoleon. Almost 30 streets are named after his generals, the avenue de la Grand Armée honours his army, the sixth arrondissement boasts a rue Bonaparte, a street where he lived was re-christened rue de la Victoire, and all Napoleon's military glory is commemorated together in the Arc de Triomphe. On top of that, twelve of his great victories are memorialised in place names: there are streets called Castiglione, Arcole, Rivoli, Pyramides (as well as a square), Aboukir, Marengo and Ulm. His most famous triumph, Austerlitz, has a street, a bridge, a port, a quay and even a railway station. Then comes Iéna with a walk, a square and a bridge and finally there are the avenues – Eylau (which is also a villa), Friedland and Wagram.

The last of these, Wagram, was fought today outside Vienna, and it was indeed the last, for Napoleon never won another major victory.

Wagram was a bloody, two-day battle fought by huge armies in terrible midsummer heat. It was especially notable for the massed artillery fire with which Napoleon buttressed the uncertain performance of his Saxon and Italian units, and for the extraordinary feats his engineers performed in bridging the Danube, which allowed the 188,000 soldiers and 488 guns of the Grande Armée to make a timely night crossing to the battlefield. The Austrian army, 155,000 soldiers under the command of Archduke Charles, was decisively defeated but withdrew intact. Six days later Austria asked for an armistice, which Napoleon granted.

Battle losses were extensive: over 32,000 killed, wounded or captured for the Grande Armée, almost 40,000 for the Austrian army. Among the Austrian casualties of war might be counted the great composer Joseph Haydn, aged 77, who died of shock and humiliation at the French occupation of his beloved Vienna.

In the peace treaty that followed the end of hostilities, the Austrian emperor Franz I was forced to pay a heavy war indemnity and to cede huge tracts of territory – including Salzburg, part of Galicia, Trieste and the Dalmatian coast – to France and its allies.

Eager to celebrate his victory, Napoleon sent for his Polish mistress Marie Walewska, installed her in the Schönbrunn Palace outside Vienna, and to his delight – and relief – quickly impregnated her, thus demonstrating that he was not sterile. The happy news prompted him to consider the prospect of a new marriage, one that would produce an heir to his empire. The news was less happy for Marie and the Empress Joséphine, both of whom would be cast aside for a new empress. She turned out to be a daughter of the Austrian emperor, the Archduchess Marie Louise, whom Napoleon married the following April.

Finally, the Russian tsar Alexander I, on hearing of Wagram and its aftermath, drew the prescient conclusion that the Austrians had been too quick to capitulate. 'People don't know how to suffer,' the tsar remarked to an aide-de-camp. 'If the fighting went against me, I should retire to Kamchatka rather than cede provinces and sign, in my capital, treaties that were really only truces. Your Frenchman is brave; but long privations and a bad climate will wear him down and discourage him. Our climate, our winter, will fight on our side.' Paris boasts no rue de la Russie.

Other action this day

1643: Royalists force William Waller's Parliamentarians to retreat but also have to retire due to lack of ammunition at the battle of Lansdowne near Bath in the English Civil War * 1943: 3,500 Russian tanks defeat 3,000 German tanks at the Battle of Kursk, the greatest tank battle in history * 1950: American forces engage the North Koreans for the first time at Osan, South Korea

6 July

The first Plantagenet king dies humiliated by his own son

1189 The River Vienne runs just south of the Loire, and on its north bank stand the grey and forbidding remains of the fortress of

Chinon. No Renaissance jewel box this château, but 400 yards of impregnable defences from the Middle Ages, dominating the river below it. Although the site has been fortified since Roman times, the oldest part of the fortress yet standing is the Fort St Georges, built by that great English king, Henry II, who died there on this day over 800 years ago.

Although the most powerful king in Europe, Henry was a victim of the famous 'Angevin Curse' which seemed to condemn members of the family to fight against each other. In 1173 his sons Henry and Richard (the Lionheart) rebelled in a vain effort to seize the lands they thought they had been promised. In this attempt they were supported by the queen, Eleanor of Aquitaine. King Henry easily quashed the revolt, mildly punished his sons and held Eleanor in gentle confinement around England for the next fifteen years.

Nine years later Henry's sons began fighting each other, as young Henry, Richard and their brother Geoffrey battled over who should rule in their father's lands in France. To make matters worse, the French king Philip Augustus encouraged this internecine warfare. Only the young Henry's death from dysentery prevented the onset of a true family civil war. Two years after that, Geoffrey and his youngest brother John invaded Richard's territory in Aquitaine, but Richard's superior military prowess soon sent them scurrying home.

Yet still Henry found no peace. In 1189 Richard allied himself with his father's arch-enemy, Philip Augustus, and invaded Anjou, the ancestral domain of the Angevin family. Together they conquered Tours and Maine. On 4 July Henry was forced to agree the treaty of Azay-le-Rideau, under the terms of which he not only had to cede much land but also had to pay homage to Philip Augustus for all his territories in France.

Now Henry retreated to his fortress in Chinon for the last time, an old man by the standards of the day (he was 56). He had been humiliated by Philip Augustus and by his own son Richard. Sick in body and spirit, Henry had to be carried to the fortress in a litter, and there he learned that among his enemies in league with the French was also his youngest son, the treacherous John. The only son who had not rebelled against him was the illegitimate Geoffrey, Archbishop of York. Henry bitterly claimed that his legitimate sons were 'the real bastards'.

Now Henry lay on a rude bed, face turned to the wall. 'Shame, shame,' he muttered, 'shame on a conquered king.'

So died Henry, the king who had ruled England and virtually the whole of western France for 35 years and who had founded the Plantagenet dynasty, which was to last 332 years – longer than any other English dynasty before or since.

Other action this day

1685: The forces of James II under Louis de Duras, 2nd Earl of Feversham, and the Duke of Marlborough defeat the rebel Duke of Monmouth at the Battle of Sedgemoor, leading to Monmouth's capture and execution ∗ 1777: During the American Revolution, 8,000 British troops under General John Burgoyne force the surrender of Fort Ticonderoga ∗ 1917: Lawrence of Arabia leads Arabian troops to capture Aqaba from the Turks during the Arab Revolt ∗ 1947: The Kalashnikov (AK-47) automatic assault rifle goes into production in the Soviet Union, to become so popular that more than 60 nations and innumerable guerrilla and terror organisations will arm their men with it and more AK-type rifles will be produced than all other assault rifles combined

7 July

The shot that started the Second World War

1937 The First World War began one morning in Sarajevo with the killing of an archduke. The Second World War began one night at a railway junction in China with the killing of a common soldier.

Twelve miles west of Peking, there is a place called Lukouchaio, where the railway line from Tientsin joins the Peking–Hankow line. It is in an area of northern China that had been ceded for commercial exploitation to Japan under a 1933 treaty. On the night of 7 July a brigade of the Japanese Kwantung army was conducting night exercises in the area. At some point, a shot rang out, and not long afterwards Japanese troops discovered the dead body of one of their comrades lying near the ancient Marco Polo Bridge.

It has never been established who killed the soldier, but the Japanese government chose to make the China Incident, as it referred to the event, a *casus belli*. It presented China with an ultimatum: agree by 18 July to hand over the two northern provinces of Hopei and Chahar or Japan would act.

The only question now was what Chiang Kai-shek, the leader of Nationalist China, would do. Over the past decade the Generalissimo had shown reluctance to tangle with the Japanese over their numerous grabs of Chinese territory, preferring to pursue civil war against the Communists while waiting for the Western powers to help him defeat both of his foes.

Some seven months earlier, however, Chiang had experienced something rarely encountered by heads of state: he had been kidnapped by one of his own generals who wanted to force Chiang to abandon the civil war and form a united front against Japan. To preserve face, it was important for Chiang to avoid giving the impression of having secured his release by making a political bargain with his kidnapper. But there was no doubt that he had.

In the face of the Japanese ultimatum, there was initial silence from Nanking, the Nationalist capital. When at last Chiang responded, it was no ringing declaration, no call to arms for his people. He did nothing beyond stating that no more Chinese territory would be surrendered to Japan, but the implication of his words seemed clear: armed resistance would meet another incursion. At least that is how the residents of Peking interpreted the broadcast of Chiang's message, for they ran into the streets cheering and beating gongs.

A few days later Japan launched the invasion of China, for which it had long planned, needing only a China Incident to begin it. Ten thousand Japanese troops crossed over the Great Wall and advanced into Hopei province. At first, the conflict was known as the Second Sino-Japanese War, but in a few years the world would come to see it as the first act of the Second World War.

Other action this day
1520: After six days of retreat, Hernán Cortés turns to win the Battle of Otumba over the pursuing Aztecs * 1863: During the American Civil War, the Union begins the first American military draft; exemptions cost $100

8 July

Ernest Hemingway's wound inspires a great novel

1918 Shortly after midnight at Fossalta on the Piave front in northern Italy, an Austrian mortar shell exploded near a lonely farmhouse that was serving as a canteen for Italian soldiers. Among the casualties was an American Red Cross driver named Ernest Hemingway, severely wounded by shrapnel. An ambulance took him to a field hospital in Treviso, where he was transferred by train to Milan and the Ospedale Croce Rossa Americana. Here young Hemingway, just nineteen years old, underwent two operations, and then did what all wounded men at war are supposed to do: he fell in love with his nurse.

She was 26-year-old Agnes Korowsky, of Washington, DC. Their affair, such as it was, proved enjoyable, but rather one-sided (his), and brief. Ernest went home to Oak Park, Illinois, in January 1919, and began the process of transforming himself into a war hero. Agnes stayed on in Italy as a nurse, and in March wrote him a 'Dear John' letter. For the world at large, however, it may have been the best way for things to turn out, because eventually Hemingway would write about his experiences – in Italy, being wounded, falling in love – and put them in a book that has one of the most memorable openings of any modern novel:

> In the late summer of that year we lived in a house in the village that looked across the river and the plain to the mountains. In the bed of the river there were pebbles and boulders, dry and white in the sun, and the water was clear and swiftly moving and blue in the channels. Troops went by the house and down the road and the dust they raised powdered the leaves of the trees. The trunks of trees too were dusty and the leaves fell early that year and we saw the troops marching along the road and the dust rising and leaves, stirred by the breeze, falling and the soldiers marching and afterward the road bare and white except for the leaves.

It is the beginning of *A Farewell to Arms.*

1758: During the Battle of Ticonderoga at Carillon on the shore of Lake Champlain, French general Louis-Joseph de Montcalm, with only 3,600 men, decisively defeats James Abercrombie's British force of 16,000 during the French and Indian War * 1943: After being tortured by the Gestapo, French Resistance hero Jean Moulin dies in a train taking him to Germany

9 July

A dismal king's death leads to war

1701 Today Prince Eugene of Savoy completed a secret night crossing of the lower Adige River with an army of 30,000 Austrians and overran a French cavalry corps at the small town of Carpi, 50 miles south of Verona. This minor confrontation was the first battle of the War of the Spanish Succession, a conflict with bizarre origins.

The cause of the war lay in the death the previous November of the weak-brained, epileptic and slightly deformed Spanish king, Charles II. Charles was rational, if dim, but his prognathous Habsburg jaw made his speech almost unintelligible and prevented him from chewing, so he subsisted on soups and slops. He was also impotent and so of course could produce no heirs. This was the real cause of the war, as competing European powers jockeyed to put forward their favourites to inherit the throne on his death or to dismantle his empire by depriving Spain of its possessions in the Netherlands and Italy.

Charles was aware of the problems that were likely to follow on his demise and became determined to settle his inheritance while he was still alive. Desperate to make the right choice but confused as to whom to choose, the befuddled king descended to the funeral vaults of the royal residence, the Escorial, and opened the tombs of his father, his mother and his first wife, kissed their mouldering faces and begged them for guidance. Finding no inspiration among the dead, he then turned to his ministers and court theologians, who persuaded him that only France would leave Spain and its possessions intact. Convinced at last, he willed his throne to a French cousin, Philippe, duc d'Anjou, grandson of France's reigning king, Louis XIV.

King Louis of course welcomed Charles's selection, but other European nations were either enraged or dismayed. Holy Roman Emperor Leopold I, also Charles's cousin, claimed the throne of Spain should revert to his own Habsburg dynasty, while England, Portugal and the Dutch Republic feared that if Louis's grandson became the Spanish king, it would lead to a union of Spain and France under a single monarch, destroying Europe's cherished balance of power.

Instead of offering compromise, however, Louis made matters worse by cutting off the Dutch and English from Spanish trade and recognising ex-King James II's son, James Francis Stuart, now living in France, as England's rightful sovereign. It was HRE Leopold, however, who fired the first shot, ordering Prince Eugene to invade the Duchy of Milan, a Spanish-controlled territory in northern Italy. And so the War of the Spanish Succession began.

The war lasted thirteen years, and featured some notable battles such as Blenheim (see 13 August), Ramillies (see 23 May) and Malplaquet. It cost an estimated 400,000 lives, confirmed the heroic stature of Prince Eugene and established that of the Duke of Marlborough. The Holy Roman Empire gained the Spanish Netherlands, Naples, Milan and Sardinia while Great Britain took over Gibraltar, Menorca and, edifyingly, exclusive rights to slave trading in Spanish America. But, despite the war, Louis XIV's grandson Philippe became and remained Spain's king as Philip V, founding Spain's Bourbon line which still holds the crown today, over three centuries later.

Other action this day

1755: French and Indians defeat British troops and colonial militiamen during the Braddock Expedition in the French and Indian War * 1810: French marshal Michel Ney takes Ciudad Rodrigo after a 75-day siege during the Peninsular War * 1850: American general and president Zachary Taylor dies from contaminated fruit eaten during an Independence Day celebration five days earlier, after sixteen months as president * 1944: American forces secure the Japanese-held island of Saipan, a battle in which of 31,000 Japanese troops, 24,000 are killed in action, 5,000 commit suicide and 921 are captured

10 July

The Battle of Britain

1940 On this morning 70 German bombers with fighter escorts took off from airfields in France and Belgium to attack a convoy in the English Channel. So began the contest of air forces known as the Battle of Britain. Hitler and his air force commander, Reichsmarschall Hermann Göring, thought it would be a quick and easy knockout punch: four days to destroy the Royal Air Force and then on to Act Two, Operation Sea Lion, the invasion of Great Britain. Invasion barges were being collected in the coastal ports of France and the Low Countries.

Indeed, the Germans had good reasons to be optimistic, for in the last ten months the Wehrmacht had conquered Poland, Denmark, Norway, Holland, Belgium and France. Only a month before, at Dunkirk, it had kicked the British army out of Europe. As for the Luftwaffe itself, while the toll on its resources from the French campaign had been heavy, it was well blooded, its morale was high and in fighter aircraft it outnumbered the RAF.

In this analysis, however, there were some factors the German high command did not – perhaps at the time could not – take into account. One was that the Luftwaffe's successes had been gained in support of ground operations and it had never carried out a strategic air campaign. Then there was the matter of British technology: outnumbered as it might be in planes and pilots, the RAF had developed a radar-based air defence system far more comprehensive than anything the Luftwaffe had ever encountered. Finally, there was the quality of the pilots of RAF Fighter Command, who would be scrambling in their Spitfires and Hurricanes to meet the invaders.

The German offensive began with daylight bomber attacks on coastal targets, such as ports, convoys and aircraft factories. The object was to lure the RAF fighters out over the Channel where German fighters could shoot them down in sufficient numbers to establish command of the air. When, in early August, it became clear that this strategy was not working, Göring gave new targeting orders: fly further inland to hit RAF airfields, radar stations, control centres and depots.

This second phase, a battle of attrition fought between the two air forces at an absolutely furious pace, came near at times to putting the RAF out of business.

German losses, however, were also very heavy. In early September, just when it appeared that the Luftwaffe, if it persisted, might be close to achieving air superiority, Hitler gave orders to switch the main effort from airfields and radar stations to the city of London, as a quicker way of bringing the British to their knees. The destruction and loss of life from these city raids was frightful, but British morale did not crumble. Moreover, the new orders simplified Fighter Command's task by giving it a chance to concentrate its forces in the defence of the new German objective. When, on 15 September, a large German raid over London lost 56 aircraft, it was apparent that the RAF was still very much in business. There would be no knockout punch.

Luftwaffe losses began to increase. By the end of the month it switched from daylight to night raids. On 12 October Operation Sea Lion, already postponed several times, was cancelled. Overall, losses by the end of October were 1,733 German planes shot down against 915 British.

As the year drew to a close it became clear that the battle was won. The invasion barges were put away. Hitler, defeated for the first time, turned his gaze eastward. And Churchill, addressing the House of Commons, said of RAF Fighter Command: 'Never, in the field of human conflict, was so much owed by so many to so few.'

Other action this day

48 BC: Pompey defeats Caesar at the Battle of Dyrrhachium in Macedonia * 1460: Rebel Yorkists capture Henry VI at the Battle of Northampton during the Wars of the Roses * 1690: The French sink eleven enemy ships without losing any of their own in defeating an Anglo-Dutch fleet at the Battle of Beachy Head

11 July

The Battle of the Golden Spurs

1302 The people of Flanders were in revolt against their overlord, King Philip the Fair of France, who had garrisoned his troops in

Flemish homes. On 18 May armed Flemings had entered houses in Bruges where the French were billeted and slaughtered anyone who could not pronounce a Flemish phrase, *scilt ende vriend* (shield and friend), which no francophone could manage.

Enraged by this so-called Brugse Metten (Bruges Matins), Philip dispatched 2,000 armoured knights plus a large troop of infantry under the command of his uncle Robert d'Artois, the greatest warrior in France, to teach the Flemings a lesson.

Desperate, the Flemings formed a motley army of about 10,000 untrained workmen and artisans, mostly from the weavers' guild, armed with pikes and staves.

When the two forces met at Kortrijk on this day, the Flemings, who knew the terrain far better than the French, took their stand on a patch of marshy ground surrounded by streams. The French cavalry tried to charge, but the horses could make no headway as their hooves sank into the soft ground. The Flemings then swarmed over the French knights before the French infantry could come forward.

The weavers and workmen had no use for the rules of chivalry: no prisoners were taken. At the end of the battle Robert d'Artois was knocked from his charger. Dropping his sword, he cried: 'Prenez, prenez le comte d'Artois, il vous fera riches!' ('Take him, take the Count of Artois, he will make you rich!') But he was instantly pierced by Flemish pikes.

In all, some 1,200 French knights were slaughtered. At the end of the day the Flemings gathered over 700 'golden' spurs from the field of battle and hung them in the vault of Our Lady's Church in Kortrijk. Ever since, this mighty victory by Flemish artisans over the flower of French knighthood has been known as the Battle of the Golden Spurs.

Other action this day

1798: The US Marine Corps is re-established, having been disbanded after the Revolutionary War * 1812: American forces holding Detroit surrender to the British during the War of 1812 * 1940: The German-dominated Vichy regime is formally established in France

12 July

Abraham Lincoln authorises the Medal of Honor

1862 Today, fifteen months after the start of the Civil War, President Abraham Lincoln authorised 2,000 Medals of Honor for Union soldiers who 'shall most distinguish themselves by their gallantry in action and other soldier like qualities, during the present insurrection'. Following the establishment of a Navy medal eight months earlier, the Medal of Honor was now America's highest military decoration for valour in wartime for all Union combatants. (The Medal of Honor was not the first American medal, as George Washington had established the Purple Heart in 1782 for bravery in action. But only three Purple Hearts had been awarded and the medal was allowed to lapse until 1932, when it was revived as a decoration for having been wounded or killed in combat.)

Although the Medal of Honor was created during the Civil War, the very first action for which it was awarded took place even before the war had begun. On 13–14 February 1861 in what is now Arizona, Bernard Irwin, a 31-year-old Army assistant surgeon, 'volunteered to go to the rescue of Second Lieutenant George N. Bascom, 7th Infantry, who with 60 men was trapped by Chiricahua Apaches under Cochise'. The citation for his Medal of Honor describes how 'Irwin and fourteen men, not having horses, began the 100-mile march riding mules. After fighting and capturing Indians, recovering stolen horses and cattle, he reached Bascom's column and helped break his siege.'

In the century and a half since it was first awarded – a span in which American troops saw action not only in their own civil war but also in Cuba, Europe and the Pacific, Korea, Vietnam and the Persian Gulf – a total of 3,408 people have won the Medal of Honor. Almost one in five of these were killed during the action in which they earned it. Astonishingly, there have been fourteen men who have received two Medals of Honor. In all the medal's history, however, only one has ever been awarded to a woman – and that not without controversy.

Mary Walker was a 31-year-old doctor at the outbreak of the Civil War, when she volunteered as a nurse (the Army hiring no female doctors). She served in Army hospitals at the First Battle of Bull Run and later at Chickamauga and Chattanooga. Occasionally she would cross enemy lines to treat Confederate civilians. In April 1864 she accidentally wandered into a group of Rebel soldiers and was taken into captivity for four months, during which time she treated female prisoners. Eventually she was traded for a Confederate officer captured by the North.

At the war's conclusion she was awarded the Medal of Honor for having 'devoted herself with much patriotic zeal to the sick and wounded soldiers, both in the field and hospitals, to the detriment of her own health', but in 1917 Congress stripped her of her medal because she had been a civilian, albeit attached to the army. Furious, she refused to return it to the Army and wore it proudly every evening until her death two years later. Finally, in 1977, the Army ordered her medal restored.

There have been a few famous winners, most particularly President Theodore Roosevelt, who received it 78 years after his death for his heroism during the Spanish-American War (see 1 July) and his son, Theodore Jr., who also won a posthumous one for actions on Utah Beach during D-Day in the Second World War. Other notables include 'Buffalo' Bill Cody, Douglas MacArthur and the future film star Audie Murphy, who was awarded the medal for action in France in January 1945. His medal citation gives some idea of the heroics demanded of winners:

Second Lieutenant Murphy commanded Company B, which was attacked by six tanks and waves of infantry. Second Lieutenant Murphy ordered his men to withdraw to prepared positions in a woods, while he remained forward at his command post and continued to give fire directions to the artillery by telephone. Behind him, to his right, one of our tank destroyers received a direct hit and began to burn. Its crew withdrew to the woods. Second Lieutenant Murphy continued to direct artillery fire, which killed large numbers of the advancing enemy infantry. With the enemy tanks abreast of his position, Second Lieutenant Murphy climbed on the burning tank destroyer, which was in danger of blowing up at any moment and employed its .50 caliber machine gun against the enemy. He was alone and exposed to German fire from three sides, but his deadly fire killed dozens of Germans and caused their infantry attack to waver. The enemy tanks, losing infantry support, began to fall back. For an hour the Germans tried every available weapon to eliminate Second Lieutenant Murphy, but he continued to hold his position and wiped out a squad which was trying to creep up unnoticed on his right flank. Germans reached as close as 10 yards, only to be mowed down by his fire. He received a leg wound, but ignored it and continued the single-handed fight until his ammunition was exhausted. He then made his way to his company, refused medical attention and organised the company in a counter-attack which forced the Germans to withdraw. His directing of artillery fire wiped out many of the enemy; he killed or wounded about 50. Second Lieutenant Murphy's indomitable courage and his refusal to give an inch of ground saved his company from possible encirclement and destruction and enabled it to hold the woods which had been the enemy's objective.

Other action this day

100 BC: Roman general and dictator Julius Caesar is born * 1191: Saladin's satraps surrender Acre to Richard the Lionheart's Crusaders * 1944: American general Theodore Roosevelt, Jr., son of President Theodore Roosevelt, dies of a heart attack one month after having earned the Medal of Honor for his heroic leadership on Utah Beach, where he was the only general on D-Day to land with the first wave of troops

13 July

Bismarck starts a war with a telegram

1870 This is a day to be noted by all editors, speech-writers, spin-doctors and the like for the splendid – or cautionary, if you prefer – example it provides of what a few word changes can do to the fate of nations.

The editor in this case was Otto von Bismarck, prime minister of Prussia, a kingdom on the verge of becoming an empire but needing just that foreign threat that would induce the remaining German states to join it. As it happened, the throne of Spain was vacant and Bismarck had recently proposed a certain German prince, a cousin of King Wilhelm of Prussia, as a candidate. France, alarmed at the prospect of encirclement by the powerful German Hohenzollerns, protested strongly. Wilhelm, having no wish for war – that would be a task for his grandson, he joked – instructed Bismarck to withdraw the candidate.

But bellicosity was in the Paris air and the Second Empire desired more than a withdrawal from its rival, Prussia. Napoleon III, believing in the invincibility of French arms, wanted a brilliant coup – diplomatic or military – that would show the world who was top dog in Europe, thereby restoring his regime's reputation at home and abroad. So the French ambassador to Prussia, Count Benedetti, was instructed to press King Wilhelm not only for confirmation of the withdrawal but also for 'assurance that he will never authorise a renewal of the candidacy'.

Benedetti went to Bad Ems, where Wilhelm was taking the waters. The king treated him with his customary courtesy, but declined to offer such a guarantee. He also refused the ambassador's request for a further audience with him on the subject. Afterwards, the king had a telegram sent to Bismarck in Berlin giving him an account of the meeting.

Bismarck read the message. Attuned to French sensibilities in the matter, he revised the account, eliminating any hint of the consideration with which the king had received Benedetti, thereby making it appear as if Wilhelm had delivered a humiliating snub. Then he released this edited version of the Ems telegram, as it is known to history, to the Berlin press and thence to the world. It was the Merlin touch.

The next day was the sacred Bastille Day in France. French papers emblazoned the now-insulting telegram on their front pages. 'À Berlin! Vive la guerre!' And so, on this flimsy *casus belli*, France declared war against Prussia on the 19th.

France lost the war, an emperor and Alsace-Lorraine. What France lost Prussia won, and her king became Kaiser Wilhelm of Germany, crowned insultingly on French soil. A great editor, that Bismarck!

1380: Constable of France Bertrand du Guesclin dies from drinking contaminated water during the siege of Châteauneuf-de-Randon ∗ 1558: Led by the Count of Egmont, the Spanish army defeats the French at Gravelines, France ∗ 1643: In England, the Parliamentarians, led by Sir William Waller, are defeated by Royalist troops under Lord Wilmot in the Battle of Roundway Down ∗ 1862: Confederate general Nathan Bedford Forrest defeats a Union army at Murfreesboro, Tennessee

14 July

The fall of the Bastille

1789 Over the centuries we have come to imagine the Bastille as a grim, grey fortress of cold stone in which innocents withered away and died, chained to the wall in bleak cells on the order of reactionary and contemptuous French kings. And when we think of 14 July – Bastille Day – we envision the heroics of a downtrodden people overcoming the king's heavily armed guards to free the hundreds of innocent prisoners inside.

The 'real' Bastille in Paris was indeed a massive medieval fortress. Built in the 14th century, it consisted of eight round towers connected by walls 100 feet high. In the summer of 1789 its governor Bernard de Launay commanded a force of 82 *invalides* (pensioned soldiers too old or decrepit to serve in the field) plus 32 men from a Swiss regiment. The fortress walls mounted eighteen 8-pound guns and twelve smaller pieces.

On Tuesday 14 July, Paris seemed ready for insurrection. Angry citizens thronged Place Vendôme, the Hôtel de Ville and Place Louis XV (today's Place de la Concorde), convinced that conservative factions were on the verge of overthrowing the nascent revolution (only the previous month had progressives opened the new French 'parliament', the National Assembly). In reaction, soldiers and cavalry tried to intimidate the mob, only to be met with stones and bricks.

Now a crowd of some 800 revolutionary Parisians, armed with muskets and cannon captured in the Invalides earlier in the day, marched on the Bastille, a symbol of royal repression. Their initial aim was to seize the fortress's guns and its large supply of powder, but de Launay felt he could not comply without instructions from the government. Now someone in the mob cut the chains to the drawbridge leading to the inner courtyard, and the crowd surged in, to be met with gunfire from the defenders. Instantly both sides were firing, but it soon became apparent that the defenders could hold out indefinitely; only one had been killed compared to about 100 of the insurgents.

Although in no immediate danger, de Launay wished to avoid more bloodshed and offered to open the gates if his soldiers were spared. The attackers gave assurances of safety, and the drawbridge was lowered. Immediately the rioters rushed in and killed three of the Bastille garrison. The crowd later hanged two others. De Launay was dragged away and severely beaten. Realising the inevitable fate that awaited him, he shouted out, 'Enough – let me die!' and kicked an assailant in the groin. He was then stabbed to death and beheaded, his head fixed on a pike and carried through the streets.

And so trickery rather than force of arms took the Bastille. Inside there were a mere seven prisoners. (One notorious inmate, the Marquis de Sade, had been transferred out ten days before.)

The start of the French Revolution is generally dated to the fall of the Bastille, but it was another three years before the abolition of the monarchy. Even then, it took a further 88 years before Bastille Day was established as a national holiday in France.

Other action this day

1223: French king Philip II (Augustus), who more than doubled the size of his nation by retaking much of France from England's Richard the Lionheart and King John, dies after a reign of 43 years * 1456: The Hungarians defeat the Ottomans at the Battle of Belgrade, in present-day Serbia * 1900: European Allies retake Tientsin, China, from the rebelling Boxers

15 July

The Crusaders conquer Jerusalem

1099 Today, with the aid of assault towers and scaling ladders, 15,000 Crusaders stormed the walls of the holy city of Jerusalem crying, 'Help us, God!' The First Crusade had triumphed.

'Jerusalem is the navel of the world', had cried Pope Urban II at the Council of Clermont four years earlier (see 18 November). His call for a holy war might seem a trifle tardy – Jerusalem had been a Muslim city for over 400 years – but it was only in 1071 when the Seljuk Turks swept down from central Asia that the city was cut off from Christian travellers. So Urban called out, and the First Crusade was launched.

Perhaps as many as 50,000 knights, soldiers and camp followers started on this great adventure, including minor nobles seeking their fortunes and peasants seeking their freedom from the feudal ties that bound them at home. For three years the weary Crusaders trudged across Europe and Asia Minor, attacked by hunger, thirst, disease, bandits and Turkish guerrillas. Finally reaching Palestine, they were roasted in their armour by the terrible heat, but still they came on. By the time they reached the Holy City in June 1099, more than half had died, deserted or simply wandered off.

When the inspired Crusaders finally breached Jerusalem's walls, the Saracen defenders fled to the Temple of Solomon, but soon the attackers had smashed through its gates. There, according to an eyewitness, 'in this temple almost ten thousand were decapitated. If you had been there, you would have seen our feet splattered with the blood of the dead ... Not a single life was spared, not even women or children. You would have seen a wondrous sight, when our poorest soldiers, learning of the Saracens' cleverness, cut open the stomachs of the slain to take from their bowels the jewels they had swallowed while still alive. A few days later the bodies were piled up in a great heap and burned in order to find coins more easily in the burnt ashes.'

When at last the Crusaders ran out of Muslims, they herded resident Jews into their main synagogue and burnt it to the ground.

Thus 15 July is the day of Christianity's greatest military victory. It resulted in the establishment of the Latin Kingdom of Jerusalem, of which the first ruler was Godefroi de Bouillon, the first Christian knight to stand on the conquered city's walls. He rejected the title of king, preferring Defender and Baron of the Holy Sepulchre, saying, 'I will not wear a crown of gold where my Saviour wore one of thorns.'

The Christian kingdom lasted for almost two centuries, although Jerusalem itself fell to the great Saracen leader Saladin in 1187 (see 2 October). Ironically, the day the Christians took Jerusalem from its

Muslim defenders was the exact anniversary of the Hegira, the day in AD 622 when Mohammed fled to Medina and which is considered the traditional beginning of the Muslim era.

Other action this day

1240: Prince Alexander of Novgorod defeats the Swedish at the Battle of the Neva, after which he will be known as Alexander Nevsky ∗ 1685: Charles II's illegitimate son, James, Duke of Monmouth, is beheaded for trying to depose and replace his uncle James II ∗ 1815: In surrendering to the British aboard the 74-gun warship *Bellerophon*, Napoleon announces: 'I come like Themistocles, to offer myself to the hospitality of the British people. I place myself under the protection of their laws,' but he is sent to Saint Helena ∗ 1918: In the last major German offensive on the Western Front, 23 German divisions of the 1st and 3rd Armies attack the French 4th Army to begin the 21-day Second Battle of the Marne, which ends in German defeat ∗ 1948: Death of John 'Black Jack' Pershing, commander of the American armies during the First World War; the only person, while still alive, to rise to the highest rank ever held in the US Army, General of the Armies, equivalent only to the posthumous rank of George Washington

16 July

The first fall of Rome

390 BC Today the city of Rome fell for the first time since its mythic founding by Romulus and Remus in 753 BC. Gallic barbarians had routed its legions in the field and now rampaged through the city, burning, looting and slaughtering thousands of Roman civilians. A few soldiers had retreated to the citadel on the Capitoline Hill, but could they save Rome from complete destruction?

Rome was still a fledgling power, a city-state at uneasy peace with neighbouring Etruscan cities and now threatened by Gallic tribes that occupied much of northern Italy. Among the fiercest were the Senones from the Adriatic coast.

In early 390 BC the Senone chieftain Brennus had led his warriors to the outskirts of the Etruscan town of Clusium (today's Chiusi), some 100 miles north of Rome. Desperate, the Clusians turned to Rome for help.

Unwilling or unable to send an army, the Romans dispatched three envoys, who demanded by what right the Senones were threatening a Roman ally.

Brennus coldly responded: 'All things belong to the brave, who carry justice on the points of their swords.' After an exchange of insults, a fight broke out during which one of Brennus's lieutenants was killed and the envoys fled back to Rome, the Senones in hot pursuit. Brennus demanded that they be turned over to him but, according to Livy, 'those who should have been punished were instead appointed military tribunes for the coming year'. Enraged, Brennus swore revenge, which was not long in coming.

By July Brennus's 40,000-strong army was marching through Roman territory. On this day six Roman legions, under the command of Quintus Sulpicius, met the Senones at the Allia river, about twelve miles north of the city. Accompanied by 'the dreadful din of fierce war-songs', the Senones smashed into the Roman right, then turned to the centre. The Romans panicked and fled, and only a handful made it back to Rome, where they took refuge in the citadel on the Capitoline Hill without even closing the city gates behind them. It was then that the Senones ran amok in the city.

For seven months the defenders on the Capitoline Hill held fast, despite repeated barbarian assaults. On one occasion the Senones tried a surprise attack at night, but the Romans were alerted by the cackling of the sacred geese of Juno and managed to throw back the invaders.

Now the Senones were struck by that curse of ancient armies, dysentery. Soon hundreds were dying and Brennus, despairing of conquering the citadel, called a brief truce and demanded that the Romans pay 1,000 pounds in gold as ransom. He then added insult to humiliation by weighing the gold using his own weights, which were heavier than standard. When the Roman commander objected, Brennus flung his sword onto the scale and disdainfully responded, 'Vae victis!' ('Woe to the vanquished!')

What happened next is open to debate. Polybius maintains that the Senones 'withdrew unmolested with their booty, having voluntarily and on their own terms restored the city to the Romans'. But the patriotic Livy tells us that, just as the Romans were preparing to hand over the gold, their exiled dictator, Marcus Furius Camillus, arrived with a fresh army. Drawing his sword, he exclaimed: 'Non auro, sed ferro recuperanda est patria.' ('It is not gold but steel that redeems the homeland.') He then chased the Senones through the streets of Rome and out of the city. The following day he routed them in a battle outside the walls, personally dispatching Brennus and earning for himself the title of second founder of Rome.

From this time forth, Rome remained inviolate and unconquered for 800 years, until it fell to the Visigoth chief Alaric in AD 410 (see 24 August).

Other action this day
1212: Alfonso VIII of Castile and Leon decisively defeats the Moors at the Battle of Las Navas de Tolosa in Andalucía, a major turning point in the war between Christians and Moors for control of the Iberian penin-sula * 1945: At 5.24am, the first atomic bomb explodes at Alamogordo, New Mexico

17 July

The end of the Hundred Years War

1453 Today, as French cannon ceased firing on a vanquished English army at Castillon, the Hundred Years War – which actually lasted for 116 years – at last came to an end.

It had all started in 1337 when Edward III of England laid claim to the crown of France through the blood of his mother, Isabella de Valois, daughter of King Philip the Fair of France. At first the English must have thought the war an enormous success with the great English victories at Crécy, Poitiers and Agincourt (see 26 August, 19 September and 11 August), but then the French had their turn with the stirring triumphs of Joan of Arc.

The Hundred Years War should have ended with the French capture of Bordeaux in 1451, but the citizens there had been ruled by the English for three centuries, ever since its duchess, Eleanor of Aquitaine, had married Henry II of England. Feeling more English than French, its people urged the English to send an army for their relief.

John Talbot, Earl of Shrewsbury, arrived at the city at the end of 1452 with a few thousand soldiers, enough to encourage the citizens of Bordeaux to force the French garrison to leave.

The following winter France's King Charles VII sent his army into Gascony, determined to wrest Bordeaux back. Under the command of Jean Bureau, 10,000 men marched to Castillon, a pro-English stronghold 30 miles to the east, and prepared to lay siege to the town. When Shrewsbury learned of the French arrival, he gathered his smaller force of perhaps 6,000 and set out to relieve Castillon.

Shrewsbury's 1,000 cavalry were the first to reach the stronghold, where they initially routed the French horse. Now one of Castillon's defenders slipped from the town to tell the earl that the French were abandoning their positions. Seeing a dust cloud from what he thought were the fleeing enemy, Shrewsbury ordered an attack, even though his infantry was just starting to reach the scene. But the dust turned out to be caused not by French soldiers but by their camp followers, who had been ordered to depart. Indeed, the French had strongly fortified their camp and had some 300 cannon ready for action. The English attack was met by withering cannon and crossbow fire.

Then the French cavalry returned to charge the beleaguered English right flank, and the battle turned into a rout. Shrewsbury was killed when his horse was felled by a cannonball and landed on top of him. Seeing him pinned to the ground and helpless, a French soldier finished him off with an axe.

So the Hundred Years War came to an end. After the defeat at Castillon, the kings of England had even less of France than Edward III had controlled 100 years before. And to this day the French remember their final victory: ever since, they have called the town Castillon-la-Bataille.

But, according to legend, Britain did gain one lasting heritage from the war. During the century of fighting, England's triumphs were primarily thanks to the longbow, the powerful weapon that could fire armour-piercing arrows two and a half feet long.

So formidable were the English longbows that the French cut off the first two fingers of any captured bowmen so they could no longer fire their bows. The bowmen's reaction to the French threat was to lift two fingers in contempt at the enemy, thus giving birth to the derisive two-fingered signal that the English use to this day to mock their opponents.

1203: During the Fourth Crusade, crusaders capture Christian Constantinople by assault, forcing Byzantine emperor Alexius III Angelus to flee into exile * 1936: Spanish officers revolt in Morocco, triggering the Spanish Civil War * 1944: Near Caen, Canadian Spitfire pilot Charley Fox strafes the German staff car carrying Field Marshal Erwin Rommel, whose injuries will keep him out of the war until he is forced to commit suicide three months later for alleged involvement in the plot to kill Hitler

18 July

The Spanish Civil War begins

1936 The Spanish Civil War began at 5.15 this Saturday morning, when, in a *pronunciamento* broadcast by radio from Las Palmas on Grand Canary Island, General Francisco Franco gave the order for the mainland garrisons of the Spanish army to rise against the Republican government of Spain.

It was a rebellion in which an array of forces – landowners, monarchists, the Catholic church, the army, the bourgeoisie, the fascist Falange party – sought to reclaim their country from an elected Republican government they judged incapable of putting down the violent political disorder afflicting the nation. So it was that during the morning of 18 July, in city after city, garrisons seized public buildings, proclaimed a state of war and arrested Republican and left-wing leaders. In response, workers took to the streets, calling for a general strike and throwing up barricades.

The Republican government of Spain faced a dilemma. It wished to put down the rebellion but found the institutions of law and order – the army and the civil guard – in the hands of the rebels. On the other hand, the forces remaining loyal to the republic were the unions and the left-wing parties – socialists, Communists and anarchists – whose victory, if it came, promised proletarian revolution. Late in the day, the government made its decision: arm the workers. As trucks sped through the streets of Madrid carrying rifles to the headquarters of the unions, German and Italian transport planes airlifted the Spanish army of Africa, which garrisoned Spanish Morocco, to mainland Spain. The fight was on.

At ten in the evening, in a radio broadcast, Dolores Ibarurri, the Communist leader known as La Pasionaria, told her listeners: 'It is better to die on your feet than to live on your knees!', then echoed the old phrase from Verdun: 'No pasarán!' ('They shall not pass!') It was to be the great rallying cry of Republican Spain.

The war lasted almost three years, during which the world learned about such things as Guernica (see 26 April), the 'Fifth Column' and the Condor Legion. Nazi Germany and fascist Italy supplied and reinforced Franco's Nationalists. Soviet Russia sent aid to the Republican Loyalists. The democracies – France, Great Britain and the United States – practised non-intervention. When Madrid fell in March 1939, after 28 months of siege, and Nationalist forces marched into the city, the crowds shouted: 'Han pasado!' ('They have passed!')

Franco was by now El Caudillo – The Leader – a designation he shared with Der Führer and Il Duce. Pope Pius XII cabled him: 'Lifting up our heart to God, we give sincere thanks with your Excellency for Spain's Catholic victory.' The Nationalist government now aligned itself with the Axis powers by joining the Anti-Comintern Pact and signing a five-year treaty of friendship with Nazi Germany. Only Russia among the great powers refused to recognise the Nationalist regime.

No precise estimates of the losses in the Spanish Civil War exist, but Hugh Thomas offered this tentative assessment: a total of 500,000 people perished in the conflict, of which perhaps 300,000 died in action, 100,000 died of disease or malnutrition and 100,000 were executed or murdered. All in all, it was good practice for the Second World War, only five months away.

Other action this day

1100: Godefroi de Bouillon, a leader of the First Crusade, dies in Jerusalem * 1545: The English flagship *Mary Rose* sinks during the indecisive Battle of the Solent between England and France * 1863: Led by Colonel Robert Gould Shaw, the 54th Massachusetts Volunteer Infantry of black soldiers attacks Fort Wagner in South Carolina, sustaining 1,515 casualties to 147 for the Confederates but proving the worth of black soldiers in combat * 1918: The American Expeditionary Force defeats the Germans at the Battle of Château-Thierry on the Franco-Belgian border

19 July

'Arrows as thickly as the rays in sunlight hit the Scots'

1333 Today, as the army of England's Edward III confronted a Scottish force determined to break Edward's siege of Berwick-on-Tweed, a Scottish knight named Turnbull, his black mastiff trotting at his side, strode out between the armies and challenged any Englishman to fight him in single combat.

At length a knight named Robert Venale marched out from the English host, his sword drawn. Turnbull unleashed his mastiff, which charged into the attack, but with one swing of his sword Venale cut the dog in two. Then the two champions closed for the kill, Turnbull unnerved by the ferocity of his adversary's attack. According to a contemporary chronicle, after only a few moments of combat Turnbull's 'left hand and head also afterward this worthy knight [Venale] cut off'. It was an ill omen for the Scots but only a foretaste of what was to come.

Scotland's king, David II, was the son of Robert the Bruce, but he was only nine years old. Edward Balliol, whose own father had been king 37 years before, disputed his right to the throne. But without the resources to make the challenge on his own, Balliol had sought the help of Edward III, who saw this as his chance to dominate Scotland. In March Balliol had marched on Berwick, then in Scottish hands, and in May was joined by King Edward with the rest of the army. By now they had dug trenches around Berwick and cut off all communication with the rest of Scotland. The siege had been a savage one, as the attackers' trebuchets hurled both great stones and the heads of dead Scots over Berwick's walls into the town. At length Berwick's commander agreed to surrender if the town was not relieved by 20 July. But by now the Scottish guardian, Archibald Douglas, had raised an army of 1,200 knights and 15,500 pikemen and was marching to Berwick's relief.

Edward had emplaced his force on Halidon Hill, a small 600-foot rise two miles north-west of Berwick, from which he could look down on the town and dominate its approaches. On this day, according to a contemporary report, Douglas and his army advanced from the west and 'marched towards the town with great display, in order of battle, and recklessly, stupidly and inadvisably chose a battle ground at Halidon Hill, where there was a marshy hollow between the two armies, and where a great downward slope, with some precipices, and then again a rise lay in front of the Scots, before they could reach the field where the English were posted.'

While Edward had only 10,000 men, his trump was his long-bowmen. He placed his troops in three divisions, every man including the king on foot, with the archers on the flanks of each division, positioned so they could support each other with crossfire. Commanding the high ground, he awaited a Scots attack; he knew the enemy had no choice since Berwick was committed to surrender if not relieved by the next day.

Douglas had arranged his three divisions with pikemen at the front. Now his men moved forward onto the marshy ground, already under fire from Edward's massed ranks of archers. Moving slowly uphill, they were easy targets. As they approached the bottom of Halidon Hill, 'arrows as thickly as the rays in sunlight hit the Scots in such a way that they struck them down by the thousands; and they began to flee from the English in order to save their lives'. One division finally closed with Balliol's front, but after a few minutes of hand-to-hand fighting they broke and ran back down the hill, still beleaguered by the English archers. A determined stand by the Earl of Ross and his Highlanders briefly held the English, but Ross was soon killed and the English knights mounted their horses to charge down after the hapless enemy, cutting them down without mercy.

The Scots suffered appalling losses. Their commander Archibald Douglas, six Scottish earls, 70 barons, 500 knights and perhaps 9,000 foot soldiers lay dead, while England's slain numbered but fourteen. Berwick surrendered the next day.

For young king Edward (he was only twenty) it was a glorious victory, the first of many during his reign. From it he learned the power of the English longbow, a lesson put to good use during the Hundred Years War and his decisive victory at Crécy (see 26 August).

Other action this day

AD 711: Moorish leader Tariq ibn Ziyad defeats the Visigothic king Roderic of Hispania at the Battle of Guadalete * 1195: Moorish caliph Abu Yusuf Ya'qub al-Mansur defeats Alfonso VIII of Castile at the 'Disaster of Alarcos' * 1744: The French defeat the Sardinians at Casteldelfino during the War of the Austrian Succession * 1808: The Spanish army of Andalucía under generals Francisco Castaños and Theodor von Reding destroys French marshal Pierre Dupont's 25,000-man force at the Battle of Bailén, killing over 2,000 and taking 18,000 prisoners, a blow from which Napoleon's efforts to dominate Spain never recover * 1943: One of only two female fighter pilot aces in history, Russian Katya Budanova bags her eleventh enemy plane just before she is shot down and killed over the Ukraine

20 July

The plot to murder Hitler

1944 'I must go and telephone. Keep an eye on my briefcase. It has secret papers in it', whispered Colonel Claus von Stauffenberg to Colonel Brandt sitting next to him. Then he quietly rose from the crowded table and slipped from the conference room while Germany's top brass made their gloomy reports to their supreme leader in his fortified bunker at the Wolfsschanze (Wolf's Lair) head-quarters in Rastenburg, in what is now north-eastern Poland. Three minutes later, at 12.42pm, the bomb that had been concealed in a shirt in von Stauffenberg's briefcase exploded, killing four people including Colonel Brandt but doing little damage to its target, Adolf Hitler. Needing more legroom, the unfortunate Brandt had shoved the briefcase to the far side of a heavy table support, miraculously shielding Hitler from the worst effects of the blast.

The 36-year-old von Stauffenberg was a career army officer born to the Prussian nobility. An early supporter of Hitler, he had partici-pated in all the Führer's major campaigns and had been severely wounded while serving with the 10th Panzer Division of Rommel's Afrika Korps in Tunisia. There in early 1943 Allied fighters had strafed his convoy, and von Stauffenberg had lost his left eye, his right hand and the last two fingers of his left hand.

It was probably in Russia, after witnessing atrocities committed by the SS, that von Stauffenberg began to lose his faith in Hitler, and by mid-1944 it was clear to all but the most fanatical Nazis that Germany would lose the war. Von Stauffenberg became a key member of a conspiracy code-named Walküre (Valkyrie) whose aim was to seize control of the government and seek favourable peace terms from the Allies to save the country from total destruction.

The plotters searched for a way to get at Hitler, and on 1 June 1944 fortune smiled on them when von Stauffenberg was made chief of staff of the reserve army, giving him access to the Führer's most important military meetings. Then he was summoned to the Wolfsschanze conference on 20 July. By this time his earlier belief in Hitler had turned to loathing. 'Fate has offered us this opportunity,' he said, 'and I would not refuse it for anything in the world. I have examined myself before God and my conscience. It must be done because this man is evil personified.' Flying to Rastenburg in the early morning, he set the bomb's ten-minute timer just before entering the meeting. Immediately after the explosion he bluffed his way through three SS checkpoints and, believing his mission accomplished, flew back to Berlin to help take over the government.

Sadly, *Walküre*'s conspirators showed an incomprehensible lack of both planning and resolve, and the plot started to disintegrate the moment it became clear that Hitler, whose legs were burned, eardrums punctured and hair singed, was not dead after all. In fact, that same afternoon he conducted his final meeting with Mussolini and bragged that God had saved him to lead Germany's revenge on the world.

Hitler's vengeance was swift and savage. When von Stauffenberg arrived in Berlin late in the day, an SS counter-coup was already rounding up most of the conspirators. At about midnight von Stauffenberg and three others were taken to a courtyard at the War Ministry and shot, the colonel shouting at the last, 'Long live our sacred Germany.' The bodies were buried nearby, but on Himmler's orders the corpses were dug up and burned, their ashes scattered to the winds.

Plotters all over Germany were arrested, tortured and executed. Eight were strangled with piano wire attached to meat hooks, their death agony filmed for Hitler's enjoyment. Some officers committed suicide, at least one by walking into no man's land at the front to be shot by the enemy, and Germany's most illustrious field marshal Erwin Rommel was forced to take poison to save his family. An estimated 4,980 people were executed while another 15,000, mostly relatives of conspirators, were sent to concentration camps. The killings continued into April 1945, even as Russians were in the streets of Berlin.

After the assassination attempt Hitler became even more morbidly suspicious and reclusive. He gulped pills offered by his doctors, his right hand suffered from severe tremors and he rarely agreed to be photographed. Nonetheless, his determination remained undiminished. All hope of negotiation vanished. In December Hitler told his Luftwaffe aide, 'We'll not capitulate. Never. We can go down. But we'll take the world with us.'

Other action this day

356 BC: Alexander the Great is born in Pella in the kingdom of Macedon * 1241: The army of Louis IX (St Louis) defeats a combined force of rebel French barons and Henry III of England at the Battle of Taillebourg during the Saintonge War * 1402: Tamerlane (Timur) defeats the Ottoman force of Bayezid I at the Battle of Ankara * 1881: Sioux chief Sitting Bull surrenders to the US Army

21 July

Hotspur dies in battle

1403

Two stars keep not their motion in one sphere,
Nor can one England brook a double reign,
Of Harry Percy and the Prince of Wales.

So did Shakespeare comment on the bitter conflict between two of England's most celebrated medieval heroes, Henry Percy, called Harry by his friends and known to us by the picturesque name of Hotspur, and fifteen-year-old prince Henry of Lancaster (the future Henry V), also called Harry, son of the usurper king Henry IV.

Hotspur came from the powerful and aristocratic Percy family that had come to England with William the Conqueror. By the 14th century the Percys were rulers of Northumberland, which formed a buffer against armed raids from Scotland. It was the Scots who gave

Hotspur his nickname for his indefatigable patrolling of the Scottish/ English border.

Hotspur and his father (another Henry) initially backed Henry IV and battered the Scots while the king was trying to subdue the Welsh. The problem was, the Welsh resisted successfully and Henry IV refused to give the Percys his promised rewards. It was only then that the Percys, capable and honourable knights, rebelled against their king. But once the rebellion had started, they determined to go all the way and take the throne of England for themselves.

On this day the conflict reached its bloody denouement, when Henry IV and his son Prince Harry decisively defeated the Percys at Shrewsbury.

The battle started with archery salvoes from both sides. An arrow caught Prince Harry in the face, not debilitating but enough to leave him scarred for the rest of his life. But eventually the larger royal forces began to grind down the Percys, prompting them to a desperate last-ditch charge that killed the royal standard bearer. But then came the decisive blow. One story is that when Hotspur raised his visor to wipe sweat from his face, one of the king's archers recognised his plume and shot an arrow that pierced his brain. According to Shakespeare, however, it was the prince of Wales himself who struck Hotspur down.

With Hotspur dead, the Percy force began to disintegrate, finally fleeing the field after three hours of fighting, to be pursued and slaughtered by the king's soldiers. Some estimate that the rebels lost 300 knights and (an unlikely) 20,000 men-at-arms, to fewer than 5,000 royal dead.

> Ill-weaved ambition, how much art thou shrunk!
> When that this body did contain a spirit,
> A kingdom for it was too small a bound,
> But now two paces of the vilest earth
> Is room enough.

Hotspur's head was set on the gate of York to discourage further rebellion, while his brother Thomas Percy was decapitated after the battle so that his could decorate London Bridge. The Percys of the time seemed to have a knack for dying in battle. Hotspur's father

Henry, who escaped from the field of battle at Shrewsbury, was eventually slain at Bramham Moor in 1408. His son died on the field at the first Battle of St Albans in 1455 (see 22 May), and his grandson was killed six years later at Towton (see 28 March).

The Battle of Shrewsbury greatly strengthened the Lancastrian hold on the throne of England and also proved an invaluable training ground for young Prince Harry, who only ever fought in one more full-scale pitched battle, against the French at Agincourt (see 11 August).

Other action this day

1770: With only 17,000 soldiers, Russian general Pyotr Rumyantsev utterly routs an army of 150,000 Turks at the Battle of Cahul, suffering only 1,000 casualties to 20,000 for the enemy ∗ 1798: At the Battle of the Pyramids, Napoleon Bonaparte defeats the Mamluks, destroying the Egyptian force of 24,000 men in less than two hours with a loss of only 200 Frenchmen ∗ 1861: A Confederate army of 22,000 defeats a Union force of 30,000 at the First Battle of Bull Run, the first major battle of the American Civil War

22 July

'Kill them all'

1208 Pope Innocent III had launched the Albigensian Crusade less than six months earlier, but already a sizeable army was marauding its way through southern France. Its aim was to extirpate the dangerous heresy known as Catharism, which not only denied the divinity of Christ, but also, in its non-authoritarian asceticism, stood in marked contrast to the corruption, worldliness and hypocrisy of the Church of Rome.

On this day the army reached the walls of Béziers in the very south of France, west of Marseille. Leading this band of opportunists, criminals seeking absolution, adventurers and religious fanatics were Simon de Montfort and his spiritual advisor, the papal legate Arnald-Amaury. At the city gates de Montfort handed the Bishop of Béziers a list of 222 Cathars to be handed over for execution. But the city leaders, not themselves Cathars, refused to provide the victims, saying: 'We had rather be drowned in the salt sea than surrender our fellow citizens.'

Now de Montfort ordered an assault, and the rampaging army began a brutal sack. There was to be no mercy for the heretics, but how, Arnald-Amaury was asked, can one tell a Cathar from the numerous devout Catholics in the population? 'Kill them all,' said the Pope's representative. 'God will know his own.'

Except for those few who managed to flee, the entire population of Béziers – 15,000 men, women and children – were put to the sword, 7,000 alone in the vast Romanesque church of Sainte-Madeleine where they had sought sanctuary.

Other action this day

1298: Edward I defeats William Wallace at the Battle of Falkirk * 1453: The 'White Knight' John Hunyadi (a Hungarian warlord) leads a spirited attack to force Ottoman sultan Mehmet II to lift the siege of Belgrade, which had lasted eighteen days * 1812: A British army under Viscount Wellington defeats the French at Salamanca in Spain * 1943: Palermo, Sicily surrenders to American general George S. Patton's 7th Army

23 July

El Cid's last great (posthumous) victory

1099 Greatest of Spanish folk heroes, knight and conqueror, scourge of the Moors, faithful defender of Christian Spain. Such is the legend of Roderigo Díaz de Bivar, known to history as El Cid, who, according to legend, today led his army to one final victory – even though he was dead.

El Cid was in fact a mercenary warlord who fought for the Moors as well as against them. Even his popular name is revealing: El Cid comes from *Cid-y*, meaning 'my lord' in Arabic. But whoever's side he was on, El Cid was one of the most powerful figures in 11th-century Spain and undoubtedly its greatest general. He played an important role in saving his country from complete Moorish domination.

Although myth makes El Cid a noble knight on a par with King

Arthur, the truth is less glorious. When he conquered Valencia from the Moors, he promised the Moorish commander ibn Jahhaf that he would be spared. But as soon as he had fully taken over the town he had ibn Jahhaf burned alive.

Many tales surround El Cid, none greater than that of his final victory on this day in Valencia, which he ruled.

In the summer of 1099 El Cid and his soldiers were bottled up in the city, under siege from King Bucar and a vast Moorish army. On 10 July a stray enemy arrow mortally wounded the great knight, but before he died he gave deathbed instructions to his generals on how to break the siege.

Following their leader's last orders, at midnight on 22 May his soldiers strapped his armoured body upright on his faithful horse Bavieca. Then the entire army rode out through the city gates, El Cid in the lead. As the noble corpse moved forward with the baggage train, the Spanish knights turned and attacked the sleeping Moors from behind.

According to the *Chronica del Cid*, an almost contemporary account, 'it seemed to King Bucar that before them came a knight of great stature upon a white horse with a bloody cross, who bore in one hand a white banner and in the other a sword which seemed of fire and he made great mortality among the Moors ... And King Bucar and the other kings were so dismayed they never checked the reins until they had ridden into the sea.'

After the Moors had fled, El Cid was buried in Valencia, where his wife Doña Ximena ruled in his stead. But when the Moors forced her out two years later, she took his body to the monastery of San Pedro de Cardeña, near Burgos, where for ten years it remained seated on an ivory chair before receiving proper burial. Not surprisingly, a superstitious cult soon grew up around the tomb. In 1919 the legendary knight's remains were transferred to Burgos Cathedral.

El Cid lives on in Spanish legend, and he is celebrated in the most famous Spanish epic poem, *El Cantar de mío Cid* (The Song of the Cid). Over 500 years later Pierre Corneille commemorated him again in his great drama *Le Cid*.

Other action this day

1885: American general and president Ulysses S. Grant dies of throat cancer at Mount McGregor, New York * 1951: French marshal Henri

Pétain dies in prison, having been jailed for treason committed during the Second World War * 1952: The Free Officers Movement led by Muhammad Neguib and Gamal Abdul Nasser overthrows Egypt's King Farouk and establishes the Egyptian Republic

24 July

Nelson loses his right arm

1797 En route to proving himself Britain's greatest admiral, Horatio Nelson survived illness and injury that would have put a lesser man out of the running.

He nearly died while on duty in the Indian Ocean, through contracting malaria. He was so badly affected that the navy sent him home to recover. Later, the British force of which he was part was decimated by yellow fever while attacking San Juan in Puerto Rico and again Nelson was lucky to survive.

Nelson suffered his first serious battle wound in 1794 when his squadron was besieging Corsica, in the hope of using it as a new base in the war against France. Infantry led the attack, supported by naval guns brought ashore to pound the enemy fortress. Nelson, then a 35-year-old captain, was in charge of the naval unit.

During the morning of 12 July the British guns were battering the enemy's positions at Calvi when suddenly a French shell exploded, showering the attackers with sand and broken rock. Something struck Nelson in the right eye, permanently clouding his vision.

Three years afterwards Nelson was hit again, slightly wounded by a shell splinter at the Battle of Cape St Vincent (see 14 February).

Later that same year the fleet was on the attack again, this time against the Spanish at Tenerife. Just before midnight on this day Nelson – by then an admiral – was trying to land when a musket ball tore through his right elbow. Immediately brought back to his flagship, he greeted his officers with astonishing nonchalance, refusing help in climbing aboard with the comment: 'I have got my legs left and one arm.' He said he knew his arm must come off, so the sooner the better. Taken to the ship's surgeon, he pointed to the dangling limb and commented, 'Doctor, I want to get rid of this useless piece of flesh here.'

In those days before anaesthetics the amputation must have been painful in the extreme, but Nelson bore it stoically. Half an hour later he was back in his cabin giving orders and writing dispatches with his left hand.

Although fighting the French almost continually for the next eight years, Nelson managed to avoid injury or illness until October 1805, when he received his final, fatal wound at Trafalgar (see 21 October).

(see 21 October)

Other action this day

1704: British admiral Sir George Rooke captures Gibraltar ∗ 1712: During the War of the Spanish Succession, French marshal Claude de Villars defeats the Austrians and Dutch under Eugene of Savoy at the Battle of Denain ∗ 1943: The first day of the eleven-day Operation Gomorrah, during which British and Canadian bombers bomb Hamburg by day and American bombers do so by night, dropping 9,000 tons of explosives and killing more than 50,000 people

25 July

Bonaparte routs the Turks at Abu Qir

1799 Invade Egypt, Napoleon Bonaparte had suggested, and strike at Britain's wealth by threatening the route to India. The members of France's Directory (the French government during the First Republic) were only too happy to support the plan, which had the added benefit of getting rid of this nakedly ambitious young general, and so it was in June 1798 that Bonaparte embarked for the Middle East.

At first, all went swimmingly. Bonaparte took the island of Malta and then landed his army at the Egyptian port of Alexandria. Then, on 21 July at the so-called Battle of the Pyramids, fought across the Nile from Cairo, his cannon destroyed virtually an entire Egyptian army of 24,000 men in less than two hours, with a loss of only 200 Frenchmen. But only eleven days later Horatio Nelson devastated the French fleet at the Battle of the Nile (see 1 August), leaving Bonaparte stranded in Egypt, with no means of resupply – or of returning to France. Then Turkey, which enjoyed nominal rule over Egypt at the time, declared war.

In February 1799, Bonaparte marched into Ottoman-controlled Syria, but after failing to take Acre he beat a hasty retreat back into Egypt. On 11 July, however, a Turkish force of 16,000 men debarked at Abu Qir Bay, fourteen miles to the north-east of Alexandria, under the command of Seid Mustafa Pasha. His troops were mainly Janissaries, a corps founded in the 14th century as an elite group of soldiers who had been kidnapped as boys from Christian families and forcibly converted to Islam. But by now they were an anachronism, resisting military reform and detested by the rest of the Turkish army. They were picturesquely dressed in baggy blue trousers and red turbans, and armed with muskets, pistols and sabres, but they had no cavalry, modern artillery or bayonets.

Once ashore, Mustafa wiped out the 300-man French garrison there and fortified his beachhead with two defensive lines a mile apart, the first on a plain, the second on a hill called Mount Vizir. The danger of his position, however, was that, should he be defeated, his men had nowhere to go except into the sea.

On 25 July Bonaparte advanced on Abu Qir with 8,000 men plus a thousand horse under his charismatic Gascon cavalry commander, Joachim Murat.

Bonaparte opened the battle by sending the bulk of his infantry against the centre of the first Turkish line, with Murat's cavalry around both flanks. The line quickly dissolved, the Janissaries retreating to the second line on Mount Vizir.

Then, when Bonaparte pulled his troops back to regroup, the Janissaries left their positions to finish off the wounded and mutilate the dead. At that moment the French cavalry charged and scattered the disorganised enemy while Murat plunged into Mustafa's tent behind the line. Mustafa got off a pistol shot, wounding him in the jaw, but Murat dashed the pistol out of his hand with his sabre, slicing off two of his fingers, and captured him. Meanwhile his cavalry swept the remaining Janissaries into the sea. The French had lost 1,000 men but the Turks suffered almost 12,000 casualties, including 5,000 drowned, and an additional 4,000 captured. Only a handful escaped.

Within three months French troops had completed the subjuga-tion of Egypt. In just over a year, Bonaparte had conquered a territory half as large as France. Within a month of his success at Abu Qir he left Egypt for home, leaving his army behind, to lead French forces against a new European coalition that included England.

Other action this day

1766: At Fort Ontario, New York, Ottawa Indian chief Pontiac agrees to a peace treaty with the British, ending Pontiac's Rebellion, which had started in 1763 * 1894: The Japanese fire on a Chinese warship, starting the first Sino-Japanese War * 1934: Austrian chancellor Engelbert Dollfuss is shot and killed by Nazis during a raid on the chancellery * 1938: Republican forces under Colonel Juan Modesto launch attacks across the Ebro to begin the decisive battle of the Spanish Civil War, which ends on 16 November with 70,000 Republican dead, wounded and captured

26 July

Eugene of Savoy escapes from France

1683 Today a young man who would become one of Europe's greatest generals fled his native city to find a career with his country's future enemies. His name was Eugene of Savoy.

Born and raised in Paris and of compelling title, nineteen-year-old prince Eugene had been devastated to be turned down out of hand by his king, Louis XIV, when he sought to join the French officer corps. Small and horse-faced, Eugene was hardly prepossessing, but the real reason for his rejection was his mother. Niece of the great Cardinal Mazarin, she had once been Louis's mistress (rumours, almost certainly untrue, circulated that Eugene was actually Louis's son) but in 1680 she was caught up in the great witchcraft scandal that rocked France, even touching the king's current mistress, Madame de Montespan. During the investigation Eugene's mother was accused of having poisoned her husband, and she had to flee to Brussels. As no French officer could be so close to such a disgraceful incident, Eugene was denied his commission.

Crushed by Louis's dismissal, Eugene today fled from Paris without the king's permission. Stopped by French agents at Frankfurt, the young prince refused to return and shortly made his way to

Vienna. There Emperor Leopold I welcomed him into the Imperial service, where he remained until his death 53 years later.

The moment Eugene had been commissioned by the emperor, he joined in the defence of Vienna, which had lain under siege from the Turks since 17 July. The Turks were routed (see 12 September), and for his fine performance in his first battle, Eugene was given his own regiment of dragoons two months later.

Eugene soon showed not only superior strategic ability but also a spirit of leadership that made men follow him. By the time he was 29 he had become an imperial field marshal.

Eugene achieved an extraordinary record in battle. In 1697 he crushed the Turks at Zenta, a victory that made Austria the greatest power in central Europe. Twenty years later he crushed them again, first at Peterwardein (1716) and then at Belgrade (1717), battles that delivered Hungary from the Ottomans. (The battle of Belgrade is commemorated by the famous 'Das Prinz Eugen Lied', 'The Prince Eugene Song', sung by German soldiers ever since.)

Between wars with the Turks Eugene partnered his great friend the Duke of Marlborough to defeat Louis XIV's France during the War of Spanish Succession, first triumphing at Blenheim (1704 – see 13 August) to take Bavaria, and again at Oudenaarde (1708) and Malplaquet (1709) to secure the Netherlands. Eugene also gained northern Italy by his victory at Turin in 1706. During his remarkable career, he was wounded thirteen times.

After his victories over the Ottoman empire in 1716 and 1717, Eugene splendidly retired to his Belvedere Palace in Vienna, but at age 71 he came out fighting one last time to defeat the French in southern Germany during the War of the Polish Succession.

The great general expired in Vienna two years later, peacefully dying in his sleep. One of his lions in the Belvedere zoo died the same night.

Other action this day

1469: Warwick the Kingmaker defeats the forces of Edward IV at the Battle of Edgecote Moor * 1634: The fortress of La Mothe in Lorraine surrenders to Richelieu's army after a siege of 141 days * 1918: Britain's top fighter pilot ace, Edward Mannock, is shot down and killed by ground fire on the Western Front

27 July

A cannonball kills a great soldier

1675 Today, as he reconnoitred his army's position, a stray cannon-ball killed the man Napoleon considered the greatest military leader in history.

Henri de la Tour d'Auvergne, vicomte de Turenne, had been born in Sedan, at the time a sovereign state of which his father was the reigning prince. His father had thought his son's constitution too fragile for a military career, but, on Turenne's insistence, at fourteen he was allowed to serve a military apprenticeship in the bodyguard of his uncle, the Dutch stadtholder (roughly, head of state) Maurice of Nassau, during the Dutch revolt against the Spanish. Promoted to captain at fifteen, he was praised for his valour during the siege of 's-Hertogenbosch in 1629. But a year later he left the Netherlands to enlist in France, since Sedan owed its loyalty to the French crown. Still only nineteen, he was entrusted with the command of an infantry regiment. By the time he was 23 he had been elevated to maréchal de camp (major general) for his outstanding courage during the 141-day siege of La Mothe.

For the next 41 years Turenne was almost continuously on the battlefield, particularly during the Thirty Years War. He successfully served Louis XIII and Louis XIV in turn. The first Louis's widow, Anne of Austria, was regent of France during her son's infancy, and it was she who made Turenne a marshal on 19 December 1643. He was still only 32.

At the conclusion of the Thirty Years War (1648) Turenne briefly joined the princely faction in the Fronde revolt against Cardinal Mazarin's restriction of the powers of the nobility, but he was later reconciled with the cardinal and commanded the French army in the Third Fronde War. It was then that he gained the permanent trust of Louis XIV by saving the fourteen-year-old king from capture at Jargeau.

Turenne continued to battle for his king, and in 1658 triumphed in a battle unusual in that although it was principally Turenne's French against the Spanish, further Frenchmen (French Fronde rebels) fought with the Spanish, and English troops fought on both sides. Allied with Turenne were 6,000 men from Oliver Cromwell's English Commonwealth but on the other side was a contingent of English royalists commanded by the Duke of York, the future James II. After winning the bloody three-hour battle, Turenne summed up the results in his famously terse report to King Louis XIV: 'The enemy came, was beaten, I am tired, good night.'

In 1675 Louis XIV was fighting yet another of his interminable wars, this one against the Austrians. Yet again the great marshal was expected to save the day. On 27 July the French and Imperial armies clashed at Sasbach, and it was here that the fatal cannonball found its mark, prompting from a dying Turenne the plaintive remark: 'I did not mean to be killed today.'

As soon as the news was known in Paris, the court went into deep mourning, Louis declaring that the French had 'lost the father of the country'. Turenne's finest epitaph, however, comes from his contemporary Voltaire, who wrote: 'The virtues and abilities that he alone had made people forget the faults and weaknesses he shared with so many others.'

Turenne's final honour was to be buried among France's kings at St Denis, but during the Revolution the cathedral there was desecrated by the republican mob and his remains were transferred to the Musée des Monuments. Finally in 1800 an admiring Napoleon had the great general re-interred in the Invalides in Paris.

Other action this day

1214: French king Philip I (Augustus) defeats John of England, Otto IV and the counts of Boulogne and Flanders at the Battle of Bouvines * 1778: Thirty British ships-of-the-line take on 29 French ships in the inconclusive First Battle of Ushant in the English Channel during the American War of Independence * 1880: At the huge cost of about 4,000 casualties, Ayub Khan's Afghan army of 25,000 warriors overwhelms a British/Indian force of 2,500, killing almost 1,000 with an additional 200 wounded, at the Battle of Maiwand during the Second Anglo-Afghan War

28 July

Talavera – turning the tide in the Peninsular War

1809 British forces won a welcome victory over the French today at Talavera, their first major engagement on the Iberian peninsula in half a year. Six months earlier, an outnumbered British army, facing a massive French advance into Spain led by the Emperor Napoleon himself, had been forced to retreat to the port of La Coruña and embark for home.

In the aftermath of that Dunkirk-like withdrawal, the British government turned to a young lieutenant general named Arthur Wellesley, gave him command of a new army, and sent him to protect Portugal, Britain's last ally on the continent of Europe, now threatened by French invasion from Spain.

Landing at Lisbon in May, Wellesley and his army quickly cleared French forces from Oporto and northern Portugal, then moved south to contend with Marshal Victor's forces, 40,000 strong, in the Tagus valley just over the border in Spain. Wellesley's army of 20,000 moved up the valley accompanied by a doubtful ally, the Spanish army of Estramadura, some 35,000 soldiers, ill-trained and poorly led.

The opposing forces met for battle along a streamed flowing southward to the fortified town of Talavera on the banks of the river Tagus. The Spanish held the right side of the Allied line anchored on the town, the British the left side extending northward up to a ridge line. Across the stream bed, Victor's French army was drawn up, mainly facing the British positions.

Tactically, today's battle was a draw but it was also a strategic victory for the Allies, for it interrupted French plans to advance on Portugal and forced Victor to retreat with his army towards Madrid.

More importantly, Talavera demonstrated that when it came to fighting the French – masters of combat across Europe for fifteen years – British arms, when properly organised and led, could prevail where all others had failed. In particular, the twelve hours of hard fighting at Talavera showed dramatically how a defensive line could defeat an attacking column, the preferred formation of the French army since the early days of the Revolution.

Preceded by a swarm of skirmishers, *tirailleurs*, to engage the enemy's attention, advancing French infantry columns displayed a momentum that seldom failed to carry the day, impressing the enemy psychologically with what Sir Charles Oman described as 'a sense of the solidity and inexorable strength of the approaching mass'.

But in Spain the French faced a different enemy, far better trained and disciplined. Wellesley, a master of defensive tactics, deployed his forces spread across a position two-deep – a formation that may eventually have inspired the phrase 'the thin red line' – allowing the maximum musketry to be concentrated on the head of an advancing column, whose firepower was limited to the soldiers in the first few ranks. Columns nearing the British line were subject to a murderous opening volley, which, when repeated as often as three times a minute, soon sent the attacking formations to the rear in disarray.

At Talavera, on a field often obscured by thick smoke, this pattern of battle prevailed time and time again in the course of a long and bloody day marked by attacks, counter-attacks, close combat, outflanking attempts and artillery fire. At one point early in the afternoon, some 30,000 French troops were drawn up to launch the main assault; when it was over, not a yard had been gained.

Later in the day the attacks ceased. During the evening the French army withdrew from its positions and moved eastward towards Madrid to gather more forces. Over the next week, Wellington took the opportunity to withdraw his forces to Portugal and prepare them for an invasion.

British losses at Talavera amounted to 5,400, over a quarter of their troop strength; French casualties were almost 7,300. The Spanish army, which played only a modest part in the battle, lost an estimated 400–500 men. Later, Wellesley would describe Talavera as 'the hardest fought battle of modern times', a considerable exaggeration. But the battle certainly marked a turning of the tide in the Peninsular War, in which, ultimately, Wellesley would lead Allied armies – British and Spanish – to drive the French entirely out of Spain by 1813.

In the meantime, for the success of his efforts this day, Lieutenant General Wellesley became Viscount Wellington of Talavera.

1914: Austria-Hungary declares war on Serbia, starting the First World War * 1920: Mexican revolutionary general Pancho Villa surrenders to the Mexican government * 1942: Joseph Stalin issues Order 227, specifying that all who retreat or leave their positions will be summarily executed

29 July

A Confederate ship is born in Liverpool

1862 In Liverpool this morning, an unfinished steam-powered vessel, bearing hastily drawn papers identifying her as the British merchantman *Enrica*, left her dockyard slip draped in bright bunting and headed down the Mersey for a 'trial run'. In addition to her crew, she had on board a number of well-dressed guests with a picnic lunch suitable for the festive occasion. But at noon a tugboat came alongside onto which all supernumeraries were speedily offloaded. Then *Enrica* turned north and disappeared into the Irish Sea.

Three weeks later, in the Azores, outfitted for war, she was reborn as the Confederate States' Ship *Alabama*, the most successful commerce-raider of the Civil War; in fact the most successful in all naval history. In the next 21 months, the CSS *Alabama* became the scourge of Northern shipping around the world. With a Southern captain and officers and an Anglo-Irish crew, she cruised some 75,000 miles, capturing, ransoming or destroying over 60 Union merchant ships, for a combined loss of $6,500,000. In all her travels, she never once put into a Confederate port, but revictualled and refuelled at places like Cape Town, Singapore and Bahia, usually with the permission of local British authorities.

Reflecting his nation's outrage, the American ambassador in London, Charles Francis Adams, strongly protested to the British government – officially neutral in the American Civil War – about the lax security that had allowed the ship to escape into enemy hands. But British dockyards had already begun producing other raiders, like the *Shenandoah* and the *Florida*, which collectively, by war's end, would destroy over 200 vessels and cargoes valued at as much as $25 million and would sink more than half of the American merchant fleet.

Alabama's spectacular string of depredations ended off the French port of Cherbourg in June 1864, when the USS *Kearsarge* caught up with her and sank her in a 90-minute battle. Among the witnesses who thronged the shore to see the clash was Edouard Manet, who painted the well-publicised event.

The genius behind the purchase and escape of the *Alabama* and other Confederate raiders was James D. Bulloch, a Georgian and experienced naval officer whom Jefferson Davis had sent to England early in the Civil War to acquire ships for the South. After the war he remained in Liverpool, but his celebrated exploits made him a hero, not only to Confederate sympathisers but also to his asthmatic – and very pro-Union – young nephew in New York City in whom he inspired a lifelong interest in naval affairs. Some years later, when the nephew began writing his first book, Bulloch provided valuable advice on matters of naval combat. The book, *The Naval History of the War of 1812*, appeared in 1882. Its author, only 23 years old but already an up-and-coming New York politician, was Theodore Roosevelt.

Other action this day

1014: Byzantine emperor Basil II defeats the Bulgarians at the Battle of Kleidion, capturing 15,000 prisoners and blinding 99 of every 100 men, leaving 150 one-eyed men to lead them back to their ruler, who faints at the sight and dies two days later of a stroke * 1030: At the Battle of Stiklestad, exiled Norwegian king Olaf IV and his army of 3,600 warriors are routed by a 7,000-man peasant force, and Olaf is killed, ending his quest to regain his throne * 1885: Italian fascist leader Benito Mussolini is born

30 July

Rome crushes the barbarians at Vercellae

101 BC Today at Vercellae, 45 miles west of present-day Milan, Roman consul Gaius Marius commanded eight legions plus some auxiliaries, totalling 52,000 men. Ranged against him was a huge if somewhat formless army, perhaps as large as 300,000, of a tribe called the Cimbri. If the barbarians could not be stopped, Rome would be in more danger than at any time since Hannibal was at its gates 115 years before.

For almost fifteen years two Germanic tribes, the Cimbri and the Teutones, who had descended en masse from Jutland seeking new lands, had been threatening Rome. These barbarians had routed Roman armies in 113 BC, 109 BC and 107 BC near Lake Geneva, killing its commander, the consul L. Cassius Longinus. But the most devastating defeat was at Arausio (present Orange in Provence) in 105 BC, when 80,000 legionaries and 40,000 Roman camp followers were slain.

But now commanding the Roman army was that redoubtable general, Gaius Marius, who had already demonstrated his fighting prowess in Spain and North Africa. He was a military innovator who had significantly improved one of his troops' key weapons, the *pilum* (a sort of javelin). Normally a pilum's iron head was fastened to the shaft by two metal nails, but Marius replaced one nail with a wooden peg so that when a pilum struck an enemy shield, the peg broke and the pilum would sag and drag along the ground, making the shield difficult to carry or manoeuvre.

Marius had also taken a new approach to raising armies, recruiting soldiers from the common people instead of only from landed families, and, according to the 1st-century historian Plutarch, 'he was in better training than any of [his soldiers], and in daring far surpassed them all'.

In his fight against the barbarians, first Marius took on the Teutones at Aquae Sextae (Aix-en-Provence) in 102 BC, inflicting some 100,000 casualties. Now, on this day the following year, he would meet the Cimbri. Plutarch tells us what happened:

> And now Boeorix the king of the Cimbri, with a small retinue, rode up towards the camp and challenged Marius to set a day and a place and come out and fight for the ownership of the country ... They decided that the day should be the third following, and the place the plain of Vercellae, which was suitable for the operations of the Roman cavalry [commanded by future dictator Lucius Cornelius Sulla], and would give the Cimbri room to deploy their numbers ...
>
> [On the day of battle the Cimbri] foot-soldiers advanced slowly ... with a depth equal to their front, for each side of their

formation had an extent of thirty furlongs [3¾ miles]; and their horsemen, fifteen thousand strong, rode out in splendid style, with helmets made to resemble the maws of frightful wild beasts or the heads of strange animals, which, with their towering crests of feathers, made their wearers appear taller than they really were; they were also equipped with iron breast-plates, and carried gleaming white shields. For hurling, each man had two lances; and at close quarters they used large, heavy swords ...

The infantry of the Barbarians came on to the attack like a vast sea in motion ... An immense cloud of dust was raised ... and the two armies were hidden from one another by it ... The Romans were favoured in the struggle ... by the heat and by the sun, which shone in the faces of the Cimbri ... For the Barbarians were well able to endure cold, and had been brought up in shady and chilly regions ... They were therefore undone by the heat; they sweated profusely, breathed with difficulty, and were forced to hold their shields before their faces. Moreover, the dust, by hiding the enemy, helped to encourage the Romans. For they could not see from afar the great numbers of the foe, but each one of them fell at a run upon the man just opposite him, and fought him hand to hand, without having been terrified by the sight of the rest of the host. And their bodies were so inured to toil and so thoroughly trained that not a Roman was seen to sweat or pant, despite the great heat and the run with which they came to the encounter.

The greatest number and the best fighters of the enemy were cut to pieces on the spot; for to prevent their ranks from being broken, those who fought in front were bound fast to one another with long chains that were passed through their belts. [Others], however, were driven back to their entrenchments, where the Romans beheld a most tragic spectacle. The women in black garments stood at the wagons and slew those who fled – their husbands or brothers or fathers, then strangled their little children and cast them beneath the wheels of the wagons or the feet of the cattle, and then cut their own throats. It is said that one woman hung dangling from the tip of a wagon-pole, with her children tied to either ankle; while the men, for lack of trees, fastened themselves by the neck to the horns of the cattle, or to their legs, then plied the goad, and were dragged or trampled to death as the cattle dashed away. Nevertheless, in spite of such self-destruction, more than sixty thousand were taken prisoners; and those who fell were said to have been twice that number.

Marius had comprehensively defeated both the Teutones and Cimbri and virtually wiped them out. No Germanic tribe would again threaten the existence of the empire for three and a half centuries.

Other action this day

AD 634: At the Battle of Ajnadayn, the Rashidun Caliphate (the Islamic empire) army decisively defeats the Byzantine empire in their first major battle * 1419: During the First Defenestration of Prague, Hussite rioters hurl the burgomaster and several other councillors from windows in the town hall to their deaths, leading to the start of the Hussite Wars * 1945: At 4.14am Japanese submarine I-58 hits the American cruiser *Indianapolis* with two torpedoes, sinking the ship in twelve minutes, killing 300 of the 1,196 men on board; the remaining 880 men float in the water without lifeboats for four days before rescue, during which time 559 more die of exposure, thirst and the most shark attacks on humans in history

31 July

The soldier who founded the Jesuits

1556 Although a diminutive man of only five feet two inches, Íñigo (in Latin, Ignatius) Oñaz López de Loyola had early decided to become a soldier, a fitting occupation for the son of a noble family. When he was fifteen he was sent by his father as a page to Arévalo in Castile in the service of a relative, Juan Velásquez de Cuellar, one of the Spanish king Ferdinand's provincial governors. There he became a fine soldier and an accomplished horseman and courtier, learning the soldierly virtues of discipline and obedience.

In 1517 Loyola became a knight in the service of another relative, the duke of Nájera and viceroy of Navarre, and fought in several minor battles in the border warfare against the French in northern Castile and Navarre. For his courage and leadership he was awarded a captaincy.

Probably unknown to Loyola, during this same year Martin Luther affixed his theses to a cathedral door at Wittenberg, igniting the Protestant Reformation. Indeed, Loyola gave little thought to religion at that time, later describing himself as 'a man given to the vanities of the world, whose chief delight consisted in martial exercises, with a great and vain desire to win renown'.

Four years later Loyola was helping to direct the defence of Pamplona, besieged by the French in their invasion of Navarre. As the siege wore on, the more senior captains saw that their position was indefensible, but Loyola, keen to achieve military glory, urged his comrades to continue the fight. But then, on 20 May, a French cannonball broke his right shin and tore open his left calf.

Now bereft of the one captain who wanted to fight on, the Pamplona garrison soon surrendered. Loyola himself was well treated by the victors and carried on a litter back to his castle in his home town of Loyola. There he voluntarily underwent unspeakable tortures on the operating table and the rack as surgeons tried to heal his leg without a resultant limp. His leg was rebroken and reset, a protruding end of the bone was sawn off and weights were attached to the damaged limb in an attempt to stretch it. Despite these measures, his right leg remained shorter than his left, and from then on he walked with a pronounced limp, ending his military career.

Now Loyola determined that if he could no longer fight for his king he would fight for his church. While attending the university of Paris he started to organise his own military force, but this was an army for Christ, moulded after the personality of its founder: militant and activist, believing that, in the name of God, the end justifies the means. By the time he was 49 that force, the Jesuits, had received official blessing from the Pope.

Like the good soldier he had been, Loyola was a workaholic, indifferent to his surroundings and personal comfort. (He is said to have lived on a diet of bread, water and chestnuts.) He ceaselessly sought and trained new recruits, and when he died in Rome on this day at the age of 65, some 1,500 Jesuit 'soldiers of the Church' were spread throughout Europe.

Other action this day

1192: Richard the Lionheart seizes Jaffa in a surprise attack during the Third Crusade * 1777: The British under General John Burgoyne capture Fort Edward on the upper Hudson River * 1917: The British attack the German lines to start the Third Battle of Ypres (Battle of Passchendaele)

1 August

Nelson routs the French at the Battle of the Nile

1798 Napoleon Bonaparte had left his fleet of seventeen ships in Abu Qir Bay near the mouth of the Nile, while he stormed through Alexandria and Cairo. He was not to know that Rear Admiral Horatio Nelson was closing in with fourteen men o' war. The great British admiral was determined to make his mark. The day before attacking the French fleet he had affirmed, 'Before this time tomorrow I shall have gained a peerage, or Westminster Abbey.'

The French line ran north to south, with shoals to the west. A few hours before nightfall on this day, in a brilliant tactical thrust Nelson sent five British ships-of-the-line around the head of the French line of battle between the enemy fleet and the shoals, while his other ships sailed down the eastern side of the line, thus attacking the French from both sides at once. The British were able to pick off the enemy ships one by one because the wind from the north prevented the unengaged French ships from sailing up to join the battle.

At about 10 o'clock at night the battle reached its climax when Admiral François-Paul Brueys's 120-gun flagship *Orient* exploded, killing almost 900 of its crew of 1,000, including the admiral himself. The British continued to attack the remains of the French fleet, finally capturing or sinking all but two of the enemy's ships-of-the-line. As Nelson proclaimed the next day when surveying the floating carnage of the battle, 'Victory is not a name strong enough for such a scene.'

The Battle of the Nile was exceptionally bloody; French casualties were over 5,000 dead and 3,000 captured, including wounded, while the victorious British sustained 200 killed and about 700 wounded, including Nelson who suffered a minor injury to the head. But later that year Nelson gained his peerage as he had predicted.

This was Nelson's first great triumph against Napoleon in an independent command, but oddly enough the battle was most famously commemorated by a contemporary bit of English doggerel that celebrates the French, not the British. The English poet Felicia Hemans immortalised the heroism of the son of the captain of the French flagship *Orient*, who tried to halt the flames of his father's foundering ship:

The boy stood on the burning deck
Whence all but he had fled;
The flame that lit the battle's wreck
Shone round him o'er the dead.

Sadly, the boy failed and went down with the ship.

Other action this day

30 BC: With rival Roman general Octavian (the future emperor Augustus) closing in, Roman general Mark Antony commits suicide, believing (incorrectly) that his lover Cleopatra is already dead * 1808: General Arthur Wellesley (later the Duke of Wellington) lands with a British army in Lisbon to start the Peninsular War * 1941: The first Jeep is manufactured * 1943: On her fourth sortie of the day, 21-year-old Soviet female fighter pilot ace Lydia Litvyakis, who downed more planes than any other woman in history with twelve solo kills and two shared, is shot down and killed by German fighters

2 August

Hannibal destroys the Romans at Cannae

216 BC Today the great Carthaginian general Hannibal Barca totally annihilated a huge Roman army at the Battle of Cannae.

Six hundred years earlier, in 814 BC, Phoenician traders from Tyre had founded a new city on the north coast of Africa (where today's Tunis stands), calling it simply 'Kart-Hadasht', or 'new town'.

Over the centuries Carthage developed into a powerful and prosperous Mediterranean power, a rival of Rome, with colonies in Spain, Sicily and Sardinia, but in 264 BC a minor encounter in Sicily grew into the First Punic War with Rome, a conflict that gained its name from the Roman word for Carthaginians, *Punici*, which itself comes from Phoenician, the language of ancient Carthage.

Hannibal was born in Carthage of noble parents during this war in 247 BC. When the conflict ended six years later, victorious Rome stripped Carthage of much of its wealth and territory. Brought up in

Carthage-controlled Spain, he learned to hate the Romans for the humiliation and impoverishment of his country, and vowed revenge.

Hannibal was an arresting man. Tall, clean-shaven, handsome and athletic, he was an outstanding swordsman and a fearless rider. His appearance revealed his Phoenician (Semitic) bloodlines, with a slightly hooked nose, curly hair and dark eyes (one of which he later lost during his fight against Rome). By 26 he was already a general.

At 29 Hannibal embarked on one of the most daring military exploits in all of history to achieve his goal of a decisive victory on Roman soil. To avoid having to challenge Rome's naval dominance of the Mediterranean, he marched his huge force – Carthaginian and Iberian foot soldiers, Numidian cavalry and 37 elephants – north from Carthago Nova ('New Carthage', today's Cartagena in Spain) and across southern Gaul. It was nearing winter when he reached the Alps, but, despite severe losses of men and pack animals, in only fifteen days he led his army through the mountains and down into Italy. Somehow most of the elephants survived.

Even in his first battles against the Romans Hannibal displayed his military genius in a series of devastating victories. He was a master of deception, one night tying lighted faggots to the horns of cattle to convince his enemies that his army was on the move when in fact they were waiting in ambush. Within two years he had covered much of Italy, leaving Rome terrified but not beaten.

In the spring of 216 BC, Hannibal moved south to capture a Roman supply depot at Cannae, a small village on the 'Achilles heel' of the Italian boot. Determined to rid Italy of the Carthaginian invader, the Roman consuls Lucius Aemilius Paulus and Gaius Terentius Varro advanced with a huge army of about 80,000 men to do battle with an enemy force of only half their size. Hoping to break the Carthaginian line with a heavy attack in the centre, the Romans massed their infantry and charged. Hannibal ordered his line to bow backward under the weight of the Roman assault, encouraging Varro to pile more infantry into the centre. Then the Carthaginian sent his two wings to envelop the concentrated Roman infantry on both sides, and his cavalry, which had already bested the Roman horse, completed the encirclement by attacking from the flanks and rear. The battlefield became a killing ground.

Up to 50,000 Romans perished in the slaughter (the near-contemporary historian Polybius says 70,000). Whatever the true number, it represented the greatest one-day loss in all of Rome's history, a massacre that was unsurpassed in any battle anywhere until the 20th century.

So great was the terror inspired by Hannibal's triumph that for centuries Roman parents would frighten mischievous children with the words '*Hannibal ad portas!*' (Hannibal at the gates!).

Other action this day

338 BC: Philip II's Macedonian army defeats the combined forces of Athens and Thebes in the Battle of Chaeronea, securing Macedonian hegemony in Greece * 1870: The *mitrailleuse*, the first machine gun to be employed in major combat, is used for the first time in battle when the 9th battery of Captain Dupré enfilades German troops at Sarrebourg (or Sarrebrück) during the Franco-Prussian War * 1939: Albert Einstein sends President Franklin Roosevelt the Einstein-Szilárd letter, written in consultation with Leó Szilárd, Edward Teller and Eugene Wigner, suggesting the development of an atomic bomb * 1943: When the torpedo boat PT-109 is rammed and sunk by a Japanese destroyer, Lieutenant John F. Kennedy saves all but two of his crew * 1990: Iraq's Saddam Hussein invades Kuwait

3 August

A victory in the wilderness

1757 A sentry staring out from the fort's ramparts would have seen a fearsome sight: in the cool half-light of a summer dawn lay the enemy's fleet, hundreds of bateaux and canoes arrayed from shore to shore, just out of cannon range, and clearly poised for landings. Today was D-day.

The attackers, a mixed force of 8,000 troops – French regulars, Canadian militiamen and Indians, all under the command of the marquis de Montcalm – had advanced by land and water to reach their objective, Fort William Henry, the British base at the head of Lake George. Now would begin one of the most famous battles of the French and Indian War, six days of fighting in which 'the cannon thundered all day and from a hundred peaks and crags the astonished wilderness roared back the sound'.

Montcalm's campaign was meant to drive the British out of central New York by capturing Fort William Henry, which stood along the critical and highly contested invasion route linking French Canada and the British colony of New York. On this first day of operations, the French encircled the fort, brought ashore their cannon and began laying out siege lines. Fort William Henry, located close to the shore, was a rough square with bastions at the corners connected by earthen walls. Within were barracks that housed the garrison of some 850 British regulars, supplemented by 1,500 colonial militiamen. Its armament consisted of seventeen heavy cannon and various mortars and swivel guns.

By 5 August, the French had completed the first parallel trench and brought up two batteries. The relentless bombardment that followed took a heavy toll on the fort's bastions and casements. At night the British lit bonfires outside the walls to reveal any surprise attack.

On the morning of the 9th, French cannon were within 300 yards of the fort's walls. With many of his own guns now out of commission, the British commander, Lieutenant Colonel Munro, contemplating the enemy's superior numbers, decided to surrender. A drum sounded from within the fort, a white flag was raised above the ramparts, and a mounted officer rode out towards Montcalm's tent. There it was agreed that under the civilised custom of European warfare the defenders, after swearing to be non-combatants for eighteen months, would give up the fort, march out with the honours of war for their brave defence, and receive safe passage under guard to the nearest British position, Fort Edward on the Hudson River fourteen miles distant.

Montcalm's Indian allies, however, were not content with such a settlement, preferring to plunder their defeated foe. The next day, as the British column, which included many wives and children of the militiamen, began the march to Fort Edward, the Indians struck, first demanding rum, baggage, clothing, money and weapons; then tomahawking any that resisted or attempted to flee. When the French finally restored order, 185 of the British had been killed and some 500 or 600 wounded or dragged away, although of this last category Montcalm's men eventually recovered 400 from the forest.

Now the Indians cleared out for Montreal, taking with them their plunder and some 200 captives. The following day the French escorted the survivors of the British column to Fort Edward. On the

16th Montcalm withdrew his forces, leaving Fort William Henry a smoking ruin. Then, as Francis Parkman wrote, 'The din of 10,000 combatants, the rage, the terror, the agony were gone; and no living thing was left but the wolves that gathered from the mountains to feast upon the dead.'

The fall of Fort William Henry, described by James Fenimore Cooper in *The Last of the Mohicans*, was a dramatic moment in the war for North America, but the success was only tactical. Had Montcalm held the fort, then gone on to attack Fort Edward north of Albany, he might have achieved the strategic purpose of forcing the British out of the entire region. But short of supplies and without his Indian allies, who provided his intelligence, he chose to retire to his own base, the French stronghold at Fort Ticonderoga, some 40 miles to the north on Lake Champlain.

The next year Montcalm inflicted an even greater defeat on the British when they attempted to capture Fort Ticonderoga. But then came British victories at Louisbourg, Fort Duquesne and Fort Frontenac. In the end, all these were a prelude to the culminating effort of the conflict, in which General Wolfe captured Quebec – and Montcalm lost his life – in 1759 (see 13 September), a deed that won both the war and the continent for Great Britain.

Other action this day

AD 881: Louis III of France defeats the Vikings at the Battle of Saucourt-en-Vimeu, an event celebrated in the poem *Ludwigslied* (Louis's Song) * 1860: The Second Maori War begins in New Zealand * 1914: Germany declares war on France

4 August

German cavalry charge into Belgium to start the First World War

1914 Today at 5.00am, just 35 days after Austrian archduke Franz Ferdinand had been assassinated at Sarajevo (see 28 June), German cavalry units swept over the frontier into neutral Belgium in the first fighting of the First World War, ending 43 years of peace among the great powers of Europe.

Although the great Bismarck had completed the unification of Germany in 1870, the country, in truth, was an amplified Prussia: the Kaiser was the Prussian king and the German army was loyal to him alone. The prime minister, too, was responsible only to him, not to the Reichstag.

Furthermore, the country had a three-tier voting system giving disproportionate weight to the rich and powerful. As the most populous European nation, this military autocracy was determined to be reckoned among the greatest of powers, and alarmed its neighbours with its military and naval build-up. Yet Germany felt itself a victim, encircled by France on the west and Russia on the east: two countries that had allied themselves solely from fear of German might. When Germany launched its attack, most of its citizens felt that they were only defending themselves.

Germany's northern sweep through Belgium was a central element in the 1905 plan developed by the Prussian general Alfred von Schlieffen. His aim was to destroy the French with a massive attack while fighting a holding action against Russia. Since heavy fortifications on the German–French border precluded a direct assault, von Schlieffen advocated sending a massive army on a quick enveloping dash through neutral Belgium. The Germans would storm past Brussels, down into France at Lille and along the coast, then swing around below Paris to catch the main French army from the rear. He thought France would be defeated in 40 days – too short a time for backward Russia to get more than a few token troops to the Eastern Front, or for Great Britain, tied by treaty to Belgium, to get its troops across the Channel. Once the French had been defeated, the German army would swing east to crush the Russians.

But nothing went according to plan. The Germans met fierce Belgian resistance at Liège, which slowed down their attack, and when they reached France in early September they found themselves facing the French army and the British Expeditionary Force. In the opening clashes of the war, at the Ardennes, the Sambre, Mons, Le Cateau and Guise, the Germans continued their inexorable advance. But at the Marne, in early September, the Allies managed to hold the line and mount a counter-attack, stalling the German onslaught and forcing them back into positions that would not change much over the next four years. In like manner, war against Russia proved far more difficult than anticipated. Despite early German victories at

Tannenberg and the Masurian Lakes, by the autumn the two sides were stalemated in the horrors of trench warfare on both the Eastern and Western fronts. Instead of 40 days, the war had another four years to run.

By the time the conflict finally ground to a halt, Germany had committed some 11 million men, of whom 1,774,000 had been killed and an additional 4 million had been wounded. Perhaps luckily for General von Schlieffen, he died in January 1913, too early to see how disastrous his great plan would turn out to be.

Other action this day

1265: Edward I defeats and kills rebel baron Simon de Montfort at the Battle of Evesham near the River Avon ＊ 1347: Edward III conquers the port of Calais after an eleven-month siege, but spares the Burghers of Calais thanks to the pleas of his wife Philippa

5 August

Farragut damns the torpedoes at Mobile Bay

1864 Today American admiral David Farragut earned his place in naval history, as well as in all future books of quotations.

Farragut commanded a Union fleet of eighteen ships during the American Civil War. As the mists evaporated on this hot August morning, the admiral led his fleet past Fort Morgan, a Confederate stronghold that guarded Mobile Bay on the Alabama coast of the Gulf of Mexico. Immediately the enemy opened fire, and the intrepid Farragut had a sailor lash him to the mast so he could use both hands to hold his telescope and see above the swirling smoke.

In addition to firing their cannon, the Confederates had laced the channel with mines (then called torpedoes), and the leading Yankee warship, the iron-clad *Tecumseh*, blew up and sank with 93 of her crew of 114. Near panic, the *Brooklyn* hove to, and Farragut's whole line hesitated, uncertain whether to attack or retreat, as the guns of Fort Morgan continued their deadly cannonade.

Refusing to be intimidated, Farragut cried, 'Damn the torpedoes! Full speed ahead', and led his warships safely through the minefield to destroy the Southern fleet waiting within the bay and forcing the surrender of Fort Morgan.

This famous victory effectively closed the last Confederate port still successfully defying the Union naval blockade, and made a major contribution to the North's march to victory.

Other action this day

AD 642: King Penda of Mercia defeats and kills Oswald of Northumbria at the Battle of Maserfield * 1716: Prince Eugene of Savoy defeats the Turks at Peterwardein * 1918: English fighters down the German Zeppelin L70 on the Norfolk coast during the final Zeppelin raid of the First World War; all 23 crew members of L70 go down with the ship

6 August

Hiroshima

1945 At 8.15 on this clear, still morning an American B-29 bomber flew over the city of Hiroshima, Japan, and dropped the first atomic bomb ever used in warfare. The resulting explosion devastated the city, killing an estimated 70,000 people, injuring as many, and destroying virtually every building within two miles of the explosion site.

The event marked the beginning of the end of the war in the Pacific. Nine days later – after a second atomic bomb was dropped on Nagasaki – Japan capitulated to the Allies, ending a three-and-a-half-year conflict that had seen some of the most savage fighting in human history.

Without the horrific shock of the atomic explosions over Hiroshima and Nagasaki, the Japanese leadership, dominated by a military clique, would not have surrendered to the Allies. Instead, their intention, as ULTRA decrypts made clear, was to continue the war until their nation, now blockaded and under heavy air attack, was wholly destroyed by invasion – or, as they dreamed, until the Allies, exhausted by the protracted and costly Armageddon, offered Japan a negotiated peace.

The Allied decision to drop the bombs was made against calculations of the losses an Allied invasion force would sustain in the Home

Islands, facing the sort of resistance that the Japanese had already shown defending Iwo Jima and Okinawa. Estimates ran as high as a million Allied casualties over another year of fighting.

The alternative was to rely on the blockade and incendiary air raids to bring Japan to surrender, a slower course of action but far less bloody for the Allies. For the Japanese population, however, the bombing raids would produce unimaginable losses, far exceeding those that had occurred in Germany. In six months of bombing raids on its major cities, Japan had already suffered as much damage as Germany had over the three final years of fighting in Europe. Indeed, in early March, a single incendiary attack on Tokyo had proved the most destructive air raid in history, killing over 80,000 people, injuring some 100,000 and destroying fifteen square miles of the city.

But on 16 July, a third option for the Allies was born. On this date, an atomic bomb was successfully tested in New Mexico. Ten days later, on 26 July, without disclosing to their enemy the new weapon's existence, President Truman, Prime Minister Churchill and Generalissimo Chiang Kai-shek, meeting in Potsdam, Germany, broadcast a joint declaration stating the conditions under which Japan could end the war.

The conditions included the total disarmament of the armed forces; Allied occupation of Japanese territory; and the establishment of a 'peacefully inclined and responsible government'. The declaration concluded with a call for unconditional surrender, without which 'the alternative for Japan is prompt and utter destruction'.

With no reply from Tokyo, the small number of Allied officials – civilian and military – who knew of the weapon's existence debated the next move in the war against Japan, a debate that involved both the morality and utility of its use. In the end, the argument that swayed those in whose hands the final decision lay – principally President Harry Truman and Secretary of War Henry L. Stimson – was the calculation that the sheer destructiveness of the weapon would shock the Japanese leaders into giving up the struggle. And in the long run, by bringing about a quicker end to the war, the use of the bomb would save more lives than it would take. Truman gave the order.

When the Hiroshima bomb elicited no reply of any sort from Japan, a second nuclear bomb was dropped on Nagasaki three days later, with destruction on a scale similar to that at Hiroshima. As it turned out, neither atomic bomb inflicted as much damage on its target as had the March incendiary air raid on Tokyo.

Even then, the Japanese War Cabinet could not reach agreement on a surrender. The civilian members were in favour of surrender on the Potsdam terms, if the institution of the emperor could be preserved; its military members firmly insisted that Japan should disarm itself, that there be no Allied occupation of the Home Islands, and that any war crimes trials be controlled by Japan.

Now, however, Emperor Hirohito intervened to demand that the Cabinet accept the Allies' terms. On 15 August, after a failed military coup, the Emperor, speaking over the radio, told his nation: 'We have ordered Our Government to communicate to the Governments of the United States, Great Britain, China, and the Soviet Union that Our Empire accepts the provisions of their Joint Declaration.'

On 28 August the first American troops arrived on Japanese soil to begin an occupation that would last until 1952. On 2 September the official surrender ceremony ending the war took place on the deck of the battleship *Missouri* anchored in Tokyo harbour.

Other action this day

1914: The start of the Battle of the Atlantic: two days after Britain declares war, ten German U-boats leave their base in Heligoland to attack UK warships in the North Sea on the first submarine war patrol in history * 1914: A single German Zeppelin, the Z VI, is damaged by gunfire and forced to land near Cologne during the first offensive use of Zeppelins * 1918: The Allies' top fighter ace during the First World War, French captain René Fonck, makes the first of 75 confirmed kills * 1945: Major Dick Bong, America's leading Second World War fighter pilot ace with 40 kills, is killed testing a P-80 Shooting Star jet fighter in Burbank, California

7 August

The Marines storm ashore at Guadalcanal

1942 'Now hear this! Now hear this! Stand by to disembark!' This was the sound you would have heard aboard US Navy transports lying in Ironbottom Bay at 6.00 on this calm, clear tropical morning. It was the sound of the 1st Marine Division going to war. Over the side, down the cargo nets, into the Higgins boats they went, company by company, battalion by battalion, as the division landed on the beaches of Guadalcanal Island. For American forces, it was the first offensive ground operation of the Second World War.

The Marines took the beaches unopposed, but that was a condition that did not last for long. Guadalcanal would prove to be the longest battle of the entire Pacific war. It was a laboratory of warfare for the Marine Corps and Army troops who fought there – and for the naval and air forces that provided crucial support – where they learned the techniques of joint combat operations required to defeat the Japanese in the excruciating jungle terrain. And learn they did, for despite the blunders and losses of the ensuing months, they survived, prevailed, and finally forced the remaining 16,000 Japanese off the island in February 1943.

Historian Robert Leckie, who was a machine gunner and scout with the 1st Marine Division on Guadalcanal, estimated that as many as 28,000 Japanese soldiers may have died in the battle, while American losses in the ground combat were about 1,600 deaths and some 4,200 wounded. Combined naval and air losses may have reached a similar total. Next to the Japanese, the toughest foe the Americans faced was the female of the anopheles mosquito: over 5,000 troops were incapacitated with malaria.

In the Marine cemetery on Guadalcanal someone scratched the following epitaph on a mess kit left by one of the graves:

And when he gets to heaven
To St Peter he will tell:
'One more marine reporting, sir —
I've served my time in hell.'

Other action this day

1543: The troops of French king François I and his Turkish allies start the siege of Nice that ends a month later with the capture and sack of the city * 1815: Napoleon is exiled to St Helena * 1819: The Spanish surrender to Simón Bolívar at the Battle of Boyacá in New Granada (now Colombia) in which Colombia gains independence from Spain

8 August

The Armada

1588 Under the inspired leadership of the admiral-buccaneer Sir Francis Drake, today the English fleet inflicted heavy damage on the Spanish Armada, wrecking the plans of Spain's king Philip II to invade.

To Philip the situation had become intolerable. The heretic English had been supporting Dutch rebels against Spanish rule, and Drake was raiding Spanish ports in the Caribbean, severely damaging the Spanish economy. Even worse, England's queen, the bastard Elizabeth, persisted in allowing Protestant heresies rather than continuing her sister Mary's return to the true Catholic faith. The only answer was invasion.

For two years King Philip had been assembling his attacking force: 22 warships of the Spanish royal navy and 108 converted merchant vessels, 19,000 soldiers, 8,000 sailors, 2,000 galley slaves, 1,000 noblemen and some 600 priests and monks. In the Spanish Netherlands another 30,000 men waited to be convoyed across the Channel.

On 28 May this enormous Armada set sail from Lisbon for England, but gales forced the fleet back into La Coruña for refitting, after which it finally set sail again in July.

On 19 July the English first sighted the Armada off the coast of Cornwall. At his home near Plymouth Hoe Drake was enjoying a leisurely game of bowls when Thomas Fleming, captain of his flagship *Golden Hind*, came galloping to report the Spanish approach. On hearing the news, Drake refused to be hurried, replying, 'We have time enough to finish the game and beat the Spaniards, too.'

Now the Spaniards sailed into the Channel, and three times English ships made fleeting contact. Their ships were faster and more manoeuvrable with better cannon, allowing them to bombard the Spanish at long range, but the Spaniards had superior numbers. The English were careful to keep their distance to avoid a full confrontation, but they were unable to inflict much damage. For a week the opposing fleets drifted up the Channel, stalemated.

Then the Spanish anchored off Gravelines, twenty miles up the coast from Calais, with the intention of picking up the extra troops from the Spanish Netherlands. At midnight on 7 August Drake changed the whole course of battle when he cut loose eight blazing fire ships filled with tar, pitch and gunpowder to drift down upon the Spanish fleet. In panic the Spaniards cut their cables to flee, at the very moment when the English fleet launched its attack.

What followed was the decisive moment in the English defence against the Armada. The Spanish fleet was completely disorganised, its formation destroyed. The English cannon started to take a heavy toll, largely without response since many of the Spanish heavy guns had been dismounted during the night. In addition, since the English were to windward, the heeling hulls of the Spaniards were exposed and vulnerable to cannon shot below the water line.

By the end of the day eleven Spanish ships had been sunk or damaged and some 2,000 Spaniards had been killed, compared to only a few hundred English. The would-be invaders knew they were beaten, and the dispersed Armada sailed north, the only way to avoid the English warships and return to Spain.

Up around Scotland and finally off the Irish coast sailed the Spaniards, but severe north Atlantic gales (what the Protestant Drake called 'the Winds of God') caused 24 ships to founder on the rocky Irish coast and further dispersed the fleet.

Eventually only 66 ships returned to Spain, and some 15,000 Spanish soldiers and sailors had perished, including the prince of Ascoli, Philip II's illegitimate son. England was safe for ever from the threat of Spanish invasion.

To celebrate the victory Queen Elizabeth ordered a commemorative medal to be struck bearing the inscription *Deus flavit, et dissipati sunt* (God blew, and they were scattered).

Other action this day

1918: Allied forces advance over seven miles, one of the greatest advances of the war, during the Allied victory at the Battle of Amiens on the first day of the Hundred Days Offensive that ultimately ends the First World War * 1944: German SS tank commander ace Hauptsturmführer Michael Wittmann, who destroyed 138 tanks, 132 anti-tank guns and a large number of other armoured vehicles, is killed near the town of St Aignan de Cramesnil when shells fired by a Sherman Firefly tank of A Squadron, 1st Northamptonshire Yeomanry penetrate his Tiger and ignite its ammunition * 1945: The Soviet Union declares war on Japan and invades Japanese-occupied Manchuria

9 August

Caesar defeats Pompey at Pharsalus

48 BC On the hot, arid plain of Pharsalus in central Greece the direction and fate of the Roman empire was determined today when Julius Caesar annihilated the army of his long-standing rival, Pompey the Great. The battle guaranteed his dominance of the Roman state but hastened the end of the Roman Republic that had been established almost five centuries before, in 509 BC.

Caesar and Pompey had once been firm allies, both opposed to the clique of knights who dominated the Roman Senate and obstructed all progress towards reform of a creaking Roman government. But Caesar's alarming military success in Gaul made Pompey fear that he would lose his position as the first man in Rome, and he was persuaded to side with the knights when in 49 BC Caesar and his battle-hardened legions crossed the Rubicon and entered Roman Italy (see 10 January).

Pompey fled the capital, accompanied by consuls, conservative senators and some of his army. Caesar now faced a two-front war, as two of Pompey's lieutenants commanded legions in Spain, while Pompey himself had holed up in Greece. Caesar showed his scorn for his adversaries with the comment: 'I am going to Spain to fight an army without a general, and then to the East to fight a general without an army.'

In Spain, after only minor fighting, Caesar persuaded the enemy legions to join him and then pursued Pompey to Greece, repeatedly offering compromise rather than battle. Perhaps because he had defeated Caesar at Dyrrhachium, Pompey underestimated his opponent's military genius. When Pompey failed to capture him during that battle, Caesar dismissively concluded that Pompey 'has no idea of how to win a war'.

When the armies faced each other at Pharsalus, Pompey initiated the battle, confident of victory with some 50,000 troops compared to 30,000 under Caesar's command. He planned to roll up Caesar's right wing with his cavalry and then crush the enemy with his superior numbers. But Caesar had hidden 2,000 of his most experienced legionaries behind his front lines. When the Caesarean wing fell back under Pompey's onslaught (as Caesar had planned that it should), Caesar's legionaries suddenly attacked the cavalry, using their javelins as spears to stab the enemy horses. Confounded by the attack, the cavalry fled from the field, enabling Caesar to outflank Pompey and start a general massacre. Knowing victory to be his, Caesar attempted to diminish the killing, calling out to his troops: 'Spare your fellow Romans!' He allowed his men to save one enemy soldier apiece.

At the close of the battle Caesar had lost just 200 men killed, but 15,000 of Pompey's troops were dead or missing, with another 23,000 captured. Surveying the enemy dead after the battle, Caesar remarked bitterly, '*Hoc voluerunt*' ('This is what they wanted'), referring to the knights' and Pompey's refusal to compromise.

Pompey escaped, but not for long. Caesar pursued him to Egypt, where an officer of King Ptolemy murdered him. When Caesar reached Egypt he is said to have wept when presented with Pompey's preserved head.

After Caesar's dictatorship and the civil wars that followed his assassination, Rome became an empire under Caesar's protégé Octavian (Augustus) and remained under the command of Roman emperors for 500 years in Europe and 600 in the east, from Constantinople.

Other action this day

AD 117: Roman emperor Trajan, who conquered more territory than any other Roman emperor, dies in Selinus in Anatolia * AD 378: Eastern Roman emperor Valens is defeated and killed at Adrianople (modern Edirne in Turkey) by the Visigoths * 1567: The Duke of Alva's vanguard arrives in Brussels to suppress Protestant heresy and moves towards independence in the Spanish Netherlands * 1945: The American B-29 *Bockscar* drops the atomic bomb 'Fat Man' on Nagasaki in Japan, killing 70,000; Japan surrenders five days later

10 August

A victory on the feast of St Lawrence inspires the building of a palace

1557 Of the thousands of battles fought throughout history, most are now forgotten, but the one fought on this day at St Quentin in Picardy left a memorial over 600 miles away that stands in gloomy splendour to this day.

Henri II of France had already been at war with Holy Roman Emperor Charles V since 1521, but in 1556 Charles abdicated his throne to go into one of history's most famous retirements, leaving Spain and the Low Countries (plus most of Latin America) to his son Philip II. But the young king – he was just 30 – was determined to carry on the war and led his small army of 5,000 cavalry and 3,000 foot to besiege the French town of St Quentin.

Hearing of the Spanish incursion, the constable of France, the duc de Montmorency, set out from Paris 100 miles away with a 20,000-strong army. To reach St Quentin, they had to come through a narrow valley, but the Spaniards were waiting in ambush and in a one-sided battle killed over half their number, while losing just 50 men of their own. Now without hope of relief, the defenders of St Quentin soon surrendered the town.

Being of a grave religious bent, King Philip was aware that 10 August is the feast of St Lawrence, that unfortunate Roman deacon who was roasted on a gridiron for his Christian beliefs. Hence, in commemoration of the great victory on St Lawrence's Day, Philip sent orders to Spain that a great palace in the shape of a gridiron should be built in the Guadarrama mountains, north-west of Madrid.

Philip intended the building to serve as a monastery for Hieronymite monks, a palace for himself and a grand burial place for the kings of Spain. To symbolise its royal and religious importance, it was constructed entirely of blue-grey granite and would be one of the largest religious buildings in the world. Its ground plan covers almost 377,000 square feet. This sombre memorial has 86 stairways, 1,200 doors and 2,710 windows.

Twenty-seven years after Philip's victory at St Quentin the palace-monastery was finally completed. It is called El Escorial. Philip died there in his spartan bedroom in 1598.

Other action this day

612 BC: The Assyrian empire comes to an end when the Babylonians, Scythians, Susianians and Medes destroy Nineveh and kill the Assyrian king Sinsharishkun * AD 955: Otto I (the Great), king of the Germans, defeats the Magyars at the Battle of Lechfeld, after which Otto's German lords raise him on their shields on the battlefield and proclaim him emperor * 1792: 20,000 Revolutionary fanatics attack the Tuileries in Paris and butcher Louis XVI's 800-man Swiss Guard

11 August

Henry V takes on the French

1415 Today 300 ships crammed with some 9,000 soldiers and assorted chaplains, bakers, servants, trumpeters, fiddlers and physicians sailed from the Solent in the south of England, determined to conquer the kingdom of France. Leading the convoy in his great ship the *Trinity* was the 28-year-old king of England, Henry V.

Convinced that his Angevin inheritance entitled him to great swaths of France, Henry had resolved to invade to enforce his claims. He knew that France was in turmoil; King Charles VI suffered from fits of madness and the country was riven by deadly internecine rivalry between Burgundians and Armagnacs.

Henry landed on the Normandy coast near Le Havre and marched a few miles east to besiege the port of Harfleur. Although defended by a garrison of only 100 men – soon reinforced by 300 men-at-arms – Harfleur proved difficult to crack. Its stout walls and 26 fortified towers held the attackers at bay while the defenders showered them with mixed sulphur and lime and poured buckets of heated earth and oil on their heads. Both French and English were severely affected by dysentery.

After a full month of siege, the English at last stormed one of the fortification's bulwarks, as Henry's guns – especially his largest, known as 'the King's Daughter' – hammered away at the walls.

Finally, on 22 September, just as Henry was preparing another assault, the garrison surrendered. A few days later, in a show of classic medieval bravado, Henry challenged the nineteen-year-old French dauphin (who was probably in Paris, certainly nowhere near Harfleur) to single combat. Not surprisingly, his challenge was brushed aside.

The conquest of Harfleur had been costly; Henry had lost hundreds of men killed or wounded and over 2,000 more to dysentery. But on 8 October he was once more on the move. Leaving a small garrison in Harfleur, he headed for English-held Calais, 160 miles to the north-east, with 900 men-at-arms and 5,000 archers.

Henry soon learned, however, that French troops barred the direct route across the Somme River. Turning east along the south bank, he was shadowed by a larger French force across the river. After marching almost 50 miles, on 19 October he finally found unde-fended crossings at Voyennes and Béthencourt.

Five days later Henry was still 40 miles from Calais, near the town of Agincourt, when he came face to face with a French force of 20,000 to 30,000 men. Determined to redress the humiliating defeats at Crécy and Poitiers (see 26 August, 19 September) over half a century before, the French blocked Henry's line of retreat. Even when he offered to hand over Harfleur and pay for damages, they stood resolute. There should be no escape for this presumptuous invader.

The next morning – Friday 25 October, the feast day of St Crispin and St Crispinian – both armies rose before dawn and assembled for battle facing each other across a recently ploughed cornfield, heavy with mud from recent rain. Henry arranged his slender force along a narrow, 1,000-yard front, flanked by thick forest on both sides. His unmounted men-at-arms were placed four deep in three dense combat formations, with Henry at the centre. On the extreme flanks were his archers with their six-foot longbows.

At about eleven in the morning, Henry gave the order for an advance as a way of provoking a French attack. After moving forward a half-mile, the archers fired their first salvo and then drove sharpened six-foot stakes into the ground in front of their position to protect them from the French mounted knights. But now the French knights charged, the English line bending under the weight of their assault. 'Cry "God for Harry! England, and Saint George!"', called out the English king (or at least so says William Shakespeare). And the line held, as his archers continued to devastate the advancing enemy infantry.

Unable to ride through the palings, the French knights dismounted and joined the men-at-arms, moving forward through the churned mud to attack the English line, as flight after flight of English arrows found their mark. Henry urged his men to one more effort:

Once more unto the breach, dear friends, once more:
Or close the wall up with our English dead!

So narrow was the field of battle that the French could not bring their superior numbers to bear. Soon the crush was so intense that the knights could scarcely raise their swords to strike. Knee-deep in mud, weighed down by heavy armour, they became easy targets for English archers who, when not skewering them with arrows, finished off fallen knights with axes and mallets.

In three hours the battle was over, the French in full retreat. But now, fearing that he lacked the troop strength both to guard the prisoners taken in the battle and to withstand an expected renewal of the French attack, Henry ordered the killing of prisoners. When his soldiers refused, he commanded his own guard of 200 to carry out the grisly massacre.

At Agincourt the French lost three dukes, 90 counts, over 1,500 knights and about 4,000 men-at-arms, plus an uncounted number of archers, servants and fighters of low station. Despite Henry's executions, some 1,500 were taken prisoner. English casualties came to about 450, with perhaps 150 dead.

By 1415 Henry was back in England, but over the next seven years he repeatedly returned to France, each time probing deeper into the country. Eventually he occupied Paris, became *de facto* ruler and forced a treaty from the French guaranteeing the crown of France for his son. His victories formed a notable part of the Hundred Years War, that intermittent struggle that had started in 1340 and would last until 1453. But for the moment France was at the mercy of the English and would remain so until the miraculous appearance of Joan of Arc in 1429.

1480: The Ottoman army breaches the walls of Otranto on the tip of the Italian heel, captures it and the following day beheads all 800 prisoners * 1809: The French under General Sébastiani defeat the army of La Mancha at the Battle of Almonacid, effectively ending Wellesley's Talavera campaign * 1880: In Columbus, Ohio, American Civil War general William T. Sherman says, 'The war now is away back in the past and you [the Civil War veterans in the crowd] can tell what books cannot ... There is many a boy here today who looks on war as all glory, but, boys, it is all hell.'

12 August

The death of King Philip

1676 Metacom, the Wampanoag leader better known as King Philip, died today in Rhode Island, shot while fleeing an early morning surprise attack on his camp by a party of colonial militia. To mark the event, his pursuers dismembered his body; his skull was taken to the nearby town of Plymouth and mounted on a stake.

The sachem's death was a turning point in a savage war that bears his name, King Philip's War, a desperate attempt by the Indians of the region to stem the spread of colonial settlement into their tribal territories. It was the first large-scale military conflict in American history. In its three-year course, English colonists fought Indians across the breadth of New England; some 500 colonial soldiers were killed or died of wounds; a similar number of settlers lost their lives or were captured; and along the outer edge of settlement scores of towns and villages were raided, destroyed or abandoned.

Since European settlers first arrived along the North American coast in the early years of the century, the spread of settlements had led to a number of small wars, among them the Pequot War in Connecticut, the Algonquin War in New York, and Bacon's Rebellion in Virginia. Like its predecessors, King Philip's War came about as a cry of outrage by the Indians over the progressive loss for many years of not just their lands, but also their freedom and their culture.

It started in June 1675 with acts of vandalism carried out in the town of Swansea to protest against the Plymouth Colony's execution of three Wampanoags on a charge of murdering a Christianised fellow tribesman. The violence exploded and quickly spread both westwards to the Connecticut River valley and northwards as far as Maine. A number of the region's tribes allied themselves with the Wampanoags. So severe was the threat that three Puritan colonies of the region – Plymouth, Massachusetts Bay and Connecticut – joined forces in defence.

Beyond fixed village fortifications like palisades and blockhouses, the colonists' main protection was their militia system, transported from their native England, requiring most males between the ages of seventeen and 60 to undergo basic military training and to be available and armed for emergencies. But now as the colonies' militias, drilled on their village greens in the fundamentals of European-style warfare, turned out to meet King Philip's threat, they encountered – not for the first time but at much greater strength and better armed – a foe that excelled in forest warfare: knowledgeable of the terrain, skilled at ambush, as swift in retreat as in attack, and with the uncanny ability to lure their enemies into traps.

To combat the threat, the colonists were forced to adapt their combat techniques to the realities of the forest. They engaged Indian scouts from neutral tribes to serve as trackers. They soon learned to prefer flintlock muskets to the slower-loading matchlocks, still the staple weapon in Europe. They found dense forests to be poor terrain for cavalry. And for greater mobility in the field, militiamen discarded their armour for lighter gear, a trend towards what would in time be called light infantry.

The colonists learned that if they couldn't catch and defeat their elusive foe in open territory, they could destroy his villages, crop lands and winter stores; a scorched-earth policy that had immediate impact in the war's first winter, as sheer hunger forced some of the tribes to leave the alliance. They also developed units of what would now be called rangers or special forces; small, aggressive bands of volunteers, especially adept in this irregular style of warfare, employing fast-moving, open formations while advancing through forests, then encircling their foe and attacking with superior force and maximum surprise.

The war's biggest turning point took place in December 1675 in the Great Swamp in Rhode Island, where 1,000 militiamen, led by a traitor Narragansett, surprised the tribe's palisaded stronghold, which they overran and burned to the ground, a crushing blow to the tribe, to the principal allies of the Wampanoags and to the Indian cause.

Altogether, it was a war of brutal and indiscriminate reprisals on both sides. In the end, the colonists won because of their considerable advantages in terms of raw numbers, resources, technologies and, not least, the ability to learn quickly from mistakes in the field. At the same time, their Indian foes were too often careless, misjudging the increasing craft of their opponents.

By June of 1678 the war was over, the tribes utterly defeated, the survivors treated with the greatest severity, and, for the first time, confined to specific tracts of land – reservations – a pattern that would become the hallmark of American policy towards the Indians as the frontiers moved westward over the next two centuries. Like many of the Indians captured by the colonists, King Philip's wife and son were sold into slavery.

As for future military conflicts, the military lessons of King Philip's War remained largely confined to those who had actually fought in it, the American settlers. Military leaders across the Atlantic for the most part remained ignorant – or simply dismissive – of the colonial experience. One memorable result of this ignorance occurred 80 years later on a forested hillside above the Monongahela River, where General Edward Braddock's expedition of British and provincial infantry was surprised and routed by a much smaller French and Indian force. Of this famous disaster, one historian observed: 'Although it had been known for nearly one hundred years, it was now more obvious than ever that the conditions of warfare in the vast and dense American forest required special techniques and practices unknown to European troops.'

Other action this day

1099: A month after the fall of Jerusalem, Crusaders under Godefroi de Bouillon win the Battle of Ascalon, the last battle of the First Crusade * 1687: An Austro-Hungarian army commanded by Charles of Lorraine defeats the Turks at the second Battle of Mohács in Hungary, ending Turkish expansion into Europe * 1759: Frederick the Great of Prussia suffers his most devastating defeat at the Battle of Kunersdorf when 60,000 Russians and Austrians rout 51,000 Prussians

13 August

How Blenheim Palace got its name

1704 A few miles north-west of Oxford in the rolling Cotswold hills stands the great palace of Blenheim, a gift by the grateful English nation to John Churchill, first Duke of Marlborough.

The bloody battle after which Blenheim is named took place on this day near the small Bavarian town of Blindheim, anglicised in English history to Blenheim. The battle was part of the War of the Spanish Succession, a struggle by a coalition of European nations to prevent Louis XIV's grandson from becoming king of Spain, thus setting the stage, they feared, for France and Spain to come together under the rule of a single king.

Blenheim was the first decisive battle of Marlborough's career, although he was already 53 at the time. It was also his first collaboration with that other celebrated general, Prince Eugene of Savoy.

The evening before the battle the Allied force camped a few miles from Blindheim. At 2.00 in the still black night, bugles summoned the soldiers out of their blankets; 52,000 Austrians, Prussians, Dutch, Hessians, Danish mercenaries and English, supported by 66 cannon. Although Marlborough was in overall command, only 12,000 troops were from his own country.

At dawn the armies marched off in a chilling white mist, and by 6.00am they had arrived within a mile of the French positions, a wide front behind the Nebel River, anchored on their right flank by the town of Blindheim. Prince Eugene moved to the Allied right, his job to pin down part of the French army while Marlborough attacked the centre.

At 8.00am both sides' cannon opened fire, and Marlborough, riding his white charger and wearing the silver star of the Order of the Garter, formed 14,000 infantry and 6,000 horse in a three-mile line opposite the French centre. Now the French commander Marshal Tallard made a fatal mistake in putting sixteen battalions of infantry in Blindheim itself, later increased to 27, leaving only nine battalions facing the Allies in the centre.

By noon Eugene's men were in position, and Marlborough ordered the advance. For five hours the opposing forces traded advantage to the crash of cannonfire and rattle of musketry, the Duke everywhere commanding and cajoling, always within range of enemy gunfire. Then at 5.00pm Marlborough's trumpets sounded the final assault; 6,000 Allied cavalry bore down on the French centre, swords raised. The weight of the charge utterly routed the French horse, which, after desultory resistance, turned and galloped to the rear. Meanwhile the French infantry was cut to pieces by Allied cavalry and foot, and on the right flank Prince Eugene was now overwhelming the French in his path.

All that remained was Blindheim itself, but the mass of French infantry there was so close packed that the soldiers could scarcely bring their muskets to their shoulders. When the Allies stormed the town, 10,000 surrendered.

By nightfall the battle was over; 12,000 of the victors lay dead or wounded, but Marlborough and Eugene between them had killed or wounded 20,000 of the enemy while taking 14,000 prisoners, 5,400 supply wagons, 40 cannon and 34 coaches filled with French officers' women.

A glorious triumph, the Battle of Blenheim secured Bavaria for the coalition, but it hardly settled the war, which dragged on for another ten years. And at the end Louis XIV's grandson was still king of Spain, although France and Spain were never united under a single monarch. Almost a century later the English poet Robert Southey penned his famous satirical lines:

> Now tell us about the war,
> And what they fought each other for ...
> 'And everybody praised the Duke,
> Who this great fight did win.'
> 'But what good came of it at last?'
> Quoth little Peterkin.
>
> 'Why that I cannot tell', said he,
> 'But 'twas a famous victory.'

Other action this day

1521: Spanish conquistador Hernán Cortés recaptures Tenochtitlán (modern Mexico City), and overthrows the Aztec empire * 1809: After Captain-General José de Palafox's determined defence with 6,000 troops

434

and the city's enraged civilian volunteers, the French are forced to lift the siege of Zaragoza after 61 days of brutal street fighting * 1937: At 9.00am the Chinese Peace Preservation Corps exchanges small arms fire with Japanese troops in the Zhabei, Wusong and Jiangwan districts of Shanghai, starting the Battle of Shanghai, the first major confrontation of the Second Sino-Japanese War

14 August

Portugal fights to keep its independence

1385 João o Bastardo he was called, John the Bastard, not for his personality but because of his illegitimate birth as son of Portugal's King Pedro I. In his early years he kept a low political profile befitting his station, especially after his half-brother inherited the throne. But then the half-brother died, and his widow Queen Leonor, whose only child Beatrice was married to Juan I of the neighbouring kingdom of Castile, was manoeuvred into recognising Juan as Portugal's new king.

Even in the 14th century Portuguese patriotism was strong, and soon a group of fervent Portuguese nationalists, led by a 25-year-old soldier named Nuno Álvares Pereira, persuaded João to assassinate Leonor's chief minister and seize power for himself. Fearing for her own life, Queen Leonor fled from Lisbon, imploring Juan of Castile to put down João's coup. In the meantime, João made Pereira his *condestável do reino* (constable of Portugal, i.e. field marshal).

Soon Juan of Castile was on the march with a massive army of 30,000 men. They succeeded in entering Portugal, but on this day met João and Pereira with their force of only 6,500, reinforced by a small contingent of English archers, on the road to Lisbon at Aljubarrota.

The battle started at about six o'clock in the evening when Juan's cavalry charged, only to be devastated by Portuguese and English bowmen. Hundreds were killed, and many prisoners were taken to the rear.

Then Juan ordered a full assault, but his larger Castilian army was squeezed between two creeks, and the Portuguese attacked from both flanks and the front. So desperate was João to bring all his soldiers into the fray that he ordered the wholesale massacre of the enemy prisoners held in the rear.

Although both sides suffered heavy casualties, soon the Castilians were in panicky flight, pursued by the Portuguese, who slaughtered thousands. As Castilian stragglers rushed through Aljubarrota, a stout baker-woman who, according to legend, had six fingers on each hand, bushwhacked and killed eight of the fleeing soldiers.

After his momentous victory João ordered built the beautiful Batalha monastery (*batalha* means 'battle' in Portuguese) to give thanks to the Virgin. He also recognised the vital help provided by the English archers, and the following May he signed the Treaty of Windsor with England, pledging 'an inviolable, eternal, solid, perpetual and true league of friendship'. The alliance is still in force today, the oldest in European history.

The Battle of Aljubarrota ensured independence for the Portuguese and a throne and glorious reign for João. Pereira's rewards were even greater, although it took a little longer for him to collect them all. Because of his military achievements, João rewarded him lavishly, and Pereira became rich enough to found a Carmelite monastery in Lisbon, where he became a friar in 1423. Five hundred years later he was declared a saint.

Other action this day

1900: An international military force captures Peking to put down the Boxer Rebellion; that night American marine sergeant Dan Daley earns the Medal of Honor by spending the night alone 100 yards in front of the Marines' line, armed with only a bolt-action rifle and a bayonet, holding off Chinese attackers until morning, killing almost 200 * 1936: Spanish Nationalists defeat Republicans at the Battle of Badajoz during the Spanish Civil War

15 August

Napoleone is born

1769 Ajaccio was a small, dusty port on the island of Corsica, only recently part of France, having been purchased by Louis XV from the republic of Genoa. But now, fifteen months later, the people still followed Italian customs, including the celebration of *ferragosto* – the feast of the Assumption – on 15 August. So the young and beautiful Letizia Buonaparte, still not yet twenty, insisted on going to Mass although she was heavily pregnant.

Returning home immediately after the service, she lay down on the living room sofa and, just before midday, gave birth to a black-haired son. There was joy in the household as Letizia and her husband Carlo celebrated the birth of a living child. Their six years of marriage had produced three previous births, but only one baby, a boy they named Giuseppe, had survived.

The proud parents named their new child Napoleone, a good Italian name in a family that had originally come from Tuscany two centuries before. In spite of his name and language (his native tongue was Italian), Napoleone was born a French citizen thanks to Louis XV's timely purchase of Corsica. But it was only when he was 27 and already firmly established as a French general that he frenchified the spelling of his name to Napoléon Bonaparte, eventually persuading his elder brother to convert from Giuseppe to Joseph.

During the next half-century Napoleon would win 60 of the 70 battles he fought, conquer most of Europe and honour his family in an orgy of nepotism, sprinkling glorious titles among his brothers and sisters. Joseph became king of Spain, Louis king of Holland, Jerome king of Westphalia, and Lucien prince of Canino. His sister Caroline became queen of Naples by virtue of her marriage to Napoleon's cavalry commander, 'King Joachim' Murat, and even Napoleon's stepson by his first marriage was made viceroy of Italy. Napoleon, of course, famously crowned himself emperor.

Other action this day

AD 778: Basque guerrillas defeat Charlemagne's rearguard commanded by the knight Roland at the Battle of Roncevaux Pass in the Pyrenees, inspiring the (false) legend that the victors had been Moors and the 11th-century *Song of Roland*, the earliest surviving *chanson de geste* ✳ 1057: The (real) Scottish king Macbeth is killed in battle by Malcolm III Canmore at Lumphanan in Aberdeenshire ✳ 1281: The *kamikaze* ('divine wind') destroys the Mongol fleet at Hakata Bay, Japan and in 1945 the Japanese rear admiral Matome Ugaki directs the final official kamikaze attack of the Second World War against American ships around Okinawa and dies in the attack ✳ 1945: At noon Emperor Hirohito announces to his people by radio what is known as the *Gyokuon-hōsō* (Jewel Voice Broadcast), announcing Japan's unconditional surrender in the Second World War

16 August

A bad day at Bennington

1777 Today's nasty encounter with rebel militia near Bennington, Vermont, marked a break in General John Burgoyne's invasion of New York, heretofore a most successful – and possibly war-winning – campaign.

Things had begun so well. Barely six weeks earlier, Burgoyne's army had sailed into Lake Champlain from Canada and captured the American stronghold at Fort Ticonderoga without a shot being fired, an event that prompted King George, when news of it reached London, to exult to his queen: 'I have beat all the Americans!'

Since then, his army's southward progress had been marked by further successes against the Americans, at Hubbardton, Skenesborough and Fort Anne – small victories to be sure (and won by narrower margins than he cared to admit), but ones he could well crow about in dispatches to London. Rebel resistance was proving slight at best.

Now camped at Fort Edward, Burgoyne's British and German regiments were within striking distance of their strategic objective: Albany, New York. But what they needed to sustain the momentum of their advance was horses, not just to mount the horseless German dragoons (whose pace on foot was greatly impeded by their heavy cavalry boots and cumbersome broadswords) but more importantly to keep the army's supplies moving over frontier trails that were proving too rough and narrow for the heavy wagons of his train. Then came intelligence to the effect that the rebels had a supply depot at Bennington – only 30 miles to the south-east and lightly guarded – where horses, draught animals and other supplies were available in suitable quantities.

So Burgoyne sent off a column of raiders, a mixed force of 800, composed mainly of the unmounted German dragoons fleshed out with grenadiers, British sharpshooters, Canadian and Tory volunteers, Indian scouts and a few pieces of artillery. To command this mission into hostile territory, he selected Lieutenant Colonel Friedrich Baum, a Brunswick officer with no experience in frontier warfare, not a word of English and orders from Burgoyne that included the phrase, 'always bearing in mind that your corps is too valuable to let any considerable loss be hazarded'.

Three days later, on the 14th, Baum's column was within five miles of Bennington. By now there were indications that the rebels were gathering in larger numbers than had been reckoned. He sent word back to Burgoyne for reinforcements, then hunkered down in a defensive deployment that spread his forces in non-supporting detachments along both sides of the Walloomsac river and up a hill-side. It rained heavily on the 15th, postponing action from either side, and Baum put the lull to use by constructing redoubts and entrenchments.

On the 16th it cleared by noon. At 3.00pm the American assault began. Devised by New Hampshire brigadier general John Stark, who now had 2,000 militia at his disposal, it was a three-pronged attack against the rear and flanks of Baum's position, followed by a main thrust down the Bennington Road. Retreat was quickly cut off and the action was over by 5.00pm, a complete victory for the rebels. Shortly thereafter, the reinforcement column numbering 600 soldiers arrived on the scene, surprising the Americans with a strong attack, but held off with the help of newly arrived militia. By night-fall, after fierce fighting, the relief column, low on ammunition, was in full retreat towards the Hudson.

The British losses sustained by both columns at Bennington totalled well over 900 killed, wounded or captured – some 15 per cent of Burgoyne's entire force. Among the slain was Baum himself.

For the Americans, Bennington was a rousing success, greatly heartening a local population so recently cowed by what seemed an inexorable British advance through their countryside. It gave the rebels a hint of what they might achieve. One of their number jubilantly declared it: 'The compleatest Victory gain'd this war.' George Washington, defending Philadelphia against another British army, expressed his elation at 'the great stroke struck by Stark at Bennington'.

For 'Gentleman Johnny' Burgoyne, the playwright-warrior, the battle at Bennington, his first reverse in America, was an embarrassing turn of events. But the outcome, while it left him with a weakened force, hardly diminished his confidence that he and his army would soon reach their strategic objective, Albany, from which vantage point they would be 'masters of the Hudson'. He could not know that the end of his campaign was very near and would occur just twenty miles short of Albany, at a place called Saratoga, where an American force of Continental regulars and regional militia would achieve the war's first surrender of a British army.

Other action this day

1513: Henry VIII and Holy Roman Emperor Maximilian I defeat the French at the Battle of the Spurs at Enguinegatte in the Pas-de-Calais * 1717: Under cover of darkness and a thick fog, Austrian prince Eugene of Savoy's army of 40,000 surprises and annihilates a 160,000-man Turkish force at the Battle of Belgrade, inspiring one of his men to write *Das Prinz Eugen Lied*, which is still sung today by German soldiers * 1780: British troops under Charles Cornwallis decisively defeat the Americans under Horatio Gates at the Battle of Camden in South Carolina

17 August

The passing of Frederick the Great

1786 Frederick the Great of Prussia died today in the early morning, sitting up in an armchair. He had lived for 74 years, five months and 24 days, and was for 46 years a king. The greatest military commander of his time, he had transformed Prussia into the most powerful nation in Europe and ensured the dominance of his family – the Hohenzollerns – who would rule Germany until defeat in the First World War.

For a man of war, Frederick was an extraordinary ruler. He was highly cultured, an accomplished poet and musician (he composed four symphonies and 100 flute sonatas). He neither smoked nor drank and paid no attention to women, including his wife, whom he totally neglected. He may have been homosexual, but essentially this mocking, detached man had little affection for people. 'He has no heart whatever', said a contemporary. Although a German, he almost invariably spoke French.

Frederick's greatness was in his supreme military ability. At 22 he saw battle for the first time, serving in the Rhineland against the French under the great Austrian general Eugene of Savoy. After becoming king in 1740, Frederick fought an almost endless series of battles, starting with Mollwitz in 1741 (see 10 April), mostly against the Austrians but occasionally against the French and Russians. His favoured tactic was the 'Oblique Order' in which he would concentrate his troops against an enemy flank, penetrate it and wheel 90 degrees to roll up the enemy line. Frederick's tactical brilliance was complemented by his startling ability, when on the brink of disaster, to turn events back in his favour.

Today most of his victories are just obscure names – Soor, Zorndorf, Liegnitz, Torgau. Some are memorable because of a specific event, like the charge of the Beyreuth Dragoons that shattered the Austrians at Hohenfriedberg. In others, the mere degree of Frederick's victory was remarkable, such as the Battle of Rossbach, where he lost only 500 men while inflicting 10,000 French and Austrian casualties, and the Battle of Leuthen (see 5 December), where Frederick's army of 35,000 annihilated 60,000 Austrians.

In reference to the Seven Years' War, when Prussia was attacked by Austria, France and Russia together, no less an authority than Napoleon said of him: 'It is not the Prussian army that for seven years defended Prussia against the three most powerful nations in Europe, but Frederick the Great.'

By his 75th year, Frederick was bent over by rheumatism and gout, frail in body but still quick in mind. His people affectionately called him 'der alte Fritz' ('Old Fritz'). He died at Sans Souci, the exquisite palace he built in Potsdam, just outside Berlin. Knowing death was imminent, he spoke to his valet Strutzki for the last time: 'La montagne est passé, nous irons mieux.' ('We're over the hill, we'll be better now.') He had planned to be buried in his beloved palace and had ordered an inscription to be carved on the base of a statue there: 'Quand je serai là, je serai sans souci.' ('When I shall be there, I shall be without care.') But his heirs had him buried in the Garrison Church nearby. Almost two centuries later an admiring Adolf Hitler kept a portrait of him on the wall of his bunker in Berlin.

Other action this day

1585: Alessandro Farnese, duca di Parma, conquers Antwerp for Spain's Philip II after a thirteen-month siege ＊ 1648: The first day of the two-day

Battle of Preston, where the Roundheads defeat the Cavaliers in the English Civil War ∗ 1943: American general George Patton captures Messina in Sicily hours before the arrival of the British general Bernard Montgomery, completing the Allied conquest of the island

18 August

The last of Genghis Khan

1227 When Genghis Khan died on this day at the age of about 65, he had created the greatest land empire in history through his great generalship and utter, barbaric ruthlessness.

Genghis Khan's given name was Temujin. He was born holding a clot of blood in his hand, a sure sign of great military prowess.

Before attaining his vast empire, Temujin first subdued the numerous Mongol tribes and brought them together into a single nation. In 1206 the conquered tribes awarded him the title of Genghis Khan, which probably means 'universal leader'.

Genghis Khan's main weapon was his formidable cavalry. Both ferocious and well disciplined, these fearsome warriors could fire an arrow with deadly accuracy from a distance of 200 yards. (Apparently, however, personal hygiene was not one of their strong points. One Persian account claims that they were so filthy that lice covered them 'like sesame growing on bad soil'. According to legend, their pungent stench signalled the approach of death even before you could see the dust or hear the drumming of hooves.)

Genghis Khan's military genius went well beyond leading his redoubtable horsemen, who were invincible in the open but who could not conquer well-defended cities. From his enemies he learned to use siege machinery such as catapults and even learned to divert rivers to flood a city and the surrounding countryside.

In victory Genghis Khan was merciless, once ordering the massacre of all those taller than the height of a cart axle. When he conquered an enemy city he either annihilated the population or sold it into slavery. At Herat in Afghanistan after a full week of carnage his army is said to have slaughtered 1,600,000 people. He told his chiefs to 'show no clemency to my enemies without a direct order from me. Rigour alone keeps such spirits dutiful.' People were not the Great Khan's only victims; he sacked major cities and razed important cultural centres such as Samarkand and Bukhara. The 13th-century chronicler Matthew Paris called the Mongols 'the detestable nation of Satan'.

But no one could deny the effectiveness of his draconian methods: by the time of his death he had destroyed the Chin dynasty of China and his empire extended from Peking to the Caspian Sea.

Genghis Khan died during his final campaign, as he was subduing the Tanguts, a vassal nation in north-west China that had refused to join him in his war against the empire of the Khwarezm Shahs in Persia.

The specifics put forward for Genghis Khan's demise are varied and, at least in one case, spectacular. Some claim he succumbed to a fatal illness such as cancer, while others maintain that he had injured himself in a fall from a horse and died from internal bleeding. Another source suggests that he was killed in battle against the Tanguts. But the grisliest (and least likely) tale says that he had taken a Tangut princess as a concubine. To avenge her people, she hid a knife inside her sex and waited for him to come to her bed at night. She then drew it out and castrated him, an injury from which he died, after which she drowned herself.

Unaware of Genghis Khan's death, the Tanguts living in their capital of Xingqing sued for peace and opened the city gates. Mongol soldiers poured inside and slaughtered every living thing in the capital.

The Mongols then took the corpse of their dead leader back to Mongolia. Along the route, they slaughtered anyone whom they met on the road 'to serve their master in the other world'. After lying in state for three months, Genghis Khan was buried on a sacred mountain called Burkhan Kaldun. As he was laid to rest, 40 slave girls and 40 stallions were killed to accompany him in the afterlife. Then 1,000 of his warriors rode over the burial site to keep it for ever secret.

Other action this day

1870: At the Battle of Gravelotte during the Franco-Prussian War, the Prussians win a Pyrrhic victory over the French, losing 20,163 dead, wounded, missing or captured, compared to the French, who suffer 7,855 killed and wounded along with 4,420 taken prisoner * 1965: In the first major American ground battle of the Vietnam War, US Marines destroy a Viet Cong stronghold on the Van Tuong peninsula

19 August

Allied disaster at Dieppe

1942 This morning at 4.45 Operation Jubilee began: Allied troops landed at the French port of Dieppe to launch a daring attack on Nazi-held Europe, the first such operation since the all-triumphant Wehrmacht had kicked the British army off the Continent at Dunkirk two years earlier. By early afternoon it was all over, a terrible disaster in which of the 5,100 men who went ashore – two brigades of the Canadian division supported by British commando units – 3,684 did not make it back, either killed or captured. Among those killed was Lieutenant Edwin Loustalot, one of 50 US Rangers taking part in the attack. He was the war's first American battle death in the European theatre.

Operation Jubilee suffered from inadequacies in almost every aspect: objective, planning, intelligence, communications, tactics and strategy. Loss of surprise also contributed to the mission's failure. Only courage among the attackers was not in short supply, but alone it could not prevail. The Royal Navy lost a destroyer and 33 landing craft, while the RAF lost 106 planes to the Germans' 46.

The raid at Dieppe was meant to be a practice run for the great cross-Channel attack that would establish the Second Front and reclaim Europe from German occupation. In its two strategic purposes, however, the raid failed either to draw off German units from the Eastern Front, where Soviet Russia was reeling under Operation Barbarossa, or to inflict heavy losses on the Luftwaffe units sent to defend the port. Finally, the utter failure of the raid went a long way towards bringing US war planners around to the British contention that the time was not yet right for a full-scale invasion of the Continent.

The German high command described the Dieppe raid as 'an amateur undertaking', but Winston Churchill was also right when he called it a 'mine of experience'. Among the valuable lessons the Allies learned this day was that for such an operation air dominance is vital; another was that the initial landings should be made not at a port, where urban warfare would be the order of the day, but on a long stretch of open beaches providing adequate room for the fast build-up of an invasion-sized force. Like Normandy, for instance.

Other action this day

1388: Sir James Douglas leads the Scots to victory over the English commanded by Sir Henry Percy ('Hotspur') at the Battle of Otterburn, in which Percy is captured but Douglas is killed, according to legend murmuring 'Earl Percy sees my fall' as he lies dying * 1399: Richard II surrenders to Bolingbroke (the future Henry IV of England) at Flint * 1779: Americans under 'Light Horse' Harry Lee defeat the British and take 178 prisoners in a surprise night attack at the Battle of Paulus Hook * 1812: The American frigate USS *Constitution* ('Old Ironsides') wins the Battle of the Grand Banks, defeating the British frigate HMS *Guerrière*

20 August

The Spartans defy the Persians at Thermopylae

480 BC Mighty Xerxes, king of Persia, the greatest empire the world had known, had resolved to conquer the stubborn Greeks, who had defeated his father Darius at Marathon ten years before. So great was his army that it took them seven days and seven nights to cross the Hellespont. (Herodotus tells us that the Persians numbered 2,500,000 men, but modern estimates suggest a more reasonable 200,000.) Knowing that all Greece was in mortal danger, a force of 7,000 *hoplites* (infantry) from several Greek city-states was rushed to meet the invaders under the leadership of the Spartan king, Leonidas. Indifferent to the odds against him, Leonidas declared: 'If you reckon by number, all Greece cannot oppose even a part of that army, but if by courage, the number I have with me is enough.' The armies clashed at Thermopylae in one of history's most heroic defences.

Thermopylae means 'hot gates', named for the hot sulphur springs nearby. It is a narrow mountain pass only 50 feet across at its widest, accommodating just a single wagon track. On one side tower high cliffs while on the other is a precipitous drop to the sea. It was through this restricted defile that the Persian army had to pass to enter central Greece. Even before the battle the location had dramatic connotations for every Greek, for it was on nearby Mount Oeta that Heracles had died, poisoned by the blood of a dead centaur.

Upon seeing the tiny Greek force, Xerxes demanded that Leonidas lay down his arms, to which the Spartan king tersely challenged: 'Come and take them.' As the defenders waited for the onslaught, one fearful soldier speculated that the Persian archers were so many that their arrows would hide the sun. 'Good', answered the Spartan Dieneces, 'then we shall fight them in the shade.'

To open the battle the Persian king ordered his Medes and Cissians to lead the charge. But the Greeks, armed with long spears and protected by large round shields, crested helmets and lower-leg greaves, were more than a match for the invaders, who had shorter spears and weaker armour, better suited to warfare on the open plains than to the narrow defile of Thermopylae. Soon Xerxes was forced to call on his élite infantry, the Immortals, but even they could make no progress against the ferocious defenders, who slew thousands of the enemy during the first two days of battle. So many Persians were killed that the front ranks had to be driven into battle with whips.

But then came treachery. A Greek traitor, Ephialtes, hoping for a rich reward, told Xerxes of a mountain path through which the Persians could send an encircling force. On the night following the second day of battle the Immortals started working their way behind the Greek position.

Once Leonidas learned that the Persians were closing in from behind, he sent all the Greek warriors except his own 300 Spartans home to defend their cities. Then he settled down with his men for a last meal, bleakly ordering, 'Breakfast well, for we shall have dinner in Hades.' He was determined to fight to the last.

At nine o'clock in the morning on this third day of battle, the resolute Spartans marched out for the final confrontation to the sound of their flutes. Despite fighting with ferocity, they were soon overwhelmed, with Leonidas among the first to fall. Finally the last defenders were surrounded on a small hill. Herodotus relates that 'they fought in a frenzy, without concern for their lives ... Most had already lost their spears, and they cut down Persians with their swords ... [they] defended themselves with daggers ... and with their hands and teeth ... while those [Persians] who had come round the mountain completed the circle.' But, despite their fanatical struggle, soon all 300 Spartans lay dead. In his anger at the stubborn Spartan resistance, Xerxes had Leonidas's lifeless body crucified, his severed head stuck on a pole.

Herodotus says that the Spartans killed 20,000 Persians at Thermopylae, no doubt an exaggeration but in any case not enough to prevent Persian invasion of the Greek mainland and the capture of Athens. Greece was saved not by Thermopylae but by the naval victory at Salamis the next month (see 22 September).

On the small hill where the Spartans made their last stand the Greeks erected a monument, now long vanished, with the inscription from Simonides of Ceos:

Go, stranger, and to listening Spartans tell
That here, obedient to their laws, we fell.

Other action this day

AD 636: Arab forces led by Khalid bin Walid defeat the troops of the Byzantine empire at the Battle of Yarmuk, taking control of Syria and Palestine, the first Muslim conquest outside Arabia * 1191: When Saladin delays an exchange of prisoners during his siege of Acre, Richard the Lionheart orders the beheading of 2,700 Muslim prisoners in full view of Saladin's army * 1710: The Austrians defeat the French at the Battle of Zaragoza during the War of the Spanish Succession * 1794: Americans crush the Blue Jacket confederation of Indian tribes at the Battle of Fallen Timbers in the Northwest Territory

21 August

Napoleon's marshal Bernadotte becomes Crown Prince of Sweden

1810 Two years earlier, Napoleon had made his favourite cavalry commander, Joachim Murat, king of Naples. Today Jean-Baptiste Bernadotte became the second of the emperor's marshals to take a royal title when he became Sweden's crown prince, taking the name of Charles John.

Born in the foothills of the Pyrenees and the son of a lawyer, at seventeen Bernadotte joined Republican France's Régiment de Royal-Marine as a private, displaying his zeal by having 'Death to tyrants!' tattooed on his arm. He first met Napoleon in Italy in 1797, after he had already become a brigadier general, having distinguished himself at the battles of Fleurus and Theiningen during the French Revolutionary Wars.

The two generals impressed each other, and in 1798 Bernadotte even married one of Napoleon's former sweethearts, Désirée Clary, who was also a sister-in-law of Napoleon's brother Joseph.

A strong republican, Bernadotte condemned Napoleon's rise to absolute power, but he finally offered his support when Bonaparte declared himself emperor in 1804. A few months later, Bernadotte's loyalty, military skill and family connections were fully rewarded when the emperor made him a marshal, and a year later he received the title of prince of Ponte-Corvo for his heroic participation in the great French victory at Austerlitz (see 2 December). He subsequently fought at the Battle of Wagram (see 5 July), but here he ordered a retreat against Napoleon's orders and was stripped of his command, a humiliation that contributed to his acceptance of the Swedish crown.

Although not a brilliant commander, Bernadotte always scrupulously obeyed the rules of war, treating both his troops and his enemies with generosity and good sense. Thus, when Sweden found itself ruled by the ageing, childless king Charles XIII in 1809, the Riksdag invited Bernadotte to become Charles's successor.

Much to Napoleon's chagrin, the new Prince's loyalties were now to Sweden rather than France, and he joined the allied forces at the emperor's bloody defeat at Leipzig in 1813.

On 5 February 1818 old King Charles finally died, and the once staunchly republican general became a conservative and autocratic king who restricted the press and put a stop to liberal reforms. Unlike Napoleon's other marshal-king – Murat was deposed and shot after seven years as king of Naples – Bernadotte ruled for 26 years until he died in bed at the worthy age of 81. Shortly before his death he smugly but accurately murmured, 'No one living has made a career like mine.' To this day his descendants still wear the crown of Sweden.

1808: General Arthur Wellesley defeats Napoleonic general Jean-Andoche Junot at Vimiero during the Peninsular War ∗ 1863: Confederate raider William Quantrill and his bushwhackers massacre 150 men and boys in Lawrence, Kansas ∗ 1920: The Miracle at the Vistula: during the final day of the Battle of Warsaw, Poland defeats Bolshevik Russia near Warsaw during the Polish-Soviet War, preserving its independence

22 August

Richard III dies on Bosworth Field

1485 England's Richard III had been king for only two years and two months, having usurped the throne from his twelve-year-old nephew Edward V, whose murder in the Tower of London he had ordered. But now a rival was raising arms in France, claiming that the crown should rightfully be his. This was 28-year-old Henry Tudor, but he, too, had only the flimsiest of claims. Although of royal blood, only through his mother could he trace his ancestry back to a king, and that was to Edward III five generations back, and his bloodline on his father's side was even thinner. His paternal grand-father had (perhaps) been married to Catherine de Valois, the widow of Henry V.

But Henry Tudor was the only living male member of the House of Lancaster and so became its champion in the Wars of the Roses, that periodic and bloody rivalry for the English crown that had afflicted the country since 1455. Gathering an army in France composed primarily of French mercenaries, Henry landed at Milford Haven in Wales on 7 August.

Attracting more supporters as he made his way through Wales (his father had been Welsh), Henry led perhaps 5,000 men by the time he met Richard's forces on this day at Bosworth Field, twelve miles west of Leicester. Richard commanded 8,000, but these included three vacillating barons: Henry Percy, 4th Earl of Northumberland, and the brothers William and Thomas Stanley.

Richard positioned his force on Ambion Hill and then brought them down to attack the enemy, calling on Percy for reinforcements.

But Percy held his forces back, and Thomas Stanley also remained uncommitted.

Desperate, Richard took the initiative, leading a charge directly against Henry himself. He succeeded in dispersing Henry's personal bodyguard and bringing down his standard-bearer, but Henry was saved by the intervention of the other Stanley brother, William, who turned his coat and ordered his men into battle, not for Richard, his king, but for Henry.

Now Richard's cause was all but lost, but even when defeat was certain, he challenged his fate. 'I will not budge a foot', he swore to his lieutenants, 'I will die king of England.' Surrounded by Stanley's soldiers, he was unhorsed and killed, reputedly by a Welshman's axe. Richard was only 32 when he fell at Bosworth Field, the last English king to die in battle. According to tradition, the crown that Richard had worn on his helmet during the battle was found dangling from the branches of a hawthorn bush. Retrieved by one of Henry's soldiers, it was placed on Henry's head to shouts of 'Long live King Henry VII!'

The Battle of Bosworth Field is one of the most significant events in all of English history. In defeating Richard III today, Henry Tudor accomplished more than he knew. His victory ended the Wars of the Roses, except for a battle against resurgent Yorkists at Stoke (see 16 June). It also brought to an end the great Plantagenet dynasty that had supplied every English king for the past 332 years, starting with Henry II in 1154. Finally, when Henry Tudor took the crown as Henry VII he began his own dynasty that lasted for 118 years and sent to the throne such notables as Henry VIII, Bloody Mary and Elizabeth I.

Other action this day

AD 408: Accused, probably falsely, of planning a coup, leading Roman general Flavius Stilicho is beheaded on orders from Emperor Honorius * 1138: English barons under the leadership of Archbishop Thurston of York defeat King David of Scotland at the Battle of the Standard * 1642: Charles I raises his standard at Nottingham to begin the English Civil War * 1864: The International Red Cross is founded by the Geneva Convention to assist the wounded and prisoners of war

23 August

William Wallace pays the price for treason

1305 For the crime of treason there was only one penalty in England. First the traitor was hanged but cut down while still alive. He was then emasculated and disembowelled and his entrails were burned before his eyes. Finally, he was decapitated and his body cut into four parts, to be hung in public places as a reminder of the fearsome wrath of the king. On this day in London the Scottish patriot William Wallace suffered such a death. His left leg was displayed in Aberdeen, his right one in Perth and his left arm in Berwick, his right one in Newcastle. His head was impaled on a spike and put on view at London Bridge.

In the late 13th century, Scotland was in leaderless turmoil. When eight-year-old Queen Margaret died, there were thirteen claimants to the throne and competing Scottish lords ravaged the country. At length the Scottish leaders asked England's king Edward I to arbitrate and the Scottish crown finally went to John de Balliol, who promptly swore fealty to Edward. For this act, John earned from his subjects the name 'Toom Tabard' ('Empty Coat'). But then John refused to send troops for Edward's wars in France, rejected his demand to cede three border castles and renounced his homage to England. This provided all the excuse Edward needed to invade the country.

Into this confusion stepped a member of the lesser Scottish gentry, William Wallace, a giant of a man (about six feet six inches), who, according to a near-contemporary historian/hagiographer, was 'all-powerful as a swordsman and unrivalled as an archer'. Furthermore, 'his blows were fatal and his shafts unerring; as an equestrian, he was a model of dexterity and grace; while the hardships he experienced in his youth made him view with indifference the severest privations incident to a military life'.

By 1296, when Wallace was about 27, he was leading what amounted to a guerrilla band against the invading English. Initially successful, he was once captured and left to starve in a dungeon but subsequently rescued by local villagers. After recovering his strength, he recruited another band of about 30 rebels and continued his attacks. Drawing ever more Scots to his banner, in 1297 he became the scourge of the English and scored a major victory at Stirling Bridge where, although heavily outnumbered, he slaughtered some 5,000 English as they crossed the river. For this triumph Wallace was knighted, probably by Scotland's future king, Robert the Bruce.

But Wallace's great triumph had been against Edward I's lieutenants rather than against the redoubtable English king. The following year Edward himself led an army of 25,000 deep into Scotland and annihilated Wallace's force at Falkirk. Wallace escaped the rout and spent the next few years alternately hiding from the English and keeping his revolt alive, at one point slipping off to France to seek aid.

Edward never relented in his search for Wallace, whom he regarded as a traitor for his resistance to his feudal overlord, which Edward considered himself to be. In August 1305 Wallace was captured near Glasgow and brought to London, where he was tried for treason and the murder of civilians (the indictment claimed he spared 'neither age nor sex, monk nor nun'). Although Wallace claimed that he was wrongly accused because he had never sworn fealty to Edward, under Edward's vengeful eye only one verdict was possible.

The man the English considered a treacherous outlaw and the Scottish a national hero was condemned to be hanged, drawn and quartered.

With Wallace dead, Edward believed he had cowed the Scots, but in fact by his barbarous method of execution he had turned Wallace into a martyr. By the time of his own death in 1307 Edward was already facing a new and far more dangerous enemy, Robert the Bruce. By 1314 Robert had reasserted Scottish independence by totally destroying the army of Edward's son Edward II at the Battle of Bannockburn, only two miles from Wallace's great triumph at Stirling Bridge seventeen years before.

Scotland retained its autonomy for centuries to come, although in 1603 its king, James VI, became James I of England, thus uniting the crowns if not the two countries. Finally in 1707 England and Scotland were formally brought together under the name of Great Britain.

1179: Saracen leader Saladin arrives at Jacob's Ford in Syria and begins the successful siege of the Christian-held castle of Chastellet * 1244: Jerusalem is sacked by the Khwarezmian Turks * 1650: During the English Civil War, Colonel George Monck forms his own regiment of ten companies, Monck's Regiment of Foot, which evolves into the Coldstream Guards, the oldest regiment in the regular army in continuous active service * 1939: Hitler and Stalin sign a non-aggression pact that lasts just 22 months, until 22 June 1941, when the German army launches Operation Barbarossa, the invasion of Russia

24 August

Rome falls to 'the licentious fury of the tribes of Germany and Scythia'

AD 410 Today the city of Rome, inviolate and unconquered for 800 years, fell to the troops of the Visigoth leader Alaric.

Alaric was a Visigoth nobleman by birth who had once commanded the Gothic troops in the Roman army, but when he was 25 he left the Romans and was elected chief of the Visigoths. From the moment he took power he was constantly at war with his former masters, first in Turkey, then in Greece and ultimately in Italy itself.

Twice he tried and failed to conquer Rome, still a great city even though the emperor of the Western Roman empire had moved his capital north to Ravenna in 402. In 410 he tried once more, demanding land and gold from Emperor Honorius in return for leaving the city in peace. The emperor unwisely refused and in August Alaric besieged the city. The defiant Romans threatened to send their army out to fight him, to which Alaric made the famous reply: 'The thicker the hay, the easier it is mowed.'

At first it seemed that Alaric would be stymied by the city's monumental walls, but the Romans had forgotten their own slave population that was ready to welcome Alaric as a liberator. Edward Gibbon describes the scene: 'At the hour of midnight, the Salarian gate was silently opened [by disaffected slaves] and the inhabitants were awakened by the tremendous sound of the Gothic trumpet. Eleven hundred and 63 years after the foundation of Rome, the Imperial city, which had subdued and civilised so considerable a part of mankind, was delivered to the licentious fury of the tribes of Germany and Scythia.'

In fact, Alaric, a Christian, spared the city's churches and, by the standards of the time, restrained his soldiers from mass murder, although St Augustine tells us of some killing and arson. Gibbon informs us that 'the matrons and virgins of Rome were exposed to injuries more dreadful, in the apprehension of chastity, than death itself'. After having occupied the city for six days, Alaric and his army marched away laden with plunder, leaving Rome poorer but intact. He died in Cosenza in Calabria just a few months later at the age of 40 and was buried, together with his looted treasure, in the riverbed of the Busento near Cosentia (today's Cosenza).

Other action this day

49 BC: Forces of Pompey the Great under Attius Varus and King Juba I of Numidia defeat Caesar's general Gaius Curio at the Battle of the Bagradas River; Curio commits suicide to avoid capture * 1572: In Paris, with encouragement from King Charles IX and Queen Mother Marie de' Medici, the duc de Guise and other Catholics murder Protestant leader Admiral Gaspard de Coligny to begin the Massacre of St Bartholomew, the greatest religious bloodbath in European history * 1812: During the War of 1812, the British defeat the Americans at the Battle of Bladensburg, and that evening 1,460 British seamen and marines enter Washington unopposed and burn the Capitol, the White House, the Treasury and the new Library of Congress * 1944: Capitaine Raymond Dronne leads the vanguard of the 2e Division Blindée (2nd Armoured Division) into Paris, the first uniformed Allied officer to enter the city, which the Germans surrender the next day

25 August

St Louis's last crusade

1270 Today in Tunis, near the ruins of ancient Carthage, in the camp of an army he had recently brought to Africa, a French king was felled by the plague, his final crusade a failure. So ended the life of Louis IX, one of France's good kings and great men. Stalwart in battle and always ready to lead his troops into action, his fatal weakness was his fervent desire to lead an army to victory in the Holy Land.

Born in 1214, Louis inherited the throne at twelve and at only fifteen commanded his army in the field, when Henry III of England launched a half-hearted invasion. This time Louis saw no combat, as Henry scurried back to Bordeaux (Aquitaine was then owned by England's Plantagenet monarchs) before a battle could be fought. Twelve years later, however, Louis soundly defeated him at the Battle of Taillebourg, personally leading his troops in an aggressive attack.

Louis was also deeply devout, and therefore for him the *summum bonum* was crusade in the Holy Land, enabling him to use his talent for war in the service of God's true religion.

In August 1248 Louis set off with 20,000 soldiers on his first crusade (known to history as the Seventh Crusade). His objective was the conquest of Egypt, the weakest link in the Saracen chain of defences across the Middle East and a county rich enough to tempt even the most devout of kings. After wintering in Cyprus and collecting a fleet, Louis arrived at the mouth of the Nile in May of the following year. In his eagerness to engage the infidel, he disembarked with a few companion knights before the main body of his army had arrived. Instantly attacked on the beach by Egyptian cavalry, Louis bravely led his men in a stout defence and drove the enemy off. Then, inexplicably, the Saracen commander withdrew his entire army into nearby Damietta but then abruptly abandoned the city, leaving the Crusaders to march through the open gates without resistance. It was the high point of the crusade.

Louis and his men settled down in Damietta to wait for the flooding Nile to recede and for reinforcements to arrive from Europe. Finally, in November they began their march on Cairo, 120 miles to the south. After trudging some 50 miles, they met their enemies at Mansourah in the pivotal battle of the crusade. Although Louis's brother was killed, the battle itself was a standoff, but soon Louis was forced to retreat as plague struck the army and it began to run out of food. Louis bravely took the most dangerous position, commanding the rearguard, but he was stricken by dysentery, becoming so ill that he could not stand. Too weak to command, faced by a superior force and with his army in disarray, he bowed to the inevitable and surrendered along with his entire army. Eventually

Louis and his richer nobles were ransomed, Louis for the spectacular sum of 400,000 livres, and he finally returned to France in the summer of 1254, having lost a fortune in money and Crusader lives.

Alas, Louis's thirst for crusading glory had not been slaked. On 1 July 1270 he embarked once again for the Holy Land, leaving France from a Mediterranean port he had ordered built some 30 years before, the small walled town with the ominous name of Aigues-Mortes (derived from *aquae mortuae* – dead waters – after the surrounding saline marshland).

Seventeen days later Louis landed in Tunis. Initially his army gained some painless victories, but the summer heat was frightful and soon plague appeared, first ravaging the army and then striking the king himself. Knowing he was dying, Louis instructed his son and successor Philip (III) to take special care of the poor. Hagiographers (and indeed historians) report that his last words were, 'Jerusalem, Jerusalem!'

Louis died on this day at the age of 56, having reigned for almost 44 years. His entrails were buried on the spot where he died (you can still visit the Tomb of St Louis there today), but his body was brought back to France in one long funeral procession, with mourners lining the roads as it passed through Italy, over the Alps and on to Paris. This great king was entombed in the Abbey of St Denis just north of Paris, historic last resting place of the kings of France.

From the moment of his burial Louis was considered a saint and people prayed for miracles at his tomb. Pope Boniface VIII canonised him in 1297, only 27 years after his death. He is the only French king ever to be declared a saint. Bizarrely, however, tradition among the local Tunisians denies that Louis fell victim to plague, claiming that he converted to Islam under the name of Sidi Bou Said and lived on for another quarter-century, to die as a saint of Islam.

Other action this day

1580: The Duke of Alba defeats the Portuguese at the Battle of Alcântara, leading to Spain's Phillip II becoming king of Portugal two months later * 1758: Frederick the Great of Prussia fights the Russians to a bloody standstill at the Battle of Zorndorf (then in Prussia, now Sarbinowo in Poland) during the Seven Years' War * 1911: Vietnamese general Võ Nguyên Giáp, victor at Dien Bien Phu and architect of the Tet Offensive, is born

26 August

The Battle of Crécy

1346 If you drive north from Paris to Calais, just beyond Abbéville you pass by the small town of Crécy. There on this day over six centuries ago the age of knightly chivalry received a wound from which eventually it would die.

Here on this showery Saturday afternoon England's king Edward III took on the might of France during the Hundred Years War with a force of some 11,000 men, including 7,000 longbowmen.

The French army was nominally under the command of King Philip VI, but in fact it was composed of too many undisciplined knights who thought of themselves as allies rather than subjects and were determined to win glory (and ransom from noble English prisoners). The number of the French force is reckoned to be somewhere between 35,000 and 60,000, but by any estimate was far larger than the English. Among the French were 8,000 Genoese crossbowmen.

The difference in bows and bowmen was critical to the battle. The crossbow had first been used in Europe in the 10th century. It fired a heavy, armour-piercing bolt, but the rate of fire was no more than two per minute. The longbow, first developed in Wales, fired a metal-tipped armour-piercing arrow three feet long that required a strong bowman, as the longbows of the time required a 100-pound force to draw. But the English longbowmen could fire five arrows a minute and more.

The French sent their crossbowmen to open the attack, but before the Genoese came within effective range the English archers responded with a murderous shower of arrows, overwhelming their enemy in a matter of minutes and sending them into full retreat. Seeing the slaughter, the French mounted knights rode down their own bowmen in their haste to attack the English, but once again a deadly shower of arrows brought down men and horses in thousands. Once the knights had been unhorsed, the English men-at-arms quickly finished them off with swords and maces. It has been estimated that in all the English bowmen fired some 500,000 arrows at the French.

The battle had its pathetic moments of 'honour'. Blind king John of Bohemia asked his captains: 'Gentlemen, as I am blind, I request you to lead me so far into the engagement that I may strike one stroke with my sword.' He then charged into battle with a French knight guiding him on each side – and was almost immediately slaughtered. (His crest of three ostrich feathers with the motto '*Ich dien*' was taken by Edward's son, the Black Prince, and is still used today by English princes of Wales.) But each new charge was met by another lethal flight of arrows, and the cavalry could not attack the longbowmen whose positions were protected by rows of sharpened stakes. Eventually darkness brought the grisly slaughter to a close.

The following day the English counted the casualties. Fewer than 100 English had lost their lives but 15,000 French and Genoese soldiers lay dead on the field and a further 1,500 French knights had been captured or killed.

With the introduction of the longbow, a new type of warfare had been invented. Never again was the charge of knights in armour to determine the course of victory. The Battle of Crécy did not, however, have much effect on the Hundred Years War, which continued spasmodically for another 107 years.

Other action this day

55 BC: Julius Caesar lands in Britain * 1071: Seljuk forces under Alp Arslan defeat the Byzantine empire near Manzikert, Armenia, as Emperor Romanos IV Diogenes is captured * 1278: Rudolf I of Habsburg defeats King Ottokar of Bohemia at the Battle on the Marchfield at Dürnkrut in Austria, making the Habsburgs one of Europe's most powerful families for the next six and a half centuries * 1813: The start of the 2-day Battle of Dresden in which Napoleon crushes the Austrians, Russians and Prussians under Field Marshal Swartzenberg while suffering only 10,000 casualties compared to 38,000 for the Allies

27 August

'The Dunkirk of the American Revolution'

1776 Sir Henry Clinton had devised a bold plan to attack the American rebels in Brooklyn: first, a night march to get around their left flank unseen; then, at dawn, holding actions to occupy their right; finally, the surprise attack from the rear that would roll up their line and send them fleeing to the river. Pleased with Sir Henry's plan, the commander-in-chief Lord Howe landed 22,000 British and Hessian troops on Long Island to carry it out.

And carry it out they did. By 11.00am today, most of George Washington's 9,500 troops defending Brooklyn were back behind their inner defence line, driven from their forward positions on a six-mile wooded ridge called Gowanus Heights. The outcome was not all British brilliance. The preparations for defence by the American commanders – including the commander-in-chief – were muddled, at best. In particular, their disposition of forces inexplicably ignored the very route, Jamaica Pass, by which General Howe brought 10,000 troops, marching in the moonlight, undetected around their flank.

So there it was, a stunning success, handily and decisively won. American losses totalled some 1,500, including the capture of two generals; British losses fewer than 400. All that remained now was to send in the final assault that would end the battle – and probably the war.

But now came a change in plans. Instead of a final assault, Lord Howe gave orders to dig trench lines, set up camp, and settle in for a siege. To this day it is not clear whether he wished to give his weary troops a rest before further action, or thought to avoid another costly frontal attack like Bunker Hill (see 17 June), or expected that the Americans, realising their perilous situation, would surrender without further bloodshed.

Whatever Howe's motives, Sir Henry, like many British officers at the scene, was incensed at losing the chance for complete victory. 'For there is no saying', he wrote later, 'to what extent the effect resulting from the entire loss of that army might have been carried in that early stage of the rebellion.'

The next day, a Wednesday, as British engineers began preparing approach lines for an eventual attack on the American fortifications, it began to rain heavily. With the rain came a strong north-easterly wind, blowing down the East River, preventing British warships in the harbour below from moving upstream behind the rebel position on Brooklyn Heights.

On Thursday, the rain and wind continued. Now, however, with his army on the brink of extinction and with it, perhaps, the entire

American cause, George Washington became the general with a bold plan. At noon a secret order went across the river to Manhattan Island for all available boats to be assembled 'in the east harbour of the city by dark'. At a war council in the afternoon, Washington revealed his plan to his key officers. As soon as darkness descended, boats began crossing to the Brooklyn waterfront from Manhattan.

Along the fortified line on the Heights, 100 feet above the ferry landing, a rearguard kept campfires burning to deceive the British, as regiments were summoned below, one by one, through the night. When his regiment was called, Private Joseph Plumb Martin remembered, 'We were enjoined not to speak, or even cough, while on the march. All orders were given from officer to officer, and communicated to the men in whispers. What such secrecy could mean we could not divine.'

Meanwhile, sentries on the Heights kept a close eye on any movement from the British lines. Back and forth across the mile-wide river the boats plied, transporting troops, horses, cannon, ammunition, wagons, tents, supplies – an entire army – to the safety of Manhattan.

At 5.00am, a number of regiments remained to be evacuated, and dawn would soon reveal the operation to inquiring eyes. Now, suddenly, a quirk of nature – or, as many came to call it, a miracle – occurred: a dense fog settled over the river to cover the final movements. Washington, who supervised every aspect of the operation, was among the last to depart. By 7.00am, when the fog lifted, the British would discover that there were no more Americans on the Brooklyn shore.

In England, news of the results on Long Island – with the rebels' escape downplayed – was welcomed with bonfires, ringing bells, and cannons fired. King George gave Lord Howe the Order of the Bath. Across the Atlantic, there was gloom and doubt. The sight of the soldiers arriving in Manhattan that morning was not inspiring: 'Many looked sickly, emaciated, cast down, etc.', one observer wrote. 'In general everything seemed to be in confusion.'

Yet what had been accomplished, as David McCullough described it, was 'the Dunkirk of the American Revolution – by daring amphibious rescue, a beleaguered army had been saved to fight another day'. And from the experience – of both defeat and escape – Washington, as commander-in-chief, would come to understand, far better than his opponents, that his army could survive the loss of battles and territory so long as he could keep it intact through timely retreat, for in this war time was on the American side.

Other action this day

479 BC: The Greeks defeat the Persians at the battles of Plataea and Mycale, ending for ever Persian hopes of conquest * 1626: During the Battle of Lutter in the Thirty Years War, Catholic League general Johann von Tilly defeats the Danes of King Christian IV, marking the decline of Denmark as a great European power * 1896: The British whip the Zanzibarians in the shortest war in history, which lasted from 9.02 to 9.40 in the morning * 1939: The first jet aircraft, the Heinkel He 178, takes its first flight

28 August

'A lovely procession, like elephants walking through a pack of dogs'

1914 With the British Expeditionary Force now safely transported across the Channel to fight in France, and the powerful German High Seas Fleet locked away in its harbours, what positive role could there be for the British Grand Fleet to play in these early days of the Great War?

Two young British commodores came up with an answer, advancing a bold plan to send a naval force deep into the Heligoland Bight to surprise and destroy German vessels returning to their ports from their regular North Sea patrols. The plan called for three submarines to surface as bait, drawing German destroyers out to sea in pursuit, where they would encounter more submarines lying in wait, while two flotillas comprising 31 British destroyers swept in behind them.

Such was the genesis of the first naval engagement of the Great War, the Battle of the Heligoland Bight, which took place today only 30 miles off the German coast. It turned out a British victory – a good beginning to the war at sea – but one that owed as much to good luck as it did to good management.

The scheme proposed by commodores Tyrwhitt and Keyes found immediate and enthusiastic support from Winston Churchill and others in the Admiralty. As a foray into German home waters, it risked bringing out the heavier ships of the High Seas Fleet, but for the Royal Navy this was part of the attraction, for there was always the hope of another Trafalgar. To that end, by the time it was approved, the plan had expanded beyond the original Harwich-based force of destroyers and submarines to include elements of the Grand Fleet at Scapa Flow, six light cruisers and five battle cruisers, all under the command of Admiral Beatty.

But two things interfered with the plan: visibility and communications. At daybreak today, as the British destroyers neared their rendezvous north-west of Heligoland, visibility had dropped below three miles, a condition that would be compounded as the morning progressed by the heavy black smoke pouring from countless funnels. Thereafter, ships from both fleets manoeuvring at top speeds often mistook a friendly vessel for one of the enemy's.

Making matters worse, the Admiralty had failed to tell Beatty where the British submarines were to be positioned the next day; and as the action began, neither Keyes, commanding the submarines, nor Tyrwhitt, the destroyers, had been informed that Beatty's force of light cruisers and battle cruisers were joining the operation. At dawn today, Tyrwhitt's lookouts sighted through the mist four-funnelled cruisers that for all they knew were the enemy's. Fortunately, a challenge was flashed and drew the proper reply.

By 8.00am, Tyrwhitt's flotillas were well into the Bight and beginning to engage the German patrol vessels. In the meantime, and with visibility now down to two miles, as many as six German light cruisers, ordered out of their harbours, joined the scene in counter-attacks that threatened to reverse the course of events. Churchill would describe what followed as 'a confused, dispersed, and prolonged series of combats'.

Then, in the early afternoon, from out of the mist, came Beatty's battle cruisers, their 12- and 13.5-inch guns bearing on the enemy. A British officer observing the scene called their sudden appearance 'a lovely procession, like elephants walking through a pack of dogs'.

The battle cruisers quickly opened up on the German cruisers, sinking two within minutes and driving the rest away. Taking advantage of the turn in the action and aware of his vulnerability to the appearance of powerful German dreadnoughts, Beatty now gave the entire British force the order to retire.

German losses for the day were three light cruisers and a destroyer sunk; another three cruisers severely damaged; and casualties close to 1,000. Britain suffered damage to one cruiser, and casualties below 100.

The victory – though hardly decisive and filled with tactical mistakes – was hailed in Great Britain as confirming the traditional British superiority in all matters naval. In Germany, the Kaiser ordered the commander-in-chief of the High Seas Fleet to avoid any undertaking that might entail the loss of capital ships, unless 'approved by His Majesty in advance'. For Germany, the naval war would now be carried out mainly by submarines and minelayers.

The two navies would meet each other in major North Sea actions twice more in the war – at Dogger Bank in 1915 and at Jutland the following year, the biggest naval battle ever fought – but the results of these future battles would only bear out what the Kaiser had already learned from today's engagement in the Bight.

Other action this day

AD 388: Usurper Magnus Maximus is executed after having lost the Battle of the Save in Croatia to Emperor Theodosius I ∗ AD 475: Roman general Flavius Orestes appoints his son, the eleven-year-old Romulus Augustus, as the last Roman emperor, after chasing Emperor Julius Nepos out of Ravenna ∗ AD 489: Ostrogoth king Theodoric defeats Italian ruler Odoacer at the Battle of Isonzo, forcing his way into Italy

29 August

Suleiman the Magnificent conquers Hungary

1526 Mohács lies on the west bank of the Danube, straight south from Budapest. It was there on this day that the great battle took place that was to change Hungary's history for over a century.

The Turkish sultan Suleiman the Magnificent had been demanding tribute from the Hungarians and when they foolishly refused to pay, he invaded with an enormous army of 100,000 men. Hungary's twenty-year-old king Louis II hastily gathered whatever troops he had at hand and, without waiting for reinforcements from other parts of his kingdom, marched down from Buda to engage the Turks.

When Louis reached Mohács in the early afternoon, he found Suleiman's vast army waiting for him in the pelting rain. Immediately Louis ordered his 4,000 cavalry to charge. Briefly it appeared that the Hungarians' insane attack might rock the invaders into panic as the Turkish line buckled under the weight of so many tons of armour plate. Immediately the Hungarian infantry, another 21,000 men, followed the mounted knights into the assault.

But not even mad courage could defeat odds of four-to-one, and the Turkish counter-attack produced an appalling slaughter. Hungarians fell and died, as the Turks gave no quarter, routinely massacring anyone they captured. Seeing that catastrophic defeat was inevitable, King Louis tried to escape but was crushed by his own warhorse when it fell on him. (Poor Louis had inherited the throne at ten, married at fifteen and was now dead at twenty. Later Hungarians wisecracked: 'Born too soon, king too soon, married too soon, died too soon.')

Over 14,000 Hungarians died on the plain of Mohács, and on the sultan's orders, 2,000 Hungarian prisoners were massacred after the battle. Suleiman then marched upriver to Buda and razed it to the ground. When he withdrew from the country, he took 100,000 Hungarian captives with him. Hungary was finished as a fighting force and twenty years later the nation was formally absorbed into the Turkish empire, where it would remain for a century and a half.

Other action this day

1350: Edward III and the Black Prince defeat the Castilians at the naval Battle of Les Espagnols sur Mer (the Battle of Winchelsea) * 1533: Conquistadors led by Francisco Pizarro execute by garrotte the Inca emperor Atahualpa in Cajamarca, Peru * 1642: At Huntingdon, Oliver Cromwell forms his first troop of cavalry – the troop comes to be named 'Ironsides' after its founder, whose nickname is 'Old Ironsides' * 1756: Frederick the Great invades Saxony to start the Seven Years' War * 1842: The British and Chinese sign the Treaty of Nanking, which ends the First Opium War and cedes Hong Kong Island to Great Britain

30 August

A future emperor destroys his rival at Lake Poyang

1363 Today two rebel forces met in a huge naval engagement, fought over two days on a vast lake in the middle of South-east Asia, with fantastic vessels and more men than Napoleon took to Russia. It was a battle that would decide the future of China.

By the mid-14th century China's ruling Yuan dynasty, founded by the Mongol Kublai Khan in 1279, was disintegrating into chaos. The economy was in freefall and crops were failing, after recurring flooding of the Yellow River. Famine stalked the land – it is said that 7 million people starved. In addition, Mongol discrimination against the Han (China's largest ethnic group) had turned resentment into full-scale revolt.

Leading one insurgent faction was Zhu Yuanzhang, a peasant who at 24 had joined a revolutionary group, married the chieftain's daughter and, on his father-in-law's death, taken over as leader. At the same time another rebel, Chen Youliang, had formed a powerful rival group and proclaimed himself king of the Han.

Open warfare between Zhu and Chen broke out in 1360. After they had battled back and forth for eight years, the stage was now set for the final reckoning. They would clash at Lake Poyang, a huge 100-mile long freshwater lake from which the Kan River leads south, while to the north is the Yangtze.

Chen made the first move in August 1368 when he advanced on Nanchang, 25 miles south of the lake, on the Kan. He had boarded an immense army of 650,000 aboard his fleet to launch an amphibious attack, but his most intimidating weapons were huge *lóu chuan*, literally 'tower ships'. Below decks these gigantic three-decked floating fortresses held space for 3,000 troops and stables for the cavalry's horses. Their top decks had iron-sheathed turrets for archers and carried trebuchets for hurling stones and molten iron. From the ships' high sterns soldiers could scale the waterside walls of cities under attack.

Despite these fearful ships, however, Nanchang's defenders managed to stand firm while urgently sending for Zhu to come to their rescue.

By the time Zhu's navy had arrived at Lake Poyang, Chen had realised that Nanchang could hold out indefinitely, so he sailed north into the lake to attack Zhu's fleet, which consisted of more numerous but smaller craft carrying only 200,000 men.

By the end of August, however, the summer heat had lowered the lake's water level, a major disadvantage for Chen's tower ships, which required deep water in order to sail. By contrast, Zhu's ships – mostly barges – were faster and more manoeuvrable, with a shallower draft. Both fleets dropped anchor in the lake, ready to fight the next day.

At first light on 30 August Zhu divided his ships into eleven squadrons, with his heavier ships at the centre and lighter ships on the flanks. While assaulting Chen's centre with his heavy ships, he attacked the wings with lighter barges armed with catapults throwing incendiary missiles. Over twenty enemy ships were set ablaze, but Zhu's own flagship also caught fire and then stuck fast on a sandbar. Chen's navy closed in for the kill, but Zhu's other ships came to his rescue, their bow waves rocking his flagship free.

Now the huge tower ships advanced, forcing Zhu to retreat into the shallows, losing some ships to the more powerful enemy and others that went aground. But Chen's ships could not follow, and Zhu regrouped, stopping the developing panic by executing his more timorous captains. He then attempted without success to surround the tower ships with his more nimble craft. Both fleets then retired from the action to carry out repairs that night.

The next morning Chen chained his ships together in a line, with the tower ships in the middle and smaller craft on the sides, planning to sail up the lake, scooping up Zhu's ships as he went. But then Zhu launched dozens of fire boats, small rafts loaded with straw laced with gunpowder and set alight, which destroyed several enemy ships and damaged many others. Chen ordered his ships unchained and opened his formation, but this enabled Zhu's more agile craft to surround his ships to grapple and board. But, although Zhu was gaining the upper hand, he could not achieve a decisive victory.

Now, with most of Chen's soldiers engaged in the naval battle, Zhu's ground forces were able to relieve Nanchang, thereby blocking the Kan River and any attempt by Chen to escape south. Simultaneously Zhu moved another army to close the straits leading north to the Yangtze. Chen's fleet was now bottled up inside Lake Poyang.

During the next month the two adversaries waited and watched,

Chen too weakened to attack but unable to flee, Zhu looking for a chance to go on the offensive. Finally, on 4 October, with supplies dwindling and his men near starvation, Chen swept through Zhu's blockading garrisons north of the lake and escaped onto the Yangtze, but there he found Zhu's fleet waiting to attack. Zhu immediately launched more fire ships, causing massive damage, and then the two navies crashed into each other, ships locking together to be swept downstream by the current. Just as Chen was struggling to break away, an arrow pierced his skull and killed him, causing his few remaining soldiers to surrender. Most of his army of 650,000 men had perished during a month of warfare, while Zhu had suffered only 13,000 casualties.

The battle on Lake Poyang left Zhu as the last remaining serious challenger to the fast-sinking Yuan dynasty. After an uneasy peace of five years, he marched on the Yuan capital at Peking, forcing the last Yuan emperor to flee. Zhu now declared himself emperor, taking 'Hongwu' ('Vastly Martial') as his reign title. He named his dynasty 'Ming', ('Brilliant'), which indeed it was. It remained in power until 1644.

Other action this day

1813: Thirty miles north of Mobile, Alabama, 800 Red Stick Creek Indians attack Fort Mims and massacre 500 settlers * 1862: General Robert E. Lee's Confederates overwhelm the Union forces on the third day of the Second Battle of Bull Run * 1914: At the four-day Battle of Tannenburg, the Germans under Paul von Hindenburg destroy Russian general Samsonov's 2nd Army, capturing 92,000, killing and wounding 78,000; only 10,000 escape

31 August

The Napoleonic dream is crushed for ever at Sedan

1870 Today the French army of Châlons found itself surrounded in the small city of Sedan in the Ardennes, in north-eastern France. Leading the beleaguered French was Napoleon III, the last emperor ever to command in the field. Accompanying the Prussian army were Crown Prince Wilhelm Friedrich, soon to become emperor of the combined German states as Kaiser Wilhelm I, and Prussia's Iron Chancellor, Otto von Bismarck, here to see the final victory in a war he had engineered (see 13 July).

For 22 years Napoleon had been the master of France, first as president of the Second Republic, then as emperor. During that time he had helped his country to prosper, but now France's position in Europe was threatened by the potential unification of the German states. In July 1870 the crafty Bismarck, who wanted the conflict as a means of drawing together some reluctant German principalities, cunningly manoeuvred Napoleon into war.

After some early French successes, the larger and better-trained Prussian army, commanded by the legendary field marshal Helmuth von Moltke, quickly got the measure of the French, defeating them at Weissenburg, Woerth, Spicheren, Colombey-Nouilly, Vionville and Gravelotte within a month. Now the French were forced to march into the Ardennes in an attempt to avoid the Prussians.

On 30 August Moltke's army caught up with the French at Beaumont, inflicting 5,000 casualties and forcing Napoleon to retreat to Sedan to resupply. But by 31 August the Prussians had completely encircled the town, cutting off all hope of reinforcements. The surrounding Prussian 3rd and Meuse Armies totalled 200,000 men to 130,000 French and also massively outgunned their enemy, by 774 artillery pieces to 564.

Desperate to break the Prussian grip, before dawn on 1 September, as Prussian artillery mercilessly pounded his positions, Napoleon ordered Marshal Patrice Mac-Mahon to attack. After initial sparring at 4.00am, the main battle started at six, but Mac-Mahon was among the first to be wounded. The French rallied briefly when General Emmanuel de Wimpffen led a spirited assault, but the arrival of fresh Prussian troops forced him back. Three valiant French cavalry charges led only to mounting casualties, with the commander Jean Margueritte mortally wounded.

Knowing that he could never continue as emperor after such a disastrous loss, Napoleon spent the day riding where the action was hottest, apparently hoping for a stray shell to end his reign in dignity. He survived unscathed, but his army was completely shattered, with 17,000 dead or wounded against half that number of Prussian casualties. On the afternoon of the following day he sent this message to Crown Prince Wilhelm Friedrich: '*Monsieur mon frère*; Not having succeeded in dying in the midst of my troops, nothing remains for me but to deliver my sword into your majesty's hands.' He thus became one of almost 100,000 French prisoners of war.

Thus 1 September marks the beginning and the end of Napoleonic glory. It was on that date in 1785 that Napoleon Bonaparte first received his commission as an artillery officer, the true start of his military success and of the Napoleonic saga. Exactly 85 years later came Sedan, the battle that ended the Napoleonic story.

Two days after the defeat, Napoleon's captors took him to Prussia, never to see France again. After a few months in regal confinement with Crown Prince Wilhelm Friedrich, he went into exile in England where he died in January two years later at the age of 64. His last words, addressed to his doctor, were: 'N'est-ce pas que nous n'avons pas été des lâches à Sedan?' ('We were not cowards at Sedan, were we?')

Other action this day

1422: Less than a month after his 35th birthday, English warrior-king Henry V dies at Vincennes outside Paris, probably of dysentery picked up on campaign * 1644: Royalists defeat the Roundheads at the Second Battle of Lostwithiel * 1939: On orders from Reinhard Heydrich and Heinrich Müller, German agents dressed in Polish uniforms pretend to be anti-German saboteurs and seize the radio station in Gleiwitz (then in Germany, now in Poland) to make an anti-German broadcast that serves as a pretext for the German invasion of Poland the next day

1 September

The Battle of Omdurman and the last cavalry charge in British history

1898 Today an Anglo-Egyptian army under Major General Sir Herbert Kitchener arrived before an enemy capital in the Sudan to set the stage for a famous victory – and the last British cavalry charge in history.

The British had occupied Egypt in 1882, seven years after having purchased the Suez Canal. Three years later, a certain Abd Allah took control of neighbouring Sudan, then a Muslim theocracy. He resolved further to expand the Islamic state, first through conquest in Ethiopia and then by invading Egypt. Feeling their interests threatened, the British dispatched Kitchener to bring Abd Allah and his Dervish army to heel.

On this day, Kitchener reached Abd Allah's capital at Omdurman, across the White Nile from Khartoum, with an army of 26,000 men, 8,000 British regulars and 18,000 Sudanese and Egyptian soldiers equipped with artillery and Maxim machine guns. Opposing him was a vast Dervish force of perhaps 50,000 men, carrying only rifles or spears. That evening, patrols from the opposing forces clashed as they tried to reconnoitre each other's positions, but these were just a foretaste of what would follow.

The serious fighting commenced the next day at dawn, as 16,000 Dervishes drove straight at the British, only to be scythed down in swaths by British artillery fire that inflicted over 4,000 casualties. Now ordering his infantry to advance on Omdurman, Kitchener sent the 21st Lancers ahead to clear their path. One of the British lancers later wrote this eyewitness report:

[The colonel] ordered 'Right wheel into line' to be sounded. The trumpet jerked out a shrill note, heard faintly above the trampling of the horses and the noise of the riders. On the instant all the sixteen troops swung round and locked up into a long galloping line.

Two hundred and fifty yards away the dark-blue [Dervish soldiers] were firing madly in a thin film of light-blue smoke. Their bullets struck the hard gravel into the air, and the troopers, to shield their faces from the stinging dust, bowed their helmets forward ... The pace was fast and the distance short. Yet, before it was half covered, the whole aspect of the affair changed. A deep crease in the ground ... appeared where all had seemed smooth, level plain; and from it there sprang ... a dense white mass of men nearly as long as our front and about twelve deep ... Eager warriors sprang forward to anticipate the shock. The rest stood firm to meet it. The Lancers acknowledged the apparition only by an increase of pace. Each man wanted sufficient momentum to drive through such a solid line ... the whole event was a matter of seconds. The riflemen, firing bravely to the last, were swept head over heels ... and ... at full gallop and in the closest order, the British squadrons struck the fierce brigade with one loud furious shout. The collision was prodigious. Nearly thirty Lancers, men and horses, and at least two hundred Arabs were overthrown. The shock was stunning to both sides, and for perhaps ten wonderful seconds no man heeded his enemy. Terrified horses wedged in the crowd; bruised and shaken men, sprawling in heaps, struggled, dazed and stupid, to their feet, panted, and looked about them.

Meanwhile the impetus of the cavalry carried them on ... They shattered the Dervish array, and, their pace reduced to a walk, scrambled out of the [crease] on the further side, leaving a score of troopers behind them, and dragging on with the charge more than a thousand Arabs. Then, and not till then, the killing began; and thereafter each man saw the world along his lance, under his guard, or through the back-sight of his pistol; and each had his own strange tale to tell.

This stirring account of the last ever British cavalry charge was written by a 25-year-old Lancer officer who, armed with a Mauser automatic pistol, shot three Dervishes himself. His name was Winston Churchill.

The cavalry charge had little real effect on the Dervish army, although five of its officers, 66 men and 119 horses out of fewer than 400 were killed or wounded. But Kitchener's heavy guns and a subsequent assault on Omdurman itself soon obliterated all resistance.

The battle was a catastrophe for Abd Allah, who lost 20,000 men killed and wounded plus another 5,000 taken prisoner. He managed to escape the slaughter, but a year later he encountered another British force and was killed in the battle. As for the British, they stayed in Egypt one way or another until Gamal Abdel Nasser kicked them out for good in 1956.

Other action this day

1339: Edward III declares war on France to start the Hundred Years War ∗ 1701: During the War of the Spanish Succession, Prince Eugene of Savoy leads an Imperial army to victory over the French at the Battle of Chiari, losing only 150 men to 3,000 ∗ 1802: In order to make the Danes surrender their fleet, British warships start a three-day bombardment of Copenhagen, firing 14,000 rounds into the city, killing 2,000 Danish civilians and destroying a third of the city's buildings ∗ 1880: 10,000 Anglo-Indian troops under General Roberts decisively defeat the same number of Afghans at the Battle of Kandahar, sustaining only 36 killed and 218 wounded compared to 2,500 casualties for the Afghans ∗ 1939: Germany invades Poland and captures Danzig to start the Second World War

2 September

Octavian crushes Mark Antony at Actium

31 BC Today at the Battle of Actium, Octavian became master of the civilised world through his decisive victory over Mark Antony. The Augustan age had begun.

First there were three who controlled the Roman empire: Octavian, Mark Antony and Lepidus. Together they avenged the murder of Julius Caesar, crushing the army of Marcus Junius Brutus at Philippi in 42 BC, a victory that left Brutus no way out but suicide (see 3 October). Then slowly Marcus Lepidus was moved aside until, in desperation, he raised an army in Sicily in an attempt to regain his authority. But even Lepidus's soldiers knew he was a lost cause and deserted, and Octavian sent him into forced retirement. Now there were only two; Mark Antony controlling the East, Octavian the West of the empire.

At first Mark Antony and Octavian maintained an uncomfortable alliance, cemented by Mark Antony's marriage to Octavian's sister, Octavia. But soon Mark Antony was openly living with Egypt's queen Cleopatra, comporting himself in the style of an Oriental potentate. He then repudiated Octavia and married Cleopatra, an act contrary to all Roman laws under which no Roman could marry a foreigner. Together he and Cleopatra followed a licentious lifestyle in ostentatious luxury, proclaiming themselves incarnations of Dionysus and Aphrodite.

Meanwhile Octavian had been winning the propaganda war, inciting fury in Rome when he read to the Senate what he claimed to be Mark Antony's will in which he left all to his children by Cleopatra, stated his wish to be buried in Egypt and revealed his intent to relocate the capital from Rome to Alexandria. This gave Octavian all the justification he needed to declare war on Cleopatra, although his real target was Mark Antony.

The two armies came together near the bay of Actium (modern Punta), on the west coast of Greece. Both Octavian and Mark Antony commanded about 75,000 troops, and each had 400–500 ships. Mark Antony's were mostly the powerful quinqueremes armed with massive rams, but Octavian's galleys were lighter and more manoeuvrable, and his crews were better trained. In command of Octavian's force was the experienced admiral Marcus Agrippa.

On the advice of Cleopatra, Mark Antony decided to launch a naval attack instead of an assault by his army. He had hoped his heavier vessels would dominate the fighting, but his ships were undermanned due to an outbreak of malaria, which made them even clumsier in their attack.

Mark Antony drew up his fleet facing west, with Cleopatra's 60 galleys behind in reserve. At first Agrippa kept his ships out of range, then used his galleys' greater agility to sweep enemy decks with arrows and catapult-launched stones. The battle was furious, with neither side able to take a decisive advantage, until some of Octavian's ships struck through the centre of Mark Antony's line. Fearful of capture, Cleopatra ordered her squadron to turn and row for safety even before they had engaged the enemy, although she might have saved the day had she committed her reserve. Seeing the queen in full retreat, Mark Antony turned and followed with a few of his galleys, leaving the rest of his fleet and his land army to surrender to Octavian.

Within fourteen months both Mark Antony and Cleopatra had committed suicide, while Octavian soon received the title 'Augustus' and ruled the Roman empire for another 45 years.

1649: After the new bishop of Castro (near today's Lazio, Italy) is murdered en route to the city, Pope Innocent X's army marches on Castro and totally destroys it, never to be rebuilt ∗ 1813: French general Jean Moreau, who helped Napoleon to power but later rebelled against his increasing autocracy, dies of wounds received fighting Napoleon six days earlier at the Battle of Dresden ∗ 1945: On board the American battleship USS *Missouri* in Tokyo Bay, Japan surrenders, ending the Second World War, in a ceremony attended by top Allied brass including the supreme commander for the Allies Douglas MacArthur, American fleet admiral Chester Nimitz, British admiral of the fleet Sir Bruce Fraser, French general of the army Philippe Leclerc, Australian general Sir Thomas Blamey, New Zealand air vice marshal Leonard Isitt and Chinese general Hsu Yung-Ch'ang

3 September

Oliver Cromwell Day

1650, 1651 and 1658 Today should be called Oliver Cromwell Day, for on it he led his Parliamentarian army to two great victories and on this day he also died.

Cromwell was a brilliant cavalry commander who rose from leading a single troop to commanding the entire Parliamentarian (or Roundhead) army. He was also a fervent Puritan who gave no quarter when it came to smiting his enemies, royal or religious, during the English Civil War. He ordered the killing of 100 of the 300-man Royalist garrison at Basing House after they had surrendered and urged the execution of Charles I. Later, in Ireland, when his men slaughtered 2,700 Royalist soldiers plus about 800 civilians, prisoners and priests after the siege of Drogheda, he called it 'the righteous judgement of God on these barbarous wretches'.

By September 1650 the first part of the Civil War was over and King Charles I beheaded, but his son Charles II had landed in Scotland. Backed by Scottish Royalists and Cromwell's erstwhile allies the Covenanters (an intolerant group of Presbyterians), he was a deadly threat to the English republican government. Cromwell, who had been battling in Ireland, immediately headed for Edinburgh at the head of an army of 5,000 horse and 10,000 foot. Failing to take the city, he retreated 30 miles east to the port of Dunbar for more supplies. But now the Scottish general David Leslie, who had so successfully defended against Cromwell at Edinburgh, thought he saw an opportunity to trap the Roundhead army and brought his force of perhaps 20,000 to Doon Hill, about two miles to the south of Dunbar, where he could block Cromwell's route back to England.

Although outnumbered (perhaps a third of his force was out of action due to illness), Cromwell determined to escape by attacking. Under cover of darkness on the night of 2 September, he secretly positioned six regiments of horse and three of foot opposite the Scottish right flank. As the sun rose the following morning, he cried out, 'Let God arise, let his enemies be scattered!' and launched a surprise assault.

The shocked Scottish flank soon started to disintegrate, and then the rest of the army broke ranks in panic. Before allowing his cavalry to pursue the fleeing enemy, Cromwell paused to sing the 117th psalm. Scottish losses were 3,000 dead and 10,000 captured, their army destroyed.

After the battle Cromwell released 5,000 wounded prisoners but marched the remainder towards England in appalling weather conditions. By the time they reached Durham, 2,000 had perished of starvation or exhaustion. There another 1,600 died, their corpses tossed into a mass grave near the cathedral.

The following year, the 21-year-old Charles II gathered a meagre force of 16,000 English and Scottish supporters for one last desperate attempt to invade England while Cromwell was still in Scotland. But Cromwell was not to be caught napping and followed Charles to Worcester with an army more than twice as big.

Charles brought the bulk of his troops within Worcester's walls, the River Severn and its tributary the Teme between him and the Parliamentarians. After reinforcing the city's fortifications, he ordered destroyed the four bridges over the rivers, including Powick Bridge, where the Royalists had defeated the Roundheads in 1642 in the first major skirmish of the Civil War.

On 28 August Roundhead dragoons captured a bridge south of the city and repaired it enough to allow troops to cross. Meanwhile Cromwell placed his artillery and the bulk of his army on the heights east of Worcester. The next day his guns opened up, repulsing a Royalist attempt to overrun them.

At dawn on 3 September, the noise of Cromwell's cannon awoke King Charles, who climbed to the top of the tower of Worcester cathedral, where he could see Parliamentarian troops pulling eight boats against the current up the Severn to make a pontoon bridge. He suddenly realised that he might now attack the enemy's exposed eastern flank and ordered his men to charge from the city, with himself at their head. For three hours the Royalists bitterly fought the Roundheads to a standstill, their king fighting on foot among them, and captured some of the Parliamentarian artillery. But when Cromwell counter-attacked, his weight of numbers forced the Royalists back into the city, Charles nearly captured.

Charles rode among his men, trying to rally them, but many threw down their arms, and his dispirited cavalry refused to make a fresh charge. Now the Roundheads surged into the medieval streets of Worcester against the remaining Royalist resistance, with dreadful carnage on both sides.

At dusk Charles realised that his cause was lost and at last consented to leave by Worcester's northern gate. After many adventures he escaped to the Continent. It had been a disaster for the Royalist cause: some 3,000 dead, another 10,000 taken prisoner, while Cromwell suffered only 200 casualties. The English Civil War was over, ended near Worcester where it had started nine years before.

Although a republican government had ruled the country since 1649, on 16 December 1653 Cromwell became lord protector of England, effectively a dictator, who dallied with the idea of making himself king. But after four and a half years of authoritarian rule, in the summer of 1658 he was fading fast, ill from malaria and a kidney infection. On 30 August a great storm struck London, which lasted intermittently for four days. By now Cromwell knew he was dying and was seemingly resigned to it. 'It is not my design to drink or sleep, but ... to make what hast I can to be gone,' he said. At three o'clock on the afternoon of 3 September – the date of his victories at Dunbar and Worcester – the old soldier and dictator died at 59.

Other action this day

36 BC: Octavian's admiral Marcus Agrippa defeats the fleet of Sextus Pompey (the son of Pompey the Great) at the Battle of Naulochus off Sicily, ending Pompeian resistance to the Second Triumvirate * 1260:

The Mamluks defeat the Mongols at the Battle of Ain Jalut in Galilee, the first time the Mongols have ever been decisively beaten * 1632: Imperial general Wallenstein suffers only 900 casualties while inflicting 2,400 in narrowly defeating Sweden's Gustavus Adolphus at the Battle of Alte Veste, the Swedish king's first ever defeat * 1780: Seventeen-year-old Jean-Baptiste Bernadotte joins the Régiment de Royal-Marine as a private; he will become one of Napoleon's marshals and then in 1810 Crown Prince of Sweden, where his family still reigns

4 September

Geronimo surrenders

1886 Today at Skeleton Canyon, cornered and outnumbered, the last great war chief of the Apaches agreed to surrender himself and his desperate band to the United States Army. Some 5,000 soldiers and 500 Indian auxiliaries and trackers had been pursuing Geronimo's tiny group of only 35 warriors for the past five months. Here, in this remote corner of the Arizona Territory near the Mexican border, the squat, broad-shouldered Geronimo conversed briefly with the tall soldierly figure of General Nelson A. Miles before returning to his encampment to collect his people for the march north to Fort Bowie and captivity.

For almost a century, Apache tribes had fiercely resisted the intrusion of European settlers into their territory. The chiefs who led them in this long guerrilla struggle of raids and retreats became legendary: Mangus Colorado, Cochise, Victorio, Nana – and finally Geronimo. But the cavalry, employing mobile columns, Indian trackers and the heliograph, proved relentless and ultimately successful. Over the years, band by band, the Apaches were hunted down, killed when they resisted, and sent away to reservations. Now it was the turn of Geronimo and his Chiricahua Apaches, whose elusiveness General Miles declared had 'never been matched since the days of Robin Hood'.

Arriving at Fort Bowie four days after their surrender in the canyon, the Apaches were herded into railroad cars for their journey to Florida and exile. They were never again to see their homeland. A thoughtful farewell touch was provided by the 4th Cavalry band, which played 'Auld Lang Syne' as the train pulled away. So at last the Apache War – the 'Geronimo war', the cavalry had begun to call it – was over; there was peace in the desert.

Still, a residual bit of resistance occurred many years later, as reported in this wire-service story filed from Tucson on 22 April 1930: 'Riding out of their wilderness hideout, high in the Sierra Madre Mountains, a band of wild Apache Indians scalped three persons, April 10, in a settlement near Nacori Chico, Sonora, Mexico, it was reported by V.M. White, a mining engineer … Armed parties immediately set out to trail the painted savages and attempt to engage them in battle before they reached their impregnable and historic cliffs. The Apaches are believed to have been led, White said, by Geronimo III, the grandson of the Geronimo who was chased by the US Army for three years during the '80s in Arizona.'

Other action this day

1260: At the Battle of Montaperti in Italy, the Tuscan Ghibellines, who support the Holy Roman Emperor Rudolf I, defeat the Florentine Guelphs, who support the Pope, Alexander IV * 1812: With only fifteen soldiers and several civilians, American captain (and future president) Zachary Taylor holds off an attack by 600 Shawnee Indians led by Chief Tecumseh at Fort Harrison in Indiana * 1870: Leon Gambetta, Jules Favre and Jules Ferry proclaim the Third Republic from the Hôtel de Ville in Paris after deposing Emperor Napoleon III, after his catastrophic loss and capture at Sedan three days earlier

5 September

Suleiman the Magnificent dies in the field

1566 Suleiman the Magnificent, greatest of all Turkish sultans, died today while attempting to put down a revolt in one of his many conquered territories.

Suleiman ruled Turkey and its empire with an iron hand for 46 years. He added Hungary to his domains and twice nearly conquered Austria. Domestically he was known as a great lawgiver, and he ordered built many of the finest buildings in Constantinople,

Baghdad and Damascus. But as he grew older he became increasingly megalomaniac, perhaps even paranoid, to the point that (on separate occasions) he ordered two of his three sons strangled for imagined treason, as well as a number of their children.

Even at 71, sick and ageing, Suleiman thought primarily of consolidating his power. When revolt broke out in Hungary he personally led the avenging army.

Setting out from Constantinople, this formidable despot marched with his army for 97 days to mount his attack on Hungary. But he was already so ill that he could not ride; he had to be taken in a carriage all the way from his capital.

By mid-summer of 1566, Suleiman was camped outside the castle of Sziget, his enemies under siege within. Eventually Turkish sappers would blow a fatal gap in the castle's walls, but the great sultan was not there to see his final triumph. On the night of 5 September he was stricken by either a heart attack or a stroke, dying in his tent. His grand vizier embalmed his body and dressed it in the sultan's finest clothes, leaving it sitting up in a litter to make his troops believe he was still alive until the siege had been successfully completed.

Suleiman's body was brought back to Constantinople where he was buried outside the great mosque he had built, known as the Suleiman Mosque, one of the largest and most beautiful in the world.

Other action this day

AD 394: The first day of the six-day Battle of Frigidus, in which Eastern emperor Theodosius I defeats Western ruler Eugenius, reunifying the Roman empire for the last time and guaranteeing the triumph of Christianity over paganism * 1839: The First Opium War begins in China * 1877: Trying to escape from prison at Camp Robinson in Nebraska, American Indian chief Crazy Horse is bayoneted and killed in a scuffle with prison guards

6 September

Barbara Frietchie defies General Robert E. Lee

1862 Today we remember the importance of winning hearts and minds.

When, on the heels of the great Confederate victory at the second battle of Bull Run, Robert E. Lee brought his Army of Northern Virginia splashing across the Potomac fords into Maryland – Union territory – he had a strategy in mind. First, he expected his forces to be greeted as liberators by a Southern-sympathising population that would eagerly rebel against the Union and join the Confederate cause. He also counted on resupplying his forces from the rich harvest of a grateful countryside. Then the army would proceed into Pennsylvania, well ahead of any pursuit, and for the first time bring the experience of war to Northern states. Finally, in Lee's grand strategic vision, these moves might offer the opportunity for some dazzling military triumph – before Philadelphia, perhaps, or near New York City – which would induce a demoralised Federal government to sue for peace.

The first sign that things might go wrong occurred today as the Confederate army wound its way through the streets of Frederick, Maryland. There, in a very public act of defiance, a woman displayed a Union flag from the attic window of her house and then loudly disputed the right of the Confederate troops to shoot it down. According to John Greenleaf Whittier's war ballad, it was 95-year-old Barbara Frietchie who showed the Stars and Stripes that day and uttered the words: 'Shoot if you must this old grey head, but spare your country's flag.' Whittier's famous account is, however, poetic licence based on a real incident: a Mrs Quantrill, another resident of Frederick, did stand with her daughter before their gate that day and insultingly wave a Union flag at the Southern soldiers in the street.

At this time, the Army of Northern Virginia, 55,000 strong, was starving, exhausted, shoeless and inclined towards pillage – 'a most ragged, lean, and hungry set of wolves', one observer called them. Despite the heavy posting of provost guards along the route of their march, a third of the troops would disappear over the next few days. Nor were the army's invading presence and the prospect of its resupply welcomed by the citizens of Maryland. Farmers left their crops unharvested in the fields and drove their cattle to safety in the mountains; merchants and tavern keepers locked their doors. The army remained famished; Maryland stayed in the Union.

None of the other goals of Lee's invasion was realised. Surprised by the alacrity of the Union pursuit, the Army of Northern Virginia never got as far as Pennsylvania, never found its dazzling war-ending victory. Instead, reduced to fewer than 40,000 through straggling and desertion, it went to ground at Sharpsburg, Maryland, fought a sanguinary draw with 75,000 Federals, and retired to war-ravaged Virginia and another two and a half years of conflict.

Given the way in which the Civil War divided families, it is not perhaps so surprising that Mrs Quantrill, the staunch Union patriot who became Whittier's 'Barbara Frietchie', turns out to have been a relative of William Quantrill, the bloodiest of the Confederate guerrillas.

Other action this day

1757: French soldier and Revolutionary Marie-Joseph du Motier, Marquis de Lafayette is born in the Auvergne * 1914: General Joseph-Simon Gallieni uses Paris taxi cabs to move French troops to the front to defend Paris at the start of the First Battle of the Marne * 1939: At the Battle of Barking Creek, British Spitfires shoot down two British Hurricanes, thinking they are enemy planes, the first British aircraft shot down in the Second World War and the first planes downed by Spitfires

7 September

'A continuous slaughter'

1812 Today the meteoric career of Napoleon Bonaparte reached its apogee and started its precipitous descent towards catastrophe as the emperor fought the Russians in one of the bloodiest battles of the 19th century.

At the end of June Napoleon had marched into Russia with an army of 530,000, the greatest concentration of troops in Europe since the Persian king Xerxes had invaded Greece in 480 BC (see 22 September). With this vast array came over 1,000 guns, 30,000 supply wagons and 28 million bottles of wine.

For weeks the army marched through the vast emptiness that was Russia, as the tsar's army refused to be drawn into a major battle. Slowly Napoleon's front-line force was reduced, mostly to guard his ever-lengthening lines of communications but also owing to sickness, accident and the occasional guerrilla ambush. By early

September the emperor's forces ready for battle were only about 130,000.

On 6 September the French army (which in fact was only one-third French, the rest being conscripts from Napoleon's empire) arrived at the town of Borodino, a little over 60 miles west of Moscow. There at last the Russians turned to fight, 120,000 strong under the command of 67-year-old general prince Mikhail Kutuzov, a fat and heavy-drinking nobleman who had lost an eye fighting the Turks but who possessed the cunning, determination and ruthlessness to match his adversary.

On the morning of 7 September Napoleon rose early and, remembering the brilliant weather at his most famous victory seven years before, he welcomed a glorious sunrise with the optimistic exclamation: 'Voilà le soleil d'Austerlitz!' ('Look, the sun of Austerlitz!') At six he ordered his cannon to open fire to start a day of frightful carnage.

Uncharacteristically, Napoleon then ordered his cavalry commander Joachim Murat to assault the Russian front, rather than attempting a flanking manoeuvre. In a costly attack, Murat broke the Russian line and seized the Rayevski redoubt, lost it again and retook it. At length the French artillery's relentless battering almost broke the Russians, but Napoleon let victory slip from his grasp by refusing to commit the French imperial guard or some 10,000 reserve troops, believing he might have to fight again the next day.

When both sides disengaged at nightfall, the stubborn Russians had lost 45,000 men killed or wounded, but these could be replaced. Napoleon had suffered 30,000 casualties of irreplaceable troops 1,500 miles from home. (In his compelling if slightly fictionalised narrative in *War and Peace,* Tolstoy calls the battle 'a continuous slaughter which could be of no avail either to the French or the Russians'.)

The following morning Kutuzov ordered a retreat, enabling the French to claim a victory and to begin the march on Moscow. But the Battle of Borodino was in fact Napoleon's greatest defeat. During the next three months his soldiers occupied a deserted Moscow which burnt to the ground around them, and then struggled back to the Polish border in the dead of Russian winter, attacked by Cossacks, guerrillas, the bitter cold and starvation. Only about 10,000 of the original force of over half a million survived the campaign. As Tsar Nicholas I later remarked: 'God punished the foolish; the bones of the audacious foreigners were scattered from Moscow to the Nieman.'

After the Battle of Borodino Napoleon's sun had passed its zenith and the emperor's days in power were numbered. As the crafty old Talleyrand said on hearing of the battle, 'Voilà le commencement de la fin.' ('There is the beginning of the end.')

Other action this day

1191: Thanks to a successful charge of the Christian heavy cavalry, Richard I (the Lionheart) defeats the Saracen leader Saladin at the Battle of Arsuf * 1776: In history's first submarine attack, the American craft *Turtle* attempts and fails to attach a bomb to the hull of British admiral Richard Howe's flagship, the HMS *Eagle*, in New York harbour * 1940: Late in the afternoon, 364 German bombers escorted by 515 fighter planes bomb London's docks, followed by another 133 bombers that night, killing 436 and injuring 1,666, on the first day of the Blitz

8 September

Nazi Germany fires the first ballistic missile at London

1944 At 7.17 this evening the British were subjected to a new and terrifying weapon for the first time, as a German ballistic missile exploded in Chiswick. Sixteen seconds later a second missile landed at Epping. These were the formidable V-2s, short for Vergeltungswaffe 2 (Vengeance Weapon 2), a designation coined by Joseph Goebbels, the German minister for propaganda.

The earlier V-1 (Vergeltungswaffe, or Vengeance Weapon, 1) was the so-called 'doodlebug' or 'buzz bomb', a jet-powered guided missile that looked like a small plane. The first had hit London on 13 June, and in total about 8,000 had been launched. Although the V-1 could carry a 1,900-pound warhead, its maximum range was only 250 miles. Furthermore, flying at only 360 miles per hour, buzz bombs became increasingly vulnerable to British anti-aircraft and fighter pilots. Consequently only about a third reached their targets.

The V-2, by comparison, was a rocket, guided by tailfins but without wings. It was 47 feet long with a 2,200-pound explosive payload. Flying at 3,000 miles an hour, it was invulnerable to both anti-aircraft and fighter plane attack.

On 6 September, Germany had launched the first V-2 at liberated Paris, but two days later the first of 1,400 of these sophisticated rockets started to rain down on Great Britain. The V-2 caused almost 10,000 British casualties, of whom nearly 3,000 were killed. Virtually all were civilians. Belgium was attacked even more vigorously, as the Nazis fired 1,665 missiles at the advancing Allies there, killing perhaps 4,500 soldiers and civilians.

Moving at supersonic speeds, the V-2 descended on its target area in silence, and the velocity was such that it could hardly be seen. In fact, initially few people understood that the mammoth explosions were caused by rockets. Concerned about possible British panic in the face of this new threat, Churchill at first refused publicly to acknowledge that Germany had such a weapon, informing Parliament only two months after the initial attack on London, after the Germans themselves had announced the existence of the V-2.

Originally the Germans had planned to launch V-2s from underground blockhouses but then turned to 30-lorry convoys to carry the rocket, equipment, fuel and operating crew. Each convoy would converge on a staging area, where the warhead would be installed. After being taken to a nearby launch site, the V-2 could be fuelled, armed and fired in an hour and a half. Since V-2s could be (and were) launched from almost anywhere, and the site could be changed for every firing, it proved impossible for the Allies to destroy the launchers; not a single one was attacked by Allied planes.

V-2s were developed in the Heeresversuchsstelle (army research centre) in Peenemünde, a village on the Baltic coast of north-east Germany. They were largely the brainchild of the brilliant German scientist Wernher von Braun, who was Peenemünde's technical director. Captured by American troops in the closing days of the war, von Braun and his colleagues were quickly moved to White Sands, New Mexico, to continue their work on rockets under different masters. Later, von Braun became chief of the American ballistic weapons programme at Huntsville, Alabama, which developed the Redstone, Jupiter-C, Juno and Pershing missiles.

Von Braun always maintained that scientific research is inherently impartial and that governments, not scientists, must bear the responsibility for the use that scientific developments are put to. Or, as satirised by the American composer and lyricist Tom Lehrer:

'Once the rockets are up, who cares where they come down?
That's not my department', says Wernher von Braun.

Other action this day

1157: Richard the Lionheart is born at Oxford * 1621: French prince and outstanding general Louis II de Bourbon, 4th Prince de Condé (the Great Condé), is born in Paris * 1796: Republican general Napoleon Bonaparte defeats the Austrians at Bassano near Venice during the French Revolutionary Wars

9 September

William the Conqueror dies in France

1087 At daybreak today William the Conqueror died at the convent of St Gervais near Rouen of an injury inflicted in battle a month before. A few days later he received a gruesome burial in the Abbaye aux Hommes at Caen.

For twenty years before his death William's main concern had been his subjugated kingdom in England, but he had in no way forgotten his original patrimony, the duchy of Normandy. Thus when a French army started to pillage his duchy in the summer of 1087, he quickly crossed the English Channel with his own troops. (Legend has it that William, who had grown very fat over the years, was further enraged on hearing that France's king Philip I had scoffed that he looked like a pregnant woman.)

On 15 August William captured and burned the French town of Mantes, 30 miles west of Paris. As flames consumed the buildings, William's horse suddenly shied away from a fiery ember and threw him violently against the pommel of his saddle, causing internal injuries so severe that peritonitis soon set in.

The injured king was moved by litter to the convent of St Gervais on the outskirts of his Norman capital of Rouen, where he lay in pain, his abdomen filling with fluid. On Thursday morning, 9 September, the tolling of the bells of Rouen cathedral awakened him.

Construing this as a divine signal, he commended himself to God and died instantly (although one Norman monk's account says that on his deathbed he bitterly repented the brutal repression he had visited upon the England he had conquered). The moment this ruthless king was dead, his servants stole his rings, jewellery and even his clothing, leaving his swollen body lying naked on the floor.

William's corpse was taken by boat and carriage to the Abbaye aux Hommes at Caen, which he had founded years before. His bizarre and macabre funeral was held on a day of blazing heat. Just as the funeral procession reached the church, a fire broke out, and the pallbearers were forced to put the coffin on the ground to fight the fire. Once the fire had been doused, they reclaimed the coffin and continued into the church.

By now William's body had become grotesquely bloated by the heat, and when the pallbearers tried to transfer it to a stone sarcophagus, it was too big to fit. As they struggled to cram it in, it burst, drenching the king's funeral clothing and creating a putrid stink that sent the mourners running from the church.

Eventually William was interred, but 500 years later rioting Huguenots dug him up and scattered his bones around the town of Caen. Some were found and replaced, but republicans desecrated his grave again during the French Revolution. It is said that only his left femur now remains in his tomb.

Other action this day

AD 9: The first day of the three-day Battle of the Teutoburg Forest, in which the Germanic tribes under Arminius ambush and annihilate three Roman legions under Publius Quinctilius Varus; on hearing of the disaster, Emperor Augustus cries out in anguish, 'Varus, Varus, give me back my legions!' * 1000: King Olaf Tryggvason of Norway is defeated and killed in the naval Battle of Svolder by an alliance of Danes and Swedes * 1528: Italian admiral Andrea Doria seizes Genoa and re-establishes the Genoese Republic * 1513: Twenty thousand English under Thomas Howard, Earl of Surrey, crush 30,000 Scots and 5,000 French allies at the Battle of Flodden Field, during which Scottish king James IV is killed

10 September

Commandant Perry defeats the British on Lake Erie

1813 The War of 1812 was not going well for the Americans – the British had burned Washington and the governor of Detroit had surrendered the town – but today Master Commandant Oliver Hazard Perry struck a blow for his country when he attacked the British fleet at Put-in-Bay on Lake Erie.

Perry, a young (28) and courageous officer who had joined the Navy at fourteen, was determined to regain not only the lake but Detroit as well from the conquering British. His fleet of ten vessels outnumbered the enemy, and his firepower was greater. The six British ships carried 63 guns, mostly long guns with a one-mile range. The principal American armament was carronades, guns that packed twice the punch but had only about half the range.

Hostilities began at 11.45am when the British ship *Detroit* fired the first salvo. In the beginning the battle went badly, as the American flagship, the 20-gun brig *Lawrence*, was too far from the enemy for effective fire, although British long guns constantly peppered the *Lawrence*, killing or wounding 83 of 103 crew members. When the *Lawrence*'s guns had all been put out of action, Perry lowered a cutter and was rowed half a mile through enemy gunfire to the *Lawrence*'s sister ship, the brig *Niagara*. Then the stricken *Lawrence* surrendered to the British.

Perry then led the *Niagara* directly into the British line so that her short-range firepower could take full effect, discharging broadsides from both sides at once. In the turmoil two enemy ships collided and were forced to surrender, while Perry's other ships ran down some smaller British vessels trying to escape.

By three o'clock the British had hauled down their colours, and Perry received their capitulation on the deck of his recaptured flagship, allegedly to show them the terrible price his men had paid for victory. Of Perry's force, 27 were killed and 96 wounded, while the British suffered 40 dead with another 94 wounded.

It was now that Perry earned his place in the American book of famous quotations by scrawling in pencil on the back of an old envelope a message to the future president, General William Henry Harrison:

Dear General:
We have met the enemy and they are ours. Two ships, two brigs, one schooner and one sloop.
Yours with great respect and esteem,
O.H. Perry

With the British fleet out of the way, American ships controlled Lake Erie, and Harrison was able to take the offensive, soon retaking Detroit. Perry became something of a national hero in America for his exploits and was soon promoted to captain. Sadly, only five years later he died from yellow fever contracted on a voyage to South America.

As for the war, with neither side able to achieve a decisive victory, it ended docilely with the Treaty of Ghent, signed in December 1814.

Other action this day
1491: One of Dauphin Charles's (the future Charles VII's) Armagnac nobles, Tanneguy du Châtel, cuts down Jean Sans Peur, Duke of Burgundy, at a peace parley on a bridge at Montereau, pushing the Burgundians into an alliance with England's Henry V and paving the way for his invasion of France * 1547: The English defeat the Scots, killing 10,000 to only 500 of their own losses at the Battle of Pinkie

11 September

The British trounce George Washington at the Battle of Brandywine

1777 Today was a bad day for George Washington and the Continental Army, and the result came close to destroying the main American fighting force and with it, perhaps, the cause of American independence.

A British army, 13,000-strong, led by generals Howe and Cornwallis, had sailed from New York, landed in Delaware, and was now marching eastwards on Philadelphia, the rebel capital, whose capture the generals hoped would end the war in America. But George Washington, with 8,000 regulars and 3,000 militia, decided to contest the issue by holding the fords along some five miles of Brandywine Creek, thereby blocking the British route of advance.

The day before the battle, when the Americans took up their positions along the east bank of the creek, they unaccountably neglected the job of reconnoitring the terrain, roads and landmarks across the creek from which the British would advance. Therefore, commanders were largely unacquainted with what lay beyond their immediate front, including the existence of fords further upstream and roads leading to them.

At 5.00am, Howe set his army in motion from Kennett Square, seven miles west of the Brandywine, sending a force of 5,000 troops straight down the main road to make a show at Chadd's Ford, and the balance of his command, 7,500 men under Cornwallis, marching north on a wide flanking manoeuvre designed to cross the creek undetected at a ford well above the American right.

Reaching Chadd's Ford at 10.00am, the smaller force opened up with artillery fire on the American positions but made no attempt to cross. Presently, a rider brought Washington news that a cavalry patrol had spotted a British column marching north along a road that paralleled the creek. The commander-in-chief's first reaction was to send forces immediately across the Brandywine to destroy the column, then prepare for a later attack from another quarter. But soon a second dispatch arrived reporting that militia sent to verify the earlier sighting had found no sign of enemy on that road. Which report was correct? Where were the enemy? No one at headquarters could say. Only much later was it discovered that the militia were unknowingly watching a different road from the one the cavalry had reported on. In any event, confused and wary, Washington called off his attack to await developments. At 2.00am a local farmer rode in to say that the British had crossed the creek, were coming down the east bank of the creek, and would soon surround Washington's army.

Washington realigned his forces to meet the threat from the north, which began at 4.00pm. Cued by the noise of Cornwallis's cannon, the British also attacked across Chadd's Ford. In a two-front battle, the fighting was fierce, and Washington rode up and down the line exhorting his men to stem the British tide. But as the action continued, the line began to sag, artillery pieces were abandoned, the militia withdrew, and as darkness fell the Americans were beaten and in full retreat. Their losses for the day reached almost 1,300, including 400 captured, and eleven guns.

Fortunately, the Continental Army managed to elude what might have been a greater disaster, for Cornwallis's troops, having marched over seventeen miles since dawn, were in no shape to pursue them further. The Americans regrouped at nearby Chester. Late that night, Washington sent news of the battle to the president of Congress in a masterpiece of understatement that began: 'Sir: I am sorry to inform you, that in this day's engagement, we have been obliged to leave the enemy masters of the field.'

So it was luck, not intelligence, that saved the Continental Army this day. But outgeneralled by Howe though he was, Washington quickly reorganised his army and kept it active in the field. Philadelphia fell two weeks later, but the event did not have the significance the British generals had hoped for. The rebels did not lay down their arms, the war continued, and the Americans spent a bitter winter at their Valley Forge camp keeping a watchful eye on the enemy occupying their capital. In the spring, the British army evacuated Philadelphia and marched all the way back to New York City, from which it had first sailed the previous autumn.

Other action this day

1297: Scottish rebel and patriot William Wallace defeats the English at the Battle of Stirling Bridge * 1697: Prince Eugene of Savoy routs the Turks at Zenta, with 20,000 killed on the battlefield and 10,000 more drowned trying to escape, at a loss of only 300 Austrians, resulting in a peace treaty that cedes Hungary and Transylvania to the Austrians * 1709: The Duke of Marlborough and Prince Eugene of Savoy chase the French from the field at the Battle of Malplaquet but suffer 22,000 casualties versus just 12,000 for the enemy, prompting the French commander the duc de Villars to write to Louis XIV: 'If God should grant us another such defeat, our enemies would be destroyed.' * 1855: In the Crimean War, the Russians sink their ships in the harbour, blow up the fortifications and evacuate Sebastopol, after which the Allies march in after an eleven-month siege * 1917: Having already survived being shot down seven times without a parachute, First World War French fighter ace (53 kills) Georges Guynemer is downed and killed by a German fighter near Poelkapelle, Belgium

12 September

Vienna is saved from the Turk as the croissant and the cappuccino are invented

1683 Today we celebrate a famous victory that saved Vienna forever from the threat of Turkish conquest and gave the rest of the world two recipes for the perfect Continental breakfast.

Ever since the reign of Suleiman the Magnificent a century before, the Turks had lusted for the great capital of Vienna, and now a vast Ottoman army a quarter of a million strong was camped around the city. Every day for two long months the guns of Grand Vizier Kara Mustafa crashed against the walls; the outer fortifications had been captured and now the Turks were tunnelling through to the inner walls. It was only a matter of time before the Austrian defences would collapse, the barbarously cruel Turkish brand of murder and rapine would begin, and the nation's Christianity would be extirpated for the glory of Islam.

So confident was the grand vizier that he complacently ignored the campfires twinkling down from the Kahlenburg Heights only a few miles north of the city. But there the Polish king John Sobieski, who had come to Vienna's rescue in return for a huge subsidy from Pope Alexander VIII, joined the Austrian army under the command of Charles of Lorraine. Acting as the Pope's emissary was the Capuchin monk Marco d'Aviano, whose job it was to ensure cooperation among the various Christian commanders.

At first light on 12 September some 80,000 Christian soldiers thundered down into the mass of Turks. The battle lasted for fifteen hours, but in the evening a devastating charge by the Polish horse completely routed the invaders, who left their guns, vast stores of food, Kara Mustafa's fabulous jewels and tens of thousands of corpses on the field. In his dispatch to the Pope, the Polish king modestly paraphrased Caesar, reporting: 'I came, I saw, God conquered.'

What remained of the vizier's army fled through Hungary towards Turkey, but Kara Mustafa reached only as far as Belgrade, where he was ceremoniously strangled with a silken cord, sent on orders from the sultan at first news of the defeat.

Vienna was saved, Christianity remained triumphant and Ottoman rule in the Balkans was badly shaken. Among the victorious troops who celebrated that evening was a nineteen-year-old prince named Eugene of Savoy who would utterly crush the Turks fourteen years later at Zenta, and who would become the greatest general ever to serve the Holy Roman Empire.

This tale of Vienna's salvation also has two remarkable culinary addenda. The first comes from Vienna's bakers, who commemorated the Austrian victory by creating a new roll in the shape of the crescent moon from the Turkish flag and christened it a *Kipfel*, German for crescent. The *Kipfel* gained immediate popularity in Vienna, and in 1770 Marie Antoinette (daughter of Empress Maria Theresa of Austria) introduced it to France when she married the future Louis XVI. Today we usually call it by the French word for crescent, *croissant*.

The second gastronomic creation of the battle perfectly complements the first. Among the supplies abandoned by the Turks as they fled the field was a vast store of coffee. Finding it too bitter for their tastes, the Christian soldiers sweetened it with milk and honey, some say at the suggestion of the friar Marco d'Aviano. In any case, the tasty drink, whose colour resembled the friar's habit, was named *Cappuccino* in honour of the Capuchin order to which he belonged. For this, and other holy deeds, Marco was beatified in 2003.

Other action this day

1847: American general Winfield Scott's army storms Chapultepec in the Mexican War * 1918: The American Expeditionary Force and 48,000 French troops under the command of 'Black Jack' Pershing start the Saint-Mihiel offensive, where 1,500 American, British and French planes combine with ground troops in the first ever large-scale coordinated air-ground attack * 1943: During Operation Oak, in a glider-based attack on the Campo Imperatore Hotel in the Grand Sasso in the Abruzzo region, German SS colonel Otto Skorzeny rescues fallen dictator Benito Mussolini from confinement without firing a shot

13 September

General James Wolfe dies while winning Quebec

1759 Early this morning, after nearly three months of frustration, British major general James Wolfe finally outwitted the French defenders of Quebec and under cover of darkness snuck an advance party up the steep heights above the St Lawrence River and onto the Plains of Abraham. He had finally discovered the unlocked back door to the great bastion. By first light his seven battalions – 4,800 men – were deployed in a battle line stretching across the mile-wide tract of open land. Now he awaited the French response. The outcome of the French and Indian War, now entering its fifth year, lay in the balance.

Since his expedition had arrived by ship in front of Quebec in late June, Wolfe had probed upriver and down but found no way to crack the stout defences behind which lay the marquis de Montcalm and a force of 12,000. Now time was running out: with winter in the offing, the British fleet would soon have to retire downriver, and so lose all chance of taking the city this year. But at last he spotted a route up the cliffs.

When the French emerged onto the plains at 9.00am, the British held their fire until the enemy was within 60 yards, then unloosed volley after volley, halting the attackers and routing them back inside their fortifications. That evening the French regulars left Quebec and retreated upriver. The fortress surrendered on the 18th. Thus, the glorious deed was done. But in the doing, Wolfe was shot three times and bled to death. His adversary, Montcalm, also severely wounded, died the next day.

The battle of Quebec was decisive. The French retreated to Montreal, which fell the next year. Canada was now British.

The battle on the Plains of Abraham became a celebrated event for many in that and later times. It inspired Benjamin West's 1776 painting 'The Death of Wolfe'. It may have added to the popularity of Thomas Gray's 'Elegy Written in a Country Churchyard', known to be Wolfe's favourite poem, whose most famous line seemed to capture both his exploit and his fate: 'The paths of glory lead but to the grave.'

Finally, we know that in the dire military situation of Korea in the summer of 1950, General Douglas MacArthur drew inspiration from Wolfe's surprise manoeuvre at Quebec to plan his brilliantly successful backdoor landings at Inchon (see 14 September).

Other action this day

AD 122: To keep barbarian northern tribes out of England, construction begins on Hadrian's Wall * AD 533: At the Battle of Ad Decimum near Carthage, Byzantine general Belisarius defeats the Vandals under King Gelimer * 1882: A British expeditionary force defeats the Egyptians at Tel el Kebir to start the British occupation of Egypt * 1942: US Marine colonel Red Mike Edson, commander of the 1st Raider Battalion, earns the Medal of Honor by his defence of Lunga Ridge ('Bloody Ridge') on Guadalcanal

14 September

Douglas MacArthur lands at Inchon

1950 Early this morning, in darkness off the Korean coast, the United States X Corps, 40,000 strong, prepared to launch one of the boldest amphibious assaults in all military history. Its purpose was to reverse an impending military disaster at Pusan in South Korea, where United Nations forces defending the republic of Korea were facing almost certain annihilation by the Communist North Korean army.

With X Corps and directing the entire operation was General Douglas MacArthur, commander-in-chief of United Nations forces, whose intention it was to land his force behind enemy lines at the port of Inchon, cut the North Korean army's supply line, and strangle the invasion that the Communists had launched so savagely on 25 June.

MacArthur's plan was extremely hazardous. It required complete surprise, and in addition the enormous tides at Inchon would allow only two hours for the initial landings. When he first proposed the operation, the US joint chiefs of staff opposed it as too hazardous. But at a strategic conference in Tokyo, MacArthur countered

Washington's assessment with a forceful argument in which he incorporated this history lesson:

> Surprise is the most vital element for success in war ... On the Plains of Abraham [in 1759], Wolfe won a stunning victory that was made possible almost entirely by surprise. Thus he captured Quebec and in effect ended the French and Indian War. Like Montcalm, the North Koreans would regard an Inchon landing as impossible. Like Wolfe, I could take them by surprise. [See 13 September.]

On 29 August the joint chiefs cabled their approval.

In the tense pre-landing atmosphere, MacArthur, aboard his command ship *Mount McKinley*, stared into the darkness. 'Then I noticed a flash,' he wrote, 'a light that winked on and off across the water. The channel navigation lights were on. We were taking the enemy by surprise.' By 8.00am, the Marines carrying out the first wave of the assault had secured a beachhead without losing a man. With the evening's tide most of X Corps was ashore and moving inland.

As their author had predicted, the Inchon landings forced the Communist invaders out of South Korea. For the UN forces, the military scene on the peninsula went from almost certain disaster to what seemed like war-ending victory. But MacArthur's feat, unlike Wolfe's, did not end the war. When UN armour and infantry moved north to destroy what was left of the retreating North Korean army, they suddenly encountered half a million Chinese Communist 'volunteers'. A new phase of the war began in which the front line see-sawed back and forth for another eighteen months. In the end, the invasion of South Korea was decisively defeated, but that success was obscured by military stalemate, endless armistice negotiations and a heavy cost in lives: 142,000 deaths in the UN forces (including over 33,000 Americans), 415,000 in the South Korean army, and perhaps 1,500,000 Chinese and North Koreans.

Other action this day

1812: Napoleon occupies Moscow * 1847: General Winfield Scott enters Mexico City to bring America victory in the Mexican War * 1852: The Duke of Wellington dies aged 83 at Walmer Castle in south-east England

15 September

Tanks are used in warfare for the first time

1916 Today, in a sector of the Western Front between the French villages of Courcelette and Flers, on the 76th day of that endless carnage called the Battle of the Somme, a secret weapon was unveiled. Its appearance was brief and the results inconclusive. But the event itself was electrifying and, literally, earth-shaking.

Thirty-two armoured caterpillar vehicles – code-named 'tanks' to preserve secrecy during their development – rumbled heavily out of the British lines heading towards the German entrenchments. Most of the machines broke down before reaching their objective, but thirteen of them, with British infantry close behind, managed to advance some 3,500 yards, punching a gaping hole in the enemy line, whose defenders – taking one look at the monstrous machines moving inexorably towards them, invulnerable to machine gun fire – fled to the rear. From above, a French aeroplane observer described one segment of the action in a message that was translated for an eager British press as: 'Tank walking up High Street of Flers with British Army cheering behind.'

The triumph was momentary, for there was no way for the British to exploit the sudden breakthrough, so the long tragedy of the Somme resumed, unaffected by the brief intrusion of technology. The Germans regained the lost territory through stubborn counter-attacks, and their high command failed to perceive the value of the phenomenon that had breached their line. On the British side, some called the attack a failure, while others pronounced it merely unconvincing or a premature disclosure of a secret weapon. There were those, however, including the British commander-in-chief General Haig, who saw a weapon that could win the war.

The development of the tank had begun in early 1915, based on the success of armoured car squadrons against German infantry attacks and on the increasingly obvious need for a cross-country vehicle that could break the stalemate of trench warfare. The project attracted the attention and enthusiasm of the First Lord of the Admiralty, Winston Churchill, who described its promise to the prime minister: 'The caterpillar system would enable trenches to be crossed easily and the weight of the machine would destroy all wire entanglements. Forty or fifty of these machines prepared secretly and brought into position at nightfall could advance quite certainly into the enemy's trenches, smashing away all the obstructions and sweeping the trenches with their machine gun fire and with grenades thrown out of the tops.'

The tanks at the Somme were designated the Mark I. They were some seven feet high and 32 feet long, with a crew of eight, a Daimler engine and a rarely achievable top speed of 3.7 miles per hour. The Mark I came in two versions which were distinguished by size of armament and inevitably nicknamed 'male', with two six-pounders, and 'female', with two machine guns.

After their Somme début, tanks with improved designs made appearances in several battles on the Western Front – Arras, Chemin des Dames, the third battle of Ypres, and St Julien. But it was in November 1917 that 300 Mark IV tanks, leading eight infantry divisions against the German lines at Cambrai, fulfilled Churchill's promise by achieving a victory whose scope, even amid tactical failures, was sufficient to convince the doubters that the future was at hand. Like the stirrup, the bow and gunpowder, the tank had transformed the practice of warfare.

Other action this day

1814: With Napoleon confined to Elba, the Congress of Vienna opens; it will determine most of Europe's boundaries for the next century * 1894: The Japanese defeat the Chinese at the Battle of Pyongyang during the First Sino-Japanese War * 1944: The 1st, 5th and 7th US Marine Regiments land on Japanese-held Peleliu in the Pacific for a victory that takes two months at a cost of 1,794 Marine and Army dead and 8,010 wounded; of the island's 11,000 defenders, 10,700 perish

16 September

A great warrior-king is born

1387 One of the few extant portraits of England's Henry V now hangs in London's National Portrait Gallery. It shows the king in profile, at first glance looking somewhat monkish, as the hat that conceals his blond hair gives him the air of a medieval canon. His face is strong, long and bony, with a large straight nose and contemplative brown eyes that would offer more justice than mercy. The anonymous artist read his subject well. England's last great warrior-monarch, Henry was renowned for his determination, bravery and justice (although he could also be brutal and contemptuous of men's lives, and piously priggish as well).

Henry was born on this day at Monmouth Castle in Wales, the son of Henry of Bolingbroke, who would usurp the English throne when young Henry was twelve years old. Thirteen years later the elder Henry died, and his son inherited the crown.

Henry spent most of his nine years as king in a largely successful attempt to crush a France already riven by civil war and saddled with a lunatic monarch, but his first battle was against rebels at home. Two months before his sixteenth birthday he fought at Shrewsbury against the Percys. It is said that Henry himself killed the famous Hotspur (see 21 July) while suffering an arrow wound to the face.

He didn't fight again for twelve years, but then, in 1415, he invaded France, first besieging and capturing Harfleur and then annihilating the cream of the French nobility at Agincourt (see 11 August).

Despite this great victory – and despite the fact that Henry now became de facto ruler of France – French opposition continued. Two years after Agincourt he took Rouen and made Normandy part of England.

During the summer of 1421 Henry was once again in the field, capturing Dreux, and in May the following year his army finally took Meaux after a siege of six months. It seems likely, however, that it was at Meaux that he contracted dysentery, that scourge of medieval soldiers. After several months of illness, he was forced to leave the siege on a litter and return to his headquarters at the château of Vincennes, just east of Paris.

Henry spent his last three weeks at Vincennes putting his dominions in order and securing the royal inheritance for his infant son (the future Henry VI), whom he had never seen. He died 2 August 1422, a month before his 35th birthday. He was, according to his brother, 'too famous to live long'.

When Henry died, his flesh was boiled from his bones to preserve it and both flesh and bones were placed in his casket, which made a stately return to London over the next two months. There he enjoyed a great pageant of a funeral, in which even his horses were led to the altar in Westminster Abbey for a final farewell to their illustrious master.

Although Henry's son was crowned king of France the year Henry died, within seven years France's Charles VII was crowned at Reims with the help of Joan of Arc and the claims of Henry's son were discarded.

Other action this day

1776: Americans led by George Washington defeat the British at the Battle of Harlem Heights * 1950: The US 8th Army breaks out of the Pusan Perimeter in South Korea and begins heading north to meet MacArthur's troops heading south from Inchon.

17 September

A bridge too far – the largest airborne operation ever

1944 With Paris liberated, Antwerp captured and the Germans everywhere on the run in north-west Europe, an intoxicating optimism ran through the Allied camp. Imbibing this spirit, the normally cautious Field Marshal Montgomery advanced a bold strategic plan that gave promise of ending the war by Christmas.

It called for a great thrust northward through Holland to get past the Siegfried Line, Germany's formidable frontier defences, and then a swing eastward towards Berlin and final victory. Not everyone among the Allied brass agreed, but General Eisenhower, the supreme commander, was willing to give Monty's plan a try; or at least the first part, a combined ground and airborne operation to get forces across the Lower Rhine River, the last great water barrier before Germany itself. The operation bore the deceptively pastoral code-name Market Garden.

Accordingly, on this sunny late summer morning, from airfields across southern England, a great armada of transport planes and gliders took off for Holland carrying 20,000 paratroopers from three Allied divisions. The mission was to 'lay an airborne carpet' behind German lines along a 65-mile corridor running north from the Allied front line to the town of Arnhem on the far side of the Rhine. The paratroopers would seize key bridges along the corridor, then hold them until the ground forces of XXX Corps came through on their way to Arnhem.

Allied planners viewed the retreating enemy as demoralised and incapable of strong resistance. They discounted intelligence indicating a formidable concentration of German units in the very area through which Market Garden would pass. At a top-level briefing for Market Garden commanders, the general commanding the British 1st Airborne Division asked how long his men would have to hold Arnhem before XXX Corps got through to them. 'Two days,' Monty told him confidently. 'They'll be up with you by then.'

On the ground it was very different. The Germans met 1st Airborne's drop near Arnhem with unanticipated quickness and ferocity. Only one battalion of British paratroopers managed to reach the town. The rest came under heavy fire and by nightfall went to ground west of the town. At the southern end, as the Guards Armoured Division leading XXX Corps got under way, its lead units were ambushed by heavy fire from anti-tank guns. The column halted while infantry was brought up to flank the ambushers and bulldozers cleared away the wreckage of vehicles. The tanks resumed their advance, but the pattern was set for a painfully slow, stop-and-go advance. When the Guards reached Eindhoven, just eleven miles from the start line, they were already 24 hours behind schedule.

In seizing their assigned bridges, the paratroopers of the 101st and 82nd US Airborne Divisions had done a remarkable job; but so had the German defenders in attacking the Allied columns that jammed the single roadway north. At the town of Nijmegen it took XXX Corps two days of heavy fighting, including an amphibious assault by the 82nd Airborne, to clear the bridge across the River Waal.

The advance continued, but time was running out. With one isolated battalion desperately holding the north end of the Arnhem bridge against 9th SS Panzer Division, the rest of 1st Airborne was pinned in a shrinking pocket, backs to the Rhine. An attempt to fly in reinforcements went disastrously awry when anti-aircraft fire forced Polish paratroopers to jump early, putting them on the wrong bank of the river.

Reduced to 2,200 from the 10,000 paratroopers who had landed eight days earlier, the 1st Airborne was almost out of food, ammo and medical supplies, and could no longer care for its growing number of wounded. Montgomery, finally realising that XXX Corps, close as it was, would not reach Arnhem in time, gave the division the order to withdraw. During the night and under intense fire, the survivors were ferried or swam to safety across the Rhine.

Operation Market Garden failed utterly. In the gallant effort, 17,000 Allied troops had been killed, wounded or captured. Arnhem proved to be, in a phrase that would become famous, 'a bridge too far'. Critics of the operation compared it to Dunkirk and the Dardanelles. The Allies would need to find a different strategy from Monty's single thrust. There would be one more Christmas at war.

Other action this day

1631: Protestant Swedes and Saxons under Gustavus Adolphus defeat the Holy Roman Empire at Breitenfeld * 1788: At the Battle of Karánsebes, drunken hussars and infantry of the same Austrian army fire on each other, mistaking each other for a Turkish force, causing over 10,000 casualties * 1862: On the bloodiest single day in American history, Union and Confederate armies suffer a combined 26,293 casualties at the Battle of Antietam, a stalemate * 1916: Manfred von Richthofen ('The Red Baron') downs his first of 80 Allied planes near Cambrai, France * 1935: The experimental German dive bomber JU-87 – the dreaded 'Stuka' – makes its maiden flight

18 September

Emperor Trajan – 'dreaded by none save the enemy'

AD 53 Today Marcus Ulpius Traianus was born in Italica, a Roman colony near modern Seville. Known to history as Trajan, in time he would become the first Roman emperor born outside Italy, and his conquests would enlarge the empire to its greatest extent.

Trajan came from a military family – his father had commanded the 10th Legion 'Fretensis' during the Jewish War in AD 76–68 and later become consul. Trajan himself had commanded the 7th Legion 'Gemina' and served under his father in Syria. By the time he became emperor at the age of 45, he had spent over twenty years in military posts or governing Roman territories such as Upper Germany.

Trajan was tall and rugged; according to his friend Pliny the Younger, he liked to 'range the forests, drive wild beasts from their lairs, scale vast mountain heights, and set foot on rocky crags, with none to give a helping hand or show the way'. Pliny also tells us that he insisted on sharing the hardships and dangers his men faced in the field and consequently was loved by them.

Trajan waged three major wars during his nineteen-year reign, the first two against the Dacians, who lived in today's Romania.

Ten years before becoming emperor Trajan had campaigned in Dacia under Emperor Domitian. The Romans had been ambushed at Tapae, and the war had ended in stalemate. Immediately afterwards the Dacian general Decebalus (Dacian for 'the Brave') had grabbed the throne on the death of the king.

On becoming emperor, Trajan decided to put the troublesome Dacians in their place and to avenge the earlier defeat at Tapae. In preparation, he transferred some legions from Germany and Britain and established two new ones, the 2nd Legion *Traiana* and the 30th Legion *Ulpia*, which brought the Roman army's total to 30, the most in the empire's history up to that time.

In early AD 101 Trajan invaded Dacia and met the enemy once more at Tapae, this time just winning a difficult battle. Trajan himself was in the thick of the fighting, and, according to the historian Cassius Dio, 'when the bandages gave out, he is said not to have spared even his own clothing, but to have cut it up into strips'.

The next winter Decebalus organised a counter-offensive but was decisively repulsed, allowing Trajan to march on the Dacian capital of Sarmizegethusa (about 200 miles north-west of modern Bucharest). Decebalus sued for peace, prostrating himself before the emperor and accepting the role of client king. When the triumphant emperor returned to Rome, however, he learned that Decebalus had again begun flouting Roman authority the moment the legions had withdrawn.

In June 105 Trajan marched into Dacia with eleven legions (about 60,000 men) plus an unknown but significant number of allies. To cross the Danube he ordered built a massive bridge on 60 stone piers, some of which still survive. A desperate Decebalus attempted – but failed – to have him assassinated.

Now Trajan laid siege to Sarmizegethusa. After a first assault was repelled, the Romans sealed off the city with a *circumvallatio* wall and then demolished the city's water pipes, forcing the Dacians to surrender.

During the siege Decebalus and a few of his followers had escaped, but Roman cavalry soon hunted them down. To avoid the ignominy of being marched to Rome in chains and then executed, Decebalus committed suicide. After seizing the Dacian treasure of 180 tons of gold and 360 tons of silver, Trajan ordered the capital burnt to the ground and established Dacia as a Roman province, the first on the north side of the Danube. (Romanians still claim descent from his soldiers and owe their language to his conquest.) The Roman empire now covered some 2,270,000 square miles.

To commemorate his triumph, Trajan ordered constructed his famous 100-foot column in Rome, with 2,500 sculpted figures in 23 spiral bands depicting scenes from the war.

Trajan's final military venture started in 114 against Parthia. He attacked through Armenia, moved on into Mesopotamia and captured Babylon and the Parthian capital at Ctesiphon (near modern Baghdad). When he reached the Persian Gulf he is supposed to have wept because he was now too old to repeat Alexander the Great's conquests in India. But at the end of 116 Mesopotamia rebelled, and Trajan withdrew. On his way back to Rome he died of a stroke on 8 August 117 at Selinus on the southern coast of Asia Minor. He was deeply mourned by his people, who saw him as the perfect ruler. According to Cassius Dio: 'He was dreaded by none save the enemy.' Even two centuries after his death the Roman Senate still prayed that each new emperor 'might surpass the felicity of Augustus and the virtue of Trajan' ('felicior Augusto, melior Traiano').

Other action this day

AD 323: Constantine defeats Licinius at the Battle of Chrysopolis and establishes his sole control over the Roman empire * 1454: 9,000 Teutonic knights with 6,000 infantry defeat 16,000 Polish cavalry and 3,000 Prussian mercenaries at the Battle of Chojnice in the Thirteen Years War * 1863: The start of the three-day Battle of Chickamauga in which Confederates defeat the North

19 September

The Black Prince captures a French king

1356 The Hundred Years War had already been running for nineteen years when the English overwhelmed their French foes today at the Battle of Poitiers, taking prisoner the king of France.

In early September the heir to the English throne, Edward, the Black Prince, led a raiding party of only 7,000 men out of English-held Bordeaux, but he soon found himself pursued by King Jean II of France with a vastly superior force. The armies fought briefly on 17 September but arranged a truce for the following day, a Sunday, when the local prelate fruitlessly tried to arrange peace. But the day of rest gave the Black Prince the time he needed to organise his army in the damp and thicketed marshland where the Clain and Moisson rivers come together south of Poitiers.

Ten years earlier at Crécy (see 26 August), the English had found themselves in a similar situation, vastly outnumbered by the French. Lack of French discipline plus the accuracy of English longbows had destroyed the enemy then, and the Black Prince, who had fought at Crécy as a sixteen-year-old, hoped to triumph with the same tactics. He positioned his men behind a thorn hedge with a ditch in front, stationing his cavalry out of sight behind a hill to the rear.

Early on Monday morning the French launched their first assault, as two French marshals led 300 German knights in a ferocious charge at a gap in the hedge in front of the English position. But English and Welsh archers armed with six-foot longbows moved out of the cavalry's path and opened fire on the horse's vulnerable flanks. Those knights not cut down by arrows were dragged from their horses and butchered by archers using hammers and daggers.

Now a wave of dismounted French men-at-arms reached the English positions, led by the eighteen-year-old Dauphin (the future Charles V), only to be forced back after a fierce fight when Prince Edward reinforced the sector under attack.

The Black Prince's weary soldiers now faced yet another French assault, led by King Jean himself. It was still anyone's battle when the Black Prince ordered his knights and men-at-arms to mount and charge through the hedge into the French line. According to the contemporary chronicler Jean Froissart, as the armies crashed together, 'King Jean with his own hands did that day marvels in arms: he had an axe in his hands wherewith he defended himself and fought in the breaking of the press.'

At this point Edward ordered his Gascon lieutenant Jean de Grailly, Captal de Buch to lead a small force of 200 mounted knights around the enemy's left flank to attack the French from the rear. Panic spread among the stunned French, and they turned to escape to nearby Poitiers, but the city gates remained firmly shut. Pursuing Gascons cut them down wholesale outside the walls.

King Jean now found himself isolated on the battlefield with his younger son and his personal retainers. Helpless, he surrendered to Denis de Morbeque, a French knight he had previously banished from France. According to the dispatch the Black Prince sent to his father (Edward III), during seven hours of fighting he had lost only 40 men to 3,000 French dead, while capturing the French king, his son, seventeen great lords, thirteen counts, five viscounts and 100 other knights.

King Jean was carried off for four years of luxurious captivity in London where he was held for a ransom of 3 million crowns. Although the Battle of Poitiers may have seemed decisive at the time, it was in truth just another blip in the Hundred Years War that dragged on for another 97 years.

Other action this day

1777: American general Horatio Gates's ragtag collection of American troops fleshed out with militia fights British general John Burgoyne's British and German regulars to a standstill at the First Battle of Saratoga * 1870: The Prussians begin the successful 132-day siege of Paris during the Franco-Prussian War * 1955: President Juan Perón of Argentina is deposed and exiled after an army-navy revolt led by democratically inspired officers fed up with the inflation, corruption, demagoguery and oppression of his regime

20 September

A triumphant deadlock for Republican France

1792 Today a French army 54,000 strong faced 34,000 invading Prussians, Austrians and French émigrés at Valmy, about 60 miles from the French border. The battle ended after four hours of shelling, the French having suffered only 300 casualties against even fewer – 184 – for their enemies. Yet this almost bloodless standoff changed both the history of France and the history of warfare.

Ever since the fall of the Bastille, France's republicans had steadily eroded the power of King Louis XVI, who had been under virtual house arrest since his abortive attempt to escape to Varennes fifteen months earlier. Europe's other monarchs felt honour-bound to help a fellow king, especially since they feared the virus of republicanism would spread to their own countries. In the forefront was Holy Roman Emperor Leopold II, whose sister was Louis's wife, Marie Antoinette.

During 1791 Leopold and the Prussian king Frederick William II had marched their armies up to the borders of France, a move so provocative that on 20 April the next year France declared war, even though Leopold had died seven weeks before.

Now Charles William Ferdinand, Duke of Brunswick took command of a combined Prussian and Austrian army reinforced by the so-called Army of Condé, a large corps of 8,000 French émigrés under King Louis's cousin, the Prince de Condé. (This patrician force included two of Louis's nephews, five dukes and innumerable lesser nobility.)

In August the allies crossed into France with the declared intent of restoring Louis's authority and crushing any who resisted. Easily capturing the northern towns of Longwy and then Verdun, Brunswick now headed for Paris.

By now two French armies were on the move. One under Charles-François Dumouriez marched south from Valenciennes to bar the road to Paris while a second under François Kellermann headed west from Metz. On 19 September the two forces joined each other near Valmy, 140 miles east of Paris. But, since the emigration of France's nobility had stripped the army of over 6,000 of its officers, this new

French army was led largely by republican volunteers rather than professionals, and many of its soldiers had little knowledge of war. But could Revolutionary enthusiasm match the invaders' discipline, professionalism and experience?

The French took positions facing west from Valmy, with Kellerman's 36,000 men on a hill in front and Dumouriez about two miles behind, with 18,000 more. In fact, the French were now further away from Paris than the invaders, but, as Dumouriez had foreseen, Brunswick could not safely march on the capital with so large a hostile force left in his rear.

On the morning of 20 September, Brunswick approached from the west with his considerably smaller coalition army – the corps with which he had crossed into France had been severely depleted by dysentery. But he was confident that the little-trained and mostly unblooded French would panic at the first serious gunfire. He moved his men into line about 2,500 yards from the French positions, and when the fog cleared about noon, opened fire with a broadside of 54 guns.

Contrary to all expectations, the French infantry held steady under the Prussian cannonade, while their own 34 guns responded. But the guns from both sides were at the limit of their range, and the sodden ground absorbed most of the impact of the cannon balls, so damage was minimal.

Now Kellerman mounted a charge, but a Prussian battery drove his men back, Kellerman himself unhorsed when his mount was shot from under him.

Then it was the invaders' turn, as Brunswick ordered his first assault, but now the French cannon bombarded the Prussians with surprising accuracy. The Prussians moved forward about 100 yards, but the French held their ground even as Prussians approached with fixed bayonets. Then Kellerman rode before his own ranks shouting 'Vive la nation!' – a cry immediately taken up by the whole front line as his soldiers yelled defiance, hats on bayonets. Abandoning hope of French panic, the astonished Brunswick could only pull his men back to save them from the relentless cannon fire.

Later he attempted one more attack, but once again the French line held firm while their artillery continued to harass the invaders. Brunswick now knew that his enemy would not retreat and that further attacks over a mile and a half of open ground would prove suicidal. Around four o'clock he withdrew from the field. Ten days later the allied coalition started to pull back across the border without having fired another shot.

Although tactically indecisive, the Battle of Valmy saved the French Revolution: the invading allies could not now reach Paris or restore King Louis to power. Present that day as an observer was Wolfgang von Goethe, who told his friends: 'From this place, and from this day forth begins a new era in the world's history, and you can all say that you were present at its birth.' How right he was – the day after the battle the French monarchy was abolished and the First Republic proclaimed, and four months later Louis was guillotined.

The Battle of Valmy not only rescued republican France but also changed the nature of European warfare. The new French army was composed largely of dedicated citizens rather than professional officers commanding conscripted peasants. The victors had been driven by patriotism, not the lash, and the astounding success of these citizen soldiers meant that France could now draw on the entire male population for its armies. From now on whole nations, not just armies, would go to war.

Other action this day

1854: In the first major battle of the Crimean War, an Anglo-French force commanded by French marshal Armand-Jacques de Saint-Arnaud and British general Lord Raglan and reinforced by Ottoman troops defeats General Menshikov's Russian army at the Battle of the Alma * 1857: The Indian Mutiny collapses with the fall of Delhi after a siege * 1870: After a three-hour cannonade and a token defence by the Pope's Swiss Guard, Garibaldi's troops enter Rome through the Porta Pia, to complete the reunification of Italy * 1916: The last day of the 108-day Brusilov Offensive in the Ukraine in which the Russians suffer over half a million casualties but defeat a combined German and Austro-Hungarian force, inflicting almost 1,500,000 casualties, including 400,000 taken prisoner

21 September

The Greeks annihilate the Persians at Marathon

490 BC The mighty Persian empire stretched from the edge of India to the Aegean, and King Darius the Great had set his sights on the still independent city-states of Greece.

Two years earlier Darius's first attempt had ended in failure when his fleet was storm-wrecked off Mount Athos, but now he was armed with a secret weapon, what amounted to a fifth column, in the Alcemaeonidae family in Athens who secretly favoured a Persian victory, hoping it would restore their political power. If the Athenian army could be drawn away from the city, perhaps Athens would fall by insurrection rather than costly invasion.

In September of 490 BC Darius landed an army of 15,000 men on the Bay of Marathon, which lies about 26 miles north-east of Athens. Frantic, the Athenians immediately sent a messenger, Pheidippides, to plead for reinforcements from the Spartans. Although Pheidippides covered 150 miles in less than two days, his mission was fruitless, for the Spartans announced that they could not march before the completion of certain religious festivals, still ten days away. The Athenians would have to face the Persians alone.

In mid-September 10,000 Greeks, including the poet Aeschylus, reached Marathon, and there for eight days uncertainly faced the invading Persians; the Athenians fearful of Persian military might, the Persians hoping to hear that, with the Greek army out of Athens, the Alcemaeonidae were overthrowing the government.

On 21 September the Greek commander Miltiades saw that the Persian cavalry had re-embarked, probably to mount a direct attack on Athens. He also learned that Persian reinforcements were on their way. He chose this moment to strike.

The Athenian infantry charged forward and were immediately counter-attacked by the Persian front line. The Greek centre bowed backwards under the assault, as the Persians hurled themselves forward, thinking the Greeks were in retreat. Then Miltiades brought his two reinforced wings around in a double envelopment, smashing into the Persian flanks.

The result was massacre. The Greeks lost only 192 men, but 6,400

Persians died on the Plain of Marathon. What was left of the Persian army fled to their ships and headed for home.

Now that the Persian threat had been stymied, what of the threat of revolt in the city? Knowing that the Alcemaeonidae could not act without Persian military support, the Greeks immediately dispatched a messenger (some say Pheidippides again) to herald the great victory. Without pause for rest or water, he ran the 26 miles between Marathon and Athens, announced the Athenian triumph ('Nike' in Greek, meaning victory) and then fell dead from exhaustion.

Almost two and a half millennia later, the Greeks commemorated this famous run by instituting the first 26-mile 'marathon' race in the 1896 Olympics, held in Athens. Appropriately, it was won in two hours, 58 minutes and 50 seconds by Spyridon Louis, a Greek.

Other action this day

AD 454: Believing his greatest general Aëtius wants to place his son on the throne, Roman emperor Valentinian personally assassinates Aëtius in his throne room, prompting the writer Sidonius Apollionaris to comment: 'I am ignorant, sir, of your motives or provocations; I only know that you have acted like a man who has cut off his right hand with his left' ∗ 1745: The Jacobite army loyal to James Francis Edward Stuart and led by his son Charles Edward Stuart (Bonnie Prince Charlie) defeats the army loyal to George II at the Battle of Prestonpans, the first significant conflict in the Second Jacobite Rising ∗ 1797: In retaliation for Captain Hugh Pigot's brutality, the crew of HMS *Hermione* mutiny, killing Pigot and eight other officers

22 September

The ruse that saved the Western world – the Battle of Salamis

480 BC Persia's mighty king Xerxes had sent his heralds throughout Greece demanding earth and water, symbols of submission, but the Athenian general Themistocles responded with a brutal symbol of his own: he had the messenger put to death for daring to make his barbarian demands in the Greek language. Enraged, Xerxes resolved to conquer those foolish enough to resist him.

Soon Xerxes had assembled a huge army, estimated by Herodotus at 2,641,610 men, but assumed by modern historians to be a more modest 200,000. To cross from Asia Minor into Greece he constructed two boat bridges across the Hellespont, and when waves destroyed them during a storm, he ordered the sea scourged with 300 lashes. He then threw a pair of shackles into the water, grandly pronouncing: 'Ungracious water, your master condemns you to punishment for having injured him without cause. Xerxes the king will pass over you, whether you consent or not!' By then the storm had abated, and his army easily crossed over on a new bridge.

In spite of the defensive league formed by the Greek city-states, the Persians rolled irresistibly forward. In August of 480 they defeated the heroic Spartans at Thermopylae (see 20 August), opening the route to Athens, which the Athenians then abandoned, leaving only a heavily fortified Acropolis. Soon that too had fallen, with all defenders slain.

The assembled Greek generals as ever bickered interminably over tactics. Some wanted to withdraw to Corinth, while Themistocles argued vehemently for a naval engagement to destroy Xerxes's fleet. At length it seemed that the Athenian had won the dispute, but only by threatening to withdraw his ships and men.

But on this day – 22 September – yet another debate erupted, and this time Themistocles took an even greater gamble with one of history's great military ruses. According to Aeschylus, who was present, he sent a slave with a secret message to Xerxes: 'The Athenian commander has sent me to you privily, without the knowledge of the other Greeks. He is a well-wisher to the king's cause, and would rather that success attend you than on his countrymen; wherefore he bids me to tell you that fear has seized the Greeks and they are meditating a hasty flight. Now then it is open to you to achieve the best work that ever ye wrought, if only you will hinder their escaping.' The slave then revealed that the Greek fleet was planning to flee that very night.

Having heard from his own spies about dissension in the Greek camp, Xerxes believed Themistocles's message and sent a squadron of 200 Egyptian ships to block the exit from the straits. The Greeks suddenly had no choice but to stay and fight.

Themistocles's brilliant plan was to lure the Persian fleet into the narrow straits between the port of Piraeus and the island of Salamis, where the enemy would have no room for manoeuvre. Although outnumbering the Greeks more than two to one, on the next day some 1,000 of Xerxes's galleys fell into the Greek trap. According to Herodotus, Themistocles delayed the final action 'until the time when there is regularly a strong breeze from the open sea that brings a high swell into the straits, which presented no difficulty to the low-built Greek ships but was harmful to the slow and cumbersome Persians, with high sterns and decks, as it made them vulnerable to the quick attacks of the Greeks'.

For seven long hours the Greeks harried the Persians. Greek triremes ran up alongside the enemy galleys, shearing off their oars, and then returned to ram or board. When day became evening, some 300 Persian galleys lay shattered on the seabed, against losses of only 40 for the Greeks.

Xerxes had remained on dry land, sitting in his golden throne high upon a promontory to watch his inevitable victory. As more and more of his ships went down, his ally Artemisia, queen of Helicarnassus, rammed and sank an enemy trireme, at which the king lamented: 'My men have become women, my women, men.'

Defeated and fearful of being cut off in Greece, Xerxes scuttled back to Persia, leaving behind an army to achieve on land what he had so conspicuously failed to do by sea. But in August the following year that army was destroyed at the Battle of Plataea.

The Battle of Salamis was much more than the first great naval battle in history. With the victory at Plataea, it ended the Persian threat for a century and a half, until Alexander the Great finally conquered the Persian empire in 331 BC. More than that, it prevented Greece from being crushed by Oriental despotism, leaving it free to develop its systems of democracy and the philosophical ideals that have pervaded Western civilisation ever since. In the words of historian Will Durant: 'It made Europe possible.'

Other action this day

1776: On Manhattan Island, British soldiers hang captured American revolutionary spy Nathan Hale, who dies with the words: 'I only regret that I have but one life to lose for my country.' * 1950: Omar Bradley is promoted to general of the Army, the highest rank in the United States Army * 1965: The UN Security Council unanimously passes a resolution calling for a ceasefire in the Indo-Pakistani War of 1965, which ends the next day

23 September

John Paul Jones has not yet begun to fight

1779 Not all battles of the American Revolution were fought in North America. On this fine late summer evening, at Flamborough Head on the Yorkshire coast of England, 1,500 people gathered at cliffside, drawn by the rumble of cannon from a spectacular naval battle taking place six miles out to sea. There, commanding a 40-gun rebuilt French merchantman renamed the *Bon Homme Richard*, the Scottish-born American John Paul Jones, the best fighting captain in the Continental navy, was taking on the British ship *Serapis*, a 50-gun frigate built for war.

For hours the ships traded murderous broadsides, Jones seeking to close for boarding, *Serapis* manoeuvring away. Outgunned, the *Richard* got the worst of the exchange. At one point the British captain called out: 'Has your ship struck?' To which Jones gave his immortal answer: 'I have not yet begun to fight!' As night fell, however, Jones managed to bring the two vessels together, and then in an extraordinary effort helped his crew swing around a nine-pounder cannon from his unengaged side so it trained on the enemy's main mast.

Finally, with both ships severely damaged and on fire, a sailor on the *Richard* managed to toss a grenade through a hatch into the *Serapis*'s gun deck, where it ignited the powder bags and blew up her main battery in an enormous explosion that brought down the main mast. Shortly afterwards, in the moonlight, the *Serapis* surrendered, three and a half hours after the action had begun.

With the *Bon Homme Richard* sinking, Jones transferred his command to the *Serapis* and, eluding British patrols, sailed her as a prize of war into a neutral Dutch port. When he reached Paris he was a hero, the symbol of French–American victory over the common foe. A grateful Louis XVI made Jones a chevalier of France.

It was a memorable encounter, and not only because of Jones's indomitable reply. Like the battle of Bunker Hill, the victory off Flamborough Head served notice that the American rebels were able to meet the best that Britain could throw at them. In England, the shock of the event, occurring as it did in home waters, called into question British naval invincibility and lent force to the anti-war sentiments of Fox, Pitt and Burke.

Finally, the dramatic outcome of the battle and the style of Jones himself, while soon forgotten in the young American republic that had won its independence, served in time as a source of inspiration for advocates of a strong professional navy, among them President Theodore Roosevelt. In 1906, at the president's direction, Jones's remains were taken from an unmarked grave in Paris and brought to the Naval Academy at Annapolis, where with great public ceremony they were interred near the inscription: 'He gave our navy its earliest tradition of heroism and victory.'

Other action this day

1459: Yorkists defeat the Lancastrians at Blore Heath during the Wars of the Roses * 1642: Prince Rupert's Royalists decisively defeat the Roundheads at the Battle of Powick Bridge in the first major cavalry engagement of the English Civil War * 1803: In the Battle of Assaye, a British and Indian Sepoy army under Major General Arthur Wellesley (later the Duke of Wellington) defeats the Mahratta army, opening the way for the British conquest of central India * 1938: British premier Neville Chamberlain flies to Munich to appease Hitler

24 September

The She-Wolf of France invades England

1326 Today a vengeful queen and her lover landed on the Suffolk coast of England at the head of an army, intent on overthrowing her husband, King Edward II.

Daughter of the formidable Philip (IV) the Fair of France, Queen Isabella had married Edward at the beginning of 1308, but a year later he publicly humiliated her at his coronation by dressing his favourite Piers Gaveston in royal purple, heavy with pearls, and giving him the queen's wedding presents.

Within three years Gaveston was dead, beheaded by some dissatisfied nobles, but the ambidextrous king had soon turned to other young men, while siring four children by Isabella. Meanwhile the country's nobility seethed under Edward's capricious rule and his support of his rapacious new favourite, Hugh the Dispenser the Younger. In 1321 several barons revolted, including a handsome 34-year-old earl named Roger de Mortimer, who was locked in the Tower of London for his troubles. But in August 1323 the resourceful Mortimer drugged one of his guards and escaped to Paris.

Two years later Queen Isabella manoeuvred herself into a diplomatic mission to the court of France, where her brother Charles VI now reigned. Bored, insulted and generally fed up with her ineffectual and ambivalent husband, she was soon enmeshed in a passionate and public affair with Mortimer, whose wife was back in England.

The liaison caused such a scandal that Isabella and Mortimer were forced to move to Flanders, and there they began to plan the invasion of England. The queen set about raising a small army of ambitious nobles and mercenaries from the Lowlands, Germany and Bohemia. She even borrowed a Dutch baron, John of Hainault, to share command of the troops.

On this day the queen's force of only 2,757 landed between Orford and Harwich on the Suffolk coast. When he learned of the invasion, Edward tried to muster his barons and their soldiers, but many refused his summons; the Earl of Lancaster did assemble his troops, but instead of rallying to the king, he marched south to join the queen and her paramour. Now London rose for the invaders, and Edward was forced to flee to Wales, where he fruitlessly searched for support until he was captured at Tonyrefail, north-west of Cardiff, on 16 November.

Isabella and Mortimer now ruled the country as regents for the fourteen-year-old prince Edward (the future Edward III). Some of King Edward's supporters like the Earl of Arundel were summarily beheaded, and Hugh the Dispenser the Elder (father of the king's favourite) was hanged. A worse fate awaited the younger Hugh: convicted a traitor, he was hanged but taken from the gallows while still conscious, castrated and disembowelled, and finally drawn and quartered.

In the meantime, King Edward was clandestinely moved to Berkeley Castle in Gloucestershire. But no matter how securely he was imprisoned, he still represented an intolerable threat to the usurpers of power.

Perhaps hoping Edward would succumb to natural causes, his

jailers locked him in a small, cold room and fed him with scraps, but his constitution was rugged, and he showed no signs of sickness or deterioration. Something had to be done.

During the night of 21 September 1327, three guards entered Edward's cell while he slept and pinned him to the bed with a table. Then one of them thrust a red-hot spit up through his anus, burning out his internal organs. This indescribably agonising method of execution both served as an evil parody of the king's homosexuality and left his body outwardly unmarked, so that it could later be laid out in state for inspection.

Edward's death – publicly explained as due to sudden illness – permitted Queen Isabella to control the state through her son, now Edward III, with her lover Mortimer acting as unofficial co-ruler.

But neither the queen nor Mortimer understood young Edward's hatred for their usurpation or his steely determination as he grew older. When he reached his majority three years later he ordered a traitor's execution for Mortimer: now he would be hanged, drawn and quartered. Meanwhile Edward sent his mother to forced retirement in Norfolk. When she died 28 years later, she was interred at the Church of the Grey Friars in London. The heart of her murdered husband was buried with her, as she had requested, whether from true repentance or deep hypocrisy no one knows. Such was the end of England's worst queen, known to history as 'the She-Wolf of France'.

Other action this day

1583: Imperial general Albrecht von Wallenstein is born in Bohemia * 1667: John Churchill, later the Duke of Marlborough, is gazetted as ensign in Charles II's Foot Guards (now the Grenadier Guards), his first military assignment * 1884: German weapons designer Hugo Schmeisser is born in Jena

25 September

One victory too few for King Harold

1066 At Stamford Bridge today, England's king Harold, leading an outnumbered army, won a crushing victory over Viking invaders. It should have been enough to ensure his reign. Instead, Harold would soon learn that one victory was not enough.

Only nine months earlier, on his deathbed, King Edward the Confessor had left his realm to Harold, the country's most powerful noble – or at least so Harold earnestly insisted. But across the Channel another pretender staked his claim: the powerful Duke of Normandy, Guillaume le Bâtard, William the Bastard.

Learning that William was preparing to invade, Harold gathered his forces near London, only to hear that a more immediate danger came from the north. The legendary Viking warrior-king Harald Hardrada of Norway – called Harald the Ruthless by his fellow Norsemen – had landed at Riccall, near York, with a force numbering some 10,000 men. Supporting him was King Harold's exiled brother Tostig.

To meet the invaders, Harold now led his army of some 5,000 mounted infantrymen out of London, heading north along Watling Street, the old Roman road. Spurring his men on at top speed, he arrived at Tadcaster on Sunday 24 September, having covered an astounding 200 miles in only four days.

The next morning was warm and sunny. Harold led his army to Stamford Bridge, which crosses the River Derwent some eight miles to the east of York. There he caught Harald Hardrada's soldiers completely by surprise, most without their chain mail, as they relaxed by the river. The first the Vikings saw of the approaching force was a huge dust cloud churned up by the horses. One Nordic source relates: 'And the closer the army came, the greater it [the column of dust] grew, and their glittering weapons sparkled like a field of broken ice.'

Harold called out to his brother Tostig, offering him an earldom if he would change sides. Hesitant, Tostig asked what reward would be offered to Harald Hardrada if he pulled back his army. 'He shall have seven feet of good English soil, or a little more perhaps, as he is so much taller than other men,' responded the English king. Rebuffed, Tostig turned back to rejoin the Vikings, who were urgently preparing for battle.

To attack the invaders, Harold first needed to cross the Derwent, but a single armoured Viking desperately defended the bridge, defeating all comers. Finally a resourceful English warrior commandeered a boat and rowed beneath the bridge. There he plunged his spear through a gap in the planks, impaling the frenzied defender.

As the English poured over the bridge, the Vikings formed a triangular shield wall, awaiting the enemy onslaught. Bloody hand-to-hand fighting lasted throughout the day, the English attacking from all sides, raining down spears and arrows. Then, according to a Norse saga, an enraged Harald Hardrada suddenly charged out in front of his men, 'hewing with both hands. Neither helmet nor armour could withstand him, and everyone in his path gave way before him.' But, just when the English line started to waver, an arrow caught him in the throat, and his life bled away on the grass.

Now Tostig rallied the demoralised Norse and reorganised the defence. Reluctant to spill yet more blood, King Harold offered a truce, but the invaders responded that they would 'rather fall, one across the other, than accept quarter from the Englishmen'. Once again the two sides hurled themselves at each other, the invaders reinforced by more Vikings from their ships, but the hammering of English swords and battleaxes forced them back, and Tostig was slain. At the end of the day, the Vikings fled back to their ships at Riccall. Of the 300 ships that had brought the invaders to England, only 24 returned to Norway.

King Harold's victory was monumental; he had so completely defeated the Vikings that they never again attacked England. But within a week he learned that two days after his triumph at Stamford Bridge, William of Normandy had landed near Pevensey in Sussex. Once again, Harold set his troops on a forced march, this time headed south, but on 14 October he was defeated and killed at Hastings, England's last Anglo-Saxon king.

Other action this day

1396: At Nicopolis on the Danube, Sultan Bayezid I leads a joint Turkish/ Serbian force to a decisive victory over a mixed army of French, Hungarians, Venetians and Knights Hospitaller which had attacked the Ottoman empire * 1780: American general and traitor Benedict Arnold flees to the British after spying for them for over a year * 1915: The French launch their first attack on the opening day of the Second Battle of Champagne, which ends 43 days later with 145,000 French casualties to half that for the Germans

26 September

The destruction of Jerusalem and its Temple

AD 70 Today Jerusalem fell to future Roman emperor Titus after a seven-month siege. The price of Jewish resistance was several hundred thousand dead, 100,000 more enslaved and the destruction of the Jews' most sacred building, the Temple.

Iudaea had been a Roman province for 60 years, but the rapacity of Roman governors, added to their insensitivity to Jewish religious traditions, had led to armed revolt. In AD 66, when some Greeks offended the local population by sacrificing birds in front of a synagogue, Jewish Zealots attacked the Roman garrison in Jerusalem, provoking an insurrection that spread across the province.

Emperor Nero dispatched future emperor Vespasian with an army of 60,000 to quell the outbreak. Within two years the uprising in the north had been crushed, its leaders escaping to Jerusalem. By 70 only Jerusalem and a few isolated fortresses like Masada remained defiant (see 15 April), but now within the city itself bloody civil war erupted among Jewish groups competing for authority. The most powerful, the Zealots, insisted that only a Jewish king descended from King David, who had reigned 1,000 years before, could rule Judaea. Even more extreme were the Sicarii, terrorists and assassins (Sicarii means 'dagger-men') who stabbed anyone advocating peace with the Romans. The conflict between these groups and more moderate ones was so vicious that, it is said, Jews had to climb over dead bodies to offer their sacrifices in the Temple.

Despite the turmoil within, Jerusalem remained impervious to Roman attack, protected by three massive stone walls. In 69 Nero had been forced into suicide and Vespasian had returned to Rome to struggle for power, leaving the Jewish war in the hands of his son Titus Flavius.

In March of 70 Titus arrived before Jerusalem with four legions. He ordered a huge trench to be dug completely around the city and then built a new wall on the Roman side of it as high as the city walls it faced. To put pressure on the food supply, he allowed Jews to enter the city to celebrate Passover but refused to let them out. Twice he attempted to negotiate with the Jewish leaders within, but was almost killed by a sudden attack.

Now Titus instituted more draconian measures; anyone caught attempting to leave would be crucified in the trench between the walls. Soon thousands of crucified bodies ringed the city.

In May Titus brought his battering rams to bear on Jerusalem's outer wall. According to an eyewitness description, the Roman battering ram was 'an immense beam, similar to a ship's mast, with one end covered with iron shaped into a ram's head; hence its name. It is suspended from another beam like a balance arm by cables around its middle, and this in turn is supported at both ends by posts fixed in the ground. It is drawn back by a huge number of men who then push it forward in unison with all their might so that it hits the wall with its iron head.'

With the first crash of ram against wall, the 600,000 Jews of Jerusalem knew they were in a fight to the death: Roman law decreed that any defender who continued to resist after the first stroke of the battering ram forfeited all his rights. Both men and women armed themselves, prepared to battle for their lives.

Nine days after the outer wall was breached, the Romans penetrated the second wall, and in mid-summer Titus turned his attention to the third wall and the Antonia Fortress on the north-eastern side of the city. Built by King Herod and named for his patron Mark Antony, the fortress had formidable towers at each corner. After repeated attacks failed, on their own initiative twenty legionaries launched a surprise night assault, killing the Zealot guards in their sleep. Now the Roman soldiers charged towards Temple Mount, where Jerusalem's famous Second Temple stood, a massive structure raised by Herod in 19 BC.

Titus had not intended to destroy the Temple but to transform it into a Roman one dedicated to the emperor; however, a legionary threw a flaming branch onto its walls, starting a raging fire that engulfed it and spread to other parts of the city. Now Roman troops charged in, obliterating any resistance. Some Jews escaped through secret tunnels while others mounted a final stand in the upper city, but by the end of September all resistance had been crushed. Titus then ordered the wholesale destruction of the city.

According to the Jewish historian Josephus, who was there, 'the wall [around the city] was so thoroughly laid even with the ground by those that dug it up to the foundation, that nothing was left to make those that came thither believe it [Jerusalem] had ever been inhabited … And truly, the very view itself was a melancholy thing; for those places which were adorned with trees and pleasant gardens were now become desolate country every way, and its trees were all cut down. Nor could any foreigner who had formerly seen Iudaea and the most beautiful suburbs of the city, and now saw it as a desert, but lament and mourn sadly at so great a change. For the war had laid waste all signs of beauty.'

Titus had succeeded: the revolt had been stamped out, and Jerusalem was once more under Roman control. But he declined a victory wreath for his triumph because, he said, 'there is no merit in conquering people forsaken by their own god'.

Other action this day

1513: In Panama, Spanish conquistador Vasco Núñez de Balboa wades into the Pacific Ocean in full armour to claim it for Spain * 1820: Indian-fighter and frontiersman Daniel Boone dies * 1941: Kiev falls to German armies under Gerd von Rundstedt after a battle of 34 days in which each side suffers 150,000 casualties but the Germans capture 450,000 prisoners * 1943: Six members of Z Force (a joint Australian, British and New Zealand commando unit) clandestinely place limpet mines on Japanese ships in Singapore harbour, sinking or seriously damaging four Japanese ships, amounting to over 39,000 tons

27 September

Three claimants, two invasions, one throne

1066 For weeks Duke William of Normandy had fretted and cursed, waiting impatiently for the weather to change. His 8,000 men were eager to fight and 600 boats lay ready at St Valéry in the mouth of the Somme, but the wind had been blowing from the north, making a Channel crossing both difficult and dangerous. But today, at last, in response to the Normans' well-orchestrated prayers, it had changed direction. William boarded the *Mora*, the fastest of his ships, and led his fleet out of the harbour for a night crossing. The invasion of England was on.

The throne of England had been up for grabs since January, when King Edward the Confessor had died childless. There were three claimants to the throne. The first was Harold Godwinson, the late king's brother-in-law, who swore that Edward had named him on his deathbed. But the English barons had no sooner agreed to support him than King Harald Hardrada of Norway claimed the crown, and in September, to make the point, led an invasion of England via northern England. King Harold's army met and defeated the Norwegians at Stamford Bridge, near York, killing Harald Hardrada (see 25 September).

Unknown to the king and his soldiers, just as they were recovering from their throne-preserving victory, on this autumn Thursday the third claimant, William of Normandy, was leading his army aboard ship.

The following morning the Normans landed at Bulverhythe on the Sussex coast. The chroniclers tell us that as William came ashore he slipped and fell on his face before his collected army, and his soldiers cried out in dismay, seeing his fall as a bad omen. Quickly springing to his feet, William opened his fist to display a handful of earth, claiming it to be a symbol of his claim to the territory. 'What astonishes you?' he asked his men. 'I have taken possession of this land with my hands, and by the glory of God, as far as it extends it is mine – and yours!' (See 4 January for Julius Caesar's use of the same ploy.)

During the next two weeks, while William was moving slowly inland, Harold turned his tired warriors south, gathering fresh troops along the way. By the time he neared the south coast, his army, like William's, numbered perhaps 8,000 men, but the English force was entirely infantry, as they used horses for transport but not in battle. William's trump was to be his 2,000 cavalry.

On the evening of 13 October Harold caught William by surprise near the town of Hastings, but it was already growing late and too dark to fight.

The next morning the two armies faced each other, Harold's soldiers protected by large shields and armed with Danish war axes, William's infantry better armoured and equipped with swords and crossbows. Behind the Norman ranks trotted his cavalry.

According to tradition, William's minstrel and juggler Ivo Taillefer begged him for permission to strike the first blow. Riding out alone from the Norman line, he insouciantly sang while he juggled his sword in the air. In response, an English warrior stormed out on foot, but Taillefer quickly dispatched him, taking his head back to his own lines as proof that God favoured the Normans. He then charged into the enemy ranks and was engulfed.

Now the battle started in earnest. At first, William's assaults made little progress against Harold's wall of shields, and William himself was nearly slain, with three horses killed under him. After repeated failure to break the enemy line he finally resorted to ruse, ordering his men to pretend to panic and escape to the rear. In spite of Harold's efforts to restrain his troops, the English line broke in triumph, eager to pursue what they saw as a defeated enemy.

While the English were streaming towards the apparently retreating Normans in a chaotic charge, William unleashed his cavalry, which ploughed into the disorganised enemy, cutting them down in hundreds.

Harold still held part of his original line, but many of the English were dead or dying. Resolutely he pulled his men behind their wall of shields, but now Norman arrows constantly bombarded them and they could not return fire as the English archers had all been routed. Before the battle could reach a conclusion, a Norman arrow struck Harold in the eye and killed him. Now, although Harold's bodyguard and a few of his housecarls (soldiers attached to the royal household) carried on the fight, most of the English panicked and fled.

William the Bastard had vanquished the English, and in the years ahead he would subjugate the Welsh and Scots, too. Enthroned in Westminster Abbey on Christmas Day 1066, he was known henceforth as William the Conqueror.

Other action this day

1810: Lieutenant General Viscount Wellington defeats Marshal André Masséna at the Battle of Busaco during the Peninsular War * 1864: The Centralia massacre: Confederate guerrilla 'Bloody' Bill Anderson and his henchmen, including a teenage Jesse James, massacre twenty unarmed Union soldiers at Centralia, Missouri * 1941: The USS *Patrick Henry* is launched, the first of more than 2,700 Liberty ships built to carry cargo during the Second World War * 1944: Leading British fighter ace Johnny Johnson scores his 38th and last kill over Nijmegen

28 September

The American Revolution ends with a victory at Yorktown

1781 At dawn today, with its concentration of forces complete, an Allied army began its final advance from Williamsburg, Virginia. By nightfall it had come within a mile of its objective, the British defences at Yorktown, held by General Cornwallis and 8,000 troops. So began a combined American–French land-sea campaign, a model of timing and cooperation that would achieve a momentous victory and bring to an end major military operations in the War of American Independence.

Throughout six years of war in North America, the British had always enjoyed the considerable advantage of command of the sea. But suddenly – and only briefly – the window of naval opportunity opened for the rebels. With his army north of New York City, Washington received word in August this year that the French admiral de Grasse and his fleet in the West Indies would sail north for Chesapeake Bay, where they would be available for operations until mid-October. The presence of a French fleet in this location would cut communications between the British armies in Virginia and New York, leaving the former force especially vulnerable to blockade and attack.

Washington set his army marching southward from New York in forced marches, accompanied by a French army under the command of General Rochambeau. Arriving in Virginia in mid-September, this force was joined by another American army commanded by General Lafayette. Meanwhile, de Grasse's fleet, 30 warships carrying more troops and supplies, arrived off Chesapeake Bay, driving away a smaller British fleet. Now a second French squadron entered the bay, bringing siege artillery from the French base at Newport, Rhode Island.

With 17,000 troops on hand, almost half of them French, Washington began siege operations at Yorktown the very next day, ordering the heavy guns brought forward and his engineers to begin laying out the first parallel siege trench, activities that caused the British to abandon several outposts. On 9 October Allied batteries began a heavy and destructive bombardment of Yorktown. On the

14th two infantry attacks seized vital British redoubts east of the main fortifications.

With no way out by land or sea and with no prospect of timely relief, Cornwallis recognised his situation as hopeless. On 17 October he requested a truce. Two days later, he surrendered his army. News of the defeat in Virginia shocked London. Five months later Parliament authorised King George to make a peace treaty with the Americans.

And so the American rebels, with crucial help from their French allies, beat the mightiest military power in the world. It was an amazing turn of events, at least as amazing as the examples offered in the old tune to which (legend has it) the British and Germans marched out of Yorktown to lay down their arms:

> If ponies rode men, and if grass ate the cows,
> And cats should be chased into holes by the mouse ...
> If summer were spring, and the other way 'round,
> Then all the world would be upside down.

Other action this day

48 BC: Roman general Pompey the Great is assassinated on orders of the Egyptian pharaoh Ptolemy XIII * AD 351: Roman emperor Constantius II crushes the would-be usurper Magnentius at the Battle of Mursa Major * 1538: The Ottoman navy under the command of the admiral and pirate Barbarossa defeats the fleet of the Holy League at the Battle of Preveza, sinking thirteen ships, capturing 36 others and killing 3,000 * 1941: Russia's Marshal Zhukov sends a ciphered telegram to the commanders on the Leningrad front and the Baltic navy declaring that families of soldiers captured by the Germans would be shot

29 September

Darius the Great is chosen King by his horse

522 BC Ever since Cyrus the Great had completed his conquests, the Persian Achaemenian empire had been the greatest the world had known, encompassing the Near East from the Aegean to the Indus River. When Cyrus died, his son Cambyses claimed the throne, but now Cambyses had succumbed to the horrors of gangrene after having stabbed himself in the thigh with his own sword while mounting his horse in Syria. This left the empire to his ambitious brother Bardiya, who many believed had stage-managed Cambyses's death.

Not everyone welcomed Bardiya as the new king, especially a group of seven of Cambyses's officers, headed by a distant cousin named Darius, who was only 28 but carried the high title of Cambyses's 'lance-bearer', as befitting a member of the Achaemenian clan. Now this cabal resolved to do away with Bardiya and replace him on the throne.

To escape the heat of the summer, Bardiya had retreated to Ecbatana, the Achaemenian kings' summer residence (now Hamadān in Iran). But the conspirators knew he must soon leave the safety of the city to return to the Persian capital of Susa, and they waited for news of his departure.

By the end of September, Bardiya was headed home but he stopped en route at the stronghold of Sikayauvatiš, near Nisaea. On the evening of this day, the seven plotters also arrived at the fortress, and, by virtue of their high rank, easily talked their way past the guards. Then, drawing their daggers, they surged into Bardiya's bedroom, where he was diverting himself with one of his concubines. Caught unawares, Bardiya desperately grabbed a broken footstool to ward off the assailants, but Darius's brother Artaphernes drove his blade home.

So yet another Persian ruler was dead, but apparently the regicides had not determined who would take his place. They settled on a novel way of selecting the new king.

The assassins mounted their horses and rode out onto the plain beyond the fortress, there to await a sign from Ahura Mazdā, the great god who ruled the world. They agreed that when the sun rose, whoever's horse neighed first should be king; when dawn broke, Darius's horse shook its head and whinnied.

As a signal from Ahura Mazdā, it was beyond dispute – Darius had been chosen. But afterwards a rumour began to circulate: that during the night, Darius's groom Oebares had rubbed the genitals of a tethered mare with his hand, and when the sun rose he had held his fingers beneath the nose of Darius's stallion, causing it to neigh. The almost contemporary Greek historian Herodotus tells us that the first thing Darius did after winning the throne was to order built a monument of himself on horseback with the inscription: 'Darius, son of Hystapes, by virtue of his horse and of his groom Oebares, won the throne of Persia.'

Now Darius was king, thanks to his co-conspirators, who had probably stage-managed the selection in order to give it the imprimatur of the god. For good measure, Darius now revealed that the cabal had not killed a king after all but only an impostor. The murdered man, he informed his subjects, was not Bardiya but a sorcerer named Gaumâta, who had impersonated Bardiya after the real Bardiya had been secretly put to death by Cambyses. As Darius ordered graven on a rock face: 'By the grace of Ahura Mazdā I became king; Ahura Mazdā granted me the kingdom.' All in all, as good a piece of political flummery as ever has been disseminated to a credulous public.

Although the beginning of Darius's reign was troubled by internal revolt, he soon stamped out all resistance, fighting nineteen battles against rebels in his first year in power. He conquered Babylon, then Sindh in India and the Punjab while expanding the Persian empire to its greatest extent. He built the great city of Persepolis and even a 52-mile canal connecting the Red Sea with the Nile. One of his few failures came in 490 BC, when he tried to invade Greece but was famously defeated at the Battle of Marathon.

Darius the Great died in his bed in 486 BC at the age of 64, king of kings for 37 years, thanks to the great god Ahura Mazdā – and his horse.

Other action this day

106 BC: Roman general Pompey the Great is born ∗ 1364: The Bretons and their English allies decisively defeat the French in the Battle of Auray, as Bertrand du Guesclin is captured, ending the Breton War of Succession (part of the Hundred Years War) ∗ 1758: British admiral Horatio Nelson is born ∗ 1941: Near Kiev, German Einsatzgruppe C starts the two-day Babi Yar massacre, resulting in the killing of almost 34,000 Jews

30 September

The Wehrmacht suffers its first defeat

1941 Moscow, Hitler's generals insisted, was the key. It was not only the capital of the highly centralised Russian government but also a major industrial centre and railway hub. Furthermore, if Moscow came under attack, Stalin would be forced to concentrate huge numbers of troops there, who could then be annihilated. But Hitler had a different aim. Not only did he wish to destroy Leningrad and Stalingrad as symbols of communism, but he also wanted his southern armies to advance on Kiev and into the Ukraine, where early on they could cripple both the enemy's industrial capacity and his production of food. It was not until victory at Smolensk in early August of this year that he allowed his generals to begin planning for a decisive assault on the Soviet capital. The delay, however, gave the Russians time to bolster their defences.

So it was that today – at last – the German central army group began its drive on Moscow, as some 750,000 men under Field Marshal Fedor von Bock launched two giant pincer movements from the south-west against perhaps a million Soviet defenders under Marshal Timoshenko. In just ten days they encircled six Russian armies, taking over half a million prisoners and more than 1,000 tanks. Moscow was surely doomed.

Then, however, on 8 October, the sunny weather vanished, as heavy rain turned roads into impassable quagmires on which even tanks were immobilised. The Germans were still over 100 miles from Moscow. Slowly they pushed forward, and two days later they reached the Mozhaysk line, the well-prepared defences the Russians had been given time to build. The same day Stalin relieved Timoshenko of his command and replaced him with Georgy Zhukov. NKVD (Russian secret police) gunmen were stationed behind the lines with orders to shoot any recalcitrant soldiers. Meanwhile, 250,000 women and teenagers had been drafted to dig anti-tank trenches around the city. On 13 October Stalin ordered the evacuation of most of the government and the Communist Party, although he remained in the capital.

For a month the German assault made only modest headway, mostly due to the impassable roads. Then, in November, Russian winter arrived, and the roads froze over. In Moscow, Stalin reviewed the traditional military parade in Red Square to fortify morale, but now German Panzers once again lumbered forward. By the 15th they had broken through the Mozhaysk line, and two weeks later some German troops were only twelve miles from the city.

But now the cold that had frozen the roads also began to freeze German soldiers, who had no winter clothing, thanks to Hitler's conviction that he could blitzkrieg his way through Russia as quickly as he had through Poland. German tanks and armoured cars also froze to a halt in temperatures of −30°C. On 5 December the Führer at last relented and allowed his army to take up defensive positions, but refused to let them withdraw. The same day the Russians unleashed a massive counter-attack at Kalinin north-west of the capital. Stalin also began to bring in an additional 100,000 soldiers and 300 tanks and pushed the Germans back to over 60 miles from Moscow. Although the Soviet counter-offensive ran out of steam in early January, by now the Russians had rebuilt their defences before the city. The Wehrmacht had suffered its first defeat of the war, and Moscow had been saved.

The Soviet victory owed more to the weather – first the rains and then the bitter cold – than to Russian military prowess, demonstrating Hitler's folly in delaying his attack while dreaming of the destruction of Stalingrad and Leningrad. In the end, of course, he conquered neither of those cities, suffering heavy defeats at both in January 1943.

Other action this day

1862: Chancellor Otto von Bismarck addresses the Prussian parliament: 'The great questions of the time are solved not by speech-making and the resolutions of majorities, but by blood and iron.' ∗ 1938: The League of Nations unanimously outlaws 'intentional bombings of civilian populations', a law violated by the British, Germans and Americans during the Second World War (although Germany had withdrawn from the League prior to the war, and the US had never joined) ∗ 1938: Returning from a meeting with Hitler, British prime minister Neville Chamberlain announces, 'I believe it is peace in our time'

1 October

Alexander the Great overwhelms the Persians at Gaugamela

331 BC Today the man who was perhaps history's greatest general destroyed the Persian empire in his greatest victory at Gaugamela, in what is now northern Iraq.

Alexander the Great had been taught by his father Philip II of Macedon and his tutor Aristotle to hate the Persians, who had been invading and harrying Greece since the time of Xerxes a century and a half before. But Alexander had also developed revolutionary ideas of his own. He was a fervent believer in the superiority of Greek civilisation and thought he had a mission to spread it to the barbarian world.

When Alexander succeeded to the Macedonian throne on his father's assassination, he inherited a kingdom, a superb army and a fledgling plan to invade the great Persian empire that ruled from Anatolia to the plains of India. In the spring of 334 BC he crossed the Dardanelles with an army of about 50,000 men, including some 7,000 cavalry, determined to conquer. 'Heaven cannot support two suns, nor the earth two masters,' he portentously announced.

Within three years Alexander had defeated many of the Persian emperor Darius III's satraps (governors of his provinces), and Darius attempted to buy him off, promising to cede substantial territory and pay 10,000 talents in gold if Alexander would return to Greece.

When told of the offer, Alexander's most senior general Parminio advised, 'I would accept it were I Alexander', to which the haughty Alexander replied, 'And so truly would I, if I were Parminio.'

Forced at last to fight, Darius now massed near the town of Arbela a vast army of perhaps 200,000 that included vicious scythe-chariots and at least fifteen elephants.

Darius picked his ground carefully. Nearby lay the Plain of Gaugamela, perfect terrain for cavalry and chariots. To ensure his victory, the emperor ordered trees felled and the ground roughly flattened in order to give his superior force a better chance of surrounding the invading Greeks.

When Alexander arrived on the high ground before Gaugamela his generals urged immediate action, but instead he ordered his troops to rest for the night while giving the impression that attack was imminent, thus fooling Darius into keeping his men up all night awaiting the assault. By the next morning the Persians were already exhausted when they went into battle.

Once the battle began, the Persian cavalrymen moved forward to charge, leaving a gap in their line into which Alexander led his own horsemen and drove them directly at Darius. When the emperor fled, Alexander wheeled to attack the enemy's flank, starting the general disintegration of the Persian army.

There are various estimates of battle casualties, none reliable, but what is certain is that the Persians suffered grievous losses, perhaps 40,000 killed, while only a few hundred of Alexander's Greeks died on the field.

Following the battle Alexander pursued Darius, but before he could catch up with him the emperor was murdered by one of his own generals. Alexander's victory at Gaugamela gave him control of what to that time was the greatest empire the world had known, but perhaps an even more important result was the spread of Greek values and Alexander's own concept, unique in his era, that the good men of the world, Greek or barbarian, should unite to rule the world for the benefit of mankind.

Other action this day

1578: Don Juan of Austria, victor at the Battle of Lepanto, dies of typhus * 1756: Frederick the Great with an army of 29,000 defeats 34,000 Austrians at the Battle of Lobositz, the first battle of the Seven Years' War * 1860: Garibaldi defeats the Kingdom of the Two Sicilies in the Battle of Volturno during the Risorgimento * 1918: Arab forces led by Lawrence of Arabia capture Damascus

2 October

Saladin reconquers Jerusalem

1187 Today the holy city of Jerusalem fell to the forces of Islam after less than a century of Christian rule.

When European Christians had first captured the city from the infidel during the First Crusade, they had established there a kingdom, but by the close of the 12th century the royal house was in steep decline. When King Baldwin IV died of leprosy, the throne should have passed to his young nephew, but Baldwin's sister Sibylla had other ideas. With her husband Guy de Lusignan she seized the crown for herself and had Guy declared king.

But Guy had neither the intelligence nor the ruthlessness of former Christian rulers, and their Saracen adversary was the formidable and experienced sultan Saladin, who had already been commander-in-chief of the Saracen army for sixteen years.

Born in Mesopotamia (modern Iraq), Saladin was a devout Muslim, totally committed to the idea of jihad against the Christians and the recapture of Jerusalem. In July 1187 he completely routed the Crusader army at Hattin (see 4 July) and then marched on the holy city. After only a short siege, it fell to the Muslim host. To the delighted astonishment of the conquered Christians, Saladin and his men treated them with kindness and courtesy rather than the indiscriminate slaughter that had followed the Crusaders' capture of the city (see 15 July).

Nonetheless, for Christians in Jerusalem and all over Europe, the fall of the holy city was considered a major catastrophe. To the Saracens, however, the date itself must have confirmed their belief in the divine righteousness of their cause, for it was also on 2 October over half a millennium before that the Prophet Mohammed had ascended to heaven from that self-same place, Jerusalem.

Jerusalem had been Christian for exactly 88 years, two months and seventeen days.

Other action this day

1780: British major John André, the go-between for American traitor Benedict Arnold, is hanged as a spy, refusing the blindfold and placing the noose around his own neck * 1851: French general Ferdinand Foch is born at Tarbes, France * 1944: German troops crush the Home Army forces of the Warsaw District who two months previously had launched the Warsaw Uprising

3 October

The battles of Philippi and the deaths of Brutus and Cassius

42 BC Ever since Caesar had crossed the Rubicon with a legion behind him in 49 BC (see 10 January), the Roman nobility had suspected he was intent on making himself king. When he defeated the official government forces of Pompey (see 9 August) and two years later made himself dictator-for-life, they had plotted his murder, determined to restore the republican government – which would have equally restored the power of the nobles themselves. But instead of bringing back the republic, the assassination triggered civil war.

On this day, just twenty months later, the armies of Caesar's principal murderers – Marcus Junius Brutus and Gaius Cassius Longinus – met those of his avengers, his adopted son Octavian (the future emperor Augustus) and his one-time general Mark Antony, at Philippi on the Macedonian coast of Greece. It was the first of two battles that would forever change the Roman empire from a mildly democratic oligarchy to fully-fledged dictatorship.

In the months leading up to the battles there were omens aplenty. According to 2nd-century historian Cassius Dio, in Rome 'meteors darted here and there; blaring of trumpets, clashing of arms and shouts of armies were heard at night from the gardens both of [Octavian] and of Antony [...] A child was born with ten fingers on each hand, a statue of Jupiter sent forth blood from its right shoulder; there were also rivers that began to flow backward [...] But [in Greece] the thing which most of all portended the destruction that was to come upon [Brutus and Cassius] [...] was that many vultures and also many other birds that devour corpses gathered above the conspirators' heads and gazed down on them, screaming and screeching in a ghastly and frightful manner.'

On the day of the first battle the two armies faced each other across the Philippi plain. 'Then one trumpeter on each side sounded the first challenge, after which all the trumpeters joined in [...] to rouse the spirit of the soldiers. Then there was suddenly a great silence and after waiting a little the leaders uttered a piercing shout and [...] the heavy-armed troops gave the war cry, beat their shields with their spears and then hurled their spears, while the slingers and the archers flung their stones and missiles. Then the two bodies of cavalry charged out against each other.'

Brutus's army soon had the better of Octavian's, killing many and burning the enemy camp, but, after a standoff, Mark Antony suddenly ordered his men to storm Cassius's camp. Unaware of Brutus's triumph and believing all was lost, Cassius withdrew to his tent with his freedman Pindarus. Drawing his robes up over his face and laying bare his neck, he ordered Pindarus to kill him. After the battle his head was found severed from his body.

The armies separated, each one part-victorious, part-defeated. For twenty days the generals eyed each other nervously, until on the afternoon of 23 October Brutus lined up his forces, once again preparing for battle. But in reviewing his troops he noticed their hesitation, especially that of his cavalry, which seemed to be waiting for the infantry to attack. Then, suddenly, one of his bravest soldiers dashed from his lines to desert to the enemy. Fearful that more would follow, Brutus ordered an instant assault.

This time Octavian's and Mark Antony's forces quickly over-whelmed Brutus's uncertain troops. Retreating from the field, Brutus grasped his sword with both hands and fell upon it, killing himself instantly. When Mark Antony found Brutus lying dead, he ordered him clothed in the best of his own robes, intent on honouring his dead opponent with a ritual cremation, but the unforgiving Octavian insisted that Brutus's head be sent to Rome for display in the Forum.

Brutus's corpse was decapitated and the head pickled in brine to be shipped to Rome. During the voyage, however, a hurricane threatened to wreck the ship and the crew, convinced that the severed head displeased the gods, threw it overboard. Back in Rome Brutus's wife Porcia killed herself by swallowing burning coals.

The Roman Republic was now dead forever and eleven years later Octavian destroyed Mark Antony's forces at Actium, to become Rome's first emperor and sole ruler of the Roman world.

Other action this day

1605: Li Tzu-ch'eng, Chinese revolutionary who dethroned the last Ming emperor, is born * 1935: Forces under General Emilio De Bono's command cross into Ethiopia from Eritrea, starting the Second Italo-Ethiopian War that ends with Italian annexation of Ethiopia * 1942: The

V-2 rocket is successfully launched for the first time from Test Stand VII at Peenemünde, Germany

4 October

The Crimean War begins

1853 Rarely since the Thirty Years War in the 17th century have nations so bloodied each other in the cause of religion. Today the Ottoman empire declared war on Russia to begin a conflict that would become the Crimean War.

In 1851 France's new president Napoleon III had browbeaten the Turks into giving France authority over Christian churches and holy places in Palestine – including Russian Orthodox ones. Russia's tsar Nicholas I of course objected, and soon Russian diplomats were in Constantinople doing the browbeating, claiming the right to manage the Orthodox Church's hierarchy in the Ottoman empire as well as to interfere whenever they felt the sultan's Christian subjects were at risk.

Now the British got into the act, persuading the Turks to resist these demands on the grounds that they were demeaning to the sovereignty of Turkey. Rebuffed, in May of 1853 Nicholas marched into the Danubian principalities of Moldavia and Wallachia (now in Romania) that, because of their large Christian populations, were under joint Russian and Turkish 'protection'. The tsar figured, incorrectly as it turned out, that the European great powers wouldn't mind Russian annexation of a little Ottoman territory.

But France, Austria and Great Britain protested loudly, and by September crowds were rioting in Constantinople against the Russian incursion. The tension was palpable, as two corrupt and dying empires, Ottoman Turk and Romanov Russian, eyed each other for the main chance. Knowing that they had the principal European powers behind them, the Turks enthusiastically declared war.

By March of the following year, after Russian forces crossed the Danube into what is now Bulgaria, France and Britain had thrown their lot in with the Turks, and eventually even the kingdom of Sardinia would send a regiment. To counter Russia's naval strength in the Black Sea, the allies concluded that their goal should include the destruction of the great naval base at Sebastopol, on the Crimean peninsula. An initial force of 51,000 soldiers – French, British and Turkish – began landings on 9 September.

Sebastopol finally fell after twelve months of slaughter – about 25,000 losses on each side, plus 80,000 civilian casualties – but the war dragged on in appalling conditions until February 1856, men dying of war wounds, of cold and most of all from diseases that ravaged all sides. (Of 23,400 British dead, only 3,400 were killed in battle.) The Crimean War witnessed some legendary if futile heroics such as the ill-fated Charge of the Light Brigade (see 25 October), and courageous British soldiers were awarded 111 Victoria Crosses. For ministering to the wounded during the conflict, Florence Nightingale became a British heroine.

Before the war began, Nicholas had contemptuously called Turkey 'the sick man of Europe', but it was the tsar who was toppled by disease, dying on 2 March 1855, some eleven months before the war's end. Some historians maintain that he committed suicide in despair over Russia's mounting losses, but it seems more likely that he succumbed to pneumonia, his exhausted body too weak to resist.

In 1856, Nicholas's successor Alexander II initiated peace negotiations, Russia conceded a few trifling border changes and fighting ground to a halt. But by then some 250,000 men on each side had died in one of the most purposeless wars in history.

Perhaps the sole beneficial result of the Crimean War was the enrichment of the English language regarding apparel. From it came the balaclava helmet, invented to combat the murderous cold and named after the town of Balaclava, where the famous battle was fought; the raglan sleeve, originally designed to be worn by the one-armed British commander, Field Marshal Baron Raglan; and the cardigan sweater, named for its inventor, British general Sir James Cardigan.

Other action this day

AD 610: When Heraclius reaches the Byzantine capital at Constantinople, the elite imperial guard deserts the usurper emperor Phocas, and Heraclius takes over the city and executes Phocas with his own hands; Heraclius declares himself emperor the next day ∗ 1777: British troops under Sir William Howe repel American attacks under George Washington at the

Battle of Germantown * 1943: US troops capture the Japanese-held
Solomon Islands

5 October

Napoleon gives the rabble a whiff of grape

1795 Today was 13 Vendémiaire, An IV, according to the French
republican calendar. Both Louis XVI and Robespierre had already
been fed to the guillotine, but hard-eyed monarchists and fanatical
revolutionaries still roamed the streets of Paris. Now royalist agita-
tors, bizarrely backed by their former enemies on the hard left, were
marching at the head of a mob of 30,000 armed and excited
protesters. Their goal: the Tuileries, where the Convention (the
republican government) was meeting. The government must fall, no
matter who was there to pick up the pieces.

In charge of security for the Convention was vicomte Paul Barras,
a brawny provincial nobleman who had helped bring about the
executions of both Louis XVI and Robespierre. As commander of
the Army of the Interior and the police, he was one of the most
powerful men in the country. He had recently begun a new affair
with a tempting 32-year-old widow from Martinique named
Joséphine de Beauharnais.

Realising that only military force could quell the mob, Barras
called on a young unemployed brigadier general named Napoleon
Bonaparte and put him in charge of the Convention's defences.
Bonaparte instantly recognised the need for artillery and ordered
Major Joachim Murat, whom he now met for the first time, to
commandeer 40 cannon and place them at key points around the
Tuileries.

In mid-afternoon the excited rabble approached. Bonaparte held
fire until the crowd reached point-blank range then is traditionally
supposed to have said, 'We'll give them a whiff of grape.' The cannon
spat out murderous grapeshot, instantly cutting down over 200 and
wounding twice as many more. The mob fled in panic, and the
government was saved.

In an uncanny way, the lives of many of the principal players from
13 Vendémiaire would be intertwined in the years to come. A year

later Bonaparte married Joséphine de Beauharnais, whom he had met at Barras's house. Barras went on to even greater power in the government but was precipitously driven from office and eventually exiled from France by Bonaparte, the general he had drafted. Murat became one of Bonaparte's most successful marshals, ultimately becoming the king of Naples. And of course in his coup d'état of November 1799 Bonaparte also destroyed the republican government that he had so well protected.

Other action this day

1805: British general Charles Cornwallis, who lost the last battle of the American Revolution at Yorktown, dies of fever in India * 1813: Brigadier General (and future president) William Henry Harrison wins the Battle of the Thames north of Lake Erie against a combined British and Indian force, killing the Indian chief Tecumseh * 1877: In the Bear Paw Mountains of the Montana Territory, Chief Joseph of the Nez Perce Indians surrenders to the American army after a devastating five-day battle in freezing weather conditions with no food or blankets * 1918: French fighter pilot Roland Garros is shot down and killed near Vouziers in the Ardennes the day before his 30th birthday; the French Open Tennis tournament is named in his honour

6 October

The Yom Kippur War

1973 War began on two fronts today, as the armies of Egypt and Syria launched simultaneous offensives against Israel. The Yom Kippur War – just nineteen days from first attack to effective cease-fire – would be primarily a tank war and involve armoured concentrations of a size not seen since Kursk and the Normandy breakout in the Second World War.

With their preparations cloaked by remarkable deception, the Arab forces achieved virtually complete surprise, catching the Israel Defense Forces off-guard and outnumbered, many of its active-duty troops at home on the holiest day of the Hebrew year, its reserves – the bulk of its strength – unmobilised.

Israel had a single division on each front. In the north, five Syrian infantry and armoured divisions, with over a thousand tanks, crossed into the Golan Heights. In the south, wave after wave of Egyptian infantry rowed across the Suez Canal to attack the forts of the Bar-Lev Line, Israel's defensive position on the east bank. By nightfall, ten Egyptian brigades – 32,000 troops – had crossed to the Sinai shore; behind them the canal was bridged in a dozen places for the massive flow of troops and armoured vehicles that would follow.

The war's opening moves looked disastrous for Israel, whose military – the Israel Defense Forces – had successfully contended with Arab forces in three previous wars. The IDF had never envisioned that Egypt and Syria were capable of mounting such large-scale attacks without their plans being detected well in advance by Israeli intelligence. Faced with what looked like impending disaster delivered by foes well equipped with Soviet weapons – tanks, planes and SAM (surface to air missiles) and anti-tank missiles – Israel called up its reserves and sent its air force to counter the armoured penetrations.

In the days that followed, the IDF suffered heavy tank and aeroplane losses but in time managed to blunt both advances with a combination of hard fighting, air power and Arab mistakes, then launched counter-attacks. By the 18th it had pushed the Syrian army clean out of the Golan and broken into Syrian territory, coming within twenty miles of Damascus, where Iraqi and Jordanian forces joined the Syrian army to save it from rout.

On the Sinai front, the Egyptian forces, reluctant to risk Israeli air attack by moving beyond their missile umbrella, lost the initial momentum of the crossing. After several days of heavy fighting, the IDF found an unguarded spot in the Egyptian line and on the 16th sent two divisions across the canal to achieve a bridgehead on the western side. Then, driving southward, this force soon outflanked the east-facing Egyptian Third Army, sealing it off from Cairo, just 50 miles away.

In the meantime, attempts to arrange a ceasefire occupied the energies of both the US and the USSR on behalf of their respective client states. Henry Kissinger, President Ford's National Security Advisor, embarked on an extraordinary round of shuttle diplomacy between Washington, Moscow, Cairo and Tel Aviv, which led to the UN Security Council's Resolution 338, calling for an end to the fighting.

A ceasefire agreement finally took effect on the 25th, by which time Israeli forces had seized the Cairo-Suez road, a key Egyptian supply route. The terms of the ceasefire called for Israel to withdraw from the canal and for Egypt to open it to international traffic.

Militarily, Israel had prevailed once again over Arab forces, although at an unexpected cost in troops and equipment. And even though they were defeated, never before had Arab armies acquitted themselves so well in the field. Thirty-five years after the event, Thomas Friedman, writing in the *New York Times*, observed that the Yom Kippur War 'was as psychologically important as it was militarily important. It wiped away Egypt's humiliating loss in the 1967 war and gave Egyptians the dignity and self-confidence to make peace with Israel as military equals.'

Other action this day

68 BC: Roman general and consul Lucius Lucullus defeats King Tigranes II of Armenia at the Battle of Artaxata * AD 105: At Arausio (now Orange in Provence) the German Cimbri and Teutoni tribes rout the Roman general Caepio and then destroy his colleague Mallius's army, killing '80,000'

7 October

Christian Europe defeats the Turks at Lepanto

1571 It is fitting that this day was a Sunday, the Lord's day, when the Christian forces of Spain, Venice and the papacy combined to destroy the Turkish fleet at the Battle of Lepanto, ending for a century the danger of Islamic conquest of Europe.

The two fleets met at dawn off the west coast of Greece. The huge European armada with 316 vessels outnumbered the Turks, who had only 245 ships. But in the 16th century naval battles were won primarily using heavily manned rowing galleys carrying soldiers who fired on enemy ships and then boarded them, and the Turks had a critical advantage in number of galleys.

In command of the Christian flotilla was Don Juan of Austria, the dashing illegitimate son of retired Holy Roman Emperor Charles V and thus half-brother to Spain's king Philip II. Although only 24, he had already proved himself against Barbary pirates. As the fleets approached each other he ordered the attack. His captains urged caution, to which Don Juan replied, 'Gentlemen, it is no longer the hour for advising, but for fighting.'

The battle lasted four hours and was decided not by the galleys and soldiers but by the Christians' sailing ships – galleons, frigates and galleasses heavily armed with cannon. The Europeans' superior firepower proved decisive, slaughtering enemy troops and sinking their galleys before they could bring their soldiers into play. When his galley was overrun, the Turkish commander dropped to his knees, offering a huge ransom in return for his life. Disdainfully a Spanish soldier lopped off his head as he knelt, then displayed it on the end of his pike.

This was the first engagement in naval history where sailing ships supplanted galleys as the primary weapon. When the battle ended, over 8,000 Christians had perished, but almost 30,000 Turks had been cut down or drowned. In addition, about 15,000 Christian galley slaves had been set free from the Turkish vessels.

The Battle of Lepanto marked the end of Turkish domination of the seas and destroyed the myth of Turkish invincibility that had been created earlier in the century during the reign of Suleiman the Magnificent. It was also a decisive experience for a 24-year-old Spanish soldier, wounded in the left hand by a Turkish bullet. He abandoned his military career, perhaps believing that a pen in his good right hand would prove mightier than the sword. His name was Miguel de Cervantes.

Other action this day

1777: The Americans defeat the British at the Second Battle of Saratoga * 1870: With Paris surrounded by the German army at the end of the Franco-Prussian War, French interior minister Léon Gambetta escapes from the city, soaring over the heads of the encircling enemy by balloon to rally his compatriots * 1944: Jewish *Sonderkommandos* (inmates working in the gas chambers) attack SS guards at the Birkenau concentration camp with axes, hammers, stones and homemade grenades and blow up two of the four crematoria; hundreds escape, only to be recaptured and executed

8 October

Backwoods hero – Corporal Alvin York

1918 Of all the American heroics of the First World War, none is more celebrated than those of Corporal Alvin York, a backwoodsman from the Tennessee mountains who single-handedly put 35 German machine guns out of action, killed over twenty machine gunners and captured 132 enemy soldiers in a single morning.

York's platoon was part of a 328th Infantry Battalion attack against heavily fortified enemy positions in the Argonne forest. At dawn on 8 October the assault began, but the Americans were almost immediately riddled with machine gun fire, pinned down and seemingly helpless. German machine guns continuously raked their position, and American casualties were heavy. In desperation, seventeen men including York's squad determined to work around behind the enemy through a concealed gully.

Miraculously they succeeded in getting behind the Germans, only to have the enemy machine gunners turn around to face them, immediately killing six of them.

By now York was the most senior man left. Here is his own account of what happened next: 'As soon as the machine guns opened fire on me, I began to exchange shots with them. There were over thirty of them in continuous action, and all I could do was touch the Germans off as fast as I could. I was sharpshooting. I don't think I missed a shot ... In order to sight me or to swing their guns on me, the Germans had to show their heads above the trench, and every time I saw a head I just touched it off ... Suddenly a German officer and five men jumped out of the trench and charged me with fixed bayonets. I changed to the old automatic and just touched them off too. I touched off the sixth man first, then the fifth, then the fourth, then the third, and so on. I wanted them to keep coming. I didn't want the rear ones to see me touching off the front ones, I was afraid they would drop down and pump a volley into me.'

Terrorised and bewildered by this American killing machine, the remainder of the Germans surrendered to York, who marched them to the rear holding a pistol to the senior German officer's head.

For his spectacular heroism York was promoted to sergeant and received the Medal of Honor directly from General Pershing, the commander of all American forces in Europe.

Other action this day

AD 314: Emperor Constantine I ('the Great') defeats his co-ruler Licinius at the Battle of Cibalae (in modern Croatia) and takes over Licinius's European territories ∗ 1856: After Chinese officials board the Chinese-owned ship the *Arrow* and arrest twelve Chinese suspected of piracy and smuggling, the British claim (falsely) that the ship is British and use the incident as a pretext to launch the Second Opium War ∗ 1862: Although the Confederate Army of Mississippi wins a tactical victory over the Union Army of Ohio at the Battle of Perryville in Kentucky, it is a strategic success for the North, as the Confederates are forced to withdraw to Tennessee, leaving Kentucky under Union control

9 October

The Lionheart heads for home

1192 On this day King Richard the Lionheart sailed for home from Acre on the Palestinian coast, after sixteen months of bloody but profitless fighting during the Third Crusade.

In the beginning the Crusade had been full of promise. Pope Gregory VIII had called for action, offering absolution to the warriors of Christianity who would fight for the reconquest of Jerusalem, fallen to the Saracens of Saladin at the end of 1187 (see 2 October). Europe's most powerful monarchs agreed to join forces and preparations were soon under way. From France came the scheming but intelligent Philip Augustus, from Germany the emperor Frederick Barbarossa, now almost 70, from England the redoubtable Richard the Lionheart and from Sicily Richard's brother-in-law, King William the Good. A massive force was gathered to crush the Saracens and return the Holy Land to the control of Christians.

But all had not gone according to plan. William of Sicily, still only 35, died even before setting off, and Barbarossa was tragically drowned crossing a river in Turkey. Richard and Philip succeeded in conquering Acre, but the victory was sullied by Richard's brutal slaughter of several thousand Saracen prisoners, men, women and children.

After Acre, on the excuse of illness, Philip returned to France to plot with Richard's brother John in dismembering Richard's French possessions. Richard continued southward towards Jaffa and finally met Saladin in battle at Arsuf in 1191, where his heavy cavalry drove Saladin's lighter horse into panicky retreat. Then the English king took Daron and led his army to within twelve miles of Jerusalem.

But there Richard had to stop. His force was so depleted that he had little chance of taking the city and even if he had succeeded, he could not have garrisoned it sufficiently to keep it.

Reluctantly, Richard turned back for Acre. On 2 September 1192 he and Saladin finally agreed a five-year peace treaty that gave Christian pilgrims free access to Jerusalem. But the only territory now in Christian hands was a thin strip of coastline 100 miles long, from Acre to Jaffa. Saladin controlled everything else.

So, a month after peace had been agreed, Richard boarded ship. The Third Crusade was over, with little achieved and much lost. Richard found only further disaster on his route home, captured and held for ransom in Austria (see 21 December).

Other action this day
1812: American forces capture two British ships, HMS *Detroit* and HMS *Caledonia*, on Lake Erie during the War of 1812 * 1864: At the Battle of Tom's Brook, Union general Philip Sheridan defeats the Confederates so quickly that it is called 'The Woodstock Races' * 1940: During a night-time air raid, German bombers hit St Paul's cathedral

10 October

Charles the Hammer earns his name

AD 732 Charles Martel – Charles the Hammer – earned his nickname today at the Battle of Tours.

In the 8th century the most aggressive and successful military power in the world was militant Islam, intent on endless conquest for the glory of Allah. In 711 the Moors crossed from North Africa into Spain to begin an occupation of almost eight centuries. Their kingdom of al-Andalus covered all of modern Portugal and Spain except Leon, Castile and Pamplona on the northern rim. Twenty years after its initial invasion, the Umayyad Caliphate, probably at the time the world's foremost military power, was again on the march.

The warlike Abd-al-Rahman had for two years been the Umayyad governor of al-Andalus. Ambitious for more territory, he now led his invading cavalry into Aquitaine in south-west France. There he easily defeated Aquitaine's duke Eudes at the Battle of the Garonne River and headed towards Tours in search of the city's reputed vast wealth.

Desperate, Eudes fled to Paris to beg for support from his one-time enemy, Charles, the de facto ruler of the Franks. Charles welcomed him with caution and agreed to help only on the condition that Eudes swear fealty to him, something that the distraught duke was only too happy to do.

Assembling an army perhaps 30,000 strong, Charles and Eudes headed for Tours. Somewhere between Tours and Poitiers they met the forces of Abd-al-Rahman, numbering about 80,000 mounted men.

Charles had positioned his force at the top of a partially wooded hill, hoping the slope and the trees would disrupt any Moorish cavalry charge. The Moors, however, believed the Frankish force was larger than it was and held back from attacking.

For seven long days the two armies nervously watched each other. The Moors trotted on their horses, magnificent with lances and scimitars but without body armour, depending on the will of Allah and their own ferocious courage to defeat their enemy. The Franks were primarily on foot but lightly armoured and equipped with axes, swords and javelins.

At last Abd-al-Rahman gave the order to charge, and several thousand horsemen galloped towards the waiting Franks. But Charles had formed his men into impenetrable squares that, in charge after charge, the Muslim cavalry could not break. The Moors knew no other battle tactic than the wild cavalry charge, and their casualties began to mount under the rain of javelins and thrown axes.

Suddenly a cry went up among the Moors. Their treasure – all they had plundered since leaving Spain – was under attack. They would lose it all. Several squadrons of cavalry turned to protect their goods. They soon discovered that the cry was false, but by then it was too late. The Franks had cut down Abd-al-Rahman, and other Muslim troops were turning from the field. The battle was effectively over.

The remaining Moorish horsemen fled back towards Spain, and the Muslim threat to Western Europe was over until Suleiman the Magnificent marched into Austria in the 16th century.

Ever after this battle Charles was known as Charles Martel for his hammering defence that broke the Moorish onslaught. Two years later Eudes died, allowing Charles to march into Bordeaux to take direct control. By 739 he had also taken possession of Burgundy, substantially enlarging his Frankish domain. Charles died in 741 at the age of 53, leaving behind a virtual kingdom that was to be enlarged into an empire 50 years later by his grandson, Charlemagne.

Other action this day

AD 680: The Umayyad caliph Yazid defeats and kills the Prophet Mohammed's grandson Husayn bin Ali and his followers at the Battle of Karbala, after which this date becomes an annual holy day of public mourning among Shi'ite Muslims * 1198: Richard the Lionheart defeats the French king Philip Augustus at the Battle of Gisors, in which Richard uses *Dieu et mon droit* ('God and my right') as a password, the motto of British monarchs to this day * 1845: The United States Naval Academy opens in Annapolis, Maryland with 50 midshipman students and seven professors

11 October

The Boer War begins

1899 War in South Africa began today, to no one's surprise. Two days earlier, the Boer leader, Paul Kruger, president of the Transvaal, had sent a message to the British Cabinet demanding arbitration on 'all points of mutual difference' between the two nations and an immediate halt to the British military build-up in South Africa. Unless his terms were met within 48 hours, Kruger's ultimatum read, his government would 'with great regret be compelled to regard the action as a formal declaration of war'. There was no response from London.

No shots were fired this first day, or the next, although this was a condition soon to be corrected, but Boer commandos rode south to launch a series of pre-emptive, over-the-border attacks before the British could begin their invasion. A participant, seventeen-year-old Deneys Reitz, who would go on to write a classic account of the war, remembered the opening scene: 'As far as the eye could see the plain was alive with horsemen, guns and cattle, all steadily going forward to the frontier.'

For the British, whose geopolitical goal was to bring the gold-rich Boer republics – Transvaal and the Orange Free State – under direct imperial rule, the prospect of war was welcome, particularly if it was the Boers who made the first move. Moreover, a recent report from military intelligence in London gave this assessment of the Boers' military capability: 'It appears certain that after [one] serious defeat, they would be too deficient in discipline and organisation to make any further real stand.'

Like so many other military adventures in history, this one was predicted to be over by Christmas. At the outset, however, the war seemed a disaster for British arms. Badly underestimating the mobility, field skills and firepower of the Boer forces, the British army soon found its border garrisons bottled up at places like Kimberley, Ladysmith and Mafeking. Then came a string of major defeats at Modder River, Magersfontein and Colenso, which gave the period 10–15 December the name 'Black Week'. In the midst of it all, a young correspondent for the *Morning Post*, Winston Churchill, was captured by the Boers and spent almost a month in a Pretoria jail before escaping.

Suddenly, it was a serious war. Now, the British field commander was replaced with Lord Roberts, large-scale reinforcements were ordered into South Africa and Her Majesty's forces reorganised with a stress on mounted infantry.

Embarrassing defeats and surrenders continued, but in the new year the tide of war began to turn. The sieges were lifted and British armies advanced onto Boer soil, occupying and annexing both republics. In October President Kruger fled to the safety of Europe. At the end of 1900, Roberts pronounced the war 'practically over' and headed home to England, leaving his chief of staff, General Kitchener, to clean up. By now, there were almost half a million troops fighting for the British, facing a Boer force that never exceeded 50,000 in the field.

With their homelands largely in enemy hands, the Boers now turned to a guerrilla war directed against the enemy's vulnerable lines of communications, which stretched far inland from the seaports. Their far-ranging commandos raided within 50 miles of Cape Town. In response, the British adopted harsh tactics, which would become all-too-familiar features of modern wars: they erected lines of block-houses – 8,000 of them, built and manned mainly by black African troops – with barbed-wire fences criss-crossing the countryside; they burned the Boer farmlands on which the commandos relied for supplies; and they herded much of the civilian population – including women and children – into concentration camps, where 25,000 of them died of disease and unhygienic conditions.

In this way, resistance was at last worn down and the Boer leadership came to realise that, in order to preserve any control over their homelands in the future, the only hope lay in ending the fighting. In May 1902 General Kitchener called a peace conference, held at the village of Vereeniging, on the Vaal river. The resulting treaty, signed at Pretoria on 31 May, brought the two former republics into the British empire as colonies, with the new king Edward VII as their sovereign; provided amnesty to all those who agreed to disarm; granted the two colonies internal self-government; and offered financial assistance for rebuilding the devastated countryside.

The historian Thomas Pakenham gave this assessment of the war: 'It proved to be the longest (two and three-quarter years), the costliest (over £200 million), the bloodiest (at least 22,000 British, 25,000 Boer and 12,000 African lives) and the most humiliating war for the British between 1815 and 1914.'

Other action this day

1531: On the border between the cantons of Zurich and Zug, at the monastery of Kappel, Swiss Reformist military chaplain Huldrych Zwingli is killed in battle against Swiss Catholics * 1746: The French defeat the British, Hanoverians, Austrians and Dutch at the Battle of Roucoux during King George's War * 1797: During the French Revolutionary Wars, the British defeat the Dutch fleet at the Battle of Camperdown

12 October

Edith Cavell before the firing squad

1915 At 7.00 this morning, in the city of Brussels, an English nurse was marched before a German firing squad. Before stepping to the execution post she pinned her skirt tightly around her legs to prevent it from flaring up on the impact of the bullets. Moments later four shots were fired, and she died instantly.

When the German army entered Brussels in August 1914, Edith Cavell, aged 49, was working as a matron at a Red Cross hospital. The Germans offered her and other nurses safe conduct to Holland, but she chose instead to remain tending the Allied soldiers wounded in the opening days of the First World War. She was arrested in August 1915 and taken before a German military court, where she admitted the charges brought against her: that she had helped some 200 British and French POWs and Belgian civilians to escape to neutral Holland.

The night before her execution, she told a British chaplain that 'Patriotism is not enough. I must have no hatred or bitterness towards anyone.' Her words became famous, but public reaction in Great Britain and the United States was not so Christian in attitude. A celebrated war propaganda poster soon appeared showing a nurse's corpse on the ground and standing above it a German officer wearing a spiked helmet, a smoking pistol in his hand. The poster's legend was *Gott Mit Uns* (God with us).

At war's end her body was brought home to England. In May 1919 her memorial service at Westminster cathedral was thronged, the streets around lined with mourners. A statue was erected just north of Trafalgar Square.

There was also a memorial to Cavell in Paris, but on 23 July 1940, after an early morning tour of the vanquished capital, Adolf Hitler, with a veteran's bitter memories of the last war, ordered the monument torn down, along with other offensive reminders of French victory.

Other action this day

539 BC: Cyrus the Great of Persia conquers Babylon * 1428: The English and Burgundians begin the siege of Orléans, which will last 207 days until

Orléans is relieved by Joan of Arc ∗ 1870: Confederate general Robert E. Lee dies in Lexington, Virginia at 63; his last words are 'Strike the tent'

13 October

The American Navy is launched

1775 The American navy was born today in Philadelphia, as the Continental Congress voted to purchase and arm two ships, giving them the mission to capture British transports carrying war supplies to the king's army in North America.

The push to create an American navy had originated in Rhode Island, which had felt, since the rebellion began six months earlier in nearby Massachusetts, the hard tactics of British cruisers directed against local merchant-smugglers. In August the state assembly had instructed its delegates to the Congress to introduce a measure calling for 'the building at the Continental expense a fleet of sufficient force, for the protection of these colonies, and for employing them in such a manner and places as will most effectively annoy our enemies'.

But in the Congress there was considerable resistance to such a measure. Delegates from Southern colonies saw it as benefiting only New England; others viewed it as too radical a move and feared reprisals by the British navy against defenceless ports along the Atlantic seaboard. The measure became stalled.

In September came a timely reminder: the Continental Army's commander-in-chief, General George Washington, finding that his forces laying siege to Boston were running out of critical military supplies, commissioned a small schooner – the first of seven, 'Washington's Navy', they were dubbed – with which to interrupt the enemy's supply line and capture cargoes of muskets, ammunition and artillery.

So, in the following month, when intelligence revealed a tempting target – two British transports sailing unescorted for Quebec carrying war *matériel* – the Congress appointed a committee of John Adams, Silas Deane and John Landon, New Englanders all, to take up the matter of a naval force. Their recommendation led to today's favourable vote.

Two weeks later, Congress went further, establishing a naval committee of seven members, which authorised the purchase of two more vessels armed as men-of-war for 'the protection and defence of the united colonies'. Before the end of the year, the Congress had ordered thirteen commerce-raiding frigates, and established a Marine Corps (see 10 November) to serve aboard the new navy's ships.

No one expected the fledgling naval force to challenge the mighty Royal Navy for command of the sea. Instead, its mission would be coastal defence and to prey on the long and vulnerable British supply line. To this end, during the war Congress authorised over 50 ships for service, most of them speedy frigates designed for commerce-raiding, midway, in size and gun-strength, between a ship-of-the-line and the smaller sloop of war.

In its first war, the American navy was an improvised, underfunded force, relying on untrained leadership and forced to compete for its sailors with privateers offering more prize money and less discipline. It has been estimated that of the 800 enemy prizes seized by American ships between 1775 and 1783, three-quarters were accounted for by privateers. Of the thirteen original frigates authorised in 1775, only seven ever put to sea, the other six being destroyed to prevent their falling into enemy hands. None was in service after 1781.

At war's end, the navy was virtually defunct, and for a period of ten years the new republic was without a naval force at all. Interest was revived, however, by the threat to American shipping posed by the Barbary pirates operating from North African ports. Then war between Revolutionary France and Great Britain broke out, imperilling neutral shipping in the West Indies.

Thus, a movement to revive the navy was born, aided in part by memorable deeds from the recent War of Independence, like Esek Hopkins's 1776 raid on Nassau Island – the first amphibious landing by American forces – and John Paul Jones's momentous 1779 victory off Flamborough Head (see 23 September). So it was that in 1794, nineteen years after the Continental Navy was born in Philadelphia, Congress created its successor, which would be known forever after as the United States Navy.

1307: On the orders of King Philip (IV) the Fair of France, hundreds of Knights Templar are arrested throughout France, prior to the suppression of the order ✳ 1812: The British defeat the Americans at the Battle of Queenston Heights in Ontario during the War of 1812 ✳ 1815: Captured trying to regain his kingdom of Naples, as he faces the firing squad the dashing Napoleonic marshal and king of Naples Joachim Murat directs his executioners: 'Save my face – aim for the chest – fire!' ✳ 1943: Italy, switching allegiances, declares war on Germany

14 October

Rommel the Desert Fox is forced to commit suicide

1944 In the old photographs we see him in a weathered leather field coat, sporting goggles on the brim of his battered officer's cap. Nazi Germany's most coveted medal, the Iron Cross, hangs from a ribbon around his neck. He is Field Marshal Erwin Rommel, who today was forced to take his own life.

Rommel was born in 1891, son of a schoolmaster. He chose a military career, and at the age of twenty, fresh out of cadet school, he joined an infantry regiment. After war broke out in 1914 his regiment fought in France, Romania and Italy. He won his first Iron Cross in September 1914 when he was wounded in France, and another in 1915, but his highest medal of the war was for action in Italy, where he won the Pour le Mérite (informally known as 'der Blauer Max' – the Blue Max), then the highest award for gallantry in action given by the Imperial German Army.

After the First World War Rommel remained in the military, just another infantry officer in a defeated army. It was only in 1933 with the rise of Adolf Hitler that his star began to rise. In 1937 he published *Infanterie greift an* (*The Infantry Attacks*), a military text-book based on his combat experiences, and came to be considered a superior military thinker. Hitler was impressed and made him commander of his bodyguard.

At the outbreak of the Second World War Rommel, by this time a major general, was commander of Hitler's field headquarters during the invasion of Poland. From this special vantage point in the fast-moving campaign, in which he accompanied Hitler both in the field and at conferences, he grasped the potential that tanks offered to the determined attacker. Even though his experience was in infantry, he now asked for an armoured division, and, with Hitler's intervention smoothing the way, received command of the 7th Panzer Division in time for the invasion of the Low Countries and France.

Once France had been subdued, Rommel was sent to North Africa as commander of the Afrika Korps. There he gained fame for his brilliant tank attacks across wide expanses of open desert, earning the nickname used by both Germans and the Allies, the Desert Fox.

Rommel used speed and surprise to outwit the British, driving them 600 miles back into Libya. He was also a master of deception, once having brooms and rags tied to the backs of his tanks to raise clouds of desert dust, making the enemy believe he had superior numbers. In June 1942 he reached his greatest success with the capture of Tobruk.

In October 1942, however, superior British numbers and firepower – plus the careful planning of the British field marshal Montgomery – defeated the German force at El Alamein (see 4 November). On learning of the Afrika Korps' imminent defeat, Hitler ordered its commander to hold to the last man, but, knowing the cause was hopeless, Rommel ignored the order. The British captured 230,000 Germans and Italians.

Returning to Germany, Rommel was still a national hero. His next assignment was to defend Normandy against Allied invasion. He wanted a mobile defence with 1,500 tanks positioned behind the beaches, but he was overruled in this disposition, and the result was just what he feared: the landings were not met with sufficient German strength to stop the attackers on the shore and drive them back into the sea.

On 4 June 1944 he went on leave to celebrate his wife Lucie's 50th birthday. Two days later the Allies landed in Normandy. Hurrying back to the front, he was wounded when an RAF fighter strafed his staff car. The injured field marshal was sent home to convalesce.

The following month Colonel Claus von Stauffenberg led a group of senior army officers in an attempt to assassinate Hitler, but the bomb he placed in Hitler's headquarters succeeded only in wounding the dictator (see 20 July). Hitler's vengeance was swift, terrible and all-encompassing.

The Gestapo suspected that Rommel might have been involved in the plot, but although he had been approached, he had refused to participate. But any connection to the bungled assassination was enough for Hitler, who ordered Rommel's death.

The only obstacle to a quick trial and execution was Rommel's stature as one of Germany's most heroic field marshals. Therefore two army generals were dispatched to call on him at his home, there to offer him a grim choice: either to commit suicide or to be disgraced in a public trial and executed, leaving his family at the mercy of the Gestapo.

On this day the generals arrived at his home in Herrlingen, near Ulm. To save his wife and son Rommel left with the generals and took poison in the staff car. The public was told he had died of war wounds, and the government arranged a solemn state funeral, which Hitler refused to attend. Goebbels, Göring and other top Nazi leaders, all of whom knew that Rommel had in effect been executed, sent odious notes of condolence to his widow. Hitler's, dated 16 October 1944, read: 'Accept my sincerest sympathy for the heavy loss you have suffered with the death of your husband. The name of Field Marshal Rommel will be forever linked with the heroic battles in North Africa.'

Other action this day

1066: William the Conqueror defeats King Harold at the Battle of Hastings ∗ 1529: After killing his prisoners, Suleiman the Magnificent leads his army in retreat from Vienna after an unsuccessful siege of eighteen days ∗ 1806: Napoleon defeats the Prussians at the Battle of Jena-Auerstädt ∗ 1890: American general and president Dwight D. Eisenhower is born ∗ 1947: In the experimental X-1 aircraft, US Air Force test pilot Captain Chuck Yeager becomes the first man to break the sound barrier

15 October

Scipio overwhelms Hannibal at Zama

202 BC Today was fought one of history's pivotal battles, when two of antiquity's greatest generals faced each other at Zama to determine hegemony of the Mediterranean world.

After the calamitous annihilation of the Romans at the Battle of Cannae in 216 BC (see 2 August), it looked as if the formidable Carthaginian general Hannibal would force Rome to sue for terms, restoring Carthage to the pre-eminence lost in the First Punic War 39 years before. But the obdurate Romans simply refused to be defeated. As Livy wrote two centuries later, 'No other nation could have suffered such a tremendous disaster and not been destroyed.'

This was Hannibal's problem. In spite of his victories, he could not force his enemies to submit. He continued to roam Italy for another thirteen years, once coming within three miles of Rome, but with no siege machinery, he could not attack the great city.

Then Hannibal's problems got worse. A young Roman patrician named Publius Cornelius Scipio had escaped the slaughter at Cannae. Now he had become a general, and, in a series of brilliant tactical engagements, he reconquered virtually all of Carthage's vast territories in Spain. Then, in 204 BC, he embarked for North Africa with an army of 35,000 to strike at Carthage itself.

Scipio brilliantly defeated the Carthaginian forces at Bagbrades, reportedly killing 40,000 men, while destroying enemy towns and cutting off Carthage's food supply. As Scipio knew it must, the Carthaginian government ordered Hannibal to return from Italy to protect the home front.

Two years later these two illustrious generals met on this day at Zama (five miles south of today's Tunis) to determine the fate of the Western world.

Hannibal's army of 45,000 infantry and 80 elephants looked stronger than Scipio's force of only 34,000. But the Carthaginian troops were largely raw and untrained, and Roman and allied Numidian cavalry came to 9,000 horse, three times the mounted strength Hannibal could put in the field.

In the early stages of the battle the Romans managed to panic the

Carthaginian elephants with the deafening blare of trumpets and horns. Then the Roman horse put the Carthaginian cavalry to flight, apparently leaving the battle to be settled by the lines of infantry. At first it appeared that the larger Carthaginian force would prevail, but while the Roman soldiers held, their cavalry came charging back into the conflict, taking the enemy from the rear. Some 20,000 Carthaginians died on the field. The defeat of Carthage opened the way for complete Roman domination of southern Europe and North Africa for over half a millennium.

A magnanimous victor, Scipio permitted Hannibal to remain in Carthage, where he was elected the country's ruler. When the two generals met shortly afterwards, Scipio, perhaps fishing for compliments, asked Hannibal who he thought were the three greatest generals in history. The Carthaginian named Alexander the Great, Pyrrhus and himself. 'And what if you rather than I had won the Battle of Zama?' asked the Roman. 'Then I would be the greatest of all,' answered the confident Hannibal.

In gratitude, the Roman Senate awarded Scipio the title of 'Africanus'. In 25 years of warfare this remarkable commander never lost a battle.

Hannibal was not so fortunate. A few years after Zama the Roman Senate decided it wanted revenge, forcing him to flee for a secret life in exile. Finally, when he reached the age of 64, his enemies found him in Bythnia. As Roman soldiers surrounded his house to capture him for return to Rome and execution, the great general escaped their clutches in the only way possible, by taking poison. 'Let us relieve the Romans of their continual dread and care', he said, 'who think it long and tedious to wait for the death of a hated old man.'

Other action this day

1894: French major Alfred Dreyfus is arrested on false charges of espionage before being wrongly convicted and sent to Devil's Island * 1917: Femme fatale Mata Hari is shot by firing squad at the Vincennes barracks in Paris after being convicted of passing military secrets to the Germans * 1945: Former Vichy France premier and collaborator Pierre Laval is executed by firing squad * 1946: Nazi Luftwaffe leader Hermann Göring commits suicide in a Nuremberg prison the day before he is scheduled to hang

16 October

The walls of Vienna

1809 As if to add a spiteful exclamation point to the humiliating treaty he had forced Austria to sign two days earlier, the emperor Napoleon had ordered the walls of Vienna to be demolished. At four this afternoon great explosions shook the city, as commanding gates and high ramparts were blown up. The Viennese were appalled, for these walls – or their predecessors – had protected them and their city since time immemorial, although now they no longer possessed real military value.

Celts had originally founded Vienna in about 500 BC, but it fell to the Romans during the reign of Augustus in 15 BC. They turned it into one of a number of military installations on the Danube guarding the Roman empire against marauding Germanic tribes and called it Vindobona, Celtic for 'White Field' – possibly in reference to the severe winter snows. Although not walled in stone, the entire site was a sturdy fortress constructed of wood.

At the beginning of the 2nd century AD these wooden fortifications were replaced by the first stone walls, but even these could not save Vindobona when a Germanic tribe named the Marcomanni sacked it sometime after AD 166. Emperor Marcus Aurelius later rebuilt the walls but died there of the plague in 180.

Somewhere around 250 Vindobona's fortifications were once again strengthened, as the city had progressed from fortified military camp to a city of about 20,000. For well over a century the walls kept out intruders, but in about 395 another German tribe pillaged the city. The walls were shortly rebuilt, but during the first decade of the 5th century a fire levelled most of the fortress.

In 433, during the Roman empire's final decline, the Eastern Roman emperor Theodosius II relinquished Vindobona altogether, allowing the Huns to take over. (According to the 12th-century German epic poem the *Niebelungenlied*, Attila was married there.) By now the name 'Vindobona' was evolving to Wenia, which in turn became Wienis and eventually today's Wien (Vienna).

During the Dark Ages Vienna was overrun several times, but in 1192 England's Richard the Lionheart was captured there on his return from crusade (see 21 December). He finally bought his release for 'six thousand buckets of silver' that went into the city treasury, to be used to rebuild the city's wall. Then, in 1251, Ottocar II of Bohemia built the first truly massive stone walls around the city. These resisted all attacks, even in 1485, when Matthias I Corvinus of Hungary occupied Vienna. To avoid a long siege, the city fathers surrendered, but the walls were never breached.

The walls' biggest test came in 1529 when Suleiman the Magnificent laid siege to Vienna with a vast Turkish army. The fortifications held firm and the Turks were forced to retreat precisely 270 years to the day before Napoleon pulled the walls down. In 1555 these medieval walls were reinforced and largely replaced by new fortifications, which protected the city for centuries, even during the summer of 1683, when once again they stymied a massive Turkish attack (see 12 September).

Then came Napoleon. He first occupied Vienna in 1805 but left the walls intact. On his return four years later, however, he ordered their destruction. Even then, remnants of the walls and their moats remained and as the city grew, they became a severe impediment to traffic.

Finally, in 1857 Austrian emperor Franz Joseph issued his famous decree 'Es ist Mein Wille' ('It is My Will'), which ordered the walls' final demolition. He had been swept to power during the revolution of 1848 and, mindful of a restless public, wanted a broad street that made the erection of revolutionary barricades impossible. But he also wanted a new boulevard as a showplace for grand imperial buildings, so the beautiful Ringstraße, the most spectacular street in what remains one of Europe's most enchanting cities, finally replaced the last vestiges of the ancient city walls.

Other action this day

1793: Marie Antoinette is guillotined during the French Revolution * 1859: Northern abolitionist John Brown and 21 followers raid Harpers Ferry Armory in a vain attempt to foment a rising of black slaves * 1939: Spitfires of 603 Squadron shoot down two German Junkers Ju-88s and two Heinkel He-111s near the Firth of Forth, the first enemy aircraft ever downed by Spitfires * 1946: Nazi leaders Hans Frank, Wilhelm Frick, Alfred Jodl, Ernst Kaltenbrunner, Wilhelm Keitel, Joachim von

Ribbentrop, Alfred Rosenberg, Fritz Sauckel, Arthur Seyss-Inquart and Julius Streicher are hanged for war crimes at Nuremberg

17 October

'Thy necessity is yet greater than mine'

1586 Today Sir Philip Sidney died of his wounds at the age of 31, knight, courtier, poet, soldier, diplomat, scholar, friend and supporter of artists and scientists, a man widely admired in his time not so much for any particular accomplishment but as the quintessence of what an Elizabethan gentleman should be.

Sidney was one of the best-connected young men in England. His grandfather was the Duke of Northumberland, one uncle was the Earl of Warwick and another was Queen Elizabeth's favourite, Robert Dudley, the Earl of Leicester. He was godson to King Philip II of Spain and son-in-law to Sir Francis Walsingham, Queen Elizabeth's secretary of state.

In spite of these spectacular relations, Sidney failed to get the state appointments he wanted after he had shown poor judgement in an early ambassadorial assignment. Fortunately for posterity, this gave him the time to pursue his literary career and other intellectual interests.

Sidney's chance to serve the queen came in 1585 when Elizabeth decided to come to the aid of Dutch Protestants in their struggle with Catholic Spain. She sent a small force under the command of Sidney's uncle Leicester, and Sidney was put in charge of a company of cavalry.

By the autumn of 1586 the rebellious Dutch and their English allies were besieging the town of Zutphen, trying to prevent the Spanish from resupplying the small garrison within. Suddenly an enemy supply train was spotted. Sidney was about to lead his cavalry into attack when he noticed that one of his men had been caught without full armour. The gallant commander threw across his own thigh piece and then thundered off into the assault.

Three times Sidney charged the enemy, but on his last attack a musket ball smashed into his leg just above the knee, shattering the bone. Seriously wounded, he managed to retain his mount and escape from the field of battle to a nearby field filled with English casualties. As he lay injured, he saw a common soldier stretched out near him, clearly on the point of death. In a moment of conspicuous gallantry, Sidney handed the soldier his own cup of water, saying, 'Thy necessity is yet greater than mine.'

Sidney's men then carried their stricken leader to nearby Arnhem, his wound already showing signs of infection. Twenty-five days later, on 17 October, he died. Subsequently he was given a state funeral in St Paul's cathedral in London, the last to be so honoured until Nelson over two centuries later.

Other action this day

1346: Edward III of England defeats David II of Scotland at the Battle of Neville's Cross near Durham * 1651: After being defeated by Cromwell at Worcester, England's Charles II flees to France, to remain in exile until 25 May 1660 * 1941: Japanese prime minister Konoye's government falls, bringing army minister and general Hideki Tojo to power

18 October

Napoleon retreats from Russia

1812 Today the 90,000 men remaining from Napoleon's Grande Armée trooped out of Moscow to begin the most famous retreat in military history.

Thirty-five days before, Napoleon and his army had at last reached the Russian capital after twelve long weeks of plodding across 500 miles of empty and desolate Russian countryside, laid waste by Russian peasants before they abandoned it.

Yet Moscow, too, was ominously quiet and empty. Indeed, only 15,000 of its quarter of a million inhabitants remained, mostly foreigners, vagabonds and criminals. The rest had deserted the city on orders from its governor.

Then came the fires, deliberately set by the Russians, which razed four-fifths of Moscow. No word came from the tsar, no surrender, no discussion of terms. Each day food became scarcer; each day there was less left to burn to fight the murderous cold.

Recognising that his plight was desperate, Napoleon appealed to Alexander I for a truce, but the tsar refused even to answer the emperor's letter. Later the tsar wrote to an ally: 'We would rather be buried beneath the ruins of the empire than make terms with the modern Attila.' Finally Napoleon understood that his only hope was withdrawal, and he gave the order to abandon the city.

Now the army tramped 500 miles in retreat, numbed with fatigue, frozen by the terrible Russian winter, with regular frosts of −25°C. As described by future American president John Quincy Adams, who was in Moscow at the time as his country's ambassador, 'The invader himself was a wretched fugitive and his numberless host was perishing by frosts, famine, and the sword.'

Badgered by guerrillas and marauding Cossacks, tracked by the main Russian armies, Napoleon's men and horses fell and died, left equally for the howling wolves. For seven weeks the army struggled on, at last reaching sanctuary in Vilna (now Vilnius in Lithuania). By then perhaps 12,000 were left, and Napoleon could only repeat his now famous observation, 'Du sublime au ridicule il n'y a qu'un pas.' ('From the sublime to the ridiculous is only a step.') The days of the empire were numbered.

Other action this day

1016: Danish king Canute defeats the English under King Edmund II (Ironside) at the Battle of Ashingdon, concluding his reconquest of England * 1663: Imperial general Prince Eugene of Savoy is born in Paris * 1945: German-born Communist spy Klaus Fuchs gives American plans for the plutonium bomb to the Russians

19 October

'Sheridan's Ride'

1864 On this Indian summer morning Major General Philip Sheridan made a celebrated ride from Winchester, Virginia, to Cedar Creek and turned the rout of his Army of the Shenandoah into a timely victory for the Union.

Returning to his command from Washington, DC, Sheridan, having spent the night at Winchester, woke to the sound of heavy gunfire from the army's encampment twenty miles away. Riding out to investigate, he encountered 'the appalling spectacle of a panic-stricken army ... all pressing to the rear in hopeless confusion'.

With two aides and twenty troopers, 'Little Phil' Sheridan began the gallop to the battlefield over roads choked with wounded soldiers, stragglers and transport. As he rode through, he shouted to them: 'About face, boys! We are going to lick them out of their boots.' They began to cheer. When a hysterical infantry colonel yelled at him: 'The army's whipped!' Sheridan replied, 'You are, but the army isn't.' An officer who accompanied him wrote: 'Sheridan, without slowing from the gallop, pointed to the front; men cheered and shouldered arms and started back.'

The diminutive Sheridan arrived at Cedar Creek at 10.30am. Riding up and down on his big, black horse Rienzi, he began to restore order to his battered army, exhorting men and officers, ordering breastworks thrown up, directing returning units back into the line and establishing a new headquarters. At 4.00pm he sent off the counter-attack that swept Jubal Early's Confederate forces from the field and carried the day.

His spectacular victory had political as well as military significance. In the war-weary North, the 1864 presidential election was only days away, with Republican president Lincoln running against his former general George B. McClellan of the anti-war Democrats, known as 'Copperheads'. With Atlanta fallen to Sherman the month before, Horace Greeley, the influential editor of the *New York Tribune*, could now write: 'Sheridan and Sherman have knocked the bottom out of the Copperheads.'

For his ride and victory, Sheridan was the hero of the hour and the toast of the Union army. President Lincoln said he had always thought that a cavalryman should be about six feet four inches tall, but 'now five feet four seems about right', unwittingly reducing the general's true height by an inch.

Like another famous rider, Paul Revere, Sheridan became the subject of an immensely popular poem. Here is the first stanza of 'Sheridan's Ride' by Thomas Buchanan Read:

> Up from the south at the break of day,
> Bringing to Winchester fresh dismay,
> The affrighted air with a shudder bore,

Like a herald in haste to the chieftain's door,
The terrible grumble and rumble and roar,
Telling the battle was on once more,
And Sheridan twenty miles away.

Other action this day

1805: The Austrians under General Mack surrender to Napoleon at Ulm after 10,000 are killed or wounded and 30,000 taken prisoner * 1813: A coalition of 430,000 Austrians, Prussians, Swedes, Russians and Saxons defeat Napoleon's army of 195,000 at the Battle of Leipzig, with 38,000 French killed or wounded against 54,000 for the Allies, in the largest battle of the Napoleonic Wars * 1914: A British attack starts the first Battle of Ypres; one German involved in the battle was *Gefreiter* (lance corporal) Adolf Hitler

20 October

Eddie Rickenbacker gets his last kill

1918 Today, with the First World War drawing to a close, Captain Eddie Rickenbacker, commander of the US 94th Aero Pursuit Squadron, flew his Spad high above the trenches of the Western Front and shot down his 26th – and final – German aircraft of the war. Over the past six months, he had become America's best combat pilot, its 'ace of aces'.

Rickenbacker was a natural in the air. Before the war, he had won fame – as well as money and influence – as one of the world's top racing-car drivers, but he had never flown a plane. When the United States entered the war in March 1917 he joined the Army with the hope of organising a flying squadron of former racing drivers, counting on their experience of operating powerful engines at high speeds to make them first-rate pilots. When the War Department proved resistant, he managed to get to France as a driver, first for General John J. Pershing, then for Colonel 'Billy' Mitchell, head of the recently formed American Air Service. Eventually, with Mitchell's help, Rickenbacker got assigned to a flying unit as an engineer, then to pilot training and an officer's commission and finally, in March 1918, to the 94th Squadron, the famous 'Hat-in-the-Ring'

Squadron. He took his first combat flight on 25 April and four days later, piloting a Nieuport, downed his first enemy plane. At the end of May, Rickenbacker was a five-victory ace.

In the course of the long war, there were plenty of aces who had more kills than Rickenbacker – Billy Bishop, the Canadian ace flying for the British, had 72, for instance, and on the other side Manfred von Richthofen had 80 – but no other pilot ever matched Rickenbacker's rate of 26 in just six months. For his feats he received the Croix de Guerre, the US Distinguished Flying Cross and the Congressional Medal of Honor.

Three weeks later, on 11 November 1918, Rickenbacker took his plane out over the front lines to see the war end. 'It was a foggy morning at the base,' he wrote years later, 'and I wriggled my way out just a half minute before eleven o'clock. I was flying down no-man's land, between the trenches of the opposing forces and they were shooting at each other just as madly as they could. And then the hour of eleven struck. The shooting stopped and gradually men from both sides came out into no-man's land and threw their guns and helmets into the air. They kept talking to each other and shaking hands and doing something for the men who had been hit ... I was only about 100 feet over no-man's land. I got out to see what I went out to see and went back home and that was it.'

Other action this day
1827: In the last major battle ever fought entirely with sailing ships, British, Russian and French fleets destroy the Ottoman fleet at the Battle of Navarino during the Greek War of Independence * 1899: At the Battle of Talana Hill in Natal during the Boer War, a British artillery-supported infantry assault drives the Boers from the field, but British general Sir William Penn Symons loses 220 men captured, 185 wounded and 41 killed, including himself, while inflicting less than half these casualties on the Boers * 1944: Surrounded by photographers in a carefully stage-managed landing, General Douglas MacArthur wades ashore at Palo Beach, Leyte to begin the successful Philippines campaign against the Japanese invaders

21 October

Trafalgar

1805 Atop his column in London's Trafalgar Square stands one-armed admiral Horatio Nelson, who won a battle and lost his life on this day in 1805 at the age of 47.

Nelson joined the navy at the age of twelve, so he had been serving for over 30 years before his years of greatness during the French Revolutionary and Napoleonic Wars. He lost an eye at Calvi helping to capture Corsica in 1797 and four years later his right arm at Tenerife. A year after that he destroyed Napoleon's fleet at the Battle of the Nile.

On this day Nelson, with only 27 ships, completely outmanoeuvred a French/Spanish fleet of 33 warships at Cape Trafalgar on the south coast of Spain.

Two days before the battle the enemy fleet set sail from Cádiz headed for Italy to resupply Napoleon's army there. The French admiral Pierre de Villeneuve hoped to slip past the British without giving battle, but Nelson caught them south of the port, off Cape Trafalgar.

While Villeneuve's ships formed a single long curving line, Nelson split his fleet into two squadrons, one with twelve ships commanded directly by himself, the other by Admiral Cuthbert Collingwood. Closing with the enemy, just before noon Nelson issued his famous signal: 'England expects that every man will do his duty.' A few minutes later Collingwood's ships were the first to engage the enemy. Then, ordering what amounted to a frontal assault on the French line, Nelson in his 104-gun flagship *Victory* led his column of ships directly at and through the opposing fleet, raking the enemy's flagship with crippling cannon shot.

Even when *Victory* became entangled with the French warship *Redoutable*, Nelson remained fully exposed to enemy fire, walking resolutely on the quarterdeck with his captain Thomas Hardy. At 1.15pm a sniper's bullet fired from the rigging of the *Redoutable* caught Nelson in the shoulder, passed through his lungs and shattered his spine. 'They have done for me at last,' murmured the dying admiral.

In indescribable pain, Nelson was carried below, to survive for another three hours. Knowing he was about to die, he beseeched Hardy 'to take care of my poor Lady Hamilton' (Nelson's mistress). At the end he murmured, 'Kiss me, Hardy.' The captain knelt and kissed his cheek, and the great admiral expired, according to legend dying with the famous words, 'I have done my duty, thank God for that.'

The Battle of Trafalgar was one of the truly decisive naval encounters in history. The French lost nineteen ships and 14,000 men killed or captured, including their admiral. British losses were only 1,690 killed and wounded, and not a ship was lost. Napoleon's last hope of invading England had been denied forever.

Nelson's body was brought back to England to receive an imposing funeral in St Paul's cathedral. There he was buried in a coffin that he himself had ordered, made from timber taken from the French warship *Orient* that he had destroyed at the Battle of the Nile.

Other action this day
1600: At the Battle of Sekigahara in Japan, Tokugawa defeats Ishida Mitsunari to start the Tokugawa shogunate that lasts until 1868 * 1940: Ernest Hemingway publishes his novel about the Spanish Civil War, *For Whom the Bell Tolls* * 1944: The Australian cruiser HMAS *Australia* is hit by the first Japanese kamikaze attack of the Second World War in the prelude to the Battle of Leyte Gulf

22 October

The Long March that changed Chinese history

1935 Today, in what is known as the 'union of the three armies', the Second Red Army joined 8,000 bedraggled survivors of Mao Tse-tung's main Communist force and the remnants of the Fourth Red Army to reach safe haven in Communist-controlled Shensi Province in north-western China. After one year and five days of retreat from the repeated attacks of Chiang Kai-shek's Kuomintang troops, the Long March was over. More than 90 per cent of the Communist army had perished, but Mao had survived, achieving in the process de facto leadership of China's Communist Party.

The previous October Mao, his pregnant wife and 100,000 soldiers of the Red Army had abandoned their capital of Juichin in Kiangsi province to start a trek of some 8,000 miles from one side of China to the other. During the next twelve months they covered some of the world's most inhospitable terrain while constantly pursued by Chiang Kai-shek's forces. It was the longest – and fastest – infantry march made under combat conditions by any army in history.

Since the Red Army had no motorised transport, the Long March was indeed a march, every man afoot except Mao himself, who was so ill from malaria that he rode the army's solitary horse. When the terrain was too difficult for him to stay in the saddle, four soldiers would carry him in a wooden litter.

Every soldier had to march with his own supplies. According to Mao's chief artillery engineer, 'Each man carried five pounds of ration rice and each had a shoulder pole from which hung either two small boxes of ammunition or hand grenades, or big kerosene cans filled with our most essential machinery and tools. Each pack contained a blanket or quilt, one quilted winter uniform, and three pairs of strong cloth shoes with thick rope soles tipped and heeled with metal.'

The army had little ammunition, less food and virtually no medical supplies. Sometimes forced to go several days without eating, many fell by the wayside due to weakness while even more died of disease.

Almost insuperable obstacles barred the Red Army's progress. At Luting the soldiers had to haul themselves over a river on a chain suspension bridge from which all the wooden slats had been removed. Later they had to cross seven high mountain ranges crested with snow, and in the heat of August they tramped across the Grasslands of Chinghai, a high plateau that was boggy with rain and infested with swarms of malaria-carrying mosquitoes. The wet ground prevented the soldiers from making fires to cook the little food they carried, and many suffered from severe dysentery from eating raw rice and vegetables.

Although China's Communists were on the point of annihilation, the Long March not only provided a stirring example of revolutionary zeal and commitment, but also gave Mao time for the political situation to change. China had already been under attack from

Japan, but Chiang Kai-shek had decided to cleanse the country of Communists as his first priority. The Long March showed that total victory against the Communists was unachievable, and by September 1937 the Kuomintang and the Communists had (temporarily) joined forces to fight the common enemy. Once the Japanese were defeated, however, the civil war was re-ignited almost immediately, and in 1949 Mao's armies took over the country, forcing Chiang to flee to Taiwan and amply demonstrating Mao's famous maxim that 'political power grows out of the barrel of a gun'.

Other action this day

1633: The last day of the three-month Battle of Liaoluo Bay in the Taiwan Strait, in which the Ming fleet defeats the Dutch East India Company, sinking four galleons and damaging another 50 ships while inflicting 400 casualties and taking 800 prisoners * 1797: Jacques Garnerin takes off from Paris in a hot air balloon and leaps into space at 3,200 feet to make the first parachute jump from an aircraft, landing safely in the Parc Monceau; almost two and a half centuries later the Russians form the first unit of paratroopers * 1962: President John F. Kennedy announces that American spy planes have discovered Soviet nuclear weapons in Cuba and that he has ordered a naval quarantine of the island

23 October

America's first combat in the First World War

1917 At 6.05 this morning C Battery of the 6th Field Artillery fired a round from its French 75mm gun towards the German trenches a few hundred yards to the front. America had truly entered the Great War at last.

Ever since 1914 the Allied powers had attempted to persuade the United States to join in the conflict against Germany, and finally, on 6 April 1917, President Woodrow Wilson had declared war. But now American troops were for the first time actually engaging the enemy.

By the time the Germans collapsed seven months later the United States had increased the strength of the American Expeditionary Force to just under 2 million men, an incredible feat of planning and logistics. Commanding US forces in Europe was General John 'Black Jack' Pershing, aged 57 when he took command but still tough and energetic, as he proved on arriving in Paris when he took a 23-year-old French mistress.

Pershing was originally dubbed 'Black Jack' by fellow officers in a derisive reference to his command of a black cavalry unit, but later it came to represent his dark, hawk-like looks and stern discipline. He had climbed the ranks of the military in part through unimpeachable connections. He had become a great friend of Teddy Roosevelt when Roosevelt was police commissioner of New York, and his father-in-law was the head of the Senate Military Affairs Committee. No doubt there was also tremendous sympathy for him because his wife and three daughters had all perished in a fire in San Francisco a few years before the war. Nonetheless he was a fine soldier, as he had demonstrated in searching out and almost killing the Mexican revolutionary and bandit Pancho Villa.

Pershing deserved and received much of the credit for the great fighting success of the American forces in Europe. In all they fought in thirteen battles and turned the tide of the war from stalemate to victory. Although light compared with the European nations that had fought since 1914, American casualties were still significant. In all over 116,000 were killed in action while another 200,000 were wounded.

Other action this day

1642: In the first battle of the English Civil War, Charles I and Prince Rupert meet Parliamentary forces under Robert Devereux, 3rd Earl of Essex in an inconclusive contest at Edgehill * 1702: British admiral Sir George Rooke leads an Anglo-Dutch fleet to victory over the Spanish in the Battle of Vigo Bay during the War of the Spanish Succession * 1738: Britain declares war on Spain to begin the War of Jenkins' Ear, named after Robert Jenkins, captain of a British merchant ship, who exhibited his severed ear in Parliament after Spanish coast guards had boarded his ship and cut it off in 1731 * 1911: In the first ever use of aircraft in warfare, an Italian pilot flies over Turkish lines on a reconnaissance mission in the Turco-Italian War

24 October

Catastrophe at Caporetto

1917 Between 1915 and 1917, on the Italian front of the First World War, there were eleven battles of the Isonzo River: a series of costly and mostly inconclusive assaults by the Italian army on Austrian positions north of Trieste. The twelfth battle began on 24 October 1917 and is usually called the Battle of Caporetto, after the place where the breakthrough occurred, which an observer described as 'a little white town with a campanile in a valley'. The battle was anything but inconclusive, but this time it was the Austrians who launched the assault and it proved to be a disaster for Italy.

The attacking forces, greatly bolstered by the presence of German divisions, knocked a fifteen-mile hole in the Italian line and then kept moving, infiltrating their forces into the rear of the Italian strong points. 'The further we penetrated into the hostile positions, the less prepared were the garrisons for our arrival and the easier the fighting', wrote a young German infantry leader named Erwin Rommel, whose exploits during the offensive won him the Pour le Mérite.

The Italian Second Army crumbled in panic, forcing the armies on either side to pull back. When the Italians finally stopped retreating eleven days later at the Piave River, they were some 80 miles to the rear of their former line on the Isonzo. The Austrians were now in a position to threaten Venice but, mercifully, had outrun their supplies. The Piave line held. In the retreat, the Italians had lost some 40,000 men killed and wounded and another 275,000 taken prisoner.

For the Allies, a few good things came out of the catastrophe at Caporetto. General Count Luigi Cadorna, an unimaginative martinet, was sacked as the Italian commander-in-chief. Then Great Britain and France, at long last recognising that the informal and haphazard direction of the Allied war effort so far was proving inadequate to the task of defeating the Central Powers, called a meeting of the Allies in Locarno, Switzerland on 5 November, at which the parties agreed to establish a Supreme War Council.

Finally, a man who wasn't even in Italy at the time of Caporetto left a vivid account of the retreat that ranks with the very best war fiction: he was Ernest Hemingway, who wrote of it in *A Farewell to Arms*.

Other action this day

AD 69: Antonius Primus, loyal to future emperor Vespasian, defeats Emperor Vitellius at the Second Battle of Bedriacum, guaranteeing that Vespasian will replace Vitellius as emperor * 1648: The Holy Roman Empire, Spain, France, Sweden and the Netherlands sign the Treaty of Westphalia, ending the Thirty Years War in which 350,000 were slain on the field of battle and 8 million civilians perished * 1915: Fighting Haitian Caco bandits, American Marine Gunnery Sergeant Dan Daly earns his second Medal of Honor for heroically attacking when the 38-man unit to which he belongs comes under fire from 400 Cacos * 1945: Norwegian traitor and wartime president Vidkun Quisling is executed by firing squad at Akershus Fortress in Oslo

25 October

Courage and calamity in the Crimea

1854 Although today's indecisive battle at Balaclava made no change to the outcome of the Crimean War, it is remembered for the magnificent if sometimes foolhardy courage of the British soldiers who fought there.

Since September, British and French troops, plus a small contingent of Turks, had been besieging the Russian naval base at Sebastopol. The British commander, Lord Raglan, had established his base fifteen miles down the coast at Balaclava.

On 25 October the Russians moved against the British base with a force of 20,000 infantry and 3,500 cavalry. A unit of 3,000 Russian cavalry riding for Balaclava descended from a ridge called the Causeway Heights and suddenly found the British Heavy Brigade of 900 horse in their path, ready to charge. Confused, the Russians halted, perhaps in an attempt to extend their line, and the Heavy Brigade thundered into their midst. Then, in the words of an eyewitness, 'almost as it seemed in a moment, and simultaneously – the whole Russian mass gave way, and fled, at speed and in disorder, beyond the hill, vanishing behind the slope some four or five minutes after they had first swept over it'.

Four Russian cavalry squadrons, however, had been detached from the main force and continued on towards Balaclava. This time, instead of meeting British horse, they found the 93rd Highlanders, splendid in their red coats and dark green plaid kilts, blocking their way. On seeing the Russians, the Highlanders' commander Sir Colin Campbell told his soldiers, 'There is no retreat from here, men. You must die where you stand.'

Campbell spread his troops in a thin line only two men deep to meet the Russian assault. The Highlanders fired two volleys as the Russians bore down on them, causing the cavalry to split in half, galloping to right and left, and finally into full retreat. Some of the younger soldiers started excitedly forward for a bayonet charge, but Campbell shouted out, '93rd, 93rd, damn all that eagerness!' The Highlanders' heroic stand was famously described by war correspondent William H. Russell in *The Times* as 'a thin red line tipped with steel', a phrase, shortened to 'a thin red line', that became a symbol for courageous British resistance against the odds.

Positioned on a high ridge, the British commander Lord Raglan could watch the Russian attacks unfold. He then saw that on the Causeway Heights the Russians had chased away a few Turkish defenders and were on the point of making off with nine 12-pounder naval guns that the British had positioned there. To save the guns, he urgently dispatched Captain Louis Nolan with orders to his cavalry leader, Lord Lucan.

Leaping from his horse, Nolan presented the orders, which read: 'Lord Raglan wishes the cavalry to advance rapidly to the front, and try to prevent the enemy carrying away the guns. Troop of horse artillery may accompany. French cavalry is on your left. Immediate.' Nolan, an intrepid horseman who detested Lucan for his timid use of his cavalry, then commented, 'Lord Raglan's orders are that the cavalry should attack immediately.'

'Attack, sir! Attack what?' demanded Lucan. 'What guns, sir? Where and what to do?' From Lucan's position in a valley, the guns on the Causeway Heights could not be seen. The only enemy position in view was a Russian redoubt at the end of the valley about a mile away.

'There, my Lord!' answered Nolan with a sweep of his arm. 'There is your enemy! There are your guns!' He then turned and galloped away, leaving Lucan still mystified.

But now Lucan summoned the general in charge of the Light Brigade of horse, his brother-in-law, the wealthy James Brudenell, 7th Earl of Cardigan, who was a quarrelsome martinet just a few days short of his 57th birthday. Lucan instructed Cardigan to lead his brigade straight into the valley between the Fedyukhin Heights and the Causeway Heights, even though the Russians were positioned on both sides and at the end of the valley, with 76 guns and twenty battalions of infantry. At first Cardigan tried to question the confused order, but then ordered the charge.

> Theirs not to reason why,
> Theirs but to do and die:
> Into the valley of death
> Rode the six hundred.

So wrote Alfred, Lord Tennyson of this famous charge of the Light Brigade. With Cardigan at their head, the British horse swept forward over a mile of open ground. Suddenly Nolan appeared, waving his sword at Cardigan, perhaps to alert him that he was attacking the wrong target, but a shell splinter brought him down before he could complete his warning.

Moving at a trot, the brigade advanced in a line 100 yards wide and immediately came under fire from the flanks. Minutes later they came within range of the Russian guns at the end of the valley, which could shoot at the British head-on. As the Russian cannon scythed down the attackers, the brigade charged on, now at the gallop. Reaching the Russian position, they cut down any gun crews that had not fled and attacked the enemy cavalry to the rear.

The Russian position destroyed, now the Light Brigade returned back down the valley whence they had come, harassed by Russian cavalry. Of the original 673 attackers, 118 had been killed and 127 wounded, with a loss of 517 horses.

Cardigan, who had fought fearlessly, survived unscathed, but on his return he ignored his men without even checking for survivors and rode off to his yacht in Balaclava harbour for a champagne dinner.

The Charge of the Light Brigade remains one of the most senseless and horrifying displays of proud courage in all of military history. Nothing sums it up better than the comment of the French general Pierre Bosquet, who witnessed the heroic debacle: 'C'est magnifique, mais ce n'est pas la guerre. C'est de la folie.' ('It's magnificent, but it's not war. It's madness.')

Other action this day

1415: England's Henry V defeats the French at the Battle of Agincourt * 1936: Hitler and Mussolini create the Rome-Berlin Axis * 1944: Japanese kamikaze planes sink the escort carrier *St Lô*, the first American ship sunk by kamikazes during the Second World War; approximately 400 more American ships will be hit and 35–50 sunk by the end of the war * 1950: The People's Republic of China enters the Korean War as huge numbers of Chinese soldiers pour across the border into Korea, crushing the Republic of Korea's 6th Division in a ten-day attack

26 October

Alfred the Great, the king who saved Anglo-Saxon England

AD 899 Today, at Winchester, died Alfred the Great, the first king of England, who against all odds saved his country from Viking conquest and unified the Anglo-Saxon kingdoms into a single nation.

The son of King Aethelwulf of Wessex, Alfred was born in the royal palace at Wantage in one of the most calamitous periods of English history. Since the end of the 8th century, savage pagan Danes had raided and plundered, searching for slaves and occupying much of the country.

When King Aethelwulf died in 858, two of Alfred's older brothers took the throne of Wessex in brief succession; the second, Aethelred, in 865. The Danes had seized York and set up their own kingdom in Northumbria, while subjugating East Anglia and Mercia and torturing to death their conquered kings. Now the Great Heathen Army advanced on Wessex, the only remaining independent Anglo-Saxon kingdom.

After capturing the royal palace at Reading, in January 871 the Danes met the Anglo-Saxons at Ashdown. It was now that Alfred first showed his prowess in war. As the two sides faced each other,

King Aethelred abruptly left the field to pray for victory in a nearby church. Impatient for battle and judging that he must strike immediately, Alfred ordered his men to charge. The result was victory – a pyrrhic one with great slaughter on both sides – but at least the Danes were temporarily halted. One of the casualties was Aethelred, who later died of his wounds. Now Alfred, still just 22, was king of Wessex, but his troubles were only beginning.

Temporarily beaten but far from subdued, the Danes resumed their raids. Early in 878 Alfred narrowly escaped a surprise attack and fled to Somerset. There, according to legend, the disguised king lodged in the rude hut of a peasant woman. Asked to keep an eye on some cakes cooking on the fire, he was so preoccupied by his predicament that he allowed them to burn. Scolded by the peasant woman, the hapless Alfred could only apologise, reproached by the lowliest of his subjects.

Despite the seeming hopelessness of Alfred's cause, recruits flocked to his banner of the golden dragon. For months he waged hit-and-run warfare before being reinforced by the militia from Hampshire and Wiltshire. Now with an army at his command, he defeated the Danes at Countisbury Hill. Afterwards, the king himself slipped into the enemy camp in the guise of a minstrel to learn their plans.

Next came the critical Battle of Ethandune. According to his contemporary, Bishop Asser: 'Alfred attacked the whole pagan army, fighting ferociously in dense order and by divine will eventually won the victory, made great slaughter among them and pursued them to their fortress [at Chippenham].' After a two-week siege, the Danes 'were brought to the extreme depths of despair by hunger, cold and fear and they sought peace'. Their king, Guthrum, and his top lieutenants agreed to be baptised and Alfred and the Anglo-Saxons took control of the south-western half of England. So great was his triumph that the Vikings claimed he must be descended from Odin, the Nordic god of war.

A year later the Vikings were chased from Mercia and in 886 Alfred reconquered London. He had stopped the Danes from conquering the whole of England and was recognised as monarch by all Anglo-Saxons not living in Danish-controlled territory. By the early 890s his coinage pictured him as king of England, rather than of Wessex.

Alfred had ordered the construction of a new minster in Winchester, to serve as a final resting place for English kings, but when he died at 50 it was still under construction, so he was buried in the old minster. The monks there, however, were much alarmed when his ghost walked in the cloister at night and transferred his remains to the new minster as soon as it was ready. Later his sepulchre was relocated to Hyde Abbey, also in Winchester, but the tombs of the Anglo-Saxon kings were destroyed when Henry VIII dissolved the monasteries in the 16th century. Pious monks collected some of the royal bones and put them willy-nilly into caskets that are now above the chancel in Winchester cathedral.

Other action this day

1800: Prussian military strategist and Generalfeldmarschall Helmuth Karl Bernhard Graf von Moltke is born ∗ 1940: The American fighter plane P-51 Mustang makes its maiden flight ∗ 1944: After four days of fighting, the Battle of Leyte Gulf ends in American victory, as the Japanese lose over 10,000 killed, four aircraft carriers, three battleships, eight cruisers and twelve destroyers in the largest naval battle of the Second World War

27 October

A flaming cross inspires Emperor Constantine at Milvian Bridge

AD 312 The emperor Constantine was camped with his army around the Via Flaminia, seven miles north of Rome. Today, as his troops prepared for battle, he looked to the sky and saw suspended there a flaming cross brighter than the sun inscribed with the Greek words Εν Τουτω Νικα (often rendered in Latin as *In hoc signo vinces* – 'By this sign thou shalt conquer'.) Understanding this as a direct message from God, he ordered a cross interwoven into the imperial standard and attached to the helmets and shields of his soldiers.

Constantine and his co-emperor Maxentius were jockeying for control of the Roman empire. Constantine held sway over Gaul, England and parts of Germany, and Maxentius was master of Italy, Spain and Africa. In 310 Constantine had taken over Spain and was now determined to seize the rest of Maxentius's territories. (The fact that the two were brothers-in-law apparently made no difference to their bloody rivalry.)

The day following Constantine's heavenly vision, Maxentius moved his troops to the Milvian Bridge, a stone structure crossing the Tiber that carries the Via Flaminia into Rome. When Constantine's inspired soldiers attacked, Maxentius was pushed back towards the city over a temporary wooden bridge that had been thrown up beside the stone one, but under the weight of the fleeing soldiers the wood gave way and many of the defenders, including Maxentius, drowned in the swirling waters of the river. As a sign of victory, Constantine had his rival's head carried on a pike throughout the city as he entered in triumph. So convinced was he that he had received divine aid that he immediately erected a triumphal arch (the remains of which still stand) that credits his success to the inspiration of God.

The Battle of Milvian Bridge was a true turning point in history. The first result was the reunification of the Roman empire under a single ruler (although another regional Caesar, Licinius, had to be overcome first, which he was in 324). But of far more lasting conse- quence was Constantine's confirmed commitment to Christianity. The year after the battle he and Licinius published the Edict of Milan that established toleration of Christianity throughout the empire.

For the remainder of his reign Constantine actively tried to Christianise his subjects. Numerous laws supported Christianity while (usually mildly) suppressing paganism. He abolished cruci- fixion as a punishment because of its symbolic significance and imposed the observance of religious worship on Sundays. He even went to war with a portable altar and commanded that his soldiers recite a special Christian prayer that he himself had written.

In 326 his mother Helena, long a committed Christian, travelled to Jerusalem where she discovered the Holy Sepulchre, the tomb of Jesus. Constantine ordered the construction of a great basilica on the spot. (Oddly, the emperor himself waited until a few days before his death to be baptised into the church.)

It was largely through the efforts of Constantine that the Western world was converted to Christianity as early and as completely as it was. If you would like to see the site of this epochal battle, you can still admire the Milvian Bridge (Ponte Milvio in Italian) and walk the Via Flaminia as it leads north from the Eternal City.

Other action this day

1644: The Roundheads defeat the Cavaliers at the Second Battle of Newbury during the English Civil War * 1858: Birth of Theodore Roosevelt, American president and colonel of the 'Rough Riders' of the Spanish-American War * 1870: French marshal François Bazaine surrenders his army of 140,000 men to Prince Frederick Charles of Prussia at Metz during the Franco-Prussian War

28 October

Richelieu takes La Rochelle

1628 Since the mid-16th century, religion and politics had been inextricably mixed in France, as Huguenots battled with Catholics not only for religious freedom but also for political independence from the crown.

La Rochelle was a Huguenot city on France's Atlantic coast. During the turmoil of the Thirty Years War it had allied itself with Protestant England at a time when France's Cardinal Richelieu – and especially his *éminence grise*, the Capuchin friar Père Joseph – were bent on suppressing Protestantism. For Richelieu, the paramount need was to unify the realm, while Père Joseph was intent on establishing the supremacy of the Catholic church.

Richelieu was determined that no rebellious strongholds would be left to challenge King Louis XIII's authority, and he ordered the besieging of the city, leading the army himself. At his side was Père Joseph, there to help suppress the Protestant heresy.

Richelieu's task was made doubly difficult by the British garrison occupying the Ile de Ré, a tiny island less than two miles off La Rochelle's coast. In June of 1627 George Villers, Duke of Buckingham had landed there with 6,000 men to reinforce the Huguenots.

Ultimately, however, disease struck Buckingham's soldiers, and he ran out of money. They made one final attack on the French-held fort of St Martin but suffered heavy casualties and withdrew from the island.

Now Richelieu strengthened his grip around La Rochelle with seven miles of entrenchments, studded with forts. He also ordered constructed a 60-foot-high sea wall almost a mile long, to prevent the English from relieving the Huguenots by ship.

The English made one final effort to break the siege, but their bombardment failed to do serious damage to the French defences and they abandoned La Rochelle to its fate.

Now Richelieu settled down to wait. To conserve their meagre supplies, La Rochelle's defenders expelled *bouches inutiles* ('useless mouths' – i.e. women, children and old people). Richelieu's troops refused to help them and they perished of cold and hunger. Meanwhile the remaining inhabitants were reduced to eating first horses, then dogs and cats and even rats.

Finally, after fifteen months of siege, La Rochelle capitulated on this day, and the triumphant Cardinal Richelieu and Père Joseph rode through the gates to a grim reception. Three-quarters of the city's 27,000 citizens had died of starvation.

Richelieu ordered the city's walls demolished but pardoned the remaining citizens, although they lost their political and military rights. They were even allowed to remain Protestants. That small freedom they retained for 57 years, until Louis XIV revoked the Edict of Nantes in 1685.

Other action this day

1664: The Duke of York and Albany's Maritime Regiment of Foot, later to be known as the Royal Marines, is established * 1922: Benito Mussolini marches on Rome with 30,000 Fascists, forcing King Victor Emmanuel III to make him prime minister * 1940: Okhi Day: after Greek prime minister Metaxas had rejected Mussolini's ultimatum, at 6.00am Italian troops cross the border from occupied Albania to invade Greece

29 October

'Forward the Mule Brigade'

1863 If ever the phrase 'in dire straits' needed a vivid illustration, it could be provided by the situation of the Union Army of the Cumberland in the autumn of 1863 during the American Civil War: 45,000 strong, badly defeated at Chickamauga the previous month, now under siege at Chattanooga, running out of supplies, its troops on half rations.

Virtually surrounding them, the victorious Confederate forces of General Braxton Bragg, at a strength of 70,000, occupied the heights and valleys around Chattanooga, commanding the city's approaches – rail, road, and water – and leaving the Union army, its back to the Tennessee River, with a single pontoon bridge to link up with a now greatly elongated supply line over difficult terrain.

A retreat from Chattanooga would have likely been a disaster for the Northern cause, losing an important strategic position and bringing on the possibility of a second demoralising defeat in the Western Theatre. So General William Rosecrans, whose leadership before, during and after Chickamauga had led to the Army of the Cumberland's present situation, was dismissed on 20 October and replaced by General George Thomas, the army's one bright star in that defeat. Thomas wired his superior General Ulysses S. Grant: 'We will hold the town till we starve.'

Grant admired the spirit of the new commander's message, but when he reached Chattanooga on 23 October, it appeared to him initially 'as if but two courses were open: one to starve, the other to surrender or be captured'. After inspecting the river above and below the city, however, Grant decided that the answer to the army's problem was to find a shorter supply route across terrain now under enemy guns. It was a route the hungry Northern troops would soon dub 'the Cracker Line'.

It was a bold operation that involved seizing Brown's Ferry, some six miles below Chattanooga, putting a bridge across, and then linking it by a road to the pontoon bridge above the city. Accordingly, on the night of 26 October, from Bridgeport, well to the south, Union general Joseph Hooker began a march upriver with a sizeable infantry force. Meanwhile, troops from the city descended the river in boats, reaching Brown's Ferry at 5.00am to capture the Confederate pickets and take possession of the heights above. By 7.00am the position was reinforced and by 10.00am a bridge was laid. Hooker's force arrived at the crossing late in the day. Now, with bridges at Brown's Ferry and Chattanooga – and a road between out of enemy fire – the 'Cracker Line' was connected.

General Bragg was surprised by the unexpected Union move-ment, and to break the new connection so vital to the Union forces, he sent four brigades down from Lookout Mountain on the evening of 28 October to attack Hooker's troops holding a position at Wauhatchie, near Brown's Ferry.

The Confederates, outnumbering the defenders, launched their attack well before dawn. The fighting was fierce, although the Union line was holding. Then something unaccountable occurred. Here is Grant's account from his memoirs:

> The night was so dark that the men could not distinguish one from another except by the light of the flashes of their muskets. In the darkness and uproar, Hooker's teamsters [mule drivers] became frightened and deserted their teams. The mules also became frightened, and breaking loose from their fastenings stampeded directly towards the enemy. The latter, no doubt, took this for a charge, and stampeded in turn. By four o'clock in the morning the battle had entirely ceased and our 'cracker line' was never afterward disturbed.

So it was that some 200 badly frightened beasts helped produce a welcome victory for the North, bringing relief at last to a besieged Union army. The event was, of course, no more than the briefest prelude to the great campaign of the next month, when Grant, Sherman and Thomas would combine efforts to free Chattanooga from the Confederate grip.

Even so, as food, clothes and ammunition flowed at last into Chattanooga, the action at Wauhatchie seemed worth celebrating, and it inspired one Union soldier to heroic poetry – or in this case parody. The historian Shelby Foote identifies an otherwise anonymous Ohio infantryman as the author of 'The Charge of the Mule Brigade'. Here is the opening stanza:

> Half a mile, half a mile,
> Half a mile onward,
> Right toward the Georgia troops,
> Broke the two hundred.
> 'Forward the Mule brigade;
> Charge for the Rebs!' they neighed.
> Straight for the Georgia troops
> Broke the two hundred.

Other action this day
1665: The Portuguese defeat the forces of King Antonio I of Kongo in central Africa, decapitating the king, at the Battle of Ambuila * 1762: Prince Henry of Prussia defeats the Austrians at the Battle of Freiberg, the last major battle of the Seven Years' War * 1956: Israeli troops invade the Sinai peninsula as the Suez Crisis begins

30 October

The last Muslim invasion of Spain

1340 What chance did a poor sultan of Morocco have against two Alfonsos – Alfonso XI from Castile, called the Just, and Alfonso IV from Portugal, called the Brave? As it turned out, not much.

When he succeeded to the Moroccan sultanate in 1331, Abu al-Hasan dedicated himself to a familiar Muslim goal: to cleanse all Spain of Christian infidels. To that end he crossed from North Africa (present-day Morocco) with a vast army, captured Gibraltar and Algeciras and then utterly destroyed the Castilian fleet in the Strait of Gibraltar when the Spaniards tried to reclaim the Rock. The entire Iberian peninsula looked ripe for the picking, for its two principal Christian states, Castile and Portugal, were enmeshed in deadly rivalry. The sultan marched his divisions north, towards Seville.

Abu al-Hasan's mistake was to forget that the Christian powers hated the Muslims even more than they hated each other. Although the two Alfonsos had long been at loggerheads about disputed territory, Abu al-Hasan's victory at Gibraltar inspired them to forge an alliance to combat the Moorish threat.

And so it was that on this day the combined forces of Alfonso the Just and Alfonso the Brave met Abu al-Hasan's Saracen army at Rio Salado just outside Tarifa, on Spain's south coast, west of Gibraltar. During the battle the Castilian Alfonso came under severe attack and was saved only by the timely intervention of the fighting Archbishop of Toledo, Gil Álvarez Carrillo de Albornoz. But the Christian forces rallied for a quick, complete and merciless victory. At the battle's conclusion they sacked the sultan's camp, killing many of his wives and his daughter and taking his sister and his son captive.

It was such a disastrous defeat for Abu al-Hasan that he was forced to flee for North Africa, never to return. This was the last Moorish attempt to conquer Spain. The Muslim jihad was over and, little by little, the forces of Christianity would reconquer all of Spain until that day in 1492 when Granada, the last Moorish stronghold, would open its gates to the army of Ferdinand and Isabella (see 2 January).

Other action this day

1270: Charles I of Sicily, the brother of France's king Louis IX (St Louis) who had died of plague, and the sultan of Tunis agree a peace treaty, bringing the failed Eighth Crusade and the siege of Tunis to an end * 1961: The Soviet Union sets off a 58-megaton hydrogen bomb over Novaya Zemlya, the largest nuclear device ever detonated, approximately 3,500 times as powerful as the Hiroshima atomic bomb

31 October

Take Jerusalem by Christmas

1917 Take Jerusalem by Christmas. That was the word from London. But now, after two costly defeats at Gaza in the spring and a British army, the Egyptian Expeditionary Force (EEF), left stalled in front of the Turkish defence line stretching 30 miles inland to Beersheba, the task didn't look so easy. Once again, as they had at Gallipoli and in Mesopotamia, the Turks demonstrated formidable skills in defending prepared positions.

So in June, for his failures, General Sir Archibald Murray was recalled to London and General Edmund Allenby, fresh from his success at Arras, was sent out to Cairo to replace him. The objective remained the same: take Jerusalem by Christmas. With discouraging news on other war fronts, Prime Minister Lloyd George wanted results in Palestine.

Not everyone in the higher reaches of British policy-making circles was in favour of an effort on the Palestine front. After the 1915 failure at Gallipoli, many doubted that such 'sideshows' were anything more than a drain of resources badly needed in the main war theatre, France. Lord Kitchener saw no strategic value in Palestine. Others, however, saw action there as a way to prevent Turkey from reinforcing other fronts. A few even advocated a far larger effort, using a naval force to land an army behind the Turks and produce a surrender by the autumn of 1917, thus freeing up the troops there for deployment to Europe in the following year.

Once in the field, Allenby got to work immediately. First, he moved his operational headquarters from Cairo to the field. Then he changed his army's command structure and overhauled its logistical establishment. Finally, he asked London for more troops, artillery and aircraft. He got three divisions, giving him a total of nine and raising the EEF's strength to some 80,000, about twice what the Turks had facing him across the Gaza–Beersheba line.

By late October, Allenby's plans were set. Using a variety of tricks – including arranging for faked orders to fall into enemy hands – he deceived the Turks into expecting a third attack on Gaza. At dawn on this date his forces struck, six divisions sent against the Beersheba end of the line. In the late afternoon, in what has been called the last successful cavalry charge in history, the Australian cavalry division charged a distance of four miles to overrun the Turkish trench lines, capturing first Beersheba's vital water supply, then breaking through the outer walls to take the city itself. By day's end, the Turks had fled.

Follow-up attacks against Gaza proved unsuccessful, but five days later Allenby threw the main weight of his army against the strongpoint at Tel Esh Sheria, near the middle of the line. Breaking through, British cavalry headed towards the coast, forcing the Gaza defenders to withdraw and splitting the enemy forces east and west. Over the month of November, as the British advance continued, there was severe fighting at Junction Station, then at Hebron. But the momentum was with Allenby's army, and on 9 December British troops entered Jerusalem, evacuated by the Turks a day earlier.

While these successes were achieved, warfare of a different sort was being waged behind Turkish lines. British major T.E. Lawrence led a group of Arab raiders intending to blow up a bridge at Yarmuk and cripple the Hejaz railway on which Turkish logistics depended. The raid turned out to be unsuccessful, but it was the first of many guerrilla actions which, coordinated with Allenby's advance, would prove highly effective at distracting the Turks on their desert flank.

Allenby's Palestine campaign was one of the few bright spots in Allied operations in 1917, and he received further reinforcements for its continuation in 1918. His efforts, however, were interrupted by the spring German offensive in France, which required the imme-diate transfer of 60 battalions to the Western Front and, thus, the postponement of his opening attacks. In the end, however, what had begun at Beersheba led eventually to the decisive battle of Megiddo in September 1918, followed by the capture of Damascus, the rout of Turkish forces from Syria, and Turkey's surrender on 30 October.

Allenby's victories of 1917 and 1918 were heady news for war-weary Britons. Some years later, in his history of the war, *The World Crisis*, Churchill gave this evaluation of the Palestine and Syrian campaigns: 'No praise is too high for these brilliant and frugal opera-tions, which will long serve as a model in theatres of war in which manoeuvre is possible.'

Other action this day

1639: Dutch admiral Maarten Tromp crushes a Spanish fleet under Admiral Antonio de Oquendo at the Battle of the Downs * 1861: Suffering from rheumatism and gout and weighing over 300 pounds (21 stone), 75-year-old Winfield Scott resigns as commander of the Union Army on the grounds of poor health, to be replaced the next day by George McClellan * 1941: At 5.25am the German submarine U-552 torpedoes and sinks the destroyer USS *Reuben James*, killing 115 of her 159-man crew, the first US Navy ship sunk by enemy action in the Second World War

1 November

The Chinese enter the Korean War

1950 The war in Korea – now in its fifth month – looked all but won, with the North Korean army shattered and in retreat, closely pursued by General Douglas MacArthur's United Nations forces, mainly the US 8th Army. Final victory seemed very near, and among the American units in the field, the word was out that the troops might get home for Christmas.

This evening, however, outside the North Korean village of Unsan, some 50 miles below the Yalu River which marked the border with China, an omen to the contrary arrived. It arrived with no warning out of the evening gloom. It came in the form of an enormous mass of enemy infantry carrying out savage assaults against forward positions in the UN line. Among the units heaviest hit was the US 8th Cavalry Regiment, which was soon surrounded on three sides, its battalions cut off from one another. Backed by rocket and mortar fire, the attacks continued through the night. With morning came the order from I Corps for the regiment to withdraw; but the withdrawal route had been cut, and the retreating column found itself ambushed. Soldiers fled into the hills to escape; many were killed or captured. Left behind as a rearguard, the 3rd Battalion was effectively destroyed.

Unsan was a shock. The 8th Army withdrew its forward units south of the Chongchon River to consolidate. Meanwhile, the enemy disengaged completely. And now it was revealed that the attackers were not North Koreans, but Chinese. Communist China had entered the Korean War.

It was a development with serious strategic consequences. The immediate and pressing question was how to proceed with the war. Some 8th Army commanders expressed misgivings about continuing the war-ending push in the face of this new and unquantifiable hazard. So did the joint chiefs of staff in Washington. US Army Intelligence, which had heretofore denied reports of Chinese troops sighted in the field, now estimated that as many as 300,000 Chinese troops might have crossed the Yalu into North Korea. If that were true, UN forces would be heavily outnumbered as they conducted an offensive in mountainous terrain, in fierce winter weather, and on a peninsula whose widening dimensions would disperse 8th Army elements well beyond mutual support. Many now asked whether a pause in the advance was indicated, whether a more defensible line should be drawn across the waist of the peninsula from which the Republic of South Korea could be protected.

It was, of course, Douglas MacArthur's war, for he had turned it around only two months earlier with his brilliant amphibious landing at Inchon (see 14 September), which had driven the North Korean forces out of South Korea. Now, on the brink of what might be his greatest triumph in a long, illustrious – and sometimes controversial – military career, he chose to ignore whatever Unsan portended and resume the push towards the Yalu.

To all doubters MacArthur had the answer. Addressing a group of I Corps officers a few days after Unsan, he said: 'Gentlemen, the war is over. The Chinese are not coming into this war. In less than two weeks, the 8th Army will close on the Yalu across the entire front. The 3rd Division will be back in Fort Benning for Christmas.' To the joint chiefs of staff in Washington, who suggested a rethinking of strategy, he cabled that abandoning the mission would be an act like 'Munich'.

On 24 November, Thanksgiving Day, he flew to Korea from his Tokyo headquarters for the send-off of what had become known as the Home-by-Christmas offensive. Two days later 180,000 Chinese troops hit the 8th Army, crumpling its right flank and forcing a confused retreat. On the east coast, X Corps – 1st Marine and 7th Infantry divisions – found itself surrounded by six Chinese divisions, some 120,000 troops, but fought its way out to an evacuation by sea. These were major reverses for the UN forces, which managed to avoid disaster only by falling back to positions near the 38th parallel.

A second Communist assault in early January 1951 – by now an estimated 500,000 Chinese troops had crossed the border into North Korea – pushed the UN forces further south. In turn, a UN spring counter-offensive restored the line along the central corridor. There, for the next two and a half years, as negotiations for a ceasefire dragged on, the conflict 'sank into a position war of trenches, bunkers and patrols', as the historian Walter Millis described it, 'strikingly reminiscent of the trench stalemate of 1915–18'.

True to form, MacArthur never conceded he was wrong about

Unsan. As his forces retreated down the peninsula, he called for more troops and the expansion of the war into China itself. In so doing, he openly defied the US president, Harry Truman, whose policy was one of limited war, and because of it the general lost his job in April.

'The object of war,' he announced on his return home, 'is victory.' But by this time, the situation in Korea didn't look winnable his way. His colleague Omar Bradley, chairman of the joint chiefs of staff, had the better analysis: to expand the conflict with China, Bradley said, was to fight 'The wrong war at the wrong time in the wrong place'.

MacArthur's successor as Supreme Commander Far East – an officer who had revered him as 'a truly great military man, a great statesman, and a gallant leader' – was General Matthew B. Ridgway. Some years later, Ridgway, evaluating the competing strategies of the Korean War, chose to compare what took place after Unsan with another famous military gamble gone wrong: 'MacArthur,' he wrote, 'was like General Custer at the Little Big Horn, who had neither the eyes nor ears for information that might deter him from the attainment of his objective ...'

Other action this day

1911: In the first-ever aerial bomb attack, Italian pilot Giolio Gavotti drops four bombs on two Turkish positions in Libya during the Turco-Italian War * 1914: German Vice Admiral Maximilian von Spee routs a British fleet under Rear Admiral Christopher Cradock at the Battle of Coronel off the coast of Chile, the first British naval defeat since the Battle of Lake Champlain 100 years and 50 days before * 1952: America detonates the first hydrogen bomb in the Eniwetok atoll of the Marshall Islands in the Pacific, yielding 10.4 megatons

2 November

American abolitionist John Brown is sentenced to hang

1859 It is said that fanatics make good martyrs, and John Brown, who today was sentenced to death for murder and treason, was a perfect example. Hawk-nosed, hard-eyed and bearded, he even looked the part he played.

Born in Connecticut in 1800, he had failed at numerous trades: tanner, land speculator, drover and travelling salesman. Moving his large family from place to place, he became a fanatical abolitionist, once demonstrating his ardour by living in a free black community in New York state. Later he moved to the Kansas Territory and led a night-time guerrilla raid against a pro-slavery community in which five men were dragged from their cabins and beaten to death.

On 16 October 1859 Brown led a ragtag bunch of sixteen whites and five blacks on a raid on Harper's Ferry, Virginia (today West Virginia). After an early exchange of shots in which two bystanders were killed, he set up headquarters in the federal armoury that his men had captured. For two days and nights he holed up there with some 60 hostages, waiting for nearby slaves to rise up to claim their freedom. By then state militia had surrounded the armoury, and on the morning of 18 October a company of US Marines under the command of Colonel Robert E. Lee and cavalry officer J.E.B. Stuart stormed it. A Marine lieutenant beat Brown to the ground with his sword, and ten of Brown's men were killed in the action, including two of his sons.

Brown was quickly taken to Charlestown (now in West Virginia) for his trial, during which he lay prone on a cot, incapacitated by the sword wounds he had received when captured. At the end of a week, on this Wednesday the jury found him guilty of murder, treason against the state of Virginia and inciting slave insurrection. He was sentenced to death by hanging.

About eleven o'clock on the morning of 2 December, Brown was brought to the field of execution, where a crowd of 1,000 waited in anticipation, along with 1,500 soldiers. He arrived riding in a furniture wagon, sitting on his own coffin, his arms tied at the elbows. On his way to the gallows he slipped a final note to one of his supporters in which he accurately prophesied: 'the crimes of this guilty land will never be purged away; but with Blood.'

Although shabbily dressed, Brown was calm and courteous. He mounted the scaffold without resistance and offered his neck for the noose. His head was then covered with a white hood.

The sheriff asked Brown if he wanted to signal the drop himself by throwing a handkerchief, but the tired old man replied: 'No, I don't care. I don't want you to keep me waiting unnecessarily.' These were his last words, spoken civilly, without emotion. Then a hush fell over the crowd until there was total silence, and the sheriff cut the rope with a sharp blow from his hatchet.

Within eighteen months Brown's cause was vindicated; the Civil War had begun, and 'John Brown's Body' soon became a favourite marching song of Northern troops.

Other action this day

82 BC: Roman general Lucius Cornelius Sulla enters Rome with his army after year and a half of civil war, shortly to become dictator * 1401: Owen Glendower begins his Welsh rebellion against Henry IV * 1963: South Vietnamese president Diem is assassinated during a military *coup d'état*, to be replaced by General Duong Van Minh ('Big Minh') four days later

3 November

The Indians attack at dawn

1791 It was a military situation tailor-made for disaster: an ill-trained force, deep in enemy territory, low on rations, weakened by desertions, beset by rain, hail, and snow, its commander so disabled by gout he had to carried in a litter, and its perimeter defences inadequate despite intelligence that hostile forces were drawing close.

This was the situation in which General Arthur St Clair's American army found itself this afternoon, encamped near the east bank of the Wabash River in Indiana. The army's mission – to deal with hostile Indian tribes of the region, while building a string of forts as a line of communications – was part of a larger effort by the United States to take control of the Northwest Territory, won from Great Britain in the 1783 Treaty of Paris.

These vast new lands, increasingly coveted by American settlers, were occupied by Indian tribes, most of whom had sided with Britain in the war and who increasingly resented the tide of white settlement. Congress, having virtually disbanded the Continental Army after 1783, now came to realise that the region would require order and protection. But what the legislators created to meet the frontier challenge was no more than a makeshift military force combining an inadequate core of trained regulars with a large complement of state militiamen and one-year recruits.

In 1790 this army, led by General Harmar, met utter defeat at the hands of the region's tribes – Miamis, Shawnees, and Delawares – an event that prompted Congress in March 1791 to authorise the raising of a new expedition, one with a distinctly punitive mission. Under the command of General St Clair, the force, 2,100 strong at the outset, included just 600 regulars, the balance being barely trained recruits and militia. Accompanied by 200 women and children, it began its advance north from Fort Washington (Cincinnati) on the Ohio River in August. The troops were described by their adjutant general as 'the offscouring of large Towns and Cities, enervated by Idleness, Debaucherie and every species of Vice', a force that could not 'have been made competent to the arduous duties of Indian Warfare'. He was right.

The army soon paused to build the first of the forts, then continued its march in late October. A second fort was constructed in November. By now, however, desertions had reduced its ranks to just over 1,000. This evening, at a camp 100 miles into the territory, near the Wabash River, the army's fate was at hand.

At dawn the next morning 1,000 Indians attacked, precipitating headlong flight by much of the militia. St Clair left his litter to send his regulars on a series of bayonet charges to disperse the attackers. But as a major noted in his journal: 'The savages seemed not to fear anything we could do. They could skip out of reach of bayonet, and return as they pleased.'

In desperation, St Clair ordered what remained of his force to make their way back to the second fort. From there, in disarray, the survivors reached Fort Washington four days later. Apart from militia desertions, the losses exceeded 900, including over 600 soldiers killed and another 260 wounded. In addition, many of the women and children perished or were taken prisoner.

If the experience of such a disaster can ever have a good side, it was this: Henry Knox, the new republic's secretary of war, concluded that the reliance on militia for frontier warfare had proved unrealistic and that a standing federal army of reasonable size was required. President Washington agreed. So did Congress, which the following March authorised a permanent regular fighting force of 5,200 troops.

The new army's commander, General Anthony Wayne, shaped his force with the strictest discipline, then led it into the Northwest

Territory on a campaign that brought what his two predecessors had been unable to achieve: victory over the Indians, in this case, the 1794 Battle of Fallen Timbers, resulting in a peace treaty in which the tribes agreed to open most of what would soon become the state of Ohio to white settlement.

But by any measure, St Clair's defeat in the Battle of the Wabash ended up being the worst American military disaster in over two centuries of Indian fighting – worse than what Braddock had encountered on the Monongahela in 1755, far worse than Custer's famous defeat at the Little Bighorn in 1876.

Other action this day

1760: Frederick the Great suffers 20,000 casualties in defeating a larger Austrian army, with 16,000 casualties, at the Battle of Torgau during the Seven Years War * 1812: Russian forces defeat part of Napoleon's army at Vyazma during Napoleon's retreat from Moscow * 1856: A British fleet shells Canton (now Guangzhou) during the Second Opium War

4 November

Montgomery defeats Rommel at El Alamein

1942 Make sure you drink a Montgomery cocktail (recipe below), for today marks the completion of a tremendous two-week battle at El Alamein, Egypt, in which the British 8th Army, under the command of General Bernard Law Montgomery, defeated the Italian–German Panzerarmee Afrika led by General Erwin Rommel.

If you were in England and read the next day's *Daily Telegraph*, you would have seen this headline: 'AXIS FORCES IN FULL RETREAT: OFFICIAL. Rommel's disordered columns attacked relentlessly. 9,000 prisoners; 260 tanks destroyed.' In America, on the eve of congressional elections, news of the victory swept politics off the front pages.

El Alamein was a most welcome feat of arms, coming as it did after the British debacles at Singapore and Tobruk, and went a long way to cement relations between the British and American military chiefs. Montgomery's victory saved Egypt and the Suez Canal. Churchill, in handsome overstatement, said: 'Before Alamein we never had a victory; after Alamein we never had a defeat.' In truth, the battle marked a turning of the tide of war, a shift that would be entirely confirmed three months later by the German defeat before Stalingrad.

Monty always had his detractors, however, who found his style of warfare too cautious and deliberate. Some years later in Harry's Bar in Venice, Ernest Hemingway invented the Montgomery cocktail, a martini made up of fifteen parts of gin to one of vermouth. This mixture, its inventor swore, was based on the ratio of his own troops to those of the enemy that Monty required before ordering an attack. Serve very cold.

Other action this day

1576: The first day of the Spanish Fury, three days of horror at Antwerp when Spanish *tercios*, enraged because they have not been paid, sack the city, killing 8,000 people * 1921: Hitler establishes the SA (Sturm-abteilung ['Assault Division'] or storm troopers), known as the Brownshirts * 1956: At 4.25am Soviet tanks open fire on Hungarian army barracks and move out across Budapest, smashing the Hungarian revolution that had started on 23 October

5 November

The general who wouldn't fight

1862 The war changed, but General McClellan didn't. So on this date President Abraham Lincoln signed General Order No. 182, which began: 'By direction of the President, it is ordered that Major General McClellan be relieved from command of the Army of the Potomac ...' George Brinton McClellan received the news two evenings later, sitting in a tent at his headquarters in Rectortown, Virginia.

McClellan had arrived in Washington, DC some sixteen months earlier, right after the Union army's shocking defeat at Bull Run in July 1861. Splendidly uniformed, a well-connected professional soldier and only 35 years old, he looked every inch the successful military leader. Lincoln picked him to command the shattered Army of the Potomac, restore it to fighting trim and lead it to some badly needed Union victories against the Confederates.

McClellan quickly rebuilt and reinvigorated the demoralised army. He proved popular with the troops, who cheered him at every opportunity. He was promoted to general-in-chief of all the Union armies. In the autumn a series of stirring military reviews took place in the capital. But parades were no substitute for success in the field and as the campaigning months passed, the president, his cabinet and the Republicans in Congress grew frustrated by the chief general's reluctance to engage in offensive operations against the enemy, whose picket lines after Bull Run were visible from the Union capital. At one point, an exasperated Lincoln asked whether he might 'borrow' the army if the general had no plans to use it.

McClellan countered the pressures on him to get moving with demands for more troops, citing intelligence estimates of enemy strength that were soon found to be highly inflated. As more government officials and committees called for action, he met them with active hostility, for he considered the war and its conduct matters to be dealt with solely by professional soldiers. He referred to politicians as the 'incapables' and Lincoln as the 'gorilla'.

The heart of the problem was McClellan's fear of risking his considerable reputation by engaging in actual combat, where defeat was always a possibility. The historian Bruce Catton summed up the general this way: 'McClellan had nearly all the gifts: youth, energy, charm, intelligence, sound professional training. But the fates who gave him these gifts left out the one that a general must have before all others – the hard, instinctive fondness for fighting.'

Finally, in April 1862, after eight months as commander, 'Little Mac' took the Army of the Potomac towards the enemy capital at Richmond, Virginia. It was a campaign that, had he pressed it, might have ended the war that year. Instead, he dawdled away all the Union's considerable advantages of numbers and initiative in an effort that ended in stalemate and withdrawal five months later. In self-defence, he cited the enemy's superior strength – which he managed to double – and the lack of support from the 'incapables', whom he accused of 'sacrificing' his army.

With his Richmond campaign a failure, it looked as if his days as commander were numbered, but after General Pope's 29 August disaster at Second Bull Run, there was simply no other senior officer deemed capable of putting the battered army back into working order. So McClellan got a second chance.

Again, he rose to the occasion, quickly refitting the army, this time setting it in motion to intercept Lee's invading army at Antietam, Maryland. There, on 17 September, the two armies fought to a bloody tactical draw. A more vigorous and better-coordinated push might have won a war-ending battle for the Union, but McClellan, in an excess of caution, never committed his reserve against an outnumbered enemy. And on the second day he avoided combat altogether, allowing Lee's battered army to slip away.

In any event, Antietam went down as a strategic victory for the Union, for it not only repelled the Confederate invasion of Maryland, but also gave Lincoln the platform of success he needed to issue the Emancipation Proclamation freeing the Southern slaves, which he did on 22 September.

And there was still a chance to secure a Union victory in the field. In early October Lincoln ordered McClellan to send his forces across the Potomac and pursue the retreating enemy. The general, however, pleading the necessity of visiting Mrs McClellan in Philadelphia, kept his army idle for three weeks before sending it south, a delay that allowed the Confederates to reach safety east of the Blue Ridge mountains.

Now, Lincoln had had enough and issued today's order relieving McClellan of command. 'Little Mac' never held another military command. His immediate successors – Burnside and Hooker – were, in turn, notably unsuccessful in attaining Union victories, but in time Lincoln found what he was looking for – a general who fights – in the slightly dishevelled figure of Ulysses S. Grant, in every way the antithesis of McClellan.

'Little Mac' ran against Lincoln in the presidential election of 1864, on the Northern Democrats' peace platform, but in the face of timely Union victories at Atlanta and Cedar Ridge – of the sort he himself had never been able to achieve – he lost in a landslide. He retired to New Jersey, where in 1877 he was elected governor and served a single term.

Other action this day

1556: Emperor Akbar defeats the Hindus at Panipat and secures control of the Mughal empire * 1757: With only 22,000 men against his enemy's 42,000, Frederick the Great trounces the French and the Holy Roman Empire at the Battle of Rossbach, losing only 550 men compared to 10,000 casualties and 5,000 captured for the foe ∗ 1854: The combined British and French armies defeat the Russians at the Battle of Inkerman during the Crimean War ∗ 1925: Russian-born British spy Sidney Reilly (the Ace of Spies) is executed in the forest near Moscow by the Russian OGPU (secret service) for espionage

6 November

The battle that saved the German Protestants

1632 Today Europe's two greatest generals, King Gustavus Adolphus of Sweden and Prince Albrecht von Wallenstein, met near the Saxon town of Lützen in a battle of which the outcome prevented the destruction of Protestantism in Germany. The victor died on the field.

Gustavus Adolphus's portraits show a man of high and noble brow, calm, speculative eyes and a long, strong nose above his moustache and narrow, pointed goatee. He was intelligent and enlightened, an inspiring leader and brilliant commander.

He had inherited the Swedish throne in 1611, seven years before the outbreak of the terrible Thirty Years War between Germany's Protestant principalities and the reactionary Catholic Holy Roman Emperor Ferdinand II of the House of Habsburg.

Wallenstein was an altogether different animal. Eleven years Gustavus Adolphus's senior, he was born in Bohemia, orphaned at thirteen and raised a Protestant by his uncle. But at 23 he cynically converted to Catholicism to strengthen his position with the Holy Roman Emperor of the day and three years later married an elderly but fabulously rich widow, whose money he inherited five years later. His wealth enabled him to provide an army at his own expense in the service of the emperor and by 1625 he had become the head of all Imperial forces, while grabbing for himself enormous swaths of Germany and Denmark. As his power grew, so did his ambitions, as he then started to trade alliances like any unscrupulous king, negotiating for advantage with Protestants and Catholics alike, finally causing Emperor Ferdinand to sack him in August 1630.

But only weeks later, seeing the cause of Protestantism in danger of collapse, Gustavus Adolphus joined the German principalities in their conflict against the emperor. Supported financially by France's crafty Cardinal Richelieu, the 34-year-old king swept across northern Germany, utterly crushing the Imperial forces under the command of Wallenstein's replacement, Johann von Tilly, at Breitenfeld, earning himself the sobriquet of the 'Lion of the North'. Desperate, Emperor Ferdinand was now forced to recall the arrogant, ambitious – but supremely talented – Wallenstein.

The morning of 6 November 1632 was cold and misty as Gustavus Adolphus launched his assault against Wallenstein's army at Lützen. His Swedish soldiers rushed to the attack singing Martin Luther's hymn 'Eine feste Burg ist unser Gott' ('A Mighty Fortress is Our God') and another hymn composed by the king himself. The fate of Protestant Germany rested on the outcome.

All day long the two forces battled, with the Swedish king leading his own cavalry, but in one fierce charge Gustavus Adolphus became separated from his men and was cut down by encircling Imperial horsemen. According to the myth-makers, his last words were a noble: 'I seal with my blood my religion and the liberties of Germany.'

In spite of his death, Gustavus Adolphus's army continued to batter Wallenstein's, capturing the enemy artillery and forcing Wallenstein to retreat in defeat. At the close of battle the king's body was found on the field and the spot was marked with a stone. Later the German people raised a monument there.

In bringing about the death of the empire's most capable enemy, Wallenstein performed a great service for the emperor, but it also meant he was no longer vital to the emperor's cause. Unwisely, he kept his army at the ready but failed to bring it to Ferdinand's support. Now considering his one-time favourite a traitor, the emperor ordered his assassination two years later (see 25 February).

Other action this day

1494: Birth of Turkish conqueror and sultan Suleiman the Magnificent ＊ 1865: The last surrender of the American Civil War: the Confederate warship *Shenandoah* surrenders to the British ship HMS *Donegal* in Liverpool 211 days after the South's capitulation at Appomattox, having captured 21 Union merchant ships since the war's end ＊ 1917: Canadian troops take Passchendaele, ending the Third Battle of Ypres after three months of fighting

7 November

The October Revolution – the Bolsheviks take over Russia

1917 Today one of the most improbable events in history took place. It was announced with this message at 10.00am, composed by Lenin only minutes before: 'TO THE CITIZENS OF RUSSIA! The Provisional Government has been deposed ...' But what had occurred during the night was no glorious uprising of workers, no pitched battle in the streets, no storming of a Bastille, only a mild and bloodless coup carried out so quietly that almost nobody resisted and very few knew it had even happened. When it was over, however, the city of St Petersburg and the government of Russia lay in Bolshevik hands.

The slightest resistance might have saved the day. The Bolsheviks had taken over the instruments of power simply by walking in and dismissing those on duty: post offices, railway stations, banks, bridges and telephone centres changed hands without a shot. When morning came, only the Winter Palace remained under the control of the prime minister, Alexander Kerensky, and the Provisional Government.

Leaving his Cabinet ministers behind, Kerensky departed St Petersburg by car and in disguise, looking for troops who would defend the government. At Pskov he persuaded some Cossack units of the 3rd Cavalry Corps to accompany him, but when the soldiers discovered that no other units would join them, they quit two hours from the capital.

Lacking sufficient forces to take the lightly defended Winter Palace by assault, the Bolsheviks ordered the artillery of the Peter and Paul Fortress to fire on the building. Of 35 shells fired, two hit their target with minimal damage. The 'storming' of the palace, later portrayed by Bolshevik historians as the epic event of a great popular rising (called the October Revolution because in Russia the old Julian calendar still prevailed), came about that night only after most of the discouraged defenders – teenage cadets – sensing that reinforcements were not going to turn up, had slunk away, and only then because, as George Kennan wrote, 'someone had inadvertently left the back door open'.

In the capital of Russia, at least, the first day of their bid for power ended successfully, if not heroically, for the Bolsheviks. In other places it was not always so easy – where there was resistance, it often prevailed – but authority, whether military or civil, showed little determination to save itself. So the improbable became reality. Within weeks, in most of the cities of central Russia, the Bolsheviks, with barely 25,000 members around the country, had taken power in the name of 100 million Russian people, most of whom had never heard of the Bolsheviks.

No one mourned the death of the Provisional Government. It had come to uncertain power in the vacuum left by the fall of the monarchy in February. It could not govern a Russia grown unmanageable under the multiple burdens of war, shortages, inflation, strikes and mutiny.

One eyewitness to the day's events was John Reed, who liked what he saw. Later, in *Ten Days That Shook the World*, he remembered how he felt the next morning: 'Now there was all great Russia to win – and then the world! Would Russia follow and rise? And the world – what of it? Would the peoples answer and rise, a red world-tide? Although it was six in the morning, night was yet heavy and chill. There was only a faint unearthly pallor stealing over the silent streets, dimming the watch-fires, the shadow of a terrible dawn grey-rising over Russia ...'

Other action this day

1811: General (and future president) William Henry Harrison defeats a conspiracy by Shawnee chief Tecumseh in the chief's absence at the Battle of Tippecanoe in Indiana * 1900: Three members of the Royal Canadian Dragoons win Victoria Crosses at the Battle of Leliefontein during the Boer War * 1944: The man Ian Fleming called 'the most formidable spy in history', Soviet spy Richard Sorge, who supplied the Red Army with information about the German–Japanese Pact, the attack on Pearl Harbor and the launch date of Operation Barbarossa (Germany's invasion of Russia) is hanged in Sugamo Prison in Tokyo

8 November

The Battle of the White Mountain

1620 It all started on 23 May 1618 with that famous farce, the Second Defenestration of Prague, during which Bohemian Protestants tossed three agents of the Holy Roman Emperor out of the first-floor window of the Hradčany Palace in protest against the Catholic Habsburgs. No one was hurt, but imperial dignity was badly bruised and Catholics and Protestants were further polarised.

Sixteen months later, the Habsburg Ferdinand II, who had been elected King of Bohemia in 1617 only to be deposed by the largely Protestant Bohemian Diet (parliament) a year later, became the new Holy Roman Emperor. Educated by Jesuits, he was a fervent Catholic and determined to restore the true faith – by force if necessary.

Then some Protestant Bohemian nobles rose in revolt, under the leadership of the 24-year-old Frederick V, the very man who had replaced Ferdinand as King of Bohemia. This gave the emperor all the excuse he needed to send in his army. It was the beginning of the Thirty Years War.

On this day in 1620 Imperial troops under the joint command of Johann Tserclaes, Graf von Tilly and Karel Buquoy met the rebel Bohemians on the outskirts of Prague in what is known as the Battle of the White Mountain. The Bohemian commander, Christian Anhalt, endeavouring to block the road to Prague, deployed his troops on the side of a hill called the Bílá Hora (White Mountain). His position looked impregnable, with his left flank protected by a stream and his right flank by a hunting lodge, while between him and the advancing Imperial army was a small brook to slow their charge.

What Anhalt had not counted on, however, was the power of faith – or at least of anger. A monk with Tilly's soldiers suddenly displayed a picture of St Mary that, he said, had been defaced by Protestants. Incensed, the Catholic troops charged across a small bridge crossing the brook and, in less than two hours, annihilated the Bohemians.

Tilly now entered Prague and hanged 27 noble leaders of the insurrection in the Old Town Square, while King Frederick and his wife fled to Holland.

Although the Thirty Years War would continue to drench Europe in blood for another 28 years, in Bohemia the Counter-Reformation was victorious as Protestantism was crushed under the heel of Rome. Prior to the battle, the Bohemians had been semi-independent. When it was over they had become an integral part of the Holy Roman, and later the Austrian, Empire, not to regain their independence for three centuries until the creation of Czechoslovakia in the aftermath of the First World War.

Other action this day

1923: Hitler leads an unsuccessful uprising in Munich, known as the Beer Hall Putsch * 1939: In Munich, Georg Elser unsuccessfully attempts to assassinate Hitler during his celebration of the sixteenth anniversary of the Beer Hall Putsch by detonating a bomb during Hitler's speech * 1942: Under Eisenhower's command, British and US forces invade North Africa, in Operation Torch * 1950: In the first jet dogfight in history, American lieutenant Russell Brown shoots down two North Korean MiGs

9 November

Napoleon's coup d'état

1799 By Revolutionary France's calendar, today was 18 Brumaire, An VIII, the first day of Napoleon Bonaparte's *coup d'état*.

Just back from his battles in Egypt, the diminutive Napoleon (he was just five feet six) was seen as a national hero. Backed by a few powerful members of government (notably Talleyrand), he donned his splashiest general's uniform – white breeches, blue coat with gold-embroidered lapels and a flamboyant red, white and blue sash at the waist – and paraded through the streets of Paris to tumultuous applause. He then entered the Tuileries to swear allegiance to one chamber of the government (the Elders) and next promptly sent 300 soldiers to 'protect' the other chamber, the Council of the Five Hundred.

The following day Napoleon boldly addressed each group, but the Council of the Five Hundred in particular turned on him savagely, and a pale and stammering Napoleon had to be accompanied from the chamber by four soldiers.

601

Having failed to charm the government with words, Napoleon did what he always did best. He sent in troops. His soldiers charged into the Orangerie, forcing the 500 members to flee through the windows.

On the evening of 10 November Bonaparte was declared First Consul; the republican government known as the Directory was over. From that day until his abdication Napoleon held supreme power in France. Six years earlier to the day, the Revolutionary government had abolished the worship of God, and on that anniversary they instituted a replacement.

Other action this day

1918: German Kaiser Wilhelm II abdicates and flees to Holland * 1925: Adolf Hitler forms the SS (Schutzstaffel or 'Protection Squad') as his personal bodyguard * 1970: General and president Charles de Gaulle dies of an aneurysm at Colombey-les-Deux-Églises

10 November

The US Marine Corps is born

1775 Today, seven months after the first shots of the American Revolutionary War had been fired at the Battle of Lexington (see 19 April), the Continental Congress authorised the creation of the Continental Marines, now known as the United States Marine Corps.

Just five days earlier, the Congress had commissioned Samuel Nicholas a 'Captain of Marines', authorising him to raise two battalions. On this day he set up his headquarters in the Tun Tavern in Philadelphia and appointed its proprietor Robert Mullan as chief recruiter. And there young men flocked, lured by the beer and the chance to serve.

By March the following year, the Marines had already executed their first amphibious assault when they captured a British island in the Bahamas. Since then they have conducted over 300 amphibious landings on foreign shores.

Deactivated at the end of the war in 1783, the Marine Corps was reinstituted fifteen years later. Marines have fought in all of America's major wars, and in most cases were the first troops to see combat.

In the early 1800s Marines fought Barbary pirates from North Africa and crushed an enemy force in Tripoli, in what is now Libya. During the Mexican War they won a major victory at Chapultepec Castle, later fancifully referred to in the Marine Corps 'hymn' as 'the halls of Montezuma'.

In connection with the American Civil War the Marines' best-known assignment was a minor one, the apprehension of abolitionist John Brown at Harper's Ferry (see 2 November). Their commander was an Army general named Robert E. Lee. In 1898, 28 Marines were among the 260 killed when the USS *Maine* blew up in Havana harbour, igniting the Spanish–American War (see 15 February). During this same war the Marines established the American base at Guantánamo Bay in Cuba.

In the First World War the Marines' most famous battle occurred in 1918 when the 4th Marine Brigade attacked the German line at Belleau Wood (see 6 June). Both before and after that war, American presidents used the Marines to quell revolutions (and support American business interests) in the 'banana wars' of South and Central America.

During the Second World War the Marines were the country's primary ground assault force in the Pacific, fighting in bloody battles such as Guadalcanal (see 7 August), Tarawa, Saipan, Guam and Okinawa (see 1 April). The bloodiest of all was Iwo Jima (see 19 February) in early 1945, when the Marines suffered 6,000 dead and 17,000 wounded while killing some 20,000 Japanese defenders.

Marines played a prominent role in the Korean War, especially in MacArthur's surprise amphibious attack at Inchon (see 14 September). They were the first American ground troops to fight in Vietnam and saw combat in the Gulf War, Afghanistan and the war against Iraq.

Today the Marine dress-blue uniform still includes a standing collar, evolved from the leather one that was part of the original 18th-century uniform. From this distinctive if uncomfortable feature comes the Marine nickname of 'Leatherneck'.

Marines like to think that 'Semper Fi', their shorthand version of the Corps motto 'Semper Fidelis' (always faithful), is their most famous slogan, but perhaps even better known is a word they coined during the Second World War, snafu, an acronym denoting confusion and chaos. It stands for 'Situation Normal, All Fucked Up'.

Other action this day

1444: An Ottoman army under Sultan Murad II decisively defeats Polish and Hungarian forces at the Battle of Varna in eastern Bulgaria as they fail in their attempt to eject the Ottoman empire from Europe * 1865: Confederate major Henry Wirz, the superintendent of the notorious Andersonville prison camp, is hanged, the only American Civil War soldier executed for war crimes

11 November

The eleventh hour of the eleventh day of the eleventh month

1918 At the eleventh hour of the eleventh day of the eleventh month an armistice, signed six hours before in French marshal Ferdinand Foch's railway carriage at Compiègne, France, took effect between the Allies and the Central Powers, bringing the First World War to a close after four years, three months and nine days of fighting.

By July the Allied armies, greatly strengthened by 42 American divisions, had contained the German spring offensives and then launched a series of powerful counter-offensives that rolled the German army back towards the Rhine.

From far-flung fronts in Italy, the Balkans, Palestine, Mesopotamia and the Caucasus, and on the seas, the war news was at last favourable for the Allied cause.

For Germany, the news was correspondingly bad. During recent weeks, the Supreme Command had acknowledged that the war could not be won, the fleet had mutinied at Kiel, and revolution was in the streets. The Kaiser had fled to Holland the day before the Armistice, and the Reichstag declared a republic. Meanwhile, Germany's allies – Bulgaria, Turkey and Austria-Hungary – had all left the war.

Across the world, the news of the armistice was electrifying. Parisians sang and cheered in the boulevards. In New York 1 million people thronged Broadway. In London one observer recalled the event: 'I stood at the window of my room looking up

Northumberland Avenue towards Trafalgar Square, waiting for Big Ben to tell that the War was over ... And then suddenly the first stroke of the chime ... From all sides men and women came scurrying into the streets. Streams of people poured out of all the buildings. The bells of London began to clash ... All bounds were broken. The tumult grew ... Flags appeared as if by magic ... Almost before the last stroke of the clock had died away, the strict, war-straitened, regulated streets of London had become a triumphal pandemonium.'

For all the celebration, the costs of the war were staggering. An estimated 65 million people were mobilised during the war, of whom 8.5 million had died, another 21 million had been wounded and 8 million were being held prisoner when the war ended. Another 6 million civilians also died.

As well as human beings, four imperial dynasties perished during or in the aftermath of the chaos. Had they tombstones they would read:

Habsburg 1282–1919
Hohenzollern 1415–1918
Romanov 1613–1917
Ottoman 1290–1922

For the Germans the end of the war brought still further losses. By the terms of the Versailles Treaty of 1919 they were made to relinquish large swaths of territory, their colonies and enormous quantities of war *matériel*. One of the few things the Germans gained during the peace process was the myth created by their generals that the German army were 'undefeated in the field' and had been 'stabbed in the back' by their own civilian government at the peace table. As the American commander General 'Black Jack' Pershing bitterly but presciently observed: 'They never knew they were beaten in Berlin. It will have to be done all over again.'

Other action this day

1861: The first aircraft carrier: during the American Civil War a Union trial balloon ascends from the converted coal barge *George Washington Parke Custis* off Mattawomen Creek on the Potomac to observe Confederate positions on the Virginia shore three miles away * 1940: The British navy launches the first all-aircraft naval attack in history, as HMS *Illustrious* launches 21 aircraft in two waves against the Italian fleet at the Battle of Taranto * 1942: The German 7th Army and the Italian 4th Army invade Vichy France

12 November

The 'Father of Modern Warfare' takes the Swedish throne

1611 Gustavus Adolphus was still only sixteen when on this day he was crowned King of Sweden, having inherited the throne – and innumerable problems – from his irascible, foul-mouthed and vicious father, Charles IX, who had involved Sweden in three wars simultaneously, against Russia, Poland and Denmark. From this unpromising stock sprang one of Sweden's very greatest kings, whose skill as an innovating general gained him the sobriquet of 'The Lion of the North'.

Although Gustavus Adolphus started and won the Polish–Swedish War in 1625, a much larger conflict, the Thirty Years War, had broken out in 1618 when the Holy Roman Emperor Ferdinand II tried to suppress the Protestant Reformation in the German principalities. For a dozen years the king watched and waited, no doubt hoping for a Protestant breakthrough that never materialised. By 1630 the Protestant cause looked all but lost as Ferdinand's great general Wallenstein recorded victory after victory.

When Gustavus Adolphus finally intervened, he launched a bold attack through northern Germany, almost immediately sweeping through Frankfurt and Mainz. That same year Ferdinand had made the cardinal error of replacing Wallenstein with Count Johann von Tilly, a highly capable soldier but no match for a military genius like Gustavus Adolphus. In September 1631 the two armies met at Breitenfeld, where Tilly, aged 72 and never yet defeated in battle, commanded the Imperial army. The king himself led his light cavalry on a charge that overran the enemy artillery. Then his cavalrymen, whom he had had cross-trained in the use of cannon, were able to turn the captured guns against the Imperial forces. The victorious Swedes inflicted some 60 per cent casualties.

Gustavus Adolphus then roared through Bavaria, taking Munich, Augsburg and Nuremberg. He again defeated the Holy Roman Empire at the Battle of Rain am Lech, where Tilly was struck by a cannonball and died of tetanus fifteen days later.

In November 1632, the king defeated a recalled Wallenstein at Lützen (see 6 November), but he was killed during the action, just a month short of his 38th birthday. Astonishingly, during his reign, Sweden had become the third-largest European nation after Russia and Spain.

Gustavus Adolphus's impact on the Thirty Years War saved the Protestant cause and alone was enough to guarantee his historical immortality. But military historians also rate him as one of warfare's most important innovators.

Thanks to his emphasis on training, his musketeers achieved outstanding firing accuracy, and their reload speed was three times faster than any contemporary rivals. Furthermore, his extensive cross-training meant that both musketeers and cavalry could handle artillery and his pikemen could fire muskets. All infantrymen were taught to ride so that, in some degree, they could replace cavalry in a desperate situation.

The king was also a great believer in integrated attacks, mixing pikemen and musketeers with his cavalry. The musketeers could pick off enemy cavalry at a distance, while their pistols were still out of range, but if the enemy horse should charge through his cavalry, his pikemen stopped them from breaking the line, behind which his own cavalry could pull back and reform.

His greatest innovation was the development of the extended line of infantry, reducing it to only six ranks of musketeers and pikemen interspersed with artillery, a formation that was far superior to traditional *tercios*, infantry squares ten to 50 ranks deep, in which the rear ranks could not sustain continuous fire for fear of hitting the men in front of them. Gustavus Adolphus's thinning of these rectangular units allowed them to cover a broader front and made them much more manoeuvrable; so successful were these linear formations that, in modified form, they were still in use through the First World War.

Gustavus Adolphus's battles and tactics were studied by many of the great commanders of the future, including Napoleon, Wellington, von Clausewitz and Patton, and many consider him the 'Father of Modern Warfare'.

Other action this day

1642: Royalist cavalry under Prince Rupert defeat the Roundheads at the Battle of Brentford * 1715: At the Battle of Preston, British government troops under the 2nd Duke of Argyll defeat Scottish rebels under the Earl of Mar supporting James Francis the Pretender, ending the last Scottish armed resistance of the revolt of 1715 * 1944: Twenty-nine British bombers sink the German battleship *Tirpitz* off the Norwegian coast

13 November

The king who started the Hundred Years War

1312 On this day at the great medieval fortress of Windsor was born a baby boy who one day would become the seventh king in the Plantagenet line, the future Edward III of England.

Tall, blond and handsome, today Edward is best remembered as the founder of the Order of the Garter, but his greatest impact on history was his obsessive claim to the throne of France, which ignited a war that would last for more than a century.

In 1328 France's King Charles IV died without sons or brothers, survived only by his sister Isabella. His cousin Philip of Valois, however, immediately persuaded the powerful French barons that he rather than Isabella should become monarch since the Salic Law ordained that only males could inherit the throne.

But Isabella had been married to England's Edward II, now dead. Their son Edward III conceded that 'the Kingdom of France was too great for a woman to hold, by reason of the imbecility of her sex', but claimed that a woman could *transmit* inheritance, and therefore the crown of France should rightfully be his. Now he added the title 'King of France' to his own. Obviously Philip (now Philip VI) did not agree, and therein lie the origins of the Hundred Years War.

Although there had been minor bloodshed since 1337, the war's first major battle took place at sea on 23 June 1340 near the port of Sluys, which lies north of Bruges near the present Belgian–Dutch border. Here Edward, in personal command of the English fleet, scored a great victory over Philip's navy, inflicting some 25,000 French casualties, including 16,000 dead. (One account insists that after the battle no one dared tell Philip the outcome until finally his court jester exclaimed: 'Oh, the cowardly English, the cowardly

English!' Asked to explain, the jester continued: 'They did not jump overboard like our brave Frenchmen.')

Edward continued intermittently to pursue the Hundred Years War, while occasionally subduing the Scots on the side. In 1346 he won another famous victory over the French at Crécy (see 26 August), and ten years later his son the Black Prince completely routed them and captured their king, Jean II (Philip had died in 1350) at Poitiers (see 19 September).

Two years after Poitiers the French were further weakened by the peasant revolt known as the Jacquerie (see 9 June), and Edward sought to take advantage by invading for the third time. Although unable to capture Paris or Reims, he forced on the French dauphin (the future Charles V) the Treaty of Brétigny, by which England took over Aquitaine, Calais, Ponthieu and half of Brittany. It was Edward's (and England's) finest hour in the Hundred Years War.

In 1369 Charles V felt strong enough to challenge England once again and resumed the war. Edward, now 57, gave command to his son John of Gaunt, but after seven years of intermittent fighting the English were forced to sign the Treaty of Bruges, by which the great English possessions in France were whittled down to only the coastal towns of Calais, Bordeaux and Bayonne. England now had less territory in France than at the beginning of the war.

The years until his death in 1377 were sad ones for Edward. His son (and foremost general) the Black Prince died a year before him (see 8 June), and France, commanded by the great knight Bertrand du Guesclin, continued to stymie the English in their attempts to take over the country.

But, despite it all, Edward persisted so fervently in his claim to the French crown that his successors continued to assert it for over 400 years. Every English sovereign called himself King of France until George III finally abandoned the claim in 1801.

Other action this day

1775: American revolutionary Ethan Allen fails to take Montreal from the British during a disastrously disorganised attack * 1814: Birth of Union general Joseph 'Fighting Joe' Hooker, commander of the Army of the Potomac, whose female camp followers became known as 'Hooker's girls', since shortened to 'hookers' * 1918: Allied forces occupy Constantinople, the capital of the Ottoman empire

14 November

'The whole city was ringed with leaping flames'

1940 At seven o'clock on this bright moonlit night, the wail of air raid sirens suddenly broke the winter calm. Twenty minutes later, as anti-aircraft fire rent the sky, the first planes of a German pathfinder squadron dropped their flares to mark the target for the following bombers. It was the start of what the Germans had dubbed Operation Moonlight Sonata – the bombing of Coventry – part of a larger effort – the Blitz – to bomb Great Britain into submission by destroying its cities, an aim that the Battle of Britain had failed to achieve.

Only six days previously, the RAF had attacked Munich, a raid that did little damage but was a psychological blow against the birth-place of the Nazi Party. Incensed, Hitler personally ordered retalia-tion, and Coventry was chosen because of its high concentration of armaments production.

Enemy bombers had first hit Coventry on 25 June when Ansty aerodrome was attacked. Then had come further small strikes, the worst in October, which left 176 dead. The city was protected – badly, as the night ahead was about to show – by 24 3.7-inch anti-aircraft guns, twelve lighter Bofors guns and 56 barrage balloons stationed at various heights to keep enemy planes too high for accu-rate bombing.

Earlier this afternoon, the thirteen Heinkel He 111 pathfinders of Kampfgeschwader (Combat Squadron) 100 had taken off from their bases in France. Guided by radio beams towards the centre of Coventry, they dropped parachute flares that hung over the city like huge glittering white chandeliers, illuminating the target for the bombers in their wake. At 7.30 the first wave – mostly twin-engine Dorniers – began dropping high-explosive bombs to knock out the city's water, electricity and gas infrastructure, crater the roads and damage roofs, making it easier for incendiary bombs to fall into buildings and set them on fire. The second wave carried the incendi-aries, some aimed at the factories on Coventry's outskirts, others targeting the city centre. The planes also released landmines suspended from parachutes that would drift down to explode just above ground level, flattening anything below.

Almost immediately fires spread throughout the city, stoked by the ancient timber-framed buildings in Coventry's historic centre. Now over 200 conflagrations blazed as one, flames rising 100 feet into the night. An eyewitness wrote: 'The whole city was ringed with leaping flames, bathed in brilliant moonlight and a few searchlights were sweeping the smoke-filled sky.' The 14th-century Cathedral of St Michael was one of the early victims, totally destroyed after incendiaries ignited its roof.

As Coventry's populace huddled in air raid shelters and cellars, wave after wave of planes droned over their heads. The 449 medium bombers carried only about 3,000 pounds of bombs apiece, so after each sortie they would return to their bases to reload. By 2.00am the anti-aircraft guns had exhausted their ammunition, having shot down only one enemy aircraft, and still the bombers came. Factories were reduced to ruins, and Coventry's streets were choked with the rubble of destroyed houses. Through the chaos, brave firefighters battled the flames, but by the next morning 26 lay dead with another 34 seriously injured.

At last, at 6.15am the all-clear was sounded, and the stunned people of Coventry began to emerge from their shelters to find vast desolation where houses and shops had once stood, the city still shrouded in smoke, with a light rain beginning to fall. The Germans had dropped 500 tons of high explosives and perhaps 30,000 incendiaries during eleven long hours. Three-quarters of the city's factories had been hit and more than 4,000 houses destroyed, with another 41,000 damaged. Over 600 shops were gone, and the trams and tramlines were so severely damaged that the trams never ran again. The death count, however, was surprisingly low for such a destructive attack – only 554 had been killed, with another 865 injured. (By contrast, the bombing of Hamburg in 1943 caused almost 40,000 deaths, and that of Dresden (see 13 February) even more.)

Devastated though it was, Coventry, as a production centre, was not knocked out of the war, as the Germans proclaimed over the radio. As it turned out, the factories suffered much less damage than the centre of the city, so while bombing attacks continued through most of the next year, bringing the total to 41 raids and 1,236 people killed, arms production was fully restored within two months of the November raid.

1263: Russian general and saint Alexander Nevsky dies in Gorodents-on-the-Volga * 1916: 'Put that bloody cigarette out.' – H.H. Munro's (Saki) last words, instants before being shot by a German sniper at Beaumont-Hamel in the Somme * 1965: At 10.48am, the first elements of Bravo Company of the 1st Battalion, US 7th Cavalry touch down at landing zone X-Ray, following 30 minutes of artillery, rocket bombardment and air strikes, to start the inconclusive Battle of Ia Drang, the first major engagement between American and regular North Vietnamese forces in the Vietnam War

15 November

Sherman's march through Georgia

1864 This morning advance units of the Union army began moving out of Atlanta, heading south-east in two columns. Behind them the city lay 'smouldering and in ruins', as their commander, General William Tecumseh Sherman, later described the destruction he had ordered. Grown tired of chasing his Confederate opponent, General Hood, and of having to protect a supply line stretching all the way back to Louisville, Kentucky, 'Uncle Billy' Sherman had decided to cut his force loose against the heartland of the Confederacy. For over a month the North would have no news of Sherman and his troops. 'I know the hole he went in at,' said his brother, the senator from Ohio, 'but I can't tell you what hole he will come out of.'

The hole he came out of was Savannah, Georgia, on 22 December. In the intervening weeks his two columns, with a combined strength of 62,000 and for the most part unopposed by rebel forces, destroyed much of what the Confederacy needed to keep fighting: crops, industry, transportation, infrastructure and morale. Sending their foragers ('bummers' in Union army parlance) far and wide, Union soldiers stripped Georgia bare, helped immensely in their task by thousands of runaway slaves who accompanied the invading forces. No army on either side had eaten so well. And what the troops didn't take, they let rot or they burned.

Sherman's march could not have been a pretty sight, but as military strategy it worked by shortening the war. It also produced one of the greatest marching songs of this or any war, 'Marching through Georgia':

Hurrah, hurrah, we bring the jubilee.
Hurrah, hurrah, the flag that makes you free.
So we sang this chorus from Atlanta to the sea,
As we went marchin' through Georgia.

Other action this day

AD 655: King Oswiu of Northumbria defeats and kills Penda of Mercia, the last pagan king in England, at the Battle of Winwaed near Leeds * 1899: During the Boer War, Boers ambush a British armoured train from Estcourt and capture war correspondent Winston Churchill * 1942: American forces secure Japanese-held Guadalcanal

16 November

The final death scene of Old Russia

1920 Today, if you had been in the Black Sea port of Sevastopol, you would have witnessed the final death scene of Old Russia, as the last White army began its evacuation from the Crimea. Greatly outnumbered and facing annihilation by the victorious Red Army, some 35,000 troops of the counter-revolutionary forces of Baron Peter Wrangel withdrew to ships that would carry them from the Crimean peninsula to Turkey. Under their protection were three times as many civilians seeking escape from revolutionary Russia. Those left behind faced firing squads, labour camps or forcible incorporation into the Red Army. The Russian Civil War had come to an end.

When, after the Communist coup of November 1917, it became clear that a police state was emerging from the political chaos and intended to carry out its revolutionary justice by means of a Red Terror, hundreds of thousands of Russians fled the Bolshevik north for Siberia, the Ukraine or southern Russia. Counter-revolutionary – White – armies were raised to fight the Bolshevik regime. The war lasted for three years, fought on both sides mainly by hastily assembled, ill-trained and poorly motivated troops. Fluid fronts stretching for hundreds of miles defied logistics. The Whites came closest to winning in 1919 when five of their armies advanced on Moscow and St Petersburg, offering the prospect of capturing both capitals. But by October the Red Army had risen to the occasion and turned them all back in defeat. Now the only White force left intact was Wrangel's army, which was forced to retreat to the Crimea.

The White cause failed for many reasons but mainly because it pursued a simple military solution to a very complex problem. It appeared to be a reactionary movement bent on restoring the old order, offering no political or economic programme with which to win the allegiance of the populations across whose lands its forces waged war. Wrangel, the Whites' best and most perceptive commander, recognised the flaw: 'We had not brought pardon and peace with us, but only the cruel sword of vengeance.'

Late in the day, the ships took Wrangel's army out of Sevastopol, once the playground of the old regime, and steamed for Gallipoli, scene of another military debacle. There the soldiers would reside in old Allied camps awaiting their dispersal around the world. As they left the harbour, Wrangel must have spoken the thoughts of many when he wrote: 'God has helped me to do my duty. He would bless our journey into the unknown ... The stars are gleaming in the darkening sky; the sea is all a-twinkle. The lonely lights on my native shore grow fainter, and then vanish all together, one after another. And now the last one fades from my sight. Farewell, my country.'

Other action this day

1161: Jin commander Zheng Jia throws himself overboard to drown after the navy of the Southern Song dynasty routs his fleet with incendiary missiles at the Battle of Tangdao on the East China Sea * 1532: Francisco Pizarro defeats the Incas and captures their king Atahualpa in an ambush against unarmed Incas in the town of Cajamarca, in which his cavalry annihilate enemy soldiers who have never before seen a horse * 1857: During the Second Relief of Lucknow during the Indian Rebellion, British soldiers win 24 Victoria Crosses in a single day

17 November

Bonaparte wins a battle that builds his own legend

1796 Today seventeen miles south-east of Verona, a French army finally forced its way into the town of Arcole on the third day of fighting. Their Austrian opponents had been defeated as much by a cunning ruse as by force, but the battle was critical to the growing legend of the French commander, Napoleon Bonaparte.

The Austrian general Josef Alvinczy was leading an army 24,000-strong to the relief of Mantua, which was under siege by the French. Outnumbered with only 19,000 men, Bonaparte planned to move around the Austrians and attack them on the flank. To do that, he had to cross the tiny Alpone River at Arcole, but the Austrians were established there in strong defensive positions guarding the bridge to the town.

Fighting began on 15 November when the French came under heavy cannon and musket fire as they approached the Arcole Bridge. As casualties began to mount, the attackers began to waver, but at that moment – at least according to legend – Bonaparte seized the French tricolour and, waving it aloft, personally led his grenadiers across the bridge, as men were cut down on either side of him.

Although the attack failed to dislodge the Austrians, Bonaparte's troops were inspired by the courage of their general. But still the French failed to pierce the enemy defences, and the fighting continued into the next day, neither side able to overcome the other. At one point Bonaparte's horse was shot from under him and he was thrown into a swamp. He was lucky to escape; his brother Louis and the future marshal Auguste Marmont dashed in and dragged him out before the Austrians could reach him.

At length, on the third day of battle, the French crossed on a bridge further south and then, when they neared the enemy, Bonaparte ordered his drummers (some reports say trumpeters) around to the Austrian rear, there to sound the attack as loudly as possible. Tricked into thinking that another French detachment was about to assault them from behind, the Austrians pulled around to deal with these (non-existent) reinforcements, leaving only a small guard to protect Arcole. Bonaparte then ordered his generals

Augereau and Masséna to advance in a pincer movement, inflicting 6,000 casualties on the enemy and at last taking the town.

When word of Bonaparte's victory reached Paris, his reputation was dramatically enhanced. Newspapers carried fulsome reports of his heroism, and the painter Louis Bacler d'Albe, who was present at the battle, created several famous panoramas of it. Other artists like Antoine-Jean Gros and Horace Vernet depicted the stirring scene of Bonaparte flourishing the tricolour as he leads his soldiers across the bridge through a hail of enemy fire. The legend of a fearless and invincible Napoleon had begun to take root.

Other action this day

AD 9: Roman general and emperor Vespasian is born * 1887: English field marshal Bernard Law Montgomery is born in Kennington, London * 1915: US Marine major Smedley Butler wins his second Medal of Honor for capturing a Cacos stronghold at Fort Riviere in Haiti with 100 men, killing 200 Cacos

18 November

Urban II launches the First Crusade

1095 The huge crowd outside Clermont cathedral in the Auvergne region of France shivered with cold, wept with religious fervour and smiled inwardly with greedy anticipation when Pope Urban II made his dramatic appeal today for a holy crusade.

'Jerusalem is the navel of the world,' declared the Pope, 'a land more fruitful than any other, a paradise of delights. This is the land that the Redeemer of mankind illuminated by his coming, adorned by his life, consecrated by his passion, redeemed by his death, and sealed by his burial. This royal city, situated in the middle of the world, is now held captive by his enemies … It begs unceasingly that you will come to its aid.'

Such was the call to arms that today launched the First Crusade to reclaim Jerusalem from the heathen Muslims and return it (and all the riches between it and Constantinople) to Christian domination.

Urban had been strongly influenced by an ascetic monk called

Peter the Hermit who had visited the Holy Land the year before. His descriptions of the miseries of the Christians and the sacrilegious insults offered to Jerusalem's holy Christian shrines inspired Urban to unite the faithful into one vast effort to overthrow the Seljuk Turks who controlled Palestine.

Offering remission of all penance for sin to all who helped the Christians in the east, Urban provoked an immediate and overwhelming response. Soon a massive force of some 4,000 mounted knights and 25,000 infantry, principally from France, Italy and the Germanic states, was headed towards Constantinople en route to the greatest Christian adventure in history.

Wearing the symbolic white cross on their breasts, the Crusaders were soon pillaging and sacking their way to the Holy Land, encouraged by their battle cry of 'Deus le volt!' ('God wills it!')

In June 1099 the Christian army, which had dwindled to perhaps 1,500 mounted knights and 12,000 foot soldiers, reached Jerusalem. On 15 July the great walled city fell to the Crusaders for a triumphant massacre and sack. The First Crusade had reached its jubilant conclusion.

Peter the Hermit, however, fared less well. He and another rabble-rousing friar, Walter the Penniless, led a 'People's Crusade' of unattached soldiers, fervent peasants, adventurous youths and unemployed criminals to Constantinople. Evicted from the city as a threat to its civilian population, this ragtag army was ambushed at Cibotus and annihilated by the Turks.

Jerusalem remained in Christian hands for less than a century, falling to Saladin in 1187 (see 2 October). In all there were nine crusades aimed at conquering or retaining Jerusalem, the last in 1365.

Other action this day

1812: The last day of four days of skirmishes around Krasny in which Russian marshal Mikhail Kutuzov inflicts 10,000 casualties on the retreating Napoleon while capturing 25,000 prisoners * 1916: General Douglas Haig calls off the First Battle of the Somme, after General Hubert Gough has ordered one last (failed) attack on the 'Munich' and 'Frankfurt' trenches; the British and French have suffered 624,000 casualties against 435,000 for the Germans in 140 days of fighting in which the Allies gain less than five miles

19 November

Kublai Khan and the Divine Wind

1274 The Mongol empire of Kublai Khan was the greatest the world had known, extending from Hungary in the west to Korea in the east, a greater expanse of territory than even Alexander the Great had won. But one country not yet subdued was Japan, and the great Mongol emperor, grandson of the fearsome Genghis Khan, was determined to bring it to heel.

The Khan sent emissaries demanding that Japan become his vassal state, on pain of invasion should the Japanese refuse. But the *bakufu* (military government) not only failed to accept the Mongol ultimatum, they refused even to reply.

Now Kublai Khan ordered assembled a huge fleet carrying 25,000 Chinese, Korean and Mongolian troops in over 800 ships. This mighty armada put to sea in November 1274 and on this day landed at Hakata Bay (near Fukuoka on Kyushu, Japan's southernmost island).

The Japanese had thrown together a hasty defence but were more accustomed to man-to-man fighting in the samurai tradition and were soon driven inland by the invaders' mass formations of warriors – but then nature took a hand.

The sailors from the invasion fleet had bitter experience with typhoons that savaged the Japanese coast. Now, at the end of the first day's fighting, thunderous storms swept in, and the sailors persuaded the Mongol generals that the only way to save their men was an immediate return to their ships. But the storm scattered the fleet, drowning more invaders than had been killed in the battle. The first Mongol invasion had failed.

Annoyed but not discouraged, Kublai Khan soon sent more emissaries, this time demanding that the 'King of Japan' come to his capital to do homage. But instead of yielding, the bakufu beheaded the six Mongol envoys on the beach at Kamakura. It was an open invitation to another invasion.

The Great Khan established a special 'Office for the Chastisement of Japan', which by May 1281 had assembled a huge invading force of 140,000 battle-hardened soldiers to be carried by a vast fleet. On

23 June the Mongols landed at several points on the Kyushu coast and again at Hakata Bay, where the defenders had built a massive stone rampart. Now the Japanese samurai fought the invaders to a standstill, in some places even denying them a beachhead. After six weeks of intense fighting, nature took a hand once more.

On 15 August a massive typhoon struck, wreaking havoc with the Mongol fleet. Many of the ship's captains re-embarked their troops and tried to reach the open sea. But ships collided and went aground and others sank with all aboard. Those invaders who swam to land were butchered, and soldiers left on shore were taken as slaves. Some reports claim that over 100,000 perished.

The Japanese gave credit for their deliverance to the god Raijin, the lord of thunder and lightning. Ever since that day they have referred to the great enemy-destroying typhoon as the Divine Wind, or *Kamikaze*.

For the next 664 years no invader set foot on Japan, until 15 August 1945, when the Japanese surrendered during the Second World War.

Other action this day

1682: Death of the dashing Royalist cavalry commander of the English Civil War, Prince Rupert of the Rhine * 1863: Abraham Lincoln gives the Gettysburg Address * 1896: Russian marshal Georgy Zhukov is born; 1942: Soviet forces under Zhukov launch Operation Uranus, a counter-attack at Stalingrad that turns the tide of battle on Zhukov's 44th birthday

20 November

Judgement at Nuremberg

1945 The Nuremberg trials opened today, with the top brass of Hitler's Nazi Germany in the dock, accused of the most heinous war crimes of the 20th century. The 21 defendants sat in two rows, white-helmeted American military police stationed behind them. At precisely 10.00am the four judges from Russia, Great Britain, France and the United States took their seats.

Before the German collapse, Winston Churchill had suggested the summary execution of Nazi government leaders, while Stalin had proposed shooting '50,000 to 100,000' German staff officers, but in late 1943 the Allies agreed to bring the Germans to trial. Nuremberg, the scene of massive Nazi rallies before the war, seemed a fitting place to determine their fate.

The defendants uniformly claimed innocence of the charges against them: either they had never done the deeds described, or, if they had, it was only to follow someone else's orders. Reichsmarschall Hermann Göring set the tone. Relaxed and confident (and 80 pounds lighter owing to the prison diet), he explained: 'We had orders to obey the head of state. We weren't a band of criminals meeting in the woods in the dead of night to plan mass murders. The four real conspirators are missing: the Führer, Himmler, Bormann and Goebbels.'

Following suit, high command chief of staff Wilhelm Keitel offered: 'We all believed so much in him [Hitler] and now we take all the blame – and the shame! He gave us the orders. He kept saying that it was all his responsibility.'

Interior minister Wilhelm Frick, who had promulgated the anti-Semitic Nuremberg laws, abolished opposition parties and looked on complacently as 'useless eaters' such as the insane and disabled were put to death, defended himself: 'Hitler didn't want to do things my way. I wanted things done legally. After all, I am a lawyer.'

Fritz Sauckel, Hitler's chief of slave labour, who had deported 5 million labourers to work in conditions so desperate that many of them died, testified that: 'I did everything possible to treat them well.'

The pornographer, sadist and Jew-baiter Julius Streicher, organiser of boycotts against Jewish businesses, helpfully explained, according to Prosecutor Jackson, that his programme for the destruction of synagogues was 'only because they were architecturally offensive'.

The other most vicious criminals in the dock were as follows:

- Ernst Kaltenbrunner, top man in the organisation controlling the Gestapo, the SD (Sicherheitsdienst – intelligence service of the SS) and the Criminal Police, had been the chief organiser of the 'Final Solution'. He had also ordered prisoners in Dachau and other camps liquidated just before the Allies would have liberated them.

- Alfred Rosenberg, the Nazi 'philosopher', had developed Germanisation policies that led to the extermination of Nazi opponents and to segregation of Jews into ghettos, facilitating their mass murder.
- Albert Speer, Hitler's architect and head of armaments and munitions, had used slave labour to boost Germany's war output.
- Arthur Seyss-Inquart had been in charge of the Netherlands when over 50,000 Dutch starved to death and another 40,000 were shot as hostages.
- Hans Frank, called the 'Jew butcher of Kraków' for atrocities he organised while governor-general of Poland, had unwisely noted in his diary: 'The Jews must be eradicated. Whenever we catch one, it is his end.'
- The once-arrogant foreign minister Joachim von Ribbentrop, now grey and bewildered, had helped plan invasions of Czechoslovakia, Poland and Russia.
- Hitler's deputy, Rudolf Hess, who in 1941 had secretly flown to England to try to negotiate a peace treaty, had previously participated in the takeovers of Austria, Czechoslovakia and Poland. Emaciated and broken in spirit, he pretended not to remember his Nazi role.

The trial lasted eleven months, with 216 sessions in court. Then, on 1 October 1946, came the verdicts: three defendants were acquitted, seven, including Hess and Speer, drew prison sentences, and the other eleven were sentenced to hang.

The executions were set for 16 October, but Göring cheated the hangman by swallowing a cyanide capsule hidden in a container of pomade the night before. After the hangings, the condemned men's bodies were incinerated in a Munich crematorium and their ashes were consigned to oblivion in the Isar River.

Other action this day

AD 284: Diocletian accuses the Praetorian prefect Aper of having killed Emperor Numerian and personally kills him in front of the troops, who immediately elect Diocletian as the new emperor * 1917: In the First Battle of Cambrai, the British use of tanks shows that the Hindenburg Line can be penetrated

21 November

A helicopter raid behind enemy lines

1970 'We are going to rescue 70 American prisoners of war', Colonel 'Bull' Simons told the 55 Special Forces 'Green Berets' facing him at the Udon Air Force Base in Thailand. 'The target is 23 miles west of Hanoi.'

Simons, a grizzled veteran with a weather-beaten face and close-cropped hair, was one of America's most formidable combat soldiers. A Ranger in the Pacific during the Second World War, he had participated in the famous behind-enemy-lines raid on the Cabanatuan prisoner of war camp. Even now, this 52-year-old warrior was astoundingly fit – he did 250 push-ups every day. Five hours after addressing his men, Simons and his heavily armed assault team boarded helicopters for Operation Ivory Coast, one of the most daring raids of the Vietnam War.

By January 1970, a half a dozen camps scattered around North Vietnam were holding over 500 American POWs, almost all of them Air Force and Navy pilots captured after their planes were downed. Usually kept in solitary confinement and atrocious conditions, they were cruelly treated and sometimes tortured. In June the joint chiefs of staff had started planning a rescue mission aimed at the Son Tay prison camp, and by August Simons and his team of Special Forces volunteers were preparing at Eglin Air Force Base in Florida. There they had built a mock-up of Son Tay and had run through 170 mission rehearsals. Now the training was over; it was time for the real thing.

On the evening of 20 November, the colonel and his Green Berets boarded two CH-53 Sea Stallion helicopters codenamed 'Apple 1' and 'Apple 2', and one Sikorsky HH-53 Super Jolly Green Giant helicopter codenamed 'Apple 3'. The men were armed with a variety of weapons: carbines and M16 rifles, M60 machine guns, M79 grenade launchers, hand grenades, Claymore mines and demolition charges. At 11.25pm they were in the air. As the choppers flew across Laos and approached Vietnam, planes from American aircraft carriers dropped flares and Nightingale firefight simulators at other locations to create a diversion.

Before dawn on 21 November the assault helicopters were approaching Son Tay, a small compound with three guard towers encircled by a seven-foot wall. The American prisoners were kept in four large buildings inside the complex.

Just after 2.00am, Apple 3's door gunners opened up at 4,000 rounds a minute on anything that moved as the chopper hovered over the compound. One of the guard towers erupted into flames under the fusillade. The helicopter then set down in a rice paddy just outside the walls, and its twenty Green Berets set up roadblocks against any North Vietnamese reinforcements that might come out from Hanoi.

Meanwhile, the fourteen-man Apple 2 assault team landed right in the middle of the compound, cut down any remaining soldiers and charged into the prison buildings to begin a cell-by-cell search.

Apple 1, the helicopter carrying Bull Simons and 21 other Green Berets, was supposed to land just outside the compound walls (there was insufficient space within for two helicopters to land at once), blow holes in the walls and provide supporting fire for Apple 2. But Apple 1 had landed 500 yards away, near a different building that was actually a barracks for North Vietnamese troops. Simons and his men immediately attacked the barracks, kicking open every door and letting loose a hail of bullets that caught most of the soldiers still in bed. In five minutes over 100 enemy soldiers were killed.

After dropping the attack team, the Apple 1 pilot had immediately taken off and only now realised his error and was returning to pick up the men. Meanwhile, Simons had dropped into a trench to wait. Suddenly a terrified enemy soldier dressed only in his underwear jumped into the same trench, unaware of Simons. The colonel instantly shot him in the chest with his .357 Magnum. Now Apple 1 collected the team and rushed them up to Son Tay.

Suddenly radio messages began coming through from Apple 2 teams searching the prison: 'Negative packages.' It meant 'we have located no prisoners'. Only later would it be learned that in July, because of the threat of flooding at Son Tay, the 65 Americans held there had been moved to another camp fifteen miles away.

With nothing more to fight for, Simons and his Special Forces team reboarded their helicopters and were airborne by 2.45am – they had been on the ground a mere 27 minutes. By 4.30am the force was back at Udon Air Force Base. The entire raid had lasted just five hours.

From one point of view, Operation Ivory Coast had been near-perfect: Simon's team of 56 men had flown into the heart of enemy territory, demolished much of a POW compound and killed more than 100 of the enemy without losing a single man – the only casualty was an Apple 2 crew member with a broken ankle. But owing to a monumental intelligence failure, the mission had completely failed in its original purpose, to free American POWs.

Over time, however, the Pentagon began to see that, despite everything, the raid had indeed been a success. It caused the North Vietnamese to bring American prisoners together from camps scattered around the country to two large ones near Hanoi, where they were no longer kept in isolation, tortured or deprived of food. Although it would be two more years until the prisoners were freed, they knew about the Son Tay raid. As one POW later said: 'The raid may have failed in its primary objectives, but it boosted our morale sky-high.' The death rate plummeted, and hundreds of lives were saved.

Other action this day

1791: Colonel Napoleon Bonaparte is promoted to full general and appointed commander-in-chief of the armies of the French Republic * 1836: Major David Moniac, the first Native American to graduate from West Point, is shot and killed by the Seminoles at the Battle of Wahoo Swamp during the Second Seminole War * 1894: Japanese general Yamaji Motoharu's troops kill 20,000 Chinese soldiers and civilians during the Port Arthur massacre, as Manchuria falls to the Japanese in the First Sino-Japanese War

22 November

Warwick the Kingmaker

1428 Today Richard Neville was born in Bisham, 30 miles west of London. By his daring exploits he came to be called by one of those magic names that echo down the centuries: Warwick the Kingmaker, the man who made two men King of England during the Wars of the Roses.

The Wars of the Roses were a series of dynastic conflicts fought for the crown between the Houses of Lancaster and York amid the anarchy of 15th-century England. The Lancastrians had ruled since the usurpation of Henry IV in 1399, but now the king was the pious and weak-minded Henry VI, who had never had effective control of the country since inheriting the throne at the age of nine months in 1422. Now great barons ruled their territories with private armies, and chaos reigned.

Richard Neville was the son of an earl, but he attained his own earldom not from his father but by his marriage to the sister of the Earl of Warwick. When he was 21 he inherited the earldom through his wife, making him the richest man in England, including the king. He was also the most dynamic and capable – and the most ambitious.

Allied with the House of York, in 1455 Warwick played a major role at the first battle of the Wars of the Roses at St Albans (see 22 May). Six years later he 'made' his first king, providing the armed muscle to help Yorkist Edward IV usurp the throne from the ineffectual Henry.

During the first three years of Edward's indolent reign, Warwick virtually ruled the country, but then Edward married Elizabeth Woodville, and soon her relatives were displacing him in the king's councils. Unable to dominate Edward, in 1470 Warwick daringly switched sides and, in a matter of months, invaded England with a force from France and restored the hapless Henry to the throne, while Edward fled to the Netherlands. Behind it all lay no loyalty to any king but Warwick's determination to be the country's most powerful man, perhaps, with luck, even to become king himself.

Only a year later, however, Edward returned to England at the head of an army. On Easter Sunday, 14 April, the armies of Edward and his former supporter clashed at Barnet, just to the north of London.

Both armies had reached the field of battle on the previous evening and had spent the night within earshot of each other. The next morning Warwick rose at four o'clock to brief his soldiers and ordered his cannons to open fire. But the day was still dark and the field was shrouded in fog, so the stones fired by his primitive cast iron artillery carried over the heads of the enemy he could not yet see.

Then, in the words of historian Paul Murray Kendall: 'Warwick signalled his trumpeters. Archers and gunners fired into the blankness of the fog. Close ahead, the trumpets of the Yorkists rang out. A great shout gave notice that they were coming on the run ... With a crash the two hosts came together out of the murk.'

In order to buoy up his men, Warwick was fighting on foot like his soldiers rather than from horseback, having ordered his war steeds taken to the rear. At first the battle seemed to turn in his favour, but then, in a mix-up in the fog, his ally Oxford's cavalry accidentally fell on his brother Montagu's flank. Amid cries of 'Treason!' Warwick's line, under severe attack from Edward, began to collapse.

Seeing that the situation was hopeless, Warwick turned to regain his warhorse behind the lines, but, encumbered by heavy armour, he was soon surrounded by Edward's soldiers. One forced open his visor with an axe, another plunged in his sword.

The next day Edward had Warwick's body, naked except for a loincloth, displayed at St Paul's in London, there for all to see that the Kingmaker was actually dead. Warwick was then buried in Bisham Abbey, but during the reign of Henry VIII the abbey was destroyed and his tomb and bones obliterated. Such was the end of the man who put two kings on the throne and died still hoping to become one himself.

Other action this day

1688: Lieutenant General 'Jack' Churchill (later the Duke of Marlborough) deserts James II's camp and joins the forces of William of Orange ∗ 1718: Near Ocracoke Island in North Carolina, American sailors lure the pirate Blackbeard (Edward Thatch) aboard the *Ranger* and kill him and most of his crew in fierce hand-to-hand fighting in which he is shot five times, stabbed more than twenty times and decapitated ∗ 1739: Six British ships of the line attack Spanish-held Puerto Bello in Panama in one of the first actions of the War of Jenkins' Ear ∗ 1890: French president and general Charles de Gaulle is born in Lille

23 November

A bright victory at Missionary Ridge

1863 Today, a Monday, Ulysses S. Grant, commander of all Union armies in the Western Theater, began the battle to lift the Confederate siege of Chattanooga. For that purpose, he had brought along the Army of the Tennessee, the very force he had led to the great victory at Vicksburg last summer and now commanded by his favourite comrade-in-arms, General William Tecumseh Sherman.

The war was in its third year and it had become clear to President Lincoln and his army planners that the path to a Union victory lay in an invasion of the Southern heartland. The possibility of such a move had been opened when Vicksburg, on the Mississippi, fell to Grant. But the next step required control of Chattanooga, a key railway junction at the eastern end of Tennessee and the strategic gateway into the Deep South.

Grant had concluded that the Union force actually holding Chattanooga, the Army of the Cumberland, was too battered and demoralised by its recent defeat at the Battle of Chickamauga to be of much use in the effort to raise the siege. Even with a newly promoted commanding general, George H. Thomas, who had won the epithet 'Rock of Chickamauga' for his sterling performance in an otherwise disastrous engagement, the Army of the Cumberland, in Grant's plan, was to be used only in support. The main effort would be Sherman's Army of the Tennessee.

On this first day of battle, however, Sherman, commanding the Union left, was unable to get sufficient forces across the Tennessee River in time to mount the scheduled attack against the northern end of Missionary Ridge, the main Confederate position around Chattanooga. In contrast, Thomas, sending in two divisions of the Army of the Cumberland against the centre, managed to turn a reconnaissance in force into a rousing, full-blown attack that pushed the Union line a full mile closer to the ridge. It was a hint of things to come.

On Tuesday, Sherman got his troops up to the high ground for an attack on what he supposed was Missionary Ridge, only to discover that through a failure of intelligence the Confederate positions lay on the far side of yet another valley. The day's only excitement was far down on the Union right, where 'Fighting Joe' Hooker led two brigades up the steep slopes of Lookout Mountain, 1,200 feet above the city, and chased the Confederate defenders off the mist-shrouded summit, a showy action that became famous as the 'Battle above the Clouds'.

At dawn, on Wednesday, Sherman finally attacked. But by now, an enemy well alerted to his intentions had strongly reinforced the northern end of the ridge. By 3.00pm the Army of the Tennessee had made little headway at a cost of 1,500 casualties. A Confederate counter-attack seemed imminent. A worried Grant asked General Thomas for a diversionary attack against the Confederate lines at the base of Missionary Ridge. Thomas gave the order: at the firing of a signal gun, four divisions of the Army of the Cumberland started across the plain. As Confederate artillery on the crest of the ridge opened up, the advancing infantry quickened their pace, then broke into a run. As they did, they began yelling: 'Chickamauga! Chickamauga!' It was a day for revenge and redemption.

The Union attack carried the first line of Confederate rifle pits, but now came under heavy musketry from a second line halfway up the ridge. It was retreat or keep on going. There was no hesitation. From his command post, Grant was stunned at the improbable spectacle of regiments clawing their way up the steep slope, flags waving, troops shouting, officers as well as men caught up in the spirit of the moment. Passing through the second line, the attackers pounded for the crest. Suddenly, blue-clad figures filled the ridge-line, firing their muskets, cheering, clapping each other on the back and pointing jubilantly at the sight of the enemy in full flight down the other side of the ridge.

Grant was always disappointed that it was the Army of the Cumberland, under Thomas, rather than his own Army of the Tennessee, under Sherman, that played the major role in the notable victory at Chattanooga. But there was glory enough to go around. Soon, Grant would become general-in-chief of all the Union armies; Sherman, succeeding him as commander in the Western Theater, would, in the following year, lead a Union army from Chattanooga to capture Atlanta and make the famous march through Georgia to the sea (see 15 November); and the redoubtable Thomas would be confirmed as the commander of a redeemed army that would perform with distinction throughout the rest of the war.

News of the victory at Chattanooga reached much of the North the next day, which was, appropriately, the last Thursday of the month – a date President Lincoln had recently proclaimed Thanksgiving Day.

Other action this day
1248: Ferdinand III of Castile (San Fernando) conquers the Moorish city of Seville * 1943: US Marines defeat the Japanese in four days of fighting at the Battle of Tarawa in the Gilbert Islands, during which four Marines win the Medal of Honor, including future commandant, David Shoup

24 November

The battles of Henry VIII

1542 The most famed English kings gained their renown primarily on the field of battle – witness William the Conqueror, Richard the Lionheart, Edward III, Henry V and Henry VII to name but a few. But the exception to the rule is perhaps the most famous of them all, King Henry VIII.

To be fair to Henry, when he was 22 he crossed into France and personally took part in the successful sieges of Thérouanne and Tournay. Subsequently he and Holy Roman Emperor Maximilian I, with an army of 30,000 men, defeated a French army one fifth their size at the 'battle' of Guinegate, an engagement so short that it became known as the Battle of the Spurs, named because the French army fled so fast that only the spurs of their heels could be seen over the dust.

But the English fought only two serious battles during Henry's reign. Both were against Scotland, both were victories, both resulted in the death of a Scottish king and both left an infant behind to inherit the Scottish throne. And Henry was at neither of them.

The first against the Scots, the Battle of Flodden, was fought on 9 September 1513. During the fighting, Scotland's King James IV was killed on the field. But the victory was due to the generalship of Thomas Howard, Earl of Surrey, as Henry was in France at the time.

On this day, 29 years after Flodden, came the second major battle, at Solway Moss, fought while Henry was in London, once again leaving the combat to one of his barons, Sir Thomas Wharton.

Here his small force of only 3,000 Englishmen met a Scottish army of 15,000, but the Scots were virtually leaderless. The Scottish king was Henry's nephew James V, who had inherited the crown at the age of seventeen months on his father's death after the Battle of Flodden. Like Henry, he had not ventured coming to the fight, instead giving command to Lord Maxwell. But Maxwell fell ill, and the remaining Scottish lairds failed to agree who would be in charge, leaving their large army without a commander.

Not surprisingly, most of the Scots turned and ran almost without a fight. The victors captured 1,200 prisoners, including 500 gentlemen, five barons and two earls, killing almost no one. Scotland was thus eliminated as a military threat for the remainder of Henry's reign.

Although James V avoided the battle, the defeat brought on a mental breakdown, and just twenty days later he died, it is said, of shame. Six days before his death, his wife Mary of Guise gave birth to a daughter, named Mary after her mother, who on her father's death became Mary, Queen of Scots.

Henry lived on for another five years, never imagining that his then thirteen-year-old daughter Elizabeth and five-year-old Mary would never meet but would in their turn become mortal enemies.

Other action this day

1729: Born in Moscow: Russian general Alexander Suvorov, who fought the Swedes, Prussians, Poles, Turks and French over a 40-year career and never lost a battle * 1857: British East India Company general Sir Colin Campbell captures Lucknow during the Indian Rebellion * 1899: Anglo-Egyptian forces under Lord Kitchener obliterate the Mahdist army of Muhammad Ahmad at the Battle of Umm Diwaykarat in the Sudan * 1929: Georges Clemenceau, prime minister of France during last three years of the First World War, dies in Paris with the last words: 'I wish to be buried standing facing Germany.'

25 November

The leper king defeats Saladin

1177 When Prince Baldwin of Jerusalem was only nine, his tutor William of Tyre made a disturbing discovery. When the young prince played with other boys, he neither flinched nor cried out when they scratched his arms with their fingernails. This was no display of royal courage; Baldwin's arms were completely numb. It was the first sign of the most dreaded disease of the medieval world, leprosy.

Four years later, Baldwin's father King Amalric I died of dysentery (or possibly typhoid fever) contracted during a siege. Despite his affliction, Baldwin was immediately crowned king by the unanimous decision of the High Court of Jerusalem.

These were perilous years for the Kingdom of Jerusalem. The Saracen leader Najm ad-Din had twice tried to invade, in 1170 and 1172, and then on his death his far more capable son Saladin had become the Sultan of Egypt. Now in the autumn of 1177 Saladin was planning his own invasion and set out with an army of 26,000 men. Rising from his sick bed, Baldwin, still only sixteen, assembled a force of several thousand infantry, 375 mounted knights and 80 Templar knights and marched out to confront the invaders.

Certain that Baldwin would not dare to attack with so small an army, Saladin ignored him and continued towards Jerusalem, allowing his soldiers to become spread out and distracted with pillaging local towns as they went. Today, on the feast day of Saint Catherine of Alexandria, Baldwin and his tiny contingent intercepted Saladin near the hill of Montgisard, only 45 miles from Jerusalem.

Saladin was taken totally unawares by the sudden appearance of the small Christian force but tried to consolidate his centre with a forward wing on each side. His soldiers, close to panic, scrambled in the confusion to form battle lines.

Baldwin, meanwhile, unsheathed a potent Christian weapon, a fragment of the True Cross. Helped from his horse (he was too enfeebled by leprosy to dismount on his own), he ordered the Bishop of Bethlehem to raise it before his troops and then prostrated himself before it. After a moment's prayer for victory, he rose and exhorted his inspired men to attack.

Helped to remount, the young king led the Christian charge. It is said that the True Cross flashed in the sunlight and that suddenly St George miraculously appeared to gallop at his side during the assault.

Baldwin's knights, reinforced by the Templars, thundered into the unprepared Saracen centre, Baldwin himself in the thick of the fray, his hands bandaged to cover the sores of leprosy. Saladin's Mamluk bodyguard broke under the charge, and the Saracen leader escaped only by fleeing on the back of a racing camel. Meanwhile the rest of his army panicked and fled, as thousands were slain.

Saladin and the surviving Saracens made desperately for Egypt, harried and ambushed by Bedouins along the way. Of the 26,000 men that he had brought to the field, fewer than 3,000 survived.

Baldwin's force had suffered 1,100 killed plus 750 wounded, but it was a small price for such a resounding victory. Believing that divine intervention was responsible for his triumph, he ordered a Benedictine monastery built on the battle site and dedicated it to Saint Catherine of Alexandria.

Two years later Baldwin and Saladin met again at the Battle of Marj Ayyun. This time the Saracens surprised the Christians, and Baldwin, unable to mount his horse because of his leprosy, escaped on the back of one of his knights as his bodyguard cut a path through the Saracens.

King Baldwin died in Jerusalem in the spring of 1185, still only 24 years old. Just two years later (see 2 October), Saladin finally conquered Jerusalem after a brief siege.

Other action this day

1758: British forces capture French-occupied Fort Duquesne during the French and Indian War * 1944: At Peleliu, Palau, American forces led by Marine general William Rupertus defeat the Japanese after a bitter four-month battle * Fête de Catherine Ségurane (Catherine Ségurane Day) in Nice that celebrates a local washerwoman who in 1543 coshes the Turkish standard-bearer, takes his flag and then stands on the city's battlements exposing her bare backside to repel the invading Turks during the siege of Nice

26 November

Napoleon escapes the Russians

1812 The Emperor Napoleon was up at two hours before dawn this morning. As first light broke, he stood on the Berezina River's east bank, peering anxiously through the winter gloom as engineers constructed an escape route for his beleaguered army.

Now in its fifth week of retreat from Moscow (see 18 October), the Grand Army was in appalling condition, encumbered with sick and wounded soldiers, overburdened with artillery and loot, its ragged columns stretching out over 50 miles in length, and in its wake thousands of stragglers and camp followers.

The force that had been the spearhead of the invasion of Russia, with a strength of 250,000 troops, was now down to fewer than 50,000 effectives, exhausted, ill-supplied, and in poor morale. Never far away was the enemy in pursuit: a Russian corps menaced the Grand Army's northern flank, while the main Russian army – 65,000 troops under the command of General Kutusov – dogged close behind. On all sides, Cossacks and armed peasant groups waited out of musket range for any opportunity to harass the vulnerable columns.

Nevertheless, over bad roads and in unusually cold weather, the Grand Army had battled and staggered its way 600 miles from Moscow, aiming now for the safety of Poland to regroup. Then came news of a new threat: another Russian army had moved ahead to seize the town of Borisov, blocking the line of retreat. When the Grand Army's advance guard took the town, it found the bridges across the Berezina River destroyed and the enemy holding the far bank in force. On 22 November the emperor gave orders for the destruction of his state papers.

But three days ago, a light cavalry force stumbled on a crossing point eight miles upstream at a village called Studienka, where there was a ford shallow enough for cavalry to use, but too deep for infantry, artillery, and the baggage train. The news was reported to the emperor, and a plan was quickly devised to bridge the river there, while drawing the enemy's forces away with feints downriver. The ruse worked, and on the 25th 400 engineers moved upstream to begin building two pontoon bridges, one for infantry, the other for artillery. In two days and a night of ceaseless activity, frequently under the gaze of their emperor, the sappers accomplished one of the great feats of combat engineering, often working in the bitterly cold water. For bridging material, they tore down the entire village of Studienka.

When the bridges were finished, at midday on the 27th, cavalry units went over to hold the western bridgehead against the enemy now alerted and closing in; then the Grand Army began to cross – troops, guns, horses, wagons – a process that took two days and nights. Owing to the enormous weight moving over the pontoon sections, the hastily constructed bridges required constant repair by the engineers. On the 28th, by the time the emperor's headquarters was moved across, Russian forces were delivering heavy attacks against the bridgeheads on both sides of the river. At last, the rearguard came across, early on the 29th. Then sappers blew up the bridges, leaving countless stragglers on the eastern bank to the mercy of the Cossacks.

Once again, the emperor's luck had held; his army had escaped its entrapment. For the moment, a mood of relief swept through the ranks. Armand de Caulaincourt, the emperor's senior aide in the Russian campaign, noted: 'After crossing the Berezina, our faces were less care-worn. For the first time, Poland seemed delightful to everyone. Vilna had become a promised land, a safe port that would shelter us from all storms, and the end of all our troubles.'

But these were dreams never to be realised. Despite its undoubted success as a military operation – even as its four days cost another 20,000 casualties – the crossing of the Berezina merely postponed the Grand Army's imminent fate. On 5 December the emperor left his soldiers for urgent business in Paris. The surviving elements of his command continued their slogging retreat, the numbers of effectives declining each day, as the numbers of stragglers behind them increased. At Vilna, reached on 8 December, the remnants of the Grand Army numbered no more than 12,000; when they passed out of Russia into Poland on the 10th, there were fewer than 7,000 soldiers marching with the colours. On the 12th Marshal Berthier, Napoleon's chief of staff, sent the emperor a report: 'The whole army is completely disbanded ... Twenty-five degrees of cold and heavy snow on the ground are the cause of this disastrous state of the army, which no longer exists.'

Other action this day

43 BC: Roman leaders Octavian (the future emperor Augustus), Mark Antony and Marcus Lepidus form the Second Triumvirate, which will last for ten years ∗ 1851: Napoleonic marshal Jean-de-Dieu Soult dies at his castle of Soultberg in the Tarn ∗ 1939: The Soviet army shells the Russian village of Mainila and declares that the shelling originated from Finland across the nearby border, an incident used to justify the start of the Winter War with Finland four days later

27 November

Clovis, the first French king

AD 511 Today in Paris the Frankish warrior-king Clovis died at the age of 45. Through guile, treachery, murder and war, he had taken control of all the Frankish tribes in Gaul to create a realm that covered most of modern France.

In AD 476 the Western Roman empire had reached its final collapse, its last emperor Romulus Augustus forced to abdicate. Gaul had fragmented into mini-states, one of which was ruled by Clovis's father, Childeric I. In 481 Childeric died, and at fifteen Clovis had inherited the small kingdom of the Salian Franks, located along the modern border of France and Belgium. Five years later he embarked upon the road to conquest.

There remained one last Gallo-Roman rump state around Soissons, 60 miles north-east of Paris. It was ruled by a *magister militum* (military commander) named Syagrius. In 486 Syagrius became Clovis's first target.

Although Clovis had only about 5,000 warriors of his own tribe, he enlisted the help of Frankish allies and marched on Soissons. There the Franks overpowered the Roman army, and Syagrius fled into exile to the Visigoths in Toulouse. But victory was not enough for Clovis, who pressured the Visigoths into turning the fugitive ruler over to him. One account says that then Clovis had Syagrius secretly stabbed to death, while another maintains that he was beheaded, but what is certain is that Syagrius was murdered and Clovis's realm almost doubled in size.

Next Clovis used cunning and ruthlessness to take over a Rhineland Frank kingdom. Knowing of bad blood between King Sigebert and his son Chlodoric, he persuaded Chlodoric to murder his father to put himself on the throne. After the assassination, Chlodoric was searching through his father's treasure chest for a gift for Clovis when one of Clovis's knights crept up behind him and split his skull with an axe. Clovis then reported to the remaining Rhineland Franks that Chlodoric had killed his father but had received a mortal blow in the process. Leaderless, the Rhinelanders accepted Clovis as king.

Now master of half of Gaul, Clovis returned to Belgium and turned on his own cousins, Ragnacaire and Chararic, who ruled the kingdoms of Cambrai and Tongres. While defeating them in the field, Clovis took both brothers prisoner. Subsequently they were brought before him with their hands chained behind their backs. 'Why', Clovis asked Ragnacaire, 'have you permitted our blood to be humiliated by allowing yourself to be put in chains? Better that you should die.' Whereupon Clovis hacked his prisoner down. Then, turning to Chararic, he said: 'Had you but helped your brother, they would not have chained his hands', and promptly executed him as well.

In 491 Clovis set his eyes to the east, invading the German state of Thuringia. Two years later he briefly abandoned war in order to consolidate an alliance with Burgundy through marriage to Clothilda, the daughter of the king. This was an unusual choice in that Clothilda was a fervent Christian while Clovis was a pagan, but the marriage would have incalculable consequences.

At first Clovis ignored Clothilda's pleas to become a Christian, but in 496 he found himself threatened with defeat by a Germanic tribe called the Alamanni, whom he fought at Tolbiac, about 40 miles east of today's German–Belgian border. According to a contemporary account, 'as the two armies were fighting fiercely, there was much slaughter, and Clovis's army began to be in danger of destruction. He saw it and raised his eyes to heaven, and with remorse in his heart he burst into tears and cried: "Jesus Christ, whom Clothilda asserts to be the son of the Living God ... I beseech the glory of thy aid, with the vow that if thou wilt grant me victory over these enemies ... I will believe in thee and be baptised in thy name. For I have invoked my own gods but, as I find, they no longer aid me; and so I see that they possess no power." … And when he said this, the Alamanni turned their backs, and began to disperse in flight. And when they saw that their king was killed, they submitted to the dominion of Clovis, saying: "Let not the people perish further, we pray; we are yours now."'

After this triumph, Clovis led 3,000 of his army to Reims for a mass baptism on Christmas Day, changing for ever the direction of religion in France.

Despite his conversion, Clovis was by no means through with fighting. Alaric II of the Visigoths was an Arian king who persecuted his Catholic subjects in Aquitaine. Using Alaric's persecutions as an excuse for attack, in the spring of 507 Clovis led his army to Vouillé, just west of Poitiers. There his army comprehensively defeated the Visigoths, and Clovis personally dispatched Alaric, although he was nearly killed by Visigoth warriors. He now added south-western France to his territories.

During 29 years in power Clovis had quadrupled the size of his kingdom to form an 'r'-shaped realm that covered most of western France, south as far as Toulouse, east almost to the Rhône, and in the northern part, covering today's Belgium and parts of what is now western Germany. In 508 he established Paris as his capital, a useful central location to keep an eye on his various conquests. There he built for himself a palace on the Île de la Cité.

Clovis's original Frankish name was Chlodovech, meaning 'glory in combat'. Latinised as Chlodovechus, it evolved into the French 'Louis' and the German 'Ludwig'. The French so revered him that nineteen future kings bore the name Louis. Despite the fact that Clovis was really a Belgian, probably born in Tournai, and his native language was Frankish German, he is considered the founder of France.

Other action this day

1770: Twelve-year-old Horatio Nelson enters the British navy, joining HMS *Raisonable* as a midshipman * 1942: The French navy scuttles its fleet of two battleships, six cruisers, sixteen destroyers, thirteen torpedo boats, fifteen submarines and nine other ships at Toulon to keep them out of German hands

28 November

Operation Overlord is determined at Teheran

1943 The Big Three leaders of the Grand Alliance began a conference today in Teheran at which they would finally settle the most important issue of the Second World War: when to launch the Allied invasion of Nazi-held Europe.

In four days of formal sessions and private meetings held at the Soviet Union's embassy, President Roosevelt, Prime Minster Churchill and Premier Stalin discussed a range of strategic issues involving every theatre of the war against Germany and Japan, now in its fourth year. But none was as important as that of a 'second front', the launching of an Anglo-American cross-Channel landing into France, a move designed to bring the war home to Germany. Overlord, as that vast undertaking was codenamed, had been in the planning stage since the end of 1941. Stalin had long pleaded for an invasion front in Europe, which offered the prospect of relief for his embattled forces on the Eastern Front. But, almost from the beginning, Overlord had been, in Max Hastings' description, 'the subject of bitter dissension between the warlords of Britain and America'.

The Americans had always pressed the view that the route to victory over Germany lay with an invasion of 'fortress Europe' launched as soon as possible. The British, however, with their greater experience in fighting German armies – gained in the First World War and confirmed more recently at Dunkirk and Dieppe – worried about the ultimate risk and cost of embarking on an enterprise directed at the formidable German coastal defences before overpowering force had been assembled. Until then, their thinking went, the wiser course was to weaken the enemy at his more vulnerable points. To the Americans this approach seemed too leisurely, too vague.

First considered for 1942, a cross-Channel invasion plan was postponed on British persuasion until the following year. In its stead came Operation Torch, the Allied invasion of French North Africa, which took place in November 1942. Then, in early 1943, at the Anglo-American meeting in Casablanca, Churchill proposed putting off Overlord until 1944 in favour of Husky, the invasion of Sicily, which took place in July 1943, followed by the invasion of mainland

Italy in September. The Americans acquiesced, again reluctantly, but began to put pressure on the British for a firm date of May 1944 for Overlord, for which the troop and equipment requirements would almost certainly cancel plans for substantial operations elsewhere.

Anglo-American wrangling about Overlord continued through 1943 at Allied conferences held in Washington, Quebec, Moscow and Cairo. Now, at the very end of the year in Teheran, FDR and Churchill hoped to resolve their differences, perhaps with help from Stalin. At the first session, Churchill said his plans for further Allied operations in the eastern Mediterranean would accomplish the goal of relieving pressure on the USSR, 'without postponing Overlord for more than perhaps a month or two'. Stalin responded by asking whether a supreme commander had yet been selected for the cross-Channel invasion. Later, Stalin turned the heat up, first by urging his partners to keep the May 1944 invasion date, then by voicing his approval of an American proposal to supplement Overlord with a second landing in southern France.

The tension over war policy between FDR and Churchill was obvious to many at the conference. Since early days, Churchill had been the senior member of the Big Three, representing as he did the nation longest at war with Nazi Germany. He also had formed a close relationship with Roosevelt dating from before the war. But at Teheran it became clear the political landscape of the Grand Alliance had changed. Now, by virtue of what Ian Kershaw called 'the unlikely combination of an indomitable Soviet fighting machine and limitless American resources', Churchill had become in effect the Grand Alliance's junior member.

By the time the conference ended on 1 December, the Big Three had confirmed the Overlord date as May 1944 (in fact, it took place on 6 June 1944). They also agreed simultaneous landings in the south of France, codenamed Anvil. For his part, Stalin promised to launch a new offensive against the Germans to coincide with Overlord, and that once Germany had been defeated, the USSR would join the war against Japan.

The next day, the Allied leaders left Teheran, Stalin returning to Moscow, FDR and Churchill heading for Cairo, where for four more days they would continue their deliberations. On their last day in Cairo, FDR informed Churchill of his choice for Overlord commander: General Dwight Eisenhower.

While the date, exact location, and other details of Overlord remained top secret, news of the Teheran agreements was announced around the world. The *New York Times* of 7 December 1943 conveyed it with these front-page headlines: 'BIG 3 CHARTS TRIPLE BLOWS TO HUMBLE REICH ... ATTACK PLANS SET. Dates Fixed for Land Drives from the East, West and South.'

Other action this day

1862: Union troops under General John Blunt defeat General John Marmaduke's Confederates at the Battle of Cane Hill ∗ 1920: At four in the afternoon at Kilmichael, Northern Ireland, 36 Irish Republican Army volunteers kill seventeen members of the Auxiliary Division of the Royal Irish Constabulary, marking a huge escalation in the IRA's guerrilla campaign

29 November

Captain Jack and the Modoc War

1872 A band of about 150 Indians from the Modoc tribe had refused to stay put on their reservation in southern Oregon, and 40 soldiers from the US 1st Cavalry Regiment, reinforced by local militia, had been sent to force them to return. Today, when the two sides met to parley, an act of violence triggered a six-month war.

The meeting took place at the Indian camp at Lost River on the Oregon–California border. The Modoc chieftain, Captain Jack (Kintpuash in Native American) had no desire to provoke a fight and agreed to return to the reservation. When he and his men began to hand over their weapons, however, one warrior put down his rifle but kept a pistol in his holster. A sergeant bellowed at him: 'Give me that pistol, damn you. Quick!' The young brave retorted that he was not a dog to be given orders. The sergeant replied, 'You son of a bitch! I'll show you how to talk back to me', and raised his gun, just as the Indian drew his pistol. Both men fired and missed. Now all the Modocs dived for the rifles they had just given up, and after a sharp exchange of gunfire that killed a soldier and two Indians and wounded several more, they fought their way out of the camp. It was the first bloodshed of the Modoc War, in which this exiguous band of Native Americans – more than half of them women and children – held out against the US Army for almost a year.

After the skirmish at Lost River, the Modocs retreated to a vast lava bed on the south shore of nearby Tule Lake, an area honeycombed with outcroppings, caves and caverns, a virtually impregnable rocky fortress ideal for hit-and-run defence. The new camp was soon to be dubbed Captain Jack's Stronghold.

Captain Jack and his 53 warriors were already in a perilous position, having shot down a US soldier, regardless of who was at fault. But they made matters worse when a few of the braves attacked and killed eighteen settlers during the retreat from Lost River. Now the Army had to take action, and did.

Four days after the Lost River clash, local militia were sent to reconnoitre Captain Jack's Stronghold, but the Modocs ambushed them, killing all 23 men. Then, two weeks later, the Indians attacked an Army ammunition wagon. In less than a month the Army had 400 soldiers in the field, ready to fight.

The first assault came on 17 January, a freezing day of impenetrable fog. When the Army tried to attack the stronghold, Modoc warriors sprang out from behind rocks and ridges, snapped off shots and then ducked back behind cover. At the battle's end, 35 soldiers lay dead, with another 25 wounded, but the Modocs suffered no casualties at all. Extraordinarily, not a single survivor reported having even seen a Modoc. When the Army pulled back, the Indians helped themselves to the guns and ammunition from the dead soldiers littering the battlefield.

Although the Modocs had been victorious until now, Captain Jack realised that their small number could not long resist and pushed for a peaceful solution. But his more bellicose braves had more ambitious plans; they urged him to agree to peace talks and then kill the Army leaders, believing that with the leaders dead, the Army would withdraw.

In the meantime the Federal government had authorised a peace commission, headed by an experienced Civil War veteran, Major General Edward Canby. After months of false starts and aborted meetings, Canby went to a parley midway between the Army encampment and Captain Jack's Stronghold. After a short period of 'negotiation', on Captain Jack's order two Modocs dashed from their hiding place among the rocks and opened fire with their rifles while

Captain Jack himself drew his pistol and shot Canby in the head and cut his throat.

This act of treachery produced exactly the opposite of what the Modocs had hoped for; the Army now brought in another 1,000 soldiers.

Four days after Canby's murder, the Army attacked the stronghold; but this time, when the soldiers charged, the Modocs slipped away through an unguarded crevice after inflicting twenty casualties.

During the next month the Modocs fought the Army twice more, the first time surprising a troop while they were eating lunch, killing seventeen and wounding eighteen. But at the second battle, at Dry Lake, the Army repulsed a Modoc attack and then charged and routed the Indians, killing five.

By now the pressures of continuous war were beginning to split the Modocs, and one group surrendered to the Army. Then, in return for a pardon for the murder of General Canby, they agreed to help capture Captain Jack. (Among those now searching for him were the wonderfully named Shacknasty Jim, Bogus Charley, Hooker Jim and Steamboat Frank.) After several months on the run, in June 1873 Captain Jack and his last 30 followers finally surrendered. Taken to Fort Klamath in Oregon, he was tried and convicted of the murder of General Canby and hanged alongside three other warriors on 3 October. The hanged men's heads were sent to the Army Medical Museum in Washington, but in 1984 the skulls were returned to the Modocs.

The few remaining Modoc were treated as prisoners of war, shipped to Kansas in freezing cattle cars, guarded at gunpoint, and finally settled on Indian Territory. Despite hardships and predatory Indian agents, the tribe survived and eventually prospered.

Other action this day

1330: Under orders from Edward III, Roger de Mortimer, previous de facto ruler of England, is hanged, drawn and quartered at Tyburn for having usurped royal power and murdered Edward II * 1612: Four British East Indian galleons defeat the Portuguese at the Battle of Swally off the Indian coast, marking the end of Portugal's commercial monopoly over India and the ascent of the East India Company * 1847: Missionaries Dr Marcus Whitman and his wife and fifteen others are killed by Cayuse and Umatilla Indians at the Whitman Massacre, starting the Cayuse War

* 1864: US cavalry kill over 150 Cheyenne and Arapaho Indians who had surrendered and were disarmed at the Sand Creek massacre in the Colorado Territory

30 November

Sweden's warrior-king is cut down

1718 Today died Sweden's warrior-king, Charles XII, shot through the head at the siege of Fredrikshald.

Charles had become an absolute monarch at the age of fourteen when his father died of stomach cancer on 5 April 1697. Despite his youth, he was exceptionally strong-willed, not to say obstinate, with a fervid belief in his country's destiny and his own moral duty to serve it. Fearless in the face of danger, he shot his first bear at eleven and became an outstanding horseman. Later in life he developed an interest in painting and architecture, could quote Swedish poetry and relished philosophical arguments. But his real genius was war.

In February 1700, when Charles was still seventeen, Denmark, Poland and Russia launched an attack against Sweden to start the Great Northern War, which was to last for 21 years. First turning his attention to the Russians, Charles marched into what today is Estonia, where his small force of only 10,000 men annihilated Peter the Great's army of 40,000 in the driving snow at Narva. (Charles was always where the action was hottest. When his fifth horse was shot under him, he laconically commented: 'These people seem disposed to give me exercise.' Later he fell into a swamp and lost his boots. When his men pulled him free, he cheerfully continued to fight in his socks. Some 15,000 Russians perished against only 667 Swedes.)

Charles continued to crush his enemies for the next nine years. He defeated the Danes, the Saxons and the Poles, capturing Kraków. Convinced of his righteous cause, he had little mercy for his defeated enemies, commenting: 'Rather let the innocent suffer than the guilty escape.' He instructed his troops to 'ravage, singe and burn all about! Make the whole district a wilderness!'

But in 1709 Charles made the mistake of attacking a vastly superior Russian force at Poltava and his army was obliterated (see

27 June). Charles escaped and fled to Turkey, where he remained for the next six years.

By the time Charles finally returned to Sweden in 1715 he had been away for fifteen years, either fighting his enemies on foreign battlefields or fleeing from them in Turkey and Poland. Extraordinarily, during all of this time he had continued to rule his kingdom *in absentia*. And the Great Northern War ground on without result.

In 1718 Charles launched a new campaign to conquer Norway (then a Danish province) to force the Danes to sue for peace. In November he brought his army before the enemy fortress at Fredrikshald (today's Halden) and surrounded the town with trenches. On this day Charles entered the trenches to get a better look at the enemy's positions. As he peeped over the parapet a bullet suddenly smashed into his head, killing him instantly.

Some thought an enemy sniper had hit him, while others thought a grapeshot bullet from a cannon had brought him down. But almost immediately rumours began to spread that someone from his own side had shot him – anyone who had kept his country in a state of war for eighteen years was bound to have enemies. The question will never be definitively answered, but most historians now believe a lucky musket shot from the enemy killed him.

The Great Northern War continued for another three years, reducing Sweden to the minor power that it still is today. Charles remains a contentious character. Some blame him for Sweden's precipitous decline from major power status, but many celebrate him as a great general and leader. More ominously, both Napoleon and Hitler looked to his example as a guide for their own invasions of Eastern Europe, and even now he is extolled by Sweden's right-wing extremists for his chauvinism.

Other action this day

1808: Outnumbering the Spanish 20,000 to 12,000, Napoleon wins the Battle of Somosierra to open the way to Madrid ∗ 1853: During the Crimean War, Pavel Nakhimov's Imperial Russian Fleet destroys the Ottoman fleet under Osman Pasha at Sinop, a port in northern Turkey ∗ 1939: Russia invades Finland to start the Winter War

1 December

Napoleon besieges Madrid

1808 Only the day before, Napoleon's army of 45,000 men had swept aside Spanish resistance at the Somosierra Pass in the Sierra de Guadarrama mountains north-west of Madrid, opening the road to the capital. Now, on the afternoon of the first day of December, regiments of French dragoons advanced through the suburbs to begin the siege of the city, which was defended by a mere 3,000 troops.

Under the pretext of reinforcing the Franco-Spanish army occupying Portugal, in early 1808 the French had started moving troops into Spain, but by February, on Napoleon's orders, they had seized several Spanish fortresses, effectively turning their ally into an enemy. Madrid had been occupied and a revolt there put down with draconian ferocity. A month later Napoleon had named as Spain's new king his older brother Joseph, whom the Spanish soon nicknamed 'Pepe Botella' ('Joe Bottle') for his bibulous habits. In July, however, the French lost an entire army – 2,000 dead and 18,000 captured – at Bailén and abandoned Madrid in panic.

By October Napoleon had seen that Spain was slipping from his grasp, so now he came in person, joining his forces at Vitoria on 6 November and arriving at the siege of Madrid on 2 December. This was the anniversary not only of his coronation in 1804 but also of his great triumph at Austerlitz a year later; perhaps he hoped that the fame of that titanic victory would bring the Spaniards to their knees without a fight, but the Madrileños turned down his demands with the warning that 'the people of Madrid will bury themselves under the ruins of their houses rather than let French troops into their city'.

Despite the bravado, Madrid was virtually indefensible, since it had no fortifications and such an exiguous defence force. But its citizens somehow fancied that they could stymie the invaders, as had the population of Zaragoza, where earlier in the year determined resistance had forced the French to lift a siege. So a Junta had been formed to organise the city's defences, and, to bolster the soldiers, 20,000 civilians had armed themselves however they could and were prepared to fight. In the words of historian Charles Oman: 'Not merely the combatants but the whole population of both sexes turned themselves with absolute frenzy to the work of fortification.' Animated crowds stripped the streets of paving slabs and built a massive-looking wall around the city.

On the evening of 2 December Napoleon positioned his guns to the north and east and then once again demanded an immediate surrender, only to receive an immediate refusal. The next morning the French began their attack.

First came a short bombardment that blasted through the paving-slab wall, splintering the slabs into chips that flew like shrapnel against the defenders. Then Marshal Victor, hero of Marengo, Jena and Friedland, ordered an infantry division to charge into the Retiro, today Madrid's loveliest park but then just a weakly defended hill with a view over the city. The few Spanish defenders were quickly overrun, and the French moved their artillery onto the Retiro, most of Madrid now beneath their guns.

At last the Junta began to realise their perilous situation. One of their generals came to open negotiations with the emperor, only to be met with contempt and the threat that, if Madrid did not surrender by six o'clock the next morning, the French would execute any man found with a weapon. The Spaniards quickly folded, and the following morning French troops marched in. Fortunately for the Madrileños, however, Napoleon forbade the usual pillage; Madrid was spared the sack to preserve it for his brother, King Joseph. There Joseph would remain until 1813, when his army – with Joseph in command – was crushed by Wellington at Vitoria, after which he scuttled back to France, never to return.

Other action this day

1640: Portugal revolts against Spain, installing John IV (of Braganza) as king * 1896: Soviet marshal Georgy Zhukov, conqueror of Berlin during the Second World War, is born in Strelkovka, Maloyaroslavets * 1941: At a Japanese imperial conference, Emperor Hirohito sanctions 'War against the United States, the United Kingdom and the Kingdom of the Netherlands'

2 December

Napoleon's greatest victory

1805 Today, a Monday, Napoleon crushed a combined Russian–Austrian army at Austerlitz, making France the dominant power in Europe.

Precisely one year earlier, on 2 December 1804, a crowd of 8,000 had jammed Notre Dame to witness Napoleon's coronation. There Pope Pius VII officiated but did not crown, as Napoleon reserved that honour for himself, famously placing the iron crown of Charlemagne on his own head and then crowning his wife Joséphine as well.

Now, on the first anniversary of his coronation, Napoleon's army of 68,000 men utterly routed a force of nearly 80,000 commanded by Alexander I of Russia and Franz I of Austria. Fought on frozen ground near a Moravian town called Austerlitz (now Slavkov u Brna in the Czech Republic), this seismic victory was called the Battle of the Three Emperors.

In the days before the battle, Napoleon had tried to make the enemy believe that he was vulnerable and wanted to avoid a fight. In reality, he was luring the Russians and Austrians into battle, intentionally weakening his right wing in the hope that if they attacked him there he could punch through the Allied centre to score a decisive victory.

Preparations for the Allied attack began early in the morning, the opening movements concealed from French eyes by dense fog. But by 8.00am the mists had lifted, and a wintry sun cast its light over the landscape, dramatically revealing to Napoleon that the enemy was advancing against his right, as planned. Ever after, that moment of revelation became known as 'Le Beau Soleil d'Austerlitz'.

For an hour the battle seesawed back and forth, as more units joined the fray. Then Napoleon split the enemy force with a determined attack by Marshal Soult against the centre and vigorously pursued both enemy halves.

Defeated and demoralised, the Allies now started a panicky retreat. In one horrific incident, when fleeing Russians headed across the frozen Satschan Lake at the south end of the battlefield,

Napoleon ordered his gunners to lob shells onto the ice, punching great holes through which men sank to their deaths in the freezing water.

Allied casualties at Austerlitz came to 15,000 killed and wounded plus 11,000 captured, compared to Napoleon's loss of only 9,000 men. It was Napoleon's greatest victory; two days later a truce was signed and on 26 December Austria withdrew from the war. The Russian army was allowed to retreat back to Russia, no longer a threat to Napoleon's dominance of Europe.

The French people reacted with unrestrained joy at news of their emperor's titanic triumph. Austerlitz became so emblematic of French victory that, 46 years later, in 1851, Napoleon's nephew Louis Napoleon chose 2 December for his *coup d'état*, becoming French dictator, and precisely one year after that the French Senate confirmed him as Emperor Napoleon III.

Other action this day

1547: Spanish conquistador Hernán Cortés dies of pleurisy near Seville * 1899: At the Battle of Tirad Pass during the Filipino–American War, a 60-man Filipino rearguard takes 52 casualties while holding off the American 33rd Infantry Regiment long enough for Filipino independence fighter Emilio Aguinaldo (to become the Philippines' first president) to escape

3 December

Operation Genghis Khan

1971 Today Pakistani jets launched Operation Genghis Khan, a surprise attack on ten Indian military airfields, to start a war that led to the birth of a new nation.

When Pakistan had first gained independence in 1947, it was formed from two geographically separated areas, West Pakistan and East Pakistan (formerly East Bengal), with India in the middle. Since then the western half had ruled the country, but in 1970, in the nation's first-ever general election, East Pakistan's Awami League won a majority in the Pakistani National Assembly. Finding the results unacceptable, Pakistani president General Yahya Khan arrested the Awami League's candidate, causing its leaders to flee to Calcutta and set up a government in exile and declare East Pakistan's independence on 21 March the following year. Four days later Yahya Khan launched Operation Searchlight, a military assault on East Pakistan. In just two months, West Pakistani troops wiped out all Bengali military resistance while massacring huge numbers of civilians, especially civil leaders, who were specially targeted. Somewhere between 200,000 and 3 million were killed, and 8 million people fled over the border into India.

In the meantime, East Bengali military units had combined with police and armed civilians to form the Mukti Bahini, a guerrilla force that launched bloody attacks from India against the West Pakistani army, causing heavy casualties. Indian prime minister Indira Gandhi publicly expressed support for the East Bengali revolt, set up training facilities for the Mukti Bahini and provided active aid with Indian army troops.

Open war with India was now inevitable, and the Pakistani government determined to launch a pre-emptive strike. They knew they could not defend East Pakistan but believed that international pressures would prevent a long war, so they planned a surprise attack against India that would give them tracts of Indian territory that could be used as bargaining chips in the eventual negotiations. The first step in what would be called the Indo-Pakistani War of 1971 was Operation Genghis Khan, the Pakistani air strike against airbases in north-west India.

Starting at 5.40 this Sunday evening, two waves of planes rose to the sky, an international array comprised of 24 F-86F Canadian-built Sabre jets, four American-built Lockheed F-104 Starfighters and eight French-built Mirages.

Caught by surprise, the Indian bases failed to scramble any aircraft, and, despite light anti-aircraft fire, the Pakistani planes damaged several runways and radar installations, although failing to put them out of action for more than a few hours. Almost simultaneously, Pakistani artillery began shelling India's western frontier, and infantry made a minor border incursion in the state of Jammu. Later, Pakistani planes launched another strike that included three B-57 bombers, one of which was shot down by Indian ground fire.

Just after midnight, Prime Minister Gandhi announced the attacks on the radio to her nation and began a full-scale invasion of

East Pakistan. At 9.00 on Monday evening, four squadrons of Indian Canberra light bombers hit eight Pakistani airfields, heavily damaging two of them at a loss of only one aircraft; within two days the Indian air force had gained total air supremacy. Then three Indian corps advanced into East Pakistan, supported by three brigades of Mukti Bahini, brushing aside the Pakistani force of only three divisions and capturing over 5,000 square miles of territory. Meanwhile, the Indian navy attacked Karachi, wrecking two destroyers.

Now Indian planes continued to hammer Pakistani positions, flying some 4,000 sorties, while the Pakistanis offered little in retaliation; their F-86s and F-6s were a generation older than India's MiG-21s, and the Pakistani high command decided to cut its losses.

In the land war, the Pakistanis launched a number of armoured thrusts against the Indian onslaught, even sending commandos on sabotage missions, but nothing could halt the Indian advance, as troops bypassed the few powerful Pakistani strongholds and were soon marching on the East Pakistan capital at Dhaka. Overwhelmed by the assault, on 16 December, less than two weeks after India had crossed the border, the Pakistani troops in East Pakistan surrendered. They had suffered 8,000–10,000 killed and wounded and lost 91,000 captured. East Pakistan had become independent; the new nation called itself Bangladesh, which in the Bengali language means 'land of the Bengalis'.

Other action this day

1800: During the French Revolutionary Wars, French general Jean Moreau defeats the Austrians and Bavarians at the Battle of Hohenlinden near Munich, forcing the Austrians to sign an armistice * 1946: From rooftops around Syntagma (Constitution) Square in Athens, Greek police and British troops supporting the Greek government open fire with machine guns on a banned EAM (Communist-controlled National Liberation Front) demonstration of approximately 250,000, leaving 28 dead and 148 wounded and sparking the Greek Civil War between the Greek government and the Communists

4 December

The Danes fight the Swedes in the bloodiest battle in Scandinavian history

1676 In his memoirs, Denmark's King Christian V listed 'hunting, love-making, war and maritime affairs' as his principal interests in life, so he must have been content when on this day he fought the Swedes in the bloodiest battle in Scandinavian history.

Christian had resolved to regain Scania, the southernmost province in Sweden, which had once belonged to Denmark. In June 1676 he invaded with 15,000 men, in personal command even though he was only nineteen. During the early months of the war he took town after town to force the Swedes out of the province, but in October Sweden's King Charles XI marched back into Scania with an army 12,000-strong.

For two months the Swedes and Danes fought only minor skirmishes, and by late autumn Christian had settled his troops in winter quarters just outside the Scanian town of Lund, twelve miles northeast of Malmö.

By 3 December the Swedes had reached the Kävlinge River, seven miles north of the town. That night the temperature dropped sharply, freezing the river enough to allow them to cross under cover of darkness between 4.00 and 5.30 the next morning. Since the Danish outnumbered them almost three to one in infantry, the Swedes' greatest strength was their cavalry, but Swedish patrols discovered that the terrain leading up to the Danish positions was unsuitable for mounted troops. Now King Charles quietly moved his infantry forward just outside the north wall of Lund without alerting the Danes' somnolent sentries. Christian's troops were taken totally by surprise, many of them drunk. Nonetheless, they managed to organise themselves for battle.

By nine o'clock a feeble Scandinavian sun at last rose over Lund. There Swedes and Danes faced each other along a half-mile front, the Swedes occupying the highest hill-ridge north of the town.

Charles now personally led his cavalry around the enemy left flank, even though his horse 'Thotten' was shot from under him. The attack forced the Danish left into a headlong retreat until they reached the river, now slightly thawed by the sun. There some Danish soldiers fled out onto the ice, only to fall through to their deaths.

With Charles's cavalry off chasing the Danish left, the remaining Danes could – and did – concentrate on the Swedish infantry, who were soon backed against the walls of Lund. At noon, however, the Danes pulled back briefly to regroup.

In the meantime, Charles returned from the river, reaching Lund at sunset, around three o'clock, and daringly rode straight through the Danish line with only two officers and three of his guards to rally his embattled infantry. Inspired, the Swedes attacked with renewed vigour. The Danes were now caught in a pincer, Charles's infantry in front of them and his cavalry at their rear. Seeing their infantry collapse, the Danish cavalry galloped off the field, leaving the foot soldiers to be cut down en masse. Finally, at five o'clock the Swedes called for a ceasefire to bring the killing to a halt. Many of the wounded froze to death on the battleground during the night.

The next day the Swedes counted 8,993 dead strewn on the field before Lund, about a third of whom were their own. This toll excludes the Danes who drowned. Counting those who died from wounds during the following weeks, almost half of the soldiers on both sides were killed.

Despite this sanguinary Swedish triumph, the Scanian War dragged on for another two and a half years without a definitive victor. The town of Lund, which had escaped more or less unscathed from the battle, was set on fire by a Danish patrol in 1678, and more than half of it was destroyed. In the end, France brokered a peace treaty, and King Charles married Christian's sister, to whom he had been betrothed before the start of hostilities. Neither Sweden nor Denmark had gained a foot of territory.

Other action this day

1783: Two months after the American Revolution had officially ended with the Treaty of Paris, George Washington bids farewell to his officers at Fraunces Tavern in New York * 1892: Spanish general and dictator Francisco Franco is born in El Ferrol, Galicia * 1942: US Marine Lieutenant Colonel Evans Carlson and his 'Carlson's Raiders' enter friendly lines at Lunga Point on Guadalcanal after a 30-day raid behind Japanese lines in which 488 Japanese were killed against sixteen Raiders killed and eighteen wounded

5 December

Frederick the Great's greatest victory

1757 During the Seven Years War Prussia's population totalled only 4.5 million, while the opposing alliance of Austria, France and Russia could draw their armies from over 100 million inhabitants. But Prussia had Frederick the Great.

Frederick was the greatest general of the 18th century, one of the greatest of any century. On this day he proved it and saved his nation from extinction.

The town of Leuthen lies just west of the Oder in land that Frederick had seized from Austria only a few years before. Here his force of just 36,000 men would face an Austrian army of 60,000–80,000. Aware of the enormous odds against his success, Frederick offered his officers the chance to leave before the battle, but none defected. The evening before the battle he laconically remarked: 'Shortly we shall either have beaten the enemy, or we will never see one another again.'

The next day, through a brilliant flanking manoeuvre, Frederick utterly routed the Austrians in a three-hour battle. Although Prussia lost some 6,000 killed and wounded, the enemy lost 10,000 killed plus 21,000 captured. And within two weeks another 17,000 dispirited Austrian soldiers surrendered almost without a fight at Breslau.

The war dragged on until 1763, sometimes favouring Frederick's enemies, but the great general always managed to extricate himself from disaster with a timely victory. As Napoleon remarked in the following century: 'It is not the Prussian army which for seven years defended Prussia against the three most powerful nations in Europe, but Frederick the Great.'

In the years ahead, the Battle of Leuthen became a totemic victory for the German people, a symbol of German superiority that would play its role in the eventual unification of the country, reverberating through the centuries to the First World War and culminating in the militarism of the Third Reich. As Frederick's contemporary, the comte de Mirabeau, commented: 'La guerre est l'industrie nationale de la Prusse.' ('War is the national industry of Prussia.')

63 BC: Cicero denounces Catiline in the Senate in the last of his Catiline Orations, forcing Catiline out of Rome and into military rebellion ∗ 1443: Birth of the 'Warrior Pope' Julius II, who personally led his Papal troops in battle and founded the Vatican's Swiss Guard ∗ 1839: American general George Armstrong Custer of 'Custer's Last Stand' is born

6 December

A Pakistani major earns the Nishan-e-Haider

1971 Today, after four days of ferocious fighting, a company commander in Pakistan's 6 Frontier Force gave his life during an Indian tank attack at the very start of the Indo-Pakistani War. For his leadership and daring – he had even fought a one-on-one duel with an Indian officer – he was awarded Pakistan's highest military honour, the Nishan-e-Haider.

Shabbir Sharif was a handsome, dark-eyed 28-year-old with a full but neatly trimmed black beard. A major in command of Bravo Company of 6 FF, he had already seen combat in the 1965 war against India. Now war had come again.

It had begun when Pakistan launched pre-emptive air strikes against Indian airbases (see 3 December). On the same day, Sharif had been ordered to cross into India in the Sulemanki sector (east of Lahore) and seize a steep artificial ridge that the Indians had constructed as a defence against invasion. Fronting the ridge was a 30-foot canal, and the ridge itself was defended by a company from the Indian army in camouflaged bunkers, supported by tanks.

Sharif's first feat of bravery came in assaulting this stronghold. After making his way through an enemy minefield (the mines probably malfunctioned) and swimming the canal, he led his 100 men in a frontal attack, while Pakistani artillery hammered the ridge, destroying three tanks. After 30 minutes of bitter fighting, during which Sharif caught a hand grenade thrown from a bunker and rifled it back through the bunker's firing aperture, the defenders pulled out, leaving 43 dead and 28 captured at the cost of only a handful of Pakistani casualties.

Sharif and his men now occupied the ridge, but that night the Indians counter-attacked with 150 men and fourteen tanks. Sharif himself set the first tank ablaze with an anti-tank rocket, and the flames from the burning vehicle sharply illuminated the accompanying enemy infantry, who then came under intense automatic weapons fire. The Indians were forced to retire, with over 40 more killed and four tanks destroyed.

The next day the Indians attacked once more and were once more rebuffed, and then, on the night of 5 December, they mounted a major assault with about 800 men.

Now an Indian major named Narayan Singh and a few of his men worked themselves close to Sharif's position. Somehow he had learned the Pakistani commander's name, and, like some medieval knight, he called out: 'Where is Shabbir Sharif? If he has the courage, he should come out right now and face me like a man.'

Sharif, being as hot-headed as Singh, stepped forward from his trench, just as someone threw a grenade that exploded a few feet away and set fire to his shirt. As a few of Sharif's men came out to quench the fire, the soldiers accompanying Singh levelled their guns. 'No firing', Singh barked out. 'This is a man-to-man fight.' He, too, then stepped out, grasping a Sten gun in his right hand.

But before Singh could raise it, Sharif leaped forward and grabbed his wrist to prevent him from bringing the gun to bear. For a few moments the two men struggled against each other, then Sharif knocked Singh to the ground and shot him in the chest with his own Sten gun. The other Indian soldiers melted away into the night.

By now Sharif and his company had been fighting for three days and nights, but still the Indians came on. The next attack came at 11.00 the following morning, 6 December. Once again, Indian tanks led the charge. Sharif manned an anti-tank gun and took out one enemy tank, but as he tried to aim in on a second, it fired, killing him and two other soldiers.

When Sharif was posthumously honoured with the Nishan-e-Haider, he became the only man to receive it not for a specific act of gallantry but for his inspiring performance over the four days up to his death. Since the first Nishan-e-Haider was awarded in 1948, only ten have been given. All the recipients died in action.

1185: Afonso I, the Conqueror, first king of Portugal, dies at 76 having gained Portugal's independence from the Kingdom of León and doubled the size of his country by reconquering it from the Moors * 1240: The Mongols under Batu Khan capture Kiev * 1608: English Civil War general George Monck is born near Torrington in Devon * 1833: American Confederate guerrilla leader John Singleton Mosby is born * 1917: After the French freighter *Mont Blanc* collides with a Norwegian ship in Halifax harbour, Nova Scotia, the *Mont Blanc*'s cargo of 2,300 tons of picric acid, 200 tons of TNT, 35 tons of high-octane gasoline, and 10 tons of gun cotton explodes in the most devastating man-made explosion in the pre-atomic age, killing 1,600 people, injuring another 9,000 and destroying the north end of Halifax, including more than 1,600 houses

7 December

Marshal Ney is executed in the gardens of the Palais Luxembourg

1815 Today Michel Ney, one of Napoleon's most illustrious marshals, was shot by firing squad in the gardens of the Palais Luxembourg in Paris.

Ney was a beefy, red-haired, tobacco-chewing man of the people. Although his mother tongue was German (he was of Alsatian origin), he was exactly the kind of soldier Napoleon most valued: brave under fire to the point of recklessness, intimate with his troops and intensely loyal.

Ney's blacksmith father had hoped for a genteel future for his son and had found him a position as apprentice to a lawyer, but at nineteen the adventurous young man ran away to join a regiment of hussars. He had already risen to the rank of general by the time he was 32, when he first met Napoleon.

Promoted to marshal three years later, Ney served the emperor loyally, participating in the great victories at Jena-Auerstädt, Eylau and Friedland, and heroically commanding the rearguard in Napoleon's retreat from Moscow, for which the emperor created him Prince de la Moskowa. He also fought courageously in the crucial defeat at Leipzig, where he was wounded.

When Napoleon was packed off to Elba, Ney allowed fat King Louis XVIII to persuade him to remain a marshal of France, and when the ex-emperor escaped, Ney vowed to 'bring him back in a cage'. But on seeing Napoleon again, he returned to his original loyalties, rejoined him for his 100 Days and commanded the left wing at Waterloo. There at the battle's end he tried to stop the rout, crying to his soldiers: 'Venez voir comment meurt un maréchal de France!' ('Come and see how a marshal of France can die!')

This reversal of loyalties engendered the special hatred of King Louis. Soon after Waterloo, Ney attempted to escape from France but was captured and returned to Paris in chains.

Tried for treason, he was sentenced to death, and on the cold, clear morning of 7 December, the bold marshal bravely faced the firing squad. Refusing a bandage over his eyes, he addressed his executioners and gave the order to fire: 'Don't you know that for 25 years I have learned to face both cannonballs and bullets? Come on, soldiers, straight to the heart ... I have fought a hundred battles for France and not one against her ... Soldiers Fire!'

Ney died a criminal in the eyes of his government but a hero in the eyes of the French people. In 1853 sculptor François Rude's vigorous statue of the great marshal was placed around the corner from the Luxembourg Gardens in the avenue de l'Observatoire in front of what today is the Closerie des Lilas, the café so beloved by Ernest Hemingway.

Other action this day

43 BC: On orders from Mark Antony, Roman soldiers execute Roman ex-consul Marcus Tullius Cicero * 1941: In a tactically brilliant but strategically catastrophic attack, at 7.55am 200 Japanese aircraft bombard the American base at Pearl Harbor, sinking five battleships, two destroyers and one other ship, damaging three battleships, three cruisers and one destroyer, and destroying 188 aircraft and damaging 155 more, while inflicting 3,400 casualties including 2,300 KIA; five US soldiers and sailors win the Medal of Honor, and the next day President Roosevelt brands the surprise attack 'a date which will live in infamy' and the US Congress declares war

8 December

A pyrrhic victory for the Japanese

1941 Today in only fourteen hours Japan launched seven nearly simultaneous attacks in a breathtakingly audacious plan to take control of the entire south Pacific. At almost the same moment that their aircraft were ravaging the American fleet at Pearl Harbor, Japanese soldiers were storming ashore in Thailand and on the northern coast of Malaya, and their bombers were hammering the British airfield on Hong Kong and American bases on Guam and in the Philippines. (The bombing of Pearl Harbor is dated 7 December because Pearl Harbor is on the other side of the International Date Line.) The last to be attacked on this long day was a tiny, wishbone-shaped coral atoll called Wake Island, which lies 2,300 miles west of Pearl Harbor and about the same distance south-east of Japan.

Only four months before, a detachment of 499 US Marines from the 1st Marine Defense Battalion had set up the first permanent garrison on Wake, accompanied by 68 members of the US Navy. In addition to their rifles, the Marines were armed with an odd assortment of firepower: six 5-inch guns taken from a dismantled battleship, twelve M3 3-inch anti-aircraft guns, eighteen .50 calibre machine guns and about 30 miscellaneous machine guns of varying calibre and condition. With them were over 1,100 civilian construction workers to help build the base.

At twelve noon local time today, 36 twin-tailed Mitsubishi G3M2 bombers caught the Americans by surprise, releasing their loads on Wake's half-completed air and submarine base. They destroyed eight of the twelve Marine F4F Wildcat fighters on the ground, killing 23 Marines and wounding eleven more, as well as killing about 25 civilian workmen. Although the Americans had been radioed the news of the attack on Pearl Harbor, they had no radar, and the pounding surf on Wake had prevented them hearing the approach of the Japanese planes.

After two more days of bombing, at dawn on 11 December an enemy taskforce of three light cruisers, six destroyers, two patrol boats and two transport ships carrying 450 men of the Special Naval Landing Force (Japanese marines) appeared off the coast.

The approaching enemy ships shelled the shore, setting ablaze several oil tanks. The American Marine commander, Major James Devereux, held fire until the Japanese were only 4,500 yards away and then opened up with his 5-inch guns, severely damaging one of the light cruisers. Then three salvos slammed into a Japanese destroyer, touching off a massive explosion in the ammunition hold that sent her to the bottom with all 167 men aboard. She was the first Japanese surface warship sunk during the Second World War.

Meanwhile, Marine captain Henry Elrod led the four remaining Wildcats against the enemy taskforce. Elrod flew directly into a flight of 22 Japanese planes, downing two Zeros and damaging two bombers. He then strafed a second enemy destroyer, dropping bombs on her rear deck, which detonated the depth charges stored below and sank the ship with all hands. But enemy anti-aircraft fire had perforated his plane's oil line, and he was forced to crash-land on Wake's rocky beach, his Wildcat a write-off. Stunned by the Americans' fierce resistance, the Japanese taskforce withdrew.

Over the next eleven days the Americans would lose their last remaining fighters, despite the Marines' near-miraculous cannibalisation and refitting of damaged planes, as the attackers incessantly bombed the island in preparation for another landing, which would come on 23 December.

Reinforced by two aircraft carriers and an additional 1,500 Japanese marines, the invasion force struck the beach at 2.45am. The two converted destroyers landing the troops were set alight by Marine guns, but the invaders were now ashore. For over twelve hours the vastly outnumbered and outgunned defenders held off the attackers, moving from place to place, often in hand-to-hand fighting. Before they were overrun, their 5-inch guns damaged two more destroyers. Without a plane to fly, Captain Elrod organised a unit of ground troops into a beach defence and repulsed repeated Japanese attacks, but he was shot and killed while throwing a hand grenade. He was posthumously awarded the Medal of Honor.

But no amount of heroics could save the American forces on Wake, and at last they were forced to surrender. Of the original force of 449 Marines, 49 were now dead with another 32 wounded. Of the Navy's 68 officers and men, three were killed and five wounded. In addition, 70 of the 1,100 civilian workers were killed. With the exception of about 100 workers whom the Japanese kept on Wake to do forced labour, all the prisoners were interned in prisoner of war camps until the end of the war. It was a pyrrhic victory for the Japanese, who had suffered almost 800 KIAs, with 1,000 more wounded. Two of their light cruisers had been damaged and two destroyers and an escort vessel sunk. Seventy-two of their aircraft had been hit, 21 of them shot down.

American planes periodically bombarded Japanese-occupied Wake for the rest of the war. (One American pilot who attacked it was future president George H.W. Bush, who flew his first combat mission there.) The Japanese garrison finally surrendered on 4 September 1945, twenty days after their nation had itself capitulated.

Other action this day

1914: The British navy sinks the German cruisers *Scharnhorst*, *Gneisenau*, *Nürnberg* and *Leipzig* in the Battle of the Falkland Islands * 1941: The Japanese invade Malaya, Thailand and the Philippines * 1941: The first day of the eighteen-day Battle of Hong Kong, in which the Japanese conquer the island, inflicting 4,500 British/Commonwealth casualties and capturing 8,500 prisoners

9 December

The story of a warrior

1944 Sometimes in reading of battles we forget the heroism of individual warriors, especially junior officers and enlisted ranks, whose actions – fighting and dying – so often turned the day. On this date, just three days after his 22nd birthday, British captain John Brunt earned his country's highest medal, the Victoria Cross, for courageous action in Italy. It was his second decoration for valour within a single year.

In December 1943 Brunt (then a lieutenant in the 6th Battalion of the Lincolnshire Regiment) was in action south-east of Salerno, where soldiers from a German tank battalion were holed up in three houses. Brunt led his section into the attack, quickly overrunning the first two, but the Germans in the third house doggedly returned fire. After half an hour of intense fighting, Brunt's men killed all the enemy within the house plus eight outside, using Tommy guns and grenades. During the action one of Brunt's men had been killed and six others wounded. Sending his section back to friendly lines, Brunt remained with two men to rescue a wounded comrade. For his actions that day, he was awarded the Military Cross. He later commented to his friends: 'I've won the MC, now for the VC!'

A year later Brunt, now a temporary captain, commanded a platoon near Faenza, 30 miles south of Bologna. It was for his actions here that he was awarded the Victoria Cross. His citation tells the story:

In Italy, on the 9th December 1944, the Platoon commanded by Captain Brunt was holding a vital sector of the line.

At dawn the German 90 Panzer Grenadier Regiment counter-attacked the Battalion's forward positions in great strength with three Mark IV tanks and infantry. The house, around which the Platoon was dug in, was destroyed and the whole area was subjected to intense mortar fire. The situation then became critical, as the anti-tank defences had been destroyed and two Sherman tanks knocked out. Captain Brunt, however, rallied his remaining men, and, moving to an alternative position, continued to hold the enemy infantry, although outnumbered by at least three to one. Personally firing a Bren gun [a light machine gun], Captain Brunt killed about fourteen of the enemy. His wireless set was destroyed by shell-fire, but on receiving a message by runner to withdraw to a Company locality some 200 yards to his left and rear, he remained behind to give covering fire. When his Bren ammunition was exhausted, he fired a Piat [an anti-tank weapon] and 2 in. mortar, left by casualties, before he himself dashed over the open ground to the new position. This aggressive defence caused the enemy to pause, so Captain Brunt took a party back to his previous position, and although fiercely engaged by small arms fire, carried away the wounded who had been left there.

Later in the day, a further counter-attack was put in by the enemy on two axes. Captain Brunt immediately seized a spare Bren gun and, going round his forward positions, rallied his men. Then, leaping on a Sherman tank supporting the Company, he ordered the tank commander to drive from one fire position to another, whilst he sat, or stood, on the turret, directing Besa [a type of machine gun] fire at the advancing enemy, regardless of the hail of small arms fire. Then, seeing small parties of the enemy, armed with bazookas, trying to approach round the left flank, he jumped off the tank and, taking a Bren gun, stalked these parties well in front of the Company positions, killing more and causing the enemy finally to withdraw in great haste leaving their dead behind them.

Wherever the fighting was heaviest, Captain Brunt was always to be found, moving from one post to another, encouraging the men and firing any weapon he found at any target he could see. The magnificent action fought by this Officer, his coolness, bravery, devotion to duty and complete disregard of his own personal safety under the most intense and concentrated fire was beyond praise. His personal example and individual action were responsible to a very great extent for the successful repulse of these fierce enemy counter-attacks.

The next day this heroic soldier was killed by a stray mortar round.

Other action this day

AD 536: Byzantine general Belisarius takes Rome during the Gothic War * 1594: Swedish warrior-king Gustavus Adolphus is born * 1824: Peruvian nationalists under Antonio José de Sucre defeat the Spaniards at the Battle of Avacucho, securing the independence of Peru

10 December

Disaster on the South China Sea

1941 Three days after the surprise bombing of Pearl Harbor, British admiral Tom Phillips's flotilla was headed for Singapore, but at 12.50am today he learned that the Japanese were now landing on the east coast of Malaya. Intent on attacking the invading force, he turned his ships – the battleship *Prince of Wales*, the battlecruiser *Repulse* and four destroyers – towards the enemy. But at dawn the sea was still quiet and empty. One crewman remembered: 'A clear blue sky, streaked with rays from the rising sun shone above, while around us sparkled the deep blue ocean, ruffled by a gentle breeze.'

At 11.00am, however, the ominous drone of aircraft broke the eerie calm; thirteen minutes later three waves of Japanese twin-engined Nell bombers swept in from astern. A sailor on the *Prince of Wales* later wrote: 'First the 5.25's [dual-purpose guns for use against ships and aircraft] opened up in all their fury, belching forth flame and death, followed later by the steady, heartening and assuring bark of the pom-poms – then silence again. The first attack had been beaten off …' The attackers had failed to damage any of the ships except for one bomb that started a small fire on the *Repulse*.

But after half an hour's lull, sixteen more Nells appeared. 'The enemy now altered his tactics and splitting up into several formations, launched a low flying torpedo attack at different angles on our port side … Once more our guns broke the uncanny silence, creating uproar, scarcely able to be borne. The foremost formations were piteously attacked and destroyed, some aft, crashing in flames into the sea before they had time to release their deadly cargo; others a victim to their own torpedoes, blew up in mid air, scattering the sea with wreckage … Our captain [dodged a few torpedoes], but alas there were too many … First a splash as the torpedo entered the water, and then a thin white line of foam defined the course. With a deafening crash the torpedo struck the *Prince of Wales* amidships …'

The force of this tremendous explosion appeared to halt the battleship, some sailors believing her to have been thrown into the air, as her speed plunged from 25 to 15 knots. Now she 'began to develop a list to port, which became so great that the guns on the starboard side could not be lowered sufficiently to fire at the low-flying Japanese planes, which now with advantage began to drive home their attacks. At this stage another torpedo struck the *Prince of Wales*, causing damage to the steering, with the result that the ship began to career about in wide circles and was unable to dodge enemy torpedoes. In order to correct the severe list to port, the starboard side was flooded and many gallant men were trapped below and drowned in this drastic attempt to save the ship.'

With the *Prince of Wales* sorely stricken, the Japanese planes concentrated on the *Repulse*, as 26 Betty torpedo bombers attacked from several directions at once. After dodging nineteen torpedoes, the *Repulse* was struck twice. A reporter on board named Cecil Brown related: 'It feels as though the ship has crashed into dock. I am thrown four feet across the deck but I keep my feet. Almost immediately ... the ship lists ... Over the loudspeaker, a cool voice [of the captain]: "All hands on deck. Prepare to abandon ship." There is a pause for just an instant, then: "God be with you." ... The torpedo-smashed *Prince of Wales*, still half to three-quarters of a mile ahead, is low in the water, half shrouded in smoke ... Japanese bombers are still winging around like vultures, still attacking the *Wales*. A few of those shot down are bright splotches of burning orange on the blue South China Sea.'

On the *Repulse*, 'men are jumping into the sea ... one man misses his distance, dives, hits the side of the *Repulse*, breaks every bone in his body and crumples into the sea ... Another misses his direction and dives from one of the towers straight down the smokestack ... Twelve Royal Marines ... jump into the water and are sucked into the propeller.' Brown leapt from the foundering ship, and, kept afloat by a life preserver, he watched 'the bow of the *Repulse* swing straight into the air like a church steeple. Its red underplates stand out as stark and as gruesome as the blood on the faces of the men around me.' Just six minutes after the first torpedo strike, she went down with the loss of one third of her 1,500 men.

The *Prince of Wales* stayed afloat for another hour, by which time one of the destroyers had come alongside to take off survivors, although 327 were killed, including Admiral Phillips.

So it was, in a battle of less than two hours' duration, the British had lost a battleship and a battlecruiser, the first capital ships to be sunk solely by airpower on the open sea. Churchill was still in bed when he was informed of the catastrophe. He later recalled: 'As I turned over and twisted in bed the full horror of the news sank in upon me. There were no British or American ships in the Indian Ocean or the Pacific except the American survivors of Pearl Harbor, who were hastening back to California. Over all this vast expanse of waters Japan was supreme, and we everywhere were weak and naked.'

Other action this day

1508: Representatives of Pope Julius II, France, Holy Roman Emperor Maximilian I and Ferdinand I of Spain conclude the League of Cambrai against the Republic of Venice * 1864: Union general William T. Sherman's army reaches Savannah, Georgia during his March to the Sea * 1949: Communists begin their siege of Chengdu, the last Kuomintang-held city in mainland China, which will force Chiang Kai-shek and his government to flee to Taiwan

11 December

'Retreat? Hell, we're attacking in a different direction!'

1950 Today the last battered survivors of the US 1st Marine Division climbed onto trucks at Chinhung-ni and headed for Hungnam to board ship. In the midst of a calamitous defeat of UN forces on the Korean peninsula, they had fought their way out of an immense trap around the Chosin Reservoir, in an incredible thirteen-day, 35-mile retreat in which they took heavy casualties but inflicted ten times as many on the Chinese forces surrounding them.

Six months earlier, the Communist North Korean army had invaded the Republic of Korea (ROK) to start the war. Within hours the UN Security Council had condemned the aggression, but the North Koreans quickly routed the ROK army and continued to smash their way south even after the United States, under UN auspices, intervened in July.

Two months later, however, in a stroke of strategic genius, UN commander General Douglas MacArthur staged an amphibious landing at Inchon (see 14 September), catching the North Koreans completely by surprise and driving them out of the south in full retreat. Confident of victory, the UN forces (US 8th Army and X Corps, comprised of the 1st Marine Division, elements of the US 7th Infantry Division and some British Royal Marine commandos) drove into North Korea towards the Yalu River, the border with China. But, in a massive intelligence failure, the American generals had not foreseen that Communist China would not stand by while its client state of North Korea was destroyed.

On 25 October an enormous wave of Chinese troops poured across the Yalu into Korea, annihilating the ROK 6th Division in just ten days. A week later (see 1 November) they smashed into the 8th Army, starting the longest retreat in US Army history. The 8th Army collapse exposed X Corps to enemy attack from all directions.

X Corps was spread out east and west of the Chosin Reservoir, its units too far apart to support each other. By 27 November two Chinese divisions had surrounded and virtually destroyed the 3,000-man unit of the 7th Infantry Division east of the reservoir; only 1,500 soldiers managed to fight their way out, while the rest were killed or captured.

In temperatures of –31°C and under heavy snow, the remains of X Corps reeled under the assault of six Chinese divisions. Now MacArthur ordered Marine major general O.P. Smith to lead a withdrawal out of the Chinese encirclement. So began an incredible fighting retreat by 22,000 Marines, spread out over a narrow, mountainous, one-lane supply road running south to the secure base at Chinhung-ni.

During the nights of 27–29 November the Chinese launched mass attacks to the sound of blaring bugles and the light of flares, glowing threads from tracer bullets criss-crossing in the dark. Northeast of the reservoir at Yudam-ni, three Chinese divisions fell on two Marine regiments, inflicting 500 casualties. With hospital tents overflowing, the less seriously wounded were laid down outside, near each other for warmth, and covered with tarpaulins and snow.

On the morning of 29 November, General Smith ordered a 900-man taskforce of Marines and Royal Marine commandos to break out down the sole road to the south. Under incessant fire from the heights overlooking the route, the taskforce lost 300 killed or wounded and 135 captured, with 75 of their 140 vehicles destroyed. The taskforce had failed, and the Marines were still surrounded, prompting Marine colonel Chesty Puller's famous if perhaps apocryphal comment: 'All right, they're on our left, they're on our right, they're in front of us, they're behind us … they can't get away this time.'

Now Smith concentrated his units to break the Chinese stranglehold. When asked if the Marines were retreating, he responded: 'Retreat? Hell, we're attacking in a different direction!' One of his regiments took 79 hours to fight their way just fourteen miles from north-west of the reservoir to the main Marine position at Hagaru-ri. Although over a third of the force was frostbitten, they managed to bring their 1,500 casualties with them.

On 6 December the Marines moved a further ten miles south down what became known as Hellfire Valley, from Hagaru-ri to

Koto-ri. During the entire 38-hour withdrawal they were either under attack or conducting their own assaults, often with hand-to-hand fighting. Helping to clear the Chinese from their path were fighter-bombers that continually blasted and strafed Chinese positions. Over 4,000 Marine casualties were flown out to safety.

On 9 December the Marines started on the final ten-mile leg of their withdrawal, from Koto-ri to Chinhung-ni, still under constant enemy attack, but the Chinese had taken staggering losses and suffered even more than the Marines from the bitter cold. Marine companies leapfrogged each other as they moved down the frozen loops of the road, artillery hammering the enemy whenever they grouped to attack. Just after noon on 11 December the last platoon piled into trucks to be transported to Hungnam and the sea. With typical Marine bravado, one lieutenant had painted on his tank: '14 more shooting days until Christmas.' For conspicuous gallantry during the battle, eleven Marines were awarded the Medal of Honor.

During this heroic retreat the 1st Marine Division's 22,000 men had suffered 718 dead, 192 missing and 3,508 wounded, plus 6,000 frostbitten casualties. In addition, US Army and British commando units had lost almost 2,000 killed and 1,500 wounded. But by the battle's end, thousands of Chinese lay frozen on the ridges around the Chosin Reservoir, rifles still slung on their shoulders, packs on their backs, shrouded in snow. Of their 120,000-man army, 25,000 had been killed and another 12,500 wounded, plus an estimated 30,000 frostbitten.

Other action this day

1282: The independence of Wales is lost for ever as Prince Llywelyn ap Gruffydd (Llywelyn the Last) of Wales is killed in battle against Roger de Mortimer, who delivers his head to English king Edward I * 1941: Hitler and Mussolini declare war on the United States * 1994: Russian forces enter Chechnya in order to 'establish constitutional order in Chechnya and to preserve the territorial integrity of Russia', starting the First Chechen War

12 December

The Crusaders' most barbarous victory

1098 For three years since Pope Urban II had urged the faithful to deliver Jerusalem from the Saracens, Crusader armies from Europe had trudged towards the Holy Land, killing and dying in equal number. Now two of their leaders were commanding the assault on Ma'arat al-Numan, a fortified town now in Syria, a few miles south of Antioch. One was one-eyed Raimond de Saint-Gilles, comte de Toulouse and marquis de Provence, at 55 the oldest and richest leader among the Christians and the first to heed the Pope's summons.

The second was Bohemond of Otranto, a blue-eyed Norman from southern Italy who was christened 'Mark' but nicknamed 'Bohemond' after a legendary giant because of his height – a contemporary recorded that 'he was so tall in stature that he overtopped the tallest by nearly a cubit [eighteen inches] … narrow in the waist and loins, with broad shoulders and a deep chest and powerful arms'.

On 3 June 1098 Raimond and Bohemond had conquered the great walled city of Antioch after a difficult siege of 21 months, the city finally falling only when a traitorous Saracen commander allowed Bohemond and his soldiers over a section of the city's walls. The Crusaders' triumphant entry was followed by the customary Christian slaughter of its Muslim inhabitants. Even then the citadel held out until, three weeks later, the Crusaders annihilated a Muslim relief force outside the city.

Although successful, the siege of Antioch had drained Christian resources. Little food was left; inside the fallen city there was none, and Crusader raids on the surrounding countryside failed to produce an adequate supply, especially when summer turned to autumn and autumn to winter. Leaving Antioch garrisoned with Christian reserves, Bohemond and Raimond now marched onward to Ma'arat al-Numan, still in enemy hands. By this time many of the invaders were suffering from starvation, with scant prospect of finding supplies in winter.

Inspired by visions of food, loot and Christian conquest, on this day the Crusaders breached Ma'arat's walls and slaughtered some

20,000 Saracens, mostly civilians, even those who had paid Bohemond to spare them. Many of the children were sold to the slave market at Antioch. But at Ma'arat al-Numan, even now no provisions could be found.

What followed was the most barbarous act in all the barbarous crusades. Frantic with hunger, Christian troops turned to cannibalism. One commander reported to Pope Urban: 'A dreadful famine tormented the army in Ma'arat and placed it in the cruel necessity of feeding on the bodies of the Saracens.' Another chronicler wrote (one hopes with some hyperbole), 'our soldiers boiled pagan adults alive in cooking-pots; they impaled children on spits and devoured them grilled'.

These monstrous acts left an indelible stain on the reputation of the Crusaders. In some Arabic dialects Crusaders are still called 'cannibals' and many Muslim writers have claimed that their heinous behaviour was driven not by starvation but by their belief that Muslims were lower than animals. Even today, the shadow of the Crusaders' bestial deeds distorts the Muslim view of the Christian West.

Other action this day

AD 627: Byzantine emperor Heraclius defeats the Persian emperor Khosrau II at the Battle of Nineveh * 1793: The French Republican army routs Catholic rebels from the Vendée at the Battle of Le Mans * 1913: Menilek II, the Ethiopian emperor who defeated the Italians, dies after a series of strokes * 1939: The Finns defeat the Russians at the Battle of Tolvajärvi, their first major victory in the Winter War

13 December

The sinking of the Graf Spee

1939 One of the most dramatic encounters in modern naval history occurred this morning off the coast of South America, as three cruisers of the Royal Navy – two British, one New Zealand – faced the pride of the German battle fleet. In an engagement that lasted just one hour and thirteen minutes, the cruisers, heavily outgunned but using their greater manoeuvrability to best advantage, managed to inflict enough damage on their opponent, the pocket battleship *Admiral Graf Spee*, to force her to seek safety in the neutral waters of Uruguay's River Plate.

The *Graf Spee*, powerfully armed with 11-inch guns, had sailed from Wilhelmshaven on the eve of the Second World War. Her mission was to be a surface raider, attacking and disrupting vital Allied shipping headed from South American ports for Europe. In her three months at sea, she had sunk nine British merchantmen; moreover, her presence in the South Atlantic had drawn some twenty French and British warships from other theatres where they were badly needed.

The *Graf Spee*'s method was to range widely across the South Atlantic and Indian Oceans, maintaining radio silence, appearing only briefly to sink a ship, then disappearing once again into the vast expanse. What might have been her tenth victim, sighted just after dawn today some 230 miles east of Montevideo, turned out to be a squadron of cruisers: *Exeter*, carrying six 8-inch guns, and *Achilles* and *Ajax*, each with 6-inch guns.

Instead of standing off and relying on its heavy batteries, which outranged those of the cruisers by 10,000 yards, the *Graf Spee*'s captain, Hans Langsdorff, ordered his ship to close for battle. In response, the squadron's commodore Henry Harwood split his ships into two groups – *Exeter* as one, *Ajax* and *Achilles* the other – each group manoeuvring separately to prevent their opponent from concentrating her fire on any one ship.

When the brief action was over, *Exeter*, with seven hits from the 11-inch guns, was completely out of action, on fire, and steering away for the British base in the Falkland Islands. *Ajax* and *Achilles* suffered heavy damage as well, but, more important, the cruisers had landed 50 shells on their opponent, inflicting significant damage to both hull and superstructure.

Turning away, the *Graf Spee* headed west for the River Plate and Montevideo harbour, *Ajax* and *Achilles* in dogged pursuit. She reached Montevideo shortly after midnight, where news of her unexpected arrival, and the presence of British warships lying in wait in international waters, was radioed around the world. From London, the Admiralty sent orders for other warships in the South Atlantic to join the two cruisers.

Learning the next day that the Uruguayan government would allow the *Graf Spee* to remain in port no more than 72 hours for repairs and medical assistance, Captain Langsdorff cabled naval high command in Berlin for instructions: Should he allow his ship to be interned; make a run for the ocean past the waiting cruisers; steer upriver for possible sanctuary in Buenos Aires; or scuttle the *Graf Spee*?

On 17 December, Langsdorff and a skeleton crew sailed the *Graf Spee* out of the harbour and, in a series of spectacular explosions, witnessed by thousands gathered along the shoreline, destroyed her in the River Plate's shallow waters. Two days later, in Buenos Aires, her captain committed suicide.

The *Graf Spee*'s presence in the South Atlantic was the first significant threat to the Allied war effort at sea. As Winston Churchill noted in *The Gathering Storm*, the victory 'gave intense joy to the British nation'. The naval historian Dudley Pope, whose 1956 book, *The Battle of the River Plate*, is still the best account, considered the effects of that victory: '[T]he fact that the *Graf Spee* was at sea ultimately affected ships sailing the oceans of the world and soldiers and airmen fighting on many battlefields; and although she was destroyed in the last days of 1939, the Allies were still reaping the benefit of Commodore Harwood's victory in 1943 and 1944.'

Other action this day

AD 522: Darius the Great defeats Babylonian king Nebuchadnezzar III en route to the conquest of Babylon * 1636: The Massachusetts Bay Colony organises three militia regiments to defend the colony against Pequot Indians, the founding of the National Guard of the United States * 1862: Confederate general Robert E. Lee triumphs over Ambrose Burnside at the Battle of Fredericksburg, Virginia * 1937: Nanking falls to the Japanese, who initiate a massacre – the Rape of Nanking, in which 200,000 Chinese civilians and prisoners of war are murdered and perhaps 40,000 women are raped

14 December

George Washington dies hard

1799 Today at about ten in the evening George Washington, America's first president and its greatest 18th-century general, died quietly in his bed at the family home at Mount Vernon, the Virginia estate originally owned by his great-grandfather.

Most of us are familiar with Washington's pivotal role during the American Revolution – his daring surprise attack at Trenton after crossing the Delaware on Christmas night (see 26 December), the unflagging leadership during the snowy winter at Valley Forge, the final victory over the British at Yorktown (see 28 September). But Washington's military career had started over twenty years before the Revolution. In 1754 he was nearly killed during skirmishes with Indians, and in May of that year he successfully ambushed a detachment of French in what is considered the first battle of the French and Indian War.

After his 1754 victory he was overwhelmed and captured at Fort Necessity, and a year later he was part of British general Edward Braddock's defeated force in the Ohio Country (although Washington himself played a heroic role in rallying the retreating forces). He also lost the Revolution's largest battle, the Battle of Long Island (see 27 August), and was later beaten at Brandywine (see 11 September) and Germantown.

During his career as commander-in-chief of the Continental Army, Washington probably lost as many battles as he won. Despite the losses and draws, as the Revolutionary War dragged on, he became his nation's indispensable man, holding together a ragged army of volunteers, always preserving it as a force to fight another day, and eventually leading it against all odds to victory.

Washington had finished his second term as president in 1797, then aged 65. Two years into retirement he was still an active and robust man who delighted in the outdoors and horseback rides around his property. One bitter cold morning in December 1799 he started the day by writing a reply to a letter from Alexander Hamilton on the subject of a military academy (eventually to be West Point – see 16 March) and then rode for several hours in the damp cold of a snowy Virginia, to return home frozen and exhausted. The next morning, suffering from a sore throat, he remained in the house to pursue farm business at his desk. Late in the afternoon, however, when the weather cleared, he went outside to mark trees for removal. At dinner he was hoarse and his cold had worsened, but he was cheerful and afterwards read aloud to his wife Martha from journals recently arrived. He refused the suggestion of medicine for his condition, preferring, he said, to 'let it go as it came'.

The next day he was unmistakably ill, suffering from fever and acute laryngitis, possibly with diphtheria. The local doctor, James Craik, ordered the former president to be bled and to gargle with a mixture of vinegar, butter and molasses.

By the morning of 14 December it was clear that Craik's prescriptions were ineffectual, for Washington was still in great pain and sinking fast. He knew his demise was imminent. For fear of being buried alive, he instructed his secretary: 'Do not let my body be put into the vault in less than three days after I am dead.'

Facing death with serenity, just before the end he murmured: 'I die hard, but I am not afraid to go.' His last words were: ''Tis well.' So departed the nation's Founding Father, still considered to be one of America's three greatest presidents, along with Lincoln and Franklin Roosevelt.

Other action this day

1751: The Theresian Military Academy is founded at Wiener Neustadt near Vienna, the first military academy in the world * 1775: Born in Annesfield, Lanarkshire, Scotland: British admiral Thomas Cochrane, who not only served in the British navy during the Napoleonic Wars but also later commanded the Chilean navy, the Brazilian navy and the Greek revolutionary navy, becoming such a legend that it is said that he was the model for the fictional Jack Aubrey by Patrick O'Brian * 1896: American general Jimmy Doolittle, who led America's first bombing raid on Japan, is born * 1931: Future British flying ace Douglas Bader loses both legs in a flying accident

15 December

Napoleon's last trip to Paris

1840 Today Napoleon entered Paris for the first time since his famous Hundred Days 25 years before, but this time he came in a coffin.

The greatest general of the 19th century and sometime French emperor had died on the island of St Helena nineteen years before, to be buried there in a triple-sealed tomb. But by now, in an attempt to curry popular favour, King Louis-Philippe had laboured for seven long years to gain British consent to allow the return of Napoleon's body to France. At last the British had agreed, and during the summer of 1840 Louis-Philippe's son, the Prince de Joinville, had been dispatched to St Helena aboard a frigate with the glorious name of *La Belle Poule* ('the beautiful tart') to bring the emperor home.

A week after the prince reached St Helena, Napoleon's remains were disinterred and the coffin was opened for two minutes. All those present testified that, like some medieval saint, he had remained in a state of perfect preservation.

Now the *Belle Poule* headed back to France. After a voyage of 43 days, she reached Cherbourg, where the defunct emperor was honoured with every pomp: one of the main squares was rechristened Place Napoléon, and the town's guns fired 1,000 rounds.

When the ship reached Rouen, the celebrations were equally enthusiastic. The central arch of a suspension bridge had been formed into an immense arch of triumph. When the *Belle Poule* passed under it, veterans showered down wreaths and laurel branches. Some aged soldiers fired salutes with their muskets while others simply bowed their heads in tears.

By the afternoon of 14 December the *Belle Poule* had sailed up the Seine to Courbevoie, just north of Paris. The next day Napoleon was brought into the city for his second funeral.

The day was bitterly cold, with eight degrees of frost and patches of snow on the ground. Despite the weather, at five in the morning the drums began to beat and the guns to boom, while over a million people jammed the three-mile route the funeral procession would take. From Courbevoie to the Arc de Triomphe, down the Champs

Elysées, through the Place de la Concorde and across the Seine, then along the quay to the Esplanade des Invalides came sixteen black horses in splendid trappings drawing the funeral carriage, accompanied by a marshal and an admiral of France. Following the cortege was an identical horse standing in for Napoleon's famous stallion, Marengo. To see the spectacle, people peered from windows, crowded rooftops, stood on ladders and even hung from trees.

The route was elaborately decorated with crowns, eagles, bees (Napoleon's emblem), banners with huge N's, wreaths and the names of Napoleon's famous victories. Banks of seats draped in imperial purple were crowded with spectators and soldiers. Thirty-two statues of French heroes and warriors had been placed on the Esplanade des Invalides – Clovis, Charles Martel, Charlemagne, Bayard, Joan of Arc and Turenne, along with some of Napoleon's marshals, like Latour d'Auvergne and Ney, roughly carved for the occasion but there to salute the emperor as he passed. Every quarter hour, cannon fired from the first court of the Invalides.

At two o'clock the cortege approached the Dome of the Invalides, to be met by King Louis-Philippe and Napoleon's 86-year-old marshal Bon-Adrien Jeannot de Moncey, who arrived in a wheelchair that had to be carried up the steps to the church. Thirty-six sailors from the *Belle Poule*, led by the Prince de Joinville, carried the coffin through the entrance.

The black-carpeted Dome was jammed with mourners, largely soldiers, and both sides of the aisle were lined with troops and Napoleon's aged veterans. Lit by 12-foot candelabras, the church's pillars held plaques with the names of Napoleon's triumphs – Rivoli, Austerlitz, Wagram, Ulm, Jena, Marengo and more. Above the plaques and extending all round the nave were dozens of flags taken from the enemy in different battles. In solemn splendour the Archbishop of Paris conducted the obsequies while Mozart's *Requiem* was performed.

Outside the church the immense crowd was still, as vendors sold a famous Napoleonic song that ran:

Premier capitaine du monde
Depuis le siege de Toulon,
Tant sur la terre que sur l'onde
Tout redoutait Napoleon.

Du Nil au nord de la Tamise!
Devant lui l'ennemi fuyait,
Avant de combattre, il tremblait
Voyant sa redingote grise.

(First captain of the world
Since the siege of Toulon,
On the earth as on the wave
All dreaded Napoleon.

From the Nile north to the Thames!
The enemy fled before him,
Before the battle he trembled
Seeing his grey greatcoat.)

It was not a day to mention Waterloo.

Other action this day

AD 533: Byzantine general Belisarius, with only 10,000 infantry and 5,000 cavalry, defeats King Gelimer of the Vandals with '50,000' men at the Battle of Ticameron * 1899: General Sir Redvers Buller's British army loses 143 killed, 756 wounded and 220 captured as the Boers defeat the British at the Battle of Colenso while suffering only 50 casualties * 1944: At 8.00am, elements of the US 6th Army land on Mindoro in the Philippines, to begin the Battle of Luzon, in which ten US divisions and five independent regiments take part, making it the largest campaign of the Pacific war, involving more troops than the US had used in North Africa, Italy, or southern France

16 December

The Boston Tea Party

1773 The colonial Americans had just about had enough. Restricted by British law from many types of manufacturing, the colonies' sole role had been arbitrarily defined by the Parliament in London as purchasers of British manufactured goods and suppliers of raw materials – except for some, like wool, in which the British had their own interest.

Britain had also given the foundering East India Company a monopoly of the colonial tea trade, including the sole right to transport the tea in its own ships.

In early December 1773 the ships *Dartmouth*, *Eleanor* and *Beaver* of the East India Company reached Boston Harbor, but a furious populace refused to allow the tea to be landed. In retaliation, the British governor Thomas Hutchinson, already hugely unpopular because of his repressive measures, commanded the ships to remain in the harbour and posted two warships to enforce the order.

Led by the radical propagandist Samuel Adams, some 2,000 Americans gathered at the wharf on the afternoon of 16 December. Then a smaller group of about 60 protestors, some disguised as Mohawk Indians, boarded the three ships and flung the cargo of 342 cases of tea into Boston Harbor.

The incident at Griffin's Wharf was not the protest of a mob but a carefully organised political response, a true act of revolution. It provoked Governor Hutchinson to close Boston Harbor, caused much suffering among the citizens of Boston, and pushed the colonies one step closer to revolution. In time, however, it became remembered as a slightly comic affair, fondly celebrated as the Boston Tea Party. For its centennial observance in 1873 Oliver Wendell Holmes wrote 'The Ballad of the Tea Party', which hinted at the radical spirit of the original day with these splendid, mocking lines:

An evening party, – only that
No formal invitation,
No gold-laced coat, no stiff cravat,
No feast in contemplation,
No silk-robed dames, no fiddling band,
No flowers no songs no dancing –
A tribe of red men, axe in hand,
Behold the guests advancing.

Other action this day

1598: Admiral Yi dies from a harquebus bullet wound directing the Korean fleet in a decisive victory over invading Japanese at the Battle of Noryang, ending the Seven Year War * 1675: At a battle called the Great Swamp Fight, American colonial militia devastate the main Narragansett Indian fort near modern South Kingstown in Rhode Island during King Philip's War, killing 300 and driving the remainder to perish in the frozen swamp ∗ 1742: Prussian field marshal Gebhard von Blücher is born in Mecklenburg on the Baltic coast of Prussia

17 December

Death of 'El Libertador'

1830 When he died today at only 47, the great liberator of South America, Simón Bolívar, must have wondered where it had all gone wrong. For 22 years he had fought to free South America from the dead hand of Spain, and how he had succeeded! But now, rejected by the very nations he had brought into being, penniless and dying of tuberculosis, he would meet his end not even in his own native Venezuela but in Colombia, in the house of a Spaniard.

Bolívar had been born in Caracas, the scion of a wealthy Creole family. When he was 21 he moved to Paris for three years, where he encountered the enlightened ideas of Europe's great liberal thinkers such as Locke, d'Alembert, Voltaire, Montesquieu and Rousseau. On a trip to Rome he vowed that he would return to liberate his own country.

From the age of 25 Bolívar fought for Venezuela's freedom, leading an expeditionary force that defeated the Spaniards in six pitched battles in what is called the Campaña Admirable. In 1813 he entered Caracas and was proclaimed 'El Libertador'.

Although Spain retook Caracas and Bolívar had to escape to Jamaica, his vision was always grand: to establish something like a United States of Hispanic America, from Chile and Argentina to Mexico. Returning from exile in 1816, his first point of attack was the Spanish viceroyalty of New Granada (a federation covering most of today's Venezuela, Colombia, Panama and Ecuador). He led a group of only 2,500 men (including a small contingent of British and Irish mercenaries) through impossible terrain to surprise the Spanish expeditionary force, defeating them first at Gámeza and then at the Vargas River, culminating in the Battle of Boyacá, where his soldiers captured 1,800 prisoners, including the Spanish commander. On 17 December 1819, eleven years to the day before his death, Bolívar proclaimed the Republic of Gran Colombia, with himself as president.

Now victory followed victory. In mid-1821 he led a force of 6,500 men in the attack against a Spanish/royalist army at Carabobo on the plains near Caracas. Breaking the enemy line, Bolívar's troops sparked a Spanish panic. At the battle's end there were fifteen Spanish/royalist dead for each of Bolívar's losses. Venezuela was free at last.

Then, in May 1822, a victory at Pichincha secured the liberation of Ecuador. Two years later he marched on Peru, where the Argentinian revolutionary José de San Martín had already chased the Spaniards into the highlands east of Lima. Realising that only Bolívar had the ability and the men to free all of Peru, San Martín left the country and the Peruvian congress elected Bolívar dictator. By December he had crushed all Spanish opposition, his able lieutenant, Antonio José de Sucre, smashing the last Spanish army on the American mainland at Ayacucho. In August 1825 Bolívar received the ultimate accolade: the Republic of Bolivia, in what had been upper Peru, was created in his honour.

Now that Spain had been comprehensively defeated, Bolívar devoted himself to his grandest dream, that of establishing a pan-Hispanic American confederation of nations, with similar political institutions and perhaps a shared army. But although a revolutionary, Bolívar was at heart dictatorial. While his ideal government was based on an elected assembly, it also included a hereditary upper house and a president for life. His elitist and autocratic policies rubbed other leaders the wrong way – especially since many of them harboured their own ambitions. Venezuelans, Colombians, Ecuadorians and Peruvians vied for power and Peru even invaded Ecuador, while other leaders staged periodic revolts. When Bolívar assumed dictatorial powers to quell the insurrections, mutinous officers tried to assassinate him. He survived only thanks to the quick thinking of his mistress, who convinced him to flee by his bedroom window while she stalled the attackers. (For this she was called 'La Libertadora del Libertador'.)

Bolívar could now see that his presence was creating more problems than it was solving, and in 1828 he resigned all his offices. Bitter, tubercular and broke (he had used all his wealth to support the revolutions), he left public life. Intending to return to Europe, he stopped with a Spanish friend in La Quinta de San Pedro Alejandrino in Santa Marta, Colombia, where he became too ill to travel. Shortly before he died he commented somewhat histrionically: 'The people send me to the tomb, but I forgive them.' His mortal remains were brought back to Venezuela with great pomp in 1942, to be interred in the National Pantheon in Caracas.

Other action this day

1619: Royalist cavalry commander in the English Civil War, Prince Rupert of the Rhine is born in Prague * 1935: On the 32nd anniversary of the Wright brothers' first flight at Kitty Hawk, South Carolina, the Douglas DC-3 makes its maiden flight in California; it becomes the main American transport plane during the Second World War, under the designations C-47 and Dakota

18 December

A father and son make military history

1912 Benjamin Davis first joined the US Army in 1898 during the Spanish–American War. Mustered out at the war's end, a year later he rejoined as a private and then gained his commission as a second lieutenant in only nineteen months. Four years later he was promoted to first lieutenant, the rank he held when on this day in Washington DC his son was born, a son whom a proud father called after himself, Benjamin Oliver Davis Jr. Years later the younger Davis would also join the armed forces, and he and his father would not only distinguish themselves on the field of battle but also attain high rank against all odds: Benjamin Davis and his son were black.

Although blacks had served in the American armed forces under Andrew Jackson a century before, and in the Civil War, they had usually been assigned lowly duties as cooks and carriers, and when in combat they had been in black units commanded by white officers. Even now, in the early 20th century, barriers against blacks were formidable. In the South, segregation laws prevented blacks from attending schools or eating in restaurants with whites, and blacks and whites could not intermarry. Only eleven years before the younger Davis's birth, President Theodore Roosevelt had caused a scandal by inviting the black scholar Booker T. Washington to the White House – the first black ever so honoured in American history.

But despite his colour, by 1932 Davis Sr. had attained the rank of colonel, and his son was determined to follow his father into the army. Recommended by America's only black member of Congress, he was accepted at West Point, but his life there was difficult. The Point's only black cadet, he was shunned by his classmates, ate by himself and never had a roommate. Nevertheless he graduated 35th in a class of 278, only the fourth black ever to attend West Point.

The first Davis to make history was Benjamin Sr., who on 25 October 1940 was promoted to brigadier general, the first black general in the history of the American army. At about the same time President Franklin Roosevelt ordered the Army Air Corps to create a black flying organisation, with a black West Point graduate to command it. As Benjamin Jr. was the only living black West Point graduate, he was ordered to begin training at Tuskegee Army Air Field in Alabama. There he became the first black officer to solo an Army Air Corps aircraft. Now a lieutenant colonel, he was given command of the first all-black air unit, the 99th Pursuit Squadron, which distinguished itself in Tunisia and Sicily. Sometimes his men flew six combat missions a day.

In the autumn of 1943 Davis Jr. took command of another all-black unit, the 332nd Fighter Group, which was known as the Tuskegee Airmen. Their primary mission was to escort American bombers over Europe, often flying into the teeth of the Luftwaffe's most tenacious defences. In 200 air combat missions, they lost only 25 bombers to enemy fighters. Davis himself flew 60 missions in P-39s, P-40s, P-47 Thunderbolts and P-51 Mustangs and won the Silver Star for a strafing run over Austria and the Distinguished Flying Cross for a bomber-escort mission to Munich. During the war the men under his command shot down 111 enemy planes at the cost of 66 of their own.

After the war, in July 1948 the elder Davis finally retired after 50 years of service at the age of 71. During the same month President Truman ordered the racial integration of the armed forces. Davis Jr., now a colonel, helped draft the Air Force plan, and the Air Force became the first service to integrate.

During the Korean War, Davis took command of the 51st Fighter-Interceptor Wing – composed primarily of white pilots. This time he flew F-86 Sabres in combat. In 1953 he achieved what his father had done in 1940 – he was promoted to brigadier general, the first black Air Force general ever.

In 1967, Davis took over the 13th Air Force, with 55,000 people under his command. By the time of his retirement in 1970 – the same year that his father died – he had become a lieutenant general, and on 9 December 1998 President Clinton awarded him a fourth star, raising him to the rank of General, US Air Force (Retired).

Other action this day

218 BC: Carthaginian general Hannibal defeats the Romans at the Battle of Trebia * 1118: The Christian King of Aragon, Alfonso the Battler, captures Zaragoza in Spain from the Moors * 1939: When 22 British Wellington bombers attack German bases in Heligoland Bight, German fighter planes shoot down ten and cripple five more, two forced to ditch before returning to Britain and three destroyed in crash landings, compelling Bomber Command to abandon day bombing for night bombing only * 1941: 610 American Marines and sailors fight off more than 5,000 Japanese invaders for over three hours before surrendering the American-held island of Guam

19 December

The Battered Bastards of Bastogne

1944 Yanked out of strategic reserve at Reims only two days before, and arriving at their destination by a most prosaic means for paratroopers – a truck convoy – four regiments of the US 101st Airborne Division, nearly 15,000 strong, took up positions this morning to form a defensive perimeter around the French town of Bastogne, now threatened by three advancing German divisions.

On 16 December the Germans had smashed through the Allied line in the Ardennes to begin the Battle of the Bulge, Hitler's last-ditch effort to avoid defeat in Western Europe. Three Panzer armies poured through the gap, heading for the key port of Antwerp and a stalemate with the Allied forces in north-west Europe. But at the shoulders of the gap, the Allied lines held, thus limiting the space through which the Germans could rush their armour westward.

And in the middle of that space lay Bastogne, the principal road junction in the Ardennes region. As long as it remained in Allied hands, Bastogne forced the Germans to move around it on a circuitous set of secondary, often unpaved, roads, while denying them all but one of the main east–west routes so crucial for the support of their fast-moving offensive.

In their eagerness to press on towards the River Meuse, the German Panzer divisions had left Bastogne behind for the infantry to take care of. Surrounded, supplied by air drops, and under heavy attack, the US 101st, together with the remnants of two combat commands – 18,000 troops in all – held the line. On the 22nd the Germans sent in a team under a white flag bearing a message for Brigadier General Anthony McAuliffe, the division's commander: 'There is only one possibility of saving the encircled USA troops from annihilation. That is the honourable surrender of the encircled town.' This occasioned McAuliffe's famous reply, 'Nuts!' – a term for which the German party required clarification.

On the 26th, tanks of the 4th Armored Division from General George Patton's 3rd Army pushed through a corridor to reach the town, bringing supplies and reinforcements. Their timely arrival meant that Allied-held Bastogne would continue the vital role it had played over the past ten days: clogging the throat of the great German counter-attack.

Meanwhile, the German offensive had been stopped short of the Meuse, brought to a halt by stiff Allied resistance, aided by snow, fog, challenging terrain, and the lack of supplies needed to sustain the advance. Frustrated with the results and furious with the 'incompetence' of his commanders, Der Führer ordered Bastogne taken. For Hitler, as one historian observed: 'The capture of Bastogne provided a convenient replacement for the lost grail of Antwerp.'

Now the heaviest fighting began as some 100,000 German troops concentrated around the town. Moving against them, however, Patton's divisions pressed northward, widening the Bastogne corridor into a salient – a bulge into the Bulge – and Allied air power continued to take its heavy toll. By 4 January it was evident to all that Bastogne would hold and the great Ardennes battle would end as an Allied victory.

When it was all over, the 101st had lost almost 4,500 men, killed, wounded, or missing. On 19 January, just a month after its arrival,

General Patton and his staff visited the scene of the airborne division's heroic stand. There they encountered a large sign that read: 'Bastogne: the Bastion of the Battered Bastards of the 101st.' Today, the town's central square is Place McAuliffe.

Other action this day

1562: In the first engagement of the French Wars of Religion, even though he is captured in a cavalry charge, the duc de Montmorency leads Catholic forces to defeat Huguenots under Louis, Prince de Condé in the Battle of Dreux * 1777: George Washington takes the Continental Army into winter quarters at Valley Forge in Pennsylvania

20 December

A Roman general becomes emperor after his soldiers lynch his predecessor

AD 69 Today marauding soldiers killed one of Rome's worst emperors with appalling brutality, leaving the empire in the hands of one of their foremost generals.

It had been a horrendous eighteen months. In June AD 68 the atrocious Nero had escaped capture and execution by his own troops only by suicide, plunging Rome into the calamitous Year of the Four Emperors. In January 69, Nero's successor Galba was brutally murdered in the Roman Forum by soldiers supporting Otho. But by April Otho was dead, another suicide after his defeat at Cremona by the army of the next claimant, Vitellius.

Vitellius was a cruel, vindictive man who was reputed to have had his own rebellious son put to death. Immensely fat, he often ate four times a day, while relieving himself with emetics between meals. According to Tacitus, 'He was the slave and chattel of luxury and gluttony'.

After only four months of power, Vitellius learned that the Roman legions in the eastern provinces had abandoned him, acclaiming their general Vespasian as emperor. Soon an army supporting Vespasian was on the march towards Rome, although the general himself remained in the east for another year. On 24 October they crushed Vitellius's legions at Bedriacum and then advanced on the capital.

On this day Vespasian's troops arrived at the gates of Rome and, after furious fighting, entered the city. Realising that his cause was hopeless, Vitellius hid himself in the janitor's quarters of the imperial palace, but the assaulting soldiers quickly discovered him. Frog-marching him to the Forum, they put him to the torture of the little cuts and then slit his throat and threw his body into the Tiber. Now Vespasian was the only would-be emperor left standing, and a fine ruler he turned out to be.

Already 60 when he took power, Vespasian was the son of a simple knight and had spent most of his life as a soldier. He first came to prominence in AD 43 during the Roman invasion of Britain, when he fought in 30 battles and subdued two enemy tribes, feats for which he was awarded *ornamenta triumphalia* (triumphal regalia) on his return to Rome. But he earned his greatest military renown while subjugating the Judaea province during the Jewish rebellion of 66. With three legions, eight cavalry squadrons and ten auxiliary cohorts under his command, he crushed the uprising at places like Gabara and the 47-day siege of Jotapata, during which 40,000 enemy were killed. (During this siege an arrow wounded him in the foot.) He also destroyed the walled city of Jericho, after which he famously tested the buoyancy of the Dead Sea by throwing some shackled prisoners in to see if they would float (they did).

Vespasian was known for his bluff, straightforward style and infectious if sometimes coarse sense of humour. Relaxed and down-to-earth, when he became emperor he dispensed with the usual bodyguard and mixed freely with Rome's citizens. After nearly ten years in power, he was nearing 70 when he caught a fever while visiting Campania. He then made matters worse by retreating to his summer residence in Reate and bathing in cold water. Suspecting that the end was near, the old commander wryly referred to Rome's habit of deifying dead emperors with the remark: 'Vae, puto deus fio.' ('Oh dear, I think I'm becoming a god.')

Vespasian tried to soldier on with his imperial duties, but on 23 June 79 he was seized with violent diarrhoea. Almost fainting, he struggled to remain on his feet, murmuring, 'Decet imperatorem stantem mori.' ('An emperor should die standing.') He then fell dead into the arms of his attendants.

During his ten years as emperor, Vespasian followed a practice of reconciliation, dispensing justice with mercy. According to Suetonius: 'No innocent party was ever punished during Vespasian's reign.' He ended the civil war and probably saved the empire from dissolution. He also embarked on an ambitious reconstruction programme in a country torn by war. Now of course the Roman empire is long gone, as are most of its buildings, but one of Vespasian's monuments is still with us – the Flavian Amphitheatre in Rome (Flavius was his original family name), which we call the Coliseum.

Other action this day

1860: In Columbia, South Carolina, the state convention votes 160–0 in favour of seceding from the United States, eventually to be followed by eleven more states, the first inexorable step towards the American Civil War * 1915: The ANZACS, Australian and New Zealand forces, with British troops are evacuated from Gallipoli, after their expedition against the Turks fails * 1941: The Flying Tigers, a unit of American volunteers in the Chinese air force, goes into battle for the first time in Kunming, China

21 December

King Richard the Lionheart is captured

1192 Richard the Lionheart was one of England's worst kings – during his reign of nine years and nine months, he spent only 179 days in England. Yet as a warrior and commander he was unsurpassed, a fine horseman, strong and courageous, always eager for battle. Today he was captured by the enemy, not on the field of battle but through the foolishness of his page – and his own.

When the great Saracen leader Saladin reconquered Jerusalem in 1187, Richard committed himself to ride to its salvation as a leader of the Third Crusade. In the Holy Land he participated in some notable victories, especially at the siege of Acre. There he was struck by scurvy but, according to legend, while he was being carried on a stretcher he still shot an enemy guard on the city's walls with a crossbow. (He also perpetrated one of history's most barbarous slaughters there when he ordered the beheading of 2,700 Saracen prisoners.)

Richard's later victories during the crusade included Arsuf and Jaffa, but Jerusalem remained in Saladin's hands, the crusade a failure in its main objective.

Richard left the Holy Land to return home in late 1192. As he was sailing through the Adriatic, a storm forced him ashore near Aquileia on the Ligurian coast of Italy. He then made the foolish decision to continue his journey on land through Austria, even though he knew that its ruler Duke Leopold V could be counted among his enemies. When the Crusaders had conquered Acre, Richard had refused to give Leopold his share of the booty and had ordered his standard thrown from the city's walls into the mud in the moat below. Leopold left in cold fury, vowing revenge.

Richard's one precaution as he entered Leopold's domains was to travel disguised as a wealthy merchant. But nearing the duke's capital in Vienna, Richard made two further mistakes. Exhausted from his time on the road, he remained in the town of Ganina for three days and sent one of his pages to purchase supplies with a pocket full of gold coins.

On this day, Richard's last in Ganina, the page ambled through the market dispensing his gold and with one of the king's gloves bearing the royal insignia carelessly tucked in his belt. Sharp-eyed agents of Duke Leopold spotted and seized the insouciant page and quickly forced him to reveal that Richard and the rest of his entourage were staying at a nearby inn.

Leopold's soldiers instantly surrounded the inn and had no trouble capturing the English king, despite his attempt to disguise himself yet again, this time as a cook in the kitchen.

For the next fourteen months Richard was held prisoner in Leopold's castle at Dürnstein on the Danube. Tradition has it that he was found by his faithful troubadour Blondel, who wandered through Europe singing a ballad that Richard and he had composed together. When Blondel passed before the castle, Richard heard his voice and responded by singing a verse of the same ballad so that Blondel would know he had found the king.

With Richard safely locked up at Dürnstein, Leopold demanded an enormous ransom for his release. The king was finally freed on 3 February 1193 for a payment of 6,000 buckets of silver, (or 150,000 silver marks), equal to 34 tons in weight. In 2008 that would have been worth a healthy £10,800,000, but in 1192 its value would have been something like £6 billion, truly a king's ransom, a price that virtually bankrupted England.

Duke Leopold did not long survive to enjoy his fortune. The Pope excommunicated him for having imprisoned a fellow Crusader, and two years later his foot was crushed when his horse fell on him during a tournament and he died of gangrene.

Other action this day
1845: The British under Sir Hugh Gough defeat the Sikhs at the Battle of Ferozeshah * 1936: The German Junkers Ju-88 bomber takes its first test flight * 1945: American general George Patton dies of an embolism at the military hospital in Heidelberg after an automobile accident on 9 December

22 December

Napoleone becomes a general after the Siege of Toulon

1793 Today Captain of Artillery Napoleone Buonaparte was promoted to the rank of brigadier general at the tender age of 24, rewarded for his heroic achievements during republican France's victorious siege of Toulon.

In late August French royalist counter-revolutionaries had treacherously welcomed an enemy Anglo-Spanish fleet under the command of Admiral Hood into the key French naval base of Toulon, just down the Mediterranean coast from Marseille. There the English had seized over 70 vessels, including 30 ships of the line, over half the French fleet. For reasons of both political prestige and military necessity, the Revolutionary government in Paris had resolved to wrest back the base and ordered a siege.

The siege began on 28 August. After several months of mutual cannonading, French soldiers at length captured the forts overlooking the port. Then, on the afternoon of 18 December, Buonaparte, still an obscure captain in charge of the French artillery, focused withering fire from the secured forts directly on the English ships moored in the harbour. Forced to evacuate, the English burned more than half the French ships on their way out. In the evening the revolutionaries reoccupied the city and shot several hundred royalists who had not fled with the English.

Based on his successful use of artillery, Buonaparte became a hero and was jumped half a dozen ranks to brigadier general. With supreme confidence he wrote to the Committee of Public Safety in Paris: 'It is the artillery that takes places; the infantry can only aid it.' But, as remarkable as it was, his dizzying rise was a bit less spectacular in 1793 than it would be today, given that Buonaparte was a trained and professional soldier. During this self-same siege of Toulon the attacking French force was commanded by three successive generals, men who before the Revolution had been, respectively, a painter, a sugar planter and a dentist.

Other action this day

1790: Russian general Alexander Suvorov storms the Ottoman fortress at Ismail in Bessarabia and pillages the city, killing 33,000 Turks, in the Russo-Turkish War of 1787–92 * 1944: Ho Chi Minh forms the Vietnam People's Army to combat the Japanese; it will later fight the French, the Americans and the South Vietnamese, defeating them all

23 December

Insurrection in the Vendée

1793 In January Louis XVI had been fed to the guillotine, but all over France there was resistance to the bloody republicanism now gripping the nation, none more dogged than that in the Vendée, a *département* south of Brittany on the Atlantic coast.

Vendéan peasants had initially supported the Revolution, but Republican excesses, the shackling of the Catholic church, and new conscription demands had now caused major unrest in this isolated and highly conservative region. By March there were riots, soon followed by bloodshed, as rebels ambushed and murdered local mayors and judges. In Machecoul, 40 men were killed in the street and 400 more were forced to dig their own graves and shot.

Armed largely with captured weapons, the insurgents formed a ragtag 35,000-man army, which they christened 'L'Armée catholique et royale'. They were led by a charismatic 21-year-old aristocrat, Henri de la Rochejaquelein, who ordered: 'Mes amis, si j'avance, suivez-moi! Si je recule, tuez-moi! Si je meurs, vengez-moi!' ('Friends, if I advance, follow me! If I retreat, kill me! If I die, avenge me!')

Now the *Blancs* (counter-revolutionaries and royalists) over-whelmed small Republican garrisons sprinkled throughout the region at towns like Thouars, Fontenay and Saumur, and then crossed the Loire to take Angers but were repulsed at Nantes.

In response, the Paris government dispatched an army of 45,000 to suppress the rebellion. Although the Blancs won the first skirmish at Chantonnay, within six months they were in full retreat.

After defeat at Cholet in October, La Rochejaquelein took most of his force towards Granville on the Channel coast in the hope of finding a British fleet and an army of French exiles, but the *Bleus* (Republicans) had already seized the port.

After failed attempts to take the town, the Blancs pulled back, but on 12 December a Republican army of 20,000 under generals François Marceau, Jean-Baptiste Kléber and François Westermann defeated them at Le Mans, killing 15,000 during the battle and the subsequent butchery of prisoners.

The insurgents, now reduced to 7,000 men by disease, hunger and Republican forays, headed back to the Vendée and reached Savenay on 22 December. After chasing away a garrison of 150 enemy soldiers, they set up in defensive positions, knowing that the Bleus were not far behind.

The first to arrive was Westermann, who immediately launched an assault but was repulsed after a short fight. At noon Kléber and Marceau rode in with the bulk of the Republican army. After one further skirmish, a heavy fog descended on the village, and the Bleus were forced to call off their attack.

Westermann wanted to strike again that night, asserting: 'I'll take care of everything. I've started this business too well to let it be taken over by someone else.' But Kléber insisted they wait until dawn, and by two in the morning, reinforced by another division, they had surrounded Savenay.

But at dawn today it was the Blancs who attacked, desperately trying to break out to the north. Although they overran the first Republican line of grenadiers, seizing 40 prisoners and two cannon, Kléber's determined bayonet charge sent them back through the town gates.

Now the Bleus attacked on all fronts and battled their way into the town, where even Vendéan women joined in the bloody house-to-house fighting.

While the Blanc cannon redeployed in front of the town church, 300 cavalry with supporting infantry launched a counter-attack, nearly breaking the Republican line. Then the Bleus swept over the defenders' battery and chased the Blancs out to the west of the town. One Vendéan captain heroically manned the last two remaining Vendéan guns to cover his comrades' escape. (La Rochejaquelein did break out and started a guerrilla campaign but was shot and killed a month later.)

A last group of 600 Blancs managed to hold a ridge in a vineyard but were surrounded and massacred to a man. Inside Savenay, the victors rounded up several hundred old men, women and children and locked them in the church, to be dealt with later. By two o'clock the battle was over.

But the killing was not. Cavalry units searched neighbouring villages and countryside for fugitives, bringing back prisoners to be tried for treason and put to death the same evening. The executions lasted for eight days, and some 2,000 people were shot. An additional 1,700 women and children were sent to Nantes, to be shot or drowned. (These were of course just a fraction of the perhaps 150,000 Vendéans who were shot, drowned, buried alive and killed in every conceivable fashion before the Vendéan war finally ended in 1796.)

Other massacres took place around the countryside. Westermann and his 'Hussars of death' shot almost 700 men, women and children in the Sem Woods. As he proudly reported to Robespierre's notorious Committee of Public Safety: 'There is no more Vendée, Republican citizens. It died beneath our free sword, with its women and its children. I have just buried it in the swamps and the woods of Savenay. Following the orders that you gave me, I crushed the children beneath the horses' hooves, massacred the women who, these at least, will give birth to no more brigands. I do not have a single prisoner to reproach myself with. I have exterminated them all. The roads are sown with corpses. At Savenay, brigands are arriving all the time trying to surrender, and we are shooting them non-stop ... Mercy is not a revolutionary sentiment.'

How right he was. Only four months later he was ordered back to Paris and guillotined for his support of the revolutionary, Georges Danton.

Other action this day
1783: George Washington resigns as commander-in-chief of the Continental Army at the Maryland State House in Annapolis * 1916: Allied forces defeat the Turks in the Sinai peninsula at the Battle of Magdhaba * 1948: General and prime minister Hideki Tojo and six other Japanese military leaders are hanged, having been found guilty of crimes against humanity

24 December

Truce on Christmas Eve

1914 In the midst of war, peace broke out today – not for long, not widely observed, but nonetheless a remarkable event – as at various points along the Western Front, fighting ceased and soldiers signalled their enemies across no man's land to arrange a Christmas Eve truce.

By October, the war on the Western Front had become a stalemate, with formidable trench lines stretching continuously across Belgium and France from the English Channel to the Swiss frontier. When attacks were launched, the gains were negligible; not so the losses in manpower.

Then, in November, the heavy rains that flooded the trenches seemed to increase the sense of deadlock, making clear to every soldier in every army that the war, which was to have been over by now, had only just begun.

So it happened that a phenomenon began to make itself known among soldiers holding the forward positions of their respective armies. It was in part camaraderie and male bonding based on their shared identity as survivors from some of the costliest fighting in the history of warfare. It was also an awareness of the contrast between the bleak and squalid world they now inhabited and the warm Christian traditions of the approaching holiday season. By now these hardened troops could see that the war would not be lost – or even changed – by a pause in the fighting.

As a result, there came about a growing number of ad hoc, undeclared ceasefires. At first, these were isolated accommodations – usually occasioned by the need for one or the other side to gather their dead for burial. But such truces defied the policies and expectations of the higher army commands. The British II Corps, for instance, felt compelled to send out this order in early December: 'Friendly intercourse with the enemy, unofficial armistices and the exchange of tobacco and other comforts, however tempting and occasionally amusing, are absolutely prohibited.'

But as Christmas drew closer, bringing thousands of presents to troops in the Allied and German armies – sent by families but also by public subscription – the tendency towards fraternisation increased. On the 18th, near Armentières, a German unit sent this message into the British lines: 'We propose having a concert tonight as it is our Captain's birthday, and we cordially invite you to attend – provided you give us your word of honour as guests that you agree to cease all hostilities between 7.30 and 8.30 ...' The invitation was accepted; from their trench line, the British troops applauded every song.

By Christmas Eve, the war had truly paused, as the dreary scene along the front lines became transformed: Christmas trees and candles were lit above the trenches, holly hung, carols sung, invitations called out across the lines; soldiers meeting, hands clasped, gifts exchanged, drinks and cigars offered and accepted.

Where the French 74th Infantry Regiment held the line, there was singing from both trench lines, 'Minuit Chrétien' by the French, 'Stille Nacht' by the Germans. The next morning a German soldier crossed to the French side to announce his comrades' wish to call a truce for the day and their request for reciprocity. The French soldiers agreed, and what resulted was described as a 'village fair', involving 'the convivial exchange of items from Christmas packages sent from home – food, tobacco, beer, wine, etc'.

A lieutenant with the 1st Warwickshires described the Christmas Day scene in no man's land: 'I awoke very early, and emerged from my dug-out into the trench. It was just the sort of day for Peace to be declared. ... I clambered up and over our parapet, and moved out across the field to look [at the enemy] ... This was my first sight of them at close quarters. Here they were – the actual, practical soldiers of the German army. There was not an atom of hate on either side that day; and yet, on our side, not for a moment was the will to war and the will to beat them relaxed. It was just like an interval between the rounds in a friendly boxing match ...'

The lieutenant posed for several group photographs taken by a German soldier. Amid the celebration, he noted, both sides seemed well aware of how their senior officers would regard the scene. In the twilight, the soldiers gradually dispersed to their respective trenches, 'but there was a distinct and friendly understanding that Christmas Day would be left to finish in tranquillity'.

After Christmas, the 'live and let live' spirit diminished, although in sectors of the front held by the British army, it remained alive at least through Boxing Day. In other areas, bad weather extended truces for a few days. But even on the front lines there were those who opposed the truces, and sometimes shots were fired to break up gatherings in no man's land. Higher commands took severer steps to end the truces: artillery pieces in rear positions were ordered to fire on enemy lines; General Joffre ordered infantry attacks for 1.00pm on Christmas Day; French planes dropped flechettes (pointed steel projectiles) on German positions. In addition, in the routine of trench warfare, front-line battalions were rotated back to the reserve line for several days of rest, and their replacement units entering the trenches had no commitment to prolonging a ceasefire with the enemy.

As military discipline was restored, full combat operations soon resumed, with costly – and unsuccessful – Allied attacks mounted in the Artois, at Ypres, and elsewhere. For the rest of the war, there were no more Christmas truces. As inspiring an event as they were in 1914, they were never repeated. Nor did they – or their memory – have any further effect on how the war proceeded for another four years.

Other action this day

1144: The Christian city of Edessa falls to a Saracen army under the command of Imad ad-Din Zengi * 1814: The Treaty of Ghent ends the War of 1812 * 1942: French resistance fighter Fernand Bonnier de La Chapelle shoots and kills Vichy French admiral François Darlan in Algiers; Bonnier de La Chapelle is executed two days later * 1943: Dwight Eisenhower becomes Supreme Allied Commander in Europe

25 December

Charlemagne is crowned emperor

AD 800 The great Frankish king Charlemagne was in Rome on Christmas Day, and where else would he attend Mass but in St Peter's Basilica? There, while Pope Leo III was conducting the service, the large Roman gathering in the cathedral began to cheer the king. In response, the Pope suddenly crowned him Imperator Romanorum (Emperor of the Romans). Charlemagne was taken entirely by surprise, later declaring that he would not have entered St Peter's had he known.

This, at least, is the story promulgated by Charlemagne's supporters, although in all likelihood Charlemagne had orchestrated his own coronation. Whatever the truth, on this day Christendom's greatest conqueror became the first Holy Roman Emperor, with dominion over all the territories he had subjugated, which meant most of Western Europe.

Charlemagne had inherited half his father's Frankish kingdom in AD 767 when he was 25, and he spent most of the years until his death in 814 battling to enlarge it. He subdued most of Italy, conquering the Lombards in the north and besting the dukes of Friuli and Spoleto in the south, although never taking full control of the area.

He smashed the Avars of Hungary, the Slavs, the Saracens (from whom he captured Corsica, Sardinia and the Balearic Islands), and fiercely suppressed pagan German tribes, especially the Saxons and Bavarians, against whom he led his army into battle eighteen times over the years.

Personally religious and a great supporter of the church (he attempted to ban dancing throughout his empire because of its supposed pagan origins), Charlemagne liked to be seen as conquering for Christianity. However, his conquests had more to do with building his empire than promulgating his religion. In one rather un-Christian moment, he ordered a mass beheading of 4,500 captured Saxon warriors.

Through his campaigns, Charlemagne united in one superstate almost all the Christian lands of Western Europe except northern

Spain, southern Italy, Great Britain and Ireland. Ironically, however, his most famous battle was a defeat, when Basques overwhelmed his rearguard at the Roncevaux Pass, a loss that inspired *La Chanson de Roland* (*The Song of Roland*), the oldest major work of French literature.

When Charlemagne was crowned, it began a sort of revival of the Western Roman empire that had lapsed in the 5th century when the last emperor was deposed by German mercenaries. Although his contemporaries would have known it as the Frankish empire or perhaps even the Roman empire (Charlemagne called himself simply *rex Francorum et Langobardum*), we now think of it as the Holy Roman Empire. In 1157 Emperor Frederick Barbarossa was the first to call it 'Holy', and the full title, *Sacrum Romanum Imperium*, was first used in 1254. Even then it was a description, not a title, as the 'Holy Roman Empire' has in fact never existed as an institution but simply as a name used by historians. The empire Charlemagne founded (or revived) lasted over 1,000 years until the abdication of Franz II in 1806, who, under pressure from Napoleon, renounced the title of Holy Roman Emperor to become simply Emperor of Austria.

Other action this day

1119: The Templars are founded as an order of knighthood, when French nobleman Hugues de Payen takes vows of poverty, chastity and obedience in the Church of the Holy Sepulchre in Jerusalem * 1683: In Belgrade, Janissaries execute Kara Mustafa, the Turkish grand vizier whose army was destroyed at the siege of Vienna on 12 September, strangling him with a silk cord and delivering his head to Sultan Mehmed IV in a velvet bag * 1837: 400 Seminole Indians led by Billy Bowlegs, Abiaca and Alligator defeat 800 American soldiers under future president Zachary Taylor at the Battle of Lake Okeechobee

26 December

Washington crosses the Delaware to surprise the Hessians

1776 Today, like Lazarus raised from the dead, the Continental Army, widely dismissed as an effective fighting force after a series of defeats around New York, emerged from the early morning gloom in unexpected strength and total surprise to overwhelm the Hessian garrison at Trenton, New Jersey, and produce a timely and crucial victory in the American War of Independence, one of the most significant in the entire history of American arms.

Reports of the army's demise – from its friends as well as its foes – seemed well founded by the late autumn. As its columns retreated southward through New Jersey, they were harried by the pursuing British and their progress was marked by increasing desertions and near-mutinies from troops who were weary, underfed and defeated. It was a force reduced to 3,400 men, a 'shadow army' in the commander-in-chief's phrase, that Washington led across the Delaware River to Pennsylvania on 7 December.

Well satisfied with his own army's autumn operations, General Howe, the British commander-in-chief, went into winter quarters in New York City, leaving some 5,000 troops in forward positions in New Jersey, a force more than adequate, he thought, to keep the local population under control and deal with whatever attacks the rebel forces might mount.

At this blackest of times, with the enlistment periods of most of his regiments expiring at the end of the year, barely three weeks away, General Washington and his generals decided on a bold, do-or-die operation: they would lead the Continental Army back across the Delaware at night and attack the isolated British position at Trenton, held by three Hessian regiments.

From spies, deserters and British sympathisers, the British military expected American attacks against Trenton over Christmas, but assumed they would be no more than the usual patrol-sized, hit-and-run affairs. When, in fact, a rebel scouting party materialised and shots were exchanged on Christmas morning, Colonel Rall, the Hessian commander, supposed that he had met whatever the Americans intended. A raging north-easter bringing heavy snows that evening furthered the impression that the garrison was safe from raids, at least while the storm lasted.

On Christmas night, Washington and his regiments, numbering 2,400 men, began ferrying across the ice-swollen river nine miles above Trenton. It was slow, dangerous work, impeded by high winds, and the last of the artillery didn't get over until 3.00am. The army marched over frozen roads in sleet, snow and freezing rain.

The force divided at one point so that it would enter Trenton simultaneously from two directions. It was 8.00am when an outpost spotted the northern column advancing through the snow and shots were fired that roused the sleeping garrison.

It was a quick but bloody action as Washington's troops fought through the village of 100 houses. Captain Alexander Hamilton positioned the artillery pieces that enfiladed the streets in which the Hessians tried to form. Lieutenant James Monroe was wounded while leading a charge to capture Hessian cannon. By 9.30 the Hessians had surrendered. American losses were light: four wounded, none killed. Of the Hessians, 106 were killed or wounded, and 918 taken prisoner. By noon the exhausted American army, with its large bag of prisoners, began returning to its positions across the river.

Washington's victory at Trenton – together with his brilliant follow-up successes a few days later at Assumpink Creek and Princeton – gave a tremendous boost to the American cause, breathing life into wavering patriots, restoring self-confidence to the army, and providing the Continental Congress with a glimpse of what its forces, poorly cared for as they had been, might after all accomplish.

Other action this day

1530: Mughal conqueror Babur dies in Agra * 1837: American admiral George Dewey, the victor of the Battle of Manila Bay during the Spanish–American War, is born in Montpelier, Vermont * 1862: General John Pemberton's Confederate troops repulse an advance by a Union army under General William Tecumseh Sherman at the Battle of Chickasaw Bayou in the first engagement of the Vicksburg campaign

27 December

'Don't take prisoners. No one should be left alive.'

1979 Today Afghan president Hafizullah Amin ordered a lavish dinner for visiting Russian dignitaries at the Tajbek presidential palace near Kabul. It was to be his last meal: the troops he had requested from Moscow were at that very moment moving in on the palace, not to protect him but to kill him.

Amin had been president only since September. In April of the previous year he and another Communist, Nur Mohammad Taraki, had overthrown the government and shot its president and his family. Initially Taraki took power, but his rivalry with Amin grew so fierce that in September 1979 Amin had him seized by the palace guard and smothered with a pillow.

Amin now suppressed opponents with the utmost brutality, wiping out rebellious villages and killing 1,000 Mujahedin (fundamentalist Islamic guerrilla fighters). To his Russian backers, he justified the slaughter with their own rhetoric – everything is moral that benefits the Revolution. 'If any tribe takes up arms it will not lay them down. The only solution is to destroy them all, from big to small! Such are our traditions.' But Amin knew he needed military help – the Mujahedin numbered 40,000 irregulars – and he appealed to Russia for troops.

By now the Politburo were worrying about their huge investment in supporting a Communist Afghanistan, as Amin consolidated his dictatorial power by distancing his regime from Russia. Worse, they thought he might be secretly approaching the CIA. It was time to get rid of him.

In mid-December KGB snipers were concealed along Amin's travel route, but the dictator's cavalcade moved at such speed that they could not get off a shot. Three days later the Russians poisoned a bottle of Pepsi Cola, but Amin's nephew drank it and was hospitalised in Moscow for what Russian doctors claimed was 'hepatitis'. Fearing assassination by his Afghan enemies but not by the Russians, Amin now moved to the Tajbek palace, ten miles from Kabul.

On 24 December Russian troops started to arrive in Kabul under the pretence of coming to Amin's aid, but their real role was to storm the presidential palace.

The Tajbek palace was on a steep, snow-covered hill overgrown with trees and shrubbery, accessible by a single road, with other approaches mined. The palace's thick walls could withstand an artillery strike. Inside, Amin kept a 200-man personal guard, and outside it was ringed by guard posts manned by sentries with machine guns and grenade launchers, reinforced by three motorised units and three T-54 tanks. The total security brigade came to 2,500 men. The Russians knew they had to rely on surprise and daring.

At 7.15pm on 27 December, 'Storm 333' flashed over the Russian radio nets, signalling the attack. The thunder of explosions rocked Kabul, as KGB units blew up the city's communications conduit, paralysing the Afghan military command. Then, as red flares burst overhead, two self-propelled ZSU-23-4 ('Shilka') guns opened fire on the palace while soldiers with grenade launchers attacked the Afghan tanks.

The assault force of 700 elite soldiers, mostly from KGB and GRU special forces, were dressed in Afghan uniforms and wearing body armour. The first armoured personnel carrier crashed through the traffic barrier on the access road, crushing the Afghan soldier rushing to close it. Now more APCs raced up the road, but the volume of fire from the palace forced the troops to jump from their vehicles and shoot at the windows. After a Shilka had neutralised a machine gun in one of the windows, the soldiers climbed up through the snow with scaling ladders, carefully avoiding the mines.

As Afghans lobbed grenades from the second floor, Russians burst through the front door into the central hallway, an officer barking out: 'Don't take prisoners. No one should be left alive.' They began working the rooms with machine guns and grenades.

One attacker later remembered: 'Suddenly a guard jumped out around a turn from somewhere. He began to shoot at me practically point-blank, from about 10 metres, and let loose a burst of about 10–12 rounds. It penetrated the hand guard and hit the magazine, and the shells flew from it. The guard stopped, frightened, and looked at me because he was shooting and I wasn't falling. He had such glazed eyes; they were right in front of me, such dark hazel, even brown eyes. He himself was dark complexioned. And I was struck dumb for a second. Then I thought that I had rounds in my chamber. And in a fraction of a second I lifted my weapon and fired. He fell.'

In one corner of the palace Amin hunkered down with his adjutant, dressed in Adidas shorts and a sport shirt. 'The Soviets will help', he said, to which the adjutant responded: 'It's the Soviets who are shooting.' After failing to get through to his military chief on the telephone, he quietly muttered: 'It's all true.'

The assault continued for 45 minutes, Amin's bodyguard slowly wiped out while stubbornly resisting. When the firing finally stopped and the smoke had cleared, the attackers found Amin lying in the palace bar, dead from a bullet or grenade fragment. A bullet in the chest had also killed his eight-year-old son, and his daughter had been shot in the leg. By the next morning the Russians had taken over all of Kabul.

On the same day that the soldiers stormed the Tajbek palace, a massive Soviet force of 80,000 men and 1,800 tanks entered the country; it was the start of a war that developed into a savage anti-Soviet *jihad*, joined by Muslim volunteers from many nations, and with secret support from the US. It would cost the Russians 15,000 dead and 54,000 wounded, while over a million Afghans would be killed. When the Russians were forced to withdraw their military forces in 1988, it left a country in chaos in which the Taliban would come to power.

Other action this day

1761: Russian general Michael Andreas Barclay de Tolly is born * 1776: Russian general Nikolay Kamensky is born * 1918: The Great Poland Uprising against the Germans starts

28 December

A prophet in his own country

1879 One of America's most controversial soldiers was born today; his career with the US Army Air Force would end in disgrace but posthumously he would become an American hero. His name was 'Billy' Mitchell.

Mitchell first joined the army at eighteen during the Spanish–American War, but after attending a flying demonstration by Orville Wright ten years later, he became a blunt and outspoken advocate of air power. As a leading member of the Aeronautical Division of the Signal Corps, in 1913 he made his first public critique of the military, testifying before Congress that the United States lagged behind in military aviation.

By the start of the First World War, Mitchell had risen to lieutenant colonel. Sent to Europe as an observer to learn how the Allies were using air power, he sometimes flew as a gunner in British and French fighter planes. Although he admired the courage of pilots who fought each other in dogfights, he concluded that: 'No number of flying machines can prevent an enemy aircraft from crossing the lines. The sky itself is too large to defend. We must plan military aviation to attack the rear areas of any enemy and destroy all means of supply.'

Promoted to brigadier general in charge of all American air combat units in France, Mitchell put his ideas into practice at Saint-Mihiel in 1918, where he led 1,500 Allied planes in the first large-scale coordinated air–ground attack in history. While 1,000 planes flew deep into enemy territory to destroy communications and supplies, another 500 strafed and bombed the German front. During the four-day battle the Allies eliminated the Saint-Mihiel salient and captured 15,000 prisoners.

In another innovation, Mitchell proposed that troops be para-chuted behind German lines 'to surprise the enemy by taking him from the rear', but the top American commander, General Pershing, thought the idea absurd.

After the war, Mitchell continued to harangue his superiors, particularly infuriating the nation's admirals by insisting that even the largest warships were 'sitting ducks' in their vulnerability to air attack and that 'the first battles of any future war will be air battles'.

In 1921 Mitchell was at last given the chance to prove his theories. In an area off the mouth of Chesapeake Bay, he conducted a demon-stration against an ex-German destroyer and cruiser. First S.E.5 fighters (single-seater biplanes) strafed the ships to simulate suppres-sion of anti-aircraft fire, and then MB-2s (biplane bombers) bombed and sank both ships. A few days later his planes sent the 'unsinkable' battleship *Ostfriesland* to the bottom in a two-day attack.

Conducted against stationary ships that could not fire back, these demonstrations were highly controversial, but Mitchell insisted that he had proved his case. He argued that a thousand bombers could be built for the cost of a single battleship – and could sink that battle-ship. He continued to call for a stronger air force, often publicly crit-icising the blinkered views of military top brass.

In 1925 Mitchell reverted to his permanent rank of colonel. Although such demotions were not unusual, his was widely seen as punishment for his outspokenness. But he was hardly chastened; that year he published *Winged Defense*, in which he repeated his claims for air superiority and predicted war with Japan and the attack on Pearl Harbor. As one historian commented: 'Again, no one paid any attention: no one – but the Japanese.'

That same year a Navy dirigible crashed in a storm, killing all on board. Mitchell now scathingly denounced the 'incompetency, criminal negligence, and the almost treasonable negligence of our national defense by the War and Navy departments'. 'All aviation policies, schemes and systems,' he wrote, 'are dictated by the non-flying officers of the Army and Navy, who know practically nothing about it.'

Such intemperate condemnation outraged America's military leaders, and Mitchell was court-martialled for insubordination and 'conduct of a nature to bring discredit upon the military service'. In the longest and most controversial court martial in US history, twelve generals (including Douglas MacArthur) sat on the jury, and among the witnesses who testified on Mitchell's behalf were fighter ace Eddie Rickenbacker, 'Tooey' Spaatz, who would later be the US Air Force's first chief of staff, and Mitchell's protégé, Hap Arnold, a future five-star general of the Air Force.

Despite such illustrious backing, Mitchell was found guilty and suspended from active duty for five years without pay. The following February he resigned from the military.

During the next ten years Mitchell continued to preach the virtues of air power, writing newspaper articles and books and addressing the House Military Affairs Committee in 1935. Already suffering from heart disease, a year later he was struck with influenza and died in a New York hospital.

Mitchell was gone, but many of his acolytes were now rising to positions of power and starting to implement his ideas. During the Second World War the US Air Force named the B-25 Mitchell bomber after him, the only American warplane named after a person. It was in Mitchell bombers that Jimmy Doolittle carried out the first raid of the war against mainland Japan in April 1942.

Other action this day

1835: Osceolo leads his Seminole warriors in Florida into the Second Seminole War against the US Army, which lasts for seven years * 1943: Canadian general Chris Vokes's infantry defeat paratroopers from the German 1st Parachute Division after eight days of fighting at the Battle of Ortona on the Adriatic front in Italy

29 December

The Jameson raid on Johannesburg

1895 Towards sunset on this Sunday evening, Dr Leander Starr Jameson, right-hand man of the great British empire-builder Cecil Rhodes, led 600 armed and mounted men on a daring raid. Their destination was Johannesburg, 200 miles away in the Boer republic of Transvaal, their mission – a wild imperial gamble in the spirit of Wolfe, Clive or Gordon – to make Britain supreme in all of South Africa.

The Jameson raid was a disaster and failed utterly in its purpose of overthrowing the anti-British Boer government of President Paul Kruger. Jameson and his men were captured miles short of Johannesburg and carted away to jail. Found on them were incriminating copies of telegrams that linked the raiders with Rhodes, the prime minister of the Cape Colony, and with his superiors at the Colonial Office in London.

It was a terrible foreign policy embarrassment for Great Britain. In another age, CNN would have had a field day. In London and Cape Town, there were official investigations and public trials. The involvement of unnamed higher-ups was suspected. It was the Iran–Contra affair of its day: there was a cover-up and deals were made. A Colonel North figure in the Colonial Office was found, who testified that he had never informed his chiefs of his dealings with the now thoroughly discredited Rhodes and the plotters of the raid. Rhodes was forced to resign.

Like John Brown's abortive 1859 raid on Harper's Ferry before the American Civil War, the Jameson raid succeeded in hastening conflict. Winston Churchill called it 'the herald, if not indeed the progenitor of the South African War'. War came in 1899 and lasted two and a half years at a frightful cost to Boers and Britons. It resulted in the Boer Republic's incorporation into the British empire, Rhodes's intention from the beginning. Jameson spent fifteen months in a British jail for leading the raid, but after the war he got Rhodes's old job as prime minister of the Cape Colony. Cecil Rhodes died in 1902, reputation in ruins, but wealth intact. He is remembered today not for his imperial mischief in South Africa but for the scholarships that bear his name.

Other action this day

1503: During a freezing rainstorm, Spanish general Gonzalo Fernández de Córdoba launches a surprise attack against a French army commanded by Ludovico II, Marquis of Saluzzo, at the Battle of Garigliano near Naples, decisively defeating them and gaining Spanish domination over the Kingdom of Naples until the Austrian conquest in 1707 * 1890: At the massacre at Wounded Knee, South Dakota, after an Indian brave fires a shot in a dispute about a rifle, American troops open fire on 350 Lakota Indian men, women and children, killing over 150 in the last major bloodshed between American Indians and US troops

30 December

Score one for the Lancastrians in the Wars of the Roses

1460 The Wars of the Roses had started five years earlier, as Duke Richard of York tried to wrest the crown of England from the befuddled Lancastrian king, Henry VI. Finally England's barons had agreed that Henry would remain king but Richard would be first in the line of succession. They had not counted on Henry's termagant wife, Margaret of Anjou, now the de facto leader of the Lancastrians, who was determined that her six-year-old son Edward would inherit the throne, even at the price of continued civil war. Now Queen Margaret had summoned the loyal Duke of Somerset to Yorkshire to lead an army to destroy the Duke of York once and for all.

Hearing of this new threat, York rallied 6,000 men and marched north from London with his seventeen-year-old son Edmund, Earl of Rutland, and his chief lieutenant, Richard Neville, Earl of Salisbury. They reached Sandal Castle, two miles south of Wakefield, on 21 December. York by now had learned that Queen Margaret's commander had a far superior force, perhaps 18,000 men, so he hunkered down in the castle, a massive structure built on top an old Norman fortress with earthworks 33 feet high. After he had strengthened its defences by positioning artillery on its parapets, it was virtually impregnable. Although York knew his force was too small to face battle, he could now wait in safety for reinforcements to arrive from the south. Meanwhile, the Lancastrians had gathered at Pontefract Castle, about nine miles away.

On 29 December York dispatched a foraging party to gather supplies, but it was spotted by the Lancastrian army and chased back to Sandal Castle. But Somerset lacked siege machinery and knew he could never reduce the fortress, so he would have to seek victory through guile rather than force.

The next day Somerset deployed about 5,000 men around the castle, in full view of the defenders. Unknown to the Yorkists, these were just the bait – another 13,000 Lancastrian soldiers were concealed in a nearby woods.

No one knows why York, against Salisbury's advice, now decided to come out to fight. He may have believed that the enemy he could see constituted the entire Lancastrian army, or he may have been trying to save some foragers who hadn't made it back inside. Some say it was simply because, as the duke had said, he could never live 'like a bird in a cage'. What is certain is that his men charged down the hill onto the level ground by a nearby river to attack.

The moment the Yorkists engaged the enemy, the hidden Lancastrians emerged from the woods to engulf both flanks. Then Somerset brought more of his men around the Yorkist rear and sealed their line of retreat.

Richard of York was in the thick of the action and saw that his men were about to be overrun. After ordering his son Rutland to escape, he rode hard at the enemy but was unhorsed and, after refusing to surrender, was hacked to death.

His son Rutland was galloping along the road to Wakefield when he was overtaken on Wakefield Bridge by one of Somerset's lieutenants, John, 9th Lord Clifford, whose father had been killed at St Albans five years before (see 22 May). As Clifford stood over him, dagger in hand, Rutland begged for quarter, to which Clifford answered: 'By God's blood, thy father slew mine and so will I do thee.' He then plunged his dagger into the boy's throat with such force that it penetrated through to the back of his neck.

It was a complete victory for the Lancastrians; over 3,000 Yorkists were slain, and the day after the battle Salisbury was beheaded for treason. The severed heads of York, Rutland and Salisbury were stuck on poles and displayed on Mickelgate Bar, the traditional ceremonial gate for kings entering York. The duke's head was adorned with a crown of paper and a sign saying: 'Let York overlook the town of York.'

But, although the red rose of Lancaster was at the moment in the ascendant, it was not long to remain there. York's son Edward now inherited his father's claim to the throne, and, with the help of the executed Salisbury's son, Warwick the Kingmaker, he bested Queen Margaret's forces in a succession of battles, to be declared king only two months after his father's calamitous defeat at Wakefield. As for the victors at Wakefield, 88 days later at Ferrybridge an arrow caught the revengeful Clifford in the throat and he died in agony (see 28 March), and Somerset was captured and beheaded at the Battle of Hexham in 1464.

Other action this day

AD 39: Born today: Roman general and later emperor Titus, who conquered Jerusalem and destroyed the Jewish Temple there ∗ 1917: The British under General Edmund Allenby push back the Turks after their four-day advance on British-held Jerusalem, the final significant fighting in Palestine until the spring of 1918

31 December

'Large ships are a thing of the past'

1942 New Year's Eve, 73 degrees north latitude. In the grey murk of an Arctic morning, fourteen British and American merchantmen steam due east through the Barents Sea, bound for Murmansk, carrying vital supplies for Soviet Russia, locked in its all-out struggle against the Wehrmacht. Suddenly, from the dimness, emerges the outline of an enemy force of vastly superior strength. In five hours of aggressive moves, the convoy's escorts, British destroyers, manage to drive off the attackers, holding them at bay until help arrives.

It is a dramatic victory for the British, for they had in fact held off the cream of the German navy: the pocket battleship *Lutzow* and the heavy cruiser *Hipper*, accompanied by six large destroyers. Beyond that, however, today's action held an unintended consequence for the entire German battle fleet.

Convoy JW 51B, nine days out from Scotland, was closely shepherded by a small flotilla of destroyers. Providing more distant cover, Force R, consisting of two British cruisers, was sailing westward out of Murmansk to meet the convoy and provide cover on the final stage of its journey. So far no sign of the enemy.

But two days earlier a U-boat had detected the convoy and signalled its course to German Navy North in Narvik. There, Operation Regenbogen (Rainbow) went into effect, the plan to intercept and destroy JW 51B. It needed Hitler's approval, but Der Führer, at his headquarters in East Prussia, was reluctant to give the go-ahead. He doubted the navy's ability to prevail in surface engagements against the British – he cited the fate of the *Graf Spee* and, more recently, that of the *Bismarck* (see 13 December and 24 May) – and beyond that he considered the loss of a capital ship to be a national humiliation. But assured by his naval advisors of Regenbogen's sure and imminent success, and preoccupied by events on the Eastern Front, Hitler gave his assent.

Shortly before 9.00am, three destroyers – unidentifiable in the poor light – are sighted sailing behind the convoy. When HMS *Obdurate* is sent back to investigate, they quickly steer away into the gloom; one, however, opens fire. Aboard the British warships, Action Stations sounds, guns are loaded, and torpedoes are set for depth and speed. Now, from where the destroyers have disappeared, emerges the enormous shape of the *Hipper*. Flotilla commander Captain Sherbrooke aboard the *Onslow* gives his orders: *Obedient* and *Orwell* to join him in confronting the enemy, *Obdurate* to return to the convoy, *Achates* to lay smoke, and the merchantmen to change course to south-east, away from the enemy.

Over the next three hours, the destroyers, with bold countermoves that threaten the imminent launch of their torpedoes, drive *Hipper* away from the convoy four times, all the while zigzagging to avoid the heavy cruiser's salvoes from its 8-inch guns. In the course of the action, however, a shell hits *Onslow*, badly damaging the destroyer and wounding Captain Sherbrooke. Smoke-laying *Achates*, hit by several shells, begins to sink.

At 11.30am *Hipper is* joined in the fray by a new and larger presence, quickly identified by the British as the *Lutzow* (sister ship of the late *Graf Spee*), carrying 11-inch guns and accompanied by three more destroyers. At almost the same time, however, shells from a new quarter begin falling around *Hipper*. Force R has arrived on the scene with its two cruisers and two destroyers. Within minutes, *Hipper* is hit three times, and a German destroyer sunk. After salvoes are exchanged between Force R and *Lutzow*, the German ships withdraw to the north, disappearing into the dark.

By 2.00pm the action is over. Two days later, JW 51B reaches Murmansk harbour unscathed to deliver its cargoes of war-critical supplies: trucks, tanks, aircraft, and fuel oil. Among its escorts, *Achates* has sunk, but heavily damaged *Onslow* eventually makes it back to Scapa Flow; for his bold and gallant leadership in the Battle of the Barents Sea, Captain Sherbrooke is awarded the VC.

The unwillingness of the German commanders to press their clear force advantage in firepower and armour – the timidity of their performance in action – was in part ascribable to their mission orders from Narvik, which included the cautionary note: 'Avoid a superior force, otherwise destroy according to tactical situation.' But this warning only reflected a far larger caution among the naval staff: Hitler's lack of faith in the German navy.

So it was that three days later, when Hitler, at his headquarters, learned the outcome of the engagement, he became furious and demanded the immediate decommissioning of the German navy's capital ships, leaving the war at sea to the U-boats and the Luftwaffe. 'Large ships are a thing of the past', he informed Admiral Dönitz, the U-boat advocate whom he had just promoted to commander-in-chief, replacing Admiral Raeder, the surface navy man who had held the post since 1928.

This, then, was the unintended consequence of the Battle of the Barents Sea: during 1943 most of the German navy's surface fleet – battleships, pocket battleships, battlecruisers, heavy and light cruisers – were decommissioned or relegated to the status of training ships or kept in port. The only one to see action was the battlecruiser *Scharnhorst*, which, in its only action of the year, was sunk by the British off the North Cape of Norway on 26 December.

Other action this day

AD 406: Vandals, Alans and Suevi break across the Rhine near Mainz as the Western Roman empire nears collapse * 1863: The first day of a three-day stalemate called the Battle of Stones River in Tennessee in which the North suffers 13,249 casualties, 31 per cent of its fighting force, while the South loses 10,266 (27 per cent), the highest level of any battle in the American Civil War * 1880: American general George C. Marshall is born in Uniontown, Pennsylvania

Index

McClellan, General George B.
6 February; 19 October;
5 November
McCullough, David 27 August
McHenry, Fort, attack on 3 March
McKinley, President William
15 February; 1 July; 2 July
Meaux, Battle of 9 June
Medal of Honor 17 April; 2 July;
12 July; 8 October; 20 October;
8 December; 11 December
Megiddo, Battle of 15 May;
31 October
Mehmed II (the Conqueror),
Ottoman Sultan 3 May; 29 May
Menelek II of Ethiopia 1 March
Metternich, Klemens 23 March
Mexican–American War 2 July;
22 February
Meyer, General John C. 1 January
Midway, Battle of 3 June
Military Cross 9 December
Miltiades 21 September
Milvian Bridge, Battle of
27 October
Mirabeau, Honoré Gabriel Riqueti,
Comte de 5 December
Missionary Ridge, Battle of
23 November
Mitchell, Colonel William ('Billy')
20 October; 28 December
Mobile Bay, Battle of 5 August
Moctezuma (Aztec king) 30 June
Modoc War 29 November
Mohács, Battle of 29 August
Mohammed 11 February
Molay, Jacques de 3 April
Mollwitz, Battle of 10 April
Moltke, Helmuth von 31 August
Monitor **(Union warship)** 9 March
Monroe Doctrine 19 June; 2 July
Monroe, President James 22 March;
26 December
Montcalm, marquis Louis-Joseph de
2 August; 13 September;
14 September

Monte Cassino, bombing of
22 January
Montereau, Battle of 29 January
Montfort, Simon de 14 January;
22 July
Montgisard, Battle of 4 March;
3 April; 23 April; 25 November
Montgomery, Field Marshal Bernard
Law 23 January; 17 September;
4 November
Montmirail, Battle of 29 January
Montmorency, Anne de, duc de
Montmorency 10 August
Moonlight Sonata, Operation
14 November
Moore, General Sir John
16 January
Moore's Creek Bridge, Battle of
27 February
Moorish conquest of Spain
29 April
Morison, Samuel Eliot 4 May
Mortimer, Roger de 24 September
Mosby, John Singleton 8 March
Moscow, Battle of 30 September
Mothe, siege of La 27 July
Mozart, Wolfgang Amadeus
15 December
Mstislav of Kiev 31 May
Mühlberg, Battle of 24 April
Mukden, Battle of 9 February
Mukti Bahini 3 December
Munda, Battle of 4 January;
15 March
Murat, Marshal and King Joachim
4 April; 25 July; 15 August;
21 August; 7 September;
5 October
Murphy, Audie 12 July
Mussolini, Benito 28 April;
18 July
Mustafa, Turkish Grand Vizier
Kara 12 September

Nagasaki, bombing of 27 March;
6 August